D0848153

The Baltic

The Baltic

A History

Michael North

Translated by Kenneth Kronenberg

Harvard University Press

CAMBRIDGE, MASSACHUSETTS · LONDON, ENGLAND
2015

This book is an updated version of the German edition, originally published as
Geschichte der Ostsee, copyright ©Verlag C. H. Beck oHG, München 2011.

Library of Congress Cataloging-in-Publication Data

North, Michael, 1954– author.
[Geschichte der Ostsee. English]
The Baltic : a history / Michael North ; translated by Kenneth Kronenberg.
pages cm
"This book is an updated version of the German edition, originally published as
Geschichte der Ostsee, copyright © Verlag C. H. Beck oHG, München 2011."
Includes bibliographical references and index.
ISBN 978-0-674-74410-3 (alkaline paper)
1. Baltic States—History.   2. Baltic States—Commerce.
3. Baltic States—Civilization.   I. Kronenberg, Kenneth,
1946– translator.   II. Title.
DK502.7.N6713 2015
947.9—dc23
2014035123

To my friends and colleagues at the University of California at Santa Barbara

Contents

Preface ix

Introduction: Trade and Cultures 1

1. Vikings, Slavs, and Balts 9

2. The Christian Mission and the Settlement of the Land 28

3. The Hanseatic League and the Monarchies 52

4. The Reformation and the Nordic Renaissance 87

5. Swedish Dominance 117

6. The Rise of Russia 145

7. Nordic Romanticism 183

8. Revolutions and New States 222

9. Sovietization versus Welfare States 262

10. Transformation and EU Integration 301

Conclusion 326

Place Name Concordance 331
Notes 337
References 355
Acknowledgments 397
Illustration Credits 399
Index 401

Preface

In the spring of 2013 my Cambridge colleague Joachim Whaley suggested to Ian Malcolm at the London office of Harvard University Press that a translation of *Geschichte der Ostsee,* which had been published in Germany by C. H. Beck in 2011, might be in order. At nearly the same time, Bradley D. Woodworth in a review in the *Journal of Baltic Studies* (2013) also recommended an English-language edition. I am grateful to Harvard University Press, and especially to Ian Malcolm, for making an English-language edition a reality. Working on this edition has enabled me to incorporate the fruits of even more recent research. The translation was supported by the International Graduate Program "Baltic Borderlands."

If the book is as readable in English as it was in German, it is the work of my congenial translator Kenneth Kronenberg, and I would like to thank him here. It was really fun to work with him, not only via email, but also face-to-face at his home in Cambridge, Massachusetts. The book gained much from the critical comments of Charlotte Hedenstierna Jonson, Kristoffer Neville, and Alexander Drost. I owe a debt of gratitude to Doreen Wollbrecht, Robert Riemer, Hielke van Nieuwenhuize, and Lasse Seebeck, who bore the brunt of the work on the final production of the book with great commitment.

This book is dedicated to my friends and colleagues at my second academic home at the University of California at Santa Barbara on the Pacific.

The Baltic

Introduction

Trade and Cultures

THE Baltic has always been a region of exchange and encounter. Since ancient times it has been populated by various language communities, with Germans, Slavs, Balts, and Finns living in close proximity. During the Middle Ages and in some cases even during modern times these populations developed into peoples and states. As a result, the political affiliations of the various coastal lands have long been subject to frequent change. Various powers gained control over the Baltic, or at least parts of the coast, for long periods of time. Sweden in the seventeenth century would be one example. At the same time, the Baltic region was the scene of intense social and cultural exchange at all levels. The intensification of communication as a result of shipping and trade and the migration of population groups fostered transformative processes, which in some cases ran counter to developing power structures. As a result, supranational cultures, such as those of the Vikings and the Slavs or the Hanseatic League, developed. The Netherlandization of the Baltic in the sixteenth and seventeenth centuries and its Sovietization in the twentieth are other salient examples. The political upheavals of 1989 were far-reaching and lent the region renewed significance. This new importance may be seen in the recent expansion of the European Union (EU) to the east and its 2009 Baltic Sea strategy.

The reawakening of political interest in the region has given Baltic studies a considerable boost. Although the Baltic had been intensively studied from the regional perspective of the inhabitants both during the interwar years and during the Cold War, scholars have lacked an interdisciplinary approach of the sort that Fernand Braudel pioneered for the Mediterranean.[1] In the 1990s, given impetus by the political changes taking place, David Kirby and Matti Klinge wrote general surveys that began to address the need for such a synthesis. Whereas Kirby viewed the Baltic region as peripheral to Europe, Klinge's essay placed the grip exerted by empires on the Baltic region at the center of his considerations. This struggle for hegemony over the Baltic was a constant motif of Alan Palmer's 2005 study as well.[2]

Since then, not only has research advanced, but also our entire understanding of the cultures and geography of the region has been transformed. This "spatial turn" has given rise to a new historical perception of the concept of region and regionalism, much as it has given other disciplines a new understanding of the processes of regional formation and of the varied functions of regions generally. Geographically, for example, regions are no longer viewed as natural entities but as the constructs of a multiplicity of actors. In place of static natural spaces in which human beings labor, we are now more interested in the transformation and plurality of such spaces that make up the complexity of our world. In addition to natural spaces, there are also historical and communication spaces and spaces of memory in which political, linguistic, ethnic, religious, economic, and social boundaries overlap.[3]

As a result, the desire for a history of the Baltic à la Braudel would take us in the wrong direction because it would presuppose an all-powerful nature that ineluctably determined the physical setting in which the peoples around the Baltic Sea lived their lives.[4] But there is no such thing as a single Baltic. Rather, there are many Baltics, which, from Adam of Bremen to Björn Engholm and the Baltic Sea strategy of the EU, have been constantly reinvented and reconstituted by trade and cultures and by the merchants and artists who have embodied these historical trends.

Contemporary place names and their derivation provide the first evidence of how the Baltic region was constructed and perceived. Although a number of chroniclers had described the inhabitants of the Baltic coast in ancient times, the first mention of the Baltic Sea in its Latin form, *mare Balticum*, is found in Adam of Bremen (ca. 1050–1085). In his history of the Hamburg church, Adam described the successful missionary work conducted by the Archbishopric of Hamburg-Bremen in preparation for further missions. In the first book, he described the mission of Archbishop Unni, following in the steps of St. Ansgar, that led him across the Baltic (*mare Balticum remigans*) to Birka.[5] In the fourth book,

Adam discussed the Baltic in reference to Einhard's *Vita Caroli Magni*. Einhard had spoken of a gulf (*sinus*) of unknown length, which at no point was more than one hundred thousand paces wide and along whose shores lived Normans, Slavs, Estonians, and other peoples.[6] As Adam explained it, the name *Baltic* derived from the fact that this gulf was called *Balticus* by its inhabitants because it stretched like a belt (*in modum baltei*) as far as the Scythian regions and Greece.[7] The sea was also known as the Barbarian Sea or Scythian Sea, after the barbarian peoples it bordered.[8] Over the course of the Livonian mission that soon followed, chroniclers and encyclopedists, such as Arnold of Lübeck, Henry of Latvia, and Bartholomew of England, began to turn their attention to the eastern coasts of the Baltic and their inhabitants,[9] but without explicitly dealing with the *mare Balticum* as a whole.[10]

In the thirteenth century, the Baltic became a well-worn pathway for pilgrims and merchants after Duke Albert I of Saxony, in 1241, granted safe passage to merchants passing from the Baltic to the North Sea, and papal nuncio Guido, in 1266, exempted from the strand law merchants and pilgrims taking the same route, saving them from plunder by coastal inhabitants. The document of 1241, it should be noted, contains the first mention of the Baltic Sea and the North Sea in Latin and Low German simultaneously (*de orientali mari ad occidentale mare, [que] Osterse et westerse wlgariter nuncupantur*).[11]

In the Netherlands, too, matters of trade motivated an interest in the geography of the region after a 1294 letter from the Dutch town of Zwolle to Lübeck spoke of the *mare orientale* in contrast to the *mare occidentale*. A hundred years later, Albert of Bavaria, Count of Holland, Zeeland, and Hennegau, granted safe passage to representatives of the Hanseatic cities—whom he referred to as *ghemeenre steden bi der osterzee* (common cities on the East Sea).[12] This is the first extant mention in Dutch, whereas the Latin *mare Balticum* is found in the writings of humanists such as Enea Silvio Piccolomini (1405–1464) when discussing the history of the heathen Old Prussians.[13] Olaus Magnus (1490–1557) also used the term in his *Historia de gentibus septentrionalibus*, although he used *mare Balticum* and *mare Gothicum* interchangeably. He did the same with *seu Finnonicum ac Livonicum* and *mare Sveticum*, and with *mare Bothnicum* and *mare Germanicum*, names he used to distinguish between particular sections of the coast. In this context, *mare Balticum* meant the southern coast of the Baltic Sea.

In the sixteenth and seventeenth centuries, the Baltic Sea became the focus of attention in both Latin and Dutch texts as a result of economic and military interests. Whereas Denmark, Sweden, and Poland battled for hegemony over the Baltic coasts and justified this *dominium maris Baltici* in their propaganda, the Netherlands attempted to protect the interests of its merchants and of shipping generally. As early as 1493, a warship out of Amsterdam rescued a ship from Hamburg from privateers who were most likely allied with Sweden. Whereupon Sweden's strongman, Sten Sture, suggested that the Amsterdamers might want to compensate him for lost profits—assuming, of course, that they wished to pursue their interests in Baltic shipping in the future (*"soe verde dese stede die Oestersche zee dochte te gebruken"*) (so far as these cities think to use the Eastern Sea).[14]

Over the next few years, Dutch concerns over Baltic trade were constant and led to the conceptualization of an *Oostersche Zee* or *Oostzee* region, which Flanders and Holland viewed as economically essential. This was happening at the same time as the disputes between Denmark and the Hanseatic city of Lübeck, which claimed a monopoly over Baltic trade that would have threatened Dutch interests in any case.[15] One interesting sidelight is that letters from the government in Brussels, which were often written in French, used a Dutch variant. Although they later used the term *Mer de Baltique* exclusively, we find earlier governmental correspondence regarding the Baltic using the terms *mer d'oost, mer de hoost,* or *mer d'Oostlande. Oostland* was a term that, in addition to the word *Oosten*, was used in contemporary Dutch sources and defined the sphere of interest of Dutch trade. Thus, for example, when discussing trade or shipping in the Baltic region, they would write, *"den uuytvoer van boter ende kaes op Oostlandt"* (the export of butter and cheese to Eastland).[16] *Oostland* was described as if it were a real country (e.g., *"de scepen, die uuyt dese landen, Spaignen, Portugael, Oostlandt ende andere landen nair Calais sullen begeren te varen"*) (the ships which from these lands, Spain, Portugal, Eastland and other lands wish to sail to Calais).[17] At the beginning of the eighteenth century, a directorate was formed for this trade (the so-called

Directie van de Oostersche Handel en Reederijen), which consisted of three merchants and three shippers. They advised the Dutch Republic on all matters relating to Baltic trade, while the Directie van den Moscovische Handel represented traders active in Russia.

In England we find such demarcations as early as the sixteenth century. There, the Eastland Company (Merchants of Eastland), founded in 1579, plied their trade with the Baltic region, while the Muscovy Company had since 1555 attempted to reach Russia by way of the White Sea.[18]

For many years the name *Oostzee* was reserved for the sea itself and was popularized by Dutch cartographers. In 1590, Lucas Janszoon Waghenaer (1533–1606) received a patent for an atlas, *Het Thresoor van de Zeevaert, inhoudende de geheele navigatie van de Oostzee, Noortzee, Westerzee ende Levantse Zee ofte Middelsee* (the treasure of seafaring, containing the whole navigation of the East Sea, North Sea, West Sea and Levant Sea or Middle Sea).[19] In 1606, another concession was granted to Willem Janszoons, *"kaartsnijder te Amsterdam"* (map engraver in Amsterdam), for an oceanic atlas, *"inhoudende de navigatie van de Oister-, Westerende Midtlansche zee"* (containing the navigation of the East-, West and Middle Land Sea).[20] Other Dutch maps used the French *Mer baltique* or, like Adriaan Veen, the Latin *mare Balticum,* with the explanation *"vulgo De Oost Zee"* (Eastern Sea, in the vernacular).[21]

Dutch politicians who, like Johan de Witt and Coenraad van Beuningen in the seventeenth century and Anthonie Heinsius during the Great Northern War (1700–1721), sent warships into the Baltic, often spoke only incidentally about "Eastern Sea matters" (*saken van de Oostzee*), although they were well-informed about the course of the war and the dangers to trade and shipping. In the peace treaties that ended hostilities between the warring parties in the Baltic, however, the Baltic was seldom mentioned because at issue were bilateral territorial concessions. Only Denmark and Sweden, in the preamble to the 1720 Frederiksborg Treaty, mentioned the damage that had been done to trade in the Baltic.

Along with political and diplomatic interest, scholarly and historical interest in the Baltic Sea and its inhabitants grew as well. We see, for example, an article titled "Baltic Sea" in Zedler's *Universallexikon,* published in 1733, which also examined the older literature.[22] The coining in 1845 of the term *Baltic languages* by the philologist Georg Heinrich Ferdinand Nesselmann (1811–1881) in his study *Sprache der alten Preußen* (Language of the old Prussians) also reflects this perspective (Eastern Sea=Baltic Sea). Nesselmann linked the names of the languages to the particular areas of settlement along the coast.

Although this tradition continued to be propagated in publications and names of associations, the increasing domination of Russia over the Baltic provinces of Estonia, Livonia, and Courland brought about a semantic transformation. While Russia initially continued to call its possessions *ostzejskij* (on the Eastern Sea), the term *pribaltijskij* (on the Baltic Sea) came into increasingly widespread use toward the end of the nineteenth century, which the Russians defined as the coastal provinces of the Russian Empire. At the same time, the term *Baltic* became attached to the German-speaking minority in the region, who tried to shield their privileges from both the Russian rulers and the local Estonian or Latvian populations.[23] After the founding of the new Baltic states after World War I, this delimitation of the word *Baltic* to the eastern coast of the Baltic came to be widely accepted in other languages, which, like English and French, had not yet undergone this semantic transformation.

The newly formed states, however, soon attempted once again to organize all of their Baltic neighbors (with the exception of Germany and Soviet Russia) into a Baltic League to advance a common foreign policy. Although this was unsuccessful, numerous initiatives aimed at researching a common Baltic past were developed in the Baltic republics and their new neighbor Poland (for example, at historical conferences, the journal *Baltic Countries*, and the Instytut Baltycki research institute).[24] By contrast, National Socialist historians such as Erich Maschke (1900–1982) painted a picture of a Germanic Baltic region, which continued to have influence even after the end of World War II.[25]

The Soviet occupation and annexation of the Baltic states and the loss of most German territories along the Baltic coast reduced interest in this region generally; emigrants and associations of expellees (*Vertriebenenverbände*) were mainly responsible for keeping alive what interest there was. New bridges were built only during the period of détente in the 1980s. As a result, Finns and Estonians began to establish relationships, and scholarly exchanges between Germany and the Baltic states intensified. In this context, Björn Engholm, prime minister of the state of Schleswig-Holstein, initiated a debate in 1988 about a "new Hanseatic League," which would form the basis for cooperation among all the Baltic countries. Engholm's program, which included cultural initiatives such as the Ars Baltica art exhibits and the Jazz Baltica music festival, was overtaken by the political events of 1989 and the dissolution of the Soviet Union. These events transformed perceptions of the region yet again. Cities and countries that had previously been considered distant, unfamiliar, and foreign were suddenly discovered to be neighbors and, despite the visible physical deterioration of the architecture and housing, were seen as culturally similar.

At the same time, politicians began making plans for the future of the Baltic region because they feared (especially in Scandinavia, where only Denmark belonged to the European Union) that they would be overtaken and marginalized by the dynamics of European unification. This is why, at the initiative of Danish Foreign Minister Uffe Ellemann-Jensen (1941–) and German Foreign Minister Hans-Dietrich Genscher (1927–), the Baltic countries and their neighbors formed the Council of the Baltic Sea States (CBSS). This organization has inspired political cooperation and the work of numerous subcommittees and nongovernmental organizations (NGOs), a result of intense consultations among prime ministers, foreign ministers, and parliamentarians.[26] The membership of all countries bordering on the Baltic plus Iceland to the west redefined the Baltic yet again—this time politically. The enlargement of the EU since 2004, to which all states bordering the Baltic, with the exception of Russia, now belong, and the EU Baltic Sea strategy of 2009, have again changed our image of the region. The goal of the Baltic Sea strategy, with its focus on the environment, trade, security, and access, is to transform the Baltic region into a model of regional cooperation within the EU.

The list of constructs of the Baltic Sea region that I have outlined—as missionary, trade, and EU model region—could be expanded more or less arbitrarily.[27] In fact, even the names for the Baltic and the present identification of the inhabitants of neighboring states with the Baltic reflect different perspectives. Whereas the Danes and Swedes call it the Eastern Sea (*Østersøen* and *Östersjön*, respectively), and the Finns use

8 THE BALTIC

Itämeri, which is a translation from Swedish and means the same thing, Estonians (logically) call the Baltic the Western Sea (*Läänemeri*). On the other hand, Russians and Poles use a version of the Latin *mare Balticum* (*More baltijskoe* and *Morze bałtyckie*). The same goes for Latvians and Lithuanians (*Baltijas jūras* and *Baltijos jūros*).

Given this background of multiple perspectives and constructs, this volume presents a new perspective on the history of the Baltic and the surrounding region. It views the Baltic region as one of cultural exchange over the centuries, with the sea both connecting and separating the peoples living along its shores.[28] The Baltic region is viewed as a contact zone within which the various cultures interact while also entering into relationships with other regions and cultures in western and southern Europe and in Asia.[29] One medium of cultural exchange has been trade, without which neither material nor nonmaterial transfers could have occurred. Merchants and traders were the first to cross the sea, and the goods that they brought with them changed the societies and cultures into which they were introduced, just as the significance of the goods was transformed in the exchange process. In addition, this exchange also affected the mind-sets of the merchants, their trading partners, and the consumers of their products. Craftsmen, artists, and scholars adopted new ideas, processed them, and passed them on, to the extent to which they had not themselves conveyed them from one coast of the Baltic to another. Coasts and port cities were close enough to be connected yet distant enough to be separated. As a result, although the people living in the hinterland may not have crossed the sea themselves, they were affected by the consequences of this contact both as producers and as consumers.[30] At the same time, trade fostered the development of states, which in turn attempted to gain control of that trade.

The manifold forms and processes of economic, cultural, and political interaction are at the center of this history of the Baltic Sea, which extends from the age of the Vikings to the EU Baltic strategy. This region is currently one of the most dynamic in the world, and it is my hope to bring it and its history to the attention of a larger public.

CHAPTER ONE

Vikings, Slavs, and Balts

Focus on Wolin

In the tenth century, Wolin, which is situated at the mouth of the Oder River, was the commercial center of the Baltic region, with a harbor, a settlement of fishermen and craftsmen, and a cemetery with richly ornamented tombs. Along a stretch of four kilometers stood large houses, many ornamented on plots of equal size, which could be reached by walking along narrow alleyways paved with wooden planks. The town was home to smithies, glass and comb makers, amber workers, potters, and boat builders. Because Wolin was well situated along trade routes, its trading partners stretched from the Rhineland in the west to Lake Mälaren in Sweden to Russia in the east. It was a seven-day overland journey from Hamburg. But merchants and travelers could take a boat from Schleswig or Oldenburg, which would get them to Novgorod in two weeks. The chronicler Adam of Bremen described Wolin's heyday:

> It is truly the largest of all cities that Europe has to offer, in which live Slavs and other tribes, Greeks, and barbarians. Even the foreigners from Saxony have received equal settlement rights, although they may not openly profess their Christianity during their stay. They all still remain captive to their pagan heresies; other than that, it would be hard to find another people more honorable and friendly in their way of life and hospitality. The city is full of wares from all the peoples of the north; nothing desirable or rare is unobtainable. Here there is a beacon, which the inhabitants call the Greek fire.[1]

The mythic city of Vineta was to be sought in Wolin; however, Wolin was unable to maintain its independence in the face of Polish kings, who controlled the mouth of the Oder. The city lost much of its importance after incursions by the Danes in the twelfth century. At this

Map 1. The Baltic region in the 9th and 10th centuries

point, Stettin (Szczecin) became the center of power of the Pomeranian princes and the leading mercantile city in the region.[2]

The Vikings

The Vikings, or Norsemen, made their first appearance in sources from the late eighth century, when they attacked monasteries in the British Isles, such as Lindisfarne on the coast of Northumberland (793) and St. Philibert at the mouth of the Loire (799). Here is how Alcuin of York (ca. 735–804) described the attack of 793 in a letter to King Ethelred of Northumbria:

> Lo, it is nearly 350 years that we and our fathers have inhabited this most lovely land, and never before has such terror appeared in Britain as we have now suffered from a pagan race, nor was it thought that

such an inroad from the sea could be made. Behold, the church of St. Cuthbert spattered with the blood of the priests of God, despoiled of all its ornaments; a place more venerable than all in Britain is given as a prey to pagan peoples.[3]

Several explanations have been given for their sudden appearance, including population pressures and land shortages that forced people to sea, the combativeness of young men, and the desire for easy plunder. Tribal leadership (chieftains) constantly had to be defended and reasserted. This not only required success in war and the reputation flowing from it, but also a large following, which a successful warrior could keep in line only by the constant distribution of spoils. The Frankish Empire, which was expanding at the time, presented an easy target for pillage. In spite of the efforts of Pippin and Charlemagne, their territory was not yet consolidated, let alone defensible at all points. Boats and nautical know-how were essential to success, and the Vikings possessed both in abundance. They were able to sail or row their seaworthy boats across the open North and Baltic Seas without having to orient themselves by coastal landmarks. With their smaller boats, they could also penetrate the interior, where nary a riverfront port was safe from their depredations.[4]

The Vikings profited greatly from the expansion in Frisian trade, whose riches they were easily able to make their own. Dorestad, at the mouth of the Rhine, and Domburg, on the island of Walcheren, had developed into trading centers where Frisian farmer-merchants no longer went to sea as a sideline but began to live exclusively from trade and craftwork. One manifestation of the intensity of this trade are the Frisian (and also English) *sceat* coins, which spread as far as Scandinavia. The Vikings attacked Dorestad regularly in the 830s and 840s. This was a call to action for the Frankish Empire, whose kings tried to protect their monasteries and trading centers while at the same time engaging some of the Viking chieftains politically by playing rivals off against each other.

But the invaders set up power bases not only in Scandinavia, but on the islands of the North Sea as well. The Danish kings, who from their base in Jutland had conquered chieftains and minor royal houses, initially controlled the neighboring islands as well as the passage between the Baltic Sea and the North Sea. They extended their influence as far as Viken and the area surrounding the Oslofjord as well as in the south to the coast of the English Channel. In the middle of the ninth century, the Danes conquered the eastern half of England, making York their headquarters. The Danes also challenged the Norwegians in Ireland, which they had settled along with the Orkney, Shetland, and Hebrides Islands. However, the Danes continued to threaten the Frankish Empire as well. After the division of the empire in 843, the kingdom of West Francia in particular was subject to Viking incursions; in 845, they rowed up the Seine to Paris, where the city was saved only by paying 7,000 pounds of silver in tribute. Fortifications in West Francia began to provide protection from the Vikings only in about 870.

The Vikings then shifted their activities to the British Isles, where the Anglo-Saxon kings had at times succeeded in shaking off Danish rule. But between the turn of the tenth century and the eleventh century, the Danes under kings Sweyn Forkbeard and Canute the Great reestablished Danish dominion over Norway and the Anglo-Saxons, who were forced to pay annual tribute to Denmark in the form of noble metals. This so-called danegeld was assessed in eight large installments between 991 and 1040, the total coming to 248,647 pounds of silver, or almost 60 million pennies.[5]

Furthermore, the East and the Baltic region presented significant possibilities for expansion and the accumulation of wealth. Pelts and furs from eastern regions were much desired in western markets in the eighth century, and the resources of the East were systematically exploited thereafter. The Svear from Sweden, known in the Slavic sources as Rus' or Varangians (Varjagi), were especially active in this trade. They settled in Staraya Ladoga—approximately 15 kilometers from the mouth of the Volkhov River—along Lake Ladoga, Lake Ilmen, and the upper reaches of the Dnieper River, where they lived in close proximity to Slavs, Finns, and Balts. They reached the Arab world by way of the Don River, the Volga River, or the Caspian Sea, where they obtained or stole large quantities of silver. This is documented by archeological evidence.[6] Arab sources, compiled by the Persian astronomer Ibn Rustah, tell of the Varangians:

> With their ships they undertake forays against the Slavs, and upon arriving, take them prisoner and bring them to the capital of the Kha-

zars and to Bolghar, where they put them up for sale. They have no seed fields, but eat only that which they export from the land of the Slavs . . . their employment consists entirely in trade in sable, squirrel, and other pelts. They sell these pelts to their customers, and in exchange they receive a small fortune in coin, which they tie to their belts.[7]

Another Arab historian, al-Masudi (ca. 896–956), described an attack on the inhabitants of the Caspian Sea in the tenth century. A Varangian fleet had appeared in Constantinople as early as 860. Byzantium responded by embracing the Varangians and concluding trade agreements with them. In Kiev, along the middle stretch of the Dnieper, another stronghold of the Scandinavians in the Slavic lands, the Byzantines founded a trading settlement with a church, whose religious services had an influence on the pagans to the north and the Slavic population. The chieftains of the Varangians surrounded themselves with Scandinavian followers, one of whom, Rurik (ca. 830–879) was the founder of the old Russian Rurikid dynasty. Rurik and his son Oleg built strongholds, which they filled with their followers to maintain control of the territory. The regional principalities of Novgorod, Pskov, Polock, and Rostov originated under Rurik's rule. The subsequent rulers of the Kievan Rus', Igor and Olga, were also of Scandinavian origin, as were their retinue, but their son and dynastic successor, Sviatoslav (died 972), represented a more Slavicized trend, as his name implies. The warriors who served in the imperial palace guard in Byzantium were not from Scandinavia alone. Slavs, Balts, and Finns were included in a cultural community with the Varangians, as can be seen in trade documents between the Kievan princes and Byzantium. Whereas the agreement of 911 contained negotiations with only fifteen emissaries of Scandinavian descent, by 944, twenty-six such emissaries and twenty-eight merchants were mentioned. Judging by the names, a large majority was Scandinavians (forty-seven), but five Baltic Finns or men of Finnish descent, one (Lithuanian) Yotvingian, and possibly one Slav were also represented. The latter were mainly employed as boat builders and possibly also as shippers in the trade with Byzantium.[8]

The Slavs

In the fourth and fifth centuries, the Germanic tribes that had settled along the southern coast of the Baltic Sea left their homes during what has become known as the Migration Period and migrated south and east. A small Germanic population remained behind. During the second half of the seventh century, Slavic tribes presumably migrated into these now more thinly settled regions. They are first mentioned in about 780 as Obotrites in connection with the battle between the Frankish Empire and Saxony. The Obotrites, who settled between eastern Holstein and the Warnow River, were joined by the tribal confederation of the Veleti, who may possibly have settled in the region earlier. The island of Rügen was populated by the Rani, whose political and religious capital was the temple at Cape Arkona, where their chief god Svantevit was venerated. Ukrani and Müritzians settled to the south along the Uecker River and Lake Müritz. Finally, we find Pomeranians east of the Oder, along with Wolins at the mouth of the Oder and Prissani (Pyritzans) to the south. To the southeast, along the middle stretch of the Warte River, was the settlement area of the Polans, who in the tenth century formed the core of the Polish Piast dynasty.[9]

The sometimes openly hostile tribal confederations not only competed with each other, they were also subject to the hegemonic claims of the Franks and the Kingdom of East Francia, which later became the German Empire, and its rulers, and to the expansion of Denmark and Poland. This created not only the potential for numerous political alliances, but also the risk of being crushed between internal and external enemies. As a result, Christian rulers did not shy away from "unholy" alliances with Slavic "pagans" against Christian states; nor did Slavic tribes turn down compacts of convenience with German and Danish kings against their Slavic neighbors or adversaries within their own tribe.

The eighth and ninth centuries were characterized by the expansion of the Frankish Empire and later by that of the Ottonians into the territory of the Obotrites and Veleti. In addition, the Danes conquered the southern Baltic coast, and the Poles annexed Pomerania. The Ottonians attempted to expand their rule, especially to the Slavic regions east of the Elbe River. Here, the margraves put in place by Otto I would conquer new territory and Christianize the Slavs. As a result, Otto founded the Bishoprics of Brandenburg and Havelberg, in 948, and the Oldenburg Obotrite mission in Holstein, in 968.

Very few sources have come down to us regarding political organization. We do know that the tribes were headed by kings, princes, or chieftains, with Obotrite kings sometimes leading the tribal confederations. Hereditary princes, who mainly came from a noble caste, were seated in fortified castles along with their retinue. They lived mainly from the taxes and services levied on the surrounding villagers. In some tribes, as with the Veleti, the people's assembly was an important institution. Among the successors of the Lutici Federation, the noble and priestly caste exercised power through the people's assembly. Here, military, political, and sacred functions were exercised by one man. The temple at Rethra, dedicated to their chief god Svarožić, served as the center of the federation and was where meetings took place.

The Slav rebellion of 983, which drove out the political and religious representatives of the Ottonian Empire, and during which the Bishoprics of Havelberg and Brandenburg and numerous churches and monasteries were destroyed or plundered, started with the Lutici. The emperor and his margraves were powerless against this uprising. At the start of the eleventh century, the Lutici Federation, in turn, became valued allies of the German kings Henry II and Conrad II in their disputes with Poland. However, by the twelfth century, the Lutici were no longer able to withstand Pomeranian and Obotrite expansion.

For many years, the Obotrite tribal princes were able to maintain their rule in alliances with the Frankish Empire and Denmark. From the time of Prince Nakon (960s), who resided in Mecklenburg Castle, we see an uninterrupted princely dynasty, which stabilized the Obotrite state based on castles, taxes, and military service. Gottschalk, the first baptized Obotrite prince, established a bishopric in Mecklenburg in the eleventh century, and he had monasteries and churches built on the properties of other castles as well. This process of Christianization and consolidation of rule was, however, interrupted by the aristocracy, which was allied with the Lutici and maintained its allegiance to the pagan cults. Gottschalk's son Henry, who returned from Danish exile in 1090, managed to reassert the power lost by his father. He built a favorably situated residence at Liubice ("Old Lübeck") in the western

region of his territorial dominion and tried to increase its prestige by
minting coins.[10]

Written confirmation of a Polish state federation has come down
to us from the 960s. It is presumed that rule became consolidated in
the ninth century among the tribe of Polans, who were agricultural-
ists (in Polish, pole=field), in the region of the later Greater Poland. The
name Poloni or Polani is first mentioned in the sources at the turn of
the tenth to the eleventh century, which probably means the territorial dominion of the Polish princes. Neither a tribe nor a land is mentioned in the sources, only the name of a ruler, Misaca or Mescheqqo.
This may refer to Mieszko I (ca. 940–992), against whom the margrave
Gero fought in the name of the Ottonian Empire. Mieszko was also
mentioned by a Jewish merchant from Spain, Ibrahim ibn Ja'kub, who
traveled throughout the Slavic lands. He reported on a certain Mescheqqo, the King of the North, whose empire bordered the Old Prussians, the Kievan Rus', and Bohemia—the land of Prince Boleslav, in
Prague. He also reported on Mieszko's war with the "Ubaba" in the
northwest, which undoubtedly meant the Wolinians, whose trade em-
porium Mieszko coveted. Consolidation of rule in the area of the Polans has been confirmed archaeologically by the discovery of settlements. Not only were numerous new fortifications built in Greater
Poland (Giecz, Gniezno, Kruszwica, Ląd, Ostrów Lednicki, Poznań), but
the populations became more concentrated in their surroundings. The
fortified castles had more than just a military function. They also developed into administrative centers and collection points for taxes and
services from the local population. This arrangement was presumably
the germ from which the population was organized into an early feudal
system to maintain the military apparatus.

The defeat by Margrave Gero led to Mieszko's integration into the
empire's system of rule, which, however, he attempted to balance out
by entering into a marriage alliance with Bohemia. But the prerequisite for this marriage was his conversion to Christianity. Bohemian military support eventuated in Mieszko's triumph over the Wolinians in
the battle for control over the mouth of the Oder. At the same time, he
consolidated his position after the death of his wife Dobrawa, in 977,
by marrying Oda, daughter of Dietrich of Haldensleben, a Saxon margrave. In return, he even supported the empire against the rebellion of

the Elbe Slavs. However, his successor and son from his first marriage, Bolesław Chrobry (967–1025), was forced to defend his succession and territory from Saxon claims before being able to play a central role east of the Elbe.[11]

Balts and Finns

The Old Prussians in the former East Prussia, together with the Couronians in Courland, the Semigallians between the Gulf of Riga and what is now Lithuania to the north, as well as the Latgallians, Selonians, and Lithuanians, all belonged to the Baltic linguistic community. The Latgallians, the largest Baltic tribe, settled the eastern and northeastern parts of what is today Latvia, while the Selonians lived in the area between the Daugava River and the Lithuanian tribes. These tribes lived in the Lithuanian highlands (*Aukštaiten*) around Vilnius and in the western lowlands (*Žemaiten*). The Baltic area of settlement originally stretched from Eastern Pomeranian in the west to the Valdai Hills and the upper Volga in the east and as far as Pripyat in the south. This area was, however, greatly diminished after the expansion of the Germanic tribes in the first centuries of the Common Era, and of the Slavs later on.

In the north, the Baltic tribes joined with the Baltic Finns, who belonged to the Finno-Ugric linguistic family. While the Finns and Karelians inhabited the area between the Gulf of Finland and the settlement areas of the Sami in the north, the Estonian tribes were distributed from the Baltic coast southward to Lake Peipus, and on the islands of Ösel (Saaremaa) and Dagö (Hiiumaa).[12] The Livonians, finally, lived south of there, at the lower course of the Daugava and as far as the Couronian areas, where they were the ruling caste. The Baltic Finnish tribes, the Voti and the Vepsians, lived in what is today northwestern Russia.

Compared with the Slavic and Germanic tribes, Baltic tribal society appears to have been less hierarchical and thus more egalitarian. Aside from slaves, mainly women and children who were abducted from neighboring peoples, the society consisted mostly of free farmers. Different approaches to social structure—possibly patterned after Scandinavian models—are to be found most prominently in western coastal regions and later in the eastern Latvian areas and in Lithuania. Here,

perhaps influenced by the Rus', the power of the tribal chieftain and
the territory ruled by him was greater than in the West. Fortified hill
settlements in Lithuania are an expression of this hierarchical pattern;
such places are much less numerous among the Latvians and Estonians.
The hilltop fortifications, which would be transformed into church par-
ishes (*Kirchspiele*) during the period of Christianization, were integrated
into larger tribal or chieftain districts at the turn of the millennium,
which meant that a single chieftain could rule over a territory with
several hilltop fortifications. Several of the large fortifications, such as
Jersika (Gerzike) along the middle stretch of the Daugava River, developed into large settlements in which lived the chieftain and his retinue. In the thirteenth century, the city of Kernave, in Lithuania, is
estimated to have had as many as three thousand inhabitants.[13]

In the ninth century, Estonians and Couronians were forced to defend themselves against the claims of Swedish Vikings—until they
themselves attacked the Swedish coast and, in the eleventh and twelfth
centuries and in 1187 even captured the capital city of Sigtuna. In the
tenth century, however, the Novgorod Varangians penetrated Estonian
territory to force them to pay tribute. In about 1030, the Varangians
took the Estonian Dorpat castle, and the Russians built Jur'ev Castle to
subjugate the Estonians. In 1061, however, the Russians were forced to
relinquish control. Both the Semigallians and Couronians came under
Russian pressure, while the northern Latgallians were forced to pay
tribute to the princes of Pskov, and the eastern Latgallians and Livonians
were forced to pay the Daugava Polocks. In the thirteenth century,
finally, the Danes conquered northern Estonia, while the Lithuanians
penetrated the regions of the Livonians and Latgallians from the south,
plunging them into war and a state of despoilment.[14]

The population was primarily agricultural, and over time they
switched from slash-and-burn agriculture to a two-field system. The
narrow strip fields that resulted determined the structure of their villages. In addition to agriculture, the farmers also raised cattle and
hunted, fished, kept bees, and practiced forestry. The Couronians, Semigallians, and Estonians, along with the Livonians, engaged in piracy
as well as trade, and much like the Vikings and Slavs, they acted as
go-betweens in the trade between the Muslim world and the Baltic and

North Seas. The Old Prussians, who lived on the Sambia Peninsula, had an especially desirable commodity in the form of amber.

Trade

Seamen and traders shaped the Baltic region by structuring it around multiethnic trading centers. As a result, a variety of trade zones arose. These included Scania in the western Baltic; the southern Baltic coast to the mouth of the Oder; the region between the mouth of the Oder and that of the Vistula, including Courland and the opposite-lying islands of Gotland and Öland; as well as the region between central Sweden and the Gulf of Finland.[15] Traders, shippers, and craftsmen from neighboring areas took part in this long-distance trade, which sometimes included trade in slaves. Frisians and Anglo-Saxons from the North Sea were among the traders as were Arab and Jewish merchants. The latter established contacts to the Arab world and by their reports were the first to draw attention to the Baltic region. Many trading centers prospered. The most important ones included Hedeby (Haithabu) at the end of the narrow Schlei Inlet (an important junction between North Sea and Baltic trade), Reric on the Bay of Wismar, Wolin at the mouth of the Oder, and Truso in the delta of the Vistula as well as Birka on Lake Mälaren, the island of Gotland, Staraya Ladoga in Russia, which was the relay point between trade in the Baltic Sea and the Black Sea. In addition, numerous smaller, often only transiently active trading centers included Menzlin on the lower Peene River and Ralswiek on the island of Rügen. Both are known only from archaeological digs. In Menzlin, for example, burial practices that included ship-like graves attest to the presence of Scandinavians in close contact with the local Slavic population, which in turn attests to the multiethnicity of even such small trading centers.

Hedeby was distinguished by an extensive area of settlement consisting of open hall houses, a harbor with jetties and palisades, as well as a semicircular defensive wall to protect against attacks from land. As in other places, trade was conducted on the jetties or landing stages, as evidenced by small archaeological finds such as coins and weights. Craftsmen in Hedeby processed imported raw materials and half-finished products. The extent of their trade was immense: cloth came from Friesland and ceramics, glass, and weapons from the Rhineland. The millstones from the Eiffel region of Germany were presumably shipped from Dorestad, while mercury and tin probably arrived from the Iberian Peninsula or England. Scandinavia supplied soapstone, whetstone, and iron, while amber arrived from the eastern Baltic. Judging from the burial practices, the ethnic composition was similarly varied, consisting of Frisians, Saxons, Slavs, and Swedes, with Danes predominating.[16] Farther to the east, Birka, on Lake Mälaren, played a role similar to that of Hedeby in trade from western Europe across the Baltic to the trading center on Lake Ladoga and on to the Volga Bulgars and the Muslim world. Craftsmen produced wares for long-distance trade as well as for local consumption, which is why Birka can be viewed as an early city center.[17] But it was also subject to attack from Danish Vikings. In about the year 1000, the island of Gotland superseded Birka. Unlike the Svear and Varangians, its farmer-merchants did not actually settle in Russia but traded seasonally and returned to the island each year. Here they hoarded the silver coins that they had amassed, approximately a quarter of the silver then circulating in the entire Baltic region and Russia, much of which originated in western European, especially in German, mints.

The importance of Ralswiek, on the southern coast of the Baltic, is evidenced by the more than eight hundred burial mounds and sailing vessels found there, along with more than two thousand Arabian coins. Other trading centers are mentioned in chronicles. Reric, which was probably located near Gross Strömkendorf on the Bay of Wismar, is a case in point. We have learned that in 808, Danish king Göttrik (Gudfred) resettled the local Reric merchants to Hedeby. And Adam of Bremen called Wolin the "largest of all cities" in Europe and stressed the presence of Slavs, Saxons, Greeks, barbarians, and members of other tribes. House plans, burial customs, and found objects also point to Scandinavian and Frisian traders. Wolin appears to have been so attractive that both the Polish state and the Danish king attempted to annex this trading center under the pretext of fighting piracy.

In fact, the line between trade and piracy was a rather fluid one, especially where intrinsically valuable objects such as slaves were concerned. Thus, for example, Slavic trader-pirates presumably stole gold

Figure 1. The Hiddensee Treasure, ca. 950

ornaments from Hiddensee and Peenemünde, which had been produced by goldsmiths in Scandinavia in the tenth century. Regular goods, on the other hand, included grain, horses, honey, wax, pelts, and amber. Weapons, cloth, and millstones came from the West, while soapstone and soapstone containers from Scandinavia. Salt was also mined or panned along the coasts of the North Sea and the Atlantic and then traded. In addition, local and regional craftsmen produced other objects such as combs.

Archaeological findings and written reports provide ample evidence of the extent of Baltic trade, while datable caches of coins allow us to draw conclusions about the volume of trade and shifts in trade routes. As one might expect, historians are very interested in the massive hordes of coins found in the Baltic region. For instance, the increase in Arab *dirham* coins toward the end of the eighth century reflects the increasing trade with the Arab world. Whereas most of the *dirham* coins have been found in the hinterland of the Old Prussian harbor of Truso, Arab coins tended to flow toward Sweden and Gotland in the ninth century. It is likely that the advance and settlement of the Varangians in Russia was responsible for this change. Silver coins from the central Asian Samanid Empire, on the other hand, were hoarded in large quantities in the northwestern Russian trading centers of Staraya Ladoga, Novgorod, Polock, and Pskov, and in the territory of the Volga Bulgars.

The finds often contain hack-silver, which, together with the scales and weights, which are sometimes found in close proximity, gives evidence of value determined by weight and trade in weighted coin and which may possibly have been influenced by Arab weighting systems.[18] Less common was the influx of Asian money into western Europe, and few caches of *dirhams* have been found even in Jutland. On the other hand, this could indicate a positive trade balance between the Baltic region and the North Sea region. It is also possible that Arab silver was smelted and reminted in Hedeby and elsewhere. In any case, toward the end of the tenth century, Arab silver became much less abundant in the Baltic region, and it completely ceased to flow into Russia after 1015.[19] The cessation of *dirham* production in central Asia may have been the reason. At the same time, silver began to move in the other direction. As a result of danegeld levies and more intensive contact, large quantities of English pennies began to flow into the Baltic region. In addition, the discovery of new silver deposits in the Harz Mountains, especially in Rammelsberg, near Goslar, and in the Schwarzwald, made possible the coining of deniers on a massive scale. The so-called Otto Adelheid pfennigs that were now minted made their way along with other deniers to Hungary, Poland, Estonia, Russia, and especially Scandinavia, to be exchanged for pelts, wax, honey, and slaves. Here they were presumably hoarded, but some undoubtedly made their way into commerce again. Thus, Swedish hoards from the time of the Vikings contain about 80,000 Arab, 45,000 English, and 85,000 German coins, evidence of a regular inflow of coinage. Moreover, the coins found in Germany indicate that deniers were produced at about 150 mints. Because the coins found in domestic German hoards are relatively rare, they have, given their function, been designated as *deniers for long-distance trade.*[20]

The epoch of the long-distance trade deniers came to an end when the need for money increased domestically in the twelfth and thirteenth centuries as cities were founded in Germany and the city elders began minting money themselves. And with that, these coins ceased to flow into northern and eastern areas as well. The deniers became lighter and were no longer accepted everywhere, only where they had been minted. Something not dissimilar occurred in the Baltic region, where the multiethnic trading centers were transformed into the political and administrative centers that were set up by princes who were coming into power in various territories. These were then integrated into the overall regional economy. The displacement of international trade from Hedeby to Schleswig and from Birka to Sigtuna, Paviken to Visby, Staraya Ladoga to Novgorod, Truso to Danzig, and Wolin to Stettin are only a few examples illustrating the effect of urban development in the Baltic region.[21]

Society and Culture

Among the Obotrites and Veleti and their successors, tribal authority in military, political, and religious affairs was in the hands of the nobility and a priestly caste. Viking and Baltic tribes exhibited comparable forms of social organization. In addition to their role as chieftains, large Viking landowners also took on priestly duties in their districts. This included presiding over the thing, the community governing assembly, and acting in the capacity of judge, making decisions in consultation with the thing. The chieftains had their own contingent of warriors, whom they had to satisfy with plunder and trade. The chieftains fought among themselves for influence, hoping to be viewed as petty kings if not kings outright. Subordinate to the chieftains were the free farmers, who engaged in agriculture and cattle breeding. They frequently became independent of their tribes, achieving economic power and respect as a result of land acquisitions or by founding villications.[22] Such farmers kept laborers and slaves (thralls) to help with the farm work. A laborer or slave might have been captured or bought at a slave market. But such involuntary labor may also have been the result of debt or punishment. Over the course of time, another caste developed intermediate between the free farmers and the slaves, that of freed slaves and their families.[23] This sort of social structure was only weakly developed among the Baltic tribes, however, where free

farmers and slaves predominated. Only later do we see tribal chieftains
with their attendant rule over territory and people.

Social caste is also reflected in the material culture, where we find
the graves of chieftains both among the Vikings and among the Slavs.
Swords, which often came from the Rhineland, are especially common
in the graves of upper-caste warriors. The blades were made of dama-
scened steel, and the artfully shaped handles and pommels are often
identified by their creator. For example, a sword from Liepe (near Ebers-
walde) bears the name Hiltipreht. In other cases, the name of the smith
is identified, such as Ulfberth. However, metal works did exist in the
Baltic region, as did communities of smiths.[24] The swords became the
basis for sagas, which in the Nordic tradition were often inscribed on
rune stones. But swords were not the only artifact that demonstrates
class. Upper-caste warriors also rode horses and wore helmets and
coats of mail, which gave them a decided advantage in battle over foot
soldiers.[25]

From archaeological findings, we also know that music, often played
with rattles, pipes, and flutes made of wood and bone, was an important
part of social life. Stringed instruments and shawms probably made their
way to the western Slavs from Byzantium and the Arab caliphates.[26]

The religious beliefs of the Vikings, Slavs, and Balts were quite
similar. Most of the tribes had a primary god, attended by secondary
gods or even a family of gods. Odin was the main god of the Vikings, a
role played by Svantevit among the Slavs. Both gods rode horses and
were attended by their retinue. Whereas, according to legend, Odin rode
the eight-legged stallion Sleipnir, the priests of Svantevit read the
divine oracle from the hoof prints of Svantevit's wondrous white steed.
The hammer-wielding Thor was the Scandinavian god of thunder,
while Perun and Perkunas played that role for the Slavs and Balts. Taara
was the comparable god for the Estonians. In addition, the Veleti wor-
shiped the sun or smith god Svarožić. Actual religious practices, on the
other hand, varied. Whereas the Balts worshipped their gods in sacred
groves, especially oak groves, the Slavs and Scandinavians built tem-
ples and carved statues. In addition, traveling merchants and warriors
carried small cult figures with them, so-called pocket gods, and wore
hammers of Thor as amulets.[27]

Unfortunately, unlike the Scandinavians, the Baltic Slavs and Balts left behind no literature or even rune stones. The rune stones of the Scandinavians generally originated during the period of Christianization, but even before then they often scratched runes onto unusually situated stones and sometimes decorated them. Several inscriptions give evidence of orally transmitted poetry about gods and heroes, not dissimilar from those later written down in Iceland. Thus, on the famous Ardre stone (no. VIII) on the island of Gotland, we see Odin riding on Sleipnir toward Valhalla with a fallen warrior. The cultural and social life of the Vikings is also depicted on the rune stones, which landowners, mostly families of high social status, often commissioned. We begin to see picture stones in the fifth and sixth centuries, depicting rosettes, spiral wheels, longboats with rowers, snakes, and dragons. Larger stones from the eighth to tenth centuries are laid out in horizontal rows and depict scenes of Viking life and of the gods. In these, manned Viking boats alternate with fabulous creatures and depictions of battles. Many of the rune stones are memorial stones to fallen warriors, in some cases commissioned by wives, who retained their heritance claims based on the inscriptions dedicated to their husbands. The later rune stones with their decorative drawings reflect the lives of pagan heroes, sometimes depicting the confrontation between the Nordic legends and Christianity. Often, however, they merely show the cross as a Christian motif with intertwined ornamentation. Some believe that this labyrinthine motif may have been influenced by the Homeric epics. Rune stones have been found, to the west, in Greenland, England, and the Faroe Islands and, to the southeast, along the Dnieper, and they attest to the extent of Viking travels and influence.[28]

But rune stones are not the sole evidence of cultural exchange in the Baltic region. Archeologists have found a wealth of material during the second half of the twentieth century that attests not only to relations between the Baltic region and the Anglo-Irish world, but also with Asia and the empires of the Bulgars and Khazars on the Volga, and in late antiquity with the Mediterranean basin. During this time, decorative patterns, such as braidwork, tendrils, and animal elements, began to appear throughout Europe, which were then reworked into local variants. At the same time as the so-called Viking style was influenced by the cultures of Ireland, England, and the Frankish Empire, Scandinavian and Byzantine motifs made their way into the Slavic regions. Snake and animal motifs played a more prominent role here, and for a long time they continued to be used on clothing among the Baltic and Finnish tribes.[29]

The particular provenance of an artifact (bracelets, for example) is often indeterminable because of the similarities in decorative and stylistic techniques from one region to another. In some cases, earrings made by Slavic silversmiths in Pomerania exhibit Byzantine influences, which must have been transmitted northward by way of the Danube region and the Great Moravian Empire. Trade spread this type of earring onward to Bornholm and Gotland. Arab jewelry patterns reached the Baltic region by way of Bolghar, the capital of the Volga Bulgars, where they were copied. Other articles of jewelry, such as temple rings, remained limited to the Slavic portions of the southern Baltic coast. Whenever we find them in Scandinavia, as we have in a woman's grave in Gotland, it is to be inferred that the woman was of Slavic origin. In addition, the rings were valued for their silver content, which explains their presence in unearthed troves. By the same token, Scandinavian clasps, which were used to both ornament and fasten items of clothing, are found in the graves of Scandinavians along the southern coast of the Baltic. Of special interest is the production in that region of combs and pottery for export, which traders and itinerant craftsmen brought to Scandinavia. The impetus for this type of pottery, which was first discovered at the Feldberg excavations in Mecklenburg and called "Meissen porcelain" because of its high quality, came from the Slavic tribes that were settled in the south and had gained access to pottery from antiquity. The Feldberg pottery developed into what is known as the Fresendorf variant, and in this form became something of a brand for the Slavic tribes, which was then copied in Scandinavia.[30]

The use and spread of combs is also a sign of cultural exchange, in this case between the North Sea and the Baltic. Comb makers in the Rhineland and Friesland, using ancient models, specialized in the production of decorative hair combs made of antler. They were first brought to the Baltic region by Frisian merchants but were soon produced in Viking trading centers, such as Hedeby, Birka, and Staraya Ladoga as well as on the southern coast of the Baltic. This, naturally, greatly diminished the need to import combs. It is presumed that Frisian comb makers settled in the trading centers along with the merchants, whereas Slavic potters continued to produce their earthenware there. The first mint masters in Hedeby probably came from Friesland as well, while Scandinavian carpenters built houses in the traditional stave construction, which were in marked contrast to the local blockhouses.[31]

The introduction and reception of western European technologies intensified over the following centuries during the missionary period and the eastern expansion of German settlement described in Chapter 2.

CHAPTER TWO

The Christian Mission and the Settlement of the Land

Focus on Eldena

The Christian mission in the Baltic region profoundly changed the physical landscape of the region. Fortified castles were built, as were churches and monasteries, which increasingly served as the focal point of new religious life. Eldena Abbey, for example, was built in 1199 in a place where Danish, Slavic, and German interests on the Baltic coast intersected. After the conquest of the island of Rügen, the Danish crown attempted to secure its new regions in Pomerania by founding monasteries. In the 1170s, with help from the Cistercian monks at Esrom Abbey, in Denmark, they built monasteries in Dargun and Kolbatz, both in the Slavic area of settlement. Out of fear of attack by the Brandenburg margrave, the monks at Dargun moved their monastery to the coast, where the prince of Rügen, a vassal of the Danish king, offered them protection. Furthermore, the Danish settlement of Wiek was within easy striking distance across the bay, and Denmark itself could be reached by boat on the open sea. In 1207, Prince Jaromar of Rügen granted rights to the Eldena saltworks, which were already being used by the monastery, as well as five villages and the forest in the still unsettled border area between the principalities of Rügen and Pomerania. Along with that, they were granted the privilege of settling Danes, Germans, and Slavs, and the right to open a tavern (*Krug*) in accordance with Slavic, German, or Danish law. A monastery market was opened in the area controlled by the abbey, which was mentioned in 1241 as a *forum mercationis* (trading center). The city of Greifswald grew from these humble beginnings. To this day, the ruins of Eldena, which "local artist" Caspar David Friedrich painted so often, reflect the architecture and ornamentation of their Danish origins.[1]

Figure 2. Eldena Abbey near Greifswald

Pagan Religion and the Christian Mission

It has become conventional wisdom to view the Baltic region as the borderlands of medieval Christianity into which the Western world expanded, transforming the local cultures by conquest, colonization, and Christianization.[2] Some historians even speak of a "clash of cultures" and base this view on the crusades mounted in the twelfth and thirteenth centuries in the eastern part of the Baltic. By doing so, they accept the Christian perspective of the chroniclers and fail to see the often multifaceted exchanges that took place in the Baltic region, or perhaps more precisely, between the world of the North Sea and that of the Baltic, where, for example, the Scandinavian kings awakened in the populace a willingness to accept Christianity.

The mission to the Vikings originated with the Franks, who at the beginning of the ninth century had subjugated the Saxons south of the Elbe and forcibly converted them. As a result, the Vikings, and especially the Danes living in Jutland, became the immediate neighbors of

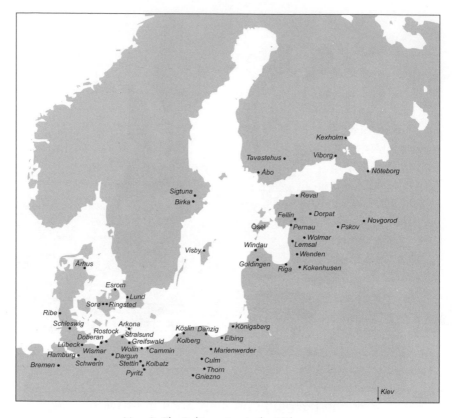

Map 2. The Baltic region in the 13th century

the Frankish Empire, although the areas north of the Elbe belonged to
no one. Whereas the Danish king, Göttrik (died 814), tried to fight off
the expansion of the Franks, others, like his son Harald (died ca. 846),
tried to find support among the Franks for their battles for succession.
Because the Franks played their opponents off against each other,
Harald's right to rule was forever questioned by his rivals. At the behest
of King Louis the Pious (778–840), he therefore decided to be baptized in
Mainz, and he returned to Denmark accompanied by a monk named
Ansgar (801–865). In spite of his mission, Harald's rule collapsed along
with his missionary venture. At the request of the Svear king, the now
unemployed Ansgar was sent to Birka, where he converted the king's
representative and persuaded him to build a church.[3] As a result of this
success, Ansgar was given the new bishopric in Hamburg, and he was

soon elevated to archbishop. His new position was short-lived, however, because in 845, Danish Vikings plundered Hamburg and destroyed his church. In Birka, too, Christian influence was soon stamped out.

Despite these setbacks, the pope gave Ansgar a new archbishopric in Bremen, from which he attempted a new mission to Denmark. This time he was welcomed with open arms and received permission to erect a church in Hedeby. The Danish king, Horic, even supported Ansgar in reestablishing the mission in Birka. The king also permitted a new church to be built in Ribe, although he refused to be baptized. Step by step, the Archbishopric of Hamburg-Bremen was able to assert and expand its religious power by the creation of bishoprics in Schleswig, Ribe, and Århus.

Nonetheless, its influence on the population remained limited. Babies were baptized with any regularity only in the British Isles, where the Vikings came into contact with Christian rulers; however, baptisms were often followed by defections from Christianity. Nonetheless, a number of Danish priests and monks, among them three archbishops, were active in England and felt the need to baptize their countrymen. These Danish-English missionaries also preached in Jutland and in Norway, which had previously remained outside the sphere of the Frankish mission. The process of Christianization received an important boost as a result of the conversion of Danish kings, who accepted Christ in an attempt to stabilize their rule. One of the first Danish kings to be baptized, in 965, was Harald "Bluetooth" Gormsson (ca. 935–985), who attempted to persuade his subjects to destroy their pagan idols. The resistance to this move was led by Harald's son, Sweyn Forkbeard (ca. 960–1014), who refused to accept the authority of the bishops of Hamburg-Bremen above that of the Danish church. His son and successor, Canute the Great (ca. 985 or 995–1035), who ruled in Denmark and England, was the first to encourage the mission. He evidenced his faith by visiting Rome and praying at the graves of the apostles. Canute won English bishops to his mission and founded dioceses in Denmark, but he did so without freeing himself from the supremacy of the church authorities in Hamburg-Bremen. His successor, the tyrannical Harthacnut (ca. 1018–1042), a ruler who was beatified despite his brutality, managed to set up an archbishopric in the diocese of Lund, which was independent of Hamburg-Bremen.

In Sweden, Olof Skötkonung (ca. 980–1022) was the first Christian king and was baptized at the turn of the eleventh century—before that, Christianity had already spread to Birka and Sigtuna, while pagan rituals were still practiced in other parts of the country. The first missionary king of Norway, Haakon Haraldsson (ca. 920–961), also known as Haakon the Good, brought his Christian faith back with him from England. His mission was, however, unsuccessful. Olaf Tryggvason (ca. 960–1000), who was also baptized in England, returned to Norway in the 990s and attempted to enforce the Christian faith by violence. Olaf II Haraldsson (995–1030), also known as St. Olaf, was more successful; he was able to build a church organization with the help of English bishops. This administrative effort created the framework for a unified kingdom; the kings of Sweden and Denmark were able to unite their territories in the same way at about the same time. The Orthodox influence of Byzantium was palpable east of the Gulf of Bothnia from Kiev to Novgorod, at least inasmuch as the paganism of the Balts and Baltic Finns did not predominate.[4]

Among the Slavs living between the Elbe and Oder Rivers, the Lutici Federation constituted the center of paganism. The Lutici put up considerable resistance to the missionaries, which culminated in the great Slavic revolt of 983. They were not, however, able to maintain themselves for long against the power of the German Empire and Denmark, let alone pressure from neighboring Obotrite and Pomeranian princes.

Over time, the Obotrite chieftains entered into alliances with the empire and Denmark. However, centrifugal forces, especially resistance to centralization and Christianization, continued to prevent state consolidation, and so in the twelfth century the Obotrite state was forced to recognize the supremacy of the empire. At the same time, the overall political climate had changed, especially after the Saxon duke, the later king and emperor Lothar of Supplinburg, began to annex various Slavic territories between the Elbe and Oder Rivers into his territorial domain. To this end, he transferred the area that would later become Mark Brandenburg to the Ascanian Albert the Bear (ca. 1100–1170), and in 1129 he gave the Obotrite territory in fief to the Dane Canute Lavard (1096–1131). Canute, who was later murdered, was followed by the Obotrite princes Pribislav (died ca. 1156) and Niklot (1090–1160), who were dependent on Lothar, who was now emperor of the German Empire. In alliance with Count Adolf II of Holstein, Niklot was able to retain his properties, which extended as far as the Peene River, even during the Wendish crusade of 1147. He did so by attempting, with papal blessings, to extend the German territorial rule of Albert the Bear and Henry the Lion (1129–1195) at the expense of the Slavs. However, Niklot did not survive the joint action undertaken against him in 1160 by Henry and Danish king Valdemar I (1131–1182). Nonetheless, Niklot's son Pribislav, who had converted to Christianity, was given this domain as a fiefdom by Henry, becoming his vassal. His domain was centered in the region around Mecklenburg, while Henry's ally, Gunzelin of Hagen, took the county of Schwerin. In 1171, Pribislav founded Doberan Abbey and provided land for the Bishopric of Schwerin, which Henry the Lion had transferred there from Mecklenburg. Pribislav's son and successor, Borwin, married a daughter of Henry's and expanded his domain, as a result of which the Niklotides became the ruling dynasty of Mecklenburg.

For many years, the Rani, who had settled on Rügen, managed to avoid Christianization. They had become wealthy through trade and piracy, with the majority of their riches flowing as tribute to the Temple of Svantevit, in Arkona. Despite their veneration of this pagan god and the great importance of their priestly caste in making political decisions, the Rani had few qualms about entering into alliances with the German and Danish kings against the Lutici, Obotrites, and Pomeranians. In 1168, however, the Danes conquered Arkona and forced the princes of Rügen to accept their land in fief from the Danish king. The newly formed church organization was then transferred to the Danish Bishopric of Roskilde. This Slavic princely house came to an end in 1325 with the deaths of Vitslav III (ca. 1265–1325) and his son Jaromar. As a result, Rügen was given to Duke Vartislav IV (ca. 1290–1326) of Pomerania-Wolgast.

Pomerania (and the region of the Pomeranians) was a coveted objective, fought over by the Poles, the German Empire, and Denmark. The margraves of Brandenburg also had designs on it. From the written sources we have available to us, such as Otto of Bamberg's travelogues, it seems that the Pomeranians were not really organized into federations of tribes. Rather, the individual tribes became concentrated in "early town communities" along the Baltic coast. During the tenth century, the Pomeranian areas of settlement were integrated into the empire of Mieszko I of Poland, and a fortified castle was then built in Danzig (Gdańsk) to protect the mouth of the Vistula. In 1000, Pomerania was integrated religiously into the state of the Piasts, when the new Bishopric of Kolberg (Kołobrzeg) was subordinated to the Archdiocese of Gniezno (Gnesen). Despite intermittent independence from the Poles—in 1046 we see a certain Prince Siemysl—it seems that starting in the early twelfth century, the Polish crown under Bolesław Krzywousty (1086–1138), also called Wrymouth, put increasing pressure on the territory of the Pomeranians.

The Polish army conquered Stettin (Szeczecin) in 1091 (and again in 1113), and the Piasts used Christianization as a means to integrate or annex Stettin into their domain. After an initial missionary attempt by a Spanish monk foundered in Wolin despite impassioned sermons, Bolesław, with the consent of the pope and emperor, called on Bishop Otto of Bamberg. Otto had previously been chaplain at the Polish court, and so he had the requisite knowledge of both language and country. On two missionary trips between 1124 and 1128, he tried to introduce Christianity into Pomerania with sermons and mass baptisms. In 1124–1125, he visited Pyritz (Pyrzyce) and Cammin (Kamień Pomorski), the seat of the Pomeranian duke, as well as the trading centers of Wolin, Stettin, and Kolberg, where he had churches built. The conversion of Domizlaus, a member of the Stettin aristocracy, brought short-term results, but the influence of pagan priests in the people's assemblies quickly vitiated those advances.

On his second trip, Otto—now supported by King Lothar—visited the western areas of Pomerania, among others the cities of Demmin, Gützkow, and Usedom, where he induced the leaders of the Slavs who were settled there to undergo baptism. Nonetheless, it took until 1140 before the time was ripe to establish a bishopric in Wolin. Duke Vartislav, however, was unable to free himself from Polish rule. In addition, like the Obotrites in Mecklenburg, he feared the power of the Danes. The Piast state collapsed after the death of Bolesław, in 1138, after which pressure on Pomerania diminished. In its place, Denmark and Henry the Lion, who had already brought the land of the Obotrites and Rügen under their control, intensified their grip. Danish influence on the continent is evidenced by the foundation of monasteries. Danish monks from Esrom Abbey founded Dargun Abbey (near Demmin), and in 1173–1174 Kolbatz Abbey, southwest of Stettin. The Dargun monks founded Hilda Abbey (Eldena), in 1199, where they sought refuge from the conflict between Denmark and Brandenburg.

After Henry the Lion lost his title of Duke of Saxony and Bavaria— he had denied his support to Emperor Frederick I (Barbarossa) for his Italian campaigns—a power vacuum resulted along the Baltic coast. In 1185, the Danes made Duke Bogislav I a Danish vassal and demanded payment of an annual tribute, which was secured by taking hostages. Because Mecklenburg had come under Danish control, Danish sovereignty now extended from Holstein to Pomerania and was recognized by King Frederick II in 1214. But Denmark had its eyes on the eastern Baltic coast, where it contended against Sweden and the Livonian Brothers of the Sword over control of Finland, Estonia, and Livonia. Danish fleets attacked Finland in 1191 and 1202, Estonia in 1194 and 1197, and Prussia in 1210. In 1206, King Valdemar II (1170–1241) and the archbishop of Lund, Andreas Sunesen (ca. 1167–1228) sailed to Ösel, mission privilege in hand, to force the local inhabitants to accept Danish sovereignty and Christianity. After Valdemar had supported the mission of Bishop Christian of Oliva (ca. 1180–1245) among the Old Prussians, he turned his attention to Estonia, in 1219, having received a privilege from Pope Honorius III, which promised him whatever pagan lands he conquered. It was said that the Danish army saw a vision of a cross in the heavens as they conquered the Estonians. The cross motif was later symbolized in the Danish flag, the *Dannebrog*. The Estonians called the place where Valdemar built a castle after the castle name, Tallinn, meaning "castle of the Danes," while the old name of the surrounding countryside, Rävala, lives on in Danish, Swedish, and German as Reval, which was the city's name from the thirteenth century until 1918. Danish power continued to expand, and for some years even Bishop Albert of Riga and the Livonian Brothers of the Sword came under Danish protection as vassals and swore an oath of fealty.

Missionary work had begun in Livonia in the 1180s when the German Augustinian canon Meinhard (died 1196) started to preach. However, it was not until Albert of Riga (ca. 1165–1229), who came to Livonia as a missionary bishop, that churches began to be built in the region. These activities included the founding of the city of Riga, in

1201, by merchants and pilgrims, and the establishment of the Livonian bishopric at the mouth of the Daugava. Albert and his coworkers
founded the Livonian Brothers of the Sword (*Fratres militie Christi Li-
voniae*), a military order that conquered Livonia and received additional
land in fief from the emperor. However, the Livonian Brothers maintained their independence only until 1237 when, as a consequence of
a devastating defeat against the Lithuanians in 1236, they were incorporated into the Order of Teutonic Knights, located in Prussia.

The Teutonic Order was a Christian military order founded in Acre,
in the Holy Land, at the end of the twelfth century. It was directly under
the control of the pope, and its original purpose was to assist and protect Christian pilgrims. In addition to its activities in the Holy Land,
the Teutonic Order was, with the support of the pope and emperor, given
a new mission in Prussia, where Polish Cistercians and Bishop Christian had been unsuccessful in converting the Old Prussians, the Baltic
tribes that inhabited Prussia. Because the Old Prussians regularly raided
neighboring Polish lands, Conrad I of Masovia called upon the Teutonic
Order to help in his fight against the pagans, and for this service he ceded
them the Culm (Chełmno) Land. The Old Prussians, who practiced po-
lygamy and bought and stole women, lived in scattered tribes. Between
1221 and 1223, crusader armies led by Polish princes had all been unsuccessful in suppressing them; each time the knights retreated, the
Old Prussians won back whatever territories had been wrested from
them. But the Teutonic Order, which from the beginning had as its goal
the conquest of the land, proved the more unyielding foe. In 1231, the
first group of Teutonic knights crossed the Vistula and erected a fortified camp, which they named Thorn (Toruń). This was followed in 1232
by the fortified castles at Culm, and at Marienwerder (Kwidzyn), in 1233.
From here they continued up the Vistula, and in 1237 the knights
reached the coast of the Baltic and founded Elbing (Elbląg). The order
then conquered other Old Prussian districts, and in 1255 they took the
Sambia Peninsula and the castle at Königsberg. After another Old Prussian rebellion, the Teutonic Order (with papal intermediation) guaranteed them their property under the condition that they accept the Christian faith and rule by the order. This so-called Christburg Peace was
broken, in 1260, when the Old Prussians rose up against the order but
were brutally defeated. At the end of the battles in 1283, the region con-

trolled by the order extended to the borders of pagan Lithuania. A large
portion of the subjugated Old Prussian population made its peace with
life under the Teutonic Order, and former chieftains and their descendants were even able to attain high positions in the order.

The Teutonic Order itself expanded beyond the borders of Prussia,
first acquiring Pomerelia. It did so in alliance with the Polish prince
Władysław Łokietek (1261–1333), also known as Władysław the Elbowhigh, who was attempting to unite the petty Polish principalities.
Władysław requested that the order assist him against Brandenburg,
which claimed dominion over the Baltic Sea. In 1308, the order drove
Brandenburg's knights from Danzig, but then, against Władysław's
wishes, the order established a base there permanently.

After the Teutonic Knights incorporated the Brothers of the Sword,
the order was kept busy in Livonia and Estonia as well. In 1242, their
attempt to extend their Livonian dominions eastward was throttled on
the ice of Lake Peipus by a Russian army under Alexander Nevsky
(1220–1263). After that defeat, they concentrated on consolidating their
rule, which was constantly challenged by the Couronians and by the
Semigallians, who were allied with Lithuania. In 1261, the order subjugated the island of Ösel, which meant that it now shared dominion
over northern Estonia with the Danish crown. This dominion seemed
consolidated—until exploitation by Danish and German landlords provoked an Estonian uprising, in 1343. Many manors were burnt to the
ground and their owners murdered. The Teutonic Order brutally suppressed the Estonians, and Denmark completely relinquished its claims
to Estonia when it sold Harrien (Harju) and Wierland (Virumaa) to the
order for 19,000 silver marks. With this sale, the rule of the Teutonic
Order was consolidated in the north, which in other places it shared
with the Archbishopric of Riga and other bishoprics. At this point, the
order was unable to make good on its ambitions in Lithuania. It did,
however, succeed in converting Prince Mindaugas to Christianity, in
1251, by supporting his expansion to the east. The Žemaiten region,
which was given to the order in exchange for its support and should
have provided it with a bridge between Prussia and Livonia, proved un-
controllable. Not until the fourteenth century did the order, with the
help of knights from western Europe, undertake annual campaigns, the
so-called Lithuanian Crusades, which, however, brought the Teutonic

Knights into confrontation with the militarily superior Lithuanian Gediminid dynasty.[5]

Denmark was not the only Scandinavian kingdom that took part in crusades and missions in the Baltic region. Sweden, which had suffered incursions along its coast by the Couronians, Estonians, and Finns, took revenge in the twelfth century by mounting Viking-like campaigns on the opposite shores. Some of these incursions—like a conjectured mid-century expedition by King Eric IX—were celebrated after the fact as the beginning of the Finnish mission. However, the mission probably started with merchants, fishermen, and peasants from Sweden and Åland, who settled in the area of Åbo.[6] It was more difficult, however, to convert the Tavastians and Karelians as the Orthodox Church and the princes of Novgorod were vying for their souls as well. The first Swedish military campaign, in 1240, under Birger Jarl (ca. 1200–1266), was foiled by Alexander of Novgorod on the Neva River (this victory earned him the epithet Nevsky), while a second expedition, in 1249, also under Birger, led to the subjugation of the Tavastians, which the Swedes then secured by building fortified castles. Another crusade to Karelia, which was celebrated in the *Erikskrönikan* (Chronicle of Eric), was undertaken in 1293 after receiving papal blessing. It led to the building of Viborg Castle. In the meantime, Swedish nobles took over the castles in Finland and were keen to secure the country by means of settlement. Novgorod, however, did not wish to relinquish its claims to Karelia and fortified its own castle, Korela (Kexholm in Swedish, Käkisalmi in Finnish). This arms race continued as the Russians placed the fortified Valaam Monastery on an island in Lake Ladoga, and the Swedes built Olavinlinna. In 1323, the military stalemate between Sweden and Novgorod was settled by the Treaty of Nöteborg, which ceded western Karelia to Sweden and eastern Karelia to Novgorod. At the same time, the two sides came to an agreement on an approximate border, which ran from the mouth of the Neva to the Gulf of Bothnia but that guaranteed Karelians access to fishing and hunting grounds, whichever side they lived on.[7]

The various territories that had been conquered during the northern crusades of the thirteenth century differed greatly in terms of their political structure. Sweden and Denmark secured their dominion over

Finland and Estonia by building fortified castles and establishing bishoprics, populating these with elites from the motherland. The situation in Livonia was complicated because five ecclesiastical territories contended with each other. These included the Archbishopric of Riga, whose archbishop was an imperial prince who ruled a region north of the Daugava that was separated by a strip of land from that controlled by the Teutonic Order. He also controlled the Bishoprics of Dorpat and Ösel-Wiek, which were also imperial fiefdoms, with the bishops exercising dominion. The small Bishopric of Courland, on the other hand, was incorporated into the order, which exercised sovereignty there. Overall, the Teutonic Order controlled the largest contiguous area, which extended from the Gulf of Finland to the Lithuanian border. After initially settling in Riga, the master of the order, in the fifteenth century, took up residence in Wenden (Cēsis), one of the sixty castles belonging to the order. The order ruled only within its territory, and in Harrien and Wierland it had to take the local knights into account, as they had been given their lands as vassals of the Danish crown. In addition, the Livonian Order was dependent on the decisions made by the grand master of the Teutonic Order, who confirmed the election of the master of the Livonians. The Livonian Order, which accepted no local recruits, initially recruited knights from Lower Saxony and then later from Westphalia and the Rhineland. By contrast, the Prussian knights of the order came primarily from central and southern Germany and from the Rhineland.[8]

Of all the mission territories that we have cited, Prussia was the area where the rule of the Teutonic Order was best organized. The reason for this was primarily that the order had acquired a closed area and did not have to fight off rivals for the rights of possession and dominion. Another factor was that its personnel, knights of the order who were sworn to celibacy, exercised their offices on a rotational basis as commanders (Komture) under the grand master or overseers (Vögte), without having to take family matters into account. The Bishoprics of Culm, Pomesania, and Samland were incorporated into the order as well, which meant that the brother priests of the order could function as bishops and canons. Only the Bishopric of Warmia (Ermland) was in a more independent position, although the grand master, who had since 1309 been residing in Marienburg, in Prussia, tried to install his friends as bishops. The brother priests were responsible not only for the spiritual care of the knights, but also for the countryside in general.[9]

Settlement of the Land

Like most of the regions of eastern central Europe, the southern and eastern coasts of the Baltic were greatly influenced by German settlement. This form of development was a result of the low population density in many regions. Landlords competed for the availability and services of peasants and therefore supported settlement on their lands in order to increase their income. Security probably also played a role because they feared Slavic uprisings and those of the pagan population, which they hoped to counter by settling German peasants on the land. Over time, the monetary interests of the landlords gained the upper hand because the settlement of rent-paying peasants and the founding of towns and cities that paid rent promised higher yields than the rents in kind and services formerly provided by the Slavic population.

In addition, German peasants arrived with a familiarity with the three-field rotation system and the plow with iron shares and moldboards, which increased the productivity of the land. As an incentive, Germans were given larger farms and guaranteed hereditary rights of use, personal freedom, and the right to administer their own villages as well as freedom from services and rents during the initial period of settlement (so-called free years) because in many places the land had to be cleared and made usable before it could be settled. Along the Baltic coast from Holstein to Mecklenburg, such resettlement of the former lands of the Obotrites made steady headway as wars had engendered serious losses among the Slavic population.

When settlers were in short supply, the resettlement of land that had returned to the wild was the most salient issue. For such land, Slavic and German peasants served the purpose equally well. Because so few settlement contracts, called location documents, have survived from Mecklenburg and Pomerania, we often have only indirect information about who settled, in what region, and when. In this respect, the Ratzeburg tithing register from the beginning of the thirteenth century is especially helpful because the tithe was the most important contribution made to the church. According to this document, at this time in western Mecklenburg in the land (*terra*) called Ratzeburg, only four of 125 villages were inhabited by Slavs. In Wittenburg the figure was four of 93 villages. At the same time, Slavic villages, such as Brüsewitz (now in the district of Schwerin), were in 1220 permitted to switch over to the German legal system. Farther east, in Mecklenburg, the percentage of Slavs engaged in tilling the land and building new settlements seems to have been larger.

In Pomerania, Dargun Abbey ministered to German, Slavic, and Danish peasants, and in 1231, Neuenkamp Abbey received the right to recruit and settle villagers of any ethnic origin. In addition, Vitslav I of Rügen (ca. 1180–1250) left the abbey 300 hides of forest to be cleared. The abbey was also granted the villages "of Craco, of Ratwald, and of Wulfer," which already existed, having been settled before 1231. Over the course of the next several decades (until 1273) a total of twenty-one villages were founded on the territory belonging to Neuenkamp Abbey, although we have no idea how many of these existed before 1231.

German, Slavic, and possibly also Danish settlers lived adjacent to each other, and the landlords tried to create a unified system of tithing. This is made clear from a document written in 1221 in which Vitslav I of Rügen and Bishop Brunward of Schwerin divided up the tithes of German settlers: after the land was made arable, Vitslav demanded two-thirds of the income. It seems that settlers from Flanders were also brought in as drainage and land improvement experts, and some settled in the central Elbe region. A few town names, such as Vlemingesdorp (Flemendorf), attest to this trend. It was founded in 1270, southeast of Barth, the seat of a Slavic knight named Goslav. Another town, Vlemanstorp, was founded in 1273, south of Demmin.

While the majority of settlers in the northern parts of Pomerania came from Holstein or Mecklenburg, several larger villages were founded in Stargard Land, which had been ceded to Brandenburg in 1236 by settlers from Magdeburg and Altmark. It is perhaps not surprising then that a city called Neubrandenburg would have been founded here "from scratch" in 1248. Mecklenburg knights, such as Detlef of Gadebusch, also expanded eastward and, as lords of the land of Loitz, founded a city of the same name. During the first half of the thirteenth century, Jaczo of Salzwedel (ca. 1180–1248) had risen to lord of Gützkow;

his sons founded the city of the same name beneath Gützkow Castle and granted it Lübeck city charter rights (Lübeck law).

East of the Oder, Duke Barnim I (ca. 1217–1278) and especially the bishops of Cammin were very active in promoting settlement. Hermann of Gleichen, who held office in the diocese of Cammin during the second half of the thirteenth century, founded not only the cities of Kolberg (1255), Köslin (1266), Naugard (1270), and Massow (1274), he also erected the abbeys at Kolberg (1277) and Köslin (1278). At the same time, the bishop urged German knights to colonize the land by giving them Pomeranian castles in fief. As a result, in 1274 the counts of Eberstein, who were related to the bishop, were given Naugard and 700 hides of land in the vicinity. German peasants settled there. Thus did the bishop expand his dominion by means of settlement, his newly built abbeys attesting to his spiritual power.

In the order's land in Prussia, new settlers are documented as peasants in village associations, owners of individual farms, and, as in all other regions, inhabitants of cities. At first, the colonists came from Mecklenburg, Mark Brandenburg, and Silesia, that is, all of the regions that had been settled earlier for the purpose of land development. Later, peasants from Culm were recruited to colonize Prussia's interior.

The peasants received farms measuring about two hides (*Hufen* of about 16.5 hectares each) of heritable land, with the peasants being required to pay cash rent to the landlord—mainly the Teutonic Order. This new Culm law was very different from the rights under which the Old Prussian peasants used their land. Their farms had not been measured by hides, but by the hake, that is, according to the manpower required or the surface area that could be worked with the help of a simple hake plow. Over time, the lands of the Old Prussians were remeasured this way as well (two to three hakes per 10 hectares). But beyond that, strong economic pressure to adapt caused the Old Prussian lands to be integrated into the hide system. In addition to the peasants in the village associations, there were also so-called small and large freemen. The small freemen were mainly Old Prussians who had accepted the rule of the order early on and as a result had retained their status. In contrast to the peasants, they paid little or no rent at all. Instead, they served the order militarily on horseback with small arms and used their free farms to support themselves. These vassals were free in comparison to the Old Prussian peasants, who were forced to pay rent on their land, although these could buy their way out and achieve the status of small freemen. The large freemen served the order by providing horses and heavier weaponry, and the order, in turn, gave manors to them. They did not work these lands themselves but settled other peasants on them, from whom they collected rent. Like the knights of the order, some of the large freemen came not only from the empire, but also from the colonized towns and cities and from the ruling elite of the Old Prussians. In the fifteenth century they would form a landed nobility.[10]

In Livonia, settlement proceeded from the fortified castles. The knights gave their vassals land in fief, which they were to farm with the help of the local population. As in Prussia, the knights of the order and the vassals came from the same regions in the empire. However, the large landowners were the ones who drove the conquest of the land. Like the Germans, the Livonians, Latvians, and Estonians were also given land in fief. The Danish crown also gave approximately two-thirds of its territory in Estonia in fief to German knights, which meant that Danish landlords came to be in the minority. Both the local population and a German "middle class," consisting of servants or craftsmen who served the order or the bishopric, settled in the area around the castles. So did the landowners. On the other hand, there were no German farming settlements in Livonia, although the order attempted to lure settlers there with the promise of a free year. These conditions appear not to have been attractive enough for many to risk leaving Prussia to start a new life in the Baltic region. Another factor was that peasants in Prussia still had ample opportunity for expansion and development. As a result, agricultural production in Livonia and Estonia remained largely in the hands of locals. Over the course of Swedish expansion into Finland, fishermen, seal hunters, and navigators were encouraged by the Bishopric of Ösel-Wiek and by the landlords to settle on the islands off the Estonian coast.

The Founding of Towns and Cities

Although villages, towns, and monasteries were founded simultaneously in many regions, many other towns and cities were founded under German law in or near earlier Slavic centers. Thus, for many years,

German and Polish historians discussed the possible continuity of the settlements. The continuities were undoubtedly more functional than geographic. This is because, setting aside the cities that were founded "from scratch," new German cities would have had to be founded at a certain distance from older settlements with Slavic inhabitants in order not to fall under older property right claims. Because the early Slavic urban centers united elements of the castle, crafts settlements, and trade, and because they attracted traders from regions west of the Elbe, we have a fairly nuanced picture of urban development in the Baltic region.

A good example of the transformation in city functions is the Slavic center of Stettin, which at the beginning of the twelfth century counted several thousand inhabitants living from farming, craftwork, and fishing, but especially from trade. Over the following decades, Stettin became the residence of princes, where a castellan replaced the people's assembly in the exercise of power. German merchants presumably began to show up in the middle of the twelfth century; in 1187, a merchant named Behringer, from Bamberg, funded construction of the St. Jakobikirche for them. It is quite possible that the fast-growing German community was granted a certain degree of internal self-governance. In 1237, Barnim I privileged the German community and transferred to it jurisdiction over the Slavic population of Stettin, power that had previously been exercised by the duke. In 1243, Magdeburg rights, which confirmed the changes that had already taken place, were officially implemented in the city. The founding of a city under German law, technically called *location*, was a long drawn out process that, unfortunately, is not well documented. Changing the location of the city in the process of refounding it—as occurred in Kolberg and Pyritz—had not been possible in Stettin. One part of the original Slavic-settled city was leveled and rebuilt according to new plans. The citizens of Stettin were subsequently able to tear down the ducal castle with the proviso that no fortified castles be built within a radius of three miles. This measure secured the city's autonomy, something that was later granted to other Pomeranian cities as well.

In contrast to Stettin, Count Adolf II of Schauenburg (ca. 1128–1164) did not link the 1143 founding of Lübeck (which was located on the peninsula between the Wakenitz and Trave Rivers) geographically with the Obotrite residence of Old Lübeck. The Lübeck law that was granted to long-distance merchants, which simultaneously privileged all trade and guaranteed the autonomy of the city council, became the model for many new cities along the Baltic coast. This did not yet apply to Schwerin, which was founded in 1160 by Duke Henry the Lion (who wanted to introduce his own Schwerin law) and constituted the oldest city in Mecklenburg. Rostock, on the other hand, received Lübeck law from Henry Borwin I, in 1218. Before that, we have evidence of the existence of the Slavic Roztoc Castle, a market, and a number of merchants, among them several from the Rhineland. The city grew quickly; after the old city was founded by 1232, we find a central city (around the Marienkirche) and a new city, started in 1252 around the Jakobikirche. What we see over the course of the thirteenth century is the founding of cities and towns in quick succession. As early as the 1220s, the cities of Gadebusch (1225), Wismar (1226–1229), and Wittenburg (1226) were all granted Lübeck rights. In 1234, Vitslav I of Rügen granted Stralsund the Rostock variant of Lübeck rights. A Slavic fisher and ferry village had previously existed along the shore of the Strelasund. Since the beginning of the thirteenth century, the princes on Rügen had promoted the settlement of German merchants, and they settled in the marketplace around the Nikolaikirche.

The city of Greifswald developed on a "green meadow" along the border between the principalities of Pomerania and Rügen. It had no Slavic predecessors and was founded in about 1210 as a saltworks and market settlement around the present-day Marienkirche. After the abbot of Eldena had for some years exercised the right to adjudicate quarrels between merchants, Prince Vartislav III granted Greifswald Lübeck rights in 1250. Another settlement already existed around the Nikolaikirche, which was followed by the new city around St. Jakobi. In 1264, the old and the new cities were united and given the right to build a wall.

Thorn and Culm were the first towns founded by the Teutonic Order in the process of conquering the lands of the Old Prussians. The document of their city rights, the so-called Kulmer Handfeste (Culm law) of 1233 became a model for other Prussian city rights, even informing Prussian settlement rights in general. By 1400, ninety-seven new cities had been founded, largely in the area around the order's fortified castles. Culm law granted citizens the right to choose judges, thereby fostering the development of city councils, boards of lay assessors, and mayors. The influence of the Teutonic Order was evident in its patronage over the parish, which meant that the order controlled who would be the pastor. Unsurprisingly, this was usually a priest brother of the order. The order generally waived its right to acquire property in the city in order not to imperil the homogeneous property and settlement structure in the community. Nonetheless, not all knight commanders of the order recognized the autonomy of the cities located in their domain. This led to numerous conflicts between town and city governments and members of the Teutonic Order in the fifteenth century.[11]

In Livonia, cities were first founded mainly on the initiative of German merchants from Visby (Gotland) until Lübeck began to exert its influence. Most of the Westphalian inhabitants of towns and cities in Livonia traveled there mainly via Lübeck. Riga enjoyed Visby city rights until 1290, when it was given Hamburg rights. The Livonian cities followed the Riga model, while Estonian cities, such as Reval (in 1248), were granted Lübeck rights by the Danish kings. These cities were closely connected to the northern German cities, and over the following centuries they were integrated into the developing Hanseatic League. In addition to cities such as Riga, Reval, and Dorpat, which were involved in long-distance trade, medium-sized towns such as Wenden, Wolmar, Goldingen, Kokenhusen, Lemsal, Roop, Windau, Neu-Pernau, and Fellin also followed this pattern. Although members of the local population could gain citizenship rights, the merchant elite and groups of wealthy craftsmen were generally recruited from among German immigrants. Over time, however, the rights of "non-German" Livonians (Estonians, Livonians, and Latvians) were increasingly limited.

Economic Transformation and Ethnic Assimilation

The founding of villages and cities according to German law brought with it many changes, not only economic and social, but also in terms of geography and the physical layout of cities. Even today, we see this in the regularity with which streets were laid out. But even in the countryside, the hide system changed the landscape. The hide, varying in

size from 17 to 40 hectares, established a locally uniform basis for cal-
culating levies on farms. Not surprisingly, the locators and the landlords had an interest in redividing both cultivated and cleared land. Instead of the more-or-less square meadows characteristic of Slavic
hamlets, the fields were frequently divided up into long adjacent parcels. This division resulted in new types of villages, such as seen in
Angerdorf- and Hagenhufendorf-type settlements. In an Angerdorf,
which had a village square (*Anger*) in the center, three to four long fields
in which the peasants were allotted strips of field were laid out adjacent to the common pasture (*Allmende*). A three-field crop rotation
system was used (one field each for summer and winter grain and one
fallow field). This involved the so-called *Flurzwang,* which mandated
the order in which crops had to be planted, because only in this way
could the land in the village be effectively cultivated. In settlements
of the Hagenhufendorf type, by contrast, each peasant was given a long
strip of forest behind his farm, which he was supposed to clear and make
arable. He could use this land in any way he chose, planting crops in
whatever order he wished. Depending on the size of a hide, which could
differ from place to place, and the fertility of the land, each peasant
was allotted one to two hides of land.

Levies were fixed but varied from village to village; but in any case,
yield (depending on the state of clearing) and composition of the land
were taken into account. For example, the peasants in Dargezin, near
Gützkow, paid rent of 22 bushels of rye, 26 bushels of oats, and 12
bushels of barley per hide or their equivalent in money, in addition to
which they had to pay one *Zinshuhn,* or chicken, per person, and linen.
Eldena Abbey demanded six marks annually from the cleared village
of Dietrichshagen, near Greifswald, and waived any further levies. The
levying of cash rent is a sign of the advancing monetization of the society because the peasants themselves had to pay the required amount
in cash from the sale of their products in the city marketplace. It was
here that the inhabitants got their foods and raw materials from the
surrounding areas. These products were produced by the peasants on
their hides, while the fruits of the farms belonging to the knights and
abbeys were largely for their own consumption.

The villages chartered under German law were inhabited by hide
peasants. They chose the village mayor, who was generally a locator

and as such had received a larger heritable piece of property (two to six hides). He adjudicated disputes in the community and was responsible to the landlords for collecting levies. The cottagers (*Kossäten*), who farmed a small piece of land and hired themselves out as laborers, occupied a place a step below the "hide peasants" on the social ladder. They also plied crafts and fished.

In addition to the economic and social differences that existed, the new settlement regions also witnessed a long-term process of ethnic assimilation between the local population and the newcomers. The power of the new German settlers often led to economic and then ethnic displacement of the Slavic peasants. The Germans dominated the new cities in any case, even though Slavic fishermen and craftsmen shared these spaces with them.

The church, whether in the form of monasteries and monks, churches, and pastors or cathedral chapters and bishops, played an active role in suppressing the remains of pagan practices, which created a pressure to conform. The Slavic nobles or aristocrats (*primores*) saw themselves confronted by a low German nobility, members of which entered the land as vassals of the Slavic princes of Mecklenburg, Rügen, and Pomerania and built knightly manors, villages, and towns. The Slavic knights merged with this aristocratic caste by entering into marriage alliances or by being granted equal legal status. In Mecklenburg or Pomerania, such actions resulted in a landed nobility, whose long-term economic position would be based on their rule over the rural population. Certain parts of the Slavic population were integrated, as were newcomers to the Baltic coast from Holland, Flanders, Holstein, Denmark, Mecklenburg, and Brandenburg. The relationships between people in the cities in particular fostered a certain cultural assimilation. Among other factors, the Middle Low German of the fourteenth century, which was the business language of the Hanseatic merchants and was used as a lingua franca in the Baltic region, served as a powerful linguistic assimilating force. According to the Pomeranian chronicler Thomas Kantzow (died 1542), the last woman who still spoke a Slavic tongue on the relatively isolated island of Rügen died in 1404. The Slavic language continued to hold on somewhat longer in southern Mecklenburg, in the region around Grabow and Ludwigslust, another Slavic refuge.

We have no evidence of actual legal discrimination in Mecklenburg and Pomerania such as that of the Wend paragraphs found in towns and cities in Brandenburg, which excluded Slavic inhabitants from certain guilds. This may indicate that the process of assimilation was already far advanced here in the fourteenth and fifteenth centuries. This may be assumed to have happened in the Prussian cities, where there was no immigration problem in the fourteenth century and room was probably made for Old Prussians and Poles and their descendants. Here, the peasants who paid hake rent and who were discriminated against in terms of property rights could switch to German law or aspire to the status of freemen, paying the same rent as Germans or performing services. The inclusion of the Old Prussian freemen in the service system of the Teutonic Order makes clear the extent to which the order was dependent on the local population. In this way, the small freemen were able to preserve their language and identity, and in the fifteenth century the commanders of the Teutonic Order still used interpreters to communicate with their Old Prussian freemen.[12] The assimilation process proceeded more speedily among the large freemen. Thus, the chronicler Peter of Dusburg (died ca. 1326) tells of the subjection and forcible conversion of the Old Prussian duke Skaumand. The order resettled him, but then in 1285 gave him a free farm in fief along with associated legal rights and compulsory military duties. We also have documentary evidence that one of his descendants, Dietrich Skomand, was granted 50 hides of land on which to found a village. According to its locator, the village was to be called Dietrichsdorf. This example illustrates the transition from the former Old Prussian leadership caste to that of the large freemen, that is, to the future landed nobility.[13]

The Brothers of the Sword encountered a special situation in Livonia. While the chronicler Henry of Latvia (ca. 1188–1259) painted a picture of a powerful, hierarchically structured local federation of enemies, archaeological findings indicate a more socially egalitarian federation of tribes in which individual leaders emerged as a result of their charisma but not necessarily because of their wealth. Furthermore, the Teutonic Order and the bishoprics were from the outset dependent on the cooperation of the local leaders, who in the thirteenth century received land for their services. Even after the introduction of the overseer system (*Vogtsystem*), the local elites continued to dominate the villages, as they had in the pre-crusade era. Little would change here, especially since the order, bishops, and cities were dependent on *local* agricultural production because of the continued lack of farming settlements ruled by German law.[14]

The blurred boundaries between the worlds of the ethnic locals and that of the Germans are also reflected in the comingling of Christian and pagan customs. In the cemeteries, burial mounds eventually gave way to Christian graves in rows, but "pagan" cremation continued to be practiced by the Couronians into the fourteenth century. It appears that the practice of placing burial objects in graves became much less common as early as the thirteenth century, although some have been found in sixteenth-century graves, especially in the form of weapons. Up to this time, sacred waters, forests, and trees continued to be venerated and animals sacrificed to the gods. Rather than a "clash of cultures," these practices point to a long period of symbiosis between different ethnic and religious traditions.[15]

This supposed culture clash becomes even more questionable when we examine the Swedish expansion into Finland that occurred at the same time as the "German" conquest of Livonia. Contrary to all glorifications of the crusade—such as that found in the *Erikskrönikan*—the archaeological sources suggest that the Christianization was much more peaceful in Finland, the slow effect of Swedish peasants who settled the area. In the thirteenth century, Swedish peasants drove the expansion of land clearing in northern Sweden, without evidence of influence by monasteries or nobles. Only toward the end of the thirteenth century do the interests of the Swedish state in consolidating its position in Finland to reap the benefits of trade with Russia dovetail with the church's interest in building its infrastructure. Novgorod responded to this strategy by building fortresses in Karelia, which served as medium-term impediments to cultural exchange. Even though the population regularly crossed the border, the Finns west of the line became increasingly Swedish and Catholic, while the Karelians became more Russian and Orthodox.[16]

This development was eventually reflected in sacral architecture as well. The transformation of the countryside effected by the construction of fortified castles, churches, and monasteries permanently changed the topography of the lands along the Baltic Sea. Pagan landscapes with their sacred waters and forests were transformed into Christian land-scapes. The new architecture served as a symbol of power and magnifi-cence, which even the local population would have had a hard time avoiding. In any case, the local Livonian population soon came to ap-preciate the advantages of such castles, which offered them protection and work and which, in turn, encouraged them to convert.[17] The first monasteries in Denmark were built toward the end of the eleventh cen-tury and in Sweden around 1100, at a time when the new faith was not accepted everywhere in the land. Prayer and spiritual discipline were meant to break the pagan spirit, a task that the mendicant orders would later take up in the cities of the Baltic region.

One expression of this new spirit was brick architecture, with the red color of the building material giving the buildings a characteristic look. This innovative building material and the techniques required to use it, which were introduced from northern Italy, were first used in the abbeys of Ringsted and Sorø, in Denmark, and the Danes later spread its use throughout the Baltic. In the cities, the mendicant or-ders helped to popularize brick by using it in their monastic complexes.[18] This new technique would reach its artistic pinnacle in the brick Gothic style of the Hanseatic period.

CHAPTER THREE

The Hanseatic League and the Monarchies

Focus on Lübeck

Lübeck, the most important port city in the Baltic in the late Middle Ages, dominated the region politically into the sixteenth century as head of the Hanseatic League. In his *Germania* (1458), Aeneas Silvius, the future Pope Pius II, wrote, acknowledging its power and dominance:

> Among all the cities, Lübeck stands out, because it is dotted with beautiful buildings and richly ornamented churches. The authority of the city is such that with a single nod it can install or depose the rulers of the mighty kingdoms of Denmark, Sweden and Norway.[1]

By the beginning of the fourteenth century, the urban area between the Trave River and its tributary, the Wakenitz, had largely been settled. This was when Lübeck, with its five large churches, the many chapels, the Holy Ghost Hospital, and city hall, developed its characteristic "look." The vernacular architecture featured the half-timbered or massively constructed brick *Dielenhaus* with its large central hall and its gable turned onto the street. As a result of its many years of prosperity, by 1400, 20,000 people lived in the densely populated city.[2]

In the fifteenth century, Lübeck and the Hanseatic League generally were dealing with Dutch and southern German competitors, and profits from trade declined. The city stagnated both economically and socially, but it retained a good deal of its wealth. The wealthy burghers who met at the Compass Society (Zirkelgesellschaft) continued to produce the councilors and mayors of the city, and to mold its social life, which, since the fifteenth century, had been enlivened by the so-called Merchants Company (Kaufleutekompanie), a society of rich parvenus.

Artisans became increasingly specialized, and this led to a final artistic flowering fostered by increased private and fraternal demand for altars and statues of saints. Preeminent masters, such as Hermen Rode

Figure 3. View of the city of Lübeck from the high altar in St. Nicholas Church, Tallinn (1481), from the studio of Hermen Rode

(ca. 1430–1504), Bernt Notke (ca. 1435–1509), and Henning van der Heide (ca. 1487–1520), worked well beyond the confines of Lübeck and had a major influence on the representational and plastic arts in the entire Baltic region.

The Hanseatic League

The Hanseatic League, originally an ad hoc association of traveling merchants, had since the thirteenth century developed into a mighty alliance of cities, which for about 300 years largely controlled trade, shipping, and politics in the North Sea and Baltic regions. The Old High German word *Hanse* meant "crowd" or "community," and in the twelfth century it designated a cooperative association of long-distance traders who mostly came from the same region or town. Many local *Hanse* associations existed before the German Hanseatic League of the thirteenth century made its first appearance on the political stage. Merchants from Cologne who operated a branch in London were the first to join together as an association. Their London branch, the Guildhall, and the goods they traded in, were granted a special privilege by the king in 1175.[3] But perhaps more important for the history of the Hanseatic League were the processes that began to play themselves out in the Baltic region during the twelfth and thirteenth centuries. These included the founding of Lübeck and many other cities in the Baltic region as Germans settled there and the founding of the Gotlandfahrergenossenschaft (German company of merchants traveling to Gotland).

The founding of Lübeck (1143–1159) provided German long-distance Baltic traders with a headquarters and enabled more local merchants from Lower Saxony and Westphalia to access markets in the Baltic region and Russia without having to trade through Scandinavian or Slavic middlemen. For many years, for example, the farmer-merchants on the island of Gotland had dominated trade with Russia. Lübeck, and the advantages it provided for German long-distance traders, represented a real challenge to the Gotlanders. The German merchants were better financed, better trained in the techniques of trade, and better organized, and they possessed a boat—the cog—with a larger carrying capacity than the Gotlanders had at their disposal. In 1161, Duke Henry the Lion

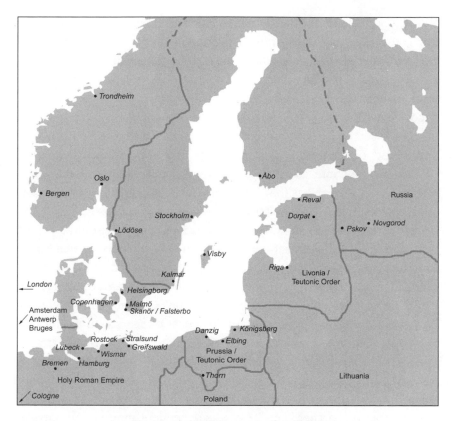

Map 3. The Baltic region in about 1400

permitted the Gotlanders to trade in his Saxon domain under the condition that German merchants be granted the same privilege on Gotland. This greatly stimulated German trade on the island. A document
from 1252, a privilege granted by Countess Margaret of Flanders (died
1285), contains the first mention of a Gotland Travelers Association
(*"universi mercatores romani imperii gotlandiam frequentantes"*). It
acknowledged visitations by an association of merchants from the
"Roman Empire" on Gotland that pursued trade both in the east and
in the west and that increasingly used its branch in Visby to gain a foot-
hold in the Novgorod market. Like the Gotlanders before them, they
erected a trading center in Novgorod, the Peterhof, which became the
Kontor (trading outpost) for the developing Hanseatic trade with Russia.
Because of its enormous hinterland, which extended all the way to the

White Sea, Novgorod became the center of the pelt trade. Trade with Novgorod was controlled from Visby, on Gotland, and this was where the surplus money was brought at the conclusion of the trading season. However, since the late thirteenth century, Lübeck had begun to vie for control of the Russian trade, and with the support of other cities it successfully argued that legal disputes in Novgorod could be appealed both in Visby and in Lübeck. With that right, Lübeck's future role as "protector" of the Russia trade was more or less preordained.[4]

A major contributor to their subsequent success was the Lübeck law with its attendant rights that served as the inspiration for other cities. Riga, for example, which had been founded in 1201 at the mouth of the Daugava by a former canon from Bremen, became a long-distance port serving Lübeck. Riga was joined in the thirteenth century by a string of trading cities along the southern Baltic coast, arrayed like pearl necklace: Wismar, Rostock, Stralsund, Greifswald, Elbing, Königsberg, and Reval. German traders had also settled in the Scandinavian kingdoms. In Denmark, schools of herring off the coast of Scania lured German traders; the same was true for southern Sweden, where German traders and artisans became commonplace in the cities, especially in Lödöse, Kalmar, and Stockholm. German miners could be found throughout the iron and copper mining districts as well. Norway was another important trading partner because it was dependent on grain imports to feed its population. Merchants from Lübeck supplied this commodity in exchange for dried cod (stockfish), which was caught in Norwegian waters and dried on wooden racks. The most important trading center was Bergen, where another Hanseatic *Kontor* was erected, the so-called German Bridge (Deutsche Brücke). From here the Lübeckers controlled trade with the Scandinavian kingdoms.

But Russia, Scandinavia, and the adjacent areas along the Baltic were not the only centers of German trade. At first, with Cologne taking the lead, they also traded with England and then Flanders. After the special privilege of 1175, the 1303 "Carta mercatoria" of Edward I promised foreign merchants, among other things, an exemption from all levies, settlement rights, legal protection from encroachment by royal officials, and the renunciation of new levies in the future—in exchange for an increase in tariffs. This last provision, the renunciation of new levies, would turn out to be the core of the privilege. When Edward III placed a duty on cloth exports in 1337 to finance the Hundred Years' War, the Hanseatic League successfully gained exemption from this levy by arguing the "Carta mercatoria." English merchants and other foreigners were forced to pay. With that exemption, the "Carta mercatoria," which originally applied to all foreigners trading in England, became a privilege of the Hanseatic League alone. They used the Guildhall as their *Kontor* and then built up the adjacent Steelyard grounds for the purpose of further exploiting their privilege.[5]

The final, and in fact most important, trade region in which German merchants were active was Flanders, where high-quality textiles were produced in large quantities. At first, the German merchants acquired these textiles at markets in Champagne and later primarily in Bruges, which because of its central location developed into the most important commodity market in western Europe. In 1252, Countess Margaret privileged the German merchants by granting them relief from customs duties. One year later, they were exempted from trial by combat, liability for the debts and transgressions of others, and from strand law and other encumbrances, which greatly bolstered the legal underpinnings of their trade. Nonetheless, conflicts between the city of Bruges and the German merchants were frequent, largely for reasons of restraint of trade. In 1280–1282, the merchants reacted by moving temporarily to the neighboring city of Aardenburg, as a result of which Bruges reaffirmed its privileges. Then in 1347, the German merchants devised a *Kontor* system of their own, which was supposed to consolidate their interests vis-à-vis the city of Bruges and the Duchy of Flanders. They did this because trade with Flanders was a matter of life and death to them; this was where they acquired the textiles that they then sold in the markets of Germany, the Baltic region, and Russia.

To successfully counter further infringements on their privileges in Flanders, in 1356 they placed the hitherto independent Bruges *Kontor* under the authority of an umbrella institution, the Hanseatic Diet, which was usually but not always held in Lübeck. From then on, the Hanseatic Diet, representing the "cities of the Hanseatic League" (first mentioned in 1358), and not the Hanseatic merchants at the various trading outposts, determined trade policy. It soon became clear that the Hanseatic League as a whole was more adroit and powerful in pressing its interests than were the groups of Hanseatic merchants, each pursuing its own special interests in its foreign trading centers. The creation of the Hanseatic Diet representing all of the Hanseatic cities marked the end of a process that had begun in the thirteenth century, when the cities began to exert an ever-increasing influence on the cooperative associations of their merchants abroad. The cities had supported them in acquiring privileges, created the necessary legal structure for their trade, and granted them legal protection. From now on, the cities of the North Sea and Baltic region that were represented in the Hanseatic League would control trade and trade policies in this region. The representatives of these cities gathered as needed in the Hanseatic Diet, which made all of the important decisions. As a result, Lübeck became the de facto capital of the Hanseatic League.[6]

New challenges in the Baltic region began to confront the Hanseatic League during the second half of the fourteenth century, which forced the new confederation of cities to prove its mettle. In 1360, King Valdemar IV (ca. 1320–1375) began to pursue a policy of Danish hegemony in the Baltic Sea and conquered not just Scania, which it had earlier lost to Sweden, but Gotland as well. Denmark raised duties and other levies for Hanseatic merchants, encumbering trade with Scania, which represented a *casus belli* for Lübeck and the eastern Hanseatic cities. After the Hanseatic League suffered an initial defeat at sea, Denmark made life difficult for the Hanseatic cities of the Zuiderzee and cut off passage through the Øresund to the Dutch cities that were loosely associated with the league. These actions struck a vital nerve. As a result, all of the Hanseatic cities from the lower Rhine to Reval joined forces with the cities on the Zuiderzee in the Confederation of Cologne. In concert, they militarily restored their privileges in the Treaty of Stralsund (1370), especially the right of unimpeded access to Denmark by land and by sea. They also received reparations stemming from the war. The Treaty of Stralsund marked the apex of power of the Hanseatic League; the supremacy of the Hanseatic cities in the Baltic trade was now uncontested.[7] However, it remained a community of interest exclusively for merchants, who used political and military means to secure only their trading privileges.

Hanseatic trade proceeded from east to west along a line dotted with their trading centers in Novgorod, Reval, Riga, Visby, Danzig, Stralsund, Lübeck, Hamburg, Bruges, and London, and its existence was based on the trade between the suppliers of foodstuffs and raw materials in northern and eastern Europe and the commercial producers of finished products in northwestern Europe. The merchants, however, went well beyond their function as middlemen between east and west, first by trading in the products manufactured by the Hanseatic cities themselves and then by penetrating deep into the Baltic hinterlands south of the coast. As a result, not only did they open up trade with Bohemia and Silesia by way of the Elbe and Oder Rivers, they also followed the Vistula through Cracow to the copper mining districts of upper Hungary (Slovakia) and connected with trading partners in the Black Sea via Lemberg (Lviv).[8]

The regions visited by these merchants depended on local demands and production. They had a large assortment of products, both mass-produced goods for daily life and luxury products for a small, wealthy clientele. The most important products were wool, woolen and linen textiles, pelts and furs, herring and dried cod, salt, wax, grain, flax and hemp, wood and forestry products (ash, pitch, tar), and beer and wine. Pelts, wax, grain, flax, wood, and beer flowed westward, where they were exchanged for needed textiles, salt, wine, metal products, spices, and other luxury goods. Fish was sold throughout the Hanseatic region.

We may have identified two interconnected economic regions in the east—on the one hand, the Russian trade region, centered in Novgorod with its pelts and furs, and on the other the Livonian urban region around Reval, Dorpat, and Riga along with the Daugava hinterland, which supplied mainly flax and hemp. Demand for furs—from expensive sable to cheap squirrel—and wax for illumination, was heavy throughout Europe. Hemp was needed for rope and flax for linen in all ports of the Hanseatic region. In eastern Europe, Flemish textiles and sea salt were in high demand. Another trade region south of Livonia was controlled by the state of the Teutonic Order and the Prussian Hanseatic cities of Danzig, Elbing, and Thorn. They made available to Hanseatic trade the products of the Lithuanian and Polish hinterland by way of the Vistula and Memel Rivers. The Lithuanian regions contributed wax, pelts, wood, and flax; Poland produced mainly grain and timber products. The latter supplied shipbuilders with wood for masts and planks; herring fisheries, breweries, and salt works needed wood for barrels, while numerous manufacturers were dependent on steady supplies of pitch, tar, and ash. The primary export product from the Prussian Hanseatic cities, however, was grain, which nourished the population living in the highly urbanized centers of western Europe. Not to be forgotten are luxury products like amber, which was gathered along the Sambian coast of the Baltic. The Teutonic Order had a monopoly on the amber trade, and they exported amber to Lübeck and Bruges, where amber turners worked them into luxurious rosaries. Salt, herring, and textiles were the most important Prussian imports.

In the western part of the Baltic, Sweden contributed iron, copper, butter, and cattle and cowhides to the Hanseatic trade, although, with the exception of metals, Sweden stood in the shadow of Denmark. Since the fifteenth century, Denmark had become an important exporter of horses, oxen, and butter. Prior to this time, Hanseatic trade with Denmark had primarily concentrated on Scanian herring, schools of which were in the fourteenth century said to be so thick that the fish could be caught by hand. During the late fifteenth and sixteenth centuries, the decline in Baltic and North Sea herring increasingly amplified the importance of Dutch herring fishers. The other important fish supplier, Norway, which at the time belonged to Denmark, was profoundly dependent on Hanseatic imports. Hanseatic merchants supplied grain, flour, beer, malt, hops, salt, and linen, and they exported primarily dried cod and small quantities of cod liver oil, walrus tooth, skins, and other goods. When, toward the end of the fifteenth century and during the sixteenth, consumers came to prefer Icelandic dried cod, Hanseatic trade with Norway receded in importance.

Trade with England, the original domain of Hanseatic merchants from the Rhineland and Westphalia, continued to be brisk. They exported Rhine wine, metals, and the dyes madder and woad to England and imported tin and English wool for the textile industry in Flanders and Brabant, and later also English textiles. The Hanseatic cities of the Baltic coast, in turn, provided wares typical of the east, including pelts, wax, grain, and wood as well as Scandinavian fish and metals. The most important market in western Europe, however, was the Netherlands. Flanders and later Brabant were not only important textile producers, they also established key trade connections with the Mediterranean basin. The Hanseatic merchants bought goods in Flemish and Brabant cities, primarily woolen textiles of high and medium quality, as well as trousers from Bruges. They also acquired spices, figs, and raisins from southern Europe. France contributed oil and wine as well as bay salt. This sea salt, harvested from the Atlantic, became increasingly important as a preservative. Prussian and especially Netherlandish ships made regular bay salt runs, then used it as ballast on the way to the Baltic, where they traded it for grain and wood for the western European market. By doing so, they undermined Lübeck's monopoly as an intermediary in trade. The Hanseatic presence in southern Europe was sporadic, except for the wine trade with Bordeaux, although the Veckinchusen family did attempt to establish trade in pelts with Venice.

In addition to products from distant trading partners, goods produced in Hanseatic cities played a key role in domestic as well as foreign trade. Products that flowed east included colored metallic goods from Aachen; Rhine wine; tools from the Westphalian lands of Mark, Berg, and Siegerland; ceramics from the Rhineland; Westphalian textiles and linen; brassware from Braunschweig; salt from Lüneburg; and beer from Hamburg.

The Hanseatic trade was organized by merchant trading companies. The most common model was the free type, in which two partners invested capital and split the profits according to the capital invested and the profits realized. Such organizations generally lasted for one to two years. The large-scale international merchants were generally involved in several companies at a time. This decreased their overall risk and increased the assortment of goods in which they traded. Relatives were often brought in as partners because they were more likely to be trustworthy, especially when it came to long-distance east-west trade. Unlike in Italy or in southern Germany, large, centrally controlled trading companies extending over several generations and including a large number of participants did not exist in the Hanseatic trade. As a result, the Hanseatic companies saw no need to introduce the double bookkeeping that was standard in Italy.

The four Hanseatic *Kontore* in Novgorod, Bergen, London, and Bruges formed a sort of higher-level trade organization. Here, German merchants lived in specially demarcated areas such as the Petershof, the German Bridge, or the walled Steelyard. Only in Bruges did Hanseatic merchants live with local hosts. Each *Kontor* was tightly structured, with aldermen (literally, older men) elected annually; firmly established statutes; and its own legal jurisdiction, counting house, and seal. The *Kontore* were important in terms of acquiring trading privileges because, with cover provided by the Hanseatic cities, they represented the interests of merchants in their dealings with the ruling elites and cities in the foreign countries in which they traded. But the *Kontore* also facilitated everyday trade by establishing a regular news and messenger system with their home cities, and the attendant correspondence, certification, and bookkeeping also helped them to raise credit. But above all, the reporting requirements regarding the Hanseatic merchants active in any given area encouraged a certain uniformity in the buying and selling of goods, which tended to limit competition among Hanseatic members.

Toward the end of the fifteenth century, Hanseatic trade experienced setbacks on all fronts. The old trading system based on privileges proved inadequate in the face of growing competition and the consolidation of the European powers. For example, the Scandinavian kings now attempted to limit Hanseatic trade for the benefit of their own merchants. At the same time, these kings played the Hanseatic merchants off against their Dutch competitors. As a result, the Hanseatic cities were drawn into Scandinavian power struggles by backing privateers in hopes of retaining their privileges. The closing of the Novgorod *Kontor* in 1494 by Ivan III was another blow, although much of its trade had already shifted to the Livonian port cities of Riga and Reval during the fifteenth century, as a result of which these cities experienced a significant upswing.

Matters were changing in England as well, where imports and exports of textiles were at the center of disputes. Internal conflicts within the Hanseatic League undoubtedly played a role, because Lübeck stubbornly demanded that England recognize its old privileges, whereas Cologne and the Prussian trading cities were ready to come to an accommodation. Be that as it may, the 1474 Treaty of Utrecht ratified an understanding with England that restored the Hanseatic privileges. As a result, Hanseatic trade in England enjoyed a final phase of prosperity up to the middle of the sixteenth century.[9]

The Dutch and the Zeelanders were locked in competition with Hanseatic cities such as Lübeck, Wismar, Rostock, Stralsund, and Greifswald because the latter saw their position as middlemen in the east-west route threatened. However, Lübeck was unable to limit Dutch access to the Baltic Sea, either by peaceful or by military means. In fact, the Prussian Hanseatic cities of Danzig, Elbing, Thorn, and Königsberg were largely dependent on Dutch freight capacity. As a result, in 1475–1476, a quarter of Danzig's shipping relied on Dutch ships, an advantage that the Dutch continued to expand and exploit.[10]

The Bruges *Kontor* had de facto been located in Antwerp since 1460 because merchants attended the Brabant trade fairs there and in Bergen op Zoom. By the time the Hanseatic merchants set about building a *Kontor* in Antwerp, in 1563, Antwerp's trade had already reached its zenith. Other Hanseatic cities like Hamburg and Bremen contributed to the decline of the German Bridge *Kontor* in Bergen by increasing their trade with Iceland and the Shetland Islands in the late fifteenth century.

Signs of Hanseatic decline were rife in the sixteenth century. Historians have cited a number of causes for this decline, including the increasing vigor of the German territorial states and the Nordic kingdoms as well as overwhelming competition from southern German trading houses and the Netherlands.[11] Nonetheless, this picture of decline contrasts markedly with the general upswing in European trade in the sixteenth century. Although the Hanseatic cities took part in this growth, a traditional trading system based on privileges proved no longer tenable. Neither Bruges, Bergen, Lübeck, nor Novgorod were the beneficiaries of this new expansion in trade, however; the future belonged to Amsterdam, Hamburg, and Danzig. Just as innovations in shipping and trade had once given the Hanseatic League an edge over the peasant-merchants from Gotland, new types of ships and the expansion of commission trade and cashless instruments of payment now overwhelmingly favored the Dutch.

The Monarchies and Unions

Danish expansion in the Baltic region collapsed in 1227 after Denmark's defeat in the Battle of Bornhöved at the hands of the northern German princes and cities.[12] At the same time, much as occurred in Poland, Denmark began to split into petty principalities after the death of Valdemar II. In his testament, Valdemar had willed parts of the land to his six sons, giving each of them independence, which proved a recipe for conflict. The weakness of the monarchy strengthened the position of the nobility, which meant that future kings would have to bend to the demands of the nobility in what was known as an electoral capitulation, which greatly limited the monarch in the exercise of his power. Thus, for example, in 1282, King Eric V (1249–1286) promised in a document called a *håndfæstning,* "the first Danish constitution," to call together an assembly on a regular basis, consisting of nobles, prelates, and court officials, the so-called Danehof (Danish court), which would be the highest legislative and legal body.

It was not until Valdemar IV that the Danish monarchy reasserted its authority with the support of the Holy Roman Emperor and Lübeck. For one thing, Valdemar redeemed the crown lands, which had been in pledge. Foreign creditors were in part paid from the proceeds of the sale of Estonia (1346) to the Teutonic Order and from special taxes. This then formed the basis for an adroit foreign policy, which, by alternating alliances with the kings of Sweden and the north German princes, attempted to establish dominion in the Baltic region.[13] The Hanseatic cities resisted this incursion, and Valdemar was forced to guarantee them freedom of trade and shipping in the Treaty of Stralsund, in 1370 (see above). When Valdemar died, in 1375, his five-year-old grandson Olaf, from the marriage of his daughter Margaret and King Haakon VI of Norway, was elected king. When Haakon died, Olaf inherited the throne of Norway as Olaf IV, which effectively united both countries until 1814. Olaf's mother Margaret assumed the regency upon his premature death in 1387 and was elected regent of both countries.

Swedish policies in the Baltic region in the middle of the thirteenth century were determined by the statesman Birger Magnusson, also known as Birger Jarl, who pursued an activist foreign policy. Although the *jarl* (or earl) was only one office under the king (though the most important office), Birger became the actual driving force in Swedish politics. This can be seen by the fact that he successfully arranged international marriages for himself and his children. His daughter became the wife of Haakon of Norway, and his son Valdemar married the daughter of the Danish king. This ensured friendly relations among the neighboring Scandinavian kingdoms. Hamburg and Lübeck were placated with royal privileges that promoted trade between Hanseatic merchants and Sweden.

Magnus Eriksson (1316–1374) pursued pan-Nordic ambitions during the first half of the fourteenth century; after he inherited the Norwegian throne, the Swedish prelates and magnates elected him king.[14] He pursued an expansionist foreign policy at Denmark's expense, and in 1332, a delegation of the estates of Scania under the leadership of the archbishop of Lund paid homage to him. In 1343, he made peace with the new Danish king, Valdemar IV, who renounced his claims to Scania, Blekinge, and southern Halland. That same year, Magnus tried to control royal succession by having his older son, Eric, elected king of Sweden and his younger son, Haakon, named king of Norway. In the meantime, he devoted himself to new foreign policy goals, and from 1348 to 1351 waged war against Novgorod for control of its trade. The monies that he squandered on this unsuccessful undertaking damaged his reputation considerably, engendering resistance among the Swedish landed nobility. Rebellion was out in the open by 1356. Young Eric Magnusson became counter-king; later, with Magnus's consent he was elevated to co-regent. This solution, however, was dashed by Eric's premature death in 1359 and the military defeat against Valdemar IV, which took Scania and Gotland away from Sweden. Haakon, his remaining son, the king of Norway, was elected king of Sweden in 1362, where he accepted his father as co-regent. Both renounced their claims to Scania and sealed their peace with Denmark when Haakon married Margaret of Denmark (1353–1412). With this new alliance, the opposition was outmaneuvered and they then sought out Magnus's brother-in-law Albert of Mecklenburg (ca. 1338–1412) to stand as a new candidate for the throne. With Hanseatic support, Albert reached Stockholm, where he was elected king. This forced Magnus and Haakon into a fight for their kingdom. Unsuccessful, Haakon had to retreat to Norway. The Swedish magnates, however, were unhappy with Albert (now King Albert), who not only raised special taxes, but also filled the most important offices with his own hand-picked agents from Mecklenburg. As a result, in 1388, they offered Queen Margaret I of Denmark and Norway the Swedish crown as well, which she then confirmed in battle a year later.

This meant that for the first time all three Scandinavian kingdoms, including their overseas and island possessions that extended from Greenland in the west to Finland in the east, were united under a single monarch. Margaret, who administered the kingdoms from Denmark, was intent on resolving the problem of succession, and in 1388 she named her grandnephew Bogislav of Pomerania (1381 or 1382–1459) heir to the Norwegian kingdom, under the name Eric. In 1396, Eric was also accepted as the heir to Denmark and Sweden. To unify the three kingdoms, and to imbue previous agreements with the universal force of law, Margaret called prelates and magnates from the three kingdoms to a meeting at Kalmar. After Eric's coronation, in 1397, the details of the future government and the foundations of the so-called Kalmar Union were set down in writing in July 1397. The original documents still exist. Of these, the so-called coronation letter and the union document are the sources most widely discussed by historians of medieval Scandinavia, primarily because of their inconsistencies. While the coronation letter reflects the monarchic desire for a *"regimen regale"* (royal regime), the union document expresses the aristocrats' interest in a *"regimen politicum"* (political regime). Because only the coronation letter had legal force, the crown was the big winner at Kalmar. The ideas advanced by the nobility and prelates contradicted those of the queen, who refused to consider them. This made the coronation letter the legal basis for the government of newly crowned King Eric.

Margaret and Eric had succeeded in creating a unified government and in creating closer connections between the kingdoms than proposed by the union document. The government, which was seated in Denmark, profited from a robust increase in royal receipts, with Scania possibly the most important crown outpost. The income from fiefs also increased, and extraordinary taxes and income from the restitution of crown land also filled the royal coffers. In addition, Eric had coins minted according to the Lübeck model, the so-called *Witten* (whites), which, because of their low fine-metal content, also brought a windfall to the treasury. Margaret's reign was strengthened by her close connection with the churches in the kingdom and with the papacy, especially in matters involving episcopal investiture. Like her father before her, this was the means by which she consolidated her influence in the councils of the realm, where the bishops largely held sway.

When Eric reached majority and he assumed control of the government, in 1400, international marriage ties began to be an issue. Although his marriage with Philippa, daughter of Henry IV of England, gave him prestige, no children issued from the marriage. As a result, the problem of succession soon became the subject of his imperial policies in the Baltic region. He sought out the Hanseatic cities as partners in successfully battling piracy in the region. With Hanseatic mediation, he was able, in 1408–1409, to resolve his conflict with the Teutonic Order, which in 1398 had occupied Gotland, claiming that it had been given the island in fief by King Albert. Furthermore, Eric adroitly played off the emerging English and Dutch competition in the Baltic region against the Hanseatic cities, which were intent on retaining their privileges. He also founded and privileged new cities, such as Landskrona, on the eastern shore of the Øresund (Sound), and he expanded Malmö's existing trade privileges. To control trade and be assured of the resultant income, fortified castles were built along the shores of the Øresund, the strategically crucial narrows between the North Sea and the Baltic Sea. All boats passing through this waterway after 1429 were charged one noble in toll. This "Sound toll," which continued to be paid until 1857, became one of the most important sources of income for the Danish crown, even though it was a constant source of conflict with the Lübeckers, who had been granted toll-free access to the Øresund in 1435.

Larger controversies, however, broke out in Sweden, where in 1434 Engelbrekt Engelbrektsson (ca. 1390–1436), a mine owner in the mining district of Dalarna province, fomented a rebellion against the Danish seneschals. To calm the situation, Eric called the union councils to Kalmar for an assembly, in 1436, which produced a conciliatory document that was based on the union document of 1397. This new agreement, however, did not come into force because the king decided to play for time. In this situation, the Danish and Swedish councils worked out a new union agreement in 1438. Eric was deposed and a new Nordic Union was formed, with Christopher of Bavaria (1416–1448), a nephew of Eric's, as king of all three kingdoms, but with the councils as the actual rulers in each.[15] But after Christopher died without heirs in January 1448, the status of the union was again up in the air. A double election was held that year. At the behest of Duke Adolph VIII of Holstein, Denmark elected his nephew, Christian I of Oldenburg (1426–1481), who founded the Danish house that ruled until 1863. In Sweden, the high nobility elected strongman Karl Knutsson (Bonde)

(1409–1470) as King Charles VIII. Historians have interpreted this election both as a struggle between union and nationalism and between
regimen regale and *regimen politicum*. However, national antagonisms
(between Sweden and Denmark, for example) were less of an issue.
More important were the power struggles among the various groups of
aristocrats for political influence in Denmark and Sweden.[16]

The union was imperiled, however, because both rulers pressed their
claims to Gotland and Norway. Karl Knutsson managed to get himself crowned king of Norway, but because he was unable to conquer
Gotland or hold his ground in Norway, the Norwegian royal council
invalidated his coronation, and in August 1450 the newly elected Christian was crowned in Trondheim. In their assemblies in Halmstad and
Bergen, the Norwegian and Danish royal councils established a new
foundation for the unification of both kingdoms—a personal union of
independent but equal parts. Impressed by the possibility of a Danish-
Hanseatic coalition, Sweden was prepared to enter into peaceful relations with the Danish-Norwegian union, and in 1457 the Swedes also
elected Christian as their king. But it was not long before his opponents
began to gain ground under the leadership of Sten Sture (ca. 1440–1503).
This opposition, backed by the citizens of Stockholm and the northern
provinces, was able to muster sufficient troops to defeat Christian at
the Battle of Brunkeberg, near Stockholm, in October 1471. Since some
members of the Swedish Council of the Realm still supported the idea
of union, neither Christian nor any other future Danish king relinquished his claim to the Swedish throne until into the seventeenth
century.

Christian was more successful in the southern part of the kingdom.
When the House of Schauenburg finally died out in Holstein, Christian was, in 1460, elected Duke of Schleswig and Count of Holstein by
the knighthood in Ribe. In 1474, Emperor Frederick III, elevated Holstein,
which was part of the Holy Roman Empire, from a county to a duchy.
The Treaty of Ribe ratified the unity and indivisibility of Schleswig
and Holstein as well as the role to be played by the Schleswig-Holstein
knighthood in ruling the land. Schleswig and Holstein were to be *"up
ewich tosamende ungedelt"* (forever together and undivided), a motto
that was dug up from obscurity during the German-Danish battles of the
nineteenth century. But in reality, after Christian's death, his sons John

and Frederick agreed to split Schleswig and Holstein in 1490–1494, which meant that the boundaries between royal and ducal prerogatives were blurred in both duchies. King John (1455–1513) had been recognized as king in all of the kingdoms, in 1488, not just in the duchies, but it was not yet clear how to reintegrate Sweden into the union.

In Sweden, royal administrator Sten Sture had so consolidated his power by the 1470s that he was for many years able to prevent King John from taking control of the government. After Denmark conquered Gotland, in 1487, the king set about resolving the problem militarily. In alliance with Ivan III of Russia (1440–1505), who was intent on expanding into Karelia, in 1493 John put pressure on Sten Sture in Finland. But after this plan failed and a cease-fire was declared in 1497, John invaded Sweden with Danish and Norwegian troops and German mercenaries and seized the throne; still, he was unable to control Sweden in the long run.

His successor, Christian II (1481–1559), who cultivated relationships with the Netherlands, tried to contain the Hanseatic merchants by encouraging Dutch shipping. He also conquered the Swedish throne by force; however, his enjoyment of the Swedish crown was to be short-lived. The opposition gathered behind the young aristocrat Gustav Vasa (1496–1560), who had escaped from a Danish prison. Gustav was elected royal administrator in 1521, and the following year he received the support of the Hanseatic cities in his effort to capture the coastal fortresses that still remained loyal to Christian. In June 1523, the Swedish parliament elected him king, which dashed any hopes that a union might be restored. By January 1523, Christian II had already been deposed by the Danish Council of the Realm. His uncle, Duke Frederick I of Schleswig, was elected king in his place. Christian fled to the Netherlands, where he received monies to acquire boats and mercenaries although he failed to create an alliance. With these forces, which had been partially decimated by a storm at sea, Christian lay siege to Akershus Fortress, outside Oslo. But Frederick managed to avoid further battles by luring his nephew to Denmark, where he captured and imprisoned him for the next twenty-eight years.

Poland, too, consolidated into a monarchy after its collapse into petty principalities in the twelfth and thirteenth centuries. The union with Lithuania changed the power relationship in the Baltic region.

After the attempts to restore the unity of the kingdom at the turn of the fourteenth century had ended in failure, Władysław Łokietek offered to unite the Piast petty principalities from his base in Cracow. He used foreign powers such as the Teutonic Order for the purpose, which in 1308 had driven the Brandenburgers from Danzig but then built permanent bases there—contrary to Łokietek's wishes. Nonetheless, he left his partially consolidated kingdom to his son and successor, Casimir the Great (1310–1370). Casimir came to a final accommodation with Bohemia when he bought its claims to the Polish crown and gained recognition of fief rights over Silesia. In 1351, Casimir also obtained Mazovia, including Kujawy, *ad personam,* that is, as his personal domain. He was especially successful in his ventures in the southeast, in Red Ruthenia. Not only did he possess old claims to Halicz and Volhynia (intermittently known as the *Regnum Galiciae et Lodomeriae*), starting in 1340, he also took advantage of a power vacuum in the region to conquer Ruthenia, Przemyśl, Halicz, and Volhynia. In the north, he arrived at an accommodation of interests with Lithuania, which took possession of Volhynia, and in the south with Hungary. Only relationships with the Teutonic Order proved difficult, and in the Treaty of Kalisz, in 1343, Casimir was forced to recognize the order's possessions in Pomerelia, Danzig, and the lands of Culm and Michelau. As a result, a reinvigorated Poland became a bulwark allied with the Roman Catholic Church against the Orthodox faiths in the southeast and against Lithuanian paganism, even though Casimir was married to a Lithuanian princess.

Casimir's nephew, Louis of Hungary (1326–1382), from the House of Anjou, succeeded him, and for a time he reigned over a personal Hungarian-Polish union. However, he saw the crown of Poland primarily as a dowry for his daughters Maria and Jadwiga (ca. 1373–1399). In exchange for succession rights for his daughters, Louis was, in the Privilege of Koszyce (1374), forced to acknowledge the constitutional rights of the Polish nobility, grant them considerable voice in all political matters, and relieve them of the burdens of taxation. When ten-year-old Jadwiga was crowned queen in Cracow, in 1384, the petty Polish nobility offered her in marriage to Lithuanian grand duke Jagiełło (ca. 1351–1434) who, as their neighbor to the east, offered a union with a larger country. Poland Christianized Lithuania, the "last pagan" European country delivered to Rome. The marriage alliance with Poland had advantages for the Lithuanians as well in that it seemed to promise that the Teutonic Order's Lithuanian crusades might finally cease. With this in mind, the grand duke, in 1385, promised that he, his followers, and the Lithuanian people would be baptized. He also pledged to assist Poland in reconquering previously lost territory. In addition, the Grand Duchy of Lithuania was to be "annexed" (*applicare*) to the Polish crown. With all of these pieces seemingly in place, Jagiełło was solemnly baptized, married to Jadwiga, and crowned king.

But the annexation of Lithuania proved unrealistic. Lithuania had conquered western Russian principalities and was six times larger than Poland; it differed religiously, culturally, and linguistically from its smaller neighbor. But over and above that, Lithuanian interests in the east and southeast proved determinative of its relationship with Poland and with the Teutonic Order. In 1362, the Lithuanian grand duke, Algirdas (ca. 1296–1377), defeated the "Golden Horde" of the Tatars, occupied Kiev, and conquered the Ukraine as far as the Black Sea. But then the grand duke of Moscow, Dmitry Donskoy (1350–1389), also threw off the "Tatar Yoke." This fact on the ground presented Lithuania with a rival who, for linguistic and religious reasons, could more easily exert influence on the Russian principalities. Lithuanian grand duke Vytautas (ca. 1350–1430), Jagiełło's cousin and an active competitor, attempted to rescue the country from its embroilment with the Tatars by entering into alliance with the Teutonic Order. In 1399, however, he suffered a decisive defeat at the Battle of the Vorskla River, which led to a partial reorientation of Lithuanian politics.

The Polish-Lithuanian union was revived in 1401 with the recognition of Lithuanian independence in the Pact of Vilnius and Radom. But at the same time, hostilities broke out again with the Teutonic Order, with whom accommodations had already been reached concerning Žemaiten (Samogitia), the strip of borderland between Prussia and Livonia. But the order was unable to subdue the native Samogitians, and so the order initiated a propaganda offensive against Poland-Lithuania, defaming its ruler as a pagan prince. Poland reacted by accusing the order of using Christianization as a pretext to expand its territory. In the end, open warfare settled the matter; in 1410, the order suffered a disastrous defeat at the Battle of Tannenberg (Grunwald).

Although territorial losses in the 1411 Peace of Thorn were modest, the propaganda war flared up again at the Council of Constance.[17]

The order's rule began to erode as the connections between Poland and Lithuania continued to consolidate. Opposition to the order grew within the nobility and the Prussian Hanseatic cities, and in 1448 they formed the Prussian Confederation, which in 1454 renounced its allegiance to the Teutonic Order and offered sovereignty to King Casimir IV (1427–1492). After a lengthy war, financed primarily by the Prussian Hanseatic cities of Danzig, Elbing, and Thorn, the western territories of the order were, in 1466, placed under the direct control of the Polish crown as "Royal Prussia." The rest of the Teutonic Order's state continued to exist until 1525 when, during the Reformation, it was transformed into the secular Duchy of Prussia, a Polish fiefdom.[18]

In the east, Poland-Lithuania was forced, in the face of expansion by Moscow, to limit itself to asserting its claims to the possessions it already had. After Vytautas's death, his title was assumed first by his cousin and later by his brother. In 1440, Casimir, Jagiełło's younger son, was elected grand duke. His underaged brother Władysław had succeeded Jagiełło in Poland in 1434, with Bishop Zbigniew Oleśnicki (1389–1455) acting as regent. After the death of Holy Roman Emperor Sigismund (1368–1437), Władysław was offered the Bohemian crown by the moderate faction of the Hussites, and he was also elected king in Hungary in 1440. After initial successes against the Ottomans, he was killed at the head of a Hungarian army at the Battle of Varna. He was succeeded in Poland by his brother, the Lithuanian grand duke who, as Casimir IV, reigned over both kingdoms, having granted privileges to both the Lithuanian and the Polish nobilities. This personal union lasted until his death, and it largely consolidated the union between Poland and Lithuania. Although the two kingdoms went their separate ways for a time under his sons, Alexander (in Lithuania) and John I Albert (in Poland), Alexander's assumption of the Polish crown in 1501 restored the old relationship.[19] Thereafter, both kingdoms elected their rulers together. In 1569, largely as a result of constant military pressure on Lithuania from Russia, the personal union was transformed into a real one. Though often unwillingly, Poland became increasingly embroiled in the conflicts that flared up in eastern central Europe, but now from a position of strength. Furthermore, aristocratic parties in

Bohemia and Hungary came to view the Jagiellonian dynasty as an important counterweight to the Luxemburgers and Habsburgers, and as candidates to the throne.

Population and Urban Society

It is difficult enough to assess the population growth at this time in Europe as a whole, but we can do little more than make educated guesses for the Baltic region. It is clear that the population in the Nordic countries increased continuously from the time of the Vikings until about 1330. But only in Norway, where peasants settled on separate farms, many of whose names have been retained up to the present, can we give a more precise estimate of the number of farms. At the end of the Viking era, there were approximately 31,500 peasant households, which we estimate to have contained five to six persons each, including slaves. It is assumed that at this time not more than 1 to 1.5 percent of the population did *not* live on farms, which means that at the end of the Viking era the population would have been approximately 185,000. In about 1330, there were 73,000 farms in Norway, and the size of the household may well have decreased to an average of 4.5 persons, which yields a peasant population of about 328,500. If we add to that another 5 percent for the nonpeasant population, that figure swells to 345,000.[20] This means that since Viking times, the population of Norway had increased continuously and that people had increasingly settled northward. The population grew in Denmark and Sweden during this time as well, but we have no direct evidence from which to calculate. Nonetheless, the Danish population in about 1300 would have been between 600,000 and 700,000 in territory that lay within today's borders, which would have meant approximately one million persons within the borders of the medieval Kingdom of Denmark. For Sweden without Finland, we estimate between 500,000 and 650,000 inhabitants at that time.[21]

The Black Death and its effects in Norway have, again, been well researched. It is assumed that the plague was introduced from England by ship sometime at the end of 1348 or early 1349, and that it spread quickly along the coast by way of Bergen. We have evidence of further waves of plague in 1370, 1371, 1379, as well as in 1391 and 1392, and

then several epidemics in the fifteenth century (1452, 1459, and 1500).
Population losses were enormous. Based on tax records from 1520, it
seems plausible that between half and two-thirds of all medieval farms
were abandoned, which implies a probable loss of population between
30 percent and 60 percent. Only in the sixteenth century do we again
see signs of population and settlement growth. The plague hit Denmark
in 1350, but the precise losses are unclear. Further epidemics occurred
in 1360, 1368–1369, 1379, 1412–1413, and 1460. One symptom of the population loss is that in about 1600, 143 medieval churches were abandoned, most of them in Jutland, where a third of the churches fell into
disuse. In Jutland, the population appears to have recovered in the sixteenth century, but it regained levels seen in the High Middle Ages only
in the seventeenth.

The plague arrived in Sweden in 1349–1350. Epidemics are also attested in 1359, 1412–1413, 1420, 1422, 1439 1450, 1455, and 1469. In some
outbreaks, the rulers also fell victim. However, the population in
Sweden began to increase again as early as the fifteenth century, and
by 1570 the population had again attained the level seen in 1300. The
population in northern Sweden increased steadily as well. In Finland,
only the coastline was affected by the plague, and as a result the population grew steadily to between 250,000 and 300,000 from 1400 through
the middle of the sixteenth century.[22]

The consequences of the plague were dramatic, especially in Norway.
The regions with the least natural farmland were most affected; there,
up to 80 percent of farms were abandoned. Fishing in the coastal areas,
which was the alternative occupation to farming, delayed the depopulation process. The plague was long considered the main cause of depopulation, but it seems that other cofactors played a role. Among other
things, the climate in Scandinavia was especially cold between 1340
and 1365, which would have impeded agriculture and possibly contributed to the abandonment of farms at higher elevations in the interior. In
addition, the individual, isolated farms inhabited by nuclear families
that were so common would have been more susceptible to plague and
the vagaries of nature than were villages in other Nordic countries.

In Denmark, on the other hand, the depopulation process seems to
have been less pronounced, but it differed from region to region. While
more unproductive regions in Jutland west of Hadersleben and Apen-

rade were abandoned, there were fewer losses in the more fertile areas near Århus and on the islands of Seeland, Falster, and Fünen. To the extent that villages and fields were abandoned, they tended to be used successfully for fattening oxen, and the coastal regions continued to offer livelihoods from fishing and trade. Evidence shows that Scania, the most fertile region in Scandinavia, suffered no population losses. On the other hand, little is known about population developments in Sweden as a whole. Whereas in Småland, 30 to 40 percent of settlements were abandoned, in Värmland only 16 to 21 percent, and in Västergöt-land and Södermanland only 5 to 10 percent of medieval farms were unoccupied.

At the same time as farms were being abandoned, eastern and northern Scandinavia were being colonized and settled. Northerly set-tlement remained brisk in Finland, for example. Divided farms stimu-lated new settlements in forests and wilderness. In addition, southern and northern Karelia and the coastline of the Gulf of Bothnia continued to be settled or resettled. These colonization efforts were promoted by Magnus Eriksson and Eric of Pomerania, kings who were interested in strengthening these regions as a bulwark against the expansion of Novgorod and Moscow. As with all land development, these settlements also brought important fiscal benefits.[23] Similar colonization efforts were undertaken in Russia as well, where, in spite of less devastating outbreaks of the plague, settlement continued northward.

The most important settlement processes, however, probably oc-curred along the southern coast of the Baltic, in the Teutonic Order's Prussian state, where northwestern areas were colonized between 1310 and 1370, after which the wilderness in the northeast was cleared. Over the course of the fourteenth century, approximately 1,400 rent-paying peasant villages were created, along with numerous smaller towns. The settlers arrived from central and lower Germany, which meant that over time the native Prussian population underwent an economic and ethnic assimilation process. Prussian freemen were able to withstand the eco-nomic and social competition the longest because the Teutonic Order gave them farmland, on which they could collect rent from peasants, in exchange for their military services.[24] More significant depopula-tion first occurred in the order's lands as a result of its conflicts with Poland (1409–1411, 1431–1435) and the Thirteen Years' War (1454–1466).

In spite of an influx of Polish peasants in the south, these settlement losses were not made good until the end of the fifteenth century.

The situation looked different in the Hanseatic cities along the coast. At the beginning, in the thirteenth century, merchant leaders and other elites came largely from the larger cities of Westphalia, which resulted in family relationships between merchants in the Baltic, especially where immigration to the eastern cities continued by way of Lübeck. Other immigrants hailed from Lower Saxony, central Germany, Silesia, and Schleswig-Holstein, while most of the shippers came from the North Sea coast. Almost all of them spoke the same language, Low German, and they could make themselves understood both in the West and in Scandinavia. The strong presence of German merchants in Scandinavia led to recurrent arguments about whether they should be tolerated as guests only during the trading season or accepted as permanent residents throughout the winter. The Danish crown pursued the former policy; in Norway, on the other hand, residence in the Hanseatic German Bridge *Kontor* became the norm. Germans were omnipresent; in Stockholm, Kalmar, and Västerås they represented up to a third of the population and played an important role on city councils. In the eastern cities, German merchants encountered Kashubians and Poles in Danzig, and the numerically predominant non-German populations of Latvians, Livonians, and Estonians in Riga, Reval, and other Livonian cities. The plague decimated the Hanseatic cities to different degrees. While a third of city councilors fell victim in Hamburg, a quarter died in Lübeck, 42 percent in Wismar, and 27 percent in Reval. Despite these losses, cities such as Hamburg, Lübeck, and Danzig saw strong population growth in the fifteenth century. By the end of the century, Danzig, with 35,000 inhabitants, and Lübeck, with more than 25,000, were the leaders, followed by Hamburg (14,000) and Riga (10,000).[25] Copenhagen and Stockholm, each with between 5,000 and 6,000 inhabitants, lagged far behind.

Because of their economic and demographic growth, the social structure of the Hanseatic cities was generally more balanced than, say, in southern Germany. In Lübeck, Hamburg, Rostock, Wismar, Stralsund, and elsewhere, there was a considerable upper class of merchants (12–22 percent of the population) followed by an artisan-trader middle class (30–45 percent), and a lower class, which in Rostock comprised more than 50 percent of the population.[26] Associations played an important role in terms of social and economic cohesion and exclusion. The upper class of council families congregated in the companies of the merchants who traveled to Scania, Novgorod, and Bergen; in the exclusive Compass Society in Lübeck; in the Brotherhood of St. George, which met in the Artushof, in Danzig; or in the Brotherhood of Blackheads in Riga and Reval. In contrast, the guilds bound the artisans together by ensuring them livelihoods. These guilds served not only to control the quality of production, they also took care of their members and their families in emergencies. At the same time, the guilds fought against maladministration and abuses of power by the merchants and their representatives; given their cohesiveness, unjust financial policies, unfair taxes, nepotism, irregularities in the election of councilors, and costly external political entanglements, guilds carried the potential for open revolt. In some cities, the guilds even managed for a time to participate in city governance—until the old council, usually with the support of other Hanseatic cities, managed to wrest control again.

Brick Gothic and the Founding of the Universities

Scandinavian architecture began to absorb western European influences as early as the twelfth century. In Norway, Sweden, and Denmark, as throughout Europe, new cathedrals were built and existing churches modified. While the Lund Cathedral, built in the twelfth century, still showed evidence of Lombard influences—by way of models in Mainz and Speyer—the thirteenth-century cathedral in Uppsala was constructed along French lines, and French master builders and masons were recruited for the purpose. Because sandstone was scarce in Scandinavia, the builders used this material only for the portals, columns, capitals, and other details, brick being used for everything else. In Trondheim, they began to build the new cathedral in the Romanesque style, but in the late twelfth century went over to Gothic, which may have been the result of communications with Archbishop Eystein, who had been exiled to England from 1180 to 1183.

The beginnings of the Cathedral of Åbo go back to the thirteenth century, when the bishopric was transferred there. In ensuing centuries, Romanesque parish churches were rebuilt, torn down, or replaced by new ones throughout Scandinavia. The reason may have been that the old ones were built of wood. This was how the grand Gothic stone churches on Gotland, which drew on both their own tradition and on a very high standard of masonry, were built. The interiors of churches were ornamented with frescoes and sculptures. In Norway, these reflected English influences. Northern German models are frequently found in southern Scandinavia, although we have seen that French stonemasons worked in Uppsala as well.

Brick Gothic, however, is perhaps most reflective of the cultural relations within the Baltic region. It developed in the North Sea and Baltic regions where sandstone and limestone were scarce, and the use of fired bricks led to a particular vernacular style. The techniques for using brick, which were first employed in Danish monasteries in the twelfth century,[27] emphasize the surfaces of the architecture in contrast to the airy, loose, and ornate forms of French or English Gothic.

Hall churches replaced basilicas, although these were sometimes restructured. This resulted in a building design all its own, which some art historians have interpreted as the bourgeois answer to the cathedral or bishop's church. The parish church of St. Marien, in Lübeck, served as the prototype for this development and as a model throughout the Baltic region. It was rebuilt as a hall church at the end of the thirteenth century.[28] The builders matched the vaults of the side aisles to those of the nave, unifying the entire church. Instead of a separate chancel that emphasized the role of the priest, they built an ambulatory, which created space for both the growing parish and for the altars of the trade and merchant guilds.

The Lübeck Marienkirche directly inspired the Nikolaikirche in Stralsund and contained five flat ambulatory spaces. Of course, numerous variations were built, such as the cathedral churches in Bad Doberan and Dargun, the Schwerin Cathedral, and the Nikolaikirche in Wismar, all of which had even more basilica-like elements. One building influenced the next, as a result of which St. Petri Church, in Malmö, and the old Church of Our Lady, in Copenhagen, have chancels echoing the one found in Stralsund's Nikolaikirche. Likewise, the Marienkirche, in Greifswald, featuring a high and wide hall church, influenced other churches in Pomerania, among them the Bartholomäuskirche, in Demmin, the Jakobikirche and Heiliggeistkirche, in Stralsund, and churches in Kolberg and Grimmen. This style reached its pinnacle with the Marienkirche, in Danzig, which was originally a basilica that over the course of the fifteenth century was transformed into a monumental hall church.[29]

But churches were not the only buildings to be constructed of brick, as is demonstrated by the late-Gothic town halls in Lübeck, Stralsund, and Stargard and by the gabled town houses throughout the Baltic region. Other exemplars are the buildings of the merchant associations and elegant merchant brotherhoods such as that of the Black Heads in Riga and Reval or the Artushof in Danzig, which took as their models castles built by the Teutonic Order.

Church interiors reflect numerous and varied cultural exchanges. Grave plates and stones from the workshops of local masons vie for space with brass grave plates of Flemish provenance. Throughout the entire Baltic region, paintings and sculptures are marked by the carving traditions of Lübeck and the ateliers of Hamburg. Thus, for example, not only did carvers from Lübeck supply altars to monasteries and cathedrals throughout Scandinavia during the fourteenth and fifteenth centuries, they were also the source for many Hanseatic cities along the southern Baltic coast. Mention should be made of the donation of an altar in Trondenes, in Norway, by Hanseatic merchants from Lübeck active in Bergen, and the altar in the Kalanti Church, near Åbo. Artists like the Lübeck master Bernt Notke received commissions from numerous wealthy clients in the Baltic region. Notable works by him include the Triumphal Cross in Lübeck Cathedral and his enormous Dance of Death and the Mass of St. Gregory, which burned along with the Marienkirche, in 1942. On the other hand, a fragment of the Dance of Death can still be seen in Reval, as can the monumental St. George in Stockholm's St. Nikolai (Storkyrkan). The latter was commissioned by the Swedish regent Sten Sture to honor himself as the savior of the nation after his victory over the Danish army at Brunkeberg.

In Scandinavia, cathedral chapters and abbots commissioned the majority of works from Lübeck workshops. But in the cities along the southern Baltic coast, corporations such as artisan and merchant guilds often commissioned religious art as well, and individual merchant families also donated altars to chapels.[30] For example, the Stralsund altar given by a merchant family named Junge was created by the circle around a sculptor of the same name, although the families were unrelated. On the other hand, the Krämer family from Wismar and the Riemers and Beutlers from Stralsund commissioned their altars for St. Marien and St. Nikolai churches in Rostock. Like the Hanseatic merchants' altar in Bergen and the so-called Mayor's Altar, the High Altar in St. Nikolai in Stralsund all came from the workshops in Stralsund that in the fifteenth century also supplied other churches in the immediate area. The renowned stalls of the Hanseatic merchants who traveled to Riga, which depict sable trapping and the Russian trade, were also carved in Stralsund.[31]

Although the altar paintings frequently evince the traditions of the renowned Hamburg studios of Master Bertram (ca. 1345–1415) and Master Francke (ca. 1380–1440), the Hanseatic cities of the Baltic made use of local painters as well. This is evident, for example, from a 1421 contract in which the painter Hennig Leptzow, from Wismar, was commissioned to supply the main altar for the Georgenkirche in Parchim. Another notable example is the famed group portrait that the first rector of the University of Greifswald, Heinrich Rubenow (1400–1462), commissioned to honor his colleagues at the universities in Rostock and Greifswald, some of whom had already passed away.

The establishment of two universities along the southern coast of the Baltic, the two oldest in northern Europe, was especially significant. Although universities were founded by sovereigns all over Europe in the fifteenth century to ensure that new generations would be educated to serve their needs, this trend was delayed in northern Europe. Thus the universities in Rostock (1419) and Greifswald (1456) were founded in a landscape otherwise devoid of such institutions. The closest universities geographically were in Cologne to the west, Erfurt and Leipzig to the south, and Cracow to the southeast.

The precise motives for the founding of these universities remain unclear, although in both cases a confluence of interests among the sovereign rulers, the city, and the church can be identified. Officially at least, the initiative came from the sovereigns, when Duke John IV and Duke Albert V of Mecklenburg, with the consent of the bishop of Schwerin and the city council of Rostock, asked the pope to approve the foundation of a *"generale studium,"* in Rostock. With church donations in hand, Duke Vartislav IX of Pomerania-Wolgast (ca. 1400–

1457) initiated similar inquiries in Rome in an effort to obtain a document for the founding of a university in Greifswald. Prior to that, the duke had disclosed his intentions to the curia, which initiated preliminary proceedings through the bishop of Brandenburg. The heart and soul of the new university in Greifswald was the aforementioned mayor, Heinrich Rubenow, who had studied at the University of Rostock.

Rubenow was made the first rector of the newly founded University of Greifswald, a post he held until his murder in 1462. Among his efforts, he used his personal fortune to support the university financially. In addition, he left the faculty of law a large library. The church supported the university with benefices, which were earmarked to pay professors of theology. The levies on four villages, which the duke allocated to the university, were raised from 600 ducats to 1,000 gulden, although the monies were never received on a regular basis. Nonetheless, the founding of the universities in Rostock and Greifswald represented a windfall in terms of prestige for the sovereigns because, like electors and kings, they now could boast of their own institutions of higher learning.

The universities consisted of four faculties (arts, theology, law, and medicine)—the theology faculty in Rostock was approved only in 1432, thirteen years after its founding—and attracted students from the region, the Hanseatic cities, and Scandinavia. Canons and members of the Teutonic Order studied here as did members of the Hanseatic elite and the nobility. Whereas Rostock's students initially came from the Hanseatic cities of Hamburg and Lübeck, and only then recruited in Mecklenburg, Greifswald's student base came from Stralsund, Greifswald, and Stettin. Students also came from the smaller Pomeranian cities as well as Danzig, the Netherlands, and from western Hanseatic cities. Several hundred students from Denmark, Norway, and Sweden also attended the two Baltic universities. They did so, in part, because the universities in Uppsala and Copenhagen were not founded until 1477 and 1479. Further competition developed at the beginning of the sixteenth century, when universities were founded in the northern half of the Holy Roman Empire, in Wittenberg (1502) and Frankfurt an der Oder (1505). As a result, the number of Danish and Swedish students declined greatly, first in Greifswald and then increasingly also in Rostock, and as a result these universities came to be viewed as merely regional or Hanseatic institutions, whose graduates would find work in the chancelleries of the Hanseatic cities and duchies and in religious institutions. Only a century later, when Pomerania belonged to Sweden, would Greifswald again attract Swedish students.

In any event, the intellectual life of the region became more cosmopolitan as a result of these universities. Thus, the first generation of university professors, even those who came from the Hanseatic region, had studied in Prague, Erfurt, and Leipzig, and in some cases even in Bologna. Peter of Ravenna (ca. 1448–1508) came to the law faculty from Italy; Bogislav X met him on his trip to Italy and recruited him from Padua. Peter taught Roman and canon law in Greifswald from 1498 to 1503, before moving on to the newly founded University of Wittenberg. He later taught in Cologne and Mainz. But even lesser known scholars such as the Greifswald jurist Johannes Meilof (ca. 1435–1505) evinced an astonishing intellectual horizon and had a career to match. He had studied both in Rostock and in Greifswald, served as rector of the Greifswald Latin school, and was a member of the faculty of arts. In the 1470s he spent time in Livonia as a legal counsel to the master of the Teutonic Order and chancellor to the archbishop of Riga. He was then called to a full professorship in the faculty of law, at Greifswald, and was later elected rector. Meilof eventually retired to a monastery, where he remained intellectually active. His private professional library, which is partially extant and consisted of numerous codices, some of which he copied out by hand from writings from Italian schools of law, attest to his continued engagement.[32]

Literature and Music

Nordic literature is generally thought to have begun with the *Edda*, which has come down to us in numerous different literary genres. In addition to the poetic *Edda* and the Snorri *Edda*, the compendium written by Snorri Sturluson (1179–1241) for young court poets (skalds), the diversity of the saga literature is impressive. In addition to the sagas about ancient families or clans, new genres of sagas about the present and about bishops and kings were also composed. There were also knightly sagas, indigenous adaptations of French or Anglo-Norman courtly material, as well as sagas based on translations of Latin vitae and hagiographies. The courts of Haakon IV (ca. 1204–1263), in thirteenth-century Bergen, and of Haakon V (1270–1319), in Oslo at the beginning of the fourteenth century, developed into centers of literary production. The *Konungs skuggsjá* (King's mirror) and the sagas about Haakon IV and his son Magnus the Law-mender (1238–1280) originated in and around the royal chancelleries. The courtly literature from western Europe also arrived in Scandinavia by way of the courts in Bergen and Oslo, where courtly romances and ballads were written in some of the fortified castles.[33]

The masterwork of old Nordic literature, however, is the *Heimskringla*, which was compiled by Snorri Sturluson between 1220 and 1241 based on a variety of older traditions. In this history of the Norwegian kings, from their mythological beginnings up to the rule of Sverre (ca. 1145–1202), he wove together biographies, speeches, verses, portraits, and miracles of the saints into a single work. In the later thirteenth century, Snorri's work stimulated others to write a chronicle about the Danish kings, the *Knýtlinga* saga. However, the actual counterpart to the *Heimskringla* were the *Gesta Danorum* (Deeds of the Danes) by Saxo Grammaticus (ca. 1150–1220). These had been commissioned by Archbishop Absalon of Lund (ca. 1128–1201) and written during the first decades of the thirteenth century. They were dedicated to his successor Andreas Sunesen and were aimed at an educated elite, whom the author attempted to impress by his quotations and allusions to Roman literature. And although this made the chronicle somewhat difficult to understand, it became a standard historical work. Shakespeare derived the material for *Hamlet* from this chronicle.

Historiography began much later in Sweden. The fifteenth-century *Cronica regni Gothorum* (Chronicle of the Reign of the Goths) written by a professor at Uppsala, Ericus Olai, is probably the first history, although its main objective was to underscore the position of Uppsala as the successor to Jerusalem and Rome in the history of salvation, thereby sealing Sweden's claim to primacy over all other Scandinavian and non-Scandinavian peoples. Later chronicles, such as the Swedish *Karlskröniken* (about 1450) and the Danish *Rimkrønike*, were less artfully written and also served mainly propagandistic purposes. The Danish rhyme chronicle was published in 1495 by a printer from Gouda in the Netherlands named Gottfried of Ghemen, and it is the earliest incunabulum in a Scandinavian language.

In addition to these works, religious literature in Latin was also of considerable importance. It consisted not only of rhymed vitae of the saints such as that of the most famous Nordic king, St. Olaf of Norway, or of the Virgin Mary, but also included such works as the *Hexaemeron* of Andreas Sunesen, a creation theology abridged for didactic purposes. The letters of the Swedish Dominican monk Peter of Dacia (ca. 1230–1289) bear important witness to the spiritual and physical torments suffered by the persecuted mystic and ecstatic Christina of Stommeln (1242–1312). Mathias Övedsson, who was educated in Paris and became the first confessor of the later beatified Bridget of Sweden (1303–1373), would become even more influential. His commentary on the Book of Revelation was read by both Nicholas of Kues (1401–1464) and Bernardino of Siena (1380–1444). In her *Revelationes*, Bridget turned her spiritual and worldly visions into a piece of literature, and after her death, Vadstena Abbey, the religious community that she founded, became a center for the study of Latin and literary production. By contrast, literature in the vernacular that has come down to us from the fourteenth and fifteenth centuries is very sparse. Apart from Peter Laale's collection of Danish proverbs, we have only a few Swedish satires from the late fifteenth century. It appears that very few works of Italian or western European literature were translated into other vernacular languages prior to the Reformation, and interest in the ancient authors began to increase only later.[34]

The situation appears to have been similar along the southern Baltic coast where, for example in the area of the Teutonic Order, Latin chronicles, such as Peter of Dusburg's *Chronicon terrae Prussiae* (Chronicle of the Prussian land) and the chronicles of Johann of Posilge (1340–1405) and Nikolaus of Jeroschin (ca. 1290–1341) and the edifying religious literature of Tilo of Culm, were read.[35]

But the North Sea and Baltic region also had a lingua franca to draw on, Middle Low German, which was understood in all the Hanseatic cities and Scandinavia. In fact, modern Finnish and Estonian use many German loanwords that came into the languages at this time.[36] Trade and urban administration required literacy, and many different types of texts were produced. One type of "organizational literature" of the time, *Hanserezesse*, from which the resolutions of Hanseatic diets could be read at later sessions, was an especially innovative medium of communication. In addition, the correspondences between merchants as well as *"Burspraken,"* the public announcements that regulated daily life in the Hanseatic cities, are also noteworthy. Private, light, and edifying literature in Middle Low German included compendiums of proverbs, satirical verse, legends of the saints, and tales of adventure, such as *Deif van Brugge* (The Thief of Bruges) and a tale of horror involving Dracula (*"Von dem quaden thyranne Dracole Wyda"*).[37] It was printed in Lübeck during the last quarter of the fifteenth century and found its way as far as Scandinavia. The publisher Hans van Ghetelen and the printers Lucas and Matthäus Brandis published not only the ominously titled *Dodes dantz* (Dance of death), in 1489, but lighter fare as well: *Dat Narrenschyp* (The ship of fools) by Sebastian Brant, in 1497, and *Reynke de Vos* (Reinecke the fox), in 1498. Other printers such as Stephan Arndes and Georg Richolff and his son Jürgen published edifying religious literature, and in the sixteenth century, they distributed the writings of the Reformation.[38]

Italian humanist influences remained sparse in the regions of the Baltic that were relatively untouched by ancient literary sources. Nonetheless, a humanist historiography did develop here. One outstanding example is the work of Albert Krantz (ca. 1448–1517), from Hamburg, who after teaching at the University of Rostock and serving as legal counsel to the city of Lübeck, became a doctor of theology in Perugia. After his return to Hamburg in 1493, he wrote a major history of northern Europe, which was published during the first decade of the sixteenth century. Three of his books dealt with the Scandinavian kingdoms (*Chronica regnorum Aquilonarium Daniae, Suetiae,* and *Norvagiae*), and three others (*Saxonia, Wandalia,* and *Ecclesiastica Historia, sive Metropolis*) with the history and church history of northern Germany. He aimed to demonstrate to the leadership of the Hanseatic League the former greatness of the Hanseatic, Low German–speaking region. Johannes Bugenhagen's (1485–1558) history of Pomerania (1518), also written in Latin, had a similar purpose.[39]

Another exception was Johannes Dantiscus (1485–1548). Born Johannes Flachsbinder into a wealthy Danzig family of brewers and merchants, he studied in Greifswald and Cracow. As royal secretary he came into contact with humanism through the court in Cracow, and he served as emissary to Vienna and Spain. Dantiscus knew Erasmus of Rotterdam and, as bishop of Culm and Warmia, wrote *Elegia amatoria* and an autobiography in Latin. Nicolaus Copernicus (1473–1543), the son of a merchant from Thorn, had a similar career trajectory. He started his studies under the faculty of arts in Cracow, and, after medical and legal studies in Bologna and Padua, he received the title of Doctor of Canon Law in Ferrara. Having returned to Warmia as a canon and administrator to the bishopric, he translated the letters of the Byzantine historian Theophylaktos Simokattes and developed the foundations of his heliocentric system. Copernicus also involved himself in issues of day-to-day politics, such as monetary reform.

The Baltic sources that have come down to us concerning music are relatively sparse. Although we do know that musicians were hired by princes and aristocrats in the High Middle Ages for entertainment and status purposes, and that in the fifteenth century musicians organized themselves in the urban centers, we have no idea what kind of music they played. The few archaeological artifacts, such as a recorder from the fourteenth century found in a latrine in Dorpat, in Estonia, tell us nothing about musical practices.[40] The building of cathedral schools in Denmark and Norway, and later in Sweden and Finland, seems to have promoted the training of choristers, with the earliest examples of notation from the *Liber daticus Lundensis* indicating the reworking of European melodies already in existence. From this time, we also find evidence of the use of organs and polyphony in religious services. Bridget railed against this "new custom" and forbade it in her order. The religious community that she founded tried to spread a *cantus sororum* (*Song of the sisters*), with new texts sung to old melodies, both within Scandinavia and to other countries. Hanseatic city registers note expenditures for musicians and organ construction. For example, in 1369 and 1399 organ builders constructed a large organ in Lübeck Cathedral, while small organs were not uncommon in parish churches. In competition with the cathedral, the citizenry of Lübeck funded musical devotions (*Marientiden*) in the Marienkirche, which led to the professionalization of training for singers and to a greater openness to polyphony (*ars nova*).

CHAPTER FOUR

The Reformation and the Nordic Renaissance

Focus on Danzig

Over the course of the sixteenth century Danzig developed into the most important port in the Baltic region. Because the Vistula River connected the city directly with the vast grain-producing Polish hinterland, it was able to exploit its geographic position and leverage the increasing demand in the Netherlands to force Lübeck out of the intermediary trade between the Netherlands and eastern Europe. With a population of 40,000, it was the largest city in the Baltic during the second half of the sixteenth century. Not only did it attract merchants and artisans from western and northern Europe, but Jews and Armenians attended its trade fairs, too, and laborers flocked to the port. Some of the latter came from along the coast, while others, such as porters, came from the hinterland. Local producers of luxury products satisfied the needs not only of the wealthy local middle class, but also of the Polish nobility. The elevated position enjoyed by Danzig, which lasted into the first half of the seventeenth century, can be gauged by the growth of the city and the new public buildings that were built by Netherlandish architects, such as the brothers Abraham van den Blocke (1572–1628) and Willem van den Blocke (ca. 1550–1628). Contemporary English travelers also took note of Danzig's importance. In his journals, for example, Peter Mundy (ca. 1600–1667) praised the city's "trafficke," "plenty," "voluptuousnesse," "pride," and "arts." *Trafficke*, by which he meant the grain trade, was the source of the wealth of Danzig's merchants, while *plenty* of cheap meat, fish, game, fruit, and vegetables were certainly to be had. *Voluptuousnesse* was evident in the extraordinary feasts and carousals in which the citizenry took part in the Artushof, and the winter and summer amusements to be sampled out in

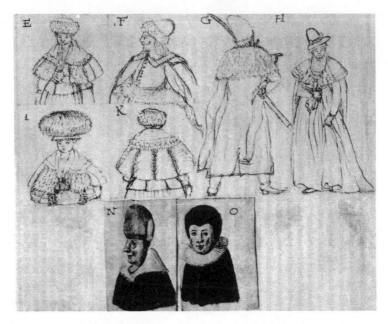

Figure 4. Women in Danzig; drawing by Peter Mundy, early seventeenth century

the country. *Pride* manifested itself in the appearance of the young women, for whom no fabrics and furs were too sumptuous. And the bell tower in Danzig's town hall, the Neptune Fountain in front of the Artushof, the wealth of furnishings in citizens' homes, and the church organs and other musical instruments attest to the high level of *artistry*.[1]

The Reformation as a Revolution in Communication

The Reformation was an event that revolutionized communication in the Baltic region and connected all neighboring peoples with each other. In Scandinavia and northern Germany, it coincided with the consolidation of territorial states—whether the Nordic kingdoms or the developing principalities. The ideas of the Reformation were spread from Wittenberg to the Baltic by a variety of media. For example, by 1520, Johannes Bugenhagen, working in Treptow an der Rega (Trzebiatów), had become very familiar with Luther's writings, and his teachings became known in Königsberg and Danzig not much later. Even before

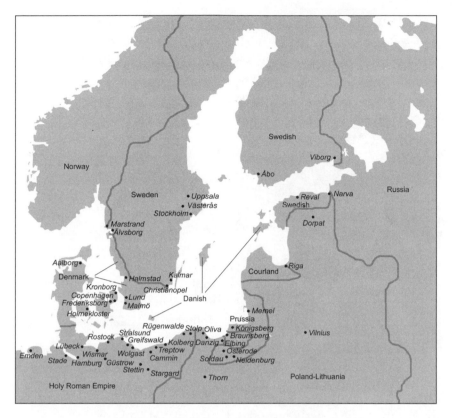

Map 4. The Baltic region in about 1590

printing presses had been set up in most of the Baltic cities over the course of the Reformation, publishers and dealers from central Germany and Lübeck were using the Hanseatic trade network to publicize Luther's works and those of other reformers.

Language was one of the crucial barriers to be overcome because Luther's written German, which was based on the official style used in Saxony, was largely unintelligible in the Baltic region, where people spoke Low German. Because of this, Luther's writings, including *To the Christian Nobility of the German Nation*, had to be translated into Low German, which proved a major turning point. They were published by Lorenz Stuchs in Halberstadt. Martin Tretter in Danzig and Hans Weinreich in Königsberg, on the other hand, published his works in High German. By the second half of the 1520s, Luther's *Small*

Catechism was available in Low German and in Danish. In 1524, the first Danish-language Bible was published for that market in Wittenberg, and the New Testament was published in Swedish in 1526. The Swedish edition of the entire Bible, based on the Lutheran Bible of 1534, was published in translation in 1541 by the brothers Laurentius Petri (1499–1573) and Olaus Petri (1493–1552) and Laurentius Andreae (ca. 1470–1552), which greatly affected the course of the Swedish written language, with numerous German loanwords and linguistic structures entering the language.

The *Small Catechism* became available in Polish in the 1530s. Initially, the lack of a written Estonian, Lithuanian, and Old Prussian seemed to be an insurmountable obstacle, but during the second half of the sixteenth century a catechism was published in those languages, which marked an important step in the creation of Baltic written languages. In Finland, the reformer Michael Agricola (ca. 1509–1557) distributed a printed primer that included liturgical texts and passages from the *Small Catechism*, which was followed in 1544 by a prayer book and his translation of the New Testament in 1548.[2]

During these early stages, the activities of itinerant preachers, some of whom had studied in Wittenberg or had met Luther and could be considered his "grand disciples," were equally important. In Pomerania, for example, the strictly orthodox University of Greifswald was sidelined, while the eastern Pomeranian city of Treptow an der Rega and the neighboring Premonstratensian Belbuck Abbey actively advanced Luther's ideas. This was where the former Greifswald student Johannes Bugenhagen, who had traveled to Wittenberg in 1521 to study, had become a priest and rector of the city's school. Bugenhagen's students included three who became monks: Georg von Ueckermünde, Christian Ketelhot (ca. 1492–1546), and Johann Kureke, who promoted the Reformation in a number of Pomeranian cities. Kureke soon began preaching against the Catholic Church's abuses and was arrested. Despite his release in the summer of 1521, the Treptow disciples found it advisable to leave their home region after the Edict of Worms, which declared Luther to be an obstinate heretic. Ketelhot traveled to Stolp, and after he was forbidden to preach there he found his way to Stralsund by way of Wolgast and several cities in Mecklenburg, where he reconnected with Ueckermünde and Kureke.

The preachers Andreas Knopke (ca. 1468–1539) and Joachim Müller traveled to Riga, and Johannes Boldewan (ca. 1485–1529), the abbot of Belbuck Abbey, who was in sympathy with the Reformation, visited Wittenberg after a brief imprisonment in Kolberg, and he later took up duties as a pastor in Belzig and Hamburg. It did not take long for the bans on preaching, which had been instigated by the Pomeranian dukes at the behest of the bishop of Cammin, to become ineffective. For example, the preachings of Johannes Amandi (ca. 1470–1530), who had left Königsberg and absconded to Stolp, soon led to riots directed against the council, which ended with the rioters' storming the church and forming a committee of twenty-four citizens of Stolp for the purpose of demanding political representation. Even the military intervention of Duke George, in November 1525, was unable to quash the Reformation process. The citizens of Stolp were then permitted to elect a preacher, Jakob Hogensee (1495–1573), who led the Reformation there.

In Stettin, Paul vom Rode (1489–1563) preached outside in the open at Luther's urging; he was soon permitted to preach from the pulpit of the Jakobikirche. After further unrest, in 1526 the council finally acknowledged him as the official preacher. From then on, numerous churches in which Catholic masses had been conducted adopted reformed services. The changeover occurred most quickly in Stralsund, the most important city in Pomerania. Even though the Hanseatic cities and the city council of Stralsund remained loyal to the old faith, the middle class of merchants and artisans, who had been incited by "subversive" sermons, managed to gain representation in the so-called Committee of 48, which broke the monopoly on power held by the council. The Holy Week of 1525 was marked by iconoclastic rampages in the Nikolaikirche and Johanneskloster, which were supported by the majority of the population. The newly formed city council recognized which way the wind was blowing and that year introduced Protestant teaching in Stralsund, which was then codified on November 5 by church and school ordinances written by Johannes Aepinus (1499–1553).

In Greifswald, the city council and professors along with priests and monks who had fled from Stralsund, managed to delay a similar process until 1531, when Johannes Knipstro (1497–1556) was granted the right to give the first reformed sermons at the Nikolaikirche. Before his hiring in Stralsund, Knipstro had already preached in Stargard. There, however, it was not until the 1530s that the Marienkirche received its first reformed preacher. Stargard's proximity to the Bishopric of Cammin and its bishop, Erasmus von Manteuffel (ca. 1475–1544), delayed the reform process. But here, too, reformed sermons spread and in 1531 were permitted by the Diet of Stettin—as long as they did not culminate in riot. Because some cities hewed to the old faith and rejected this decision, the dukes of Pomerania-Stettin and Pomerania-Wolgast realized that a unitary policy was unavoidable. They recruited Bugenhagen for the purpose. Bugenhagen had, as official pastor in Wittenberg and a confidant of Luther's, already written church ordinances for Braunschweig, Hamburg, and Lübeck. The diet, which had been invited to Treptow in December 1534 to enact Reformation policies, was unsuccessful because the duke and the nobility were unable to agree to the secularization of the abbeys. Nonetheless, the church ordinance edited by Bugenhagen was printed in Low German in 1535. At the same time, Bugenhagen, with ducal support, visited church communities in the cities of Stolp, Rügenwalde, Schlawe, Stettin, Greifenberg, Wolin, Neuenkamp, Ueckermünde, Greifswald-Eldena, Anklam, and Pasewalk to discuss financial questions and to establish policies for paying pastors and funding schools and charities. Tasks for the future included training pastors and creating a church administration with three superintendents-general at the head.[3]

Protestant ideas made their way to the Danish trading centers of Copenhagen and Malmö in the 1520s. Numerous German merchants lived there, and so these cities were receptive to itinerant preachers and pamphleteers. However, it was not until King Christian III (1503–1559) defeated the exiled King Christian II in the so-called Count's Feud (1534–1536) that Denmark converted to Protestantism and Catholic bishops were divested of their offices.[4] From now on, Lutheran bishops (superintendents) would see to the training of pastors along Lutheran lines. At the same time, Bugenhagen was called on to write a Danish church ordinance analogous to the ones he had written in Germany, in which he placed secular authorities at the head of the church. The Danish king was declared the highest representative of the church and was made responsible for the religious life of his subjects. Accordingly, Christian III regularly involved himself in theological questions

as well as church administration. Among other things, he named ex-
ponents of the Reformation, such as Frands Vermordsen and Jörgen
Jensen Sadolin, as Lutheran bishops in the dioceses of Lund and Fünen,
and he called Peder Palladius (1503–1560), who had been trained in Wittenberg, to teach theology at the newly founded University of Copenhagen. In addition, he was able to integrate the majority of Catholic
priests into the new Lutheran church.[5]

In Sweden, Gustav I Vasa called the Diet of the Realm together in
Västerås in 1527, where the decision was made to convert to Protestantism, thereby declaring the church to be independent of Rome. By
affirming the claims of the nobility to secularized church property—
the nobility was to get back all of the land with which it had endowed
the church since 1454—Gustav was able to win over the majority of the
estates to his church policies. The king, who reserved two-thirds of
this church property for his own use, now headed the church, and by
filling the ecclesiastical offices, he integrated the church personnel
into the incipient state. In 1531, Laurentius Petri was named archbishop
of Uppsala, and in addition to translations, Petri created the church
ordinance of 1571, which regulated religious life in Sweden and paved
the way for the Protestant-Lutheran state church in 1593. But it took
some time for the population to accept the new liturgy. The Swedish
mass was introduced in 1536, but it was not until 1544 that the veneration of saints, requiem masses, pilgrimages, and open-air crucifixes
were eliminated.[6]

The situation looked completely different in Prussia. Whereas the
last grand master of the Teutonic Order, Duke Albert of Prussia (1490–
1568), came under the sovereignty of the king of Poland in 1525 and
transformed his territory, Duchy of Prussia, into a model of the new
faith, the situation in Royal Prussia was very mixed. Itinerant preachers
were especially active in the cause of church reform in the large cities
of Danzig and Thorn. Although King Sigismund I (1467–1548) of Poland
had banned Lutheran writings in 1520, by 1522 the city council of
Danzig had come under considerable pressure from the citizenry to convert to Lutheranism. Because the council was unable to make a decision, social and religious riots broke out in 1523, which led to the investing of Lutheran preachers in five of the six parish churches in
Danzig. In 1525, the old council was overthrown and replaced with a

reform-minded new council that promised to act on the political, social, economic, and religious demands that were being articulated. In 1526, however, Sigismund intervened and restored the old council. The Protestant faith was banned; however, a new committee was established, the so-called Third Order, in addition to the council and the bench (the representatives of the craft guilds).[7]

Nonetheless, because of Danzig's proximity to the Protestant Duchy of Prussia, the forces of the Reformation could be held up for only so long. Among other things, Protestant preachers often infiltrated Catholic churches in the countryside, where they cautiously spread the new ideas. Only when the Polish Catholic Stanislaus Hosius was named bishop of Culm (1549) and Warmia (1551) against the wishes of the Prussian estates did this convince the Prussian estates to convert to the Reformation in 1556. They did not, however, receive the religious privileges that were granted only to large cities like Thorn, Danzig, and Elbing (1557–1558) and a number of smaller cities. These cities subsequently set about training a Protestant elite. In addition to the University of Königsberg, which was founded in 1544, they also founded academic institutions in Danzig (1558) and Thorn (1568). One had already been founded in Elbing in 1535. The schools were also reorganized. The pastoral Lutheran churches included elementary schools, and the St.-Peter-und-St.-Pauls-Kirche in Danzig even had a Calvinist school. A Protestant drama was written to inculcate students with the values of the new faith.[8]

Along the eastern Baltic coast, in Livonia, religious housecleaning was closely connected to the foreign policies of Denmark, Sweden, Poland, and Russia. As a result of the clash of interests between the Livonian branch of the Teutonic Order, the cathedral chapters, and the Hanseatic cities, the specific political and religious configuration on the ground was complex and conflicted. The work of preachers such as Andreas Knopke laid the groundwork for the relatively easy acceptance of Lutheranism, at least in Riga and Reval, where preachers sermonized to indigenous communities in Estonian and Latvian. Knopke even compiled a songbook in Low German, which included twenty-two of Martin Luther's songs. The Teutonic Order's state in Livonia, whose power generally was on the decline, nonetheless posed a problem. In contrast to the Duchy of Prussia, the master of the order, Wolter von

Plettenberg (ca. 1450–1535), would not countenance the Reformation or the secularization of the Teutonic Order's state. Nor was Margrave William of Brandenburg, Duke Albert's younger brother, willing to fulfill the hopes that the city of Riga and the adherents of the new faith had placed in him. As a result, Protestantism spread in the absence of actual political decision making.

The religious situation was overshadowed by Russia's increasing power, which under its new ruler, Ivan IV, known as "the Terrible" (1530–1584), had expanded to the southeast (Kazan, Astrakhan) and to the west, which brought Russia into potential conflict with the countries along the Baltic. In fact, Russia's invasion of Livonia, in 1558, brought Poland-Lithuania into the picture as it had entered into an alliance with the Teutonic Order only a year earlier. After Ivan conquered Narva Castle, other fortifications fell into Russian hands as well. In this situation, the master of the order, Gotthard Kettler (1517–1587) decided, in 1561, to cede Livonia to Poland but to acquire Courland for himself and his family as a hereditary Polish fiefdom. The only city able to assert its independence during the following two decades was Riga. By contrast, the city of Reval and then the knights of northern Estonia felt constrained to swear homage to and become vassals of King Eric XIV of Sweden (1533–1577).

Denmark was on the move as well. Here, King Frederick II (1534–1588) had in 1559 acquired the Bishoprics of Ösel-Wiek and Courland (diocese of Pilten) for his brother, Duke Magnus of Holstein (1540–1583), who represented Danish interests. Accordingly, Denmark initially fought alongside Poland against Sweden to achieve preeminence in Baltic trade. Narva, now in Russian hands, became the new privileged trading center, where English merchants plied their trade alongside those from Holland, Denmark, and the Hanseatic cities. The Swedes used privateers in an attempt to block this trade to force it to go through Reval, which they controlled. Skirmishes between the Swedish fleet and those of Denmark and Lübeck ended in 1566, when three Lübeck and eleven Danish ships were lost in a storm off the coast of Gotland. But even earlier, Denmark had tried to strengthen its position in the Baltic region by blocking the Øresund. This time, however, the Polish king came to the defense of the Prussian Hanseatic cities—especially Danzig—which were dependent on unimpeded shipping. The other

Hanseatic cities, in pursuit of their own interests, launched a new peace initiative, which was initially unsuccessful. It took the efforts of the emperor and his emissary Kaspar von Minckwitz to induce Denmark and Sweden to the negotiating table, where they signed the Treaty of Stettin in 1570.[9]

In the Livonian theater, where Ivan IV had once again taken the initiative in the 1570s in alliance with Magnus von Holstein, Sweden and Poland achieved supremacy over Russia only in 1581–1582. In 1584, Sweden formed the Duchy of Ehsten out of the four Estonian territories of Harrien (Harju), Wierland (Virumaa), Jerwen (Järva), and Wiek (Lääne). Polish forces under King Stephan Báthory (1533–1586) pushed back against Russian influence from the south and forced the Russians to renounce their claims to Livonia in the Truce of Yam-Zapolsky in 1582. However, fighting between Russia and Sweden continued until the Treaty of Teusina, which was signed in 1595. Religious allegiances underwent a change once again because of the Russian invasion and the increased engagement of Poland. Even before 1582, the Russians had built Orthodox churches and monasteries in eastern Livonia, where they tried to convert the peasantry.

The representatives of Rome and the Jesuits who followed Polish king Stephan Báthory into Livonia were more successful in combating the spread of Protestantism and of Orthodoxy. Their base of operations was Vilnius and the university that had been founded there in 1579. Jesuit colleges were also founded in Riga and Dorpat, and the Protestants were forced to relinquish St. Jacobs Church in Riga to the Catholics for their masses. The Catholics founded a bishopric in Livonia, with its center in Wenden. The religious freedom that had been proclaimed in documents was abrogated, and Lutheranism became a merely tolerated religion. When the city council of Riga attempted to introduce the Gregorian calendar, in 1584, the citizenry revolted and forced the Jesuits from the city. It took military intervention in 1589 by the Polish-Lithuanian Great Chancellor Lew Sapieha (1557–1633) to restore the old council, which then introduced the Gregorian calendar. In addition, churches founded by the Jesuits had to be restored to them. By teaching the Latvian language and publishing a Catholic catechism in Latvian, the Catholic mission created the underpinnings of a multiconfessionalism that has shaped the region to the present day.[10]

Religious diversity and multiethnicity were closely connected, especially because the Reformation triggered migration throughout Europe. Thus, for example, religious persecution in western Europe induced Dutch Mennonites to relocate to the Baltic. This particular peasant migration largely involved Frisian Mennonites, who had been settled in Royal Prussia since the middle of the sixteenth century. Because of their success in reclaiming the river island of Danzig, royal and noble landowners along the Vistula were keen to recruit Mennonite settlers to their lands. The Mennonites were able to enter into long-term rental agreements and enjoyed certain personal liberties. They formed the core of a uniquely independent and self-possessed wealthy peasantry in Poland.[11]

Artisans constituted the second group of immigrants. In addition to emigrating northward, Calvinist textile manufacturers from the southern Netherlands also settled in large numbers in cities along the Baltic. Much as in Leiden, they revolutionized the production of textiles in Königsberg and Danzig by introducing dyeing and the manufacture of light-weight woolens. Dutch immigrants also revived the arts of silk weaving and passementerie, with Mennonites the main passementerie makers.[12] The third important group of Dutch immigrants consisted of merchants, factors, and bankers. They settled in the Baltic ports, sometimes permanently and sometimes not, with quite a few acquiring citizenship. Of course, most of the Dutch merchants lived at the center of the Baltic trade, which was in Danzig.[13]

Englishmen and Scots were also active as traders, with the English tending toward the wholesale trade and Scots engaging in retail and peddling. In addition, the Scots were overrepresented as mercenaries in Scandinavian armies. In large part, they were attracted by the promise of profit from trade or war booty, but at home the sporadic persecution of Scottish Presbyterians, followers of John Knox, played a not inconsiderable role as well.[14]

Integration into the World Economy

As described earlier, Hanseatic trade suffered setbacks on all fronts at the turn of the sixteenth century. The old trading system based on privileges proved inadequate in the face of growing economic competition

and the increasing power of the European monarchies. One particular
rivalry existed between the Hollanders and Zeelanders, on the one hand,
and Hanseatic cities, such as Lübeck, Wismar, Rostock, Stralsund, and
Greifswald, on the other, which saw their position threatened in the
intermediary trade and freight transport along the east-west route. One
important prerequisite for the expansion of Dutch shipping and Dutch
business in general during the fifteenth century was the natural environment itself. Because their mediocre soil and the high cost of drainage
made grain cultivation unprofitable, the Dutch concentrated on alternative products. The peasants specialized in livestock husbandry and
dairy farming; they also cultivated industrial crops and fodder crops
such as flax, madder, and rapeseed along with tobacco, hops, and tur-
nips. Many of these products were sold mainly to businesses in the
cities. Fishing and shipping, which were traditional activities, were also
expanded. The Dutch traded their own products to finance their continuous need to import grain. Over time, they garnered fairly significant shares of the market for their beer, textiles, North Sea herring,
and a number of cheaper knockoffs or variants of branded Flemish and
Hanseatic products.[15] The increasing demand for freight capacity for
the burgeoning trade opened the door to the Baltic for the Hollanders
and Zeelanders. By 1580, half of all Danzig imports and exports were

Table 4.1   Sea traffic with Danzig (number of ships arriving at or departing from Danzig, 1460–1583)

Port or country of origin	1460 arrivals	1475–1476 arrivals	1530 departures	1583 arrivals	1583 departures
Netherlands	11	160	235	1,070	1,045
North Sea coast	2	—	1	234	231
Hamburg	—	2	13	30	28
Denmark	2	5	34	107	87
Schleswig-Holstein	7	6	2	142	125
Sweden	97	96	35	81	77
Lübeck	59	168	24	63	57
Baltic coast	50	106	79	199	172
Prussia	—	2	169	148	141
Livonia	30	25	9	43	43
Other	5	96	53	103	93
Total	263	666	654	2,220	2,099

transported by Dutch ships, and the proportion of Dutch shippers in the Baltic trade grew from 60 percent to 70 percent during the seventeenth century.

Starting in the sixteenth century, the Baltic cities began to limit their assortment of wares, concentrating on the export of bulk products, such as grain and wood. The productive regions in the Baltic hinterlands became ever more closely integrated into the overall European economy. The most important western European imports included herring and salt. Foreign contemporaries, such as the seventeenth-century English ambassador George Downing, viewed such economic success in the Baltic trade with misgivings. Thus, in a letter he wrote, "The herring trade [of the Dutch] is the cause of the salt trade, and the herring and salt trade are the causes of the country's having, in a manner, wholly engrossed the trade of the Baltic Sea for they have these bulky goods to load their ships with thither."[16] Although herring was praised as the "golden food" of the Dutch, their Baltic trade and economy generally were not based on it alone.

The Baltic trade was of such central significance to the Dutch economy for such a long period of time that they rightly viewed it as the *moedercommercie* (mother of all commerce). The grain imported from the Baltic region fed approximately one-third of the Dutch population and freed up Dutch agriculture for more profitable production. In the end, that trade enabled the Dutch to find a footing in completely different areas of commerce. For example, the Dutch were able to exploit their Baltic grain monopoly when crops failed in western and southern Europe toward the end of the sixteenth century. As a result, they came to control not only grain and wood exports from the Baltic, but also the export of western manufactured and luxury products in the other direction. The Hanseatic cities in the Baltic region had to make do with a small proportion of the east-west trade because of their higher freight tariffs and lower transport capacities, although they continued to dominate trade and shipping within the Baltic itself.[17]

The second important Baltic export, wood, was, like its byproducts pitch, tar, and ash, used in shipbuilding and other types of production. Dutch shipbuilding was already innovative. But this cheap supply of shipbuilding materials, to which were added flax and hemp

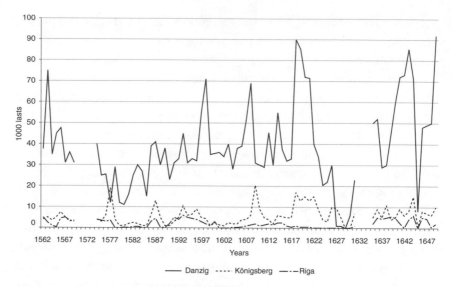

Graph 1. Grain shipments through the Sound (Øresund) in 1000s of lasts, 1562–1649   *(E. Opgenoorth [1994], p. 132)*

for sails and rope, ensured that Dutch shipping rates would be low as well. Herring processing required large quantities of manufactured barrel staves, so-called clapholts, from the Baltic, while other businesses, such as soap makers, were major consumers of potash from Danzig and Königsberg.

Dutch dominance, which was based on their trade in grain, timber, and forest products and the shipping capacity needed to make that trade flow, remained unrivaled until the second half of the seventeenth century, when the English Baltic trade began to surge. Over the course of the sixteenth century, Dutch imports of grain alone grew from approximately 19,000 lasts in 1500 to 80,000 lasts in 1567. A last of grain, it should be noted, was approximately two metric tons, varying somewhat from location to location. The volume of trade, especially grain trade, continued to increase in the waning years of the sixteenth century and the beginning of the seventeenth, but it then diminished during the second half of the century.[18]

The development of a ship called the *fluyt* (flute) or fly-ship, which according to one popular legend was first built in 1590 in Hoorn, is credited with sparking the Dutch boom in the Baltic trade. The fly-ship conferred a number of advantages on Dutch shipbuilders and shippers. It was built of light wood, and it was constructed in large numbers based on a standardized design. It was also suited to many different uses. The standardization of design decreased not only production costs, but operational costs as well. In the following century, the fly-ship became the model for Baltic shipbuilders because Dutch shipwrights brought their know-how with them when they were hired by the shipyards of Altona, Copenhagen, Stockholm, Danzig, Riga, and later even St. Petersburg to modernize the local industry. Hanseatic shipbuilding guilds forbade Dutch shipbuilders from being hired or even presenting their know-how, which slowed down the adoption of new state-of-the-art technology.

The export curves for timber and forest products such as potash, pitch, and tar, which served the needs of shipbuilders and businesses in western Europe, approximated those of grain exports. They had risen since the end of the sixteenth century and reached a high point in the 1630s and 1640s, after which they receded. They then grew continuously after the last quarter of the seventeenth century, which often brought about significant changes in the importance of the various ports and hinterland areas. Although Danzig remained the most important port for the export of grain and wood over the entire period, other ports exceeded it from time to time for certain products. These included the ports of Königsberg (wood), Riga (wood, flax, hemp), and Narva (wood) as well as smaller Swedish (tar), and Finnish (tar) ports.[19]

Another important factor was the use of resources of the Russian hinterlands, which, however, often changed hands. As long as Narva remained under Russian control during the First Northern War (1558–1583), Russian grain continued to be exported to the west through that port; after Narva came under the control of Sweden, the Russian government banned grain exports to inconvenience its enemies. However, merchants and producers continued to export flax and hemp from western Russia via Riga, while the Russian government promoted export via Arkhangelsk, although shipping from this port was rarely profitable because of the higher freight costs.

Like the textile trade, "domestic trade" within the Baltic generally continued to reside in Hanseatic or English hands. Hamburg and Lübeck continued to control the Baltic trade, especially to the ports of

Danzig, Königsberg, Riga, Reval, Viborg, and Stockholm, to which they shipped textiles, spices, salt, and sugar. Good examples are the branches that merchants from Lübeck founded in the eastern Baltic. While Reval had been the dominant market for some time, after the Russians conquered Narva (1558), which cut Reval off from its Russian hinterland, the Lübeckers switched their trade, first to Viborg and later to Narva. At the same time, exports from Riga increased, with Lübeck merchants in the lead, depending on the products being traded. While Riga's exports of flax and hemp, ash, and tar reached western European and especially Dutch markets, primarily by way of the Øresund, Lübeck became the almost exclusive trader in leather, skins, and tallow. Thus, for example, the merchant Wolter von Holsten obtained leather, skins, flax, tallow, and wax from Riga, while shipping textiles and herring on the return trip. For one thing, the profitability and relative stability of the Riga trade was attractive to Lübeck merchants as the constant threat from Swedish privateers had made trade with Narva increasingly risky. On the other hand, in the late sixteenth century, the expanse of Riga's hinterland extended into White Russia and Lithuania and offered an almost unlimited supply of these products.[20]

Sweden traded largely by way of Lübeck, with the Swedes exporting metals, butter, furs, and skins in exchange for textiles, salt, retail goods, and spices. The copper export ban, which had been in place since the beginning of the sixteenth century, had a negative effect on profits, while textile imports from Lübeck increased. It was not until the end of the sixteenth century that copper exports increased along with the export of osmond (iron).[21] Trade with Denmark was conducted both by sea and by land; while Hamburg and Lübeck supplied Denmark with retail goods, beer, hops, and textiles, major Danish exports included horses and cattle. Exports of cattle grew annually from 20,000 head in about 1500 to 50,000 in about 1580. Not all were consumed in Hamburg or Lübeck, however; a large percentage found their way to the Netherlands.[22] In addition, with the shift in the herring banks to the Kattegat and North Sea during the second half of the sixteenth century, in particular to Ålborg and Marstrand, two new centers of the fishing trade began to supply the Baltic region with fish to make up for shortfalls in North Sea herring imports from the Netherlands.

Initially, English textiles were sold in the Baltic region largely by way of Hamburg, although English textile merchants had long been seeking privileges to market their cloth (known as a *staple*) along the North Sea and Baltic coasts. A group called Merchant Adventurers, which already had a branch in the Netherlands, opened one in Emden in 1563, and in 1567 it negotiated a ten-year privilege with the Hamburg city council for the right to settle and trade. As a result, trade with England came to be conducted almost exclusively through Hamburg. The Hamburg office became indispensable to the Merchant Adventurers when they lost the Antwerp market during the Netherlandish revolt against Spain. Against this backdrop, the Hanseatic League tried to find a way to regain most favored status in the British Isles. As a result, the Hanseatic diet in Hamburg demanded that the Merchant Adventurers close their office after expiration of the privilege, to which England responded by excluding Hanseatic merchants from the center of the textile trade at Blackwell Hall, in London. In this situation, the counts of Eastern Friesland and Emden along with the city of Elbing offered the Merchant Adventurers a new home base that would protect them from Hanseatic repression.

The representatives of the Hanseatic League pulled out all the stops in their battle against the English, even attempting to have the emperor and the imperial diet expel the English from the Holy Roman Empire. After the imperial diet expelled the Merchant Adventurers in 1597, the English banned all trade with the Hanseatic cities. The Merchant Adventurers, however, continued to ship their textiles to the empire, using middlemen in the Netherlands, Bremen, and Hamburg.[23] By the beginning of the seventeenth century, Hamburg was no longer willing to knuckle under to pressure from Lübeck, and after the arrival of the English textile fleet, in June 1611, the council privileged the English branch, which also received the approval of the emperor. Although Lübeck went on the offensive in an attempt to regain its privileges, it was unable to obstruct the English merchants, especially since they had in the meantime also founded a branch in Elbing on the southern coast of the Baltic.

In 1577, after the Polish king Stephan Báthory instituted a trade blockade against Danzig and rerouted Polish exports through Elbing, a new organization of English Baltic merchants, the Eastland Company, applied to the Elbing city council for a favorable staple. Elbing was very interested in permanently taking English trade away from Danzig and was prepared to offer a very generous privilege. The contract with the Eastland Company excluded English merchants from provisions of the Hanseatic guest laws, essentially putting them on an equal footing with the citizens of Elbing. In addition, the city and the Eastland Company agreed to pay to maintain the port conjointly out of customs revenues. At the end of the sixteenth and beginning of the seventeenth centuries, more than half of all the ships sailing from Elbing were bound for England. Most of the imports were textiles, while traditional imports such as salt and herring played little or no role at all. However, Elbing was not in a position to compete with Danzig as an import center over the long term. This was because the main consumers of English textiles, the Polish nobility, mainly sold their grain in Danzig since Elbing had only a small commodity market, which meant that they now had to acquire textiles in a sort of "triangular trade." It was only a matter of time until the English textile merchants began to import their wares directly through Danzig. The Swedish occupation of Elbing (1626–1635) finally enabled Danzig to acquire the English staple. In 1628, the Polish Sejm ordered the dissolution of the Eastland Company in the Polish-Lithuanian Commonwealth and named Danzig the sole port of entry for English textiles.[24]

Grain and the Manorial Economy

The Baltic trade, and especially the growing western European demand for grain, changed the economic and social structures in the region. This trade stimulated the expansion of the noble manorial economy, concentrated the movement of goods in a few large centers along the Baltic coast at the expense of inland cities, and made local Baltic merchants dependent on Dutch traders.[25] Each year, during the first high water on the Vistula, hundreds of boats and rafts floated grain, timber, and other forest products down to Danzig, where they were first warehoused and then exported over the course of the spring and summer. During the previous year, merchants from the Netherlands and Danzig had bought the grain "on the stalk" from peasants and landowners to ensure their ownership of the harvest. Over the course of the sixteenth century, annual grain exports increased from approximately 10,000 lasts to 20,000 and even 40,000; the record years were 1563 and 1598, when 60,000 to 70,000 lasts were booked. At the same time, Danzig was the largest recipient not only of western European goods such as herring, salt, and textiles, but also of southern European luxury items, which the noble landowners traded for grain.

The expansion of the manorial system has generally been attributed to the favorable geographic position of the territories in the Baltic's hinterland area and of the rivers that drain into the sea. This is more or less correct as far as it goes. The transition from production for the sole use of the nobility and their households to production for the larger market marks the actual beginning of the manorial economy. However, we must distinguish between two types of manorial economy: on the one hand, the manorial production associated with the export market and foreign demand, and, on the other hand, the manorial economy supported by the domestic market and domestic demand.[26] Foreign demand, such as that for rye in Amsterdam, also affected prices in the domestic market and the regions and demesne farms that satisfied that demand.[27] This is why the impact of the foreign and domestic market on the development of the manorial economy cannot easily be teased apart— an effort made all the more difficult because of the scarcity of source material for scholars to consult. But overall, we may reconstruct the following economic trends based on the pricing of agricultural products. First, grain prices fell for many years up to the first decade of the sixteenth century. This was followed by an increase in economic activity that lasted until the end of the sixteenth century. A depression occurred between 1600 and 1620, after which an economic boom in grain prices took place from 1620 until about 1640 or 1650, which was associated with the Thirty Years' War.[28]

A number of important developments in the manorial economy in the Baltic region may be interpreted as a reaction to economic ups and downs, especially in the demand for grain, but certain other developments were less important. In the fifteenth century, for example, the economics of grain had little affect on the development of the manorial economy in Holstein. Nor did the upswing in economic activity stimulate the manorial economy equally in all regions during the second decade of the sixteenth century. Only in Holstein and in various parts of Poland did farms expand production for their own purposes. Rather than living from the rents and other levies collected from their peasants, landowners produced grain on land specifically set aside and worked for that purpose, the so-called demesne farms (*Vorwerke*).[29]

Traditionally, the early beginnings of the manorial economy in Poland have been explained by grain exports, even though—according to Andrzej Wyczański's estimates—less than 10 percent of Polish agrarian output was ever exported.[30] Another region with an early manorial economy was Mazovia, whose geographic position in the hinterland area of the Vistula was especially favorable to export.[31] The main grain exporter during the sixteenth century was Royal Prussia, whose agrarian structure was characterized by small demesne farms under ten *Hufen* (hides) in size (a *Hufe* or hide being a variable measure, but equal to about 16.5 hectares) belonging to noblemen, but also by large peasant farmsteads. These large farms were the ones that turned the highest profit from the export of surplus grain.[32]

A more nuanced picture is provided by another Baltic region, the Duchy of Prussia. Not only were there fewer grain surpluses in this region, in addition, most of its output was destined for the domestic market. For example, the ducal administrative districts of Osterode and Soldau earmarked the majority of their rye for local markets; only 45 percent of rye produced in Osterode and 36 percent of that from Soldau reached the export market in Elbing. Grain production was not the only agricultural activity engaged in by the peasantry or the demesne farms, which means that the manorial economy was not necessarily a grain monoculture.[33]

Economic factors seem to have been critical to the expansion of the manorial economy. Land and labor were the most important production factors, and these factors were inversely proportional. Thus, while the demographic decline during the late Middle Ages (which repeated in the seventeenth century) created a labor shortage, it also had the effect of increasing the available land. As land became more plentiful in relation to labor, the landowners, who in the late Middle Ages derived most of their income from rents in the form of money and products, suffered considerable losses on both accounts.

And because the landowners were not able to pass along rent increases to their subjects, whose value relative to land had increased, the only way they could maintain their standard of living was to increase agricultural production on their own land. The East Elbian nobility did this by taking control of the abandoned land in the region, which as late as the sixteenth century made it possible for them to develop demesne farms without having a lasting negative impact on the land use of the remaining peasantry.[34]

To a great extent, land and geographic factors determined how the manorial economy developed. These factors included soil quality and climate along with natural resources, such as forest products and fish, that were perhaps more easily harvestable. The farms were also very diverse. Thus, livestock was extremely important in Schleswig-Holstein, on the Danish islands, and in the Duchy of Prussia; in the late sixteenth century, cattle and swine played a dominant role in Schleswig-Holstein and Denmark.[35] Other important activities included forestry, freshwater fishing, and brewing. Beer was brewed increasingly on the manors, which supplied the inns and taverns in the villages. In general, the noble manors were less diversified than the demesne farms, which meant that the expansion of grain production was of great importance to them. But even toward the end of the sixteenth century, some noblemen continued to produce only enough grain to satisfy their own daily needs and to live almost exclusively from the rents paid by their subjects.[36]

The peasants performed compulsory labor (corvée) on the demesne farms. With the expansion of the manorial economy, the amount of corvée labor increased in Mecklenburg, Pomerania, and Prussia from one day per week in the mid-sixteenth century to three days at the beginning of the seventeenth. Only in Poland and Holstein, the regions that pioneered the manorial economy, did landowners demand four or five days per week at the beginning of the seventeenth century.[37] To ensure peasant labor, the peasants were legally bound to the soil. Between thirty and fifty years after the expansion phase, laws were passed that barred freedom of movement (Schollenband). These laws were in effect even during periods in the sixteenth century when the population increased and there was no dearth of peasants and settlers. At this point, the peasants were no longer able to give notice and move on; at best they could buy their freedom. This was how serfdom developed.

Denmark, especially the islands of Fünen and Seeland, was a special case. There, freedom of movement had been banned (*vornedskab*) since the end of the fifteenth century—in the absence of a manorial economy. By this method, the Danish nobility made certain that the peasants paid their rents and other levies. Similarly, the Polish diet sitting in Petrikau decreed at an early date (1496) that peasants could leave the land only if they could produce a replacement.

In Holstein, the ability to leave the land was limited in 1524. In 1575, we find the first use of the term *Leibeigene* (serf) in Holstein in the context of the "serf Heinrich Bonhoff," who absconded to Lübeck, taking horses and cattle from Waterneverstorf manor.[38] In Mecklenburg, a police decree of 1572 put an end to the flight of peasants from the land and the legalization of their residence in cities—at least on the books. Pomerania followed suit in 1616, with a provision for Pomerania-Stettin that sanctioned servitude.[39] Before they could offer their services to other peasants or landowners, the children of peasants were forced to offer their labor to their landlord. Whether and to what extent landlords made use of such forced rent depended on the overall availability of labor in the region.

In the Livonian territories, manorial claims on the person had by the fifteenth century become anchored in the principle *schult ofte maen* (debt or man), which meant that an earlier master could demand that an escaped peasant be handed over or that his debt be worked off. In practice, however, it was very difficult to press such claims because the places where a peasant might find safe harbor were many. In addition to the five ecclesiastical territories, namely the Bishoprics of Courland, Ösel-Wiek, and Dorpat, the Archbishopric of Riga, and the area controlled by the Livonian Order, the large cities of Reval and Riga also provided relatively safe refuge. As a result, the territorial rulers, such as the bishop of Ösel and the local nobility, began to negotiate extradition treaties. From time to time, Reval and Riga agreed in principle to extradite peasants who had fled, but without agreeing to binding provisions.[40]

How the manorial economy and corvée labor were implemented in the Baltic region depended on the attitude of the nobility and of the individual noblemen. We often find that a particular notion of manorial lordship was implemented by noblemen who were members of closely interconnected family networks or by aristocratic officeholders. The goal was to create a farm that functioned as a closed unit under the control of one person or family. Thus, for example, in Holstein as early as 1488 the intent was expressed as follows: *"minen ganssen hoff tho Equelstorpp mit alle siner thobehoringe unde upkamyngen, alse nomentlyken mit den dorperen unde guderen . . . mit allen lansten unde inwoneren jegenwardisch unde thokamende"* (My entire manor at Egelsdorf with all its belongings, namely the villages and farms with all lands and inhabitants present and future).[41]

This lordly mentality—this being the earliest expression of it we have been able to find—was manifested in numerous farm purchases and put on the record, especially when the purchases involved prominent noblemen such as Heinrich Rantzau (1526–1598), the governor appointed by the Danish king, or Jan Zamoyski (1542–1605), the grand hetman of the Polish crown. In the sixteenth century, farms were bought because they were increasing in value, which meant that economic investments and investments in social prestige could be combined.

The purchase of the Holmekloster manor on Fünen is especially well documented. Rantzau spent two years trying to buy that property. Finally, in 1568, the Danish king gave his consent—in exchange for 55,000 taler. Rantzau renamed the manor Rantzausholm and had a plaque installed at the entrance, the text of which documents the dynastic goals of the purchase:

> Coat of arms of the Rantzaus and Halles. Heinrich Rantzau, Johann's son, Breide's grandson, Cai's great-grandson, purchased this farm with surrounding villages for himself and his heirs, family, and descendants during the eight-year Swedish war from Frederick II, King of Denmark, and the high nobility of the kingdom, and had it named Rantzausholm. In the Year of our Lord 1568, in his 43rd year.[42]

But even petty noblemen were ineluctably driven to expand their own economic production when they inherited a farm. This was the case with the Pomeranian nobleman Jacob Wackenitz, who established his farm in Trissow between 1570 and 1575.[43] But none of his efforts satisfied his ambition to live in accordance with his elevated estate. Over and over again, he felt it necessary to take out small loans in

Görmin and from the Marienkirche in Greifswald. In effect, of all the
nobles, members of the petty nobility were probably the most disad-
vantaged by the manorial economy, and they, in turn, put the most pressure on the few subjects over whom they had control.

How did the peasants react to these increased demands? And to what
extent were they in a position to hinder the expansion of the demesne
farms? The majority of East Elbian peasants could only delay the increases in demanded corvée labor, as exemplified by the peasants of
Kummerow in the district of Demmin, who were able to do so for several decades.[44] To the extent they were successful, the peasants negotiated corvée contracts that set out compromises in terms of the labor
demanded of them. But such agreements, to the extent they were negotiated, were always contested by the landlords, who almost always
had the greater leverage. Nonetheless, the peasant did not "function"
solely as labor or as a "subsistence unit," as Witold Kula's feudal model
suggests. Generally, a peasant would not perform corvée labor himself,
but he would have a family member or his laborers do it for him. That
is why the peasants competed with each other and with the noble landowners on the rural labor market. This did not, however, encourage the
monetization of work relationships since the day laborers worked for
bread and beer.[45]

The Renaissance in the Baltic Region

The princes and the estates competed with each other in the arts as
well, which is evident even today in the craft and artistry on display
in numerous castles and manors. The culture of the princely courts was,
however, superior to that of the nobility. Netherlandish influence is evident in architecture, sculpture, and painting. Dutch architects and artists, such as Anthonis van Obbergen (1543–1611), Willem van den Blocke
and Abraham van den Blocke, the painters Hans Vredeman de Vries
(1527–1607) and Isaak van den Blocke (1575–1628), and the copper engravers Claes Jansz. Visscher (called Piscator) (1587–1652) and Willem
Hondius (ca. 1598–1658), among others, worked for a variety of clients
in both Copenhagen and Danzig. In the sixteenth century, Denmark
developed a pronounced predilection for "Italian" architecture, which

arrived either directly or through the Netherlands. For example, Jan Jorisz van der Schardt, from Nijmegen, received his architectural training in Italy, and he probably designed the observatories built by the astronomer Tycho Brahe (1546–1601) on the island of Ven (Hven) in the Øresund. Hans van Steenwinckel the Elder (ca. 1550–1601), who was born in Antwerp, also worked for Brahe. During the Netherlandish revolt against Spain, the family fled to Emden, where Steenwinckel built the city hall. In 1578, van Obbergen recruited him as his assistant in the construction of Kronborg Castle. Thereafter, Brahe instructed Steenwinckel in geometry and astronomy, which led to a confluence of stylistic traditions and disciplines.

Steenwinckel used this training when he became architect to King Christian IV (1577–1648), for whom he renovated existing fortresses on the Swedish and Norwegian coasts and laid out the fortified town of Kristianopel (1599). He was especially proud of his work in Halmstad, where he is memorialized with a gravestone.[46] His sons Hans the Younger (1587–1639) and Lourens (1585–1619) were involved in almost all of Christian IV's building projects in the early seventeenth century. Their contribution is not, however, completely evident because the king wanted to give the appearance of having himself been the architect. Hans van Steenwinckel was undoubtedly involved in building the royal chapel in Roskilde, and with his brother in working on the bourse in Copenhagen. He was also involved in designing the round tower of the university church.

Views of Copenhagen from the beginning of the seventeenth century show numerous new gabled houses in the Dutch style, of which only a few have survived. Even public buildings, such as the orphanage, the bourse, and dwellings for seamen and textile workers, were built according to the "progressive" Dutch style. Frederiksborg Palace, which testified to Christian IV's royal ambitions and prestige, attempted to meld Danish traditions with elements of the European Renaissance. Dutch art played a central role in this effort. Three large commissions—the Neptune fountain of Adriaen de Vries (ca. 1556–1626), the sculpture gallery of Hendrik de Keyser (1565–1621), and the tapestries designed by Karel van Mander (1548–1606)—are representative of the best Dutch art of the period. Some of the holdings are probably from

the early seventeenth century because in 1607–1608 Christian IV
sent his agent Jonas Charisius on an expedition to the Netherlands to
purchase paintings and musical instruments.[47]

Netherlandish architects were also busy in Sweden, where they
helped build the fortifications of Gothenburg (1603–1607) and Kalmar
(1613). Members of the de Besche family were initially architects before they began investing in metallurgy.[48] Only in Poland, and especially in Danzig, was the influence of Dutch Renaissance architecture
as great as in Denmark in the sixteenth century.[49] Here, approximately
twenty artists spread the architectural forms developed in the spirit of
Dutch mannerism. The ornamental style propagated by Hans Vredeman
de Vries and Cornelis Floris de Vriendt (ca. 1514–1575) came to epitomize art in Danzig after the 1560s. Perhaps the most outstanding example is the Red Hall in Danzig city hall, designed by de Vries between
1592 and 1596 and later embellished with Willem van der Meer's decorative fireplace. Other buildings representative of the new style in
Danzig include the Green Gate (possibly constructed by Hans Kramer
between 1564 and 1568), the High Gate with its decorative friezes by
Willem van den Blocke (1588), the Golden Gate of Abraham van den
Blocke, built between 1612–1614, and the Great Arsenal, built by van
Obbergen between 1600 and 1605. Danzig was frequently only a way
station for artists on their way to Cracow, Lublin, or Breslau. The ar-
tistic pace set by Danzig was emulated in neighboring cities in Royal
Prussia and Warmia, and in cities such as Vilnius and Königsberg. Thus,
Willem van den Blocke worked on the tombs of Duke Albert of Ho-
henzollern and his wife in Königsberg, and on a comparable memorial
in Alba Iulia in Transylvania, which was created in his workshop in
Danzig.[50]

Anthonis van Obbergen, who arrived in Poland from Denmark in
1586, deserves further mention in this context. He led the reconstruction of Danzig City Hall (Rechtstädtisches Rathaus) and built the
armory and the Old City Hall (Altstädtisches Rathaus), with artists
such as Vredeman de Vries contributing ornamentation.[51] Native
Danzig artists, such as the copper engravers Ägidius Dickmann (1593–
1648) and Jeremias Falck (1610–1677), learned their craft in western Europe, or at least spent a few years working there. In addition, the office
of master builder was given exclusively to Dutch architects between

1563 and 1666. The first, Reinier van Amsterdam, built the Green Gate in 1568, which was inspired by the city hall in Antwerp; the last, Peter Willer, was a student of Jacob van Campen (1596–1657), who built the renowned city hall in Amsterdam. Outside of Danzig, the work of Dutch architects may also be seen in Elbing, Thorn, Neidenburg, Braunsberg, Pillau, Königsberg, Memel, and Riga.[52] Dutch and northern German architectural books were distributed through Danzig, and sculptures and funerary architecture were also spread from there to Denmark and Sweden and in the southeast to the Polish Republic of Nobles.[53] Flemish tapestries ordered by Polish magnates also came by way of Danzig, with citizens of the city advising the king or the high nobility and then placing the orders.[54]

All of the Netherlandish painters and architects active in Danzig had in common that they did commissions for the city or private clients, not, as in Holland, to satisfy popular demand.[55] Even native Danzigers, such as Andreas Stech and Daniel Schultz, made their livings catering to the patrician class or the Polish nobility. The mass-produced pictures that we find in the estates of simple Danzig citizens seem to have been imported, although their provenance cannot generally be determined. By contrast, well-to-do citizens furnished and decorated their homes in the Dutch manner. Many appear to have copied Dutch interiors wholesale. The furniture was similar, and "histories" and "landscapes" hung on the walls alongside maps. Unfortunately, what has come down to us has not been examined closely enough or is simply inadequate to establish whether a change in taste from religious history to landscapes took place, as is easily discernable in the Dutch Republic.[56] As far as we can tell based on the few indications that we have, one commonality was the revival of the guild tradition, and here the influence of Dutch immigrants is quite important. In 1592, twenty-eight Netherlandish painters, led by Hans Vredeman de Vries, petitioned the city council for approval to form a painters' guild—which became a reality twenty years later. A painters' guild was also formed in Thorn in 1621.

Dutch artists were also active in Mecklenburg and Pomerania, alongside Italians who had previously worked in Silesia. During the second half of the sixteenth century, Renaissance art was broadly emulated in many parts of Mecklenburg, especially under Duke John

Albert I (1525–1576) and Duke Ulrich (1527–1603). In fact, these dukes converted the fortified castles of their ancestors into Italianate palaces and employed both domestic and foreign artists in their courts. An early example is the princely court in Wismar, built in the style of the Italian Renaissance in about 1553 or 1554, which, similar to the later Gadebusch Castle, was richly ornamented with terracottas from the workshop of Statius von Düren, a Dutchman working in Lübeck.

Probably the most important palace was that at Güstrow, built beginning in 1558. Here, Franz Parr (died 1580), the master builder of Italian descent who had constructed the façade of the palace in Brieg in the Italian style and was later called to Sweden by King John III, constructed a building commissioned by Duke Ulrich with façades decorated in a mannerist Renaissance style. The intent was to give the public the impression of a palace that had developed organically over several centuries, for which purpose he imitated Italianate and French stylistic elements. At the end of the century, the Dutchman Philipp Brandin (ca. 1535–1594), who had earlier converted the palace in Schwerin under commission from John Albert, expanded Güstrow Palace to include four wings. Ulrich, who was inspired by the Renaissance court of King Frederick II of Denmark (Kronborg), again commissioned Brandin to design an epitaph for the donor of the Güstrow Cathedral and his wife (Henry Borwin II and Dorothea) as well as a burial monument for himself and his two wives, Elisabeth of Denmark and Anna of Pomerania.[57]

The Flemish painter Peter Boeckel (ca. 1530–1599) also worked on the burial monument. Boeckel, originally from Antwerp, had already worked on the chapel in Schwerin Castle, in 1561, and he painted a number of likenesses, among them a half-figure double portrait of the duke and his wife. John Albert, like other Pomeranian dukes, was also inspired by Protestant Saxon architecture. For example, the chapel in Schwerin Palace followed the chapel in Torgau Palace, and the local stone carvers Simon and Georg Schröter supplied a reproduction of the pulpit and a sandstone altar, whose crucifixion was copied from a Dürer woodcut. The duke also ordered a painting cycle from the workshop of Lucas Cranach; unfortunately, we do not know whether it ever made its way from Wittenberg to Schwerin.

The Croy Tapestry, woven in 1554 by Peter Heymans in Stettin is undoubtedly the single most important piece of Reformation art on the

southern coast of the Baltic. It was made on the occasion of the marriage of Philipp I of Pomerania-Wolgast and Maria of Saxony, and it was
also meant to call up memories of the Reformation. It contains portraits of members of the Saxon-Ernestine and Pomeranian princely
houses along with those of Luther, Melanchthon, and Bugenhagen. It
was presumably designed by Lucas Cranach the Younger (1515–1586),
who was inspired by his father's paintings. The tapestry was willed to
the University of Greifswald in 1683.[58]

In Stettin and Wolgast, the nobility took up residence in Renaissance
palaces as well. When expanding his residence in Stettin, Duke John
Frederick (1542–1600) tore down medieval buildings that were part of
the palace. Between 1571 and 1582, he built a palace complex with four
wings and an inner court reminiscent of Italian and southern German
Renaissance buildings. The only original piece remaining from Wolgast Palace, which was destroyed in about 1820, is a stone coat of arms
from the workshop of the Dutchman Paul van Hoove, who in the 1540s
offered his services in Lübeck, advertising that he could work in the
"ancient manner."

Representations of the nobility were to be found in manor houses,
of which unfortunately only a few have survived from the Renaissance. Numerous such manors fell victim to a wave of new building
in the nineteenth century. The most important exemplar still standing
is Ulrichshusen, located south of the Malchiner See, which Ulrich, the
baron of Maltzan, had built in 1562 atop the remnants of an old fortress. Despite displaying some medieval elements, Ulrichshusen is
among the earliest aristocratic buildings from the Renaissance in
Mecklenburg and Pomerania. In Pomerania, a later building type,
represented by Spantekow Castle and the moated castle of Mellen-
thin, was built in the second half of the sixteenth century.

Church decoration begins to reflect the Reformation only toward
the end of the sixteenth century. This is true not only of converted
buildings and decorations commissioned by the dukes, but of churches
in the Hanseatic cities and parish churches in the countryside as well.
The Renaissance altarpieces and especially the pulpits demonstrate the
growing importance of sermons in religious services. Thus, in 1587
three council families in Greifswald together donated a pulpit to
St. Marien, which was produced in Rostock. This city was where the

Antwerp master Rudolf Stockmann had set up his workshop, which specialized in epitaphs as well as wooden and stone pulpits of the type that can still be admired in St. Marien parish churches in Rostock and Güstrow.

Wall epitaphs were a new form of memorialization of the dead that were installed in churches in Mecklenburg and Pomerania. In addition to memorials for deceased princes, such as the bronze epitaph cast by Wolf Hilger in Freiberg in 1569 for Philipp I of Pomerania-Wolgast, epitaphs in Stralsund (St. Nikolai) commemorated the reformer Christian Ketelhot and in Greifswald (St. Nikolai) the superintendent Jacob Runge. Achim von Rieben, who died in 1582, was commemorated in Anklam as well, with an epitaph made in 1585 by the renowned sculptor Philipp Brandin.[59]

CHAPTER FIVE

Swedish Dominance

Focus on Stockholm

During the seventeenth century, Stockholm underwent major urbanization that transformed the Swedish capital into a metropolis befitting an ambitious monarchy. In 1632, Swedish politicians harbored qualms about inviting the other European monarchs to attend the funeral of King Gustavus Adolphus. Stockholm was a rather scruffy little town at the time, but by mid-century, the city had been redesigned and laid out along geometric lines. In addition, the towns of Norrmalm and Södermalm had been built up as well. The central administration that was created in 1634 needed new buildings for its growing personnel, while the enlargement of the country's fleet required wharves, docks, and workshops. The merchants' quarter of Skeppsbron was founded to accommodate Sweden's growing copper and iron exports. Although Stockholm was not the largest city in the Baltic region, its attractiveness as a residential, administrative, and mercantile city drew inhabitants from the rest of the region and beyond. Between 1620 and 1668, the city quadrupled its population to 40,000. According to Schering Rosenhane, the governor of Stockholm, 443 foreigners were actually given citizenship rights. In addition, migrants from Germany, the Netherlands, Scotland, France, and Russia were attracted by the abundance of work. The most successful, such as the Dutchmen Louis De Geer (1587–1652) and Jakob Momma (1625–1678), demonstrated their status by building palaces outside the city in Södermalm, while the city center, apart from the noble palaces, came to be dominated in part by functional buildings in the Dutch style. Calvinist Sunday services, generally forbidden in a Lutheran state, regularly drew 200 parishioners.[1]

Figure 5. View of the city of Stockholm, copper engraving by Willem Swidde, 1693

The Battle for Dominion over the Baltic Sea

Sweden played a key role in several theaters of war in the Baltic during the seventeenth century.[2] It was a major player in the Thirty Years' War, first in northern Germany and then in large parts of the Holy Roman Empire, and also in Poland, and Livonia. In addition, the rivalry between Denmark and Sweden led to persistent skirmishing over Scania and Seeland. In the end, Sweden achieved dominion over the Baltic, which Denmark had long exerted as a result of its control of the Øresund. Sweden benefited from its effective war fleet, which was largely captained by sailors from the Netherlands.[3] The country also boasted an oversized army and a network of more than 100 fortresses.

In northern Germany, the battles of the Thirty Years' War were waged mainly in Mecklenburg and Pomerania. Danish ambitions in northern Germany were the original reason the Holy Roman Emperor had sent his troops northward, fresh from their success in Bohemia, in 1624. Danish king Christian IV, whose mother Sophie came from the ducal House of Mecklenburg, and whose brother Ulrich served as the administrator of the Bishopric of Schwerin, attempted to control the mouths of the Elbe and Weser Rivers. With the emperor threatening, Christian, as duke of Holstein and colonel of the Lower Saxon Circle, formed a defensive alliance with Mecklenburg dukes Adolf Frederick I of Schwerin (1588–1658) and John Albert II of Güstrow (1590–1636), both of whom were relatives.

Map 5. The Baltic region in 1648

The ensuing battle at Lutter am Barenberge, in 1626, was a defeat for Christian, and it cleared the way for imperial troops to control northern areas. While Christian extricated himself from this debacle at the Treaty of Lübeck (1629), without losing too much territory, Adolf Frederick and John Albert were less fortunate. They were deposed by the emperor, and Albrecht von Wallenstein (1583–1634) was first given their territory as a pledge and then received Mecklenburg as a fiefdom. Wallenstein attempted to reform the territorial administration and to limit the participation and influence of the estates. Among other things, he introduced the "contribution," a permanent tax to finance the army. Wallenstein's ambitions as "General of the Oceanic and Baltic Seas" were not limited to Mecklenburg. His larger intention was to play a major role in the region by building up the imperial Baltic fleet and revitalizing the Hanseatic League. This provoked Gustavus Adolphus, who had already successfully enforced his claims against Poland, both in Livonia and at the mouth of the Vistula.

Pomerania had more or less accepted its fate without putting up a fight and had been occupied by imperial troops in 1627, and this was one of the reasons why Sweden intervened in northern Germany. Only the city of Stralsund had defended itself, first with Danish and then with Swedish assistance. After an armistice was concluded between Sweden and Poland, with French intercession, the Swedish army, in 1630, landed on the island of Usedom near Peenemünde and relatively quickly occupied Pomerania and parts of Mecklenburg. The Swedes advanced rapidly to the south, where they encountered imperial troops. Although Gustavus Adolphus was killed at the Battle of Lützen (1632), the Swedes came away with a victory. In the hands of Lord High Chancellor Axel Oxenstierna (1583–1654), to whom newly crowned queen Christina (1626–1689) had entrusted the affairs of state, the army was transformed into an effective instrument of power. Oxenstierna's hegemonic pretensions in Germany collapsed only when Sweden and her allies were defeated at the Battle of Nördlingen, in 1634.[4] Once Sweden's fortunes had changed, imperial troops exploited the power vacuum to plunder in the north between 1637 and 1639, and again in 1643. In addition, quartering and feeding Swedish and imperial troops was economically disastrous to the region, and population losses due to disease and death were one consequence.

In the 1648 Treaty of Westphalia, Sweden was given dominion over the mouths of the Elbe and Weser Rivers (the Bishoprics of Bremen and Verden). In Mecklenburg, the Swedes received Wismar, Poel, and Neukloster, and in Western Pomerania the cities of Stettin, Greifswald, and Stralsund, including the islands of Rügen, Usedom, and Wolin. Brandenburg was forced to make do with the Bishoprics of Minden and Halberstadt, though it was given to expect Magdeburg after the death of the present archbishop, which it received in 1680. Brandenburg also received parts of Eastern Pomerania and the Bishopric of Cammin, acquiring Bütow and Lauenburg from Poland in 1657. Pomerania, Sweden's most important territory in the Holy Roman Empire, increasingly became an object of contention as it was claimed by both old and new enemies in Poland and Brandenburg. Starting in 1675, for example, Brandenburg waged war against Sweden and conquered Swedish Pomerania, but then it was unable to consolidate its victory in the Treaty of Saint-Germain-en-Laye in 1679.

Swedish intervention in the Thirty Years' War had been made possible by the Truce of Altmark (1629), which had been brokered by France to allow its Swedish ally to take up positions against the emperor. This truce put a temporary halt to skirmishes between Sweden and Poland in Livonia and the southern Baltic coast. King Gustavus Adolphus conquered Riga in 1621, a feat that his father, Charles IX (1550–1611), had repeatedly attempted but without success. In 1617, he signed the Treaty of Stolbovo with the newly elected czar Michael I of Russia (1596–1645), who ceded East Karelia and Ingria to Sweden. After annexing Riga, Sweden also occupied Dorpat in 1625, which gave it a major say in the political life of Estonia and Livonia.

In the Truce of Altmark, which was in effect for five years, Poland was forced to renounce parts of Livonia. At the same time, Sweden was given control over the mouth of the Vistula, which gave it a portion of the customs duties in Danzig. Sweden imposed levies on other Baltic ports as well, which overall proved crucial to financing the Swedish military. However, Swedish control of the Vistula led to a decrease in Polish grain exports. Nor was Sweden able to secure an alliance with Russia against Poland.

For a time, the Nobles' Republic of Poland-Lithuania was able to maintain its position in the face of Swedish expansion, although Polish king Władysław IV (1595–1648) had to renounce the Polish house of Vasa's claims to the Swedish throne.[5] The uprising by the Zaporozhian Cossacks in the 1640s under Bohdan Khmelnytsky (ca. 1595–1657) led to the loss of Polish-Lithuanian territories east of the Dnieper River, which then came under Russian protection. In 1654, Smolensk fell into Russian hands as well. At about the same time, the new Swedish king Charles X Gustav (1622–1660) from the House of Palatinate-Zweibrücken renewed hostilities with Poland. His goal was to control the entire Baltic coast from Stettin to Riga. To counter that, the Swedish armies swept across the Oder into Poland from the west, while a Baltic army advanced on Lithuania from Riga. Polish king John II Casimir (1609–1672) fled, and the Swedish king considered ways he himself might assume the Polish crown. In this situation, both Sweden and Poland cast about for

new allies. One potential ally was Frederick William of Brandenburg
(1620–1688), who was able to negotiate sovereignty over the Duchy of
Prussia in exchange for his support of Sweden. However, when the war
began to favor Poland, he switched sides and had his former lord re-
confirm his sovereignty over Prussia. At the same time, Russia, under
Czar Alexis (1629–1676), used this unsettled situation to conquer parts
of Livonia while also laying siege to Riga.

In the 1645 Treaty of Brömsebro, Sweden had received the islands
of Gotland and Ösel, the Norwegian provinces of Jämtland and Härje-
dalen, and Halland (pledged for thirty years)—and her ships were no
longer required to pay tolls through the Øresund.[6] The new king Frederick III of Denmark (1609–1670), however, thought he saw a potential
benefit to the Swedish hostilities in Poland: he might be able to regain
territories previously lost to Sweden and perhaps even take his past ob-
jectives, Bremen and Verden, away from them as well.

But in the winter of 1657, the Swedes opened up another front and
conquered Seeland, which they reached by way of the Baltic, which had
frozen over. And in a truce in February 1658, which culminated in the
Treaty of Roskilde, Denmark was forced to cede Scania, Blekinge, Halland, Bornholm, Bohus, and Trondheim to Sweden. But when Sweden
resumed its acts of war, conquered Kronborg and laid siege to Copenhagen, the Netherlands could no longer countenance Swedish dominance in the area and sent a replacement fleet to relieve Copenhagen.
It was only a matter of time before this stalemate would force a peace.
In the Treaty of Copenhagen, Trondheim and Bornholm were returned
to Denmark, but the eastern Danish provinces remained in Swedish
hands.[7] Poland, Sweden, and Brandenburg reached a settlement in the
Treaty of Oliva, in May 1660, with John Casimir renouncing his claims
to Livonia and to the Swedish crown, while all parties recognized the
sovereignty of Brandenburg over the Duchy of Prussia. In 1661, Sweden
and Russia agreed to the restoration of the status quo, while Poland
ceded Smolensk and adjacent territories to Russia in the Treaty of Andrusovo in 1667. Sweden had achieved dominion over the Baltic Sea,
while Poland and Denmark were the big losers, both territorially and
politically.

Administration and the Estates

The Swedish military state administered its territories and subjects very unevenly, in part because the Swedes took seriously the historical traditions of the various regions. In Sweden itself, the crown forced the peasants and church to pay taxes for the upkeep of the military machinery. However, the high nobility paid no taxes and, in addition, profited from land given to it for (military) services. In the new administrative ordinance of 1634, which Axel Oxenstierna put forward, the high aristocracy also laid claim to the highest offices of the central administration: the supreme court, chancellery, treasury, council of war, and admiralty. The king chose his council from among these noblemen. *Ius indigenatus* applied to all of these offices, that is, the officeholder had to be of noble Swedish birth.

Financially, apart from monies acquired through taxation, the Swedish army and navy relied on exploitation of the occupied territories. However, Sweden was able to appropriate customs duties at Prussian ports only until 1635, and the income from Pomeranian and Mecklenburg ports was rather modest as well. The occupations of Jutland, Bremen, and Verden, on the other hand, greatly increased Swedish income. In addition, Sweden's French allies supported the country financially, and war reparations awarded by the Treaty of Westphalia brought in another 5 million riksdaler, of which 3 million were used to pay the troops. But these monies were insufficient for the long term, and by 1650 the ability of the country to raise finances was limited due to poor harvests, food shortages, and high prices. Peasant revolts began to break out that year, and there was even a "rebellion" in the diet, when a coalition of representatives of the cities and the petty nobility demanded manorial "reductions," the retransfer back to the crown of crown lands that had gone into private (noble) possession. This movement would determine the course of political debate during the reign of Charles X Gustav (1622–1660). However, it was left to his successor, Charles XI (1655–1697), to enforce the confiscations in order to increase revenue and free up new resources for the army. The military reform of 1682 acknowledged the hereditary land rights of the crown peasants (*skattebönder*), but from now on four farms would be forced to pool together to supply one foot soldier with equipment and food.

At the same time, peasant land was expanded such that the peasants would work approximately a third of the land, while the aristocracy, the crown, and the church would each cultivate a third. The free peasants were also represented in the diet, and the king regularly sought their support to counterbalance the power of the aristocracy.[8]

In Western Pomerania and Eastern Pomerania, the new sovereigns, Sweden and Brandenburg, had strengthened the hand of the estates in the constitution of 1634. The details were negotiated individually with each of the estates and were set down for Eastern Pomerania in 1654 and for Western Pomerania in 1663. When a king of Sweden entered the government in his capacity as duke of Pomerania, he acknowledged the right of participation of the estates in the affairs of the land. The representation of the estates in the diet was based on the noble manors and the city magistrates. The so-called *Landkasten*, the main treasury of the estates, gave them a certain degree of financial independence. The 1663 agreement also acknowledged the autonomy of the Pomeranian cities whose autonomy had already been established in 1634. Now the estates had their own laws behind them. They rejected the competence of Swedish courts and Swedish laws to adjudicate in their affairs. In the Treaty of Westphalia, Sweden had assured itself of an appeals court for its possessions in the Holy Roman Empire, called the Wismar Tribunal, which generally followed the Imperial Chamber Court but was otherwise independent of it. Soon, however, the nobility began to criticize the "relative independence" of the tribunal, accusing it of favoring the peasantry.[9]

As Sweden became more absolutist toward the end of the seventeenth century, the Swedish territorial lord raised taxes in the provinces in order to support the upkeep of the state as a whole and keep it solvent. One part of this effort involved the geometric division of Pomerania as part of an effort to create a land registry for the purpose of taxation. Even though the Pomeranian registry maps created between 1692 and 1709 were never used for taxation purposes, largely because of the Northern Wars, they nonetheless provide a historically significant picture of Swedish Pomerania in about 1700.

The registration of land in Livonia had taken place as early as the 1680s and 1690s. This had been undertaken in connection with the reductions of manors, that is, the return of formerly royal lands from the nobility back to the royal domain, where they could serve the fiscal needs of the crown. As early as 1641, the important Swedish families, especially the Oxenstierna, Banér, Horn, and de la Gardie families, had owned two-fifths of the arable land in Livonia and farmed that land on large latifundia. In 1680, sixteen Swedish families of the high aristocracy owned almost half of the manors. After the conquest, they had appropriated lands from the Poles and their noble clientele and systematically expanded and supplemented their holdings. The manor reductions, however, affected not only Swedish landowners, but Estonian and Livonian aristocrats as well.[10]

Whereas the Estonian knights had voluntarily sworn fealty to Sweden in 1561, thereby retaining their privileges, it was not until the 1630s and 1640s that the Livonian estates were recognized as a political factor. Unlike the Estonian council, however, the one in Livonia did not function as a supreme court because such a court had been established in Dorpat in 1630. In contrast to the Swedish territories along the southern coast of the Baltic, long-standing resistance by the councils in Reval and Riga and by the Estonian council made it impossible for the Swedes to establish the Dorpat court as the highest court of appeal for Livonia and Estonia, a role played by the Wismar Tribunal.

In 1678, Charles XI confirmed the privileges of the Livonian Knighthood and agreed not to proceed with land reductions without the approval of the Livonians. At the same time, the Livonians let it be known that they had no objections to the reductions of Swedish property. But by the 1680s, reductions went beyond those of large Swedish properties that represented approximately a third of the cultivated land. Because no agreement could be reached with the Livonian estates about how to apply the reduction laws to the property of the aristocracy, the king decreed the reduction of all land that had been donated by the crown. This also included the former property of the Livonian Order. In Estonia, where the continuity of ownership had often been interrupted, a good third of the manors were declared subject to reduction during the 1680s. Nonetheless, the king granted the owners temporary usufruct of the manors that he had bestowed. In Livonia, resistance to the impending loss of approximately four-fifths of the manorial land was considerably greater, even though it primarily affected Swedish owners. The result was a series of supplications and protests, associated with the name of the Livonian estate delegate Johann Reinhold Patkul (1660–1707). However, he was no more successful in pressing the case for the knighthood than the estates had been at the diet. By contrast, the king had his sovereignty rights confirmed at the diet of 1693, and one year later he did away with the sovereignty of the Livonian estates. This entire exercise provided a financial windfall: the manors that had been reduced in Livonia brought in 2.75 million riksdaler, while the Estonian reductions brought in another 42,500. The political measures, on the other hand, seem to have had less effect, especially because the Northern War made them unenforceable. But Patkul, who allied himself with the Polish and Russian side against Sweden, paid a heavy price.[11] When Sweden invaded Poland and Saxony, it forced Polish king August the Strong (1670–1733) to hand Patkul over to Swedish authorities. In 1707 in Poland, he was broken on the wheel and decapitated.

In Denmark, defeat at the hands of Sweden, in 1658, had initially strengthened the estates. The Royal Council, which represented the high aristocracy, managed to expand its authority when it elected the new king after the death of Christian IV in 1648. Now the Royal Council would rule on all important political and economic questions affecting the kingdom.[12] As a result, the new king, Frederick III, was forced to adhere to the guidelines set by the estates, especially since military conflicts continued to eat up large sums of money that could be made good only by raising taxes. At the same time, the crown's debts to merchants in Copenhagen and to German and Dutch banks continued to grow. Because of the catastrophic defeat, the king was unable to repay the debts he had run up since the Treaty of Copenhagen. Shortly before the state went bankrupt, he tried to find a solution by playing the estates (the nobility, clergy, and citizenry) off against the high aristocracy, which had monopolized the noble offices on the Royal Council. The citizens of Copenhagen, who were the king's most important creditors, used the king's maneuver to challenge the privileges of the nobility, including the awarding of offices and exemption from taxation. As a result, the high aristocracy, which was in any case no longer able to guarantee the king's credit, was put on the defensive. Given the aristocracy's weakened position, the king was able to push through the heritability of the crown and his role as supreme decision maker. This autocratic rule was given legal imprimatur as *enevaelde* (absolutism) and would remain the basis for the sovereignty of Danish kings well into the nineteenth century. The new laws acknowledged existing property rights; however, they did away with the aristocracy's tax exemption at the same time that they gave the citizenry the right to acquire property and serve in public office. Property throughout the kingdom would now be taxed based on the tax registers, while the crown settled its debts by selling its demesnes. The monies that were realized were used to finance a standing army. The sovereignty of the aristocracy was eliminated by administrative and judicial reforms, with the new code of law, the Danske Lov of 1683, becoming the basis for the administration of justice. The power relationships in the countryside, however, did not change because the peasants continued to be dependent on their landlords and because manorial privileges were acknowledged in law.[13]

Only Poland-Lithuania remained a republic of nobles. The kings came to understand the limits of their sovereignty at the latest when Mikołaj Zebrzydowski (1553–1620) led the nobility in rebellion (*rokosz*) in 1606, although the uprising eventually failed. At the same time, the magnates (high nobility) were able to consolidate the primacy of their power among the estates. Although military conflicts with Sweden and the associated losses and distractions limited the king's room to maneuver, there was, unlike in Denmark, no alliance with the cities and petty nobility out of which a reform or stabilization program might have emerged. On the contrary, groups of magnates were consistently able to manipulate the resolutions of the diet to their purposes by buying the votes of the representatives to the provincial diets. The vetoes of these representatives effectively destroyed the parliament, or Sejm. As a result, no standing army was established, and other reform projects were defeated by the *rokosz* of Jerzy Lubomirski (1616–1667) in 1665. Those who advanced the "nobles' democracy" model were not interested in strengthening the power of the monarchy, and even the victories of King John III Sobieski (1629–1696) against the Turks in the Battle of Vienna in 1683 did nothing to stem the ultimate decline of Poland-Lithuania.[14]

In this respect, the paths taken by the Prussian lands went in different directions. While Royal Prussia, which was a part of the Polish-Lithuanian Commonwealth, sent its own representatives to the Sejm, the estates in the Duchy of Prussia, which were under Polish vassalage, met among themselves. As in the Republic of Nobles, the members of the Royal Prussian nobility attempted to undermine the power of the cities in the diet. However, they managed to undermine only the smaller (royal) cities, which they forcibly excluded from the diets in the early 1660s. On the other hand, the nobility's efforts were in vain when it came to larger cities such as Danzig, Thorn, and Elbing, although they tried to play these cities off against each other. Nonetheless, there were points of common interest such as the efforts to preserve Royal Prussia's various privileges. Above all, the nobles sought to retain the *ius indigenatus*, which ensured their access to higher offices. This included the clerical rank of bishop, which, like the secular offices, also assured a seat in the senate—the upper chamber of parliament. Apart from that, only nobles represented Royal Prussia in the Sejm. At the same time, the city syndics were often present at parliamentary sessions, where they tried to advocate for the interests of the cities. Because of its financial power and the extraordinary monies that it provided to the kings, Danzig had a great deal of influence, especially because the king received half of Danzig's customs duties (*Pfahlgeld*).[15]

The estates ruled in the Duchy of Prussia supported by the Polish crown. Although, Prussia and Brandenburg were united in a personal union in 1618, Polish sovereignty was preserved.[16] Profound changes did not occur until after 1657 or 1660, when Frederick William, "the Great Elector," after achieving sovereignty in external political matters, no longer needed to consider the domestic political needs of his Polish neighbors. That is also why he could now pay even less attention to the interests of the Prussian estates in pursuing his arms policy than he had earlier in Cleves, the County of Mark, and Kurmark. The Prussian estates resisted bitterly any demand to finance a standing army by insisting on their estate liberties. At the beginning, the so-called long diet (1661–1663) refused to recognize Brandenburg's newly acquired sovereignty rights, while the cities also rejected demands for taxation during times of peace. In 1670–1671, the estates refused to pay any taxes and began looking to Poland to support their position. In both instances, Frederick William quashed the resistance by military force. Among other measures, the spokesman for the opposition, Hieronymus Roth (1606–1678), a merchant and alderman from Königsberg, was arrested and imprisoned for life, whereupon the estates accepted taxation. In 1671, the authorities in Warsaw even kidnapped Christian Ludwig von Kalckstein, a captain from East Prussia who had sought support from the Polish king, tortured him, and then executed him in 1672. Military force was used to compel the payment of the *Hufen* tax, which the estates had not approved. The right of the estates to approve taxes was now little more than formal, and the last time they asserted this right was in 1704. After that date, taxes in Prussia were permanent. Frederick William I then took the final step when he introduced a general land tax (*Generalhufenschoss*), and from then on he completely ignored the aristocracy's exemption from taxation.[17] In the 1680s, the Great Elector ignored the interests and protests of the estates in other Brandenburg provinces as well. When the Pomeranian estates were unable to agree on the introduction of a city excise tax in 1682, he arbitrarily forced it on the cities by electoral decree.

Dutch Dominance in Trade

The Dutch dominance in the Baltic region that was a hallmark of the sixteenth century continued to grow in the seventeenth.[18] Although their grain trade in particular was adversely affected in the 1620s by the Swedish occupation of the Vistula delta, the Dutch continued to expand their trade in the Baltic region, in part by varying their offerings. The Dutch even overtook the English as the leading textile exporter, and they were the leading exporters of spices and exotic southern fruits as well. Grain exports saw robust gains up to the middle of the seventeenth century, after which they went into longer-term recession during the second half of the century.[19] Many possible reasons for this decline have been adduced. Joop Faber, for example, has explained it by the growing grain production in western and southern Europe, on the one hand, and as a result of population decreases in western Europe, on the other, resulting in weaker demand on the Amsterdam market. The relative increases in grain production in France and the southern Netherlands, for example, are consistent with this interpretation. However, causes internal to the Baltic region must also be considered. These include the destruction of productive capacity resulting from the Swedish-Polish wars and the decline in agrarian productivity consequent to the crisis in the Polish manorial economy during the second half of the seventeenth century. The demand for grain presumably increased in the Baltic cities as well.[20] Another factor is that in the 1650s, the English made efforts to hinder Dutch access to the Baltic region, and later used the Navigation Acts to ban Dutch shipping between the Baltic and English ports. This had the effect of reducing the Dutch share in shipping. At the same time, Sweden began a serious program aimed at building up its merchant fleet and at promoting regional shipbuilding (in Narva, among other places), all with the intention of making Sweden independent of the Dutch and their ships.

The decline in grain exports hit Danzig hard. It lost its dominant position to other ports such as Elbing, Königsberg, Riga, Pernau, and Narva, all of which were able to pick up a share of the trade. At the time, western interest increasingly pivoted from grain to Baltic flax, hemp, timber, and forest products. Königsberg, for example, exported timber products, including barrel staves (clapholt), thin oaken boards called *Wagenschoss*, planks, barge planks, and floorboards. The barrel staves were especially prized by the Dutch because they were crucial to the production of herring barrels. From about 1597 to 1639, Königsberg was the leader in terms of barrel stave export, after which Riga took the lead.[21] *Wagenschoss*, a split oak product used primarily in shipbuilding, was a somewhat different matter. Here, Königsberg's export figures initially lagged behind those of Danzig, and later, from the 1620s, behind those of Courland. In the later seventeenth century, exports of *Piepenholz* (pipeholt) for wine casks, floorboards, and planks grew, with Riga becoming the largest exporter. In about 1700, Swedish ports also began to export timber; during the following century, they along with Finnish and Russian ports came to dominate that sector. This development was largely driven by the introduction of Dutch fine-cut milling technology, which greatly increased productive capacity. Other forestry products, such as ash, pitch, and tar, were at least as important as timber. Ash provided western European industries with the alkali needed for dyeing, bleaching, and washing textiles, but it was also used in soap making, glass manufacture, and the processing of saltpeter. The amount of ash exported through Danzig and Königsberg increased rapidly during the first half of the seventeenth century, a level subsequently approached only at the end of the century. Pitch and tar, which were needed in shipbuilding and house construction, initially came from the hinterlands of Danzig, Königsberg, and Riga, before pitch and tar production shifted to Sweden and Finland. Two tar-producing regions were especially important: eastern Bothnia with the cities of Vasa, Uleåborg, and Gamlakarleby, which exported what was called Stockholm tar because that was the port from where it was shipped; and Karelia, whose chief port was Viborg.[22]

This shift occurred primarily because of the over-exploitation of Polish and Prussian raw materials. Ash, pitch, and tar production required enormous quantities of raw timber, and the producers systematically stripped this resource. For example, one "ship pound" of potash (approximately 170 kilograms) required 177 cubic meters of timber because a cubic meter of oak contains only 0.62 kilograms of potash. As a result, the annual exports of potash out of Danzig, which came to 19,700 ship pounds in the 1630s, were derived from 3,5 million cubic meters of timber.[23] Because this practice so endangered the health of the forests, the Duchy of Prussia tried to assume control of the exploitation of its forested lands. Increasingly, it chose to protect the forests rather than cut them down. This opened the western European market to entrepreneurs working the very abundant Swedish and Finnish forests, even though these were not as easily accessible as the Prussian resources had been. One result was that Königsberg shipped less and less timber to the west over the course of the seventeenth century and came to rely on flax and hemp exports. Because of its vast expanse of hinterland, however, Riga became the most important port for flax and hemp. In fact, a sawmill and linseed oil mill were erected in Riga using Dutch capital.

Iron and copper were also among the industrial raw materials that were exported, primarily by Dutch entrepreneurs, Louis de Geer prominent among them. As early as 1618, de Geer had mobilized credit for Sweden in the Netherlands, primarily out of his own pocket. Sweden was to repay this credit in the form of copper, which came primarily from the rich pits in Falun.[24] Together with his brother-in-law Elias Trip and Elias's brother Jacob, de Geer hoped for a windfall from his Swedish copper monopoly. Because large amounts of copper were required at the time for weaponry, especially cannons, this source seemed especially attractive as it would allow Amsterdam to circumvent Lübeck, which had been where copper was traditionally traded. De Geer's business partner was Willem de Besche, who had moved to Sweden in 1614 and was operating a brass factory (copper and zinc) in Nyköping and an iron works in Finspång. This business association greatly expanded the brass trade and weaponry manufacture, which de Geer took over when he settled in Sweden in 1627. He built up a metal empire in Norrköping and surroundings, consisting of iron foundries and brass and weapons manufacturing. He sold his products (cannons, munitions, and guns) on the Amsterdam market, and after Sweden became involved in the Thirty Years' War, he armed the Swedish army. Following his example, other Dutchmen, most notably Jakob Momma, became involved in the iron and brass trades while also operating mines in the north of Sweden. Weapons were usually the most important end product, and Momma supplied cannons and grenades to the Swedish military. However, this intensive interaction between the Swedes and the Dutch did not prevent Sweden from trying to become economically independent of the Netherlands. Protectionist measures permitted only a small number of ports to trade abroad, which meant, for example, that tar producers and traders in ports other than Stockholm were driven to smuggling. Because Swedish shipping capacity was inadequate, Sweden tried to privilege ships from its Baltic provinces by reducing customs duties on them. This measure led smaller merchant cities and companies to build their own merchant fleets. Thus, for example, merchants from Narva began to move a growing proportion of their timber, flax, and hemp products to western Europe on their own ships. And so even though Swedish relations with the Netherlands improved as a result of the shipping agreement of 1679 and an alliance in 1681, the groundwork was laid for the emergence of merchant fleets from Estonian and Livonian ports.[25]

The Crisis in the Manorial Economy

The wars of the seventeenth century had brought with them widespread destruction and depopulation so that the ratio of population to land changed in favor of the land, large areas of which were now available to the fewer peasants who remained. At the same time, reduced demand for grain in western Europe changed the terms of trade such that the manorial lords suffered considerable losses of income during the second half of the seventeenth century. This agrarian crisis left the lords with two options. The first was to reduce production on their own demesnes by transforming corvée services into monetary payments, thereby transferring the risks of production and sales to the peasants. The other option was to expand production of goods and reduce production costs to make up for declining income. In the process, the manorial lords increased the services required of the peasants, who were already required to work for them every day. This crisis behavior on the part of the landlords crippled economic activity and the material well-being of the peasants while undermining the foundations of the manorial system. The economic crisis thus quickly became a crisis of the manorial economy as a whole.[26]

Symptoms of this crisis included a decrease in the area under cultivation and therefore in the grain harvest, a drop in the overall cattle population, a reduction in the size of peasant plots, and the general impoverishment of the peasantry, which brought about their mass flight from the land. These symptoms of crisis, however, differed from region to region. While we certainly see this happening on Polish manors, those in Schleswig-Holstein seemed to have been less affected by the crisis. The reason for this reduced susceptibility may have been that production here was less dependent on a grain monoculture than in Poland. In addition, the manors responded to the depression in grain prices by increasing dairy farming, a new, more crisis-resistant endeavor, which, as a result of the use of pasture land, actually increased agricultural production. Not only did butter and cheese production return the highest profits during the grain price depression of the seventeenth century, the lessor of the cattle, the so-called Hollander, generally assumed sole responsibility for the risks associated with producing and selling his milk products.[27]

By contrast, the noble manors in Poland had only their brewing monopoly to fall back on. Breweries were an important source of income in the entire Baltic region, along with sawmills, lime kilns, and brick works. Many of the manors lacked peasants who could pay rent and provide labor. In Royal Prussia, for example, only 823 peasants remained on the demesnes in 1664, compared to 2,712 before the war. If they were unable to attract new settlers, the owners had to work their own demesnes, plowing the lands deserted by the peasantry. They hired farmhands to do the labor and brought gardeners (*Gärtner*) and cottagers (*Kossäten*), who were several steps below the peasants in social status, into the production process.

Administrative measures were used in an attempt to stem the flight of the peasantry. As a result, we find that regions that suffered population losses enacted regulations limiting the mobility of the peasantry. In Livonia, for example, such regulations were enacted in 1632 and 1645, and the police ordinance of 1668 decreed the status of serfdom for all manorial peasants and their descendants.[28]

In Mecklenburg and Pomerania, which had, on average, lost half of their population and in some regions up to two-thirds, the peasant ordinances of 1646 and 1654 legally tied peasants to the land, a practice that had a long history in the region, and transformed them into serfs. In Pomerania in 1645, the Swedish occupation force acknowledged Pomerania-Stettin's 1616 peasant ordinance along with the serfdom it mandated. This laid the groundwork for the expropriation of the peasants, even though the manorial lords did not make maximum use of expropriations because of the labor shortages at the time.

The 1670 peasant ordinance of Swedish Pomerania once again confirmed the right to corvée labor, which was important because peasant families and manorial lords were rivals for the labor of peasant children. Just how critical this labor was to the economic survival of the parents may be seen from the reports of visits to the villages belonging to the city of Greifswald in 1701. These show an average of three helpers of whom a peasant could make use, including one farmhand and two of his own children above the age of twelve. Had he not been able to exploit his own children, he himself would have had to perform the required corvée labor of up to four days a week. This would have been in addition to the work he did on his own plot—clearly an untenable situation.[29]

By contrast, many demesnes in both Denmark and Schleswig-Holstein and in the Duchy of Prussia had an overabundance of peasant labor at the beginning of the seventeenth century. As a result, the number of peasants who were forced to perform corvée labor was limited to those who were necessary to maintain production. Additional profits were realized by raising rents. In addition, the demesnes gained direct access to a considerable portion of the peasants' production in the form of monetary levies, thereby once again shifting the risks associated with production and sales to the peasantry at a time when grain prices were low. In addition, in the Duchy of Prussia the introduction of the so-called high money rent (*hohe Zins*) gave the demesnes the ability to forestall the ongoing devaluation of monetary rent.

After the increases, the rent per farm again came to 10 to 15 bushels of rye, whereas in the mid-sixteenth century the rent had been only 6 bushels because grain prices were higher.[30] However, during the second half of the seventeenth century, efforts to monetize rural labor relations by replacing corvée labor, which we see on some demesnes and manors in Schleswig-Holstein, began to falter.[31] Because of the agrarian depression and the depopulation caused by the Thirty Years' War and the wars with Sweden, monetary levies were changed back to corvée labor for the majority of the peasants. On the one hand, the manors and demesnes needed all available labor and oxen power to restore their own lands; on the other hand, the noble land owners in particular wanted to compensate for decreased income by expanding production and making it less expensive. As a result, they increased the burden of corvée labor on their subjects. The effect was that in about 1700 the large majority of peasants performed corvée labor in Schleswig-Holstein, Swedish Pomerania, and the Duchy of Prussia. On royal demesnes and noble manors in Prussia, the figure was between 80 and 85 percent; in Swedish Pomerania approximately 70 percent.[32] Corvée labor differed from place to place, not only between the demesnes and manors, but also from manor to manor. In the following century we see both an increase and a decrease in corvée peasant labor. New standards would have to await the agrarian and demesne reforms of the second half of the eighteenth century. Whether peasants were spared corvée labor depended on several factors. Only those peasants who were able to sell a large proportion of their products at local markets would have been able to pay rent in monetary form.

Netherlandish and German Cultural Influences

Swedish dominance in the Baltic region led to a wide array of cultural imports in Europe's northern reaches. During the Thirty Years' War,

Swedish armies brought not only valuable plunder from Prague and Munich, but the cultural revival of the monarchy also drew large numbers of artists from the Netherlands as well as from France and the Holy Roman Empire. Queen Christina (1626–1689) also commissioned artworks from foreign artists, including a cycle of thirty-five paintings by the Antwerp artist Jacob Jordaens (1593–1678), which depicts the life of Psyche.[33] The Netherlandish sculptor Artus Quellinus (1609–1668) also sent important clay models, without ever setting foot in Sweden.

Among the painters who did travel to Sweden, Sébastien Bourdon (1616–1671) had already made a name for himself in Paris before becoming Christina's court painter in 1652. Although he stayed in Stockholm for only about a year, his appointment gave his career a boost that led to his post as rector of the French Académie Royale. Another painter, David Beck (1621–1656), came from Delft and had earlier worked at the courts in England, France, and Denmark before painting portraits in Sweden. Jürgen Ovens (1623–1678), who was born in Schleswig, received his training in the Netherlands. He stayed in Stockholm only briefly, painting portraits at the court before returning to Holstein and Amsterdam, where he later painted visiting Swedish aristocrats. David Klöcker Ehrenstrahl (1628–1698), originally from Hamburg, also studied in Amsterdam. He was hired by Carl Gustaf Wrangel, the governor-general of Swedish Pomerania, to paint at his court. Wrangel took Ehrenstrahl along with him to Stockholm, where he became the protégé of Maria Eleonora of Brandenburg (1599–1655), the widow of Gustavus Adolphus. She even financed a seven-year study trip to Rome and Venice. While in Rome, Ehrenstrahl was taken under the wing of Queen Christina, who was staying there at the time. He returned to Stockholm in 1661 and became court painter, but he also worked in Gottorf and Güstrow. Ehrenstrahl attempted to organize his studio like that of Peter Paul Rubens. However, he was unable to find enough assistants in Stockholm to make this possible. In the late 1670s, he received royal permission to operate an "academy" free from guild interference, a very unusual privilege at the time.[34]

André Mollet (died 1665) is notable as a major figure among garden designers. Mollet had previously worked at the Tuileries in Paris, and he designed a number of gardens in and around Stockholm. He also published a theoretical tract on pleasure gardens.[35]

More important—because they are still visible today—are the works that architects left in Sweden. Simon de la Vallée (1590–1642), whose father had been a master mason at the Palais de Luxembourg in Paris, arrived in Stockholm from the court of Stadtholder Frederick Henry of Orange (1584–1647) in The Hague. Because de la Vallée was murdered in 1642, he was unable to see most of his projects to completion. The most important of these was the Riddarhus (House of Nobility), whose exterior was designed by the Amsterdam architect Justus Vingboons (ca. 1620–1698), who worked in Stockholm from 1653 to 1656. It is probable that de la Vallée's success was at least partly due to his having trained both his son and Nicodemus Tessin the Elder (1615–1681) in architecture. These two architects were largely responsible for the spread of Netherlandish classicism in Sweden and other parts of the Baltic region.

Nicodemus Tessin came from a family active on the Stralsund city council and during the occupation of Stralsund he became friendly with several Swedish commanders. After helping to build the fortifications of Stralsund, his path led him to Sweden, where, in the 1630s, he became an engineer specializing in fortifications. He worked for both Queen Christina and Chancellor Oxenstierna. In the early 1650s, Tessin continued his education in the Netherlands, Paris, and Italy. After returning to Sweden, he redesigned, among other things, the city of Arensburg on the island of Ösel for Count Magnus Gabriel de la Gardie (1622–1686), a man with a seemingly insatiable appetite for building projects. This particular project, however, appears never to have been brought to fruition. In 1661, Tessin became the master architect for the city of Stockholm, and in 1663 he succeeded de la Vallée as architect to the royal palace. Other commissions included Kalmar Cathedral (1660) and the palaces built for Gustaf Bonde, Schering Rosenhane, and Seved Bååt. For each of his projects, Tessin used a different mix of styles. While the palaces built for the aristocracy were based on French models— possibly earlier designs by Jean Marot—Kalmar Cathedral had a more Roman cast. De la Vallée, by contrast, had built St. Catherine's Church, in Stockholm, in the Netherlandish style. Tessin's final commission,

the Swedish Riksbank, sited a Roman-style palazzo in the center
of Stockholm. Drottningholm Palace, which Tessin built for Hedwig
Eleonora, the dowager queen, incorporated Venetian Palladian
elements.[36]

Many other architects and master builders were active in Sweden
and the Swedish Baltic provinces in redesigning hundreds of cities and
towns, thereby placing the stamp of Swedish cultural hegemony on the
landscape. Although numerous style elements originated in France,
Italy, and Germany, the most important influences, especially in the
Baltic provinces, were Dutch city planning and Dutch baroque classicism. And of course, the Dutch played a considerable role in this process. Thus, long before de la Vallée and Tessin began working in Sweden,
for example, the Dutch merchant and entrepreneur Louis de Geer had
master mason Jürgen Gesewitz build his residence in Stockholm, which
was closely patterned on the Mauritshuis of Jacob van Campen in The
Hague. It is therefore not surprising that de Geer's palace was depicted
along with other aristocratic palaces in the large collection of engrav-
ings titled *Suecia Antiqua et Hodierna* produced by Erik Dahlbergh
(1625–1703). Subsequently, a number of other Dutch merchants, including van Eijck, Momma, Wesenberg, Simonsz, Insen, Mijtens, and
van der Noot, settled in de Geer's vicinity.[37] Their palaces were also
ornamented with gardens in the Dutch style, and Dutch specialists were
hired to design them.

Swedish merchants were, of course, very impressed by the residences
and gardens commissioned by de Geer and his Dutch neighbors. Joachim
Pötter-Lillienhoff, for example, had a palace built on Södermalm by
Johan Tobias Albinus based on Jakob Momma's residence. And it goes
without saying that these palaces were decorated with Dutch and
Flemish paintings and contemporary sculptures. Diplomats and merchants such as Peter Spierinck and Michel le Blon acted as cultural
agents between Dutch painters and the Swedish court and high nobility.
Carl Gustav Wrangel, who was not only a military commander, but had
also made a name for himself as governor-general of Swedish Pomerania, engaged Harald Appelboom, a Swede residing in The Hague, to
advise him on the construction of his residence in Skokloster. Appelboom bought paintings at Dutch auctions and fitted the rooms of
the residence with tapestries, gilded leather walls, and furnishings.

Another Swedish agent in Amsterdam, Peter Trotzig, supplied building materials and architectural books.[38]

Cities in Finland, Estonia, and Livonia also employed Netherlandish architects and city planners. Around the middle of the seventeenth century, more than twenty cities in Finland were redesigned to one extent or another. It was not, however, always easy to change medieval structures. Sometimes, as was the case with Narva, the architects received an assist from conflagrations, which allowed them to alter the layout of the city. Such was also the case in Pernau. On the other hand, Tessin's innovative plan was never implemented in Arensburg.[39] In Narva, an attempt was made to try something completely fresh with a newly designed exchange and city hall. The Narva exchange, which was designed by Johann Georg Heroldt, from Freiberg, followed closely an unbuilt design for a city hall in Amsterdam proposed by Philip Vingboons (1607–1678), and the city hall in Maastricht, the Netherlands, by Pieter Post (1608–1669). In all probability, the city fathers of Narva were motivated by the wish to "have built a beautiful house with an exchange and shops and packing houses for the furtherance of trade and commerce as in other well-furnished cities."[40] Heroldt may never actually have seen a Dutch city hall, but he would have been aware of Dutch classical architecture from the books and prints that were available in local architectural libraries. The architect who designed the city hall in Narva, Georg Teuffel (ca. 1610–1672), had traveled in Holland. As a result, the exchange and city hall had significant stylistic commonalities.

Baltic cities were also transformed architecturally by the palaces of Swedish aristocrats that were built in the Dutch classical style. Jakob Staël von Holstein (1628–1679), who owned a large collection of architectural books, was especially active in this field. In Reval, von Holstein designed both the residence of the Swedish governor, Fabian von Fersen, and in the 1670s the palace of Axel von Rosen, who, after studies in Uppsala, Leiden, and Paris, was named vice president of the supreme court in Dorpat.

Comparable palaces may be found in Riga. These include the residence of the notary Johan Reuter, the façade of which reflects Dutch motifs. In other words, architectural ideas from the Netherlands were spread far and wide—with Dutch architects doing much of the work.

And Dutch merchants played an important role as patrons and models for future customers—as did the architectural tracts already mentioned. Architects also drew up plans for specific types of functional buildings, such as that of the new university in Dorpat, the Academia Gustaviana Adolphiana (1632), and the academic building in Pernau, possibly designed by Nicodemus Tessin, the Younger (1699). But the Dutch style, adapted to Swedish circumstances, was seen well beyond the Baltic provinces. For example, we find Swedish cultural influences in Silesia, and these are not based solely on Sweden's military presence during the Thirty Years' War. The Gnadenkirchen (Churches of Grace) in Hirschberg (Jelenia Góra) and Landeshut (Kamienna Góra), which were built in the early eighteenth century for the Protestants, were copies of the Church of St. Catherine in Stockholm, which was built in the Dutch style. But in Silesia the Protestant Gnadenkirchen would have stood out in a Catholic baroque milieu.[41]

Sweden also recruited important scholars to further its intellectual ambitions, and their intellectual networks spread Swedish influence throughout the Baltic region. Axel Oxenstierna and Louis de Geer, for example, invited John Amos Comenius (1592–1670) to Sweden in the 1640s. Prior to that, Comenius, escaping imperial repression, had found a safe haven with the Moravian Brethren in Lissa (Lezno). With Comenius's assistance, de Geer intended to found an ambitious academic program on his estate in Finspång. In order not to be too far from the Moravian Brethren, Comenius settled in Elbing, which at the time was occupied and administered by Sweden. This move intensified contacts not only with Sweden, but also with scholars in the North Sea and Baltic region, such as Samuel Hartlib (ca. 1600–1662) and John Dury (1596–1680), both centered in Elbing, with Dury, a Calvinist, agitating for the unification of the Protestant churches.

René Descartes (1596–1650) was lured to Sweden from the Netherlands at the behest of Queen Christina in 1649; however, he died in Stockholm the following year. In 1666, Sweden recruited Samuel Pufendorf (1632–1694) from Heidelberg to the new University of Lund, in Scania, which had been wrested from Denmark. Pufendorf had already acquired an international reputation as an important natural philosopher. Other Swedish universities also recruited professors who had studied in the Netherlands. In fact, half of the professors at the University of Uppsala between 1640 and 1660 had studied in Leiden, as had many of those recruited to the University of Åbo, founded in 1640. Almost all Danish mathematicians and physicians had studied in the Netherlands, as had the faculties at the new University of Dorpat and the old University of Greifswald. These included, among others, the physicians Johann Kölner and Christoph Otto Oeseler, theologians Johann Michaelis and Nicolaus Dassow, and the jurist David Mevius.[42]

This cultural transfer between the Netherlands and the southern coast of the Baltic was not mediated by the Swedish presence alone. The fact that so many Dutch merchants did business out of Danzig was critical. The number of Dutch factors in Danzig alone, who controlled trade and placed credit and exchange transactions for companies in Amsterdam, grew to between forty and fifty by the middle of the seventeenth century, and later to seventy-five. One Dutch immigrant even tried to found a discount house like those in Amsterdam, but stiff resistance from the Danzig city council quashed his plans.[43]

There were also close artistic connections much like those we have already seen for architecture in the late sixteenth century. Danzig artists, such as the copperplate engravers Ägidius Dickmann and Jeremias Falck, learned their trades in the Netherlands or worked there for at least a few years.

But in comparison to the Netherlands, there was little mass demand for art along the southern coast of the Baltic. To the extent that artists attempted to set down roots, they did so in a few large city centers. One explanation may be that, in comparison to the Netherlands, the Baltic region was much less densely urbanized. One might even say that the region was in the process of de-urbanization as a result of the depopulation of the Baltic hinterland and the conversion of land to agrarian purposes. Another explanation may be sought in the tension between the culture of middle-class city dwellers and that of the aristocrats who lived outside the cities. Elements of aristocratic clothing and lifestyle spread to the cities so that even the Danzig Mennonites succumbed to the seductions of color and silk.[44] One long-term consequence was the aristocratization of urban culture, which the bourgeois culture of the cities was unable to withstand. It should be noted that this aristocratization (or refeudalization) was a pan-European phenomenon, at least where it affected the urban upper crust. This process can be found in the Netherlands and in the Polish-Lithuanian Republic of Nobles as well.[45]

Much like their Swedish counterpart, the high Polish nobility ordered tapestries and luxury goods from the Netherlands, especially from the Delft tapestry seller Maximilian van der Gucht, who also supplied the Swedish aristocracy.[46] The farther east we go in the Polish-Lithuanian Republic, the more influences from different cultures tend to collide. Thus, we find many Dutch paintings in aristocratic art collections—but housed in buildings that doubtlessly reflect the Catholic baroque architectural tradition brought into Lithuania by the Jesuits. To the extent that the Polish Catholic line of the Vasa dynasty emulated these trends, we may even speak of a Vasa baroque tradition. At the beginning of the seventeenth century, Italian architects designed church buildings that were based on the Jesuit Church of the Gesù in Rome. One outstanding example is the Chapel of St. Casimir, in Vilnius Cathedral, which was built by King Władysław IV Vasa (1595–1648) and decorated by Constantino Tencalla (1610–1647) to commemorate the Lithuanian grand dukes and Polish kings. The "most Italian" church is the St. Peter and St. Paul's Church, which was designed by the Cracow architect Jan Zaor (active ca. 1638–1676) and decorated in the 1670s and 1680s with more than 200 ornaments, reliefs, and sculptures by the Italian sculptors Giovanni Pietro Perti (1648–1714) and Giovanni Maria Galli (1625–1665).

The Jesuit university founded in Vilnius in 1579 served as the impetus for the building of other colleges in the region, including at Dorpat. The Jesuit presence in Dorpat was, however, challenged and pushed back by the foundation of the Academy (the later University) of Dorpat by King Gustavus Adolphus of Sweden.[47] The Jesuits had a similar intention when they built their secondary school (*Gymnasium*) in Braunsberg (Braniewo) in a Prussian Lutheran milieu. But overall, at least where the aristocracy was concerned, Catholic and Lutheran beliefs tended to blur; in spite of different confessional identities, they tended to read the same edifying literature, such as Philip Kegel's *Twelve Spiritual Devotions*, which was published in numerous Swedish (i.e., Protestant) editions but was originally compiled from Jesuit sources.[48]

Italian, French, Dutch, and German traditions are also evident in music. King Christian IV, for example, sent his court musicians, including Melchior Borchgrevinck (ca. 1570–1632), Mogens Pedersøn (ca. 1583–1623), and Niels Mortensen Kolding to study in Venice, from where they returned with books of madrigals. As ambassador from Paris, Magnus Gabriel de la Gardie brought six violinists with him to Stockholm in 1647. They, of course, brought along their repertoires. The court organist and conductor of the court orchestra, Andreas Düben (1597–1662), who originally came from Leipzig and had studied under Jan Pieterszoon Sweelinck (1562–1621) in Amsterdam, soon emulated them. Johann Valentin Meder (1649–1719) had a similar career. The son of a cantor, Meder first studied theology in Leipzig and Jena, but he was soon hired to sing with court orchestras in Eisenach and Gotha. He arrived in Copenhagen in 1674, after engagements in Cassel (1672), Bremen (1672–1673), Hamburg (1673), and Lübeck (1674). In 1679, as cantor at the *Gymnasium* in Reval, he produced a musical play, and his presence is attested in Riga in 1685–1686. After that, he was engaged by the Marienkirche in Danzig, where he composed an opera. In about 1700, Meder made his way to Königsberg by way of Braunsberg, and then to Riga, where he was cathedral organist and cantor until his death in 1719.[49] And although this unsettled life—Meder had major differences with the Danzig city council—was probably not typical for most of the composers in the Baltic region, they would all nonetheless have had to contend with the disparate demands and whims of princes and those of city and church employers. By their numerous contacts, composers, such as Dieterich Buxtehude (ca. 1637–1707), bridged the various musical cultures. Buxtehude was the son of an organist from Oldesloe, in Holstein, and a Danish mother. He grew up in Helsingborg and Helsingør, and he played the organ at local churches before finally taking a position at the Marienkirche in Lübeck in 1668. Buxtehude's organ style was determinative of the northern German school. The connection between Saxony and Denmark was also quite close as evidenced by Heinrich Schütz (1585–1672) and his student Matthias Weckmann (1616–1676). Weckmann began his career as an organist in Dresden in 1638, and he assumed the same position in Nykøbing, Denmark, in 1642. Like Schütz, he returned to Dresden, and between 1655 and 1674 he was a composer and organist at St. Jacobi in Hamburg.

After a study trip to Italy, Schütz also led the Dresden court orchestra, but from 1633 to 1635 and 1642 to 1644 he held similar positions in Copenhagen, where he composed festive music for the court. In his *Geistliche Chor-Music* (1648), he demonstrated how Italian contrapuntal compositional models could be integrated with German poetic texts. By doing so, he became involved in a controversy that had been ignited in Danzig between Paul Siefert (1586–1666), organist at the Marienkirche, and the Italian court conductor Marco Scacchi (1600–1662) at the royal court in Warsaw. While Siefert complained bitterly about the present state of musical composition and blamed Italian composers and their rich melodies and bass lines for the decline, Scacchi poked fun at Siefert's supposed musical transgressions in his 1643 tract "Cribrum musicum ad triticum Siferticum" (Musical sieve for Siefert's wheat).[50] A few years later, Scacchi continued his polemic by publishing the comments of numerous colleagues who either directly or indirectly supported his position. As early as the reign of Sigismund III, Italian musicians took an active part in the musical life of Danzig and Königsberg, where they composed for royal orchestras. In about 1650 it was common to find Italian singers making their way from Dresden to Stockholm (to the court of Queen Christina) and other cities and courts in northern Europe. Manuscripts and printed compositions were in circulation there, although the music created in the northern German cities generally did not travel far. On the other hand, compositions by central German and especially Italian composers were well received by court orchestras in Stockholm and Gottorf.[51]

CHAPTER SIX

The Rise of Russia

Focus on St. Petersburg

When Peter the Great founded his capital at the mouth of the Neva River in 1703, his intention was to create an "imperial Amsterdam" better suited to the purposes of international trade than Archangelsk on the White Sea, which often froze over. Although the Swedes had in the early 1600s built a small settlement called Nyen on land that was to become St. Petersburg, Peter had plans for a new city, which, like Novgorod before it, would be the terminus for all western European trade with Russia. By the end of the eighteenth century, St. Petersburg, with a population of 220,000, had developed into the largest city on the Baltic Sea, outgrowing all other trading centers, including Copenhagen (101,000), Stockholm (76,000), Königsberg (55,000), Danzig (40,000), and Riga (30,000). In 1793, about 29,000 foreigners lived there, with Germans the largest group. Although the English dominated the foreign trading companies, German artisans, teachers, scientists, and artists as well as soldiers and court and military officials played a leading role in the development of the modern city as Peter imagined it should be. Over the course of the eighteenth century, Italian and French architects fashioned an assemblage of imperial edifices in the baroque and classical styles, starting with the Peter and Paul Fortress on Zayachy Island, that are the hallmark of the metropolis to this day.[1]

Territorial Transformation

The beginning of the eighteenth century marked a political turning point in the Baltic region, with Russia increasing its influence, while Sweden and Poland-Lithuania receded as powers. Roughly at the same time, when the Holy Roman Empire, England, and the Netherlands were busy trying to stop France from gaining supremacy in western

Figure 6. St. Petersburg, Senate Square with a statue of Peter the Great, drawing by Benjamin Patersen, 1799

Europe during the War of Spanish Succession (1701–1713), Russian czar Peter I (1672–1725), recently elected Polish king Augustus II (1670–1733), and the new Danish king Frederick IV (1671–1730) seized the apparent opportunity presented by the sudden death of Swedish king Charles XI and started the Great Northern War (1700–1721). Peter the Great wanted his empire to have direct access to the Baltic and, with it, to increase his direct stake in Baltic trade. Frederick IV wished to conquer Holstein-Gottorp, a close ally of Sweden, to expand his royal control in Schleswig and Holstein. And Augustus the Strong of Saxony, finally, had entered into alliance with Denmark and the czar with the intent of reclaiming Livonia for Poland. However, the young Swedish king Charles XII (1682–1718) struck back with support from the English fleet, and Denmark was forced to accept the status quo ante at the Peace of Travendal (1700). In 1700, Sweden defeated the Russians at Narva and then the Saxons and Russians on the left bank of the Daugava River. The Swedish army marched across Courland to Poland, occupied Warsaw, and drove Augustus from Cracow. As in earlier battles, Sweden

occupied the lowlands of the Vistula along with the cities of Elbing and
Thorn. Danzig attempted to maintain its independence, but it was
forced to join the Confederation of Warsaw, which deposed Augustus
as Polish king and elected the candidate supported by Sweden, Stanisław
Leszczyński (1677–1766), voivode of the Poznań voivodeship.[2] Danzig
enjoyed the backing and support of England and the Netherlands, while
Frederick I in Prussia took a neutral position. In the period following,
Sweden occupied Saxony in 1706, forcing Augustus to renounce his
claim to the Polish crown in the Treaty of Altranstädt. At the same
time, Reinhold Patkul was extradited and sentenced to death. Charles
XII's attempts to conquer Russia by creating an alliance with the Cos-
sack hetman Ivan Mazepa (1639–1709) and the Ottoman Empire were
shattered at Poltava in 1709. Although the king found safe harbor in
the Ottoman Empire, no effective military support was mounted. After
his return by way of Stralsund, Sweden continued to fight against Denmark and Norway, but in 1718 the king was killed in the siege of Fredriks-
hald. Starting in 1709, the Russian army besieged the fortress of Riga,
which held out until July 1710, when, after terrible sacrifices on the
part of the population of Estonia and Livonia, the garrison surrendered.
The cities of Pernau and Reval capitulated the same year. The knighthoods (*Ritterschaften*) and cities submitted to the Russian czar, but they
were permitted to retain their privileges. These events ended the war
for Estonia and Livonia, with population losses due to war and bubonic
plague having taken an extremely heavy toll.

After Sweden's defeat, Denmark exploited Swedish weakness militarily. In 1711, the Danes besieged Stralsund. The landing of Swedish
troops under General Magnus Stenbock provided temporary relief for
the region, but when Stenbock withdrew to the west and burnt the
Danish city of Altona, in 1713 Russian troops leveled Wolgast.

When Stettin fell in 1713 and Stralsund in 1715—by then, war-
profiteering Brandenburg-Prussia had joined with Russia and Denmark—
Sweden's time as a great power was over. Denmark occupied Western
Pomerania, and Wismar capitulated in 1716. Nonetheless, Wismar and
Western Pomerania north of the Peene were returned to Sweden in 1721,
and it kept them until 1815. Its ships, however, were now subject to
Danish duties whenever they passed through the Øresund. Brandenburg-
Prussia assumed control of the southern part of Western Pomerania,

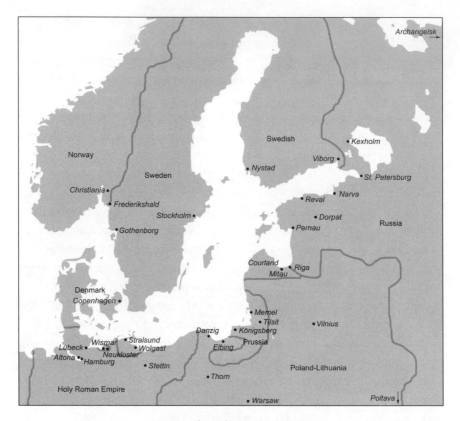

Map 6. The Baltic region in 1721

including Stettin and the islands of Usedom and Wolin, for which Frederick William I was, however, forced to pay 2 million taler. Sweden retained its possessions in Mecklenburg (Wismar, Poel, and Neukloster), which it pledged to Mecklenburg in 1803.

Mecklenburg remained divided. After the Thirty Years' War, Duke Christian Louis I (1623–1692) ruled Mecklenburg-Schwerin and Duke Gustav Adolph (1633–1695) ruled Mecklenburg-Güstrow. The dispute over succession that ensued upon Gustav Adolph's death (he had no male offspring) was finally resolved in the Hamburg Compromise of 1701. Mecklenburg-Schwerin was taken over by Duke Frederick William, who was friendly with Prussia; Adolph Frederick II received the smaller Mecklenburg-Strelitz. As a result, two houses were to rule Mecklenburg during the eighteenth century, while Sweden and Brandenburg-Prussia divided up sovereignty over Pomerania.

In Poland, the returning Augustus II found a land ravaged by plunder and forced tributes. Although he renewed his alliance with Peter I, in 1715 he was forced to avail himself of the Confederation of Tarnogród, one of whose goals was to remove the king from the throne. The presence of Russian troops led to a compromise that forbade the king from permitting either the presence of Saxon troops in Poland or the involvement of "foreign" ministers in the Polish-Lithuanian Republic. Russia became the guarantor of the Polish constitution, whose inviolability was further underscored in agreements with Prussia, Austria, and Sweden. This marked the end of the Polish-Lithuanian Republic as an independent factor in European politics, and it was subsequently wholly dependent on Russian military support. For example, during the War of Polish Succession (1733–1738), the Russian military decided in favor of the Saxon candidate for king, Augustus III (1696–1763), against Stanisław Leszczyński, who had been elected by the diet.

Pressured by the English crown, which wanted unfettered access to trade with the Baltic, Russia and Sweden signed the Treaty of Nystad, in 1721, which put an end to the Great Northern War. Sweden ceded the provinces of Livonia, Estonia, and Ingria to Russia, along with a portion of Karelia. These territories included the cities and fortresses of Riga, Dünamünde, Pernau, Reval, Dorpat, Narva, Viborg, and Kexholm, along with the islands of Ösel and Dagö. Russia returned to Sweden the areas of Finland that it had occupied and paid war reparations of 2 million riksdaler. In addition, Swedish merchants were permitted to continue buying grain in Baltic ports up to a value of 50,000 rubles, without paying duty.[3]

Russia also strengthened its influence over the Duchy of Courland, which was under Polish suzerainty and faced succession issues because of the duke's lack of offspring. Whereas Prussia wanted Courland to be independent of Russia, efforts were made in Poland to incorporate it, which ran contrary to Russia's plans. Russia proposed Count Ernst Johann von Biron (1690–1772), a favorite of Czarina Anna, as the next duke, and he was elected by the nobility of Courland in 1737. However, Biron fell out of favor after the death of the czarina and was banished to Siberia, while Poland offered several new candidates. Nonetheless, he was eventually able to reassume power and even ensure that his son Peter would succeed him.

The relatively long peace was punctuated by the Seven Years' War (1756–1763) in which Prussia, under Frederick II in alliance with England, battled France, Austria, Saxony-Poland, and Russia. Russia occupied East Prussia, which paid homage to the empress in 1758. At the same time, Russia, responding to Prussia's incursion into Saxony, used Poland as a staging area for war. Poland was sacrificed ten years after the end of the war, with the former combatants Prussia, Russia, and Austria dividing up Polish territories, thus enabling them to renounce claims each had to their territories. After the 1763 Treaty of Hubertusburg, Russian troops remained in Poland and were crucial to the election of Stanisław August Poniatowski (1732–1798) to the Polish crown. However, Empress Catherine's former favorite did not turn out as hoped. After Poniatowski initiated reforms in the Polish state, Russia and Prussia united in supporting the aristocratic opposition to the king. Alarmed by increasing Russian influence, a group of disaffected aristocrats joined together, in 1768, to form the Bar Confederation. This alliance received such support in Poland and even from outside the country that it took Russian troops years to defeat it. Prussia and Austria, fearing that Russia might become the sole ruler over Poland, joined with Russia in 1772 and partitioned approximately a third of Poland among themselves. Prussia received Royal Prussia, Warmia, and the adjacent southern Netze district. Danzig and Thorn remained part of Poland, but these cities were separated from their hinterland in Royal Prussia, which gave a decisive advantage to Elbing, transforming it into the most important port in the region. Russia now secured Polish Livonia (Latgallia) and the Lithuanian regions up to the Daugava River. Austria received parts of Lesser Poland and Galicia. The shock of partition gave a boost to reform efforts, and for a time Poland profited from rivalries between the partitioning powers. Russia, however, responded to the core reform, the Constitution of May, adopted in 1791, by intervening yet again. This time, Russian troops supported the opponents of what they characterized as a "Jacobin constitution." In the partition agreement between Russia and Prussia in 1793, the latter received Danzig and Thorn as well as Greater Poland and parts of Kujawy and Mazovia, which were spliced together to form the new administrative division of South Prussia. Russia, for its part, secured the remaining eastern territories of Lithuania, which extended to the south as far as the Bug and Dnieper Rivers. This time, however, the Polish population did not accept the partition decree without opposition. Rebellion broke out under the leadership of Tadeusz Kościuszko (1746–1817), which was, however, put down by the partitioning powers after a lengthy military campaign. Russia came to an agreement with Austria regarding the final partitioning of Poland, to which Prussia agreed. The great powers divided the remaining territory of the Republic along the Memel, Bug, and Pilica Rivers, and in a secret article in the final Treaty of Partition in 1797, they declared "the necessity to abolish everything which could revive the memory of the existence of the Kingdom of Poland."[4] As a result of this agreement, Prussia absorbed the territories bordering it to the east and southeast as far as the Memel, Bug, and Vistula Rivers. This territory was given the name New East Prussia and was administered together with East Prussia and West Prussia (that is, the former Royal Prussia).[5] However, Prussia would enjoy its territorial gains for only another ten years. Napoleon's triumphal march across Germany, Prussia's defeat, and the treaty negotiated between Napoleon and Czar Alexander at Tilsit (Sovetsk) in 1807 resulted in Prussia's demotion to a power of second rank. It was forced to give up not only Danzig, Thorn, and the Culm Land—with the exception of the free city of Danzig—but it also lost its acquisitions from the second and third partitions of Poland. All of the other territories were integrated into Napoleon's newly created Duchy of Warsaw.

Constitution and Administrative Reforms

The territorial changes described in the previous section brought about fundamentally new administrative arrangements among the states. The various new rulers responded very differently to their new acquisitions. Structural changes also occurred in the interior regions of the Baltic states as a result of land gains and losses. The new Russian (formerly Swedish) Baltic provinces are a case in point. When Russia took control in Estonia and Livonia, it granted the Baltic Germans a large degree of political autonomy and acknowledged their sovereignty over the Estonian and Latvian peasants, who were mainly serfs.[6] The basis for this arrangement was the 1710 Capitulation of Estonia and Livonia, which acknowledged the privileges of the knighthoods of the conquered territories. For Czar Peter I, keeping the estates from opposing Russian rule was a prerequisite for economic recovery in the region. In addition to acknowledging the rights of the knighthoods, the capitulation also strengthened the right to religious convictions in accordance with the Augsburg Confession, the status of the Protestant-Lutheran state church, and German self-administration and its legal system. As a result, the German language was sanctioned, even though only 10 percent of the population spoke it.

The knighthoods closed themselves off until the middle of the eighteenth century by establishing registries—in Livonia in 1747 and in Estonia in 1756—that set a limit on the number of noble families. In Estonia, the number was set at about 120 families and in Livonia at about 170 families. As in Courland, these families achieved an exclusivity that had always been denied them under Swedish rule. Only in Livonia were owners or renters of manorial farms accepted into the nobility. The diet, which had the right to enact laws and taxation policies, and before which all registered nobles had to appear, was the body through which the autonomy and self-administration of the nobility was expressed. In Livonia, nonregistered owners of manorial farms had a seat at the diet, as had the city of Riga. The power of the noble families rested on their participation rights, and especially on their right to hold the most important judicial, administrative, and ecclesiastic offices.

The Russian crown, however, also had its representatives in the Baltic. After Peter the Great named his confidant Aleksandr Menshikov (1673–1729) governor general of the conquered provinces, separate provincial governors were appointed in Livonia and Estonia to oversee the levying and administration of taxes as well as trade matters and censorship. These administrative ties were strengthened after Catherine I (1687–1727) became empress. A law commission was set to work on the legislative unification and reach of the czarist empire. Representatives of the noble families and the cities took part in this effort, and together with the Finnish representatives and those of the former Polish-Lithuanian territories in the Ukraine, they defended the rights of the provinces against those of the Russian Empire. After Russia's successes in the wars against the Ottoman Empire, Catherine intensified her reform efforts, and in 1775 she introduced a new provincial ordinance. It initially came into force in Russia alone, but it was extended to the

Baltic provinces in 1783 and, like the introduction of the Russian head tax, bound these provinces closer to St. Petersburg. In their provincial narrow-mindedness, the nobility was initially pleased that it continued to be exempt from taxation, and that taxes were largely borne by the Estonian and Latvian population. In addition, the allodification of the manorial farms (these became actual property) was welcomed by the nobility. The cities, however, resisted as their privileges had been eliminated in 1785, when Russian municipal ordinances were introduced. On the other hand, the latter led to freedom of trade and, for example in Riga, laid the groundwork for industrialization during the following century. Although Czar Paul I (1754–1801) restored the old city and provincial constitutions when he was enthroned in 1796, he also introduced the Russian military recruitment law in the provinces, which meant long-term service in the Russian army to any young man caught up in its net.[7]

The situation in Prussia was very different. Only a few small parts of what had belonged to Sweden had to be integrated into the state after 1715; however, the government was faced with the reconstruction and reorganization of East Prussia, primarily as a result of the plague and war. Between 1708 and 1710, bubonic plague and other epidemics wreaked havoc in the northeastern part of East Prussia (and in Estonia and Livonia). Attempts at resettlement were hindered by administrative abuses, which engendered a certain desire for reform in the central government in Berlin. In any case, the new king, Frederick William I, viewed the remaining rights of the estates as an impediment to the rational organization of the country. One of his solutions was to restrict the diets to paying homage to the ruler when he took the reins of government. In the following years, he initiated a program of fundamental reforms.

The system of taxation in particular was a thorn in the side of the reformers. Because property taxes were calculated by *Hufen* (i.e., by size) without taking into account their fertility and state of cultivation, there was no rational basis for the taxes that were levied. As a result, a commission headed by Karl Heinrich zu Waldburg (1686–1721) created a land register between 1714 and 1719, and a land tax based on the quality of the land was introduced. The introduction of this general land tax did away with the nobility's exemption from taxation, while at the same time transforming land held in fief into allodial land, that is, into property. The most important domestic political decisions were made by the War and Domain Chamber, and as such it was responsible for the resettlement of those regions most affected by plague and war. In addition, the lands belonging to the princes (the so-called *domanium*) were reorganized. Rather than have the districts (*Ämter*) administered and used by district administrators (*Amtshauptleute*), a general lease (*Generalpacht*) was introduced. Lessees, often wealthy citizens, took over the demesnes for their use, but they had to pay a fixed sum for the privilege. Because they were permitted to increase the productivity of the demesnes, they also introduced innovations.[8] The reorganization of the demesnes, like the tax levies, supported Prussia's militarization, which was anchored in the cantonal system introduced by Frederick William I. Army regiments were granted particular districts, so-called cantons, from which they could draft the sons of peasants. At the same time, their landlords became their superior officers.[9] In the 1750s, the districts declined in importance and were replaced by new administrative units. District administrators were replaced by district commissioners (*Landräte*), who regulated the affairs of the nobility and their subjects. In the end, the state's interest in maintaining a constant pool of soldiers led to agrarian reforms. Here, the state had a progressive effect on the demesnes, although it also tended to favor the interests of the nobility. In 1763, efforts began to be made to eliminate corvée labor on the demesnes, and, in 1773, serfdom was *formally* abolished, although the services continued to be performed. In 1799, these services were decreased by three-fourths. A quarter remained in order to make it easier for the demesnes to adapt to the changed economic conditions.[10]

In Royal Prussia, by contrast, reform efforts concentrated on the administration of the larger cities. As in earlier times, the battle lines continued to be drawn between the city councils and the members of what was known as the Third Order, that is, the representatives of artisans and merchants. Although members of the Third Order occupied some city offices by the end of the seventeenth century, in the eighteenth century complaints increased that the city councils and the aldermen no longer represented the interests of the citizens. City committees no longer consisted of men active in trade but of those educated in the law, and these individuals ruled over the cities as a professional elite. After the Third Order aired these complaints and presented them to a royal commission, constitutional reforms were made that expanded its members' scope of authority and reserved for merchants a third of the seats on city councils and boards of aldermen.[11] Comparable reforms took place in Elbing and Thorn, although the riots in Thorn were confessional in nature and did not result in political demands.

The partitions of Poland posed greater administrative challenges.[12] For example, West Prussia was created in 1772 from lands acquired by Royal Prussia, to which was added Prussia, in 1793. Whereas in West Prussia and East Prussia, a so-called *Oberpräsident* was the highest appointed administrative official, South Prussia was administered by the Silesian provincial minister. Finally, Friedrich Leopold von Schroetter was responsible for New East Prussia, having already served as *Oberpräsident* in East Prussia and West Prussia.[13] But with the occupation of Polish territories, the former voivodeships ceased to exist, and the state took over the royal demesnes and leased them out. Repopulation measures increased the number of German settlers in the region, and the integration of new lands was reflected in both increased recruitment and the construction of fortifications.[14]

Sweden was forced to adapt in completely different ways. It focused less and less on the eastern Baltic region, concentrating on Sweden proper; thus, its perspective became increasingly national. The defeat of Sweden in the Great Northern War and the early death of Charles XII caused a multitude of political disruptions. Upon the king's death in 1718, his sister, Ulrika Eleonora (1688–1741), abolished the hitherto absolutist form of government and, as Swedish queen, set out to create a new form of government. Her government was tied to the consent of the Council of the Realm (Riksrådet), which in turn was elected by the diet. The diet had the right to veto decisions by the council, and it also decided on legislative matters and taxation. When the queen relinquished her throne in favor of her husband Frederick I of Hesse (1676–1751), nothing changed in terms of the apparent powerlessness of the king. The Council of the Realm set policies, especially under Arvid Bernhard Horn (1664–1742), who reduced government deficits by pursuing disarmament and mercantilist economic policies, thereby promoting Sweden's economic recovery.[15] One of his first measures was to enact the Product Decree, which privileged Swedish merchant shipping to the detriment of Dutch and English carriers. Another was the founding, in 1731, of the Swedish East India Company, in Gothenburg, for which Dutch seamen had to be recruited.

In spite of their success, Horn's policies, which were supported by the so-called Caps Party (Mössorna) in the diet, did not find favor with all. Their opponents, the Hats (Hattarna), which represented the interests of younger military officers and officials, were intent on fomenting a new war with Russia, and they toppled Horn. Although they failed in their military undertakings, the Hats were not permanently discredited. Even with the help of a number of aristocrats, Queen Lovisa Ulrika (1720–1782) failed in her attempt to remove the Hats from power. Although the Caps returned to the government in 1765, it was not until 1772 that Gustav III (1746–1792) was able, in a coup, to assert the competence of the monarch to set policy guidelines. According to the new form of government of 1772, the members of the Council of the Realm, who were appointed by the king, were left with only an advisory function when it came to decisions made by the king.[16] As in the seventeenth century, the diet would now be convened solely at the discretion of the king.

Impressed by western European physiocrats, Gustav III initiated a comprehensive reform program. He loosened controls on international trade while at the same time creating a state monopoly in spirits, which proved to be a windfall for the treasury. Like other European states, Sweden now granted religious tolerance, which attracted merchants—Jews among them for the first time—and artisans from other countries. He also granted the peasantry the right to own property; previous land consolidation laws had made it possible for them to partition off their individual strips or pieces of land from those of the village community. A decision was made in 1789 to award property, which bought the king the support of the peasantry. And like kings before him, he used this support as a counterweight to the nobility. Just how successful he was may be gauged by his murder, in 1792, at a masked ball in Stockholm at the hand of aristocratic conspirators. Because the peasants were also permitted to acquire land from aristocrats, their land holdings increased during the nineteenth century. By contrast, during the eighteenth century, labor rent increased on numerous manorial farms, including in Scania, as agricultural production increased. Only later was corvée labor eventually transformed into monetary rent.[17]

The Swedish reforms were undoubtedly influenced by the enlightened absolutism of the Danish kings, which had so benefited Denmark during the eighteenth century. Among other measures, laws tying the peasants to the land (*stavnsbåndet*) were abrogated in 1788, and in 1781 a law was passed that enabled the peasants to lay claim to their property in the communities in which they lived. Because the king of Denmark had unlimited power, he was also able to tame the nobility. While an old nobility by birth remained prominent, he also privileged a new nobility by service, whose highest ranks were above those of the hereditary aristocrats. They were closely bound to the crown by fief. These aristocrats included entrepreneurs and men of German origin, who, like the counts Andreas Peter Bernstorff, Christian and Ludwig Reventlow, and Ernst Schimmelmann, sought to reform the monarchy economically and financially. Earlier, Johann Friedrich Struensee (1737–1772) had been able to initiate an avalanche of reforms because, as personal physician to the mentally ill Christian VII, the German-born Struensee had come to exert a considerable influence. Censorship was abolished, state administration completely reorganized, and free trade introduced. The condition of the peasantry was also improved. Despite his good relationship with the queen (he was also her lover), Struensee was unable to withstand the onslaughts of his political opponents— in part because of a lack of support from the king—and in the end he paid for his temerity and reform-mindedness, first with his right hand and then with his head.[18] Some of the reforms were rescinded. At the same time, Danish was made the preferred language, over German, in official and military matters. Nonetheless, the reforms could not be permanently or completely reversed. On the contrary, Crown Prince Frederick (1768–1839), who assumed the regency over his father in 1784, continued to drive the reform process. Beneficiaries included both urban businesses and the Danish merchant fleet, which as a result of Denmark's political neutrality was the actual winner in the wars between Britain and France, the American War of Independence, and the Fourth Anglo-Dutch War (1780–1784). The profits from Danish shippers and merchants flowed into Copenhagen—but also into smaller merchant cities such as Odense, Albørg, Århus, Helsingør, and Flensburg—and were instrumental in the capital's economic and cultural renaissance.[19]

The Upswing in Baltic Trade

Baltic trade boomed during the eighteenth century. The duties collected for passage through the Øresund may be gauged by the fact that the number of ships passing through the Sound grew steadily throughout the entire century. Even the War of Polish Succession, which weighed heavily on Danzig, and the Seven Years' War caused only minor and brief downturns. Despite short-term fluctuations, Baltic trade remained essentially stable.

Dutch trade with the Baltic during the eighteenth century grew slightly at a time when other sectors, such as herring fishing and commercial production, lagged. If not for the Baltic trade, the Dutch economy overall would have fallen even further behind the expanding English economy than was already the case. Dutch ships continued to dominate the Baltic trade over almost the entire eighteenth century, even though their share declined from 50 percent (1711–1729) to 27 percent (1771–1780). The English and Scandinavians filled the gap: English shipping increased to 26 percent (1771–1780) and Scandinavian to 28 percent (1771–1780). The English benefited from the structural changes taking place in the Baltic region, where the demand for textiles and colonial products replaced that for herring and salt.[20] Accordingly, English ships now supplied the new Russian port of St. Petersburg with English textiles and colonial reexports such as sugar, coffee, and tobacco. Swedish ships took over the transport of timber and forest products from the Baltic region to Great Britain.[21] If we analyze shipping traffic through the Øresund between the Baltic region and the ports of destination, between 1784 and 1795 Amsterdam outstripped all other western European ports in that regard (including London, Hull, Bordeaux, and Lisbon).[22] However, even shipping nations not known for their Baltic trade, such as France, increasingly sent ships there. Not only did they supply Königsberg, St. Petersburg, Stockholm, Danzig, Stettin, Copenhagen, and Lübeck with wine, salt, and colonial products, but they also returned with products important to their own domestic shipbuilding industry, including wood, forest products, and

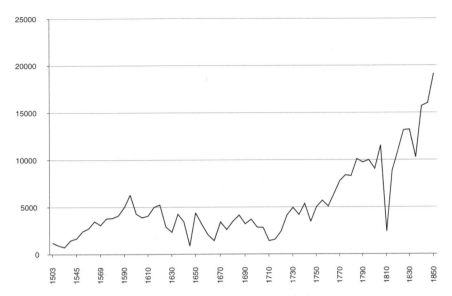

Graph 2. Ship Passages through the Sound (Øresund), 1503–1845   *(J. Ojala, "Research Potential of the Database and Guidebooks," presentation at the Baltic Connections Conference, Denmark, October 29–31, 2007; P. Borschberg and M. North, Asia Europe Journal 8/3 [2010]: 279–292)*

metals.[23] The reexport of French and other colonial products (coffee, sugar, cotton cloth) through Hamburg to the Baltic region should not be underestimated. This trade was conducted using Dutch merchant ships and, increasingly, those sailing out of Hamburg.

To measure the importance of the Baltic region to the Dutch and English economies, we must compare imports from there with those from other regions. While the entire volume of English trade between 1701 and 1800 grew from 4.37 million pounds sterling to 20.42 million pounds, the individual regions shared unequally. For example, the Atlantic region (West Indies, America, and Ireland) registered the most explosive growth, from 1.21 million pounds sterling to 8.94 million pounds, with 43.8 percent of imports coming from the Atlantic region. The proportion of trade with Asia was relatively small at the beginning of the eighteenth century (10.9 percent); by the end of the century this trade made up about a fifth of English imports. The proportion from the Mediterranean region decreased from 21.3 percent (1701–1710) to 10 percent (1791–1800). The North Sea–Baltic region is of particular interest. At the beginning of the eighteenth century (1701–1710), this

Table 6.1 Provenance of English imports, 1701–1800 in millions of pounds sterling (official values in constant prices of 1696)

	Asia (East Indies)	Mediterranean Sea	North Sea and Baltic Sea			Atlantic Ocean			
			Total	North Sea	Baltic Sea	Total	West Indies	America	Ireland
1701–1710	0.48	0.93	1.75	1.22	0.53	1.21	0.64	0.28	0.29
1711–1720	0.74	1.35	1.65	1.12	0.53	1.71	0.93	0.41	0.36
1721–1730	0.96	1.56	2.05	1.39	0.66	2.16	1.27	0.56	0.33
1731–1740	0.97	1.55	2.24	1.46	0.79	2.45	1.40	0.67	0.38
1741–1750	0.98	1.29	2.14	1.28	0.87	2.68	1.32	0.76	0.61
1751–1760	1.05	1.51	2.23	1.15	1.09	3.41	1.82	0.86	0.73
1761–1770	1.48	1.41	2.63	1.29	1.35	4.95	2.79	1.13	1.03
1771–1780	1.53	1.61	3.06	1.40	1.65	5.30	3.01	0.87	1.42
1781–1790	2.67	1.77	3.60	1.55	2.05	5.85	3.27	0.83	1.74
1791–1800	4.43	2.05	5.00	2.11	2.89	8.94	5.06	1.57	2.32

From E. B. Schumpeter (1960), Table 6.

trade contributed 40 percent of imports; that figure had decreased to about 25 percent during the ten-year period between 1791 and 1800. If we distinguish between the North Sea region and the Baltic region, we see a long-term decrease in imports from the North Sea, which is slightly, but not completely, compensated for by growth in the Baltic trade. English imports from the Baltic region, in comparison to English imports overall, rose significantly more (by fivefold) than total imports (by fourfold).

This trade dynamic is also reflected in shipping traffic. Here, shipping to the East Indies increased slightly and traffic across the Atlantic more strongly, whereas trade with the Mediterranean region decreased significantly and traffic between the North Sea and the Baltic region decreased slightly. When we look at differences between North Sea and Baltic shipping, we again see a decrease in northwestern Europe and an increase in shipping traffic with the Baltic region. Also clearly visible is the importance of trade in mass-produced goods with the Baltic, which required relatively more shipping capacity than such trade was worth by weight.

A reconstruction of Dutch imports in the 1770s yields a comparable picture. At 17 million guldens, the Baltic region ranked just barely behind Great Britain, Asia, French colonial re-exports (each 20 million guldens), and the Western Hemisphere (Atlantic) with 18 million guldens.[24]

The evolving role of the Baltic region in the world economy also reflected structural changes that had occurred there, with the most important Baltic ports being those belonging to the Russian Empire, especially St. Petersburg. Nonetheless, Danzig, not to mention Stockholm, which was privileged by the Swedish state, continued to play an important role. Stockholm's trade was so successful that in 1765 it relinquished its previous monopoly on the tar trade and allowed Finnish ports to traffic in tar, which greatly increased Finnish shipping. Merchants from Stockholm and Gothenburg used credits given to iron producers to stimulate exports to western Europe through its ports.

Gothenburg also grew in importance as a result of the founding of the Swedish "Ostindiska companiet" in 1731. It was especially active in the tea trade with China and organized tea imports in the Baltic region.[25] The company even smuggled tea to Britain.[26] Ships from Danish

162   THE BALTIC

Table 6.2   Dutch imports in the 1770s

Imports from	Value in millions of gulden per year	Percentage of total imports (%)
Southern Netherlands and Germany	10	7
Northern Europe	22	15.3
Baltic region	17	
Other	5	
Great Britain	20	14
Colonial re-export	5	3.5
France	5	3.5
Colonial re-export	20	14
Iberian Peninsula	16	11.2
Mediterranean	7	4.9
Western Hemisphere	18	12.6
Asia	20	14
Total	143	100

From Vries and van der Woude (1997), p. 497.

ports also increased their trade with the Baltic, although much of the upswing in trade was due to Denmark's neutrality.[27]

After the 1721 Treaty of Nystad, Danzig once again became a supplier of grain to Europe such that annual grain exports (1721–1730) came to about 36,000 lasts. This trade dropped to only 20,000 lasts in the 1740s and 1750s, but in the 1760s it topped 40,000 lasts. Danzig also remained an important exporter of timber products, but it was able to defend its leading role in the Baltic only with respect to potash. Danzig ships were involved in about a tenth of the shipping to western Europe.[28]

However, ships coming from the west increasingly sailed to Königsberg, Riga, St. Petersburg, Narva, and Viborg. One advantage of these ports was their specialized assortment of wood products. A snapshot of the Øresund is illuminating. The most valuable export goods were the thick balks (beams) used in both ship and house building, which came from Narva and Riga, and then at the end of the eighteenth century increasingly from Memel and its Lithuanian hinterland. Planks were thinner and were offered at most of the ports. Planks may also be distinguished from the even thinner deals, which were available from ports in the Gulf of Finland, but also from Memel and Danzig. Smaller staves were used primarily to make wine casks; these were prefabricated mainly in the hinterlands of Memel, Danzig, and Stettin. In terms of size, masts were the largest timber products, and they came primarily from Riga.[29]

The ports of destination for timber exports document the demand for timber in Amsterdam, although the traffic to English ports was even greater. In Bordeaux and other French ports, barrel staves for French wine and cognac exports were even bigger sellers. Pitch and tar from Sweden and Finland were important imports as well. Dutch merchants were especially interested in Riga's exports, which included ash, flax, hemp, linseed, and hemp seed, while the English shopped for different types of timber. The Dutch dominated the Riga trade into the 1770s, with English merchants and ships catching up with the Dutch in about 1780 as a result of their greater timber imports.[30]

After the founding of St. Petersburg, Dutch and especially English ships dropped anchor there. No Russian merchant fleet existed yet; at the most Russia had only a few ships, captained mainly by Dutch sailors.[31] The main trade—if we exclude supplying the new court with western European luxury goods—was in flax and hemp, with hemp export coming in at double that of Riga after the 1740s. There was also a demand for tallow in western Europe, which had mainly been obtained from Arkhangelsk, and for Russian leather. Timber exports were banned by the Russian state in 1754, and it was only after this ban was lifted in 1783 that St. Petersburg again became a more important timber exporter.[32] However, the most important export product from

Table 6.3   Wood exports from the largest Baltic ports, 1787
Estimated value in 1,000 reichstaler

	Viborg	St. Petersburg	Narva	Riga	Memel	Danzig	Stettin
Balks	—	3.3	573.3	287.7	755.4	97.9	13.3
Planks	135.1	316.5	101.1	45.4	1.9	1.1	5.8
Deals	80.8	40.6	15.3	1.3	127.6	120.4	0.8
Staves	—	1.0	—	1.7	29.3	33.0	85.9
Masts	—	13.0	1.9	71.5	26.1	0.7	—
Other	2.0	5.3	5.2	52.3	39.1	97.8	18.6
Total	217.9	379.7	696.8	459.9	979.4	350.9	124.4

From H. C. Johansen, in (1992), pp. 17–35, here pp. 26–27.

St. Petersburg was pig iron, whose production had greatly increased since the 1730s and had even outstripped English output. In about the middle of the eighteenth century, before the English Industrial Revolution gained steam, Russia had been the largest European iron exporter, exporting 75 percent of the iron it produced, primarily to England.[33]

Because exports from the Baltic region were worth more than the imports from western Europe, western European countries were regularly forced to make up the difference in precious metals. In the eighteenth century, for example, approximately two million reichstaler were transported annually from western Europe to the Baltic region. These monies went to producers in the hinterland, but they also flowed farther east in the Russia trade. During the expansion of English -Russian trade in the eighteenth century, St. Petersburg and Riga registered, without doubt, the largest export surpluses. As a result, much of the precious metal sent to the Baltic ended up in those cities. England paid for most of its purchases with Dutch coins or with bills of exchange drawn on Amsterdam. The bills of exchange, which could be used to make cashless payments in Baltic ports, came due in Amsterdam, and the cash flowed from there to the merchants and then on to the producers in the Baltic region.[34]

The Establishment of a Cultural and Communication Space

The large cities such as Copenhagen, Stockholm, Riga, Reval, and Danzig, but even the countryside, belonged to a communication space that stretched from Lübeck and Hamburg in the west to St. Petersburg and Moscow in the east. In addition, the port cities ensured cultural exchange with western Europe, notably with the Netherlands and Great Britain. Books and journals provided contact with the Holy Roman Empire and western Europe, as did personal relationships. While students from the Russian Baltic provinces studied at universities in the empire, the aristocratic estates, pastorates, and schools in the east provided a market for the skills of academics from the west.

Because of their published works, so-called *Hofmeister* (literally court masters) are the best attested group. They were hired to educate the children of the nobility, but they also worked in the homes of merchants in the cities. For a scholar, a position as *Hofmeister* marked a first career step. The German-speaking population in Estonia and Livonia generated between seventy and eighty *Hofmeister* positions annually, which meant that a university graduate from the empire had good income prospects, although competition was fairly stiff for these positions.[35] The social status of a *Hofmeister* (or *Literat*, as they were sometimes called) in Estonia and Livonia was considerably higher than in the empire, where they were often merely viewed and treated as common personnel.[36] Such treatment would have been out of the question in the Baltic provinces, where all of the domestics were either Latvian or Estonian. Open positions were announced not only by the Baltic students, but also by professors to whom Baltic landowners turned either directly or by using a previous *Hofmeister* as a go-between. Once hired, the *Hofmeister* began what was generally a six-year stint as an educator in one or several manors, which might lead to a permanent position as a pastor or *Gymnasium*-level teacher, assuming that all went well. In many cases, these teachers became fully integrated into Baltic society; other *Hofmeister*, however, left their positions in frustration and sometimes published their grievances, complaining loudly about the supposedly barbaric conditions in Livonia.

Those who remained in Estonia and Livonia often served as the vehicle for Enlightenment ideas, on the one hand developing ideas for reform and, on the other, taking great pains to master the language, culture, and social mores of the indigenous Latvian or Estonian population. This professional group was at least in part responsible for the identity that developed among the local Baltic population beginning in the eighteenth century. After a few years as a *Hofmeister*, most who applied were given positions as pastors or schoolmasters, pastors being in especially short supply as well. As a result, a good half of all pastors in Livonia did not come from there, and few were born in the Baltic region or had attended school there. Many of those who came from afar ended up staying in Livonia.[37]

Just how quickly a career could develop is exemplified by the scholar and Enlightenment figure August Wilhelm Hupel (1737–1819), who after his studies in Jena and three years as a *Hofmeister* in Estonia was ordained in Riga in 1760, and who shortly thereafter received a pastorate in Ecks (Äksi), in the vicinity of Dorpat.[38] It is possible that he had help from compatriots, as the notary of the city of Dorpat, Christian

G. J. Mylius, was the son of the mayor of Jena, Heinrich Ernst Mylius. Also perhaps in his favor was the twenty-three-year-old Hupel's willingness to marry the widow of his predecessor, who was ten years older than he and the mother of four children. Not long thereafter he was offered other pastorates, and he decided in favor of Oberpahlen (Põltsamaa), where he stayed for four decades and turned the place into a rural center of the Enlightenment.

But other prominent individuals were later appointed to positions in the Baltic region as well: Johann Gottfried Herder (1744–1803) as a member of the clergy in Riga, and Johann Georg Hamann (1730–1788) as a teacher in a merchant family's home. Economic support from the Berens family enabled both Herder and Hamann to publish their works. Hamann soon returned to Königsberg, while Herder set out on his academic peregrinations, initially as a traveling companion to the Berens family. Nonetheless, his stay in Riga and the works he first published there would permanently change the image of Livonia and Estonia in Germany.

Other young academics started as *Hofmeister*, later becoming school headmasters before being appointed to a pastorate. However, the opposite sequence or simultaneous positions as a teacher and pastor were also possible. For example, many headmasters at the Riga Lyceum had taught in private homes or ministered to a flock. New generations of scholars were trained not only in Jena and Leipzig, but also farther west in Giessen and Göttingen. Königsberg was a major training ground, largely because of the light cast by Immanuel Kant (1724–1804), but also because of its forward-looking recruitment policies. For example, the university managed to recruit former Göttingen students such as Christian Jakob Kraus (1753–1807), who remained there for many years. Kraus taught state economics (*Staatswirtschaftslehre*), following in the intellectual footsteps of Adam Smith. He thus became a trailblazer for liberal economic ideas, which were taken up by landowners and state administrators over the next several decades.[39] Many Königsberg students wrote extensively. Thus, Gottlieb Schlegel (1739–1810), who was born and studied in Königsberg, published more than fifty works as headmaster of the cathedral school in Riga. In 1780, he withdrew to a pastorate, but then ten years later he became a professor at Greifswald and assumed the superintendency.[40] To the extent they had studied law, a small number of *Hofmeister* were able to make the jump to a judgeship or to the office of city notary. One example was Justus Friedrich Zacharias, who was born in Thuringia but studied in Leipzig.[41]

In the eighteenth century, students from other parts of the Baltic tended to study at the universities in Jena, Halle, and Leipzig, except for the Finns, who studied in Åbo and Uppsala. Students at Halle became acquainted with Pietism, which was favored by the nobility and clergy in the Russian Baltic provinces and later made headway among the rural population as a result of the work of the Bohemian Brethren. The University of Göttingen became very popular during the mid-eighteenth century. A case in point is Peter Forsskål (1732–1763), the son of a pastor in Helsinki, who switched from Uppsala to Göttingen. In 1759, he published an anonymous pamphlet titled *Tankar om Borgerliga Friheten* (Thoughts on civil liberty), in which he demanded equal rights for nonaristocratic members of society—including access to higher state offices that had previously been reserved for the nobility. Although the pamphlet was banned and published again only after the French Revolution (1792), it brought about the temporary elimination of censorship in Sweden. Forsskål took part in a Danish expedition to the Orient along with fellow Göttingen graduate Carsten Niebuhr (1733–1815), a mathematician and cartographer. The expedition had been financed and equipped for scientific purposes in 1761 by King Frederick V. Unfortunately, Forsskål, like all of the other scholars on the expedition, succumbed to malaria. Niebuhr alone returned from Arabia and India. He described the lands he had visited as comprehensively and objectively as he could in *Reisebeschreibung nach Arabien und andern umliegenden Ländern* (Description of travels to Arabia and other surrounding lands).

On the other hand, the scholar and scientist Johann Beckmann (1739–1811), who after his studies in Göttingen undertook numerous travels, especially to the Netherlands, which he documented meticulously, took a teaching position in mathematics, physics, and natural history at St. Peter's Gymnasium in St. Petersburg. From here, he traveled to Sweden and Denmark in 1765, and he continued his studies under Carl Linnaeus (1707–1778) in Uppsala. In 1776, he was appointed to a professorship in economics at Göttingen, where he remained until

his death. Beckmann coined the term *technology* in 1772, and he was
the first to teach and write about it. Because the Swedish university in
Dorpat had closed in 1710, St. Peter's Gymnasium and the Academy of
Sciences in St. Petersburg served as the most important educational institutions in the region.

A lack of universities was also why the duke of Courland founded
the Academia Petrina, in Mitau (Jelgava), a small residence city that
he hoped to transform into an intellectual center. He appointed internationally respected scholars to professorships, and they brought their
scientific networks with them to Courland. One of these was the Swede
Johann Jacob Ferber (1743–1790), who had studied mineralogy at Uppsala and later pursued research in Berlin, England, France, Italy, and
in the mines of Bohemia and Hungary.[42] He was a member of numerous
scientific societies and academies, and his network of correspondents
was vast, among them Johann Bernoulli (1744–1807), who even visited
Ferber in Mitau. Ferber, who as a reviewer for the *Allgemeine Deutsche
Bibliothek* (ADB) was in close contact with its founder and publisher
Friedrich Nicolai (1733–1811), wrote to him in September 1777, "I do
not lack for prospects in my fatherland; however, I gladly remain in Germany."[43] What did Ferber mean by Germany? In contrast to other Baltic
residents, he did not consider his fatherland to be either Livonia or Estonia, but Sweden. Germany, namely the area where German served
as the language of communication, constituted the region that Nicolai
actively served with the publication of the ADB. Although Sweden
promised its sons good career prospects, the scholarly world of the empire, specifically the German-speaking lands, seemed to him more interesting than Sweden, especially in its Couronian manifestation. For
example, the intelligentsia of Mitau enjoyed the political freedom afforded it by its Polish sovereigns. Among other things, Courland differed markedly from Russia, Prussia, and Sweden in terms of censorship. A Swede teaching in Courland remained largely unrestricted as
a professor at the Academia Pietrina, as a member of the German literati, and as a fellow of the republic of scholars.[44]

Probably even better known than Beckmann and Ferber was the historian and political scientist August Ludwig von Schlözer (1735–1809).
After studies in Göttingen and Wittenberg, Schlözer spent some time
in Stockholm and Uppsala, and then eight years in St. Petersburg, first

as a teacher in a private home and then as an adjunct at the Academy of Sciences. Upon his return to Göttingen, Schlözer pursued research in the Slavic languages. He edited and translated the *Nestor Chronicle* and promoted research into the Nordic and Slavic worlds, which in his opinion embodied a kind of state of unspoiled innocence that western European culture had long since lost. In this respect, he and Herder were of like minds, seeing the folkishness of the Latvians and Slavs as an expression of cultural purity. This state of innocence was to be found especially in the folk song (*Volkslied*), a word that he coined, and he published collections of such songs. The collecting of folk songs became an important touchstone among peoples with smaller populations searching for a national culture and identity. Thus, Henrik Gabriel Porthan (1739–1804), a professor of rhetoric at the University of Åbo, published Finnish folk songs in his five-volume *De Poësi Fennica*, laying the groundwork for the collection and researching of Finnish folk poetry, which in the next century culminated in the publication of the *Kalevala*, compiled by Elias Lönnrot (1802–1884) from old folkloric sources. At the same time, the Couronian provost Gotthard Friedrich Stender (1714–1796), who received his training in Riga, Jena, and Halle, wrote a Latin grammar, and in 1774 he composed the *Augstas gudrības grāmata no pasaules un dabas* (A book of high wisdom on the world and nature), a sort of encyclopedia of peasant lore, while the East Prussian pastor Christian Donalitius (1714–1780) wrote one of the first poetry cycles in Lithuanian, titled *Metai* (The seasons).[45]

Hupel's publications *An das Lief- und Ehstländische Publikum* (To the Livonian and Estonian public) and *Nordische Miscellaneen* (Nordic miscellanies) should be seen in this context. Hupel propagated a German-Estonian-Latvian-Russian multilingualism, while at the same time informing the educated world about the Baltic provinces and Russia.

On the other hand, Sweden retained an influence in the study of science in the Swedish province of Pomerania. Both the government in Stralsund and the Swedish-born professors in Greifswald exerted a cultural influence on the region. Before this influence was felt, however, Swedish policies were required to make it possible. One of the first Swedish professors at Greifswald, the jurist Christian Nettelbladt (1779–1843), who in numerous publications tried to prove the superiority of the

Swedish scholarly tradition, ran up against opposition from his colleagues. The professors recruited from Pomerania, in particular, agitated against the appointment of Swedish-born candidates. The
Stralsund-born Johann Carl Dähnert (1719–1785) held positions as librarian, professor of the history of science, and later of Swedish constitutional law. As secretary of the Royal German Society, he was at
first suspicious of Swedish candidates. In founding a number of scholarly societies and journals, such as the *Critische Nachrichten* (Critical
notices), Dähnert and others tried to advance the Enlightenment in
Pomerania and to create a basis for intellectual understanding with
Sweden. His 1763 speech "Die uralte Gemeinschaft zwischen dem
Schwedischen Reich und Pommern als ein Vorspiel der glücklicheren
neueren Verbindung" (The age-old community between the Swedish
kingdom and Pomerania as a prelude to a happier newer association)
constituted an expression of his efforts, which were also promoted by
networks of freemasons, as Dähnert was the master of the "Zu den drei
Greifen" masonic lodge. This is why, as rector, he was able to implement, with the consent of Friedrich Carl Sinclair, the governor general
and chancellor of the university, the university reforms advanced by
King Gustav III. In addition to a curriculum oriented toward practice,
these reforms included the positive reception of Swedish science. As
of 1773, the University of Greifswald received a copy of every new
Swedish publication. Although some of the reforms foundered on faculty opposition, scientific and cultural relations between Greifswald
and Sweden became increasingly institutionalized toward the end of
the eighteenth century. Among other things, this included establishing
a professorship in Swedish literature associated with the office of university librarian, a position that went to the Swedish poet and philosopher Thomas Thorild (1759–1808).

Greifswald's growing popularity among Swedish masters and doctoral students, however, elicited some protestations from Swedish
universities. As a result, the number of Swedish masters students in
Greifswald was limited to ten per year. Overall, the Swedish-Pomeranian
elites increasingly came to identify with Sweden. When the French Revolution began, many of the more critical among them called for reforms
consistent with Swedish enlightened absolutism. As a result, as late
as the first decade of the nineteenth century, Greifswald and Stralsund

became bastions of Swedish intellectualism, which was defended as a counterweight to French ideas by authors such as Ernst Moritz Arndt (1769–1860) and Friedrich Rühs (1781–1820), the author of a history of Sweden.[46]

But without the media revolution of the eighteenth century, these personal networks would have been much less effective. In addition to the books that charted unexplored territory and found an expanding readership, periodicals on all manner of subjects began to appear. Journals were published in all of the sciences and disciplines, although their readership was often small, sometimes astonishingly so. One particular genre was the so-called *Intelligenzblatt* (Information sheet), which—originally intended as a pennysaver, an advertising vehicle—developed into a medium for noncommercial information. Some of these periodicals, taking their cue from English weeklies, dealt with moral questions and morality. The most famous of these, the *Hamburger Patriot*, was also read in the Baltic region during the first decades of the eighteenth century. Some journals, such as Wieland's *Teutscher Merkur* (German Mercury) and Nicolai's *Allgemeine Deutsche Bibliothek*, attracted subscribers in the Baltic and recruited correspondents from among the scholars in the region. Friedrich Justin Bertuch's *Journal des Luxus und der Moden* (Journal of luxury goods and fashion) attracted subscribers as far distant as Copenhagen, Libau, Riga, Königsberg, and Danzig. The same held true for newspapers, of which the *Hamburgische unpartheyische Correspondent* (Hamburg impartial correspondent) had the largest readership in the region. In Danzig, for example, where the first weekly newspaper was founded in 1619, people were still dependent on the *Hamburgische unpartheyische Correspondent* for daily political news in the eighteenth century. Other newspapers with large readerships included the *Gazette de Leyde*, the leading Dutch newspaper, and the *Danziger Anzeigen* (Danzig advertiser).[47] The *Danziger Anzeigen* reported on the importation and sale of western European art works, furnishings, and the like, but it also featured articles in an entertainment section, some of them of English provenance. In fact, the reform pastor Samuel Wilhelm Turner felt called upon to publicize English culture and science and founded his own periodicals for the purpose (such as the *Danziger Wochenschrift*). He also published translations of Edmund Burke's diaries for his Danzig readership.[48]

Other periodicals, such as the *Historische und Gelehrte Neuigkeiten* (Historical and scholarly news), which was published in 1782 as *Deutsche Zeitungen* and in 1795 as *Danziger Zeitungen*, joined the *Königliche Westpreussische Elbingische Zeitung von Staats- und Gelehrtensachen* (Royal West Prussian Elbing newspaper for state and scholarly matters) and the *Thorner Deutsche Zeitung von Politischen Gelehrten und Ökonomischen Sachen* (Thorn German newspaper for political, scholarly, and economic matters) (1796–1799) in informing the public in Royal Prussia before and after the partition of Poland.

In Königsberg, various book dealers put out competing newspapers. In addition to the *Königliche privilegierte Preussische Staats-, Kriegs- und Friedenszeitung* (Royally privileged Prussian state, war, and peace newspaper), known as the *Hartungsche Zeitung* after its publisher, Johann Heinrich Hartung (1699–1756) also published the *Wöchentliche Königsbergsche Frag- und Anzeigungs-Nachrichten* (Weekly Königsberg request and advertising news), later to be called the *Königsberger Intelligenz-Zettel* (Königsberg Information Sheet). The book dealer Johann Jakob Kanter (1738–1786) countered with his *Königsbergische Gelehrte und Politische Zeitungen* (Königsberg scholarly and political newspapers), to which he successfully recruited Kant and Hamann as correspondents.[49]

In Estonia, Livonia, and Courland, the publishing of periodicals had two purposes. First, it aimed to establish contact with the larger literary public in the empire, and, second, it served a cultural purpose to solidify a sense of identity. From among the multiplicity of short-lived periodicals, which was characteristic in Germany at the time, August von Kotzebue's (1761–1819) *Für Geist und Herz* (For spirit and heart) stands out. This journal reported on his many activities, such as the founding of an amateur theater in Reval.[50] Before its publication, Kotzebue had also published a Livonian version of the German women's periodical *Iris*, which was eventually merged into *Für Geist und Herz*. This journal consisted of short, sentimental poems, short dramas, and stories, the themes of which mirrored Kotzebue's successful dramas. In addition to more serious periodicals, such as the *Patriotische Unterhaltungen* (Patriotic entertainments), published by Karl Philip Michael Snell, we should also mention Hupel's *Nordische Miscellaneen*, which was published between 1781 and 1798. Hupel felt motivated to

provide news, "which concerns the history, world description, constitution, rights, morality, customs, housekeeping, products, trade, and
the like of Russia, Livonia, Estonia, and Courland," and to describe
these to a larger public not only in Germany, but also within the Baltic
provinces themselves and in Russia. The *Mitauischen Nachrichten von
Staats-, Gelehrten- und Einheimischen Sachen* (Mitau news of state,
scholarly, and local matters), edited by Johann Georg Hamann, and the
Journal de Mitau pursued similar purposes.[51] In Courland—as elsewhere in the region—people also read the German-language *St. Peters-
burgische Zeitung*, which was founded in 1727 on the initiative of Peter
the Great.

In the eighteenth century, regional dailies, and journals, such as
Lærde efterretninger (Scholarly news) (1720–1836), *Litteratur-, Kunst-
og Theaterblade* (Literature, art and theater paper) (1798–1799), and
Vetenskapsakademiens handlingar (Acts of the academic sciences)
(1739–1974) sprouted up like mushrooms in the cities of Denmark and
Sweden, as did moral weeklies and information sheets that circulated
both regionally and sometimes even beyond. These included the oldest
still published Danish newspaper, *Berlingske Tidende* (Berling's times)
(1749), along with *Københavns Aftenpost* (Copenhagen evening post)
(1772–1812), and *Stockholms Posten* (1778), which was founded in Stockholm by Johann Henric Kellgren, magister at the University of Åbo,
the book dealer Johann Christoph Holmberg, and the board of trade
member Carl Peter Lenngren. Holmberg also published *Ekstra-Posten*
(Extra post) (1791–1795), which, like all daily newspapers, was inspired
and influenced by the events of the French Revolution, and was the
first Swedish newspaper to print the "Marseillaise." *Dagligt Alle-
handa* (Daily miscellany) (1769–1849) had been published earlier in
Stockholm, and other daily and weekly papers had appeared in Gothenburg, Lund, and Gävle. The Swedish propaganda organ from the
time of Sweden as a great power, *Ordinari Post Tijdender* (Ordinary
post times) (1645–1760), is also worthy of note.[52]

Important newspapers in Swedish Pomerania included the *Stralsun-
discher Relations Courier* (Stralsund messenger) (1689–1702 and 1747–
1754) and the *Stralsundische Zeitung* (1771–1934). Professors at the University of Greifswald also published journals that catered to the needs
of scholars with news and information from Sweden and the province

of Pomerania. These included Christian Nettelbladt's *Schwedische Bibliothec*, which touted Sweden's pioneering role in the sciences and law, and the journals edited by the previously mentioned Johann Carl Dähnert, such as *Pommersche Nachrichten von gelehrten Sachen* (Pomeranian news of scholarly matters) (1743–1748) and *Critische Nachrichten* (Critical news) (1750–1754).[53]

The most exciting and entertaining medium in the eighteenth century was theater. The explosive growth in German-language theater extended to the Baltic provinces. As in the residence and trade cities of the empire, Reval and especially Riga became centers of the performing arts. In Riga, the theater was financed in 1772 by Baron Otto Hermann von Vietinghoff (1722–1792), a high official and entrepreneur. He modeled his venue on Dalberg's theater in Mannheim and theaters in Vienna. Ordinances about reading rehearsals and how rehearsals were to be held show just how professionalized the theater had become and how similar the repertoire was to that in the empire.[54] In addition to works such as Johann Elias Schlegel's *Triumph der guten Frauen* (Triumph of the good women), Gotthold Ephraim Lessing's *Minna von Barnhelm* and *Emilia Galotti*, and Goethe's *Clavigo*, French comedies were especially popular for a time. However, they were later replaced by August Wilhelm Iffland's sentimental plays, such as *Verbrechen aus Ehrsucht* (Crime of ambition), *Die Jäger* (The hunters), and *Die Mündel*, and Kotzebue's *Menschenhaß und Reue* (Misanthropy and repentance), *Das Kind der Liebe* (The child of love), and *Die Indianer in England* (The Indian exiles).

As elsewhere in Germany, musical theater was very popular. Offerings included *Jagd* (Hunt) by Johann Adam Hiller and Benda's *Medea*. In the 1780s and 1790s, they included André Grétry's *Zemire und Azor*, Carl Ditters von Dittersdorff's *Doktor und Apotheker* (Doctor and apothecary) and *Das Rothe Käppgen* (Little red riding hood), Paul Wranitzky's *Oberon*, and Mozart's *Zauberflöte* and *Don Juan*. Beloved pieces from this genre, such as *Die Jagd*, *Medea*, *Doktor und Apotheker*, and *Die Zauberflöte*, were staged by almost all theaters from Amsterdam in the west to St. Petersburg in the east to Vienna, Graz, and Trieste in the south.[55]

The theater scene in Reval, the city that Kotzebue would later use as his springboard to literary success, appears to have been especially lively. After finishing his studies in the law, Kotzebue took a position in St. Petersburg as private secretary to Governor General Friedrich Wilhelm Bauer (1731–1783). Because Bauer also headed the German theater in St. Petersburg, he gave Kotzebue his first opportunity to prove himself. In 1783, Kotzebue became an assessor in the Reval high court, and two years later president of the magistrate of the Governate of Estonia. To stage his plays, Kotzebue founded an amateur theater that provided the young playwright, director, and actor a ready experimental stage. His effect on the social and cultural life of Reval was to be long-lasting. After his departure in 1809, the theater and the "Actien-Club" (stocks club) joined forces to form a *Geselligkeitsunternehmen* (conviviality undertaking), which in addition to theater productions also featured a dance hall, billiard room, and reading room with newspapers from Germany.[56] Developments in Danzig were comparable to those in Reval, although the city lacked an author of Kotzebue's stature. Konrad Ernst Ackermann (1712–1771) and his renowned theater troupe were resident in Danzig in 1755–1756, but they also played further afield in Königsberg. Ackermann, who had revolutionized theatrical productions in Hamburg in the 1760s, followed in the footsteps of the Schuch'sche Truppe (Schuch's troupe), which entertained the public in cities along the route from Breslau to Königsberg. Caroline Schuch (1739–1787), the proprietor of the theater, concentrated efforts in the area roughly bounded by Danzig, Elbing, Königsberg, and Mitau. Königsberg was where the theatrical group was headquartered, but from August to November it regularly staged dramas, operas, and ballets in Danzig. Toward the end of the century, the public was especially receptive to Kotzebue's and Iffland's comedies and dramas. So prominent had Iffland become that on August 3, 1801, a new theater built on the initiative of a wealthy Danzig merchant played Iffland's *Vaterhaus* (Paternal house) in honor of King Frederick William III's birthday.[57]

Denmark and Sweden were quite similar in this regard. Initially, itinerant troupes of actors would play in one city or another. In Copenhagen, René Montaigu, the head of the French troupe, received approval in 1722 to found the Comédie en langue danoise, which was a going concern for a time. The writer and professor Ludvig Holberg (1684–1754) wrote comedies in Danish for the Comédie such as *Den politiske Kandestøber* (The political tinsmith). Mostly, however, French comedies were staged in Danish translation, such as Molière's *The Miser*, which was the theater's inaugural offering. But like so many such endeavors, the theater soon ran into financial problems. In 1748, the purpose of the theater was reconceived, and toward the end of the eighteenth century the building designed by the rococo architect Nicolai Eigtved saw the inauguaration of the royal theater encompassing all of the performing arts, including ballet, opera, and drama. It was at this time when the idea of a national theater began to take hold in Denmark, although it was not until the turn of the century that pieces were written and staged in the Danish language.[58]

The first Swedish theater company was formed in Stockholm in 1737 with a performance of Carl Gyllenborg's (1679–1746) *Svenska Sprätthöken* (Swedish gentleman rogue). Queen Lovisa Ulrika, however, tended to favor French theater in Stockholm, and it was not until the reign of Gustav III that Swedish theatrical talent began to be promoted. After the founding of the Royal Swedish Opera, a short-lived theater was founded in 1787, which was officially taken over and refounded by the king in 1788 after the first director had fled his creditors. But an independent Swedish repertoire had yet to be written.

The performance of music underwent a similar evolution in the cities of the Baltic region. It took a long time for concerts with professionally performed music to be viewed as an independent art form.[59] Evenings of sacred music had been introduced, such as those held at the Marienkirche in Lübeck under Buxtehude and in other churches. And concerts were performed at the courts and on the initiative of music lovers, with composers in the service of churches and cities. In the 1720s, Georg Philipp Telemann (1681–1767) organized public concerts in Hamburg, as did musical societies such as the short-lived Gesellschaft Musizierender (Society of music makers) in Copenhagen.

Reports from cities throughout the Baltic region, including Stralsund, Greifswald, Danzig, Königsberg, and Riga, demonstrate that the nobility, the elite functionaries, academicians, and merchants made music together in amateur ensembles. In addition, itinerant virtuosos, such as the blind flute soloist Friedrich Ludwig Dulon (1769–1826) and the organist Abbé Vogler (1749–1814), enriched the musical mix. Even the Seven Years' War had an enlivening effect on music across borders. For example, the classical works of the Viennese repertoire became known in Königsberg because Austrian prisoners of war staged concerts. But much more influential was the role of music publishing, especially of scores, which introduced the musical tastes of Vienna and central Germany to the Baltic region. The availability of scores, in particular, meant that this new music could be played in the home. The mobility of musicians was also important, and the courts competed for the services of musical luminaries. The czar's court, for example, recruited the renowned soprano Elisabeth Mara (1749–1833) as a singing teacher after her engagements in Berlin, Leipzig, Munich, Vienna, Dresden, Paris, and London.[60]

In Sweden at the beginning of the eighteenth century the office of court conductor was still in the hands of the Düben family, but during that century new ideas were introduced by Johan Helmich Roman (1694–1758), who had been promoted by Gustav Düben the Younger (1659–1726). Roman had studied in England under Johann Christoph Pepusch (1667–1752) and gotten to know the vibrant, Italian-influenced, London musical scene. Later, as second conductor of the court orchestra, his compositions spread the music of the Italian baroque in Sweden. Johann Gottlieb Naumann (1741–1801) also brought German and Italian influences to Sweden after completing his training at the Dresdner Kreuzchor and in Italy. He became conductor at the Dresden court in 1776. Shortly thereafter, he was recruited to the Swedish court and was commissioned by King Gustav III to write the score for the king's drama *Gustav Vasa*. This piece became the Swedish national opera. In spite of its success, Naumann returned to Dresden by way of Copenhagen and Berlin. The Berwald family, especially the symphonic composer Franz Berwald (1796–1868), had a perhaps even longer lasting influence. His forebears had been flutists with the Schleswig Orchestra and at the court in Schwerin and later in Russia, while his father, Christian Friedrich Georg Berwald, had been a violinist in the royal orchestra in Stockholm.[61]

Art Collections and Palaces

Dutch paintings were collected throughout the Baltic region, and so-called art cabinets were created to house them. Princely and bourgeois collectors took an active interest in Dutch art, and this interest was further stoked by art dealers, connoisseurs, and the media as well as through travel.[62] In Mecklenburg, Duke Christian Ludwig II of Schwerin (1683–1756) built a princely residence whose art collection ranked among the most important in Europe. In making the Grand Tour in his youth, he had visited numerous western European cities and been especially impressed with Dutch art. As a result, he decided to develop an art collection in Schwerin, an undertaking not uncommon in other German residence cities, such as Salzdahlum, Düsseldorf, Dresden, Cassel, and Karlsruhe. In addition to purchasing works by Rembrandt and Van Dyke, the duke's agents also bought Dutch and Flemish genre paintings by well-known painters of the seventeenth century at the art markets of Amsterdam and Hamburg. These included peasant scenes by David Teniers and Adriaen van Ostade; landscapes by Nicolaes Pieterszoon Berchem, Jacob Ruysdael, and Herman Saftleven; and animals and landscapes with herders, riders, and soldiers by Jan Weenix, Paulus Potter, Philips Wouwerman, and Adriaen van de Velde. The duke especially admired the still lifes of Jan Davidsz. de Heem, Jan van Huysum, and Rachel Ruysch. From among the genre painters, he acquired masters from the last generation of the Golden Age: Gerard ter Borch and Gabriel Metsu, Gerrit Dou, Frans van Mieris, Willem van Mieris, and Caspar Netscher.[63] He also commissioned contemporary masters, such as Balthasar Denner, Antoine Pesne, and Charles Maucourt, and especially the French painter Jean-Baptiste Oudry, who, among other works, produced for him a large-scale painting of a menagerie of exotic animals. Large sums of money were invested in artisanal products as well, especially gold and silver, that would add to his prestige.

Dutch and Flemish paintings served as the foundation of the royal art chambers and private collections in Denmark. The art dealer and later royal gallery keeper Gerhard Morell (ca. 1710–1771) played a central role. Since the beginning of the 1750s, he had been acquiring significant paintings for the royal collection. His purchases in 1763 were especially spectacular, filling out the collection in anticipation of the construction of a new gallery at Christiansborg Palace. Christiansborg, in Copenhagen, had been constructed in the 1730s under King Christian VI according to plans drawn up by the German architect Elias David Häusser (1687–1745). The palace, which included a theater, riding arena, and church, reflected the new self-image of Denmark after the

Great Northern War, which included rebuilding Copenhagen into a European metropolis after the fire of 1728.[64]

In designing the royal gallery, Morell tried to ensure that the various schools were represented with characteristic subjects. Accordingly, it contained large-scale historical paintings as well as landscapes, still lifes, and genre scenes. Morell had been introduced to the court by the royal *Oberhofmarschall* (administrative official at the court), Count Adam Gottlob von Moltke (1710–1792), himself an important collector and connoisseur and president of the Copenhagen Art Academy.[65] He advised other notable Danish collectors and seems to have served as something of an arbiter of taste because the collections in Copenhagen are all very similar in composition to that of the new royal gallery. Dutch painters of the Golden Age found their way into the homes of Copenhagen court officials, officers, attorneys, professors, and merchants, not to mention artisans (goldsmiths, masons, barbers, and bakers), by way of auctions.[66] Collecting art demonstrated connoisseurship and gave evidence, to one's peers, of exquisite taste. In Sweden, Carl Gustaf Tessin, the leading politician of the Hats Party and descendent of the architect of the same name, promoted the collecting of western European art,[67] while Stanisław August Poniatowski, in Warsaw, and Catherine the Great, in St. Petersburg, went to great efforts to establish art galleries of their own and to fill them with their latest acquisitions.[68] In addition, almost all port cities in the Baltic boasted private collectors of paintings or natural history cabinets, which were described by visiting travelers.[69]

The homogenization of taste under western European influence is also reflected in interior design and decor. As occurred throughout Europe, we see an evolution in the use of living spaces. Whereas previously, the few rooms available tended to be multifunctional, increasingly we see larger houses with many rooms, each with a specialized function. The furnishings and decor became more refined, according to the use to which a room was put. Journals and *Intelligenzblätter* made wealthy consumers aware of the latest French and English styles, with residence and merchant cities leading the way. While members of the nobility, bureaucratic elites, and the merchant class pioneered these new styles, they were soon emulated by members of other classes, spreading from the cities to the rest of the Baltic region. The result was a homogenization of living space regardless of the city. Homes in Copenhagen, Danzig, and Riga all had a similar feel, but this sameness was to be found in smaller cities as well, such as Stralsund and Greifswald.[70]

A number of different architectural trends are to be seen in the princely and aristocratic residences. These range from late baroque and rococo styles to early classical designs, which appear at the same time in many different places in the Baltic region. Frederick II, duke of Mecklenburg-Schwerin (1717–1785), made a name for himself with the construction of a new residence in Ludwigslust. Frederick built Ludwigslust on the site of his father's hunting palace in the form of a late baroque planned city in which the palace and church stood opposite each other, and the city was located to the side, with its streets laid out in a network. Both the church and the palace were based on designs by the Schwerin court architect Johann Joachim Busch (1720–1802), who melded early classical building elements with baroque forms. A park with a pond, fountains, and cascades was built behind the palace.

In the Duchy of Mecklenburg-Strelitz, the new residence city of Neustrelitz was built from designs pulled more or less from the same hat. In addition to the palace, the city was designed in a radiating star shape, with a square marketplace in the center. The plans for Ludwigslust and Neustrelitz were part of the European aristocratic mindset that sought to play out its princely rule on a grandiose stage.[71] This mind-set was mirrored in the countryside in the redesign of aristocratic manors. The most imposing baroque building was that erected by the Hannover diplomat Hans Caspar von Bothmer (1656–1732), near Klütz. But other manor houses, such as Vietgest, continued to be built in the baroque style as late as the end of the eighteenth century, as classical architecture was adopted in the construction of such houses only in the nineteenth.

The cities along the eastern shore of the Baltic faced very different issues. In St. Petersburg, for example, a growing population lived largely in wooden hovels. Thus, Peter the Great ordered his chief architect, Pyotr Yeropkin (ca. 1698–1740), to redesign the area along the southern shore of the Neva, and together with the architects Mikhail Zemtsov (1688–1743) and Ivan Korobov, he designed a radial street plan. While Zemtsov's bell towers punctuated St. Petersburg's skyline, Bartolomeo

Francesco Rastrelli (1700–1771) redesigned the palaces, including the
Winter Palace, in a rococo style. Czarina Elisabeth favored his buildings as did Ernst Johann von Biron, the Duke of Courland, who had
Rastrelli build palaces for him in Courland, including those in Mitau
(1738–1740) and Ruhenthal (Rundāle, 1736–1740). Many of the palaces
of the nobility also give evidence of Rastrelli's designs.

When Catherine II took the reins of government in 1762 she undertook a building program that would finally give St. Petersburg the look
of a major European metropolis. Russian early classicism, a new building
style, was first seen in buildings like the Academy of Arts, built by Alexander Kokorinov (1726–1772). The palaces built by Antonio Rinaldi
show how this style matured, as does his renowned Chesme Column,
erected to commemorate the Turkish sea battle that took place there.
Ivan Starov (1745–1808), a student of Kokorinov, was another Russian
architect working in the classical style. Among other things, he built
Tauride Palace (1783–1789) along Roman lines for Prince Grigory Po-
temkin (1739–1791). The Italian Giacomo Quarenghi (1744–1817) and
the Scotsman Charles Cameron (1743–1812), who had studied in Italy,
were also important figures. Both brought a deep understanding of ancient architecture to Catherine's building project. Quarenghi is known
for the Academy of Sciences, the Hermitage, and the Smolny Institute,
while Cameron built Tsarskoye Selo and Pavlovsk.[72]

Italian baroque architecture also reached Estonia through commissions by Peter the Great. He hired the Roman architect Nicola Michetti
(1675–1758) to build Catherinethal Palace (Kadriorg) in Reval and later
for other projects in St. Petersburg. Artisans from Stockholm, Reval,
and Riga worked alongside Russian and Italian artists to build and dec-
orate the palace. An even larger boom, in rococo architecture, took place
in Estonia, but only during the second half of the eighteenth century.
The palaces and manorial residences of Johann Schultz, who as governmental architect of Estonia built not only the governor's palace in
Reval (Toompea Palace), but also designed and outfitted the manorial
residences at Kaltenbrunn (Roosna-Alliku) and Saue, stem from this
period.[73]

One example of the growing wealth of property owners as reflected
in architecture is the restyling of Oberpahlen Castle (Põltsamaa) into a
rococo palace by the former officer Woldemar Johann von Lauw. Among

other acts, he had parks, bridges, and artificial islands designed and constructed. He hired the painter Gottlieb Welté (ca. 1748–1792) from Mainz to do the wall paintings. Welté was probably also involved in porcelain manufacture, but he is famous for his wall paintings. F. H. Barisien, the court painter and curator of the ducal gallery in Mitau, was also recruited from Dresden to Riga by way of Russia. He was commissioned to paint views of the palace and its surroundings as well as portraits of the imperial family for the painting cabinet in Oberpahlen Palace.[74]

One final example: In Poland-Lithuania, the fire that destroyed Vilnius made it possible to lay out the city completely anew. This task, assumed by the architect Johann Christoph Glaubitz (ca. 1700–1767), gave Vilnius a late baroque look that worked equally well for all confessions. He built the bell tower of the Catholic St. John's Church, provided the Basilius city gate with a pediment motif of the Holy Trinity, renovated the Russian Orthodox Church of the Holy Ghost, rebuilt the Protestant-Lutheran church, and designed the interior of the Great Synagogue. In addition, he renovated the Orthodox cathedral in Polock (Polotsk) and worked in Dünaburg (Daugavpils) as well.[75] Here, as elsewhere in the Baltic region, artistic ideas trumped confessional and ethnic differences.

CHAPTER SEVEN

Nordic Romanticism

Focus on Helsinki

Sweden's defeat in the Finnish War (1808–1809) forced the country to cede its Finnish territories to Russia. Finland became an autonomous grand duchy under Russian rule, although its legal and administrative system was based on Sweden's. In this situation, both merchants and Finnish aristocrats agitated for Helsinki as their new capital. The city was closer to St. Petersburg, and Sweden would have less influence than it had on the old capital, Turku, which was still the largest and wealthiest city in Finland. Czar Alexander I (1777–1825), who had provided the impetus for many new building projects in the classical or imperial style in St. Petersburg, favored the new capital. The military engineer Johan Albrecht Ehrenström (1762–1847), who drew heavily on the example of Habsburg Vienna, was given the task of designing it. The destruction of so many wooden buildings during the Finnish War made it possible to redesign Helsinki's layout from the ground up. Ehrenström recruited Carl Ludwig Engel (1778–1840) to the reconstruction committee. Engel, who had studied with Schinkel at the Bauakademie in Berlin, was very familiar with how motifs from antiquity had been integrated into the architecture of Great Britain, and he also knew the buildings designed by Quarenghi and Cameron in St. Petersburg. Ehrenström and Engel's ideas for the new city met with the approval of the czar, who wanted Helsinki to symbolize the connection between Finland and Russia. Accordingly, the planned north-south axis was given the name Unioninkatu (Union Street). At the center of the neoclassical architectural complex, which still exists, stands Senate Square, with its senate building, Helsinki Cathedral, and the university. The relocation of the University of Åbo (founded 1640) to Helsinki in 1827 served a programmatic purpose as well. In the 1820s and 1830s, the important governmental and administrative buildings, several

Figure 7. View of Helsinki from the yachting, Albert Edelfelt, 1899

barracks, three hospitals, three churches, a theater, a hotel, and residences for the governor general and military commander were built in the city. These thirty neoclassical buildings, of which twenty are still in use, reflect Russian, Italian, British, and German architectural influences.[1]

The Napoleonic Wars

The French Revolution and the Napoleonic Wars led to considerable changes in the Baltic region as well. Although revolutionary ideas were often well received in urban and academic circles, actual revolts and uprisings, if not initiated by the lower classes, were limited in scope. Occasionally, the rulers and aristocracy attempted to advance their interests by co-opting the demands of other social groups. Thus, for example, Gustav III of Sweden had used the grievances of the peasantry to break the power of the aristocracy and advance his reformist and absolutist program.[2] His murder by a clique of aristocrats, therefore, did nothing to advance the cause of liberty. Intellectuals who were critical of aristocratic rule, such as the philosopher Thomas Thorild, were forced to flee Uppsala for Swedish Pomerania to escape arrest.[3] But events in France had their greatest repercussions in Poland, where the king and the aristocracy set in motion a cooperative reform process to prevent even greater losses of power. The May Constitution of 1791 provided for a hereditary constitutional monarchy, but this provision was resisted and defeated by the great powers Russia, Austria, and Prussia. Objecting to the constitutional, but not to the monarchical, provision, in 1793 they took the opportunity provided by the attempted reforms and the resistance generated to them within Poland to so diminish Poland's territories that it virtually ceased to exist. The 1795 uprising by Kościuszko and his followers was the last straw, and Poland as a political entity was wiped off the map.[4]

The maps of other countries were also changed by the territorial gains made by the revolutionary and Napoleonic armies. How these changes manifested depended on whether the country in question was viewed as an ally of France or of Great Britain, its enemy. Just how quickly the overall political climate could change is demonstrated by the situation along the southern Baltic coast.[5] While the Hanseatic cities and Mecklenburg remained neutral in the coalition wars against revolutionary and later Napoleonic France, Sweden at first took the side of Russia and Britain. After the Treaty of Basel, in 1795, Prussia left the anti-French coalition, forming a neutrality zone in northern Germany that lasted until 1806. In this situation, Sweden attempted to increase its ability to raise war financing by pledging Wismar to Mecklenburg, in 1803, and by taxing its subjects in Swedish Pomerania. Prussia, on the other hand, sought to occupy Swedish Pomerania itself, and in the fall of 1805 even tendered an offer to the Swedish government. Sweden was more than ready to sell but not to its enemy Prussia. The buyer most favored was Russia. But when the Pomeranian estates refused to raise and finance a militia to defend the land, Gustav IV Adolf (1778–1837) led a coup, the purpose of which was to integrate Swedish Pomerania into the Swedish kingdom, while at the same time breaking the resistance of the estates. On June 18, 1806, the king nullified the estate constitution for Swedish Pomerania and decreed the Swedish constitution and Swedish law in its stead.

Less than two months later, on August 6, 1806, Emperor Francis II abdicated and the Holy Roman Empire ceased to exist. The empire's collapse was preceded by the founding of the Confederation of the Rhine, under French leadership. However, Sweden was unable to exploit

Map 7. The Baltic region in 1815

the seemingly favorable power vacuum in the north. Prussia's reentry into the war and its catastrophic defeat at the hands of the French at Jena and Auerstedt in October 1806 led to destabilization of the supposed neutrality zone.

After the defeated bands of Prussian troops fled to Mecklenburg territory, French troops occupied the Duchy of Mecklenburg-Schwerin despite its neutrality. On November 6, the French conquered Lübeck, where Prussian General Blücher had retreated with his troops, and on November 19 they took Hamburg, and then Bremen, on November 20. Because France now controlled large portions of the coasts of the North Sea and Baltic, Napoleon declared a continental blockade against England, on November 21. This blockade included a ban on trade and correspondence, the confiscation of English books and goods, and the arrest of British subjects. It also aimed at preventing shipping traffic between England, its colonies, and the European continent. These protectionist measures, however, could be implemented only in cooperation with the states and mercantile interests that were affected by them, which proved unworkable at best.

The merchants of Hamburg moved their operations to the neutral Danish city of Altona. Tönning was another city on the North Sea that was suitable for transshipping English goods to Hamburg, from where they made their way to the trade fairs in Leipzig. From Leipzig, the goods traveled by land to Poland and Russia. The English depot on the island of Heligoland (in operation since 1807) became a major center for smuggling to northern Germany.[6] This was important because in 1808 Denmark joined the continental blockade, and as a result Tönning could no longer serve as a haven for smugglers. In addition, ships from Hamburg frequently plied the route between Great Britain and Russia, including to Sweden and other Baltic ports, especially between 1807 and 1810. As a result, Britain's exports to Sweden grew steadily. From there, English goods were exported to Stralsund. In addition, the Prussian government secretly promoted smuggling through Prussian ports such as Stettin, Danzig, Königsberg, and Memel. Trustworthy merchants placed orders in Britain, and Prussia then captured their ships on the pretext that they carried enemy cargo. These goods were channeled into the Prussian economy. As a result, traffic into the port of Königsberg from England increased steadily, from where the goods continued on to the trade fairs in Leipzig.

By contrast, Lübeck's shipping traffic collapsed completely in 1807 and did not recover for a number of years. In contrast to Hamburg and other Prussian ports, Lübeck's share of the smuggling traffic was negligible, especially since it was under strict French customs control and because its port had been converted for use by the French navy.[7]

In Mecklenburg, the French army occupied Wismar, where it confiscated Prussian, English, and Swedish goods warehoused there. In order not to imperil good trade relations with Sweden, the Wismar city council bought back the Swedish ships slated to be destroyed for 300 louisdor (approximately 2,100 reichstaler), and the merchants of Wismar acquired the confiscated goods. Despite this attempt to prevent escalation, Sweden reacted to the continental blockade with a trade blockade against Mecklenburg ports. Traditional Swedish imports such as iron ore, copper, limestone, building timber, tar, potash, alum, and vitriol disappeared, which meant that the businesses that needed them suffered considerable losses. On the other hand, Mecklenburg was able to sell its grain to allied Denmark. At the same time, the Bay of Wismar offered favorable havens for the smuggling trade, which was often plied by ships flying a North American flag. Spices, coffee, cotton, and even English coal reached Mecklenburg by this route. Under pressure from the French, the Schwerin government attempted to interdict smuggling by banning the departure of vessels as soon as British ships were found to be approaching the Mecklenburg coast.

The Spanish revolt against Napoleonic rule, and the war against Austria (1809), loosened the French occupation along the North Sea and Baltic coasts. This resulted in a considerable upturn in Wismar's economy because alongside trade with Russia and Denmark, it could now deal in English goods on a grand scale, often using forged certificates (supposedly for North American products). When Sweden went over to Napoleon's side in 1809, shipping with Swedish ports revived. The situation in Swedish Pomerania, where France and Sweden had agreed to an armistice in 1807, was unique. Here, the continental blockade was very difficult to implement, especially as the Swedes had retreated to Rügen, while French control was by no means airtight. It became simply impossible to ensure continuous, uninterrupted monitoring of the continental blockade along the entire Baltic coast.

To address this weakness, Napoleon issued the Trianon and Fontainebleau decrees (August 5 and October 18, 1810), which attempted to get to the root of the smuggling trade by other means. These included certificates of exemption (licenses) for which large sums were to be paid, the levying of high customs duties, and the public burning of English goods.[8] Licensing fees and customs brought growing sums of money into the French treasury, which reflected a limited volume of trade with England.

The changes were more serious along the northern and western coasts of the Baltic. Here, Denmark had joined the alliance of armed neutrals Sweden, Prussia, and Russia. The British attacked, and a sea battle ensued off the coast of Copenhagen, which forced Denmark to the side of Great Britain. In the medium term, however, the British

achieved precisely the opposite, namely a military alignment with Napoleonic France. In 1807, this led to renewed military action by Great
Britain, during which its fleet bombarded Copenhagen for three days.
In response, Denmark officially allied itself with France, but when the
French adventure in Russia collapsed, in 1814, the Danes found themselves on the losing side.[9] For a relatively long period of time, Sweden
had been the only country to support Britain. But after 1806, it became
embroiled in a war with Russia (1808–1809), which for a time forced it
into an alliance with France. In the process, Russia gained control over
Finland, including the Åland Islands and Lapland. At the same time,
supporters of France toppled King Gustav IV Adolf and reintroduced a
more liberal constitution. His uncle, Charles XIII (1748–1818), became
the "transitional king," while French marshal Jean Baptiste Bernadotte
(1763–1844) became crown prince and then Charles's successor. Bernadotte, who founded a new dynasty, switched to the anti-French coalition just in time, in 1813. As a result, Sweden's territorial losses were
limited. In compensation for Finland, Sweden received Norway, which
after a personal union with Denmark lasting several centuries was
ceded to Sweden in the Treaty of Kiel in 1814.[10]

Denmark had to make do with Lauenburg, which had for a brief time
belonged to Prussia, and 2.6 million taler in compensation. However,
the duchies of Schleswig-Holstein along with Iceland, Greenland, and
the Faroe Islands remained under Danish dominion. Prussia bought
Swedish Pomerania from Sweden for 3.5 million taler and united it with
Eastern Pomerania. The dukes of Mecklenburg were elevated to grand
dukes and received a portion of French war reparations. Prussia received
other territories from the Duchy of Warsaw, which Napoleon had created, while the larger portion, the Kingdom of Poland, was united under
the Russian czarist empire as so-called Congress Poland.

New Constitutions

Because of these substantial territorial rearrangements, all of the countries in the region were confronted with the problem of how to integrate new territories into their states. To negotiate satisfactory solutions, the new governments usually made generous concessions, which,
under changed circumstances, often proved unworkable and even had

explosive consequences in the long run. Russia under Czar Alexander
I, who emerged as victor from the Napoleonic wars, appeared to be especially liberal, offering Finland and Poland an attractive package of concessions. The czar was persuaded to do so by both Finnish and Polish
advisers. In 1809, Gustaf Mauritz Armfelt (1757–1814) left Stockholm
after the dethronement of the Swedish king and entered into service to
Russia. In St. Petersburg, he chaired a commission for Finnish affairs
that paved the way for the annexation of Finland. The idea was that by
conceding a special status to the Finnish population, the population
would be won over to Russian rule. Outwardly, a governmental council
and a Finnish-constituted government that was called the Senate, set
up in 1816, and which functioned simultaneously as the supreme central authority and supreme court of the new grand duchy, gave Finland
the semblance of independence. But the czar named the senators. Because government and administration were in the hands of Finns,
and because the Russian governor general did not intrude on the grand
duchy's internal affairs despite commanding the Russian troops and
chairing the Senate, St. Petersburg and Helsinki quickly came to view
their interests as one and the same. Although a diet of the estates still
existed, after 1809 it would not be convened again until 1863.[11]

In Poland, Prince Adam Czartoryski (1770–1861), who at times
served as de facto Russian foreign minister, advanced the idea of a relatively independent Poland under Russian protection. Although the czar
was not opposed in principle, the other victorious powers at the Congress of Vienna, especially England and Austria, prevented this dream
from becoming reality. Once again, Poland was partitioned into the
Prussian grand duchy of Posen, the Russian kingdom of Poland (i.e.,
Congress Poland), and the Austrian free city of Cracow, with the majority of Poles now living under Russian rule in Congress Poland. But
even Congress Poland had a constitution that was relatively liberal in
comparison to other European states. It had, at least nominally, its own
government, a council of state, parliament, a Polish bureaucratic apparatus, and an army. However, Grand Duke Constantine, a brother of the
czar, was supreme commander of the army, and a Russian commissar
controlled the government. As a result, internal policies were limited
in scope, mainly dealing with educational and economic reforms.[12]

Structural changes were also seen in Denmark and Norway. In Denmark, royal succession had, since 1665, been regulated by the *Lex Regia*, which legitimized autocratic rule, thereby excluding the estates from participation in the government. On the other hand, the estates of Schleswig-Holstein had been guaranteed their rights in the 1460 Treaty of Ribe, and these rights had never been formally abrogated. One of the central questions of the day was the extent to which the *Lex Regia* applied to the duchies, and therefore to the rights of the estates as well. Because of its multiethnic composition at the time, the Danish state as a whole could, despite its small size, best be compared to the multiethnic Habsburg Empire. Although the various nationalities (Danes, Germans, Frisians, Icelanders, etc.) continued to express their loyalty to the monarch, the dynasty, and their immediate homeland,[13] their identification with the state as a whole was increasingly shaken by the crisis of legitimacy of Danish absolutism. Under the terms of the Congress of Vienna, Holstein, which had belonged to the Holy Roman Empire until its dissolution in 1806 and then became part of Denmark, was after 1815 allocated to the German Confederation. As a result, the duke of Holstein (that is, the Danish king) was bound by Article 13 of the Federal Act, which prescribed a constitution for each state in the confederation. This resulted in a convoluted constitutional question within the Danish monarchy, which later developed into the so-called Schleswig-Holstein Question.[14] If Holstein alone had been granted a constitution, then the unitary government of the state as a whole would have been imperiled, and conflict with the nobility of Schleswig-Holstein guaranteed, as the nobles had been demanding a single, unified constitution for Schleswig *and* Holstein.

In Norway, the estates provided themselves with a constitution as Norway was in the process of separating from Denmark. It was largely based on the American and French constitutions. Norway was administratively autonomous, and the Norwegian parliament established internal policies. The Swedish king, who had also been elected king of Norway, had authority in only foreign and military policy. Finances, taxes, and legislation were the province of the parliament, the Storting. As a result, the Storting developed into an important counterweight to the royal prerogative.[15]

In the 1830s, the compromises worked out in the various countries along with the constitutions established by moderate governmental policies would be shaken to their foundations by revolutionary movements and by new actors on the political stage who no longer felt bound by the old agreements. The latter became evident when Czar Nicholas I distanced himself from his brother's reforms, and his autocratic stance made dialogue with the non-Russian populations in his empire impossible. The Decembrist Revolt of 1825, in Russia, served only as a prelude to the November Uprising of 1830–1831 in Poland. The French Revolution and the Belgian independence movement triggered a war that took almost a year for Russia to win. Whatever residual autonomy Cracow and Posen continued to enjoy was lost as a result of the integration of these territories into Prussia and Austria. From now on, Congress Poland would be on a very short Russian leash. As a result, not very much happened in Poland during the revolutionary year of 1848, and it was not until the 1863 January Uprising that Russian rule was again challenged, though unsuccessfully. Russia was quite successful in containing and co-opting critical ideas; among other things, it was able to redirect the revolutionary enthusiasm of Finnish students into Finnish cultural patriotism.

By contrast, radical nationalism spread throughout Denmark, which was primarily directed against Prussia and the German Confederation. The catalyst was the so-called Schleswig-Holstein Question, which consumed both Danish and German revolutionaries from 1848 to 1851. The nationalism of the revolutionaries' positions was undoubtedly a way of blowing off steam in disappointment over the dashed hopes for a constitution in Denmark and Schleswig-Holstein, but nationalist yearnings soon became the focus of public discussion, not only in Denmark, but in all of the German states as well.[16] This nationalistic wave manifested itself in the promulgation of an Eider-Danish doctrine, in 1842, which demanded that Denmark's borders extend to the Eider River, and that Danish-speaking members of the estates assembly make their mother tongue the language of the proceedings. Finally, Danish nationalists held a Danish-Schleswig fraternal celebration on the Skamlingsbanke near Kolding in 1843. The opposing nationalisms, which allowed only for a Danish Schleswig or a German

Schleswig-Holstein, were bound to lead to a violent eruption, in part fed by the crisis of legitimacy of the absolutist state. This dynamic fed the Revolution of 1848. Whereas in Denmark, a liberal cabinet based on the Eider-Danish doctrine emerged as a result of pressure from the street, in Kiel, a provisional government that aimed to retain the rights of the land (i.e., the old privileges of the territory) was formed that became conjoined with the movement for the "unity and freedom of Germany." From the perspective of Copenhagen, the provisional government in Kiel was viewed as a faction of conservative putschists, which governing officials believed they could deal with handily. However, the Frankfurt parliament recognized the provisional government and announced elections for the national assembly for Schleswig and Holstein as well. In effect, the duchies were treated as part of German federal territory—without a formal international agreement. This was tantamount to silent annexation and catapulted the conflict to an international level.

Prussia received a mandate from parliament to intervene militarily against Danish troops fighting for the unity of the Danish state as a whole (*Helstaten*). This created a precedent for cross-border military action—and this in a politically sensitive region in which British and Russian interests were at stake. A pragmatic proposal to bridge the conflict was advanced by British prime minister Palmerston (1784–1865), namely to divide Schleswig along language lines. This proposal, however, proved unworkable in the face of surging nationalist feelings. Nationalism was, however, unable to forestall growing British and Russian counterpressure.[17]

As a result, on August 26, 1848, Prussia agreed to a seven-month armistice because it had largely been unsuccessful against the Danes on land, and Denmark had a pronounced naval edge. This armistice, signed in Malmö, came as a shock. The defeat of the German nationalist movement in this first armed conflict was all too glaring, occurring as it did in a region that had for years embodied the hopes and ambitions of the nation as a whole. The revolution had not been victorious; the old diplomacy carried the day. The renunciation of all national claims to Schleswig, which was forced on Germany by the European great powers, also pulled the rug out from under the liberals and their

reform strategy. This was because the national assembly could claim
to be a serious negotiating partner with Prussia and Austria only as
long as the latter two countries were threatened with a continuation
of the revolution. In Denmark, the events led to the proclamation of
the first democratic constitution, in 1849, which was based on the principle of separation of powers (*Gewaltenteilung*).[18] Thereafter, the process of integrating Schleswig into the Danish kingdom continued—
including its separation from Holstein—and was codified in the national
constitution of 1863. But to do so also meant to break with European
agreements. This resulted in violent protests on the part of the German
nationalist movement, which demanded that the duchies be liberated
from Denmark.

While the mid-sized German states demanded that Schleswig-
Holstein be brought into the German Confederation by force, Prussia
and Austria were willing to insist only that the Eider-Danish constitution be abrogated. Because Denmark rejected an ultimatum to that
effect, Prussia and Austria occupied Schleswig and then advanced toward Jutland. Because the German populace eagerly awaited the opportunity to celebrate a resounding victory, Otto von Bismarck (1815–
1898) and his minister of war, Albrecht von Roon (1803–1879), attacked
the redoubts of the fort at Dybbøl, on April 18, 1864, in what was the
key battle of the Second Schleswig War. Although the Danes were defeated, a conference ended without a clear result. However, the passivity
of the great powers gave Bismarck a free hand to continue the war, which
lasted until October 30, 1864. The Danish king renounced his dominion
over the duchies, ceding them to Austria and Prussia, which administered the duchies in condominium. After its loss of Norway, in 1814,
and the duchies fifty years later, Denmark had shrunk to the status of
a small state in the Baltic region, and Germany had enlarged itself at
Denmark's expense.

National Movements

The national movements in the Baltic region went through various
phases and fulfilled different functions. Ideally, the process progressed
from the construction of a national identity set forth by individual

intellectuals to educational campaigns that galvanized a mass movement, culminating in national independence with a national state. In
other countries, national self-discovery triggered a process of social
integration.

In Denmark in particular, but also in Sweden, the discovery of the
past had a significant compensatory function, with the loss of great
power status and the lack of political participation in late absolutism
often being covered up. Writers such as Adam Oehlenschläger (1779–
1850), who was inspired by Weimar classicism and Jena romanticism,
played a crucial role. Oehlenschläger saw himself as an intermediary
between German and Nordic literature. In 1829, the Swedish poet and
bishop Esaias Tegnér (1782–1846) hailed Oehlenschläger with laurels
as the "King of Nordic poetry," in a ceremony at the University of
Lund.[19] In formerly Danish Scania, the enmities of the past were to be
patched over by a future unity of all Scandinavia. The conservative
monarchist alternative was the popular movement of Nikolai Frederik
Severin Grundtvig (1783–1872), who with his polemical journal *Danne-
Virke* (Danes' work) intended to forge national unity based on king,
people, fatherland, and language.[20]

The ideas embodied in pan-Scandinavianism were propagated from
Denmark to Sweden at meetings of students, who undoubtedly realized that the loss of Finland would never be reversed. The Swedish monarchy, however, had the advantage that Swedish territory, the Swedish
populace, and state power were now congruent. Liberal reforms advanced the cause of political participation. Historians, artists, and
writers went to work creating a new Swedish identity based on language, history, and landscape.[21]

Pan-Scandinavianism did not, however, make much headway in
Norway or Finland. The primary task as the Norwegians saw it was
to create a written language of their own in contradistinction to
that of the Danes. Much like the Brothers Grimm and other writers
throughout Europe who collected folk legends and fairy tales, the philologist and lexicographer Ivar Aasen (1813–1896) elaborated a written
language called *landsmål* (land tongue) that was based on the dia-
lects of peasants in the interior of Norway. *Landsmål* developed into
nynorsk (new Norwegian), which is now used by about 15 percent of

the population. The majority of Norwegians, however, use *bokmål* (book tongue), which was adapted from written Danish. A predilection for oral traditions was consistent with an interest in folklore as expressed in open-air museums and stave-church romanticism.

The search for national identity was complicated in Finland, especially because public and cultural life were still controlled by the Swedish-speaking bureaucracy. In opposition, the Finnish national movement came up with Finnomania, which discerned the roots of Finland in its peasantry. The question then became which Finnish dialect should be standardized as the official language of the Finnish state. In the end, three men largely determined the direction of the new Finnish language: the poet Johan Ludvig Runeberg (1804–1877); the philosopher and statesman Johan Vilhelm Snellman (1806–1881); and the physician, poet, and philologist Elias Lönnrot. Although romantic impulses emerged from the Swedish intellectual milieu at the Finnish University of Turku, they appear to have begun bearing fruit at the latest after the university was moved to Helsinki. Even though Runeberg continued to write poetry in Swedish, he marveled at Finland's nature and landscape. He was especially taken with folk literature, from which he attempted to distill specifically Finnish characteristics. Snellman propagated the new ideas. In addition to his activities as a rural teacher, he also published two newspapers—one in Finnish for the peasantry and another in Swedish for the middle classes. However, the most important of the three was almost certainly Elias Lönnrot. On his numerous field trips, Lönnrot collected songs, laments for the dead, legends, and magical incantations from all parts of Finland, from which he compiled the national epic, the *Kalevala,* which in its final form consisted of fifty songs with almost 23,000 verses. Much of the material stemmed from Karelia, which Lönnrot and his colleagues saw as the cradle of Finnish culture. The study of Finnish was institutionalized in 1828 with a professorship at the University of Helsinki; it was, however, not until 1864 that Finnish became the official language of instruction.

Other important developments—for some of the smaller languages as well—included the founding of a Finnish literary society and the establishment of Finnish language circles in the provinces. As Finnish became more widely accepted by the educated middle classes, the defenders of the Swedish language began to organize, especially in the bureaucracy and among peasants and landowners of Swedish descent. These so-called Swecomanes touted their superiority and insisted on Swedish as the official language in schools and institutions of higher learning. The first purely Finnish-language lyceum was founded in Jyväskylä in 1858; however, it was not until the 1880s that secondary schools and lyceums throughout the country began to train a new generation of Finnish-speaking bureaucrats.[22]

Compared with the cultural ferment seen in Finland, nationalist ideals found little purchase in Estonia or Livonia, although the indigenous Estonian and Latvian populations had already been "discovered" at the end of the eighteenth century. Echoing Herder, the private teachers and *Hofmeister* who had immigrated to the Baltic from the west viewed the local populations as essentially equal members of the European family of peoples. In addition, the middle classes, consisting of pastors and physicians, promoted a new image of the Estonians and demanded improvements in their economic and social situation, especially in the form of agrarian reforms. They were joined by "Estophiles," culturally engaged Baltic Germans, and Estonians who had risen into the middle class. Their writings would culminate in the national movement of the second half of the century, while also serving as a cultural mediator between the urban middle class and the Estonian peasantry. Much like in Finland, a Latvian literary society (Latviešu Literāriskā Biedrība) was formed in 1824, largely by Couronian pastors, while in Dorpat, the Estonian physician Friedrich Robert Faehlmann (1798–1850) founded the Learned Estonian Society (Õpetatud Eesti Selts). The Estonian national epic, the *Kalevipoeg*, was written by Friedrich Reinhold Kreutzwald (1803–1882), a member of Faehlmann's circle. As in Latvia, collections of folk songs were published as well.

However, the main political concern of Estonians and Latvians was to secure equality with Baltic Germans, both in schooling and before the law. The liberalized pass ordinance of 1863, which granted the peasantry freedom of movement, brought about greater mobility. Southern Estonia was where most of the activities were concentrated. The effect of political publications such as *Perno Postimees* (Perno postman), the first Estonian newspaper published in Pernau in 1857, or the Latvian *Mājas Viesis* (House visitor) in 1856, should not be underestimated.[23] In

St. Petersburg, Latvian students published a paper called *Pēterburgas Avīzes* (1862–1865), which agitated against Baltic German hegemony and recommended that Latvians and Estonians enter into an alliance with the Russian-speaking population. Such lines of discourse also took place within the Estonian national movement.

The moderates, who viewed the cultural activities of the Baltic Germans and cooperation with them as potentially profitable, made Dorpat the center of Estonian intellectual life and gave voice to their position. Johann Voldemar Jannsen (1819–1890), the founder of *Perno Postimees*, began publishing a new newspaper, *Eesti Postimees*, in Dorpat in 1864. The radical position was represented by Carl Robert Jakobson (1841–1882), who together with the art professor Johann Köler (1826–1899) agitated from St. Petersburg for emancipation within the Russian Empire to overcome the dominance of the Baltic Germans. However, after their attempts to publish a newspaper were quashed by the Russian censors, Jakobson concentrated on education, model agriculture, and the creation of an Estonian literature. One result was the founding of the Society of Estonian Literati (Eesti Kirjameeste Selts). Jakobson refused to take part in a song festival commemorating the freeing of the peasantry because he disapproved of the role played by German pastors. Nonetheless, song festivals have been a regular fixture celebrating national sentiment in Estonia since 1869 and in Livonia since 1873.[24] Estonian and Latvian developed into modern cultural languages by precisely this literary process. Societies that focused on specific interests also reflected these developing national cultures. Farmers, volunteer firemen, teetotalers, and singers joined such societies at the local level for mutual assistance or just to socialize, and these societies soon blossomed into larger associations with regional and even national memberships. Thus, for example, the Latvian Society (Rīgas Latviešu Biedrība), founded in Riga in 1868 to promote the interests of Latvian businessmen and merchants, became a major center for the movement of national awakening.[25] In 1862, activists in rural Estonia began collecting donations for the construction of an Estonian-language lyceum (Eesti Aleksandrikool, named after Czar Alexander), which garnered support throughout the country. Taken as a whole, these activities, which were independent of the Baltic Germans and of Russian control, gained in significance.[26]

By contrast, the Lithuanian national movement was hindered by press censorship and a ban on meetings. Over the course of the January uprising of 1863, Russia had even banned the use of the Latin alphabet for Lithuanian, which for the next forty years was forced to use Cyrillic letters. In addition, a Lithuanian-language newspaper, *Auszra* (Dawn), first published in 1883, had to be published in East Prussia and, like Lithuanian books, smuggled into Lithuania. Pressure put on Lithuanian Catholicism by the Russian Orthodox state church was especially strong. Schooling was a first step to conversion. Similar tendencies toward Russification have also been found in Estonia (1880s) and Livonia (1840s), where many Estonians and Latvians were persuaded to convert to Russian Orthodoxy by the promise of land ownership.[27]

Agrarian Reforms and Industrialization

The issue of agrarian reform had emerged in public discussions about economic reform since the end of the eighteenth century. Reformers fought on a variety of fronts, depending on the legal framework in force in a particular locality. Basic personal freedom of the serfs was a major issue in Denmark and Schleswig-Holstein, but perhaps even more so the economic independence of manorial landowners and village communities. But this was not an issue in Sweden and Finland where, as on the northern Danish coast, a free peasantry with property rights already existed. Here, social stratification, especially the progressive pauperization of the small peasantry and subpeasants (i.e., the *Gärtner, Kossäten, Kätner, Büdner,* and *Insten,* who had only small pieces of land, if any), were burning issues. In Estonia, Livonia, and Lithuania, by contrast, German- and Polish-speaking manorial landowners were dealing with dependent Estonian, Latvian, or Lithuanian populations. Along the southern coast of the Baltic, finally, the question arose regarding the extent to which the various agrarian laws in effect in Pomerania, West Prussia, and East Prussia were reconcilable with Prussian reforms, or whether the removal and expropriation of the peasantry would continue as in Mecklenburg.

The earliest stirrings of reform are found in late absolutist Denmark, where suggestions had been circulating since the 1750s to improve agriculture, including in *Danmarks og Norges Øconomiske Magazin*

(Denmark and Norway's economics magazine). Politicians, manorial landowners, and businessmen, such as Andreas Peter Bernstorff, Christian Ditlev Reventlow, Johann Ludwig Reventlow, and Ernst Heinrich Schimmelmann, attempted to combine agricultural reform with protections for the peasantry. Model manors based on English prototypes, such as those of Caspar Voght (1752–1839) in Flottbek, near Hamburg, were supposed to set the tone, but the realities were very different. In 1786, a land commission began work to determine how corvée labor might be transformed into a rental relationship throughout the country.[28]

In Schleswig-Holstein, the manorial landowners allowed their demesnes to be separated and subdivided. The peasants who were forced to do corvée labor, the *Hufner* and so-called *Kätner* (cotters), were freed from serfdom and in exchange for a payment received their land with buildings and inventory on the separated fields. The demesne field (*Hoffeld*) was auctioned off in parcels or rented, and the peasants now paid an annual land rent.[29] However, laws regarding separation, subdivision, and the freeing of the serfs did not apply to the manors of the nobility. Consistent with enlightened absolutism, laws tying the peasantry to the soil were abolished in the Kingdom of Denmark in 1788. However, the knighthood of Schleswig-Holstein did not vote to abolish serfdom until 1797 (by a vote of 53 to 1), which would go into effect on January 1, 1805. The serfs were given their freedom and generally became hereditary (*Erbpächter*) and temporary leaseholders (*Zeitpächter*) on their former holdings. The services that had previously been required were dropped, unless they were part of a rental agreement. This was generally the case only for the subpeasantry. Generally, the manorial landowners switched their operations over to farm laborers and day laborers, and the much-feared labor scarcities never occurred.[30]

As a result of being freed from the three-field crop rotation system imposed by the village community (*Flurzwang*)—by 1807 approximately three-fourths of all agricultural land was no longer subject to this system in insular Denmark and about half in Jutland—economically independent farmsteads came into being that were now located in the middle of their fields.[31] This was when the now-typical agricultural landscape with quickset hedges began to take shape. Up until this time, a peasant's fields were distributed over the entire acreage of the village.

As a result of this mixed location (*Gemengelage*), the village community had used the crop rotation system to regulate the sequence in which individual strips of field could be worked. When this system was abolished, the peasants gained economic autonomy, as a result of which agricultural production increased significantly. At the same time, the consolidation that took place in Holstein spread to the manorial farms in Mecklenburg, where it contributed to increases in farming productivity.

The situation in the countryside in Norway, Sweden, and Finland, on the other hand, was not changed by administrative measures. In all three countries, a process took place in which land was increasingly concentrated in the hands of a small number of manorial landowners and peasants, while the number of small peasants and subpeasants, including the cotters, increased disproportionately. Over the course of the nineteenth century, the ability of these people to feed themselves and their families depended largely on the decision of others to emigrate. The agricultural productivity of the land was so low, especially in Norway and Finland, that emigration seemed the only way out. In Finland, the peasants were idealized as the bulwark of the nation while the cotters were largely ignored. While the integration of the cotter class into the Finnish process of nation-building was openly discussed, it was only in the twentieth century that cotters became small peasants with land of their own.[32]

In the Russian Baltic provinces, pastors influenced by Enlightenment ideas, along with Estophiles, prepared the groundwork for agrarian reforms. Although the peasant ordinances of 1802–1804 had validated the laws tying the peasantry to the soil, new laws promulgated in 1816, in Estonia, and in 1819, in Livonia, freed the serfs. The manorial landowners, however, continued to own the land, which forced the now independent peasants to sign rental agreements to farm that land. As elsewhere in Europe, crop failures, starvation, and revolts led to new agrarian laws in Livonia (1849) and Estonia (1856), which allowed the peasants to acquire land and regulated its acquisition. The peasant renters could now acquire land with the public credits they received. At the same time, the land that had up to that point been farmed by peasants was transferred to the peasants as property after ceding one-sixth to the landowners (so-called *quota land* or *sixth land*). The previously predominant natural rent or labor rent eventually gave way to money rent. This resulted in economically viable and productive units that could compete on the open market with the manorial farms. This was especially successful with crops such as linseed and for cattle and horse breeding. Vodka distilling to meet the demand in Russia proved extremely profitable. Mixed location was abandoned in most villages in the 1860s, and the land used by the peasants in common was divided up among them.[33]

Whereas a portion of the Estonian and Latvian peasantry was well on its way to commercially successful agriculture, the Lithuanian serfs were emancipated only in 1861—the same year as in Russia. But the economic power of the manorial landowners remained untouched, and the peasants remained dependent. The situation went from bad to worse when the Polish-Lithuanian uprising of 1863 was suppressed because Russian authorities now made it more difficult for Lithuanian peasants to acquire land. In addition, as part of the policy of Russification, Russian colonists moved into the region, which after 1864 triggered a wave of emigration to America.

The policy of the Prussian state was twofold. On the one hand, there was a progressive aspect to the reforms it initiated regarding the demesnes; on the other hand, as trustee of the country at large, it tended to bend to the interests of the nobility. The elimination of corvée labor, in 1763, meant the end of subservience to the manorial landowners, and after 1799, the peasants were required to perform only a quarter of the services to the demesnes previously demanded. This quarter was kept in place to allow the demesnes to adapt to the changed economic regime.[34] Between 1799 and 1806–1807, approximately 15,000 peasants became owners of their own farms. In exchange for their exemption from corvée labor, the peasants' payments to the state rose from 1671 taler, in 1803, to 117,646 taler, in 1808, which ensured significant government surpluses.[35]

In terms of the noble manors, it took Prussia's defeat at the hands of France, that is, a catastrophic failure on the part of the Prussian nobility, to give the Prussian bureaucracy the necessary powers to implement reforms. These were introduced with the edict of October 1807, which freed the serfs. The remaining corvée labor was transformed into cash payments. Further reforms regulated the transfer of property (land, buildings, and inventory), which would henceforth be paid for in cash over a period of thirty to fifty years. In East Prussia, the transfer of land was limited in scope. For the peasants who came under this law, it meant that their obligations would now be discharged in monetary form. However, these terms were also an added burden, increasing their obligations by almost 40 percent, which in many cases could be paid only if their harvests and the overall business climate were good.[36]

Corvée labor continued in Swedish Pomerania until 1810, even though the Swedish king had abolished serfdom as part of a coup, in 1806. But even after it was eliminated, the noble landowners retained the right to recruit farm laborers. Although they were legally free, they had to offer their services to their former lords first. More significant, however, was the fact that no ordinances were enacted to protect the peasantry. As a result, peasant expropriations and removals were common, and by 1846 fewer than half as many peasants worked the land as in 1780. In Eastern Pomerania and Western Pomerania south of the Peene River, an area that came under the edict of 1807, the transfer of property and the transformation of services into cash payments was slow. Because the manorial landowners were able to exclude from this process peasants who lacked the horses or oxen needed for plowing, the social and economic differences among the peasants began to widen. Nonetheless, by 1838, 10,744 peasants had come under the new regulatory measures in Pomerania, and these peasants paid their masters 724,954 taler in exchange for cattle and equipment. Unsurprisingly, these farms became considerably more productive than previously. However, approximately 3,500 peasant farms disappeared because the landowners appropriated the land—creating several thousand cotters and farm laborers in the process. That is, to the extent that peasants did not take over other farms, they became cotters or farm laborers. This ensured a surplus of laborers who either owned very little land or none at all; in the 1850s they often left the country to escape poverty. A first wave of emigration to Russia and to the United States, many to Wisconsin, had already occurred when the Lutheran and Calvinist churches were forced to unite in the Prussian provinces in 1817.[37]

The situation of the peasants was even more dire in Mecklenburg. Here, serfdom was abolished only in 1820, with many of the former serfs simply being thrown off the land by their masters. Laws creating a heritable rent relationship between the former serfs and their masters were not enacted in Mecklenburg-Schwerin until the 1860s, whereas in Mecklenburg-Strelitz such laws had already been enacted in 1824. Here, too, those without land sought refuge in the New World. But perhaps more important was the migration within Germany, with Mecklenburgers and Pomeranians swelling the burgeoning metropolises of Berlin and Hamburg, and then at the end of the century the industrial Ruhr region as well.

In most cases, agrarian reforms were not directly associated with increases in agricultural productivity, especially during the agrarian depression between 1816 and 1826. Agrarian production did increase somewhat later, especially in Denmark and in Schleswig-Holstein, where agricultural exports boomed after 1829. Grain was shipped to England, which became Denmark's most important agricultural market. Exports quadrupled between 1830 and 1870, and increasing prosperity allowed peasants to specialize in areas such as dairy, cattle raising, and sugar beet cultivation. Steamship lines were founded to satisfy the English demand for Danish foodstuffs. With the expansion of the German railroad network toward the end of the nineteenth century, Denmark had another very profitable market at its doorstep.[38]

Comparable developments in grain production are seen only along the southern and southeastern coasts of the Baltic, where noble manors and mid-sized farms were able to export to England after the repeal of the Corn Laws in 1846. This was also associated with a structural transformation in planting. While grain often comprised more than 90 percent of the harvested crops in traditional three-field farming, this figure was reduced to about 70 percent toward the end of the eighteenth century as a result of increased flax and vegetable cultivation. But during the nineteenth century, the proportion of grain dropped even further, to approximately 50 percent. The percentage of leaf crops, such as potatoes, clover, and feed and sugar beets, increased, largely because increased animal husbandry increased the demand for feed. This transition to the new crop rotation system that allowed the land to be cultivated all year (in the three-field rotation system one part always lay fallow and was used only for pasturage) was largely completed during the second half of the century.[39]

Livestock became the most important source of agricultural income in East Prussia and West Prussia. Horse breeding (at Trakehnen, among other places) increased because of the growing need for draft animals in both urban and rural settings and in the military. In addition, large-scale dairy and cattle farms were started for the first time, and again because of expanded rail connections they were now able to supply more distant markets. The same applied to hog farms.

Meat production was the most important source of income in Pomerania, with hogs, beef cattle, and oxen leading the way, while dairy farms shrank in importance, due largely to the longer distances to the end consumers. The peasants in Mecklenburg, on the other hand, increased their beef cattle stocks while also increasing milk production. In 1907, 257 creameries supplied the needs of neighboring large cities. The peasants also earned additional income by operating brickworks, distilleries, and mills.

Industrialization arrived in all of these countries relatively late. In Denmark, the food industry (slaughterhouses, creameries, and breweries) developed only toward the end of the nineteenth century, with most of the products making their way to local markets. Sweden, which had traditionally specialized in timber harvesting and processing, began to concentrate on iron and steel production, which then fed a growing mechanical engineering industry. Swedish inventors, such as Gustav de Laval (1845–1913) (steam turbines and milk centrifuges), L. M. Ericsson (1846–1926) (telephones), Alfred Nobel (1833–1896) (explosives), and Sven Gustaf Wingqvist (1876–1953) (ball bearings), secured Swedish monopolies on the world market. Large banking houses such as the Wallenberg family's Enskilda Banken financed the Swedish economy and with their investments fostered the industrialization of Norway and Finland.[40]

Both Norway and Finland produced industrial goods, but in the nineteenth century they also provided services to the booming world economy. For example, while Norwegian timber and Finnish timber and tar were crucial to English shipbuilding and industrialization generally, their merchant fleets transported a significant percentage of the goods produced. Originally, these countries exported timber mainly to England, but increasingly, Norwegian sailing vessels concentrated on the so-called tramp trade in the Atlantic. Although by 1860, the competition from steamships had largely eliminated any cost advantage enjoyed by sailing vessels in the Baltic Sea, this mode of transport was still extremely profitable on transatlantic routes. Used ships could still be bought for good prices or built at small shipyards using local timber and carpenters. The switch from sailing vessels to steamships was very capital intensive, and the decision to make the transition depended on local circumstances. Large ports, such as Copenhagen and Stockholm, switched over to steam relatively early. Bergen soon came to depend on steamers as well in order to protect its fish sales in European markets. But more provincial ports, which had specialized in different sorts of routes, initially saw little reason to make the change.[41]

In Finland, it took until the twentieth century for steamships to eclipse the traditional sailing vessels. Here, the sailing ships had specialized in the transport of timber and tar through the Øresund to western Europe, but then they increasingly shipped freight in the Black Sea and Mediterranean. In the 1870s, Finnish shippers were a factor in the freight revolution across the Atlantic, transporting grain from New York, Philadelphia, and Baltimore to Ireland and to British ports on the North Sea as well as petroleum to western Europe and even into the Baltic region. They also handled timber exports (especially pine) from the southern United States and Canada.

Shipowners and skippers came from the west coast of Norway, where fishing and fish processing were being done on a large scale. In Finland, the shipowners were often merchants and owners of sawmills as well. Peasants from the Åland Islands became increasingly competitive merchant shippers;[42] much the same occurred along the Estonian coast, where skippers and shipbuilders became shipowners. And local maritime schools trained local seamen in the basics of navigation.

Norway and Finland made ample use of their natural resources as they industrialized. Norway in particular used waterpower not only to produce electricity, but also to build up its electrochemical industry. Aluminum manufacture was at the center of these endeavors. In Finland, timber was the raw material and engine of industrialization, with timber and tar exports leading to the processing of pulp and paper. From there, it was only a small step to the manufacture of paper-processing machines.

In the Russian Baltic provinces, the expansion of the railroad net-work served as a powerful impetus to trade and transport because port cities could now be connected both with each other and with the hin-terland. A direct connection between Riga and Mitau was opened in 1868. In 1870, this was followed by the line from Baltischport (Paldiski) to St. Petersburg by way of Reval and Narva. The construction of rail-road lines worked in favor of the port cities through which they ran. Once Riga was connected with the hinterlands of Ukraine and southern Russia, it suddenly became a major player in grain exports. The popu-lation almost tripled between 1871 (103,000) and 1897 (282,000), reaching 520,000 in 1913. Riga recruited its population primarily from the coun-tryside. Libau (Liepāja) was also able to improve its relative position by exploiting its railroad connection, while Reval grew into the second most important Russian port for imports after St. Petersburg. Indus-trialization kept up with urbanization. In addition to the textile in-dustry (cloth factories), timber and metal processing also played a role, especially in the shipyards and in wagon building.[43]

In Lithuania, by contrast, the industrial potential remained largely unexploited. Further to the south and southwest, Königsberg, Danzig, and Stettin shipyards and related industries formed an industrial center. Here was built the first Stettiner Eisenschiffswerft (iron shipyard) in 1851. In 1857, it became the Stettiner Maschinenbau-AG Vulcan, which in the following years built locomotives as well as warships. The Vulcan shipyard, which employed 3,600 workers in 1882, built not only war-ships, but also passenger ships, including the two-propeller ocean liner SS *Kaiser Wilhelm der Grosse*. Stettin developed into the most impor-tant port in the region and, because of its connection to Berlin and the volume of goods that passed through it, eclipsed even Lübeck, not to mention Rostock and Wismar.

Beginning in 1896, the supply of iron from the iron works in Stettin to the machine and shipbuilding industries was improved by the Sile-sian steel magnate Guido Henckel von Donnersmarck (1830–1916). The iron works processed Swedish ore. A cement factory, copper works, coking plant, and tar and ammonia factories were added to the com-plex. Bernhard Stoewer (1875–1937), a manufacturer of motorcycles and typewriters, began to produce automobiles, motor boats, trucks, buses, and airplane motors as well.

From an Estate-Based to a Class-Based Society

Over the course of the nineteenth century, the Baltic region experienced
not only a population explosion, but also the creation of a society based
on classes. This process was complicated by ethnic and social identities. The number of subpeasants increased everywhere because of
agrarian reforms, and during the second half of the century, the industrial workforce increased as well. In Denmark, the population grew
from 1.5 to 2.5 million (in Schleswig-Holstein alone, from 0.6 million
in 1803, to 1.4 million in 1901); the Swedish population grew from 3.5
to 5 million and the Norwegian from 1.5 to 2.25 million. Finland's population almost tripled to approximately 2.6 million in 1900. The Russian Baltic provinces also saw enormous population increases, but not
all population groups shared equally in this trend.

Because of delayed industrialization, the ability to feed growing populations lagged behind in most countries, forcing many people to emigrate. In Scandinavia in particular, the death rate had decreased to such
an extent that at the beginning of the twentieth century Scandinavians
had the longest life expectancy in Europe. But most of the people still
lived in the countryside, not in cities. Denmark alone saw an increase
in urban population from 20 percent to 39 percent. The rate of urbanization was still very low in Norway (from 12 percent to 28 percent)
and especially in Sweden (from 10 percent to 21 percent). Nonetheless,
a portion of the growing rural underclasses began to be integrated into
the cities in Denmark, where the industrial and services sectors offered
employment.

The low level of urbanization in Sweden was also the result of its
decentralized industries, which tried to locate close to the sources of
critical raw materials. Initially at least, the burgeoning subpeasant population brought with it considerable problems. Between 1850 and 1914,
more than 1 million people left Sweden; only Ireland and Norway saw
higher rates of emigration. By about 1900, a large proportion of the rural
underclasses had found work in industry, which meant that the industrial working class increased rapidly. The labor movement began to
swell after suffrage was expanded. Although women generally were
granted the right to vote only in 1921, economically independent, tax-
paying (i.e., unmarried) women or widows had been permitted to vote

in municipal elections as early as 1861. The expansion of mandatory education also favored the organization of unions, which in 1913 lobbied for and helped enact the National Pension Act, which established old-age pensions not just for industrial workers, but also for the entire population.[44]

In Norway as in Sweden, the peasant underclasses either emigrated or found employment in factories, and here merchant shipping provided additional opportunities for work. Between 1850 and 1910, approximately 70,000 Swedes migrated to Norway, where most of them found work in shipping.[45] Unlike the rural underclasses, the new industrial workforce lived primarily in the cities and coastal regions. The situation in Finland was comparable, where the labor movement attempted to ensure itself seats in parliament. At the same time, however, it was promoted by the Russian administration as an instrument against the more nationalist Finnish middle class, which had its eyes on an independent Finland separate from Russia.

However, the problem facing the Finnish cotters, who supported the socialists in the first parliamentary election (1907), was not resolved. It would continue well into the interwar years, when the law transformed cotters into small peasants. Although issues of national identity had not yet been permanently resolved, the Nordic labor movement exerted a major influence on the development of society in these countries.

Socialist parties were established in all of the states. These included the Dansk Socialdemokratisk Partiet (DSP, 1876) in Denmark, Det norske Arbeiderparti (DnA, 1887) in Norway, Socialdemokratiska Arbetarepartiet (SAP, 1889) in Sweden, and Suomen Työväenpuolue (1899, after 1903 Suomen Sosialidemokraattinen Puolue, SDP) in Finland. In Sweden and Norway, the unions and the party of labor were virtually identical. Upon joining a union, one also became a member of the respective Socialist Party, and vice versa. On the eve of World War I, all of these parties had achieved key positions in their countries and were represented in parliament: they comprised one-third of parliamentarians in Sweden and a quarter in Denmark and Norway. And during this period, all of these parties took what is called a revisionist line, that is, they renounced revolution and the dictatorship of the proletariat. The German SPD served as their model, and they more or less adopted its policies and stances. Worker protection laws and tariff agreements were passed or enforced by means of strikes, and the unions came to be recognized as the official representatives of the workers.[46]

The situation was very different in the Russian Baltic provinces, where agrarian reforms together with demographic changes and internal migration patterns led to considerable structural transformations. This is illustrated most strikingly by the development of Riga from a middle-class, mainly German trading center into a multiethnic industrial metropolis. Not only did the population of Riga increase from 102,600 in 1867 to 507,600 in 1913, but its ethnic composition changed fundamentally as well.

Latvians displaced Germans as the dominant nationality during this period, while the Russian element remained approximately stable. A glance at the structure of the labor force makes another transformation clear. While Germans continued to be well represented in the bureaucracy and free professions despite their general decrease in the population as a whole, the proportion of German artisans, merchants, and providers of other services decreased. Latvians became more prominent in these sectors and in industry generally. Russians were equally active in administration, trade, industry, the manual trades, and other services. The Jewish population became more prominent in the free professions and as merchants.

Comparable developments occurred in the university city of Dorpat and in Reval, which was an administrative center. In 1897, Estonians were the predominant group in both cities (more than 60 percent), while Germans made up only 16 percent of the population. The Russian and

Table 7.1   Ethnic population movements in Riga, 1867–1913 (%)

	1867	1881 Nationality	1881 Language	1897	1913
Germans	42.9	31.0	39.4	25.5	13.5
Latvians	23.6	32.8	29.5	41.6	41.3
Russians	25.1	19.7	18.9	16.9	19.5
Jews	5.1	12.2	8.4	6.5	6.6
Other	3.3	4.3	3.8	9.5	19.1

From U. v. Hirschhausen, *Zeitschrift für Ostmitteleuropa-Forschung* 48/ 4 (1999): 482.

German populations of Reval were similar, while the Russian presence in Dorpat was much smaller.[47] Out in the countryside, by contrast, the changes did not seem especially significant because during the entire nineteenth century Estonia was already 90 percent Estonian, while Latvians were the predominant population group in Livonia (about 80 percent). The transformation was much more dramatic in the cities, especially in Riga, where Germans felt caught in a pincer by the progressive Russification of the region, the Latvian nationalist movement, and the industrial labor movement (social democracy). For Latvians social mobility in the industrial society fostered a Latvian movement. Latvian agitation was directed first against the Germans and then the Russians. Both Latvians and Russians cultivated anti-Semitic stereotypes, which found ready acceptance among the Germans, who were feeling threatened in any case.[48]

The Baltic Art Worlds

The arts in the Baltic region in the nineteenth century were first and foremost influenced by neoclassical architecture, then during the second half of the century by romantic painting conjoined with the search for a Nordic artistic ideal. At the turn of the nineteenth century, St. Petersburg set the pace with its emulation of the culture of Napoleonic France. As we have seen with Helsinki, neoclassical influences gained currency in the Baltic region through the work of English, Scottish, and Italian architects. One example is Elley Palace, in Semigallia, south of Mitau, which was built in about 1800 by Giacomo Quarenghi for Jeannot Medem (1763–1838), the brother-in-law of Duke Peter of Couronia. The Berlin Bauakademie was also involved, as can still be seen from the city plan of Helsinki laid out according to a design by Engel, whose intention was to acquaint Finns with a new type of architecture, educate the taste of the populace, and improve the skills of the country's artisans.[49] A comparable neoclassical ensemble can be found only in the university city of Dorpat, where Johann Wilhelm Krause (1757–1828), who originally came from Silesia and was trained in Leipzig, gave the reopened university a unique and imposing face to the world.[50] He began with the Institute for Anatomy in 1805 and he followed that up with the library, which he built in 1806 among the ruins of the cathedral church. He then built the grandiose main building in 1809 and the observatory in 1810. As a draftsman, Krause was highly eclectic, taking inspiration from both the city views of minor Swiss masters and the formal language of the rococo. He attempted to harmonize these influences with the natural surroundings and manors that he found in Estonia and Livonia so as to locate the region within the culture of the European Enlightenment.[51]

Fascination with things Italian had a long history in Denmark, Russia, Sweden, and Finland. This trend was best embodied by the sculptor Bertel Thorvaldsen (1770–1844), who created his most important works not in Denmark but in Rome. At about the same time, the Nordic romanticism, developed by the painter Jens Juel (1745–1802) and his Pomeranian students Caspar David Friedrich and Philipp Otto Runge (1777–1810), came to life at the Danish Academy of the Arts. Friedrich, who was born in Greifswald, studied from 1794 to 1798 under Juel in Copenhagen, before moving on to Dresden, where he did most of his work. Runge, who originally came from Wolgast, underwent much the same training, before moving on to Hamburg. During the second half of the century, painters and their customers began to idealize the *Volk* and the landscape, and these idealizations were reflected in contemporary romantic and historical paintings. Thus, while Ilya Repin (1844–1930) painted images from Russia's past and the peasant present, in St. Petersburg, the Estonian portraitist Johann Köler was also painting landscapes depicting life in the Estonian countryside.

One of the intermediaries between western European, Scandinavian, and Russian art was the Finn Albert Edelfelt (1854–1905). He had studied in Antwerp and Paris, where he came in contact with other Danish and Swedish artists. Under the influence of the Barbizon school in Paris, Danish painters settled in Skagen—where the North Sea and the Baltic meet. The so-called Skagen painters dedicated themselves to exploring the possibilities inherent in the interplay between light and water, while at the same time painting the local inhabitants at work and at leisure in a realist style. Members of this group, including Michael Ancher (1849–1927), Anna Ancher (1859–1935), Viggo Johansen (1851–1935), P. S. Krøyer (1851–1909), Marie Krøyer (1867–1940), Christian Krohg (1852–1925), Carl Locher (1851–1915), Karl Madsen (1855–1938), and Laurits Tuxen (1853–1927), became the precursors of Danish impressionism.[52]

In the 1880s and 1890s, Edelfelt became an honorary member of the St. Petersburg Academy and moved to Russia, where he received commissions from the czar's court. Edelfelt recruited numerous Finnish artists to take part in exhibitions of Scandinavian art in Russia. This Finnish-Russian relationship was exemplified by an 1898 exhibition at which a new group of Russian artists calling itself Mir Iskusstva (world of art), which consisted of Alexandre Benois (1870–1960), Konstantin Somov (1869–1939), Dmitry Filosofov (1872–1940), Léon Bakst (1866–1924), and Eugene Lansere (1875–1946), made its debut. Russian artists began to visit their Finnish colleagues, and during the first decades of the twentieth century these visits included stopovers in other Baltic countries as well.

Akseli Gallen-Kallela (1865–1931), who is probably the most famous Finnish painter, had also studied in Paris, but in the wake of Lönnrot's *Kalevala*, he began to see his calling as the creation of a Finnish national style. In 1900, he painted frescoes for the Finnish pavilion at the Paris World Fair that expressed the desire for national independence. His works had previously been shown in Berlin in 1894, along with those of Edvard Munch (1863–1944).[53]

Painters from the Baltic region also received training and exhibited their work throughout Germany. One example is the Swedish painter Anders Zorn (1860–1920), who in 1881 interrupted his studies at the Royal Academy in Stockholm and traveled throughout Great Britain before spending time in Paris. The German portion of his career began in Munich, then the most prominent German city for exhibitions and the art trade. The sales exhibition at Munich's Glass Palace brought him fame and commissions. In 1891, Zorn won a gold medal at the Glass Palace for his painting *Im Freien*, which made his career. However, Munich artists viewed the participation of "outsiders" in "their exhibition" with a jaundiced eye. In response to this parochialism, artists of what has come to be known as the Munich Secession (1892) welcomed important Swedish artists as full members. However, a number of Swedish artists, such as Karl Nordström (1855–1923), left Munich to create a national style of landscape painting of their own. Under the influence of Max Liebermann, Zorn also cast his eye toward Berlin and Hamburg, where Alfred Lichtwark, the new director of the Hamburg Kunsthalle, had begun collecting contemporary Nordic art. In Hamburg, Zorn made a name for himself more as a graphic designer than as a painter, however. Much as had happened with his Norwegian colleague Edvard Munch in the 1890s, Zorn's breakthrough came in Berlin, where the National Gallery bought his *Sommerabend* (summer evening) and patrons swamped him with portrait commissions. Zorn returned to Sweden in 1911.[54]

For aspiring young artists in the Russian Baltic provinces, the Russian Academy of the Arts and the art school at the University of Dorpat were the places to learn the rudiments of their craft. The university itself collected art and provided both professors and students opportunities to display their work. Those who did well often went on to study at German art academies. For example, the academy in Düsseldorf, which specialized in both (religious) historical painting and landscapes, attracted Scandinavians and Americans along with Baltic Germans. And the development of a Latvian middle class meant that aspiring artists had the economic means to pursue their training, even though there was little interest in their work in Latvia itself at the time.[55]

Matters had changed for the next generation of artists, which included Jānis Rozentāls (1866–1916), Vilhelms Purvītis (1872–1945), Ādams Alksnis (1864–1897), and Jānis Valters (1869–1932), who studied in St. Petersburg with the intention of creating a new Latvian national art. They used the artistic ferment taking place in Riga, infused with the spirit of Art Nouveau, to develop a landscape and genre style of their own. But their work was not well received. With paintings depicting the life of the people piling up in their studios, Purvītis moved to Reval and Valters to Dresden. While Purvītis later taught at the academy in St. Petersburg, Valters trained aspiring artists under the name Johann Walter-Kurau. Rozentāls was able to support himself as an illustrator and taught at the art school in Riga; in 1915, he followed his Finnish wife to Helsinki, where he died.[56]

The most important Lithuanian painter (who was also a composer) was Mikalojus Konstantinas Čiurlionis (1875–1911), who had initially studied at the music academy in Warsaw, and then at the conservatory in Leipzig, before studying fine arts in Warsaw. He lived in Vilnius in 1907–1908 and then in St. Petersburg. One of his peculiarities was that many of his paintings incorporated musical terms such as *Sonata of the Sea* (Jūros sonata).[57]

Over the course of the nineteenth century, music in the Baltic region became progressively more commercialized, as had already happened in Great Britain and central Europe toward the end of the eighteenth century. Music became increasingly important in European life, and many individuals pursued musical training. Although the music that reached the Baltic from the south was greatly favored, a push was also made to seek out indigenous musical traditions—or to invent them. Musical societies, some of which had already been formed in the eighteenth century so that amateurs and professional musicians could play together, began to perform concerts in public. Concerts for chorus and orchestra, evenings of chamber music, and concerts with a mixed instrumental and vocal repertoire became a regular feature of social life in cities such as Christiania (Oslo), Odense, Copenhagen, Århus, Åbo, and Helsinki. As a result, increasing numbers of people with no professional aspirations sought out musical training, something of a break with tradition as such training had previously been the province of professionals at the courts, in military and other orchestras, or in theaters in Copenhagen and Stockholm. In Denmark, music became part of the school curriculum in 1814. Private schools came into being, and the Copenhagen Conservatory was founded in 1867. In the middle of the century, as many as thirty-four private music schools were opened in Stockholm and Christiania, and starting in 1858, the Royal Music Academy of Stockholm began to train students in voice, instrumental technique, and theory. The goals pursued by Martin Wegelius (1846–1906) were especially ambitious when he founded the Helsinki Music Institute in 1882. This forerunner of the present-day Sibelius Academy sought to elevate the artistic level of the country as quickly as possible, for which purpose he recruited renowned teachers such as Ferruccio Busoni (1866–1924). While successful in Finland, a comparable institution founded in Norway failed to prosper.

All in all, these countries were able to create their own musical cultures out of a mix of many disparate elements. Future composers either emerged from royal court orchestras, had studied in Germany (mostly in Leipzig), or had moved to the Nordic countries from northern Germany.[58]

Thus, for example, the founder of Danish romanticism, Friedrich Kuhlau (1786–1832), fled Germany for Denmark ahead of advancing Napoleonic troops. In addition to classical instrumental works, he also composed music for the play *Elverhøj* (Elves' hill), for which he used traditional Danish and Swedish ballads. One of Kuhlau's arrangements was later adapted for the Danish national anthem. The composer and conservatory director, Johan Peter Emilius Hartmann (1805–1900), cultivated a romantic "Nordic" style to counter German influences. In contrast, the classical symphonies of Niels Gade (1817–1890), who was trained in Leipzig, had a greater following in Germany, while his dramatic cantata *Elverskud* (Elf-shot) and the ballet *Et Folkesagn* (A folk tale) satisfied Nordic yearnings.[59] Norway recruited a number of musicians, including Carl Arnold (1794–1873) and Friedrich August Reißiger (1809–1883), from Germany, while the Norwegian violin virtuoso Ole Bull (1810–1880) was extremely successful on the European continent. Bull convinced Edvard Grieg's (1843–1907) parents to send their gifted son to Leipzig to receive training. Grieg went on to imbue Norwegian music with a spirit that demanded to be taken seriously. Thus, he successfully used motifs from folk music to express certain themes.[60]

For many years, the leading Swedish musician was Franz Berwald. He composed orchestral and chamber works, operas, operettas, and cantatas, but he had greater success in Germany than in his homeland. The next generation of Swedish composers, including Ludvig Norman (1831–1885), August Söderman (1832–1876), and Andreas Hallén (1846–1925), was especially influenced by their studies at the Leipzig Conservatory, which exposed them to German music, including that of Mendelssohn. On their return home they tried to found a Swedish national school and even a national opera.[61]

The Finnish musical tradition, as represented by Fredrik Pacius (1809–1891), also came from Germany. Born in Hamburg, Pacius had studied under Louis Spohr, in northern Germany, but later, in the 1820s, he took a position as violinist in the Stockholm court orchestra. In 1834, he was offered the music directorship at the University of Helsinki. There, he founded a musical tradition based on cantatas and patriotic songs, among them the Finnish national anthem "Vårt land" (Our country), or "Maamme" in Finnish. His successor, Martin Wegelius, who had also studied in Germany, systematized musical training in

Finland. One of his students was Jean Sibelius (1865–1957), who, after a brief stay in Berlin in the 1890s, wrote compositions that were inspired by the world of the *Kalevala*. He later came to be viewed as the national composer of Finland.[62]

How literary styles developed in the Baltic region can be seen both in writings for the national movement and in theatrical productions.[63] The old court theaters with their troupes of foreign actors were, as elsewhere in Europe, transformed into national theaters. In addition, private theaters were founded that catered to a broader public, among them the Nya Teatern in Stockholm (1842), and the Casino (1848) and Folketeatret (1857) in Copenhagen. At the end of the nineteenth and beginning of the twentieth centuries, Stockholm and Copenhagen built magnificent new theaters. The Finnish National Theater (Suomen Kansallisteatteri) was built in 1902 in an Art Nouveau style. In Reval, the Estonia Theater, designed by the Finnish architects Armas Lindgren (1874–1929) and Wivi Lönn (1872–1966), competed for attention with the German Theater by the Russian architects Alexey Bubyr (1876–1919) and Nikolai Vasilyev (1875–1958). In Riga, the already existent German theater was joined by a Russian (1902) and Latvian theater (1908).

The works that reached the stage continued to be infused by the romantic spirit, such as plays by Adam Oehlenschläger and other Scandinavian authors. Oehlenschläger, for example, wrote a cycle of Nordic tragedies, including *Håkan Jarl* (1808) and *Axel og Valborg* (1810), that were influenced by Shakespeare and Schiller. Johan Ludvig Heiberg (1854–1928), formerly a professor of Danish in Kiel, introduced light theatrical entertainment to a broader public. It was also at about this time that Denmark's most renowned author and playwright, Hans Christian Andersen (1805–1875), made his debut, in 1829, with the play *Kæjlighed paa Nicolai Taarn* (Love in Nicolai Tower). Heiberg's successes were noticed in Sweden, where the Nya Teatern emulated his vaudevillian style.

The Comediehuset was founded in 1849 in Bergen, Norway, followed by Det Norske Teater, which Ole Bull wanted to transform into a national theater. This was where playwrights Bjørnstjerne Bjørnson (1832–1910) and Henrik Ibsen (1828–1906) obtained their first practical experience in the theater. Bjørnson in particular was captivated by the notion of a Nordic identity, which would also require a new Norwegian language.

Relatively early, he began to tackle problems in family relationships in such plays as *De Nygifte* (The newlyweds), themes that later blossomed forth under Ibsen's masterful hand.[64]

Initially, Ibsen found inspiration in Icelandic sagas and Norwegian history, as such plays as *The Feast at Solhaug* (1855) and *The Vikings of Helgeland* (1858) attest. In 1864, Ibsen left Christiania and spent twenty-seven years in Italy, which was where his most important works were written. *Brand* (1866) and *Peer Gynt* (1867) may be viewed as dramatic poems for a reading public. An abridgment of *Peer Gynt* was set to music by Edvard Grieg and was performed to great acclaim in Christiania and later in other cities. Ibsen's work came to be increasingly naturalistic, as evidenced in plays such as *A Doll's House* (1879), *Ghosts* (1881), and later *The Wild Duck*, which premiered in 1884. But toward the end of the nineteenth century, the Swedish playwright and novelist August Strindberg (1849–1912) began to eclipse Ibsen. Strindberg had begun his career entirely in the Swedish romantic tradition, bringing medieval themes to the stage. Pacifist and emancipationist ideals infused his early novels and the collection of short stories titled *Getting Married* (1884), for which he faced charges of blasphemy. In the 1880s, Strindberg, too, became more naturalistic in his dramatic style with plays such as *The Father* (1887) and *Miss Julie* (1880). Later, he also began to exhibit more mystical, expressionistic, and surrealistic tendencies.

The Baltic Sea as a Summer Resort

The arts and literature greatly influenced people's awareness of the Baltic and its landscape. In the nineteenth century, Caspar David Friedrich became associated with a new romantic image of the Baltic coast, while the pastor and Greifswald professor Ludwig Gotthard Kosegarten (1758–1818) described the charms of the island of Rügen and of the Baltic Sea generally in his sermons and literary works. At about the same time, physicians began to recommend seaside sojourns for their city-bound patients because of the clean air and restful atmosphere, and the romance of the Baltic encouraged summer visitors to the region.

Spas had been a fixture in Germany since the sixteenth century, and "taking the waters" became especially fashionable in the eighteenth. Seaside resorts, on the other hand, came into being in larger numbers in England in the 1770s and 1780s. The resorts at Brighton, Harwich, Margate, Southampton, Weymouth, and Plymouth were the start of a new bath culture, and so it should be of little surprise that the physicist and satirist Georg Christoph Lichtenberg (1742–1799), upon returning to Germany from a trip to his beloved England in 1793, asked, "Why does Germany not yet have a single large public resort by the sea?"[65] His question touched off a debate about the relative advantages and disadvantages of the North Sea versus the Baltic Sea as sites for such a facility. Whereas the proponents of the North Sea praised its higher salt content, those arguing for the Baltic cited its lack of tides and relatively consistent water temperature. In any case, Samuel Gottlieb Vogel (1750–1837), the personal physician to Grand Duke Frederick Francis I of Mecklenburg-Schwerin (1756–1839), took the opportunity to propose that the duke settle the matter by building a resort on the Baltic.

When Frederick Francis and his entourage took their first bath at Heiligendamm, at Doberan, it broke the ground for an entirely new movement.[66] Over the next several years, residences, public buildings, and cultural spaces were built, among them the parlor building (1802), the prince's palace (1806–1809), and the pavilions, which were designed by Carl Theodor Severing. Bathhouses and lodgings were built to accommodate the increasing numbers of Baltic tourists. During the first half of the nineteenth century, Heiligendamm was visited by an average of 1,200 guests per year, although not all of them took to the water. One reason was probably that the presence of the local ducal family and other members of the European high aristocracy was every bit as much of an attraction. At the same time, Heiligendamm began to see competition. Seaside resorts sprang up like mushrooms along the North Sea and Baltic coasts. Heiligendamm was followed by Norderney (1797), and then Travemünde (1802), Boltenhagen (1803), Wangerooge (1804), Warnemünde (1805), Spiekeroog (1809), Grömitz (1813), Cuxhaven (1816), Putbus (1816), Cranz (1816), Zoppot (1819), Graal-Müritz (1820), Heringsdorf (1824), Swinemünde (1824), Binz (1825), Helgoland (1826), Büsum (1837), Juist (1840), and Borkum (1850).

In the eastern Baltic, Russian bathers had been visiting local seaside resorts since about the 1820s and 1830s.[67] After it became difficult for

Russians to travel outside the czar's empire, many who could afford it headed to the coastal cities of Finland and the Baltic provinces. Residents of St. Petersburg spent summers in Helsinki or along more southern stretches of the sea. A tourist infrastructure came into being with characteristic wooden hotels in places such as Pernau, Hapsal, Arensburg on the island of Ösel, Hanko in southern Finland, and Öregrund on the eastern coast of Sweden. Over time, these ramshackle hotels were replaced by stone buildings; in some cases, magnificent luxury hotels were built, as in Saltsjöbaden (near Stockholm), Kulosaari (near Helsinki), Skodsborg on the Øresund, Binz on the island of Rügen, Heringsdorf on Usedom, and in Zoppot (near Danzig). Yacht clubs were established all over and they regularly held regattas, and yachting pavilions came to epitomize the "look" of the Baltic coast, giving the resorts a maritime flair. Sailing, an activity borrowed from England, was closely connected with the arming of fleets and the increasing prestige of navies before World War I. A good example is the port city of Kiel, which was later built up to accommodate the German navy and, especially under Emperor William II, the rapidly growing fleet of warships. Regattas had been held regularly on the Kiel Fjord since 1882. In 1887, officers and naval officials founded the Marine-Regatta-Verein (Naval regatta society), which William II, as honorary chairman of the society, named the Kaiserliche Yacht-Club. Both the emperor and his brother Heinrich regularly attended so-called Kiel weeks and promoted sailing as a sport.

In Russia, the czar's family lent the sport similar prestige by sponsoring the imperial River Sailing Society of St. Petersburg. Before World War I, it became fashionable for reigning monarchs to meet by the sea. Thus, Nicholas II and William II met on the island of Björkö in 1905, and two years later in Swinemünde. And in 1908, King Edward VII of England traveled in his yacht to Reval to pay a courtesy call on his cousin Nicholas II.[68] Nicholas's father, Alexander III, had also been a sailing enthusiast, who together with his wife Dagmar often spent summers sailing among the skerries (small rocky islands) of the Gulf of Finland. He had also owned a summer house in the vicinity of Kotka. But commoners took to the sea and enjoyed the clean air with equal abandon. The upper middle classes built summer cottages on skerries off the coast of Finland and Stockholm, while less wealthy members of the middle class found accommodations with fishermen and boatmen. These skerries and the romance surrounding them became an important motif in Baltic art when Anders Zorn began painting summer life outside Stockholm and Albert Edelfelt captured the mood of these rocky outcroppings in Uusimaa.[69] It may be said that while nature inspired the artists of the north, their work, in turn, encouraged a completely new form of development in the region.

CHAPTER EIGHT

Revolutions and New States

Focus on Riga

By the eve of World War I, the port city of Riga, which to that point had been shaped largely by a German middle class and foreign merchants, had become a multiethnic industrial metropolis with a population exceeding 500,000. This changed the settlement patterns and architectural look of the city considerably. The new railroad lines that connected Riga with its Russian hinterland invited industrialization. And the growing workforce had to be supplied with lodgings, food, drinking water, and energy. At the same time, industrialists and bankers clamored for villas to show off their importance. As a result of all this activity, between 1900 and 1914, numerous German-Baltic, Latvian, and Jewish architects created a self-contained Art Nouveau ensemble on the outskirts of the medieval old city. The revolution of 1905 marked a turning point, with Art Nouveau replacing the previously predominant eclecticism. In addition to the decorative style of architects such as Heinrich Scheel (1829–1909), Friedrich Scheffel, and Mikhail Eisenstein (1867–1921), the father of the pioneering Russian film director, Latvian architects such as Eižens Laube (1880–1967), Konstāntins Pēkšens (1859–1928), Jānis Alksnis (1869–1939), and Aleksandrs Vanags (1873–1919) worked in a specifically national variant of Art Nouveau that was greatly influenced by Finnish architects. This style included the use of local building materials and ethnographic decorations. One example is the meeting house of the Riga Latvian Society designed by Laube, which, despite its imposing size, is decorated with only a few paintings by the artist Jānis Rozentāls.[1]

Figure 8. Art Nouveau building in Riga, Alberta jela 2; architect: Mikhail Eisenstein, 1906

The Revolution of 1905

Russia's defeat in the Russo-Japanese War of 1904–1905 permanently changed life in the Baltic region. After the Russian naval base at Port Arthur surrendered to the Japanese in early 1905, the Russian Baltic fleet, which had been based at Libau, was destroyed by the Japanese navy as well in May 1905. The Russian Empire appeared on the verge of imploding. The political opposition began to articulate its demands, and the regime saw itself forced to make compromises. In addition to loosening censorship and decreeing greater tolerance, repressive measures, such as the ban on the Latin-based Lithuanian alphabet, were lifted. Although the various opposition groups had been communicating with each other within the Russian Empire, it took the events of Bloody Sunday, January 22, 1905, when the military gunned down hundreds

Map 8. The Baltic region in 1923

of unarmed demonstrators, to trigger mass protests throughout the country. But many and varied interests vied for public support. On the one hand, strikes and demonstrations buoyed the social democratic movement. But moderate reform groups, the so-called constitutionalists, also gained ground. Their aim was to use this favorable moment to reform the Finnish parliament and press for the participation and autonomy of Estonians and Latvians in the Baltic provinces, among other goals.

In Dorpat, the Postimees group (named after the newspaper of the same name) attempted, under the leadership of Jaan Tõnisson (1868–ca. 1941) and with the help of Estonian associations and the Estonian Progressive People's Party, which Tõnisson founded, to disempower the German-Baltic knighthood along with the Russian bureaucracy.

The center of the unrest was Riga, where the Marxist Latvijas Sociāldemokrātiskā Strādnieku Partija (Latvian Social Democratic Workers Party) became the leading political grouping and demanded a parliamentary democracy for all of Russia. It believed that the Russian and Latvian proletariat would fight on the same side, whereas the smaller left-wing group Latviešu Sociāldemokrātu Savienība (Latvian Social Democratic Union) demanded its own Latvian state, including Latgallia. The peasantry exerted powerful pressure of their own, not only going on strike during the harvest season, but also rampaging through the villages and estates burning barns and manor houses after Sunday religious services. The situation escalated through the fall and winter of 1905, when numerous manors were destroyed and their owners murdered. These events marked the end of Baltic-German authority in the region. It was not until January that Russian troops arrived; they pacified the Baltics, brutally meting out indiscriminate punishment. Many intellectual critics went into exile.

The question of national autonomy was discussed at a congress of delegates in Riga in December 1905. At the same time, a national congress, held in Vilnius, demanded independence for Lithuania, although there were major disagreements about the future size of the country. For example, would Poland, White Russia, and the Ukraine be part of a greater Lithuania along the lines of the Polish-Lithuanian Commonwealth? Questions such as these would occupy center stage until an independent Lithuanian state came into being.

More pragmatic forces prevailed in Finland. Finnish socialists wanted to use the general strike called by the Russian socialists in October 1905 to press for parliamentary and voting reforms based on universal suffrage and equal and secret balloting. Pointedly, they elected a revolutionary government by polling all of the adults who happened to be in the marketplace in Helsinki at that particular moment.[2] In November 1905, the czar entrusted the senate with the task of reorganizing parliamentary rules. Although the socialists refused to cooperate, within a relatively short time the senate came up with radical parliamentary reforms that gave women and men equal voting rights—although the czar continued to appoint the government, that is, the senate. The first free elections yielded some parliamentary surprises. The Finnish-language Constitutionalists, the so-called Young Finns, won 26 seats, while the Swedish-language People's Party took 24. But the real victors were the socialists with 80 seats, well ahead of the nationalist (anti-Swedish language) Old Finns with 59 seats. The party system that was created at that time remains largely in place today. Because none of the four groupings had a parliamentary majority, they were forced to work together, which often led to short-term coalitions.

However, ongoing Russian attempts to control the country caused problems for the parliamentarians. Among other things, Czar Nicholas II attempted to torpedo Finnish autonomy and the parliamentary system by dissolving parliament, and these efforts greatly reduced what the Finns could accomplish. The decree of 1910 that all Finnish laws had to be confirmed by the Russian Duma, met with considerable resistance. The Social Democrats were the chief beneficiaries as they could now link social emancipation to demands for national independence.[3]

Fundamental changes were going on in Norway at almost the same time as the revolutionary events in the Russian Empire. Since the beginning of the century, Sweden and Norway had fought over Norway's consular representation. Because they could not agree, the parliament (Storting) decided to establish Norwegian consulates abroad. The king rejected this solution, whereupon the Norwegian government resigned. Because no new government was elected, the Storting dissolved the union with Sweden, on June 7, 1905, arguing that the king had neglected his duties. Sweden refused to recognize Norway, but in the Convention of Karlstad, it was forced to agree to dissolution. In the same year, the Norwegian people elected Prince Carl of Denmark as king of Norway, who, as Haakon VII (1872–1957), became the progenitor of a new Norwegian royal dynasty.[4]

World War I and Independence

The Baltic region was relatively peaceful during World War I. While the British and the German fleets blocked each other after the Battle of Jutland, Russian warships undertook no larger campaigns. Russia concentrated on defending its capital, since 1914 renamed Petrograd. Although smaller naval battles took place in the vicinity of the Åland Islands, both the Russian and the German Baltic fleets remained relatively inactive at their bases in Kronstadt and Kiel, respectively. The Russian invasion of East Prussia in 1914 was successfully brought to a halt by the German Eighth Army, and in a rollback, German troops occupied Courland and Lithuania, including Kaunas and Vilnius. The Germans viewed the outbreak of the February Revolution of 1917 in Petrograd as interested observers. The German military high command permitted Vladimir Lenin (1870–1924) to cross German territory on his way to Finland Station in Petrograd. The revolution would permanently change the power relationships in the former provinces of the czar's empire. Various coalitions of forces and interests battled for control. On the one hand, the Finns, Estonians, Latvians, Lithuanians, and Poles wanted to throw off Russian rule, while the various Russian revolutionary and Marxist groups throughout the region agitated for world revolution. And then there were the old elites in Russia and the Baltic region, who together with Western Allies and German occupiers attempted to restore the status quo as it existed prior to World War I. What mattered to the Western powers was to support their old Russian allies, and to stem the spread of the revolutionary movement. In their occupation zones, the Germans, under the command of General Paul von Hindenburg (1847–1934), attempted to create vassal states in which the non-German populations—Lithuanians, Latvians, Poles, Russians, White Russians, Tatars, and Jews—would serve the interests of the German Reich.[5]

But the Bolsheviks and their supporters beat them to it, taking power first in Latvia, then temporarily in Estonia, and, in January 1918, in Helsinki and southern Finland as well. Finland and Estonia declared their independence on December 6, 1917, and February 24, 1918, respectively. At the same time, the German army, coming from Riga, conquered Latvia and Estonia and approached the Finnish border. Here, a Russian government-in-exile of the Whites had established itself in the Finnish northwest around Vaasa, while Finnish government troops under Carl Gustaf Emil Mannerheim (1867–1951) successfully fought alongside the German Baltic division for control over the south of Finland. Finland's independence from Russia could no longer be denied. However, German influence grew and led to the election of a Finnish king from the Hohenzollern dynastic circle. Lithuania, which was under German rule, declared its independence on February 16, 1918, and offered the crown to German Prince Wilhelm von Urach; however, the

German military government refused to recognize him as King Min-daugas II, and in Finland, Friedrich Karl von Hessen's ascent to the throne was to be short-lived. The republicans prevailed, and the new republican constitution of June 21, 1919, gave Finland the trappings of a stable democratic state.[6]

In accordance with the Treaty of Brest-Litovsk, signed in March 1918, the Baltic countries remained in Germany's sphere of influence, although Soviet troops took large portions of these territories after the German November Revolution. In Lithuania and Latvia, local Bolsheviks and revolutionaries joined together, constituting the countries as Soviet republics. Large portions of Estonia also came under Bolshevik rule. This alarming situation led to the involvement of the victorious powers in the war, especially Great Britain, which supported the Estonian troops under General Johan Laidoner (1884–1953) in repelling the Soviet advances. Lithuania was also liberated from the Bolsheviks, while Latvia at one point had three rival governments—a nationalist government, one friendly to Germany, and another allied with the Soviet Union. But here, too, the nationalist government was able to drive out Soviet troops with German and Estonian support. The nationalist Latvian government, however, soon found itself under invasion by the White forces in the Baltic region under General Bermondt-Avalov (1877–1974), which threatened the territorial integrity of Latvia.[7]

In the end, neither Germany nor Russia was able to maintain its influence in the eastern Baltic region. States proclaimed their independence and then concluded peace treaties with Soviet Russia. Estonia and Latvia agreed to draw their borders according to where the majority of the respective nationalities were located. On October 14, 1920, Finland and Soviet Russia concluded a peace treaty in which Finland received a land corridor from Petsamo to the Arctic Sea, which brought it as close as thirty kilometers from Petrograd. In the southern Baltic region, the Treaty of Versailles ceded a corridor through West Prussia to recently resurrected Poland that connected it to the Baltic. This was when Danzig became an independent, free city. In the east, Poland at first recognized Vilnius as the capital of Lithuania, but then occupied it and declared it a Polish city. Kaunas subsequently took on the functions of a capital; Lithuanian bands then conquered the Memel territory and integrated it into the Lithuanian state. Other territorial disputes were to be resolved by plebiscite. One such dispute concerned Schleswig, where the border between Denmark and Germany was redrawn—but not the East Karelian border between Finland and Russia.

Another disputed area was the Åland Islands, where a popular movement demanded annexation to Sweden. A Swedish invasion escalated the issue, forcing Finland to bring the matter before the League of Nations. The compromise ceded the Åland Islands to Finland, but in return it had to guarantee that Swedish would remain an official language and that the islands would be demilitarized.[8]

But cooperative initiatives were also undertaken among the successor states to the Russian Empire. As early as 1917, the liberal Estonian politician Jaan Tõnisson had been talking about forming a Baltoscandian Confederation, a union of 30 million people that would stabilize the Baltic region. But neither Denmark nor Norway could imagine such a Baltic alliance, and the Swedes were not interested in giving up their highly profitable neutrality. Finland's foreign minister, Rudolf Holsti (1881–1945), revived the idea in 1920, when he invited representatives of Estonia, Latvia, Lithuania, and Poland to a conference in Helsinki, and during its second session presented plans for a "Baltic League." However, after Vilnius was occupied in a Polish raid, and the Vatican recognized the city as part of Poland, no further joint actions were undertaken because, among other things, Sweden and Poland did not share the same interests. Finland increasingly flirted with Swedish-style neutrality, whereas Estonia and Latvia concluded a defense pact in 1923 and made political overtures to Lithuania.[9]

Internal Politics

Because of its autonomous status and suffrage reforms, a democratic state was created in Finland after a brief transition. Estonia, Latvia, Lithuania, and Poland, on the other hand, had to invent completely new political, economic, and even cultural structures. The elaboration of democratic constitutions was constantly impeded by changing majorities in parliament and extraparliamentary actions, including shows of force on the street. As a result, these states tended toward instability. As early as 1920, a constitution came into effect in Estonia that provided for a parliament to be elected every three years by all citizens voting by secret ballot. The prime minister was also head of state. In the beginning, the Social Democratic and Socialist Parties received the most votes, and Juhan Kukk (1885–1942) became prime minister. In the following election (1923) the conservative parties gained the majority and the conservative momentum increased, especially after the (illegal) Communist Party attempted a putsch in 1924 and was subsequently discredited. The conservative camp increasingly gained the upper hand. The right wing won the 1934 elections, with Prime Minister Konstantin Päts (1874–1956) and General Johan Laidoner staging a coup that nullified the Estonian parliament. Päts was now free to rule by decree.

In Latvia, proportional representation and the lack of major political parties meant that governments changed constantly and were always dependent on new and generally unstable coalitions. As a result, Kārlis Ulmanis (1877–1942), who had been prime minister for many years, used the opportunity, like Päts, to dissolve parliament. His stated justification was the danger from the right. As a result, the parties no longer had any room to maneuver, and in fact many of their members were simply arrested. In Lithuania, democratic institutions lasted only until 1926, with the Lithuanians mainly electing Social Democrats, the Lithuanian Popular Peasants' Union, and Christian Democrats to parliament. A military coup that year installed Antanas Smetona (1874–1944) as president, a position that he had held in 1919 as first president of Lithuania. Augustinas Voldemaras (1883–1942) became prime minister and ruled Lithuania with an authoritarian hand until he was deposed by the president, who subsequently ruled alone. In this, Smetona was supported by the Nationalist Party (Tautininkai), which he had founded.[10]

Conditions in Poland were similarly unstable until Józef Piłsudski (1867–1935), exploiting the general distrust in the parties, led a coup in 1926 with the support of the unions. Parliamentary government (sejmokracja), which many considered incompetent, was to undergo "sanation" (sanacja). Although the parliamentary system remained formally intact, the power of the parties was greatly reduced. Just prior to the 1930 elections, the members of the political opposition were arrested and Piłsudski claimed victory—whereupon he expanded the prerogatives of his office and changed the constitution, which by his death in 1935 was essentially tailored to his person. Piłsudski's "educational dictatorship," which mixed Polish nationalism (to the detriment of other nationalities) with socialist elements, was continued after his death by the so-called colonels' regimes. The resultant internal political paralysis made Poland, like the other Baltic states, easy prey for Germany and the Soviet Union. Unresolved economic and social problems paved the way for authoritarian regimes, whose policies stymied progress for years.

As a result, the achievement of independence in the Baltic and central European states after World War I is often touted as a glorious success, but that view inadequately reflects the realities on the ground. The examples of Denmark, Norway, and Sweden demonstrate that the reforms could have gone in another direction; because of their neutrality they were the real victors in World War I. During the war, these countries had profited enormously by supplying Germany and Austria as well as Great Britain and France with important war matériel, such as grain and timber products. But economic prosperity does not necessarily equate with political stability, although none of these countries experienced anything approaching civil war. On the contrary, in both Denmark and Sweden power shifted from royal prerogative to parliamentary decision making and finally to the rise to power of social democrats and socialists—without the form of government ever changing. In 1920, in Denmark, the Venstre Party, which had strong peasant support, and the Social Democratic Party held the balance of power, but in 1924 the Social Democrats took the helm. Thereafter, a succession of minority governments ruled the country.[11]

In Sweden, the socialists attained a ministerial position for the first time in a coalition government in 1917, and, in 1920, Hjalmar Branting (1860–1925) was elected the first Social Democratic prime minister. No clear majorities existed that might have decided the long-term conflict between the bourgeois and leftist parties. As a result, governments changed rapidly.[12] The growth of the labor movement was largely the work of the unions and the increasingly strong cooperatives. Originally organizations meant to provide a vehicle for economic self-help, the cooperatives came to represent a way of doing business based on mutuality, independent of the capitalist system. In this sense, the labor movement promoted the cooperatives as a way of overcoming capitalism.[13]

There were certainly foreign policy disagreements. For example, while Sweden and Finland contested the Åland Islands and took the matter to the League of Nations, Norway laid claim to Spitsbergen. But in 1920, the League of Nations allowed the Soviet Union to continue mining operations there. To this day, Norway and Russia continue to wrangle over legal interpretations, such as those involving Norwegian environmental laws. And from Spitsbergen, Norway sought to lay claim to the coast of Greenland, which provoked tensions with Denmark. But in 1933 Oslo recognized the decision of the International Court of Justice in Denmark's favor.

The Nordic countries also differed from those in the Baltic region in terms of threat potential. With their historical memory of conflict with their Russian neighbor, Sweden and especially Finland favored a policy of armed neutrality, whereas Norway and Denmark felt less threatened. Only when Hitler came to power in Germany were all of these countries moved to coordinate their foreign policy, although they all failed in the end, save for Sweden, to protect themselves from German or Soviet invasion.

In terms of internal politics, Norway, Sweden, and Finland elected to follow prohibitionist policies much like those in effect in the United States. In 1919, Norway and Finland banned the production and sale of alcohol, while Sweden, where a ban on alcohol was defeated in a referendum, chose to ration alcoholic beverages. Because, as in the United States, alcohol consumption failed to decrease, largely because of bootlegging and illegal stills, Norway by the end of the 1920s adopted the Swedish system of a state alcohol monopoly with very high prices, and Finland followed suit in the early 1930s. Only Denmark continued with more relaxed policies toward alcohol consumption.

Public health programs were another area that garnered attention during the economic depression of the 1930s. In 1933, for example, the Swedish Social Democrats and the Peasant Party reached a historic compromise that linked protectionist pricing for agricultural products with social welfare policies and job creation. This led to the *folkhem* (people's home) policies of Social Democratic prime minister Per Albin Hansson (1885–1946), which combined older philanthropic concepts with nationalistic models, such as the German *Volksgemeinschaft* (people's community), which the Nazis would later use to their own ends. The leap from the social democratic ideal of a "people's home," comprising a family of good people in a good state, to the exclusion of "unhealthy social elements" was not a great one. The need for racial hygiene was generally accepted in parliament—as in society as a whole—because it seemed to make plausible a connection between criminality and alcoholism, among other things, and genetic degeneration. Social scientists and politicians Gunnar Myrdal (1898–1987) and his wife Alva (1902–1986) played a significant role in the 1930s in the Swedish eugenics movement, which culminated in sterilization laws during the Hanssen administration, that allowed physicians to sterilize individuals against their will.[14]

The political situation evolved very differently along the southern Baltic. Here, a revolt by sailors in Kiel helped bring about the end of the German Empire, and with it a change from a monarchical to a republican form of government. In November 1918, workers' and soldiers' councils ruled almost everywhere along the coast, and in the 1919 elections, social democrats emerged victorious throughout the region. On the left, in addition to large majorities for the Social Democratic Party (SPD), the Independent Social Democratic Party (USPD) and the Communist Party (KPD) won small percentages of votes. On the other side were the liberal German Democratic Party (DPP) and the German People's Party (DVP), whose success varied greatly from region to region. The right wing was represented by the German National People's Party (DNVP). The most recent Prussian constitution had given the provinces—and therefore Schleswig-Holstein, Pomerania, West Prussia, and East Prussia—relative autonomy. The election results in the provincial parliaments differed widely. Despite significant losses, the election of 1921 left the SPD as the dominant party in Schleswig-Holstein, although the DNVP and DVP made considerable gains. In the following years, middle-class and peasant voters began to move to the right of the political center.[15]

In Pomerania, the DNVP had received the most votes as early as 1921, and it kept its leading position until the end of the Weimar Republic. Its fortunes were similar in West Prussia, whereas in East Prussia the SPD was not outpolled by the DNVP until 1925. The situation in Mecklenburg was idiosyncratic. The grand duke went into exile in Denmark, where he abdicated. This paved the way for an entirely new order. The new government, formed by the SPD, DDP, and USPD under the leadership of former Reichstag parliamentarian Hugo Wendorff (1864–1945) (DDP), dissolved the noble assembly of estates and abolished the

police powers of the manorial landowners. Their estates, however, remained untouched, and even the former grand duke was given much
of his property in a resignation agreement.

In elections for the constitutional parliament, the SPD, which carried 47.9 percent of the votes, entered into a coalition with the DDP.
Wendorff at first retained his position as prime minister; he was succeeded by the Social Democrat Johannes Stelling (1877–1933). In addition to basic free speech and association rights, the new constitution
established the separation of church and state, guaranteed universal suffrage, and mandated compulsory and free education. In addition, landless citizens were favored in any settlement projects. The conservative
parties, such as the DNVP and DDP, were completely opposed to this
latter provision, as was the Landbund, which represented the interests
of owners and renters of manors. In any case, because the civil servants
of the grand duchy were still in office, and because many of the intended
reforms failed and the treasury often lacked sufficient funds, there was
little trust in the new political regime. As a result, the SPD experienced
catastrophic losses in 1924, which led to a DNVP-DDP government
under Joachim Freiherr von Brandenstein (1864–1941). Even the Communist Party emerged strengthened from the elections. However, as everywhere in Germany, a certain economic and political stability began
to be felt between 1926 and 1929, which brought the SPD-DDP coalition back to power under Paul Schröder (1875–1932).[16]

Agrarian Reforms

Agrarian reforms were on the agenda in most of the Baltic countries
after World War I. Problems left unsettled from the abolition of serfdom
were to be resolved. At the same time, the new states were intent on
gaining the loyalty of their citizenry by promising land. And it was obvious that the privileges of the former ruling classes could not be spared
in the process. Even in Denmark, land reform prevailed, with large
manor farms confiscated and distributed to former peasants. The Venstre Party, which represented the interests of the peasantry, had worked
hard for these reforms. As a result, the amount of arable land under
cultivation increased steadily into the 1930s, when more than two-
thirds of the land was used for agriculture.

In 1918, Finland finally enacted legislation that enabled the cotters to acquire their land. The state underwrote this process with credits. Another piece of colonization legislation, enacted in 1922, enabled the state to take private land by eminent domain for settlement purposes. State-owned lands were also made available. Over the course of the 1920s and 1930s, the cotter problem lost salience because many had by then become landowners.

Large-scale social upheavals took place in Estonia, Latvia, and Lithuania. A new Estonian land ordinance of October 1919 created a state land reserve, which received all properties formerly belonging to the crown, the aristocracy, the church, and other corporate entities. Only cities, communities, and benevolent and educational institutions were permitted to retain their land. The new proprietors were given the land on hereditary leasehold. The state gave preference to veterans of the Estonian war of liberation and to the families of the fallen. A state agricultural bank was established to give poor settlers investment credits. This rapid transfer of land to Estonian nationals was crucial to the success of the program because Estonian peasants came to feel that they were fighting for their own land against the Soviets and Germans. In 1925 and 1926, new laws established peasant land ownership rights and mechanisms for compensating private landowners.[17]

In Latvia, land reform efforts and the creation of a land reserve began in earnest only after the end of the war of independence in 1920. Here, the former owners were granted the right to continue operating moderate-sized farmsteads, with no single owner having more than 50 hectares. Lithuania, on the other hand, had already impaneled a land reform commission in December 1918. In addition to large landholdings, all Russian colonists who had been given land by the Russian government in 1904 saw their land expropriated. At the same time, all volunteers in the Lithuanian army who owned less than 10 hectares were promised a large land allocation. In 1922, finally, the land reform laws stipulated the expropriation and subdivision of all private farms greater than 80 hectares in size. The Lithuanian land reforms gave priority to the landless and those with little land, which encouraged small holdings.

Land reforms lagged in Poland, largely because the parties were unable to agree on whether expropriations should or should not be compensated. It took until 1925 for Poland to enact permanent land laws, which, on the one hand, established a state land reserve consisting of former state and church lands along with private holdings in excess of 180 hectares, and, on the other, encouraged the voluntary subdivision of large farms.[18]

The land distribution program was enormous, at least in Estonia and Latvia. In Estonia, almost all large landholdings were expropriated, at least 50 percent of the entire area of the country. Between 1919 and 1936, 52,560 new farms were created on about 600,000 hectares. The state continued to cultivate 400 farms as model farms. At the same time, peasants were encouraged to settle on and cultivate new land. The reforms in Latvia, where 54,129 new farms and 9,754 new lease relationships were created, were similarly far-reaching. In addition, 50,539 farms already in existence were given additional land. Overall, about 144,000 peasant families benefited from land redistribution. In Lithuania, 249,170 hectares were distributed among 23,370 landless peasant families, and another 104,210 hectares went to Lithuanian army volunteers. The previous owners were allowed to keep 163,570 hectares, and 86,000 hectares were earmarked to enlarge extremely small farms. In Poland, on the other hand, little land was redistributed relative to the total arable land. Nonetheless, even here, 783,796 farms were enlarged during the interwar years.[19]

The reforms fundamentally changed the structure of land ownership in the Baltic states. By the end, there were hardly any landless peasants. The situation seems to have been most evenhanded in Estonia, where farms with 5–20 hectares (42.4 percent) and 20–50 hectares (34.8 percent) predominated and together represented 77.2 percent of the arable land. In Latvia, the situation was comparable, at least in terms of the farms with 5–20 hectares (44.6 percent); there were fewer larger farms, however. Even in Lithuania, small farms with 5–20 hectares predominated, whereas in Poland farms with less than 5 hectares predominated, and the large farms, that is, peasants having more than 50 hectares (0.6 percent), worked fully 40 percent of the arable land.[20]

The land reforms did not, however, automatically increase agricultural production. Initially, agricultural productivity dropped when the large farms were liquidated, eventually recovering over the course of the 1920s. This upswing in the Baltic countries was at least in part the result of the increase in the supply of land, whereas many small Polish peasants continued to eke out a subsistence living.

In Mecklenburg and Pomerania, the revolution completely changed the social and political power relationships on the land. The peasants, mostly hereditary leaseholders, and the cotters (*Büdner*) wanted to expand the area under cultivation, which was hindered by the agrarian structure dominated by the manorial farms. Accordingly, after the revolution of 1918 both the national government and the government of Mecklenburg-Schwerin turned their attention to settlement reforms, which were also meant to reform agricultural property relations. In Mecklenburg, state, not manorial, land was initially made available to expand peasant land. Only when land prices collapsed, in 1924–1925, did the large landowners begin to sell land to the settlement societies. But now the new settlers were increasingly less able to come up with the monies necessary to pay for buildings and inventory let alone for the land itself. Whereas in Mecklenburg-Schwerin, between 1919 and 1932, only 3,901 new positions were created in agriculture, the situation in Pomerania was more favorable. Here, new settlement was to have the additional benefit of increasing the German population in the German-Polish borderland. Thus, during the Weimar Republic, 8,734 agricultural positions were created on 130,858 hectares, which, at an average size of 100 hectares, was far larger than in Mecklenburg. Nonetheless, many of the settler villages were forced to abandon their cultivated land during the agrarian crisis of the late 1920s. Because of the seemingly hopeless situation, more than 7,000 villagers left the Pomeranian district of Köslin in 1928–1929 and tried their luck in the cities.[21]

Manorial landowners, who were severely shaken by the new political realities, tried to provide support for family members by making use of the already existent unions of noble families.[22] The economic crisis of 1927–1928, which was brought about by a decline in agricultural prices and led to a decline in land prices, marked a watershed. The easy credit of previous years and the current deterioration in sales turned into an existential crisis for many.

In the Baltic region during the interwar years, agriculture became a profound factor in people's emerging identities. Not only did Nobel Prize literature laureates such as Władysław Reymont (1867–1925), from

Poland, the Norwegian Knut Hamsun (1859–1952), and the Finn Frans Eemil Sillanpää (1888–1964) glorify rural life, but to the now increasingly citified population, the Nordic cult of the summer house among the coastal skerries came to symbolize a return to the simple life. The motives of summer vacationers were not inconsistent with the ideas of "people's health" or a "healthy country" that were being propagated on the right and the left of the political spectrum. In any case, these ideals stood in marked contrast to what were seen as the vices of city life. And they were given renewed currency by the Great Depression with its large-scale business failures, which caused massive unemployment and flight from the cities along with agricultural collapse. While the leaders of the peasantry in Denmark mobilized their followers to march on Copenhagen, in Finland the radical right wing Lapua Movement even attempted a coup. In contrast to the Baltic countries or Poland, where authoritarian regimes came to power, the Nordic democracies were by now so well entrenched that they were able to withstand the crisis. In Germany, on the other hand, the National Socialists (NSDAP) benefited from the radical right-wing peasant movements and the anti-Semitic and anti-capitalist Rural People's Movement in Schleswig-Holstein.[23]

The NSDAP used the social contradictions in the rural areas between farm workers, peasants, and landowners in Mecklenburg and Pomerania to paint themselves as the tribunes of the farm workers. The former farm worker Friedrich Hildebrandt (1898–1948), who since 1925 had been Gauleiter of Mecklenburg, represented the interests of the rural laboring population so convincingly that he fell into disfavor with Hitler. But the popularity of the Nazis rose, and in the provincial parliamentary elections of June 1932, the party took 49 percent of the votes and formed the government. Nazi propaganda in rural Pomerania garnered the party 48 percent of the vote in the 1932 election to the Reichstag, their second highest percentage after Schleswig-Holstein (an increase from 24.3 percent in 1930). The party increased its percentage to 56.3 percent in March 1933. It should be noted, however, that because of the Nazi terror campaign neither the KPD nor the SPD was able to take part in the election on an equal footing.

Industry and Crisis

Industrial development was uneven in the Baltic region during the interwar years. Whereas the Nordic countries experienced growth, especially during the 1920s, that catapulted them into the circle of leading industrial nations, the Baltic states initially underwent a deindustrialization process associated with their independence from the Russian Empire. Before World War I, large proportions of new industries were concentrated in St. Petersburg, Reval, and Riga. In Riga in 1913, almost 90,000 workers were employed in 372 factories, especially in the shipbuilding, machine building, rubber, chemistry, and textile industries. With the revolution and the loss of the Russian market, the large shipyards and other concerns, such as the Provodnik rubber factory, which employed several thousand, either closed or so reduced production that only a third of their former workforce remained on the job. In Estonia, the number of employees in the industrial sector decreased for the same reasons, from 46,000 (1913) to 31,000 (1921). As a result, industry was increasingly constrained and began to reduce its sights to servicing the needs of the local market.[24]

In the Nordic countries, by contrast, not only did per capita incomes increase, industrial production did as well. Most of the industries there concentrated on the export market and so were dependent on an open global economy and free trade. In the 1920s, as protectionist sentiments increased, the companies attempted to maintain their positions by entering into cartel agreements and forming monopolies. In so doing, they were able to make use of a long-standing tradition of cooperation. For example, the recovery in the Scandinavian paper and pulp industries was associated with a process of concentration that involved agreements over unitary marketing strategies. But even before Finnish independence, the newly founded Finnish cartel of cellulose manufacturers (Finncell) began to do the same. The Sulfite Pulp Suppliers (SPS) was a cartel founded in 1930 by Swedish companies, which soon included companies in Finland, Norway, Germany, Czechoslovakia, and the Memel region. In addition to Scandinavian wax paper and newsprint cartels, Scandinavian companies also controlled the international timber trade.

The most important companies in the electrical industry, ASEA and L. M. Ericsson (LME), attempted to increase their domestic market by buying other companies and entering into marketing agreements, with ASEA concentrating on the high-voltage sector and LME on the low-voltage sector. On the world market, international cartel agreements were also concluded with Siemens and AEG. The rise and fall of Ivar Kreuger's (1880–1932) match cartel was spectacular. He controlled three-quarters of global match production and was able to create a match monopoly in various countries through favorable loans. But the onset of the Great Depression meant that Kreuger was unable to refinance the loans, and the company collapsed in 1932.[25]

One political strategy much used to create jobs in Scandinavia during the global economic crisis was Keynesian deficit spending. Other strategies included limiting imports in order to favor domestic agriculture and instituting social welfare programs. In Denmark, the labor movement entered into an agreement with the peasantry, which was represented by the liberal Venstre Party, to cope with the economic crisis. While the liberals agreed to a ban on lockouts and to various job creation provisions, the Social Democratic government devalued the Danish krone and introduced protective tariffs in order to promote domestic agricultural exports. Among other things, bridge building projects were initiated, including the bridge over the Little Belt, which connects Jutland and the island of Funen.[26]

In Sweden, cooperative agreements between workers and employers led to a decrease in labor strikes. The Saltsjöbaden Agreement, in particular, which was signed between Swedish employers and the unions in 1938, created a spirit of trust that has been a hallmark of Swedish labor policy ever since.[27]

In the Baltic states, on the other hand, the first task was to rebuild industry, and only later to deal with the Depression. As a result, during the second half of the 1920s, the labor force in Estonia increased to 35,000. It continued to grow to 49,000 in 1936 and to almost 60,000 in 1939. The five most important industrial sectors were textile processing, food processing, the paper industry, the metal industry, and timber processing, which were later superseded by the chemical industry. Oil shale mining in the northeast of Estonia created a productive chemical industry. Nonetheless, Estonia remained an agricultural country that mainly exported foodstuffs, timber, flax, paper pulp, and textiles. Machinery, chemicals, raw cotton, and sugar continued to be imported from Germany or Great Britain, with Germany increasingly buying petroleum products to fuel rearmament.[28] Overall, products exported from the various Baltic countries were similar so that even Latvia, which had successfully rebuilt its industrial sector, exported mainly agricultural products. Lithuania, too, concentrated primarily on foodstuffs.[29]

Along the southern coast of the Baltic, Danzig had long ago lost its importance as a port city. Because it was cut off from its Polish hinterland as a result of its new status as a free city, it could do little to recover economically. In Pomerania and Mecklenburg, industry continued to feel the effects of the war. Industrial production fluctuated between recession and short-term stabilization during the entire Weimar period. Both raw materials and orders were in short supply. Germany had been divested of its merchant fleet to pay for war damages, and it was unclear how shipping and trade would now be conducted. The shipyards laid off workers and operated on reduced hours. In Stettin, which because of its role in building warships had experienced a real boom during World War I, the Vulcan shipyard decreased its workforce from 7,500 to 1,300 and ceased operation completely in 1928. After the Weimar Republic had regained some flexibility in its foreign policy as a result of the Locarno Agreement and the Dawes Plan, which readjusted Germany's reparations, the country once again began building smaller ships at the Neptun shipyard in Rostock. The shipyards in Stettin began to hire again and experienced a short-term boom in locomotive production. As a result, the Oderwerke alone was able to hire 2,400 workers. However, the Baltic shipyards were at a pronounced geographical disadvantage when compared to those in Hamburg and Bremen. In 1932, the Neptun shipyard declared bankruptcy. In Stettin, the Stoewer auto plant and Bernhard Stoewer's sewing machine and bicycle factories had to close as a result of the Great Depression. Only the fertilizer and chemical industry, which supplied Pomeranian agriculture, survived, although its production was half what it had been before World War I. The food industry, including large mills, sugar refineries, distilleries, and fish processing plants, also survived. During the middle of the 1920s, the textile, furniture, and paper industries even experienced something of an upswing.

In Mecklenburg, the small aircraft factory founded by Ernst Heinkel (1888–1958) in 1922, continued to expand. Orders came from the Soviet Union, and the speed records set by his He70 added to the company's prestige. Between 1929 and 1932, Heinkel increased its workforce from 360 employees to 1,000. Heinkel's success presaged Rostock's importance in Germany's later rearmament efforts.[30]

High levels of unemployment, which had been a not insignificant driving force behind the Nazis' electoral successes, also determined the party's initial policies. The Nazis had to deliver on employment. Although job creation programs had been tried earlier, including one that trained underemployed fishermen to knot carpets in Freest, near Greifswald, the majority of these initiatives had failed because of a lack of funding. The Nazis, however, initiated numerous and comprehensive job-creation programs—heedless of the state of the treasury. In Pomerania, for example, this included projects such as the creation of road, rail, and water networks, including the Autobahn that connected Berlin and Stettin, and the Rügen Causeway between Stralsund and the island of Rügen. The introduction of the draft and the labor service also relieved unemployment.

Germany's policy of rearmament also lured people from the farms to work for high wages in the armaments industry. One example was the expansion of the aircraft industry in Mecklenburg. In addition to Heinkel, which developed the He111 bomber in Rostock and increased the number of employees to 9,000 in 1938, Dornier began production in Wismar, and other aircraft builders opened factories in Ribnitz, Neubrandenburg, and Schwerin. At the Neptun shipyard, 4,000 workers were rehired to build U-boats and minesweepers. The population of Rostock grew from 93,530 in 1933 to 122,344 in 1939. Other cities in the region also attracted inhabitants, which in turn greatly stimulated the construction industry. Trade and services increased accordingly.

Societies and Minorities

The economies developed differently in the various Baltic countries, with some regions experiencing greater prosperity in the years between the world wars. In Scandinavia, for example, the standard of living generally rose despite fluctuations in growth. Homes began to be supplied with electricity, and many families could now afford telephones or radios. Tourism increased, and in Sweden the number of automobiles increased from 21,000 in 1920 to 249,000 in 1939. The rising tide of consumerism extended to culture, and Scandinavians avidly followed northern European movie stars such as Asta Nielsen (1881–1972), Greta Garbo (1905–1990), and Ingrid Bergman (1915–1982). Although Denmark had inherited a German minority in northern Schleswig, and Swedes and Finns argued over which language should be the national language of Finland, Scandinavia was generally spared conflicts among minorities. Matters took a different turn in the Baltic countries, where Estonians, Latvians, and Lithuanians replaced German and Polish-Lithuanian elites along with the Russian military and bureaucracy. Economic changes, such as land reform, also changed the social and ethnic structure of these countries. According to the Estonian census of 1934, for example, Estonians (88.2 percent) were joined by Russians (8.2 percent), Germans (1.5 percent), Swedes (0.7 percent), Jews (0.4 percent), and others (1 percent).[31] Germans and Jews tended to live in the cities, while Russians and Swedes were primarily concentrated in certain settlement areas.

While the Baltic German agrarian elite was weakened as a result of the 1919 land reform, land redistribution greatly benefited the Estonian peasants and subpeasants. From that point on, agriculture was controlled by Estonian families. The German middle class was to some extent still able to assert its economic clout in the cities. For example, in 1939 approximately a quarter of all factories were still in German hands. Nonetheless, the Estonian middle class now dominated the cities. While Estonians were now able to climb the ladder in industry, crafts, and trade, the bureaucracy, military, and educational system offered advancement as well. Most of the lawyers and physicians in the country were also Estonian. The constitution of 1920 granted Estonian women equal rights, which swelled membership in women's organizations. While women had been actively involved in the 1919 constitutional assembly, very few were subsequently elected to parliament.[32]

The constitution of 1920 also ensured that minorities obtained cultural autonomy in that it guaranteed school instruction in their mother tongues. In addition, a law guaranteeing minorities self-administration in cultural affairs also granted them the right to their own cultural

institutions. And these institutions were permitted to appoint their
own officials and teachers, a provision of which both the German and
Jewish minorities made use. Estonia differed from its neighboring
states in terms of the liberality of its cultural arrangements, although
the Latvians passed a law that permitted minorities to set up their
own educational facilities.[33] The Baltic Germans made use of this
provision as well, and they were able to gain official recognition of
their private German school, the Herder Institut, in Riga. As a result,
Baltic Germans such as Paul Schiemann (1874–1944) became involved
in minority rights issues at the European level.[34] In Latvia, nonetheless, where Russians, Jews, Germans, and White Russians made up almost a quarter of the population, minority cultural self-determination
began to come under attack in the 1920s and would intensify during
the 1930s.[35]

The spectrum of minorities in Lithuania was broad, where Jews outnumbered Poles, Russians, White Russians, Latvians, and Germans in
making 16 percent of the overall population. However, the Lithuanian
population was at a marked disadvantage because their educational institutions had been suppressed for so long, and they were unable to compete effectively with Jews, Poles, and Germans for jobs. As a result, the
Lithuanian government put a great deal of effort into education in the
cities, which sparked migration into urban areas. Because of this,
whereas in 1897 Lithuanians made up only 11.5 percent of the population of the cities, in the 1930s they constituted more than 50 percent—
even though the economy was too weak to provide them all with work.
This situation encouraged the development of a Lithuanian chauvinism
that was directed against the most successful national minority, the
Jews. Jewish officers served in the army and members of the Jewish
community also occupied high positions in the ministries. In 1919, the
Jewish minority had, in addition to educational and language rights,
also been given wide latitude in terms of religious observances, welfare, taxes, and state support, rights that the constitution gave to all
minorities only in 1922. However, almost all of these concessions were
eventually rescinded after the putsch of 1926. Jews were also overrepresented in the political opposition, including in the Communist Party
because, as under the Bolsheviks, they tended, as members of a formerly

persecuted minority, to be attracted to an ideology that promised equality.

The situation of the Polish elites was comparable; their properties were confiscated, while at the same time anti-Polish sentiment put them under increasing pressure after the occupation of Vilnius in 1920.

Literature and Architecture

During the interwar years, the Baltic region was culturally torn between the creation of national cultural identities and the integration of western and central European cultural norms. Writers and composers sought to hold onto, or find inspiration in, national (often folk) roots during a time of rapid change. But in the new Baltic states, such "indigenous" approaches first had to be created. At the same time, a small artistic elite proved itself ready to dispense completely with nationalism and to work in the musical or architectural trends that were developing internationally. In literature—as already mentioned—works that glorified rural life, such as Reymont's *The Peasants* (1924), Hamsun's *Growth of the Soil* (1920), and Sillanpää's *Meek Heritage* (1919), garnered Nobel prizes. These writings exemplify the former trend. By contrast, the Norwegian author Sigrid Undset (1882–1949) paved the way for realism with her *Kristin Lavransdatter,* a novel set in the Norwegian Middle Ages for which she was awarded the Nobel Prize as well. The Swedish poet Erik Axel Karlfeldt (1864–1931) also sought inspiration in the distant past for his neoromantic poems that drew themes from local legends and the Bible. In 1931, Karlfeldt was posthumously awarded the Nobel Prize for his work.

The Baltic states were also faced with the task of standardizing their written languages. In Estonia, the linguists Johannes Voldemar Veski (1873–1968) and Johannes Aavik (1880–1973) took the approach of borrowing from Finnish and coining neologisms. Estonian writers did not generally immerse themselves in folkish traditions; to the contrary, the Siuru circle founded by Marie Under (1883–1980) shocked contemporaries by exploring eroticism. In the 1930s, the "sorcerers" of the Arbujad group—Heiti Talvik (1904–1947), Betti Alver (1906–1989), and Bernard Kangro (1910–1994)—mixed neoclassicism and formalism in their poetry. By contrast, Estonian prose authors like Anton Hansen Tammsaare (1878–1940) realistically described life in the countryside and cities while probing the problems of human existence. Estonian-language theater came into its own; the Estonian Theater, in Tallinn (formerly Reval, its name was changed in 1918), was soon joined by other theaters both in that city and throughout the country. Over time, European operas and ballets became part of the repertoire alongside popular plays such as Hugo Raudsepp's (1883–1952) *Mikumärdi.*[36]

Naturally, the popularity of literature depended on how successfully schools taught their students. Literacy had already increased markedly during the second decade of the twentieth century, and by the time the Republic of Estonia was founded, a good 90 percent of the population could read. In the countryside, however, many students never went beyond elementary school, even in the 1930s. Training at the secondary level also improved, and as a result, the number of students at the University of Tartu stabilized at about 3000 after a rapid increase in the 1930s.

In Latvia, as early as 1920, the government of Kārlis Ulmanis undertook to develop the country's own authentic national culture. Education was at the center of his efforts, and schooling became mandatory for children between the ages of 8 and 14. One of the technical schools in Riga was transformed into the University of Latvia. Among other things, philologists laid the groundwork for a Baltic philology, publishing a Latvian grammar (*Latviešu gramatika*) in 1922, the four-volume Dictionary of the Latvian Language (*Latviešu valodas vārdnīca*) between 1923 and 1932, and an introduction to Baltic philology (*Ievads baltu filoloģijā*) in 1921 and 1936. These works helped to consolidate written and literary Latvian.[37]

Art schools and music academies were also founded. Influential writers began to return as soon as Latvia became independent. These included Jānis Pliekšāns (1865–1929), who wrote under the name Rainis, and his wife Elza Rozenberga (1865–1943), whose pseudonym was Aspazija, both of whom returned from exile in Switzerland in 1920. Both Rainis and Aspazija had belonged to the New Current group (*Jaunā strāva*) which, inspired by Marxism, attempted to awaken Latvians by describing realistically the plight of the Latvian peasantry.[38] In 1897, Rainis was deported to Russia as a result of his participation in strikes;

while in prison, he translated Goethe's *Faust* into Latvian. Upon his return to Latvia, he portrayed the 1905 revolution in the play *Uguns un nakts* (Fire and night), which was not, however, performed until 1911. By then he and his wife had had to leave the country again, but even in Switzerland they continued to write in Latvian.

After independence, Krišjānis Barons (1835–1923), who had been the first to collect and publish Latvian folk songs, was again celebrated as the father of Latvian literature. His disciple, Kārlis Skalbe (1879–1945), wrote poems full of love for the Latvian homeland and glorified the simple man. He also had opinions on the role that Latvian literature should play: "Even in those days, when the dream of a Latvian state hovered before us, the idea emerged that we must develop and support our own national culture."[39]

Lithuania was even more intent on creating a national identity. The leading proponent was Vincas Krėvė-Mickevičius (1882–1954), who transformed folk songs into literary Lithuanian and also glorified distant Lithuanian history in his plays. These efforts looked to pagan traditions as models of identity. Each year, the playwright Petras Vaičiūnas (1890–1959) produced a play on precisely such themes.

But perhaps the most important artistic medium was architecture, which made use of both national traditions and international models. In many places, attempts were made to redesign the cities to accommodate population growth. Toward the end of the nineteenth century, individualism and eclecticism had introduced a certain complexity into the urban spaces that necessitated the redesign or reconfiguration of the street plans. At the same time, leaders wanted public buildings, such as city halls, to make a statement.

For example, Sven Wallander (1890–1986) redesigned Stockholm's main street, Kungsgatan, with uniform buildings, which he intended to punctuate with Europe's first skyscrapers. However, these were never completed as they were deemed out of keeping with the rest of the cityscape. At the same time, architects worked on building housing cooperatives for the growing working population. Stylistically, architects increasingly modeled their work on styles found within the Scandinavian countries. Copenhagen city hall, built by Martin Nyrop (1849–1921) in 1905, became a model for the renaissance in brick architecture. Stockholm's city hall was finally opened in 1923, a time of growing prosperity;

it had been designed before World War I by Ragnar Östberg (1866–1945).
Its high tower made it visible from both land and sea, and it came to
symbolize the city, while the inside of the building is more reminiscent of a renaissance palace with its many galleries and halls. At almost the same time, the new Skandia Theater, designed by Gunnar
Asplund (1885–1940), and Ivar Tengbom's (1878–1968) Stockholm concert hall pointed the way toward the more practical approach exemplified by the New Objectivity, although the interiors remained largely
classicist. The state library, with its stringent geometries, marked the
end of neoclassicism.

The modernistic concepts of Le Corbusier (1887–1965) were emulated
in Sweden by Uno Åhrén (1897–1977), while in Denmark architects fell
under the influence of Bauhaus and the 1927 Stuttgart architectural exhibition of the Deutscher Werkbund (German Association of Craftsmen).
In the 1930s, functionalism was given new impetus by the preoccupa-
tion of the Myrdals with demography, as did the idea of the *folkhem*.
Swedish architects and builders came to believe that functionalism in
architecture could provide solutions to social problems. Numerous
buildings, such as the Student Union at the Royal Institute of Technology in Stockholm (Sven Markelius [1889–1972] and Uno Åhrén, 1930),
the concert hall in Helsingborg (Sven Markelius, 1932), and the National
Social Insurance Board building in Stockholm (Sigurd Lewerentz, 1932),
all reflect this spirit.

All of this new building was especially important to the housing
policies of the Social Democrats. They created several new housing
areas with both residential blocks with separate homes and blocks with
row houses. The most radical experiment was initiated by Alva Myrdal
and a group of professional women, which consisted of a collective house
built by Markelius where the problems of child care and housework
were resolved by the women collectively. It included a restaurant and
nursery school together with washing and cleaning personnel.[40]

Norwegian architects took their cue from what was going on in
Sweden. Independence from Sweden in 1905 triggered a wave of public
construction, much of which was built in an eclectic style. New buildings included not only the National Theater in Oslo, but also public
hospitals and sanatoriums. The new city hall, which was designed in

1930 by the architects Arnstein Arneberg and Markus Poulsson, was also designed to reflect the identity of the country and represented an amalgam of older romantic nationalist approaches and the new functionalism. Because of the German occupation of Norway, however, the city hall was not officially opened until 1950.

The Finnish architect Alvar Aalto (1898–1976) was especially influenced by Asplund and Markelius, although he had himself grown up imbued with nationalist romanticism and Nordic classicism. Aalto's transition to modernism is evidenced by his library in Viborg (Viipuri), the interior of which is characterized by natural materials, warm colors, and light lines. In 1941, Aalto accepted a visiting professorship at MIT, and during the postwar years he built important buildings in Finland and throughout Europe.

In Estonia, modern city planning began in 1913 when Eliel Saarinen (1873–1950) designed a Utopian plan for Tallinn, which was bursting at the seams at the time.[41] However, his plan was defeated by the spatial realities of the medieval city. A year earlier, Saarinen had built the Credit Bank, which, like Stockholm's new Kungsgatan, gave Tallinn's new business district a modern look. The Estonian state began to build its public buildings in the functionalist style, and the limestone that was used in construction gave this style a specifically Estonian character. This is evident in the firehouse in Tallinn, built by Herbert Johanson (1884–1964). Toward the end of the 1920s and into the 1930s, Lithuania, too, tried to lend its new capital city of Kaunas a metropolitan character with public buildings constructed in the functionalist style.

Very little in the way of new architecture was built in Riga immediately after World War I. During President Ulmanis's administration (after 1934) an attempt was made to minimize the German architectural presence, and as a result large-scale plans were made to redesign downtown Riga. Although the renowned architect Eižens Laube criticized this plan, the new finance ministry (1937–1939), which was designed by Aleksandrs Klinkāvs, and the monumental palace of justice (1936–1938) by Frīdrihs Skujiņš were in fact built. The new design for a Riga city hall complex was based on recent projects in Stockholm and Oslo and envisioned an oversized building with a triumphal arch and a 150-meter-high tower. However, when the Nazis invaded Latvia in 1941, they destroyed the city hall (along with the house of the Brother-hood of Blackheads and St. Peter's Church), which put an end to such planning and much else besides.[42]

In painting, a small group of Latvian expressionists centered around Jēkabs Kazaks (1895–1920) and Jāzeps Grosvalds (1891–1920) attempted to imbue Latvian painting with its own language. Latvian art devel-oped in many directions, with the state promoting a "folkish national art," which most of the leading artists rejected. The abstract paintings of Roman Suta (1896–1944) were influenced by the French Cubists and Russian constructivism. Gustavs Klucis (1895–1938), on the other hand, made a name for himself early on in the Russian constructivist avant-garde and later as a communist agitprop photographer. Mark Rothko (1903–1970), who came from a Jewish family in Dvinsk (Daugavpils), had already emigrated to America with his family in 1913, where he became a major force in modern art.[43]

Along the southern Baltic coast, architecture remained split between traditionalism and modernism; in Schleswig-Holstein in particular, buildings were characterized by a return to the traditional building ma-terials and styles of the *Heimat* and rejected historicism and eclecti-cism. Numerous homes, apartment buildings, businesses, and admin-istrative buildings were built in this provincial variant of the Hamburg brick renaissance. Because so little Bauhaus architecture had been built in northern Germany, buildings continued to be built in this "of-fending" style throughout the Nazi period. The architects remained the same, but they now built homes for Nazi organizations, including the Neulandhalle in the Adolf-Hitler-Koog (1936), as well as barracks and military facilities in the more acceptable brick style.[44]

Mecklenburg was more progressive in that functional public build-ings were constructed along Bauhaus lines, including schools, hospi-tals, and public housing. Resort architecture also reflected construc-tivist approaches, such as the casino built by the Rostock city building director Gustav Wilhelm Berringer in Mecklenburg.

The most important artist working in the region was undoubtedly the sculptor Ernst Barlach (1870–1938), who lived in Güstrow from 1910. Not only did he create his most renowned antiwar sculptures there, but in the 1910s and 1920s he also wrote influential dramas, such as *Der tote Tag* (The dead day), *Der arme Vetter* (The poor cousin), *Die*

Sintflut (The flood), and *Der blaue Boll* (Squire Blue Boll). In the 1920s, Barlach received numerous commissions to design memorials, such as those in Güstrow Cathedral (*Der Schwebende*), in Kiel (*Der Geistkämpfer*), and the group of figures in Magdeburg Cathedral. At first the Nazis courted him because his art appeared compatible with their blood-and-soil ideology. When he turned them down, however, the party began a defamation campaign against him. Several hundreds of his works were removed from museums as examples of "degenerate art," as were the *Geistkämpfer* and the Güstrow memorial, which was consigned to the smelter. Barlach died of a heart attack in 1938 in Rostock.

Music

In the world of music, the Baltic region was still mired in late romanticism. Carl Nielsen (1865–1931), whose compositions were written in the style of Brahms and Mozart, had a great influence on musical life in Denmark. This style, though it may be distinguished from German late romanticism, nonetheless rejected the modernism of the twentieth century, which limited its reception in central Europe. Nielsen's followers sought to find a third way between German late romanticism and the Viennese school. Some, such as Knudåge Riisager (1897–1974) aligned themselves with Stravinsky and Les Six, in Paris, while others, such as Finn Høffding (1899–1997) and Jørgen Bentzon (1897–1951), hewed more to the German classicism of composers such as Paul Hindemith (1895–1963).[45]

Undoubtedly, the most influential force in Swedish musical life was Wilhelm Stenhammar (1871–1927), who left an indelible mark on modern Swedish concert music as a pianist, conductor, composer, and chamber musician. Among other works, Stenhammar wrote violin romances, two piano concertos, and the Symphony No. 2 in G minor. His hymn *Sverige* was so popular that the public came to view it as something of a second national anthem. Stenhammar and Wilhelm Peterson-Berger (1867–1942) were proponents of a Scandinavian ideal, and, influenced by Grieg and Sibelius, they tried to create a Nordic music. Peterson-Berger composed the opera *Arnljot* for the Swedish national opera, and it was intended to transport listeners back to the time of Sweden's Christianization in about 1000. Probably the best-known

Swedish composer outside the country was Hugo Alfvén (1872–1960), whose Swedish rhapsodies became very popular. The symphonic composer Kurt Atterberg (1887–1974) was another prominent musician, whose works were directed by Nikisch, Furtwängler, and Toscanini. Some of his operas were first performed in Germany. The late romantic style, however, continued to predominate for several decades until the composers who began coming into their own in the 1930s developed a more neoclassical approach.[46]

In Finland, despite the heavy weight of tradition left by Sibelius, modern composers, such as Ernest Pingoud (1887–1942), Väinö Raitio (1891–1945), and Aarre Merikanto (1893–1958), began to make a name for themselves in the 1920s. Pingoud, a Russian émigré who had studied in Germany in 1906 and 1911, became a pioneer of modernism. Each year between 1918 and 1925 he performed an orchestral concert of his own works in Helsinki, which consisted of symphonic poems along with symphonies and other works. His ballet *La face d'une grande ville* was performed throughout Europe. Pingoud and his contemporaries were, however, confronted with a largely uncomprehending Finnish public, and this applied to potential patrons as well. The upper social classes, which one might have thought receptive to modernism, stopped attending, and only Yrjö Kilpinen (1892–1959) and Uuno Klami (1900–1961), who continued to compose in the tonal tradition, could claim any listenership at all for their song cycles and orchestral music.[47]

As part of its education program, the Estonian state founded musical institutions in Tallinn and Tartu. A new generation of Estonian composers was trained there; until then, most had received their training in St. Petersburg. One of the first graduates of the Tallinn Conservatory, Evald Aav (1900–1939), wrote the first Estonian opera, *Vikerlased* (The Vikings), which had its premiere in 1928 in the Estonia Theater.

The tradition of national song fests continued. These gatherings were held every five years, and the last one before the war (1938) saw almost 100,000 singers take part. In Riga, Jāzeps Vītols (1863–1948) wrote Latvian symphonic choral music, which was later augmented with instrumental and orchestral music. Foreign conductors were also influential, and as a result, the national opera, which was founded in October 1919, decided to open with a performance of *Tannhäuser*. Wagner

was an important force in the musical life of Riga until the end of the
1930s.[48] In the 1920s and 1930s, Latvian composers such as Alfrēds
Kalniņš (1879–1951) and his son Jānis Kalniņš (1904–2000) composed
numerous operas.[49]

In Lithuania, independence changed where music students studied.
Whereas the older generation had received its training in St. Petersburg,
Warsaw, and, like Čiurlionis, even in Leipzig, the new Lithuanian state
granted stipends for studies in Paris, Prague, and Berlin. Nonetheless,
the majority of composers, such as Juozas Gruodis (1884–1948), Kazimieras Viktoras Banaitis (1896–1963), and Balys Dvarionas (1904–1974),
continued to study in Leipzig, as did a large number of Lithuanian in-
strumentalists and singers. The new trends such as neoromanticism,
impressionism, and expressionism, which were represented in Leipzig
by Sigfrid Karg-Elert (1877–1933) among others, attracted students from
abroad. Other composers, such as Vladas Jakubėnas (1904–1976), studied
in the master classes given by Franz Schreker in Berlin, and they also
absorbed ideas from the likes of Arnold Schönberg and Paul Hindemith.
Upon their return, musicians who had studied in Leipzig and Berlin
did a great deal to enliven musical life in Lithuania, an influence that
did not, however, survive the world war.[50]

World War II

The world war destroyed the social fabric and economic prosperity that
had developed in the Baltic region despite the authoritarian regimes that
came to power in the 1930s. In terms of foreign policy (and militarily)
the countries along the Baltic could do little to counter the resurgent
losers in World War I: Germany and the Soviet Union. The Scandinavian states preferred a policy of neutrality, hoping that the international
community could guarantee their safety. But in the end, Denmark felt
the need to sign a nonaggression treaty with Germany. In the Baltic, a
common foreign policy was long hindered by differences in how the
countries related to the Soviet Union and Germany. Until the mid-
1930s, Estonia and Latvia viewed the Soviet Union as their main potential enemy; later, Germany would come to be viewed as an increasing
threat. At this point, the Latvian military would have been prepared
to fight alongside the Soviet Union against Germany. At the same time,

however, the antagonism between Lithuania and Poland remained and was even exacerbated by the German-Polish Nonaggression Pact of 1934. This led to an alliance among the Baltic states in which they agreed on a common foreign policy—but with no obligation to provide mutual military assistance. By the end of the 1930s, these states tended increasingly toward Germany, despite their stated neutrality, because they hoped by so doing to provide a check against Soviet influence.

Against this backdrop, the German-Soviet Nonaggression Pact, in August 1939, shocked the international community because this agreement between archenemies turned all foreign policy considerations on their head. On September 1, Germany attacked Poland, and by the middle of the month Soviet troops had occupied eastern Poland. In a secret supplementary protocol, the two powers had divided Poland and the Baltic into spheres of influence, and the Soviet Union saw an opportunity to regain the provinces that Russia had lost between 1918 and 1920. The strategy was simple. Finland and the Baltic states were offered mutual assistance pacts, which were contingent on the construction of Russian military bases along the coasts and of airstrips inland. In September and October of 1939, the Baltic states bowed to overwhelming Soviet pressure and ratified the agreements, which severely limited their ability to act on their own. At the same time, the Soviet Union and Germany concluded a border and friendship treaty that not only sanctioned the division of Poland, but also provided the German regime a propaganda tool that enabled it to offer to repatriate Germans living in the Baltic. Nazi functionaries agitated for the "Return to the Reich," and in October about 80,000 Germans left the Baltic for Germany. While the Estonian public gave voice to their naïve pleasure at finally having "gotten rid" of the Germans, most of them were settled not only in occupied Poland, in the so-called Warthegau, but also in West Prussia. The purpose of this settlement policy was to increase the percentage of Germans in Poland, thereby supplanting the Polish population.[51]

Only Finland rejected the Russian mutual assistance pact along with Soviet territorial demands. The consequence was the Winter War, in which the Soviet Union attempted to make good on its claims. The Finns put up stiff resistance in Karelia, but in March 1940 Soviet troops overwhelmed the vastly outnumbered Finnish forces, which had received no help from the Western powers. In the end, Finland had to cede Karelia along with Viborg to the Soviet Union and agree to a Russian base on the Hanko Peninsula in southwestern Finland at the entrance to the Gulf of Finland.

The German conquest of Denmark and Norway began in April 1940. The goal was to secure raw materials from Norway and Sweden, especially Swedish ores, for the German arms industry. The port of Narvik became strategically important because of the materials shipped through it. To better control Norway, the Germans simply conquered Denmark along with it. Denmark capitulated without offering much resistance, and in exchange for supplying foodstuffs was permitted a certain degree of autonomy that allowed the government to stay in office. The Norwegians, led by King Haakon VII, fought the invaders with the support of the Western Allies, but they were unable to prevail. The king and the government went into exile, and German Reichs-kommissar Josef Terboven (1898–1945) was installed as head of state. Vidkun Quisling (1887–1945) and the Norwegian Nasjonal Samling Party (National Gathering) collaborated with the Germans. From then on, Norwegian aluminum production was under direct German control, and heavy water began to be produced in anticipation of a German atomic bomb. Nazi Germany demanded that Norway supply raw materials, including iron ore, and metals such as aluminum, copper, and nickel as well as ferroalloys and minerals. In exchange, the Reich was to supply Norway with coal because Britain no longer shipped coal to Norway.[52]

Sweden bought its territorial integrity by supplying crucial war matériel, especially iron ore and ball bearings. It also placed its shipping capacity at the disposal of the German war economy. Because of its neutrality, many political refugees were able to find asylum there. The majority of the Danish Jews found refuge in Sweden, while in Norway the police arrested the Jews they found and handed them over to the German occupiers.

While the German Wehrmacht was conquering France in the summer of 1940, the Soviet Union created facts on the ground in the Baltic states. On June 14, the Red Army occupied Lithuania, and two days later Foreign Minister Vyacheslav Molotov (1890–1986) gave the ambassadors of Estonia and Latvia an ultimatum, which forced them to form Soviet-friendly governments and to allow Soviet troops free access. Once the Soviet troops were strengthened in Estonia, Stalin's envoy, Andrei Zhdanov (1896–1948), dictated to President Päts the composition of the new cabinet and demanded new elections. These elections were won by a newly formed left alliance under the leadership of the Communist Party, terrorist tactics having intimidated all potential opposition candidates. The new parliament proclaimed Soviet power in Estonia and expressed the "desire" to be admitted as a member republic of the USSR. Päts was forced to resign, and, like Laidoner and other military and political leaders of the former Estonian Republic, was deported to the Soviet Union and arrested. On August 6, the Supreme Soviet decreed the admission of Estonia as the sixteenth republic in the Soviet Union. Latvia and Lithuania, where total compliance had been achieved at an equally breathtaking pace, had previously "joined" the Soviet Union. Private property, banks, and industries were nationalized in all of the states.[53]

The new Estonian regime began with the forced collectivization of agriculture and increased peasant production quotas. All signs of resistance were severely punished. In addition to numerous executions, the new rulers deported about 19,000 persons between the summer of 1940 and the summer of 1941, half of them in June 1941 alone. These deportations had been ongoing since May in Moldova, the Ukraine, White Russia, Lithuania, and Latvia. "Counterrevolutionaries," former members of the military and security apparatus, landowners, entrepreneurs, clerics, and Polish refugees were removed from the eastern territories under Soviet occupation and taken to Siberia—that is, assuming that they survived the starvation and violence. Given these population losses—in Latvia 15,400 people were dragged off during the night of June 14 alone (out of a total of approximately 35,000 Latvians deported)—it is perhaps understandable that Wehrmacht soldiers would have been greeted as liberators when they marched into Riga on July 1.[54]

Almost at the same time, Lithuanian nationalists risked an uprising against the Red Army and the Soviet occupational administration. They used the opportunity afforded by the German invasion to settle scores with the Soviet system and its representatives. Exiled Lithuanians, in particular sympathizers with National Socialism who founded the Lithuanian Activist Front, urged the population to support the German army, while at the same time propagating anti-Semitism. Because the Soviet occupational administration contained a number of high-ranking Jews, they became the target of anti-Soviet propaganda. On June 22–23, 1941, the day that Germany attacked the Soviet Union, Lithuanian nationalists initiated a pogrom against the Jewish population of Kaunas. Systematic mass shootings conducted by the SS and Wehrmacht detachments took place from June to November, "turning the first six months of the German occupation (June to December) into the most murderous period in the modern history of the Baltic littoral."[55] Soviet war prisoners were also murdered, and during the first half year a good 90,000 Jews and 200,000 Soviet prisoners of war fell victim to the German occupation.[56] Furthermore, in November 1941, 5,000 Jews were transported by train from Breslau, Vienna, Munich, Berlin, and Frankfurt to Kaunas, where they were shot. This paved the way for the Nazi mass murder of Jews in occupied Poland, Lithuania, Latvia, and the Soviet Union.[57]

In Latvia, the German occupiers reported on October 15 that 30,025 Jews had been killed, and that the rest had been interned in the Riga ghetto. The German authorities and their Latvian helpers attributed these killings to the "spontaneous rage" of the Latvian population at the role played by Jews in the most recent deportations. This explanation conveniently ignored the fact that the June deportations from Latvia included about 5,000 Jews.

The small local political elites who had survived the first year of Soviet rule identified with the German occupation. In 1941, the Nazis established the so-called Reichskommissariat Ostland, which included the Baltic states and White Russia. Hinrich Lohse (1896–1964) was appointed Reichskommissar for the Ostland, and Latvian politicians led their own "local administrations" under him. The situation in Estonia was by far the most favorable to the indigenous population because Alfred Rosenberg (1893–1946), who was born in Reval and had been appointed head of the Reich Ministry for the Occupied Eastern Territories, believed that the Estonians had the greatest potential for being Germanized. This Germanization would supposedly be accomplished by German colonists, in particular by the resettlement of Baltic Germans who had earlier returned to Germany proper. These projects, however, were scuttled by the war. The hopes of the Nazis that their military machine would defeat the Soviets at Leningrad were dashed in September 1941, when a blockade lasting some 900 days stalled.

By June 1941, Finland had also gone to war against the Soviet Union, and the Finns reconquered Finnish territories and parts of East Karelia that had been ceded to Russia in 1940. To demonstrate their independence, however, Finland refused openly to support the German blockade of Leningrad. The German invasion of the Soviet Union ground to a halt in January 1943, by which time German personnel and war matériel shortages had become abundantly evident. The Germans then used intense pressure to recruit Estonian and Latvian men into the SS divisions.

However, despite anti-Soviet sentiments in Lithuania, the SS failed in its recruitment efforts. As a result, soldiers were mobilized in Latvia and Estonia in 1943. But a portion of the Estonian soldiers potentially available to the Germans for recruitment joined the Finnish army in their battle against the Red Army. The large-scale Soviet offensive in January initially forced the Germans to retreat to the Lake Peipus-Narva line, but at the same time this triggered further mobilization efforts in Estonia. Urged on by radio addresses from the last prime minister of the Republic of Estonia, Jüri Uluots (1890–1945), 38,000 men assembled under arms and attempted to prevent the Soviet occupation of Estonia. They were successful for about six months, but between the end of July and September 1944, the Red Army conquered one Estonian city after another.

In Latvia, about 140,000 Latvians along with the remnants of the Wehrmacht defended the northern part of Courland from the Red Army. But by the summer and fall of 1944, between 120,000 and 150,000 Latvians had fled west, and many eventually emigrated to North America.[58] Some went underground and fought as partisans against the occupation troops, as happened in Lithuania and Estonia as well.

To escape Soviet occupation, 70,000 Estonians fled across the Baltic to Sweden and Germany in late summer 1944. In Sweden in particular, Estonians and Latvians created a Baltic intellectual life in exile, founding newspapers and publishing houses. Most Lithuanians, on the other hand, hoped eventually to emigrate to the United States.

In the summer of 1944, Finland was still trying to halt the Russian invasion, but then used the opportunity to negotiate a separate peace with them. The Finns knew that they had the support of the Allies, who did not want Russia to expand its influence at the expense of Finland. In any case, at the armistice negotiations, in September 1944, Finland accepted the old borders of March 1940 and also had to give up the Petsamo corridor. In 1944, about 400,000 Finnish Karelians were again evacuated and were to be resettled to the west of the new border. The Soviets gave up their base on Hanko and agreed to a military base on the Porkkala Peninsula with fifty-year usage rights; the base was returned to Finland in 1956. After the armistice, the Finns joined the Allies and began to drive the Germans from Finnish Lapland toward Norway, where Norwegian troops with Allied support caught the Germans in a pincer. German troops did not, however, capitulate until May 8.

The Baltic states had no choice other than to return to the Soviet sphere of influence. This decision was forced on them by the large number of Soviet troops present in the newly formed Baltic military district, which also included Kaliningrad (the former Königsberg). Some of the countries also lost territory of their own. For example, Estonia was forced to give up territories east of the Narva River and south of Lake Peipus, and Latvia the Abrene district, which was incorporated into the Russian Soviet Federative Socialist Republic. Vilnius and the Memel district, on the other hand, were restored to Lithuania.

Larger shifts in borders occurred in the southern Baltic region. Here, the Red Army had, in January 1945, taken not only Warsaw, but also Tilsit, in East Prussia. In fact, during January it had penetrated as far as Eastern Pomerania. Danzig was defended until March; Königsberg held out until the beginning of April, by which time the city had been almost totally destroyed. The situation became increasingly chaotic as refugees were now streaming westward from all parts of East Prussia. The Red Army cut off part of the route along which the refugees were traveling, and only a brief halt in the Russian offensive allowed many of the refugees to flee by ship to Mecklenburg or Schleswig-Holstein. Whether and to what extent cities were destroyed depended largely on the resistance mounted by the German Wehrmacht. For example, in a number of cities, such as Rostock, Grevesmühlen, and Wismar, orders to destroy bridges were ignored. The Wehrmacht defended Stettin longer, and Friedland and Neubrandenburg until the Red Army overwhelmed their forces, which led to the widespread destruction of these cities. Greifswald was spared because the Wehrmacht there surrendered without a fight. By the end of April, Russian troops occupied Pomerania and Mecklenburg, where they were met by the British forces coming from the west. On May 2, 1945, the Wehrmacht capitulated in this region. On May 7, British field marshal Bernard Montgomery (1887–1976) and Russian marshal Konstantin Rokossovsky (1896–1968) entered Wismar in triumph.

All of the Baltic territories that had been controlled by the Wehrmacht during the war now came under Soviet rule, with the exception of Denmark and British-occupied Schleswig-Holstein. During the war, the Soviet Union had received assurances from the Western Allies that Poland would be shifted to the west at the expense of Germany. This was sanctioned by the Potsdam Conference, and as a result eastern East Prussia became part of the Soviet Union and western East Prussia along with Danzig, West Prussia, and Eastern Pomerania were placed under Polish administration. To the extent that the Germans had not already fled these areas, they were now forced to resettle in a much diminished and occupied Germany.

Mecklenburg, Western Pomerania, and Schleswig-Holstein all experienced massive influxes of refugees. As a result, during the postwar period, a total of about 1.2 million people had to be integrated into Schleswig-Holstein and approximately 900,000 into Mecklenburg and Western Pomerania. In addition, several hundreds of thousands of so-called displaced persons—forced laborers and prisoners of war along with former concentration camp inmates—were located in the region.[59]

Except for the 1944 armistice between Finland and Russia, which was ratified as a peace treaty in 1947, no general peace treaty was signed after World War II. The antagonism that had existed between Nazi Germany and the Soviet Union was soon transformed into a tense relationship between the Western Allies and the Soviet Union and its satellite states. To the extent that countries had a choice, they considered various options for creating alliances. For example, in May 1948, Swedish foreign minister Östen Undén (1886–1974) floated the idea of a Scandinavian defense union that would be independent of the great powers. This alliance never came into being because Sweden was not prepared to give up its neutrality, while Norway and Denmark believed that they could achieve such defense capabilities only with Western support. Given the choice between an alliance with neutral Sweden and membership in the North Atlantic Treaty Organization (NATO), Denmark and Norway opted for the latter.

Poland once again became a Baltic nation, receiving a coast line of about 400 kilometers. This did not, however, mean that it instantly became a maritime nation: the new inhabitants—all of whom came from the Russian-occupied districts of eastern Poland and were forced to settle along the coast—had no familiarity with the ways of the sea.

[CHAPTER NINE]

Sovietization versus Welfare States

Focus on Tallinn

As soon as the Red Army took Tallinn, in 1944, the Soviet Union did all it could to place its stamp on the Estonian capital. Streets and squares were renamed, street signs appeared in both Estonian and Russian, and the city was divided, in the Soviet manner, into districts called *rayons*. The Russians planned a governmental quarter in the Stalinist style, but these plans were never implemented after the dictator's death in 1953. Instead, prefabricated housing blocks were built in the suburbs of Tallinn, which offered living quarters to Russians and Estonians who otherwise would have found lodgings hard to find in the older parts of the city. Soon, the charms of the decaying medieval old city were recognized as potential tourist draws. Once ferry service connected Tallinn with Helsinki in 1965, the number of Western visitors grew to more than 90,000 by the end of the 1970s. Finnish companies even built a luxury hotel to Western standards, the Viru, for Finnish "vodka tourists." The beginnings of a cultural life also returned. Artists and architects were for the first time able to exhibit their unconventional works and ideas.

The 1980 Olympic sailing competition held off the coast of Tallinn was meant to demonstrate the city's attractiveness as a gateway to the West, although many nations boycotted the games in response to the Soviet invasion of Afghanistan. At the same time, mass protests by young Estonians over the cancellation of a concert were directed against the growing Russian population, whom many felt were overrunning the country. In 1987, Tallinn was the site of a large demonstration on the forty-eighth anniversary of the Hitler-Stalin pact. A year later, the Estonian song festival that was held in an open-air theater attracted an audience of 300,000. It inaugurated the so-called Singing Revolution in the Baltic republics.[1]

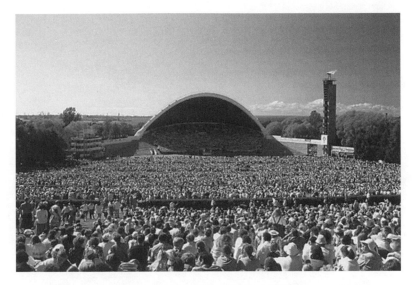

Figure 9. Estonian Song Festival in Tallinn

The Sovietization of the Baltic Region

During the Cold War, the differences between the Nordic countries and the regions along the eastern and southeastern coast of the Baltic, which had been evident as early as the 1920s and 1930s, began to deepen. While Sweden and Denmark leveraged their economic successes of the interwar years and used their experience to create a welfare state, the formerly independent Baltic states were forcibly integrated into the USSR, and Poland and occupied East Germany came under Soviet control. Finland was forced to tilt toward the Soviet Union, while Schleswig-Holstein took part in the West German economic miracle after the British occupation came to an end. As a result, the political climate in the Baltic region was largely determined by the Soviet Union and the response by the Scandinavians to Soviet influence, which reflected the intensifying conflict between East and West.

The Sovietization of the Baltic region took many forms, depending on how the Soviets and their representatives responded to local circumstances. But regardless, the structures and changing political directions followed closely the decisions of the Central Committee of the Communist Party of the Soviet Union, which were communicated by

Map 9. The Baltic region in 1948

local governors and executed largely by the military and the secret
police. While the new Baltic Socialist Soviet Republics were integrated relatively easily, the Russians first had to establish rule by the
Communist Party, both in Poland and throughout the Soviet occupation zone. In Poland, as elsewhere in the eastern, central, and southern
European countries that were liberated and dominated by the Soviet
Union, the mechanism by which this was accomplished was the so-
called government of national unity. The Communist Party assumed
key positions in these governments, including the interior ministry,
and made it difficult for competing parties to take part in elections. In
1948, the Polish Workers' Party (Polska Partia Robotnicza) was forcibly
united with the Polish Socialist Party (Polska Partia Socjalistyczna) to
form the Polish United Workers Party (Polska Zjednoczona Partia Ro-

botnicza). After "nationalist elements," such as Władysław Gomułka (1905–1982), were cleansed from the party, the new hard-line Stalinist rulers Bolesław Bierut (1892–1956) and Jakub Berman (1901–1984) ensured that Soviet directives would be followed. But the upheaval that followed Stalin's death also called into question the rule of the Polish Stalinists. In February 1956, Bierut heard Nikita Khrushchev's (1894–1971) "secret speech" at the twentieth party congress, in which he denounced Stalin's crimes. Bierut died in Moscow the next month under circumstances that have never been clarified. In June, workers in Poznań (Posen) went on strike and held demonstrations. Although the army brutally suppressed the protests—fifty-six died in the ensuing fights—the disturbances led to a power struggle within the party leadership. Gomułka, who had just recently been released from house arrest, gave a speech before the party central committee in which he demanded wide-ranging democratization. The Communist leadership in the Soviet Union gave its consent to this change in leadership. This allowed Gomułka to pacify the population by promising reforms such as slowing down the industrialization process, lifting agricultural quotas, and putting an end to collectivization. But the heavy industrialization that had been pushed by the Communists favored industry to the exclusion of everything else. The agricultural sector, smaller industries, and housing were ignored, which resulted in food and housing shortages and trigged resentment among the people. Censorship was briefly lifted, but even after it was reintroduced the Polish people enjoyed much greater freedom in relations with the West and Western culture than those in other Eastern bloc countries.[2]

In the Soviet-occupied part of Germany, three so-called initiative groups, which were led by Communist Party functionaries Walter Ulbricht (1883–1973), Anton Ackermann (1905–1973), and Gustav Sobottka (1886–1953), who answered to the Soviet Military Administration of Germany (SMAD) and were or had been trained in Moscow, were given the task of creating a new political and administrative structure. At the end of June 1945, a new government for Mecklenburg and Western Pomerania was installed under Wilhelm Höcker (1886–1955), a member of the SPD who before 1933 had been president and vice president of the provincial parliament. The position of first deputy was filled by

Hans Warnke (1896–1984), who until 1933 had been head of the KPD district leadership and chairman of the KPD faction in the Mecklenburg parliament. In addition to KPD functionary Gottfried Grünberg (1899–1985), other, initially nonpartisan politicians such as former mayor of Güstrow Heinrich Heydemann (1881–1973) and former minister for education and culture Richard Moeller entered the government. Some of these politicians later became members of the Christian Democratic Union, or CDU. The name of the new political subentity was contested because the government wanted Mecklenburg–Western Pomerania to remain a *"Land"* (i.e., state), while the SMAD wanted to call it a "province" and used this term in its orders. But after March 1, 1947, the SMAD decreed that the name "Western Pomerania," which unlike formerly independent Mecklenburg had been a part of Prussia since 1815, be expunged because the Allied Control Council (i.e., the Four Powers) had ordered that the state of Prussia be dissolved, citing its history of "militarism and reaction."

Once in the government, the KPD members went about expanding their spheres of authority and powers. For example, Hans Warnke, who was already first vice president and had control over the Department of the Interior with responsibility for the police and administration, also assumed control of the personnel department and the departments for land reform, propaganda, justice, and the administration of state-owned companies. With these competencies, Warnke was able to control the further development of the country, while the head of the government increasingly became little more than a figurehead. Furthermore, the SMAD discussed routine problems with the KPD leadership before delivering instructions to the government.

By its decree of June 10, 1945, the SMAD had consented to the founding of antifascist and democratic parties in the Soviet occupation zone, while at the same time retaining the right of control over the organizations so created. The SPD, CDU, and the liberal LDP thus joined the KPD as legal parties. But in Schwerin, for example, the local military administration rejected the SPD's choice of first chairman, Albert Schulz (1895–1974), who had been an active and popular SPD functionary in Rostock before 1933. Significantly, they also rejected the city of Rostock as the seat of the party. But they did accept a second list of leaders that included Carl Moltmann (1884–1960) and Xaver Karl (1892–1980), both of whom were viewed as willing to make compromises. And in fact, on April 7, 1946, the SPD and KPD were united into a single party with the election of Moltmann and Kurt Bürger (1894–1951) of the KPD as coequal chairmen. Even though 25,000 to 30,000 SPD members either resigned or emigrated to West Germany as a result of this union, the new Socialist Unity Party of Germany (Sozialistische Einheitspartei Deutschlands, SED) now had a clear organizational advantage over all other parties. For example, of the 551 local CDU groups that had existed up to August 1946, the SMAD approved only 154 in order to prevent the CDU from competing on an equal footing in the upcoming local elections. The LDP, which was founded in January 1946, was kept from registering its local groups for the same reason. By contrast, mass organizations that supported the SED were encouraged. These included the Free German Trade Union Federation (Freier Deutscher Gewerkschafts- bund, FDGB), the Free German Youth (Freie Deutsche Jugend, FDJ), and Peasants Mutual Aid Association (Vereinigung der gegenseitigen Bau- ernhilfe, VdgB), into which were organized new peasants who had been settled on recently freed up agricultural land.

Local and provincial elections were meant to legitimize the SED's leadership claims, especially since local elections and elections to the constitutional conventions had already taken place in the American sector in May and June 1946. Because candidates could register only in those places where their parties were registered, the CDU competed in only 237 communities and the LDP in 65 in the local elections held on September 15, 1946. As a result, the SED claimed 69.9 percent of the vote. Unsurprisingly, the CDU came in with only 16.7 percent and the LDP with 10.5 percent. Although the CDU and LDP *together* elected more representatives than the SED in larger cities such as Schwerin, the SMAD ruled that the mayor of the city should come from the largest party—which was usually the SED. Despite overwhelming official backing, the SED won only 49.5 percent of the votes in the October 20, 1946, parliamentary elections, while the CDU took 34.1 percent and the LDP 12.5 percent. The SED was assured an absolute majority only after the Peasants Mutual Aid Association threw in its 3.9 percent of the vote. Until the dissolution of the province in 1952, the prime min- isters in the Soviet zone were all from the SED: Wilhelm Höcker, Kurt Bürger, and Bernhard Quandt (1903–1999).

Although the provincial parliament, in 1947, adopted a new constitution for Mecklenburg based on a united Germany and a parliamentary democracy, the SED largely purged the opposition, including within
the party, and set the party on a Stalinist course. The next provincial
elections were held in 1950 along with local elections and elections to
the People's Chamber of the German Democratic Republic (GDR),
which had been founded in 1949. In these elections, all parties were
forced to join the National Front of the German Democratic Republic,
which determined which parties would get how many seats—before
the elections even took place. The Mecklenburg parliamentary elections were contested by 44 SED candidates, along with 11 from the CDU
and 11 from the LDPD, the successor to the LDP. In addition, the SED
had founded two new allied parties, the National Democratic Party of
Germany (Nationaldemokratische Partei Deutschlands, NDPD) and the
Democratic Farmers' Party of Germany (Demokratische Bauernpartei
Deutschlands, DBD), and five or six of their representatives ran as well.
In addition, the mass organizations competed for another three seats.
However, the history of Mecklenburg as a province ended three years
later, when the GDR leadership did away with provinces altogether and
created the districts of Schwerin, Rostock, and Neubrandenburg in the
north. This reorganization along Soviet lines reflected the centraliza-
tion of the GDR in that all decisions were henceforth to be made in the
Politburo and in the Central Committee of the SED in Berlin.[3]

In the Baltic Soviet republics, the Communists did not even bother
taking other parties into account. Despite some anti-Soviet resistance,
their dictatorship was airtight.[4] Although their membership was small,
the Communist parties in these countries grew rapidly as a result of
Russian "imports." Native Estonians, Latvians, and Lithuanians who
had grown up in Russia and joined the Communist Party of the Soviet
Union were sent to the new Soviet republics along with Russian members of the party for the purpose of building party structures in those
countries. The first secretary of the party was always an Estonian, Latvian, or Lithuanian, but the second secretary was always a Russian.
The first secretary of the Estonian Communist Party, Nikolai Karotamm
(1901–1969), however, was accused of bourgeois-nationalist tendencies
in 1950, and he was purged—a fate that awaited other politicians in Soviet satellite states, including Gomułka. He was replaced by Johannes

(Ivan) Käbin (1905–1999) who, though born in Estonia, had returned to the country with the Soviet occupiers. Even after the relative thaw after Stalin's death, there was little room for more independent politics in the Baltic republics. Eduards Berklāvs (1914–2004), in Riga, came to understand this when he spoke against the increasing influence of Russia and the suppression of the Latvian language. In a power struggle he lost to Soviet-trained Arvīds Pelše (1899–1983), Berklāvs and hundreds of his supporters were purged from the party. Pelše made sure that the Latvian Communist Party toed the Russian line. Lithuania was the only country that developed a modicum of independence. There, Communist Party head Antanas Sniečkus (1903–1974) was somehow able to survive the twists and turns of Kremlin politics from 1936 into the 1960s and 1970s and create some small space for independent action. The Communist parties grew rapidly in all three states because party membership promised better careers and earning potential to new university graduates.[5]

Although Soviet influence was not as direct as in the Baltic states, Russia also had a pronounced effect on Finland, whose politicians paid close attention to Russian interests. Not satisfied with their military base on the Porkkala Peninsula, to the west of Helsinki, the Soviet Union forced Finland to sign a friendship, cooperation, and assistance pact in 1948. In it, Finland gave assurances that it would not allow its territory to be used by others for attacks on the Soviet Union, and should Finland's own defense capabilities prove inadequate, it would accept Soviet "assistance." Ratification of the pact gave Finland greater room to maneuver internally such that Finnish president Juho Kusti Paasikivi (1870–1956) was able to force the Communists out of the government under the pretext of a purported coup attempt. A year earlier, the Soviet Union had forced Finland, like Poland, to reject Marshall Plan recovery assistance, a program that gave Denmark $276 million, Norway $254 million, and Sweden $107 million. Paasikivi's successor, Urho Kekkonen (1900–1986), convinced the Soviet Union that Finland was an indispensable ally, which gave the country even more room to maneuver. As a result, Finland was able to join the United Nations in 1955, and the Nordic Council, which Iceland, Denmark, Norway, and Sweden had founded in 1952. As an intermediary between East and West during the Cold War and, in 1975, as host of the Conference on Security and

Cooperation in Europe, Finland amply demonstrated its indispensability. Even so, the Soviet Union had an ongoing presence in Finnish politics in the form of its ambassador and the KGB, and many of the country's political decisions were made with a nervous eye toward Moscow. As a result, works critical of the Soviet system, such as those of Alexander Solzhenitsyn, could not be published in Finland.

Sweden's neutrality also provided some cover for Finland because the nonaligned Swedish-Finnish bloc reassured the Soviet Union, while at the same time providing something of a forum for exchanges among the various political systems in the Baltic region. In addition, Sweden had a profound effect on Finnish economic policies because the Finnish mark was pegged to the Swedish krone. And the successes of the Swedish welfare state were to some extent copied in Finland because that model offered a third path between capitalism and socialism.[6]

Collectivization and Industrialization

The Soviets applied their social model of collectivization to the Baltic region (where people generally favored land reform). For example, even in Schleswig-Holstein a bill was advanced in 1949 that would have expropriated all agricultural land in excess of 100 hectares and compensated its owners. The law was never passed because large landowners voluntarily gave up a total of 30,000 hectares. In the Soviet sphere of domination, however, reform was aimed not only at large property holdings, but also at economically strong family farms (*kulaks* in Soviet terminology). Their destruction, so the reasoning went, would usher in a social revolution in the countryside. In Estonia, land expropriations resumed in 1944 where they had left off in 1941, and two-thirds of arable land was distributed to landless peasants, with preference given to veterans of the Red Army and their families. *Sovkhozy*, or Soviet state farms, were started on the remaining land. But this was only the first step. In 1947, the Politburo in Moscow decreed the collectivization of agriculture in the Baltic republics. Because of resistance, the Soviets first applied political pressure coupled with higher taxes; when that failed to achieve the desired results, they used physical force and deportations. Those who refused to work on *kolkhozy*, the collective farms, landed in work camps, and women and children were sent to remote regions of the Soviet Union. By the beginning of the 1950s, 90 percent of land in Estonia had been collectivized, and wealthy peasants had disappeared from the villages.[7] Agricultural production and productivity plummeted and recovered only slowly. The collectivization process was similarly brutal in Latvia and Lithuania, with more than 40,000 Latvians and 30,000 Lithuanians deported. The process collectivized 90 percent of Latvian land, but only 62 percent of arable land in Lithuania.[8]

In Poland, collectivization began in 1948 and quickly led to a collapse in agricultural production. After food shortages sparked mass protests in 1956, collectivization was stopped and the peasants were allowed to return to and work their own land.

From 1944 to 1946 Mecklenburg–Western Pomerania was forced to deal with the ongoing problems of hunger, refugees, and homelessness, while at the same time trying to bring about economic and social reform. The expropriation of large farms and companies and their redistribution to peasants and workers promised a new social order and at the same time acceptance by the majority of the population, who benefited from these measures. Attempts were also made to come to terms with the burgeoning refugee problem. As a result of flight and expulsion from Eastern Pomerania and the other eastern regions now under Polish administration, approximately 1.2 million refugees had arrived in Mecklenburg–Western Pomerania, of whom 922,000 stayed, pushing the total population to 2,166,000 in 1949. As a result, the land reform measures of September 1945 seemed an ideal way to integrate the refugees. In this expropriation, leading Nazis, high functionaries, and all property owners with more than 100 hectares lost their land along with livestock and inventory. The properties of the now powerless Junker class (with 2,199 manorial farms, 1,157 farmsteads, and 472 former state demesnes in Mecklenburg–Western Pomerania) were absorbed by the state land reserve, from which about 114,000 families received land. This meant an increase of approximately 77,000 new peasants, a considerable number of whom had been displaced from eastern areas. This measure alone greatly increased the popularity of the KPD-SED.

Nonetheless, the beginnings were very difficult. In 1945, only 10 percent of new peasants began to work their land parcels, which were on average 9.6 hectares in size, because of a lack of seed, inventory, stalls,

and housing. As a result, most of the new peasants eked out a bare subsistence and were unable to contribute to feeding the country. By 1949,
about a quarter of those who had left the cities to work the land had
given up and gone back. The food situation deteriorated further as a
result of the fight against peasants who owned more than 20 hectares.
Arbitrarily increased quotas, criminal proceedings, and the destruction
of their credit organizations in the Güstrow show trials of 1950 demor-
alized the most competent of them, many of whom fled to the West.
Their properties along with the abandoned farms of recent settlers were
added to the state agricultural sector.

As part of the collectivization of agriculture mandated by the Central Committee, agricultural production cooperatives were created into
which the peasants were forced to merge their farmland. Resistance
was initially considerable and after June 17, 1953, led to the collapse of
many of the production cooperatives. A different approach was attempted in 1960, and long-established peasants were encouraged to join
the production cooperatives by "agitation committees." The next steps
included the unification of so-called people-owned property (state-
owned farms), the agricultural production cooperatives, and the "gardeners' production cooperatives" under a single umbrella cooperative
and the formation of an agro-industrial complex. This maneuver fundamentally changed social relations at the village level. The differences
between peasants and farm workers were leveled, and everyday life increasingly came to resemble the regimentation of the factory. The technical schools now trained agricultural leaders for the agro-industrial
complex and its constituent companies.[9]

The Soviet Union also left its stamp on the economy of the Baltic
region through its forced industrialization policies, which were supposed to transform agrarian regions into industrial ones. In Estonia,
for example, mechanical engineering and metallurgy were strongly encouraged and complemented the oil shale and chemical industries,
which had been expanding since the 1930s. As a result, the number of
workers employed in the metal and electrical industries in Riga increased markedly. The workforce was recruited from rural areas, augmented by migration from Russia. These policies urbanized the landscape while simultaneously changing the ethnic composition of the
countries. At the same time as the population of Riga increased from

580,000 (1959) to 915,000 (1989), the proportion of Latvians in the city decreased from 44.6 percent to 36.5 percent. The Russian workforce began to dominate and received preferential treatment in the prefabricated housing blocks. Similar Russian ghettos developed in Estonia as a result of the industrial expansion of Narva and Kohtla-Järves.

Later, the Soviet Union began turning its attention to regional specialization and the division of labor. From now on, the republics were to contribute to the overall economic plan by producing specific products and raw materials, a process controlled by the all-union ministries. This was, for example, the mechanism by which Moscow coordinated and controlled Estonian oil production from oil shale and its use to run power plants.[10] In Poland, a law adopted in January 1946 mandated the nationalization of industry, and, in 1947, the private sector was limited to 20 percent of total national production and 10 percent of the workforce. After Poland rejected Marshall Plan assistance, its economy was tied completely to that of the Soviet Union, and Poland was forced to sell its products at below world market prices. During the first six-year plan (1950–1955), Poland adopted the Soviet industrialization model of a command economy, with an emphasis on heavy industry. After his reinstatement as first party secretary, Gomułka, however, proclaimed a specifically Polish path toward socialism.

The transformation of the industrial sector within the Soviet occupation zone was radical. Shortly after the end of the war, the Red Army confiscated industrial products, began to disassemble factories and ship them to Russia, and forcibly drafted technical specialists to work in the Soviet Union. The German aircraft industry, which had been built up along the Baltic coast as part of German rearmament efforts, was liquidated. In addition, the occupation force expropriated numerous companies, transformed them into state-owned enterprises (such as the Boizenburg shipyard and the leather works at Neustadt-Glewe), or continued to run them as Soviet stock corporations, as happened with the Neptun shipyard. At the same time, numerous small-scale producers, automobile and bicycle repair shops, and retail stores and hotels were returned to their owners. The shipyards along the Baltic coast were refitted for Soviet needs and soon became a new and important industrial sector. The demands for reparations by the USSR as set down in the Potsdam Agreement gave to the Soviet Union the entire German military and merchant fleet, including ship wrecks off the coast. Given the scarcity of raw materials, recovery, repair, and re-fitting of ships were deemed more profitable than building new ones. But in any case, a robust shipbuilding industry would have been impos-sible to re-create until German war reparations had been fully paid in 1953.

The restoration of the shipyards changed the Baltic coast. The once charming seaside resort of Warnemünde made way for the largest in-dustrial facility in Mecklenburg–Western Pomerania, the bustling Warnow shipyard. The population of the town grew from 5,800 in 1945 to 16,000 in 1949, while the employment figures during the same pe-riod increased from 99 to 5,160. About 40 percent of the workers re-cruited from throughout the Soviet occupation zone were from else-where. Overall, by the mid-1950s, about 40,000 workers were employed by the shipbuilding industry and its suppliers. At this time, the ship-yards began to specialize in the production of particular types of ships. The Neptun shipyard, for example, built ships under 6,000 tons; the shipyard at Warnow specialized in larger freight vessels. The Mathias-Thesen shipyard, on the other hand, constructed customized ships for particular functions, such as railroad ferries, refrigerated vessels, and passenger ferries. The Volkswerft shipyard, in Stralsund, built only one model, the fishing trawler, which it designed specifically for the So-viet market. Smaller shipyards, such as the Elbe shipyard in Boizen-burg, catered to the same market: of the 560 ships that it built between 1950 and 1989, 350 were delivered to the Soviet Union.

The food industry was also crucially important. Sugar refining and milk and meat processing expanded, as did fisheries and the fish can-ning industry. In addition to traditional coastal and inner-bay fishing, trawlers ventured far out into the North Sea and the North and South Atlantic. Toward the end of the 1950s, about 1,500 persons were em-ployed in fishing and 11,500 in fish processing. Although state-owned companies and fishing cooperatives constituted the mainstay of the industry, the private sector, made up of 140 companies, also played an important role.

During the 1970s and 1980s, industrial employment in the northern districts of the GDR grew slowly even though the nuclear power plant in Lubmin; the Nachrichtenelektronik Greifswald, a company that specialized in telecommunications technology; the fertilizer plant in Rostock-Poppendorf; the Mukran ferry port; and the pharmaceutical producer in Neubrandenburg had all begun production. Tourism was also a growth industry for the region, with the Baltic coast attracting some 3.5 million visitors annually.[11]

The Welfare State

As a result of World War II, the political center of gravity in the Scandinavian countries—as in most of Europe—shifted toward the left. The Social Democrats, who had been in power in Denmark and Sweden before the war, were able to assert their dominance for the next several decades and realize their goal of building a welfare state. The parties in both countries harkened back to a long tradition of social legislation that was inspired by Bismarck's reforms. In Denmark, the conservative Danish parliament of the 1890s copied the German system by passing pension and health and accident insurance legislation. In 1933, the various elements of a social-reform system were consolidated, forming the foundation of the welfare state that would take shape later. From 1956 onward, all Danes received a state pension. This was followed, in 1961, by social welfare provisions, and in 1973, statutory health insurance was added as well. The situation in Sweden was, if anything, even more Utopian. Here, parliament provided the population with a series of benefits in quick succession: 1946, state pension; 1947, child benefits; 1951, three weeks of vacation; 1953, general health insurance; 1954, alcohol treatment; 1956, social welfare; 1956, 45-hour week; 1959, supplementary pension; 1963, four weeks of vacation; 1966, 42.5-hour week; 1969, rent subsidy for children; 1970, 40-hour week; 1974, 90 percent paid sick leave; and 1978, five weeks of vacation. It is small wonder that Swedes view their country as heaven on earth.

Not only did the Danish and Swedish systems provide for the welfare and social well-being of their citizens, the ethos penetrated much deeper into these societies. It established behavioral and social norms for the individual as much as it affected the taxation system. All members of society were to be treated equally. As a result, every citizen had an equal right to cradle-to-grave state benefits. In contrast to, say, Germany, state benefits were financed by taxation and not by contributions paid by the individual for social insurance. As a result, state expenditures rose from 23 percent (1950) to 50 percent (1970) of gross national product, while at the same time individual taxes increased from a quarter to one half of income. The welfare state also brought about an explosive increase in public sector employment. While Denmark employed only 160,000 in the public sector in 1950, by 1970 that figure had swelled to 444,000, of whom 200,000 worked in the areas of health care and social welfare. Although the welfare state was originally invented by the Social Democrats, the idea was never questioned by either the liberal or conservative parties in Denmark.[12]

In Sweden, the welfare state was augmented with a large measure of social planning carried out by the government, unions, and employers. The overall goal was to integrate the entire population into a single work process. The unemployed were given extra training and help in relocating, which favored migration to the large cities. Salary and taxation policies encouraged both married partners to seek employment, which necessitated comprehensive childcare. The Swedish model depended on high rates of industrial growth, which led to increased demand for labor in already densely populated conurbations. As a result, a large number of Finns moved to southern Sweden to take advantage of higher wages, joining internal migrants from the north, including the Sami (Lapps). It was only a matter of time before migrant workers had to be recruited from southern Europe. High real wages led to an increase in the standard of living. Class structures and traditional working environments began to dissolve; society appeared "more equal" and the *folkhem* (people's home) ideal a good deal closer to realization.[13]

However, the first oil crisis of 1973–1974, caused when the Organization of Oil Exporting Countries (OPEC) suddenly tripled the price of crude oil, led to disillusionment with the belief in continuous growth and wealth distribution. Although the Scandinavian countries attempted to deficit spend their way out of the crisis, this solution worked only for so long. As national debt and taxation rates grew, the consensus upon which the entire system was built began to be questioned. In Denmark, the anti-tax party of attorney and politician Mogens Glistrup (1926–2008) began to make headway and challenge the older established parties.

Another fundamental assumption of the welfare state, namely that the economic and social conditions in which its citizens lived were homogeneous, simply was no longer true. Scandinavian societies were becoming increasingly multiethnic and multicultural as a result of the influx of migrant workers and political refugees, but this left the welfare state hard-pressed to satisfy the needs resulting from this new reality. In addition, after Denmark's entry into the European Union in 1973 (at the same time as Great Britain), the ability of the non-EU member Scandinavian countries to control economic policies became more limited. Under pressure from globalization, the Nordic governments soon adopted many of the neoliberalism policies of deregulation favored by the United States.

At the same time, Scandinavian companies brought highly creative and high-quality products to the world market. In Denmark, small companies had success with unique inventions and then expanded quickly. For example, Mads Clausen's (1905–1966) Danfoss Group developed an automatic valve for refrigeration plants and later a thermostat for heaters, which in the 1960s made it one of the largest Danish companies. Danfoss now has branches and production facilities all over the world. Similarly, Lego blocks made Godtfred Kirk Christiansen (1919–1995) world famous. The Danish pharmaceutical and food industries found ready markets throughout Europe. The traditional shipping companies were also expanded, with Møller-Maersk becoming the largest container shipping company in the world and one of the most important logistics companies as well.[14]

Sweden has had similar success with Tetra Pak, now the largest food-packaging company in the world, and IKEA. The devaluation of the Swedish krone by 10 percent (1977) and 16 percent (1982) assisted these companies greatly as their competitiveness had been dampened by taxes and bureaucratization. The auto manufacturers Volvo and Saab profited from the devaluation as well. Older Swedish companies, such as the appliance manufacturer Electrolux, the energy company Vattenfall, and the telephone producer Ericsson, also expanded at this time.[15] The Finnish company Nokia also became an important player in the telephone market. Nokia's success was part of the evolution of Finnish industry away from traditional timber processing and paper to new product lines. At the end of the nineteenth and beginning of the

twentieth centuries, Nokia specialized primarily in paper products
for the British and Russian markets, before moving on to rubber products, such as boots and tires, along with the production of cables. In
the 1970s and 1980s, it added communications systems for the military and car telephone systems. As a result, by 1981 Nokia had posi-
tioned itself to start the first Scandinavian mobile telephone network
(Nordisk Mobiltelefon), although it took until 1987 for the production
of mobile telephones to catch up with the network that was already in
place. Finnish shipbuilding also began to specialize in icebreakers and
oil drilling platforms. The Finnish ceramics industry was internationally respected, as was its glass manufacture. And the Finnish construction industry operated very profitably in the socialist countries, where, for example, it built the new port of Muuga northeast of
Tallinn.[16]

In the 1950s, the Finns traded largely with the Soviet Union because
the Finnish-Soviet trade agreement was based on trade rather than reparations. As a result, Finland became the main supplier of metal and
mechanical engineering products to the Soviet Union, while trade with
its prewar trading partner Great Britain slumped. Later, Finland increased its trade with Sweden and the Federal Republic of Germany.
West Germany became the most important trading partner for all of
the countries in the Baltic region, although less than 10 percent of West
German trade was with this region. The GDR, on the other hand, did
more than half of its foreign trade with the Baltic countries; Finland
and Poland 40 percent, Sweden and Denmark a third.[17]

The expansion in intra-Scandinavian trade was encouraged by the
European Free Trade Association (EFTA), which the Scandinavian countries together with Great Britain had founded in 1960 partly in reaction to the European Economic Community (EEC). Because Finland was
so dependent on the Soviet Union, it abstained from joining. Nonetheless, Great Britain and Denmark soon applied to join the EEC, but their
initial application was vetoed by French president Charles de Gaulle
(1890–1970). Negotiations resumed only after his resignation in 1969,
and both countries were finally admitted to the European Community in 1973. This move, and the increasing enlargement of the European Community, constituted serious blows to the EFTA, which even
Finland's full membership could not offset.[18]

A Divided Cultural Landscape

Because of the blocs that had been formed, cultural life in the Baltic region remained divided. But the divide was not merely between East and West, but equally between the writers in the Eastern countries and their compatriots in exile. Those who remained at home used whatever space was available to them in the interstices of the system or, as in Poland, systematically attempted to expand that space. Nonetheless, cultural policies were not set in stone either; rather, they alternated among suppression, loosening (thaws), and indifference, and as a result artists were faced with an ever-changing kaleidoscope of rules and regulations that made creative work difficult.

During the Stalinist era, the majority of Baltic authors who had set the direction of literature in the new states during the interwar years were in Western exile because their writings were now viewed as "bourgeois" or "reactionary." A few writers had returned from Moscow; the regime attempted to recruit others. Thus, the "critical realist" and future Stalin Prize recipient, Andrejs Upits (1877–1970), reorganized the writers' association, and the established author Vilis Lācis (1904–1966) was rewarded for his loyalty with two Stalin prizes and the position of minister of the interior. To have one's work published, membership in the writers' association was mandatory, as was the consent of the General Directorate for the Protection of State Secrets in the Press (Glavlit), the official censor.

During the immediate postwar period, the key works of Baltic literature were published elsewhere. Sweden was the most important outlet for exiled Estonian authors. One of the most productive was Bernard Kangro, who wrote works in all genres. Karl Ristikivi (1912–1977) was another extremely creative and productive exile who wrote a number of historical novels, among them *The Tallinn Trilogy* (1938–1942). However, most of the Latvian and Lithuanian exiles, such as Henrikas Radauskas (1910–1970), perhaps the most important Lithuanian writer of the twentieth century, and the Lithuanian-born Polish Nobel Prize laureate Czesław Miłosz (1911–2004), lived in the United States.

A number of younger writers in the Baltic Soviet republics began to make their voices heard after the thaw following Stalin's death. In

1958, Jaan Kross (1920–2007), for example, published a collection of poems under the title *Söerikastaja* (The coal concentrator), in which he described his experiences in the coal mines of Vorkuta, where he had performed forced labor. In his best-known book, *Keisri hull* (The czar's madman), Kross slipped into the identity of an imprisoned and supposedly mentally unsound Baltic German aristocrat named Eberhard von Bock, who tells the czar—and therefore also his readers—uncomfortable truths about the Russian autocracy. Poets such as Artur Alliksaar (1923–1966) and Jaan Kaplinski (1941–) were also popular with readers. Mati Unt (1944–2005), whose stories take place in the university city of Tartu, had more than a hundred plays to his credit and was one of modern Estonia's most productive dramatists and theater directors.[19]

In Latvia, the writers Ēvalds Vilks (1923–1976), Jezups Laganovskis (1920–1987), and Visvaldis Eglons-Lāms (1923–1992) used the space afforded by the thaw to write short stories that criticized both openly and in veiled language everyday Soviet life and the abuse of office by functionaries. Poets such as Ārija Elksne (1928–1984), Vizma Belševica (1931–2005), and, in the 1980s, Māra Zālīte (1952–), developed their own language and a public eager to read them. The most-celebrated Latvian poet of the 1970s and 1980s, however, was Ojārs Vācietis (1933–1983), the self-styled "Latvian Yevtushenko."[20]

Lithuanian authors, like their colleagues in Latvia and Estonia, were subject to censorship and the dictates of the writers' association, membership in which assured them a living. Accordingly, they constantly navigated their way between conformism and self-expression. The poet and ardent Communist Eduardas Mieželaitis (1919–1997) was so good at the game that he was awarded the Lenin Prize, in 1962, for his cycle of poems titled *Žmogus* (Man). This award marked a seal of approval for the careful modernization that was taking place in poetry. Other poets, such as Sigitas Geda (1943–2008), Tomas Venclova (1937–), Jonas Juškaitsi (1933–), and Judita Vaičiūnaitė (1937–2001), began to publish innovative poems that represented a clear break with socialist realism. Because the underground used this greater cultural openness to launch a publishing offensive, writers once again found themselves on a short leash during the 1970s, especially after the public demonstrations against the Soviet regime. As a result, the writers named above could not be widely read in Lithuania until the 1980s and later—in Russian translation—beyond the country's borders as well.[21]

Polish writers had considerably more independence, and after 1956 at the latest they developed in a variety of directions, producing works of very high quality. Jerzy Andrzejewski (1909–1983) wrote an acclaimed novel titled *Popiół i Diamant* (Ash and diamond) that described the trauma experienced by the postwar generation. He was joined by poets such as Zbigniew Herbert (1924–1998) and playwrights Sławomir Mrożek (1930–2013) and Tadeusz Różewicz (1921–2014).

In Scandinavia, the prewar traditions of writing at first continued more or less unchanged. In Denmark, the works of Martin Andersen Nexø (1869–1954), with his novels set in working-class milieus, and those of Johannes V. Jensen (1873–1950) are examples. Jensen was awarded the 1944 Nobel Prize for Literature for his literary work. The generation of writers born after the war, such as Leif Davidsen (1950–), Bjarne Reuter (1950–), and Peter Høeg (1957–), have since the 1980s enjoyed international success in translation.

In Finland, literary output was still strongly influenced by the Nobel laureate Sillanpää and the experiences of the Winter War. Unsurprisingly, Väinö Linna's (1920–1992) *Tuntematon Solitas* (The unknown soldier) enjoyed great popularity. Mika Waltari (1908–1979) also made a name for himself outside Finland with his historical novels. After the 1950s, Paavo Haavikko (1931–2008) and Eeva-Liisa Manner (1921–1995) were important poets and playwrights. Manner was also an accomplished translator of German- and English-language literature.

In Sweden, Harry Martinson (1904–1978) and Eyvind Johnson (1900–1976) successfully continued their prewar careers. With works such as *Vägen till Klockrike* (The road) and *Hans Nådes Tid* (The days of his grace), they transported their readers back to the Middle Ages. Martinson and Johnson shared the 1974 Nobel Prize for Literature. Other important literary figures included Sven Delblanc (1931–1992), who was born in Canada, and Torgny Lindgren (1938–), both of whom wrote about the impoverishment of rural life in Sweden in the 1930s. Sara Lidman (1923–2004) described her own childhood in a remote village in *Hjortonlandet* (Cloudberry land), and country life was also the subject of Sweden's most successful author, Astrid Lindgren (1907–2002), who is perhaps best remembered for her Pippi Longstocking series.

The Scandinavians were even more successful on the silver screen. Before the war, Scandinavian actresses received top billing, but in the 1950s Ingmar Bergman (1918–2007) became a director of international importance, working with actors such as Max von Sydow (1929–) and Liv Ullmann (1938–). His films, including *Wild Strawberries* (1959), *Persona* (1960), *Cries and Whispers* (1973), and *Fanny and Alexander* (1982), express the melancholy and self-doubt that pervade an oppressive Protestant world. Since the 1980s, the Finnish brothers Mika (1955–) and Aki Kaurismäki (1957–) and the Danes Lars von Trier (1956–) (*Europa trilogy*) and Gabriel Axel (1918–2014) (*Babette's Feast*) have brought Scandinavian film back to the world's attention. In Poland, Bergman's contemporaries included Andrzej Wajda (1926–), Roman Polański (1933–), and Krzysztof Zanussi (1939–). Wajda's film rendition of Jerzy Andrzejewski's *Ash and Diamond* was a factor in Poland's political and social awakening in the late 1950s, and his films often dealt with the effects of Stalinism. His *Man of Marble* and *Man of Iron* depict the labor unrest at the Gdansk shipyard and the Solidarity movement's early successes. Unsurprisingly, these films were little shown in the Baltic states.

The visual arts in the postwar Baltic republics were constantly under pressure to conform to Soviet dictates. Depending on their artistic traditions, artists responded very differently to the situations in which they found themselves. The boundary between what could be displayed in public and what was forced underground was fairly fluid. The underground art scene in Moscow was very influential in the republics. At different times, new artistic trends began to appear in Estonia, Latvia, and Lithuania that depended on the interplay between the artists' traditions and the contacts they were able to establish with other artists. In the 1970s and 1980s, for example, Estonian artists were in contact with their counterparts in Finland and the rest of Scandinavia, while in Lithuania, artists were confronted with the more progressive art and literature of Poland that ran counter to their own country's Catholic tradition. In Poland, the constructivist painter Henryk Stażewski (1894–1988) in Warsaw, and the surrealist Tadeusz Kantor (1915–1990) in Cracow, had the freedom to work in a modernist style, and they cultivated relationships with members of the Paris avant-garde and exhibited in western Europe.[22]

In the late 1960s, Estonia became an innovative center for print-making and continues to host the Tallinn Print Triennial. In Latvia, artists such as lithographers Ilmars Blumbergs (1943-) and Boris Ber-zins (1930-) began making a mark in the 1980s. After the war, Esto-nian painting initially took its cue from Paris, and specifically the work of Léger, Matisse, and Dubuffet. But then in the 1970s, art students An-dres Tolts (1949-2014), Ando Keskküla (1950-2008), and Leonhard Lapin (1947-) began, under the influence of pop art, to produce geometric paintings, which they showed at an exhibition called Soup 69, named after Andy Warhol's famous Campbell's soup cans.

Painters in Latvia tended to produce monumental paintings into the 1980s until painters such as Aija Zarina (1954-) and Ieva Iltnere (1957-) questioned the purpose of such canvases. Lithuanian artists admired German expressionism, but later they evolved toward neo-expressionism. Photorealist works were exhibited in Estonia first, and Latvian artists followed suit. In Lithuania, this trend led to "new doc-umentalism," which combined with expressivist tendencies. The pent-up creativity felt by Latvian and Lithuanian artists led to a number of artistic modes of expression, especially in the 1980s, ranging from per-formance art to the installations of Ojars Petersons (1956-), Juris Pu-trams (1956-), and Oleg Tillbergs. Lithuania also produced the concep-tual artist Mindaugas Navakas (1952-).

The pathways by which artistic ideas spread from one place to an-other are often obscure, primarily because in the 1940s and 1950s, in particular, artists were often suppressed.[23] For example, the group in Tartu that included the surrealist Ülo Sooster (1924-1970) was arrested in 1949 and sent to a work camp. After his release, Sooster moved to Moscow, where he shared a studio with Ilya Kabakov (1933-) and be-came one of the most important intermediaries between the Moscow underground and the Estonian art scene. In about 1970, a group called Visarid, which included the artist Kaljo Põllu (1934-2010), began trans-lating and distributing Western art criticism in the art cabinet at Tartu State University—until authorities suppressed the group because of the politics that informed this criticism. Art collectors, such as the Esto-nian Matti Milius (1945-), began to collect art works from beyond the borders of the republic as well. Over time, he collected more than 1,200 nonconformist artworks from Armenia, Estonia, Latvia, Lithuania, the Ukraine, and Russia. After 1975, he showed works by Lithuanian and Latvian artists in unconventional exhibitions in Estonia as well as his Estonian works in Latvia and Armenia.[24]

After 1945, architecture became a major art form in Denmark, Sweden, and Finland, with inspiration often coming from the interwar years. In these countries, economic growth and prosperity made it possible to build Utopian constructions. In Sweden, the optimistic spirit associated with the building of the welfare state was reflected in city planning. Under a social democratic system, all cities should be equally livable and accessible to all citizens, regardless of social status. In Stockholm, this led to a succession of city plans with names such as "City 62," "City 67," and the like, which were often accompanied by large-scale demolition. Fortunately, the economic slump of the 1970s and protests by a sensitized public put a damper on these mammoth projects. Nevertheless, several architectural masterworks were built. These include the series of five office buildings designed by David Helldén (1905–1990) at Sergels torg, with their crystalline glass and metal construction, which created both a rational urban structure and gave Stockholm a distinctive skyline.[25]

The great Finnish architect Alvar Aalto was also involved in various city planning projects after the war, such as the reconstruction of Rovaniemi after German troops largely destroyed this northern city. Aalto's buildings, such as the Rautatalo business and office block, the Pension Bank building, the cultural center in Helsinki, the Church of Imatra, and the paper mills in Kotka, reflect his deep identification with his Finnish homeland as well as the needs of his clients. One spectacular example of how nature can be used is the Temppeliaukio Church, also known as the Rock Temple, which was hewn out of solid bedrock by the brothers Timo Suomalainen (1928–) and Tuomo Suomalainen (1931–1988) in the 1960s. The planners of the garden city of Tapiola, to the west of Helsinki, attempted to create a suburban Utopian environment that would attract people away from the capital. The project was all too successful—as the daily traffic jams between Tapiola and Helsinki attest.

The Dane Arne Jacobsen (1902–1971) took another path. Rather than tie his architecture to the natural surroundings, he began experimenting with geometric forms in the 1950s, which resulted in such public build-ings as the school in Gentofte and several apartment buildings. Jacobsen also became involved with product design, designing a series of "Danish" chairs with names reflecting their form, including the Drop, Egg, and Swan chairs, which were very successful. The SAS Royal Hotel is the most successful synthesis of his ideas on architecture and de-sign. In addition to Jacobsen, the Finnish designers Kaj Franck (1911–1989), Tapio Wirkkala (1915–1985), and Timo Sarpaneva (1926–2006) made "Scandinavian design" synonymous with simple sophistication the world over.[26]

By contrast, the legacy of intrusive Soviet architecture weighed heavily upon any innovation that might have arisen in the Baltic states. Although forced to live with stylistic imports, individual architects tried time and again to create a more personal mode.[27] For example, Alar Kotli (1904–1963) and Henno Sepmann (1925–1985) built an amphi-theater for the Tallinn song festivals, which, though monumentalist, fits nicely into the landscape. At the same time, the architects of the Tallinn school attempted to revive the functionalism of the 1930s, but a lack of state contracts forced them to build private homes at the pe-riphery of the city. In Vilnius, the architect Vytautus Čekanauskas (1930–2010) gave artistic flair to the suburban settlement of Lazdynai and the Center for Contemporary Art.

The most important contemporary composer in the Baltic region is undoubtedly the Estonian Arvo Pärt (1935–). His colleagues Witold Lutosławski (1913–1994) in Warsaw, and Krzysztof Penderecki (1933–) in Cracow not only drew on Polish traditions but also incorporated in-fluences from contemporary Western music. Pärt's reception in the So-viet Union and in western Europe demonstrates clearly the fluctuations in Soviet cultural policy that artists were forced to endure. One of the preconditions for making a living as an artist was membership in the All-Union Society of Composers, which Pärt joined in 1957. But his sponsors soon became disillusioned with him, especially after he com-posed the first Estonian twelve-tone work titled *Nekrolog*. He was ac-cused of "formalism" after its premiere in 1961. However, an oratorio titled *Maailma samm* (Stride of the world), which he dedicated to the Twelfth Party Congress of the Communist Party of the Soviet Union, pacified many of his critics. His experimental works subsequently became very popular, which the Society of Composers viewed with evident misgivings. But this did not keep the Soviet Estonian Ministry of Culture from commissioning Pärt's works. In 1968, however, his religious vocal symphonic work *Credo* got him into political hot water again despite public approval of the piece. He then began experimenting with new compositional techniques that harkened back to medieval Ars Nova, and his composition *Tintinnabuli* (Little bells) did much to improve his standing within the bureaucracy. The piece was well received both in the Soviet Union and abroad. Nonetheless, Pärt emigrated to Israel in 1980, and he later moved to Berlin, which greatly increased his audience in concert halls and the media. The Latvian violin virtuoso Gidon Kremer (1947–), who also emigrated, did much to make Pärt's work known, both on his tours and through his recordings.[28]

Pärt's contemporaries, the Lithuanian Osvaldas Balakauskas (1937–) and the Latvian Pēteris Vasks (1946–) had to wait until independence before they gained a larger audience for their music. The Baltic region is also home to a great tradition of choral music, which in the twentieth century served as a medium of national self-discovery and spoke to a public very different from that attracted to modern composers. Gustav Ernesaks (1908–1993) founded the State Academic Men's Choir (Riiklik Akadeemiline Meeskoor) and regularly conducted the Estonian song festivals that take place every five years. In the 1950s and 1960s, about 30,000 singers took part; by 1980 that figure had grown to almost 300,000. This growing interest constituted an expression of Estonian self-discovery during an era when foreign influences threatened to overwhelm their society. The program contained songs by Estonian composers. Gustav Ernesaks's "Mu isamaa on minu arm" (My fatherland is my love) with lyrics by the poet Lydia Koidula (1843–1886), which was sung at the conclusion of the song festivals, became the unofficial national anthem of Estonia. Together with the Latvian and Lithuanian song festivals, these major events ushered in the Singing Revolution of 1988. In 2003, UNESCO included these festivals in their "intangible cultural heritage" list.[29]

Independent of national self-discovery through choral music, a jazz scene developed in the Baltic states that was clearly in opposition to the regime. While the Communist Party branded jazz as a product of

Western decadence well into the 1960s, at least in Lithuania it became a sign of a burgeoning cultural life; until his emigration to Israel in 1987, Slava Ganelin's (1944–) free jazz trio was integral to this movement. In Tallinn, jazz fans organized festivals in the 1960s at which local, Russian, and Western musicians shared the stage. In Norway and Denmark, by contrast, musicians were able to tie into prewar traditions, that is, from before the German occupation. While musicians such as Arne Domnérus (1924–2008) made Swedes aware of new trends in jazz, Copenhagen, with its Jazzhus Montmartre club, became the real center for jazz in the Baltic region. This was largely the result of an influx of American jazz musicians, such as Stan Getz, Oscar Pettiford, Kenny Drew, Dexter Gordon, and Ben Webster, who played with Danish musicians. For example, the pianist Kenny Drew founded a very influential trio with the percussionist Alex Riel (1940–) and the bassist Niels-Henning Ørstcd Pedersen (1946–2005). From 1991 onward, the Jazz Baltica Festival in Schleswig-Holstein provided an outlet for jazz musicians from the entire Baltic region.

The Swedish pop group ABBA was yet another expression of the region's musical vitality. The group consisted of Swedish singers Benny Andersson (1946–), Agnetha Fältskog (1950–), Anni-Frid Lyngstad (1945–), and Björn Ulvaeus (1945–), who after winning the 1974 Eurovision song contest for their hit "Waterloo" went on to phenomenal success throughout the world. Although Poland was the only Iron Curtain country in which their songs were played freely, *ABBA: The Movie* (1977) had a limited release even in Moscow. ABBA records were produced in the Soviet Union under the Melodia label and commanded a high price on the black market. Their influence on Soviet pop musicians, who freely covered ABBA songs, was immense. Scandinavian radio stations were another important cultural intermediary, as was Finnish television, which could be viewed in Estonia and sometimes in other countries as well. The American-financed Radio Liberty and Radio Free Europe offered programming in Estonian and other Baltic languages, too.

Decline and New Beginning

Soviet rule in the Baltic along with the power of the Communist parties in Poland and the GDR appeared rock solid and immutable in the
1960s. The political classes in the West had come to terms with this
fact and tried with a policy of détente to improve relations with their
Eastern bloc neighbors. Nonetheless, signs of unrest, such as the Prague
Spring in 1968, continually poked through the apparently monolithic
façade. Even as the Soviet Union and its satellites attempted to sup-
press the idea of "socialism with a human face," the regime was able
to ensure compliance for only so long. The ongoing deterioration in the
economic situation proved a great impediment to long-term stabilization. Because all of the socialist countries attempted to generate foreign currency earnings by exporting to the capitalist West, they, too,
began to feel the changes taking place in the world economy. The
Western credits that they accepted to improve the economic situation
of their citizens quickly evaporated, leaving behind shortages. And television and radio made it painfully clear to the population that their
quality of life was substantially inferior to that of their neighbors to
the west and north.

But initially it was the students and not the workers who took to
the streets in Poland and throughout Europe in 1968. The precipitating
event in Poland was the cancellation by the Polish Theater of the drama
Dziady (Forefathers' eve), which Adam Mickiewicz (1798–1855) had
written in 1824. The banning of this play, in which Mickiewicz roman-
ticized a suffering Polish nation, sparked massive protests by Warsaw
students, who were soon joined by students in other university cities.
These protests were suppressed by the police and militia, and political
dissidents such as Jacek Kuroń (1934–2004) and Karol Modzelewski
(1937–) were arrested. At the same time, Minister of the Interior
Mieczysław Moczar (1913–1986) fomented an anti-Semitic campaign,
which was, among other things, intended to weaken Gomułka's leadership of the party. Jewish civil servants lost their jobs, and a large proportion of the Jewish population, which after the mass killings of the
war numbered only 40,000, emigrated. The events in Czechoslovakia
briefly stabilized Gomułka's position, primarily because the Soviet
Union could not afford the consequences of another power vacuum.

While he concentrated on foreign policy and a relaxation in Poland's relationship with West Germany, the economic situation continued to erode. Shortly after the Federal Republic and Poland signed the Warsaw Agreement, in which Germany recognized the Oder-Neisse border, protests by shipyard workers broke out in Szczecin, Gdańsk, and Gdynia in December 1970. Gomułka was forced to resign and was replaced by Edward Gierek (1913–2001), in whom many placed high hopes. Gierek promised the workers material improvements, which he financed with credits from the West. However, any hopes that he had of repaying these loans with Polish products from a more efficient and modernized industry did not materialize. By 1975 at the latest, Poles came to the sobering realization that conditions would only deteriorate further. The government's attempt to increase subsidized food prices by 60 percent elicited enraged protest from workers and had to be rescinded almost immediately. The dissidents founded the Komitet Obrony Robotników (KOR, Committee for the Defense of Workers), through which they would attempt to articulate and press their demands. Then in 1978, Cracow cardinal Karol Józef Wojtyła (1920–2005) was elected pope, which drew a great deal of international attention to Polish Catholicism. In 1979, Pope John Paul II visited his homeland.

Unfortunately, material conditions in the country did not grow in step with the population's progressive political awakening. Increases in meat prices in the summer of 1980 triggered political demonstrations. The workers considered founding their own unions because they distrusted those approved by the state. The firing of the politically active crane operator Anna Walentynowicz (1929–2010) by the shipyard managers provided the spark that led to a strike and the occupation of the Lenin Shipyard, in Gdansk, which led to further waves of strikes. Led by the electrician Lech Wałęsa (1943–) and supported by the KOR, the workers negotiated with a government delegation the right to form free trade unions. This was the beginning of the Solidarity Union (Solidarność), whose membership swelled to 10 million workers within a very short time. Even the party leadership proved ready to compromise after Gierek's resignation because they realized that economic collapse could be prevented only with the cooperation of the workers. However, with the support of Moscow, Polish general Wojciech Jaruzelski (1923–2014) organized a coup and, on December 13, 1981, he proclaimed martial law. Tens of thousands were arrested and locked in internment camps. Solidarity was banned, although several of its leaders escaped and continued their activities in the underground. International condemnation of martial law in the "East bloc" was resounding, with professional organizations and colleagues of interned friends petitioning and demanding their release.

Because the economic misery of the country had not changed, and because it was now almost completely dependent on the Soviet Union to supply the necessities of life, Jaruzelski loosened the repressive measures he had instituted. Wałęsa was released, in November 1982, and the following year he was awarded the Nobel Peace Prize. The pope again visited his homeland, and unofficial discussions began to take place between the regime and the opposition. However, these attempts at reconciliation were scuttled when Polish intelligence agents murdered Father Jerzy Popiełuszko (1947–1984), a popular priest who was allied with Solidarity. Again, the regime was discredited. But this time the Soviet Union demanded reforms and dialogue between the government and the opposition.[30]

People throughout the Baltic saw what was happening in Poland— and they identified. Similar protests had already broken out in Lithuania in the 1970s. The most dramatic protest against Soviet rule was undoubtedly the self-immolation of a student named Romas Kalanta, which led to mass protests at his burial, in 1972. Catholic priests in particular worked in the underground, where, for example, they published a history of the Catholic Church in Lithuania, including all of the repressive measures instituted by the regime. They also circulated petitions among the populace to demand that churches be built and old ones that had been turned into museums or concert halls be reconsecrated. The papal election that brought Wojtyła to the papacy increased the confidence of the oppositional movement. Although the number of actual dissidents remained small, in 1979 on the fortieth anniversary of the Hitler-Stalin Pact, thirty-seven Lithuanian, four Latvian, and four Estonian dissidents sent a "Baltic appeal" to the United Nations in which they demanded publication of the secret protocol that had divided the Baltic countries into German or Russian spheres of control.[31] In Tallinn, the cancellation of punk rock concerts, in September and October 1980, led to a youth revolt during which students demonstrated in front of party buildings with the banned Estonian flag and demanded better cafeteria food and heated classrooms. The government responded by announcing prosecutions, whereupon forty leading Estonian artists and intellectuals wrote a protest letter to *Pravda* and the Estonian party newspaper in which they complained about socioeconomic problems, the people's economic well-being, and alcoholism, but especially about the increasing Russification of the country. However, it took the environmental catastrophe after the Chernobyl nuclear accident, in 1986, to breathe resolve into the anti-Russian protests in Estonia.

The environment and peace were also major items on the agenda of the opposition in the GDR. When Erich Honecker (1912–1994) took power in 1971, the state at first seemed on solid ground. After concluding the Basic Treaty of 1972, which defined the relationship between the Federal Republic and the GDR, East Germany gained increasing political recognition in non-socialist countries. Within the country itself, a new generation of citizens had grown up that believed the official promises that their standard of living would improve, and tried as best they could to enjoy their free time in their gardens. But to make up for the lack of consumer goods and building materials, citizens were forced to cultivate ever wider personal networks. And in fact, citizens of the GDR, like their socialist neighbors, were master improvisers and organizers, and their standard of living was the highest in the entire East bloc.

But whenever East Germans looked at West German television, it quickly became apparent that standards of living on the opposite sides of the Elbe were diverging, and not converging as promised. Although the Tenth Congress of the SED, in 1981, decreed a new economic growth strategy, it proved illusory because it increased considerably the cost that people paid for energy. Foreign debt grew, especially in relation to the Federal Republic, which the GDR tried to limit by increasing exports and reducing imports. Shortages of everyday products soared, especially since production targets in the outdated factories often went unmet. People's living situations deteriorated as well because their old buildings were increasingly unfit for habitation and new buildings often remained unfinished because of shortages of building materials.

Thousands of complaints were sent to the party leadership and state bodies about the lack of necessities and inferior dwellings. One complaint from the Lubmin nuclear power plant near Greifswald, a supposedly model facility, caused a furor because it was sent directly to the Council of State and demanded rapid solutions to food short-ages and complained that consumer goods like clothing and washing machines could not be bought by people holding East German cur-rency. These and other goods were available only to those with West German (i.e., "hard") currency. Once the petition reached the Polit-buro of the SED, the party not only failed to deal with the problem, but also put pressure on party members, whom it blamed for not having the situation under control. Nonetheless, an attempt was made to improve the availability of necessities in Greifswald to defuse the situation. But the upshot was that fewer and fewer people were pre-pared to continue to submit to the dictatorship's party discipline.

Since the 1980s, environmental and peace groups had been meeting under the aegis of the Protestant Church. It was difficult for even the intrusive apparatus of the Ministry for State Security to monitor these groups effectively. Although the environmental damage in the northern parts of the GDR was less than in the south because of the lower level of industrialization, many of the rivers in the region had been turned into cesspools as a result of runoff. Numerous lakes, such as the Tol-lensesee and the Schaalsee, were ecologically dead. The ecology groups planted trees in areas undergoing development and held regular semi-nars on ecology. A bicycle demonstration against the planned route of the Wismar-Schwerin highway elicited a response from the security ap-paratus, which denied all bicyclists access to Schwerin. At least as im-portant were the church-sponsored peace groups, which, after introduc-tion of mandatory military preparedness training in 1978, fought for disarmament in both the West and the East with the slogan "Swords into plowshares." Loosely organized, they largely eluded state control. As a result, the state attempted to destroy the groups from within by planting informers and spies or to get the leaders of the church to limit "uncontrolled activities."[32]

Once Mikhail Gorbachev (1931–) became general secretary of the Communist Party of the Soviet Union, in the mid-1980s, the overall political climate changed considerably. While he tried to change the political structures of the Soviet Union with his policies of *glasnost* (openness and transparency) and *perestroika* (restructuring) and supported reform processes in other socialist countries as well, no one expected a loosening of the relationship between Moscow—the center—and the Soviet republics—the periphery. And in fact, attempts were made to intensify the economic relations and deliveries mandated by the Soviet economic plan.

For example, phosphate mining in Estonia was to be expanded to produce artificial fertilizer. When this plan was publicly revealed by the popular television program *Panda* in February 1987, it triggered a firestorm of indignation among Estonians. This "phosphate war" proved to be an important step on the path to Estonian independence. For the first time, broad sections of the population became politically engaged, overcoming the cynicism and apathy that had plagued them for so long. Now Estonia itself, its natural heritage and its people, were threatened by Russian plans and the expected influx of Russian workers. As a result, the resistance was not limited to the environmental movement but affected even members of the party. Party functionaries such as Edgar Savisaar (1950–) and Arnold Rüütel (1928–) began to take part in the protest movement. From that point on, there was no stopping it. On August 23, the anniversary of the Hitler-Stalin Pact, several thousand demonstrated in Tallinn.

At the end of the year, activists founded the Society for the Preservation of the Estonian Cultural Heritage (Eesti Muinsuskaitse Selts), which attempted to reclaim parts of Estonian history that had been suppressed. In April 1988, the blue, black, and white national flag of Estonia, which had been the symbol of the country in the interwar years, was hoisted over Tartu—without the authorities stepping in to prevent it. In June, Estonian flags were in such abundance at the Old Town festival, in Tallinn, that the Supreme Soviet of Estonia felt forced to recognize the tricolor as the national colors in order to avoid confrontation. A month earlier, associations of "culture creators" (i.e., writers, composers, artists, etc.) had demanded that Estonian rights be expanded, and this was linked to a sharply worded criticism of the Estonian Communist Party. At the same time, Savisaar founded the Popular Front of Estonia (Rahvarinne), whose aim was to accelerate the democratization process. Enormous and boisterous demonstrations were held in August of that year, again on the anniversary of the Hitler-Stalin Pact, whose secret protocol had in the meantime been published in newspapers. The song festival, which was attended by about 300,000 Estonians, included political speeches demanding Estonia's independence from the Soviet Union.[33]

In Latvia, the political awakening occurred during the summer and fall of 1987, when demonstrations were organized to commemorate the mass deportations of 1941, the Hitler-Stalin Pact, and the Latvian declaration of independence of 1918. The Popular Front of Latvia (Latvijas Tautas Fronte) was founded in June. In Lithuania, a freedom league organized demonstrations during the same time period, which the police generally dispersed; a demonstration on October 23, 1988 was brutally put down. Responding to internal and international criticism, Ringaudas Songaila (1929–), dubbed "Cement Head," was forced to step down as first party secretary and was replaced by the more flexible Algirdas Brazauskas (1932–2010). Sajudis, the popular reform movement that had been founded in June, became more radical, no longer demanding autonomy but Lithuania's unconditional independence.[34]

Initially at least, the Soviet leadership under Gorbachev had no strategy for dealing with the demands for autonomy and independence coming from the Baltic republics. After lengthy deliberations, Gorbachev suggested a revision of the all-union constitution, on October 6, 1988, that would reduce the participation of the individual republics. In response, the popular fronts demanded legislatively guaranteed economic self-determination and called on their people to sign a petition to that effect. In no time, they gathered more than 3.7 million signatures. Moscow then sent members of the Politburo to the Baltic republics to inform the local authorities that the purpose of *perestroika* had actually been to strengthen the Soviet Union. But on November 16, the Estonian Supreme Soviet voted to declare Estonia a sovereign country and to place the all-union bodies under Estonian law. Latvia and Lithuania declared autonomy half a year later, and they were soon joined by other Soviet republics. When Boris Yeltsin (1931–2007) declared the sovereignty of Russia in 1991, the Union of Soviet Socialist Republics ceased to exist.[35]

In March and April 1989, the Baltic popular front candidates won their elections to the Congress of Peoples Deputies of the Soviet Union. In Moscow, they worked together with the elected representatives of other republics to demand that the newly convened People's Congress recognize the existence of the secret protocols contained in the Hitler-Stalin Pact and condemn them outright. In May 1989, an assembly of representatives met for the first time. It established the Baltic Parliamentary Group and shortly thereafter a Baltic council of ministers was constituted to attempt to coordinate foreign policy. To commemorate the fiftieth anniversary of the Hitler-Stalin Pact, the Baltic assembly organized a 600-kilometer-long human chain, on August 23, that stretched from Tallinn through Riga all the way to Vilnius. This act, in which almost 2 million people took part, was meant to demonstrate to the world the desire of the Baltic peoples to be independent.

At about that time, the situation along the southern coast of the Baltic had taken an unexpected turn. In Poland, the regime was finally forced to recognize that the necessary economic reforms—by 1988, foreign debt had grown to $45 billion—could be achieved only with the cooperation of the unions. The terms of this cooperation were negotiated in lengthy discussions between February 6 and June 24, 1989, by the government, the party, and representatives of the Solidarity movement, with the advice of Tadeusz Mazowiecki (1927–2013), who was a confidant of John Paul II. The precondition for these discussions was the right to form free unions again, which the government conceded to immediately. Because the Polish United Workers' Party (PZPR) was not yet prepared to give up power, the negotiators agreed to a two-chamber parliamentary system. In the Sejm, 35 percent of the seats were to be subject to free elections; in the Senate all of the seats would be openly contested. In the subsequent June elections, Solidarity won almost all of the open seats in the Sejm and came to dominate in the Senate. Because the PZPR continued to be in the majority, however, General Jaruzelski was elected president on July 19, by a one-vote margin. His candidate for prime minister, however, was defeated. The final obstacles were removed for the election of Mazowiecki as the first Catholic prime minister of Poland in fifty years when the Soviet Foreign Ministry gave assurances that the Soviet Union would not interfere in internal Polish affairs.[36]

The reform efforts in the Soviet Union and the rapid changes in Poland were echoed in the GDR as well. The East German leadership, however, remained obdurate. Nowhere was this made clearer than in a tone-deaf remark by the GDR's chief ideologist, Kurt Hager (1912–1998).

When asked about possible changes in the GDR, he replied "If your neighbor puts up new wallpaper, would you feel obliged to wallpaper your home as well?" To ensure that its citizens could no longer be infected by Soviet reforms, in November 1988 the government banned the mailing and distribution of the Soviet magazine *Sputnik* in the GDR. This led to numerous protests by longtime subscribers, who had used it to keep up with cultural and political events in Russia. The sour mood in the country was reflected in the flood of applications to leave the GDR; in the district of Rostock alone, the number increased from 677 on January 1, 1983, to 1,365 on January 1, 1985, peaking at 2,839 on December 31, 1988. By May 7, 1989, when local elections were held, the people's discontent would have been obvious to any nonpartisan observer. In Dresden, the party functionary in whom many had placed their hopes, the later (and last) prime minister of the GDR, Hans Modrow (1928–), falsified the election results. But this was not the only such incident. In Rostock, the secretary of the SED district leadership, Ernst Timm (1926–2005), handed to Greifswald mayor Klaus Ewald a sheet of paper on which were written the results of the election—several days before it was held. And those were the figures subsequently reported in Rostock.

Matters took a sharp turn during the summer of 1989 when Hungary began dismantling the barriers along its border with Austria. Citizens of the GDR soon congregated at this southwestern boundary of the Warsaw Pact, setting up camps close to the border. They also occupied the West German embassy. On August 19, 600 citizens of the GDR crossed the border into Austria, and the refugees in the embassy were given exit permits because the Hungarian government was no longer prepared to take responsibility for them. This led to a virtual siege of West German embassies in Prague and Warsaw. Although the "hole in the border" more or less sealed the fate of the GDR, its sclerotic leadership went ahead and staged pompous celebrations on the fortieth anniversary of the GDR's founding, on October 7, as if nothing had happened.

In East Berlin, members of the peace movement and others formed the New Forum to articulate the people's yearning for civil rights, and soon local groups began meeting in private homes throughout the country. On September 4, demonstrations were for the first time organized in Leipzig to press for reforms. Although this demonstration was broken up by the Volkspolizei (people's police), starting on October 9 demonstrations were held each Monday in Leipzig. Peace vigils were also held regularly in churches in all of the northern cities. After one of the prayer vigils, on October 16, 300 participants in the city of Waren left the church and held a candlelight demonstration in the city center. This demonstration was followed by another in Greifswald, on October 18, with several thousand marchers. Although the party leadership was nervous, they reported back to Berlin that "the situation is stable." The day after the demonstration, the party secretary in Greifswald, Günter Köhler, promised the district party leadership that he would ensure the peace, "so that we may implement the decisions of the 9th Congress of the Central Committee in good quality." By now, the phrasing had become formulaic and increasingly divorced from reality. Despite the surface normalcy, Köhler awaited directives from above, unsure of how to handle the situation. But no directives arrived: the Politburo in Berlin, now under the leadership of Egon Krenz (1937–), who had on October 18 replaced Erich Honecker as general secretary, was simply no longer competent to act.

Demonstrators in all cities—and not just in Berlin and Leipzig— forced the party leadership in the districts of Schwerin, Rostock, and Neubrandenburg to enter into dialogue with representatives of New Forum and the Protestant Church. But it was too late. Party members began to leave the SED en masse, and younger party functionaries toppled the three leading secretaries in the northern districts in what was essentially a palace revolution. On November 9, when Politburo member Günter Schabowski (1929–) announced at a press conference that East Germans would be permitted to cross the borders, the regime's days were numbered. In all cities, roundtables were held in an attempt to ensure a peaceful and democratic transition. The former allies of the SED, the CDU and LDPD, left the National Front, and new parties such as the Social Democratic Party (SDP) were founded just as preparations were being made to hold new elections to the People's Chamber in the spring of 1990. At the same time, human rights activists attempted to prevent the destruction of evidence by the Stasi, the much-feared secret police.

The elections held on March 18, 1990, were won by the Alliance for Germany (48 percent), which was a coalition consisting of the CDU and two new parties, the German Social Union (DSU) and Democratic Awakening (DA). The SPD trailed far behind with 21.9 percent of the vote and the PDS, which had been formed from what remained of the SED, received only 16.4 percent. The electoral alliance of the liberals (BFD) received 5.3 percent, while "Alliance 90" and the Greens appeared on different lists, which doomed their electoral chances. CDU member Lothar de Maizière (1940–) was elected prime minister, the last leader of the German Democratic Republic.

In addition to deciding on a new communal constitution for the GDR, the state (Länder) system was reinstated on July 22, 1990. On October 3, 1990, the former districts of Schwerin, Rostock, and Neubrandenburg became the federal state of Mecklenburg–Western Pomerania—and the German Democratic Republic was officially merged into the Federal Republic of Germany.[37]

The Baltic republics were markedly affected by developments in Poland and the GDR, and they continued agitating for their independence, distancing themselves from the Soviet Union in small ways. Names of plazas such as Freedom Square in Tallinn, which the Soviets had renamed Victory Square, were restored. And Estonia switched from Moscow Time to Eastern European Time. In addition, the Popular Front of Estonia announced its intention to form an independent state in a neutral, demilitarized "Baltoscandia." One step in this direction was the declaration by the Supreme Soviet of Estonia that the incorporation of Estonia into the USSR in 1940 had been illegal and as such was null and void. In the spring of 1990, the popular fronts gained the majority in elections to the supreme soviets in the Baltic countries. New governments were formed, headed by reform communists such as Edgar Savisaar in Estonia, Ivars Godmanis (1951–) in Latvia, and Kazimiera Prunskiene (1943–) in Lithuania. On March 11, 1990, the first freely elected Lithuanian parliament, renamed the Lithuanian Supreme Council, declared Lithuania's independence from the Soviet Union. Estonia and Latvia followed suit on March 30 and May 4, respectively, with a carefully formulated resolution that marked the beginning of a transitional period on the way to full independence. While the Baltic states proceeded to make their case for independence internationally, a Russian opposition formed, which, together with hard-liners in the Kremlin, attempted to strangle any moves toward independence.

Even Gorbachev, in attempting to stabilize his own position, closed ranks with the conservatives in the party leadership and allowed the military, secret police, and Interior Ministry a free hand. They, in turn, hoped to use the fact that world attention was focused on the Near East in the aftermath of Iraq's invasion of Kuwait to initiate actions in the Baltic. In Latvia, bombs detonated in front of military installations provided the pretext for troop increases. At the same time, a Latvian National Salvation Committee was formed, which Moscow invited to "save" the country—that is, instigate a coup.

However, when the Lithuanian government collapsed after it decreed price increases, the Lithuanian National Salvation Committee declared, on January 12, 1991, that it had taken control of the country. Soviet troops occupied strategically important points and killed fourteen people, who had placed themselves, unarmed, between the television tower and the troops. The situation remained tense, but the next day Boris Yeltsin, the chairman of the Supreme Soviet of the Russian Federative Socialist Republic, visited Tallinn to show his support for the democratization process—although he had no actual authority to do so.

Western governments were appalled at the bloodshed in Lithuania, and the European Parliament blocked food assistance to the Soviet Union valued at $1 billion. Gorbachev, who barely a year earlier had won the Nobel Peace Prize for supporting the peaceful reunification of Germany, saw his reputation plummet. His hapless attempt, after days of silence, to make local military commanders responsible for the escalation, undermined his authority both in Moscow and in the Baltic republics. Although the reaction in the West ensured that the Red Army put a halt to its actions, the terror campaign initiated by special police units (OMON), who committed murders in both Lithuania and Latvia to intimidate the population, continued unabated. But in the end, the coup carried out against Gorbachev in August 1991 allowed the Baltic states to extricate themselves from Russian control.

Gorbachev was placed under house arrest in the Crimea, but the amateurish organization of the coup leaders allowed Boris Yeltsin to grab political power in Moscow. With this development, Estonia and Latvia declared the transition period over and announced their independence. That same month, the Nordic countries and the members of the European Union recognized the independence of the Baltic states, which, upon recognition by the United States, were admitted to the United Nations in September.[38]

[CHAPTER TEN]

Transformation and EU Integration

Focus on the Øresund Bridge

As it has throughout recorded history, the Øresund (Öresund in Swedish) remains the gateway from the Atlantic Ocean and North Sea into the Baltic region. Over the centuries, ships of almost all European countries have sailed through the Sound, making it a place of cultural memory for these seafaring nations. The control that Denmark exerted over the Øresund, which it sought to enforce with its fortifications at Kronborg, was the cause of bitter struggles among Denmark, Sweden, Poland, and Russia, conflicts that the Netherlands and England joined, intervening on different sides depending on their trading interests. The Sound became less of a point of contention between Denmark and Sweden during the twentieth century, but the dedication of the Øresund Bridge, on July 1, 2000, gave this evolution a new symbol. When King Carl XVI Gustav of Sweden (1946–) and Queen Margrethe II of Denmark (1940–) opened the bridge, the Sound took on a whole new meaning for the twenty-first century. Since then, Danes have moved to Scania, where they find more affordable housing than at home, in numbers never seen before. And today, about 14,000 Swedes commute to work by train from Malmö to Copenhagen. The building of this bridge has made it possible for politicians and citizens to envision a new Øresund identity that may eliminate old national stereotypes. The founding of Øresund University, a consortium of four Swedish and eight Danish institutions that together develop degree programs, maintain libraries, and share students and researchers, marks an important step in this direction.[1]

Building Democratic Structures

Over the past two decades, the Baltic region has experienced a radical transformation unlike any in its history. While the former socialist

Figure 10. Øresund Bridge

countries underwent political and economic changes designed to prepare them for membership in the European Union, the Scandinavian countries were also forced to deal with European Union (EU) norms and legal structures in their negotiations with the EU. The Baltic Sea, which had been a major locus of the East-West split, became an inland sea, a northern Mediterranean, around which all the old borders disappeared, but where new ones were erected, a process acutely associated with the formation of multiple identities. The democratization of Poland and the Baltic states in such a short time is surely remarkable. While internal strife and external forces—often in

Map 10. The Baltic region in 1992

the form of defeat in battle—marked the slow centuries-long process
of democratization in most European states, the democratic transformations taking place along the southern and eastern Baltic coasts occurred almost simultaneously and at breakneck speed. The situation
in the former GDR was in many ways the least complicated. There, the
newly formed German federal states were incorporated into the democratic structure of the Federal Republic, a government created under
the guidance of the victorious Western powers after World War II.

Local elections took place on May 7, 1990, and parliamentary elections in the state of Mecklenburg–Western Pomerania on October 14,
1990. The CDU won the elections (38.3 percent) ahead of the SPD (27.0
percent) and the PDS (15.7 percent). The FDP received 5.5 percent of the
votes, the Greens 4.2 percent, the former opposition groups in New

Forum 2.9 percent, and Alliance 90 2.2 percent. Because these parties ran separately, not one of their members was elected to parliament. Despite their thin majority, the CDU and FDP formed a coalition government that was faced with the enormous task of building or rebuilding. Alfred Gomolka (1942–) of the CDU became minister president, and the newly constituted parliament chose Schwerin over Rostock as the seat of government.

In the spring of 1990, parliament passed laws to modernize the universities and reform education. Perhaps even more important were the structural and economic policies over which the new government had only limited control. High levels of personnel turnover made the government's work difficult. In 1992, the CDU forced Gomolka to resign and replaced him with Berndt Seite (1940–). Other ministers were either fired or resigned. Longer-term stability in terms of policies and planning were achieved only with the "grand coalitions" between the SPD and CDU between 1994 and 1998, and then again after 2006, with a "red-red" (i.e., SPD and PDS) government taking control between 1998 and 2002.[2]

In Poland, Mazowiecki's government first had to free itself of the Communist bureaucracy and make legal and democratic changes to the constitution. This was done under the leadership of the Solidarity Union. But during the presidential elections of 1990, in which the rather more conservative Wałęsa faced off against the more liberal Mazowiecki, the stage was set for a split in Solidarity, from which a number of political parties emerged. The most important of these, the Freedom Union (Unia Wolności) formed the government after the first free parliamentary elections, in 1991. They were, however, decimated in the following elections. While the Communists successfully transformed themselves into a social democratic and Europe-friendly party (the SDP), numerous small, often very transient, parties to the left and right also rose from the political ferment. Occasionally, as with Andrzej Lepper's (1954–2011) populist Self-Defense of the Republic of Poland (Samoobrona Rzeczpospolitej Polskiej), they used extra-parliamentary tactics to appeal to their following. In parliament, new ruling coalitions were constantly being cobbled together, with seven different cabinets in quick succession between 1991 and 1997. Aleksander Kwaśniewski (1954–), who defeated acting President Wałęsa, in 1995, and was reelected in 2000, offered stability.[3] After an interlude that saw the nationalist and anti-European Kaczyński brothers (Lech, 1949–2010 and Jarosław, 1949–), who represented the Law and Justice Party (Prawo i Sprawiedliwość, PiS), the Civic Platform of the Republic of Poland (Platforma Obywatelska RP) has since 2007 governed in a coalition with the moderate Polish Peasants' Party (Polskie Stronnictwo Ludowe), under Prime Minister Donald Tusk (1957–), until he became president of the European Council. In 2010, Bronisław Komorowski (1952–) replaced Lech Kaczyński, who was killed in an airplane accident.

In the Baltic states, ever-changing majorities and prime ministers were a hallmark of the transformation process as well. In Estonia, the new Pro Patria and Res Publica Union (Isamaa ja Res Publica Liit) won the 1992 election, and their chairman, the young historian Mart Laar (1960–), became prime minister. The writer and film director Lennart Meri (1929–2006) became president. Although governments changed numerous times during the second half of the 1990s, all of the center-right governments focused on political and economic reforms.

In Latvia, the new political leaders attempted to continue the legacy of the interwar years in that they reintroduced the constitution of 1922 along with several other laws from the old independent Latvia, but with minor changes. This was the work of Valdis Birkavs (1942–), whose conservative Latvian Way (Latvijas Ceļš) had won the election. Nevertheless, the second half of the 1990s saw a revolving door of new populist parties and short-lived governments. The alienation of the parties from the people and their consequent lack of interest were surely factors in this electoral instability. Only under the conservative coalitions led by the New Era (Jaunais laiks) und Unity (Vienotība) Parties under Valdis Dombrovskis (1971–) and Laimdota Straujuma (1951–), respectively, did Latvia achieve political and economic stability and became a member of the Eurozone.

The Lithuanians, on the other hand, preferred continuity with Soviet times. Vytautas Landsbergis (1932–) and his Sąjūdis, which grew out of the Reform Movement of Lithuania, were defeated in the elections of 1992, with the renamed post-Communists, the Democratic Workers Party—and later the Social Democratic Party of Lithuania (Lietuvos Socialdemokratų Partija)—taking these elections. Their leader, the last Communist Party secretary, Algirdas Brazauskas, was elected president in 1993. In Lithuania, the president was given more power under the constitution than in the two neighboring states. But the party landscape was unstable and just as confused because so many new parties were founded between 1994 and 1997. Eleven governments came to power between 1990 and 2001, and only in the twenty-first century did larger coalitions consisting of several parties provide greater stability. Brazauskas's immediate successor was Valdas Adamkus (1926–), who had studied and spent time in the United States. But after a brief interlude, in 2001 he again took the reins of power, becoming prime minister in a larger coalition government. Only in 2008 did the Christian Democrats of the Homeland Union (Tėvynės Sąjunga) replace the Social Democrats, who returned to power in 2012 under Algirdas Butkevičius (1958–).[4]

Despite the political fluctuations and skepticism, the democracies created in the states that have undergone transformation have proven remarkably robust. If we analyze their consolidation at various structural levels and examine the actors and political culture, Estonia, Poland, and Lithuania appear quite firmly established. In terms of the constitutional rule of law, they and the states of western Europe differ little. Latvia, however, continues to have problems with its judicial system, and the battle against corruption and organized crime has not yet been won. On the other hand, we should not expect to see democratic institutions in Russia in the foreseeable future.[5]

While new political institutions had to be built and economic reforms undertaken, the relationship between the Baltic states and Russia, which still maintained troops in these countries, continued to be a source of political turmoil—especially because so many Russian-speakers lived in these countries. Although Russia removed its troops from Poland and the Baltic states between 1993 and 1994, relations with Russia remained tense, and as a result these countries came to feel that NATO membership offered a certain level of security. Russia under Vladimir Putin (1952–) built a threatening arsenal that put a damper on any moves that the new governments might be inclined to make. One point of contention remains the relatively large Russian-speaking population, to whom Latvia and Estonia had initially denied full political rights. Latvia established 1940—the year after the Hitler-Stalin Pact—as the cutoff year for claiming citizenship, which meant that all those who arrived later were ineligible. However, one of the prerequisites for membership in the European Union was the liberalization of citizenship rights, and so Latvia was forced to end this restriction. Estonia was similarly restrictive and initially granted citizenship only to those who had been citizens in 1940 and their descendants. All others had to pass a language test to be naturalized, and only about a quarter of the Russian-speaking population of Estonia passed that test. About as many decided on Russian citizenship; others are still citizens of former Soviet republics and a relatively large number are stateless. While numerous Russian families, such as the communities of Old Believers on Lake Peipus, had been living in Estonia for generations and were well integrated, many others had a hard time finding a place in the new society.[6] Both Latvia and Estonia started programs to help Russians integrate, including language instruction, although they seem to have had little success to date. Only Lithuania, where 80 percent of the population is Lithuanian, has been able to integrate its Russian and Polish minorities with relatively little disruption.

Economic Transformation

All of the former Baltic Socialist republics initiated fundamental economic reforms, including revitalizing outdated and unproductive industries and developing new products for markets other than the Soviet Union. This was a painful process because the number of jobs had to be adjusted to the need. This "shock therapy" was first tried in Poland and was initiated by its finance minister, Leszek Balcerowicz (1947–). There was no other choice but to privatize the economy given an inflation rate of over 600 percent and foreign debt exceeding $42 billion. This was the only way to ensure aid from the International Monetary Fund (IMF). Among other measures, the reform package ensured that unproductive state-owned businesses would no longer be kept alive with credits. The national bank would no longer be allowed to extend credit to the state or to flood the country with banknotes. In addition, the złoty was made fully convertible, and all limits on foreign investment were removed. The IMF supported the transformation process by providing $1 billion along with a short-term credit of $720 million. The World Bank granted further credits to modernize the Polish export industry. Foreign governments and banks followed suit, writing off a portion of Poland's foreign debt.

The social costs of these reforms were considerable because about 1.1 million Poles lost their jobs when state-owned businesses collapsed. But in 1992 alone, about 600,000 new privately owned companies were established, which provided 1.5 million jobs. Because the former state-owned agricultural collectives were equally unproductive, the increasing unemployment provided another opportunity for Lepper's populist Samoobrona Party. Even though Balcerowicz and his colleagues eventually lost support and some of his reforms were watered down, shock therapy ensured that Poland's economic growth over the next decade far surpassed that of all other former socialist countries, and that Poland itself weathered the financial crises of the early twenty-first century relatively unscathed.[7]

In the former GDR, on the other hand, the transformation was accomplished by economic, currency, and social union with the Federal Republic of Germany, and it has since been eased by transfer payments. As a result, the country as a whole inherited not only the appalling condition of buildings and industrial plants, it was also forced to deal with "hidden" unemployment due to the fact that far more people worked in the shipbuilding industry and agriculture—the two economic sectors that dominated the Baltic—than were necessary. The same applied to the administration, schools, and the unproductive security apparatus. In addition, there was the task of privatizing state-owned property and enterprises, which was overseen by the Treuhandanstalt (Trust Agency), which was founded for the purpose. Of the 239 enterprises in Mecklenburg–Western Pomerania, 118 were sold, 14 reprivatized, 20 turned over to the communities, and the rest liquidated. Although not all of its decisions have proven correct over time, without the Treuhandanstalt it is hard to imagine how the East German economy could have been restructured.

The changes in agriculture were significantly more fundamental with regard to the number of jobs because here agricultural production had to be returned to the village level. The agricultural reform law (Landwirtschaftsanpassungsgesetz) of 1990 liquidated most of the agricultural production cooperatives or transformed them into different legal entities. When individual farms that had been forced to collectivize were given back to their owners, this did not, however, trigger a proliferation of smallholder farms. Large and mid-sized farms have been the rule, especially now that a 100-hectare piece of land can comfortably be worked by two people. And productivity is now higher than it is in many of the preunification federal states, with organic farming adding considerably to this growth. But the downside is the decrease in overall agricultural employment from 180,000 (1989) to about 20,000 (2006), and the increasing abandonment of the countryside as the remaining population ages. With young people, especially women, leaving the countryside for the cities, and with many migrating to the old federal states, the birth rate has decreased drastically as well.

The industrial sector had also hired many more people than it needed, something most clearly demonstrated by the transformation in the shipbuilding industry. Approximately 55,000 workers had been employed in shipbuilding and associated industries, and—much like in the West German shipbuilding industry in the 1980s—many of these workers had to be let go. In Mecklenburg–Western Pomerania, the outdated factories with their dependency on the Soviet Union as their primary customer made privatization difficult. As one might expect, the Treuhandanstalt had a hard time finding buyers for the shipyards. In the end, the agency sold the Wismar Mathias-Thesen shipyard and the diesel motor factory in Rostock to Bremer Vulkan AG, the Warnow shipyard in Warnemünde to the Norway-based engineering firm Kvaerner, and the Peene shipyard in Wolgast to the Hegemann Group. The shipyard in Stralsund was privatized by a consortium led by Bremer Vulkan AG, which used state subsidies primarily to keep from going bankrupt. The investors changed after the collapse of the company; nonetheless, the shipyards have proved problematic for the country, especially after the collapse of world shipping in 2008. Further layoffs followed, and the only bright spot in an otherwise distressed industry has been the building of specialized ships (rather than container ships).

The firm Deutsche Seereederei, which specializes in ocean shipping, had toward the end of the GDR been strangled by interference by the party and the state security apparatus, and it, too, underwent considerable changes. In 1993, the Hamburg shippers Horst Rahe and Nikolaus W. Schües took over its forty-seven ships and 3,000 employees and successfully restructured the company into a hotel and tourism company. In the fishing industry, the number of employees dropped from 1,000 (1990) to only about 350 today. This was followed by decreases in the fish processing industry. Nonetheless, traditional companies, such as Rügenfisch, in Sassnitz, have been able to survive, and Euro-Baltic Fischverarbeitungs GmbH (a fish processing center) has demonstrated the ability to hold its own in the food industry.

Western Pomerania was especially hard hit when the nuclear power plant at Lubmin, near Greifswald, was decommissioned. It would have required enormous sums of money to bring it up to West German safety standards. Still, the dismantling of nuclear power plants and other nuclear facilities has given at least some of the former employees new possibilities at Energiewerke Nord, a company founded for precisely that purpose. In addition, Lubmin will become an important energy hub because it is the endpoint of the Nord Stream gas pipeline that has been built between Vyborg, in Russia, and Germany.

In the Baltic states, Estonia followed the Polish model and opted for shock therapy, whereas in Lithuania reform Communists chose to proceed more slowly. Latvia also applied shock therapy, although the government continually interrupted the process, which led to deficits that are proving almost impossible to repay. In 1992, Estonia underwent currency reform, introducing the krone (tied to the German mark), although the IMF had advised that the country remain in the ruble zone because it was so dependent on the Russian economy. As a result, Estonia was left with no choice but to modernize its economy and integrate it into the world economy. Devaluation of the currency reduced inflation, which had been over 100 percent, to a mere 23 percent by the end of 1996, which largely put an end to the black market economy.

Both Latvia and Lithuania initially tied their currencies (the rubelis and talonas) to the ruble. They introduced their own convertible currencies, the Latvian lat and Lithuanian lita (pegged to an international basket of currencies or the US dollar), only in 1993, and they experienced similar successes in terms of economic growth and inflation reduction. The social consequences, however, were considerable. The retired population found that because of inflation they were unable to survive on their pensions, which undermined trust in the new democracies. Because they worked disproportionately in crumbling state factories, the Russian-speaking industrial workers were as hard hit by unemployment as the former employees of collective farms in the countryside. At least in the rural areas, the employees of collective farms (or their descendants) received back the land that they had owned prior to Sovietization, although much of the land now lay fallow. It took some time for farmers to put together larger and more workable tracts, either by purchase or rent, that could then be productively farmed by machine. Because the government at first did not withdraw agricultural subsidies, relatively many Lithuanians continued to work in agriculture. In addition to the state farms, many other state-owned enterprises were privatized, with telecommunications being among the more successful sectors.

New tax provisions made the Baltic states an attractive and profitable place for western European investors. Nonetheless, the collapse of the Russian currency together with the Asian financial crisis greatly impeded their economic recovery at the end of the 1990s. But in the early twenty-first century, on the eve of EU membership, their economies rebounded such that in 2005–2006, the Baltic states experienced an astonishing growth rate of 10 to 12 percent. This boom was led by the burgeoning IT industry in Estonia, and in Lithuania by the chemical and electronics industries (laser devices). However, a large portion of this growth was the result of consumption, with the new elites openly flaunting their Western lifestyles.[8] Among other things, a boom in home building was encouraged by advantageous credits offered by Scandinavian banks, which had the largest market share in the region. The consequences were evident during the global financial crisis of 2008, when the economy suddenly collapsed and Latvia was saved from insolvency and currency devaluation only by an infusion of money from the IMF.[9]

Interestingly, Finland also suffered considerable adjustment problems in large part because it was so dependent on the Soviet market. When the Soviet Union collapsed, Finnish exports dropped by 40 percent. At the same time, like other Scandinavian countries, Finland suffered the consequences of the deregulation of the financial markets. The Nordic countries had embraced this deregulation in the hope of once again becoming internationally competitive. The result was an economic boom that was largely based on private consumption financed on credit. As a result, the export crisis of 1990–1991 caught the government and the people completely unprepared. In November 1991, Finland devalued the mark, which in turn increased the cost of servicing the national debt. At one point, Finland's foreign debts were almost 75 percent of its gross national product, which meant that interest payments imperiled the entire national budget. The economic crisis that developed was severe; the gross national product decreased by 15 percent and unemployment rose to 20 percent. The banking system almost collapsed under the weight of bad loans and the state was forced to step in to prevent an economic disaster. In the end, Finnish taxpayers paid 40 billion marks for the irresponsible loans issued by their banks that would never be repaid. The unions, shocked by the crisis, were now for the first time prepared to cooperate in a recovery program to decrease the national debt. At the same time, the crisis made many Finns recognize that greater integration into the European economy might have benefits.[10]

Sweden only reluctantly came to a similar recognition when it slipped into a severe recession in 1990, independent of the collapse of the Soviet Union.[11] Here, too, the economy had been fueled by a credit-financed real estate and stock boom and the growth of the financial sector. The bubble burst, dropping gross national product by 5 percent (1990–1993) and raising unemployment to 10 percent, a record level for Sweden. The National Bank of Sweden was forced to rescue the currency, and the government was forced to bail out the banks. The so-called Stockholm solution was later copied by European governments on a grand scale during the financial crisis of 2007–2008. After a period of strong growth during the second half of the 1990s, growth slackened at the beginning of the new millennium. Its once leading telecommunications industry proved vulnerable; Ericsson, for example, became profitable again, but only after it merged with Sony in 2004. Nonetheless, Sweden recovered relatively quickly— much as it weathered the financial crisis and depression of 2008 thanks to its public sector and export industry. Except during the most recent international financial crisis, Denmark alone was spared business downturns; but it never experienced an economic boom either.

Contrary to what the previous remarks regarding the effect of the collapse of the Russian market on Finland and the Baltic states may have suggested, these countries did not find new trading partners overnight after 1990. Exports to Russia decreased faster than imports, which primarily consisted of energy and raw materials. As a result, Russia remained the most important trading partner for Latvia and Lithuania into the mid-1990s, supplying oil, fuel, minerals, and metals. Whereas Lithuania did relatively little business with its other Baltic neighbors, Finland, Sweden, and Germany became Estonia's most important trading partners. Although Poland and Germany expanded their already intensive trade connections, business with the other Baltic countries remained below 10 percent of total foreign trade. Germany is the most important trading nation for Denmark, Sweden, and Finland, while only about one-fifth of its trade is with other Baltic countries. In both Lithuania and Latvia, Germany has replaced Russia as the most preferred trading partner; only Estonia does more business with Finland than with Germany. Overall, business within the Baltic region increased dramatically after Poland and the Baltic states joined the European Union. As a result, EU exports to the Baltic increased more quickly than to the southern EU states, which underscores the importance of the Baltic Sea as an inland sea of the European Union.[12]

The European Union's Baltic Enlargement

The collapse of the Soviet Union posed fundamental challenges to the Nordic states over and above the economic problems that they themselves had caused. The old paradigms that had guided Swedish and Finnish foreign policy no longer seemed appropriate and required rethinking. The former Baltic Soviet republics and Poland soon aspired to integration into the West, which offered protection from Russia but met with some resistance in the EU because of the member nations' concerns about Russia. Sweden, on the other hand, considered a number of different models before setting its sights on EU membership.

In 1992, Sweden broached with Finland the possibility of a common Nordic defense strategy that, in theory, would be independent of the United States, the European Union (which was dominated by Germany and France), and Russia. But the Finns, who had just worked out a new framework agreement with Russia that replaced the old "friendship treaty" of 1948, proved skeptical, and Sweden therefore shelved these plans. But Finland, too, needed time to reorient its foreign policy from

East to West. Nonetheless, EFTA members Norway, Sweden, and Finland applied for EU membership. After complicated negotiations, the Finns and Swedes voted to join the EU, while the Norwegians did not. On January 1, 1995, Finland and Sweden together with previously neutral Austria joined the EU. The fact that a country could be economically integrated into Europe *independent* of its policy of neutrality was interpreted by the Finns as giving them heretofore unimaginable freedom. In practice, this meant that they soon assumed their traditional role as broker between East and West, taking the initiative to give the EU a strategic "northern dimension." Much to Sweden's annoyance, this enabled Finland to assume rhetorical leadership in the Baltic, a region that in the next round of EU enlargement talks gained greater political weight. In addition, Finland's integration into the EU was facilitated by its membership in the Economic and Monetary Union and its introduction of the euro, while Sweden, and for a long time Denmark, were seen as more complicated to integrate. Only in the twenty-first century did Sweden decide to pursue EU and Baltic integration equally, which went a long way toward encouraging the development of the European Union's Baltic Sea strategy.[13]

After Sweden and Finland joined the EU, Estonia, Lithuania, and Latvia applied for membership as well. At first, only Estonia was invited to take part in accession talks, along with Poland, the Czech Republic, Slovakia, Hungary, and Slovenia. This momentary exclusion provided the stimulus that Lithuania and Latvia needed to do their "homework" to meet EU requirements. In addition to harmonizing its legislation, Latvia, like Estonia, was faced with the problem of how to deal with its Russian-speaking population. In 1993, Estonia and Latvia invited the Organization for Security and Cooperation in Europe (OSCE) to assess the situation of the minorities onsite. Reluctantly, the Baltic states agreed to remove all barriers that discriminated against speakers of Russian. Lithuania had to agree to decommission the nuclear power reactor at Ignalina, which was of the same design as the one in Chernobyl. As soon as these conditions were met, on May 1, 2004, the Baltic states along with Poland, the Czech Republic, Slovakia, Hungary, Slovenia, and the Mediterranean countries Cyprus and Malta became members of the European Union. Joining the Schengen Accord, in December 2007, marked another step in the integration process by eliminating all internal border controls. While borders within the EU and the Baltic region disappeared (with the exception of the Kaliningrad Oblast), the new EU members assumed the important function of monitoring the EU's external eastern border.

In 2008, the parliaments of the Baltic states ratified the Treaty of Lisbon, which established new guidelines for cooperation in the European Union. Membership of the Baltic states and Poland in the European Union gave regional cooperation new impetus, which came to fruition in 2009 when the EU's Baltic Sea strategy was adopted. Most of these states, however, were not at first able to introduce the euro. Only Estonia, with its strict austerity measures and despite the financial crisis, was able to gain access to the Euro zone, on January 1, 2011. Latvia followed in 2014 and Lithuania will join in 2015.

NATO membership proved equally daunting. While Poland was accepted during the first round of enlargement in 1999, the United States offered what was called the US-Baltic Charter, which acknowledged the efforts of the Baltic states to achieve membership and held out the prospect of military cooperation.

In general, the Baltic states were not considered defendable, but perhaps more importantly, Russia viewed NATO membership as a threat, and no one wanted to provoke Russia unnecessarily. On the other hand, the Baltic states did everything they could to prove their worthiness by cooperating with NATO peace missions, including those in the Balkans. They also formed joint army and navy units and increased their military spending. After the attacks of 9/11, the Baltic states were finally given a hearing by the George W. Bush administration, and in March 2004 they were admitted to NATO as members of the "new Europe." Their governments immediately sent units to Iraq and Afghanistan. In 2006, NATO held its summit in Riga. Although Russia remains uneasy about the integration of former Soviet republics into the Western defense alliance, NATO and the EU are attempting to relax the situation by offering "privileged partnership."[14]

Not only has NATO and EU membership brought the new states a measure of political security, it has also led to the harmonization of their legal systems. And the economic advantages resulting from expanded funding opportunities should not be overlooked. Among other measures, the European Union helps fund numerous projects in the

Baltic region, appropriating about 15 billion euros for the purpose. Funding from the European Structural Funds may be the most important source. The Structural Funds (European Regional Development Fund, ERDF) finance projects targeted at the structural convergence of regions and regional competitiveness, while the European Social Fund (ESF) is mainly involved in training people. The Cohesion Fund, finally, is primarily dedicated to the integration of regions by means of trans-European transport networks and aims to integrate states and regions with different per capita incomes. Other funds are made available by the European Agricultural Fund for Rural Development and the European Fisheries Fund. All of the new EU member states, including constituent entities such as the German state of Mecklenburg–Western Pomerania, receive considerable assistance from Brussels.

The funding program INTERREG, which has been in existence since 1989, supports cross-border cooperation. It differs from the funds named above in that the monies used for common projects involving several institutions must come from at least two EU member states such that their positive economic, social, and cultural effects can be seen on both sides of the border. As a result, INTERREG funding has had a long-term effect on cooperation in the EU. In the border regions, the first item on the agenda was to gain a cooperative knowledge of each other before actual concrete projects involving businesses, schools, and cultural institutions could be considered. In the Baltic region, in particular, cross-border cooperation on both sides of the Baltic Sea led to a real boom in new enterprises. Not only are people in the Øresund region in the western Baltic working together, people in Swedish West Bothnia are now working in the Kvarken Council with their Finnish neighbors in East Bothnia. Other interesting examples of cooperation include that between Finland and Russia in Karelia and the greater Baltic "Euroregion." In the latter, the southeastern shore of the Baltic (Poland, Lithuania, and the Kaliningrad exclave of Russia) constitutes an effort to carry out a sort of mini-EU Baltic Sea strategy along with the Danish island of Bornholm and the Swedish island of Öland.

Cooperation has been especially intensive in Pomerania, a regional cooperative effort in existence since 1992 that includes, along with Western Pomerania and northeastern Brandenburg, the Polish province of Western Pomerania (Województwo Zachodnopomorskie), on the right bank of the Oder River, and to the north the Swedish province of Scania (Skåne). The most important ferry connections between Scandinavia and central Europe are concentrated in this region, and the exchange of goods between the regional economies takes place here as well. Ever since Poland joined the European Union, Polish businesses have been locating to the west of the Oder and have contributed to the development of areas of Western Pomerania and Brandenburg that had previously lacked infrastructure. As one might expect, many of these cooperative ventures involve the relocation of businesses to these areas, and the integration of the labor market and the credit sector.[15] In addition, cultural and youth exchanges, including concerts in Stettin and Greifswald and the building of German-Polish schools, are important to the region because they serve to undermine prejudices and build trust among young people.[16]

Cooperation and Integration

Even before EU integration and the availability of public monies from Brussels, intensive cooperative ventures had emerged around the Baltic that both reinvented and reconstituted that geographical space.[17] In addition to a frequently invoked common cultural heritage, current issues such as the environment, transportation, education, and science have led to a regional consciousness that has been shaped by both state and nonstate actors.

The most important state council is the Council of the Baltic Sea States (CBSS), which was founded in 1992 on the initiative of Germany and Denmark. In addition to the countries that border the Baltic, members include Iceland and Norway and, since 1996, Russia as well. Its founding document, the Copenhagen Accord, gave the council a broad mandate as a forum to foster coordination and cooperation in developing policies in the Baltic states, organized around summits of heads of government and meetings between European ministers. The presidency rotates annually among the member countries, with the foreign minister of the country in question coordinating its activities. Areas of responsibility include environmental protection, economic development, energy, and security, as well as education and culture, which the council, its subcommittees, and nongovernmental organizations work on together.

Environmental policy constituted one of the first areas of cooperation because the fouling of the Baltic Sea made cooperation among the adjacent states urgent.[18] As early as 1974, these states signed the Helsinki Convention and pledged to clean up the Baltic Sea. Since the early 1980s, the Helsinki Commission (HELCOM) has conducted studies and issued recommendations to those responsible for policy in the EU. The framework for this is called Agenda 21, an action plan to foster ongoing development in the Baltic region, on which the states adjacent to the Baltic Sea, the EU Commission, and various governmental and nongovernmental organizations have been cooperating. Their mandate until 2015 is to study climate change, sustainable consumption and production, sustainable urban and rural development, and the innovations necessary for sustainable development. Cooperative efforts under the Baltic Sea States Subregional Cooperation (BSSSC), in which districts, states, oblasts (Russian administrative districts), and provinces are represented, and under the Union of the Baltic Cities (UBC), are crucial because implementation always takes place at the local or regional level.

Education, the sciences, and scholarship in the Baltic region are especially important.[19] The Nordic countries are at the forefront of education, and other states have specialized knowledge-intensive services to offer. One example is Skype, which was developed in Estonia. At the same time, an East-West and South-North education gap promotes a brain drain of well-educated people not only in the direction of western and northern locations, but also from the universities into private enterprise. Turning this around will require a high level of collaboration among the institutions of higher learning. EuroFaculties at the universities of Tartu, Riga, and Vilnius as well as in Kaliningrad and Pskov have successfully introduced the ideas of constitutionality and democracy to these transformation states. At the same time, student and teacher exchanges have brought about a knowledge transfer in the field of economics, while at the same time imparting democratic values. Collaboration among universities, such as the Baltic University Program (BUP) and bilateral cooperative arrangements, has led to a revitalization of the universities along the southern and eastern coasts of the Baltic. These educational communities have benefited from ongoing contacts with European and global scientific communities.[20] Several of these networks have continued unchanged after the initial transformation phase; others, such as the Baltic Biotech Forum, have carried on under different names, in this case ScanBalt.

Such associations dedicated to particular areas of research are financed by the EU and the Nordic countries, but at the same time, Baltic research has itself been institutionalized. Master's programs in Baltic studies (Tartu) and Baltic Sea region studies (Turku) no longer concentrate on specific disciplines, such as geology, hydrology, or ecology, but offer future decision makers solid training in the social sciences and cultural affairs. Doctoral programs specializing in the Baltic Sea have also become firmly established, with the "Baltic Borderlands: Shifting Boundaries of Mind and Culture in the Borderlands of the Baltic Sea Region" graduate studies program at the universities of Greifswald, Lund, and Tartu taking the lead. This international program trains doctoral candidates from Denmark, Sweden, Finland, Estonia, Lithuania, Latvia, Belarus, Ukraine, Poland, Germany, the Netherlands, and Spain.

Another field that combines visions of the future with security policy and collective memory is that of energy. This is one area where the removal of borders is especially visible in the Baltic region. The flow of energy does not stop at national borders; where impediments are encountered, it circumvents them. This is the problem facing the Nord Stream project between Vyborg, in Russia, and Lubmin, just to the east of Greifswald. Originally called the North European Pipeline, the project was a joint venture between the Russian company Gazprom and the Finnish company Fortum. After the initial feasibility studies were concluded in 1997, which demonstrated the potential for an underwater pipeline, in 2001 the idea acquired the status of a "project of common interest" in the energy dialogue between the European Union and Russia. In 2005, Gazprom bought Fortum's stake in the project, while the German energy companies BASF-Winterhall and EON-Ruhrgas entered the consortium. Rather than exploiting the oil fields beneath the Barents Sea, ever since the pipeline was completed in 2012, the gas has been piped from the Yuzhno-Russkoye field in western Siberia to Germany and will later flow from there to Denmark, the Netherlands, and potentially also to Great Britain. Initially, there was resistance to the

project in the Baltic states and Poland, which were not yet members of
the EU when the project was on the drawing boards and thus felt excluded. But at the same time, the Baltic states continue to be dependent on Russia for their energy supplies. In Finland, a debate ensued
about the possible ecological consequences of the underwater pipeline,
while the Swedish newspapers viewed the pipeline as a security and
political threat. Among other issues, a gas pipeline in the Baltic would
undoubtedly mean a heavier Russian naval presence. Nonetheless, in
2009 the Swedish government approved the laying of pipes along the
bottom of the sea to the east of the island of Gotland.

Even so, the region remains dependent on Russian energy sources
since there is no uniform EU energy policy; nor does any such policy
exist among the countries adjacent to the Baltic Sea. To establish one
will be an important task of future European and regional integration.
Furthermore, an internal network for distributing energy is needed in
the Baltic region. Estlink, a set of undersea power cables linking Helsinki and Tallinn, marks a beginning. Similar networks between Lithuania and Sweden and between Lithuania and Poland are in the planning
stages. One planned gas pipeline between Helsinki and Tallinn would
connect Finland to a Baltic pipeline network that was built during the
Soviet era. Another subject of research and planning is the use of renewable energy. Latvia, which gets 32 percent of its energy from renew-
ables, especially hydropower and wood, long ago exceeded the overall
EU target of 20 percent (by 2020).[21]

The problem of shipping in the Baltic Sea is closely connected to
that of energy because 9 percent of freight traffic and 11 percent of global
oil transport occurs in this small area. As a result, tankers make up
one-fifth of the ships crisscrossing the Baltic, and they transported 251
million tons of oil in 2009. Although freighters and container ships are
still the most numerous, accounting for more than two-thirds of Baltic
Sea traffic, the seemingly insatiable demand for energy in Russia and
the Baltic states means that oil imports will continue to grow. Helsinki
has now become the largest oil distribution terminal in the Baltic region. The fact that Finland does more than 80 percent of its foreign trade
by sea demonstrates the importance of the Baltic Sea as a transport
route. With between 3,500 and 5,000 ship passages per month, it remains
one of the busiest waterways in the world. Despite the most recent eco-

nomic crisis, the number of ships passing through the Sound and the Belt increased considerably from 51,600 (2006) to 62,700 (2009). These figures are from the Automatic Identification System (AIS), a tracking system initiated by HELCOM in 2005 to increase safety and avoid collisions in the Baltic Sea. The very narrow and sometimes shallow channels, along with the high levels of traffic, make navigation challenging. As a result, HELCOM now makes navigational recommendations, suggests deeper channels, and has launched programs to reduce maritime pollution (especially CO_2 emissions and oil spills) and to prevent accidents.[22] To improve maritime safety for ferry services, which still make up about 5 percent of the traffic, the EU countries along the Baltic instituted a program called Surveillance Cooperation Baltic Sea (SUCBAS) that monitors the sea to prevent environmental accidents and terrorist attacks, while also guarding against smuggling and human trafficking.

While gaps in energy supply and maritime safety demonstrate that cooperation between countries remains incomplete, the different national cultures of remembrance both encourage and impede regional integration processes.[23] On the one hand, politicians and artists invoke a common Baltic cultural heritage, mainly for the purpose of attracting tourists, while, on the other hand, the differing memories of the various Baltic neighbors intersect, both in terms of collective and individual memory. In areas such as the Øresund region, cross-border cooperation has gradually broken down old animosities, in some cases resulting in new identities. However, in Poland and the Baltic states politicians have harped on old stereotypes to gain entry into the European Union and NATO. For example, in 1994, Estonian president Lennart Meri spoke of the "50-year-long night of Soviet occupation," while at the same time serving up an old narrative of "700 years of bondage" (under the Germans). Individual memories regularly collide with acts of official historical interpretation, and not only when, as in 2007, a Soviet war memorial (the so-called Bronze Soldier of Tallinn) was relocated to the outskirts of the city. It also happens when the various parties discuss energy and foreign policies.[24]

By contrast, individual memory is often tinged with nostalgia—even about the socialist era in the Baltic or along the southern Baltic coast— that is completely understandable in a time of upheaval.[25] At the same

time, individual memory is very fluid and, like the politics of commemoration, it often softens as its political goals are achieved. The openness
of cultural memory has, together with the desire for "events," led to
new integrative identities by invoking the past. One example is the
"Modern Hanseatic Days" sponsored by the "new" Hanseatic League
(an association of 175 cities in fifteen countries), which enables a city
like Kaunas to recall its mercantile glory in the fifteenth and sixteenth
centuries while promoting itself within Lithuania and throughout Europe and the world.[26] Another example is the rediscovery and acceptance by Swedes of their past, especially the role of the country as a
major player along the southern Baltic coast. The Swedish political and
economic domination of the Baltic during the seventeenth century can
now be reenvisioned through the lens of the modern welfare state, and
even celebrated. As a result, we see a public reevaluation of the era when
Sweden constituted a great power, one that had been downplayed in
the years since.

The Baltic as a Model Region

At the beginning of the twenty-first century, the cooperative euphoria
felt throughout the Baltic during the 1990s fell prey to a certain disillusionment. The Baltic region had successfully constituted itself as a
region and no longer had to prove its existence. But when the states
joined the European Union, they became subject to the everyday bureaucracy that is a reality of EU life. Brussels began to make decisions
about future regional activities, and the different regions began competing for EU funding. Against this backdrop, cooperation between
neighboring states became increasingly attractive after 2006–2007 as
a means of having a larger regional voice within the EU as a whole.[27]
This was initiated by a group of seven European parliamentarians from
Finland, Estonia, Latvia, Germany, and Great Britain, who in 2006 submitted a memorandum to the president of the EU Commission, José
Manuel Barroso (1956–), regarding ways to improve cooperation between
EU institutions and Baltic organizations. Over the next two years, initiatives and appeals poured in, which had the effect of placing the Baltic
region on the political agenda. Lithuanian foreign minister and chair

of the Council of the Baltic Sea States (CBSS) Artis Pabriks (1966–) demanded that the Baltic region's identity as a region be enhanced:

> We don't look alike, we don't speak one language, we don't live in
> one country and we don't have a joint team in world ice hockey cham-
> pionship. But we share the Baltic Sea, a common history, values and
> spirit of dynamism, skillfulness and creativity. However, what is
> important—we share the same dreams about our region's future: to
> be competitive, stable, advanced and always a developing region.[28]

One year later, his Latvian colleague and successor as chair of the
CBSS presented what was called Project Balticness, which viewed the
Baltic Sea as the artery giving life to the entire region and sought to
convey a sense of cultural belonging by sponsoring photographic exhibitions and jazz concerts. Discussions around the Baltic Sea strategy
gained political weight as a result of the new non-socialist government
that was elected in Sweden in 2006, which gave the Baltic region unusual priority because Sweden would soon assume the presidency of
the EU. Thus, Minister of European Affairs Cecilia Malmström (1968–)
of Sweden declared that the Baltic region would become Europe's stron-
gest growth region, a goal that would be achieved by even greater integration. But in contrast to such efforts in the past, the elaboration of
the strategy would not be left to the bureaucrats in Brussels alone. The
strategic plan was developed in an extensive consultation process in
which the various stakeholders in the Baltic region had a major say. A
first "stakeholder conference" was organized in Stockholm in September 2008, where substate and nongovernmental organizations were
represented, and where they could articulate their interests and ideas.
The eight EU member states along the Baltic were joined by non-EU
members Russia, Belarus, and Norway, thirty-one regional institutions,
forty-eight intergovernmental and nongovernmental organizations, and
forty-nine representatives from the private sector, among them scientists and businessmen and women with suggestions for a "bottom-up
process." The goal was to ensure that many regional institutions would
be involved in the EU's Baltic Sea strategy.

Given the ideas that were submitted, the most important priori-
ties included, first and foremost, the protection of the fragile Baltic

ecosystem so that the long-term, sustainable development of the region can be ensured.[29] The HELCOM action plan for the Baltic Sea
provided the model. It called for a decrease in nitrate discharges; the
maintenance of biodiversity, including fisheries; and the development
of the Baltic Sea region as a model region for clean shipping.

The second goal, making the Baltic Sea region prosper, was to be
achieved by eliminating the existing differences in innovation between
states on the western and northern Baltic coast and those on the eastern
and southern Baltic coast. Efforts are to include overcoming trade
barriers, especially in terms of the research and development potential of the region, by encouraging cooperation between businesses
and universities.

Education and science along with tourism and health will play an
important role in making the region more attractive and improving its
accessibility, which is a third major goal. Here, the stakeholders af-
firmed that a number of different approaches must be taken to increase
environmental awareness and build up the identity and image of the
region with the aim to make education, research, and culture goals of
the strategy.[30] Accessibility also implies that the Baltic states have access to energy networks, and that the division of Europe in terms of
transportation be overcome.[31] Rail Baltica, which will connect Warsaw
and Tallinn at speeds of 75 miles per hour, is an example of the priority projects being implemented. Expansion of the railroad lines would
also strengthen the connections between the region and Asia.

The final goal in this plan—to make the Baltic Sea region a model
of maritime security—is conditional on sustainable environmental development and the HELCOM action plan. Another important effort is
the cross-border battle against organized crime and securing the EU's
external borders. It is clear that this can only occur with the cooperation of non-EU countries, including Russia, Belarus, and Norway.

After the European Commission approved the EU Baltic Sea strategy
on June 10, 2009, the European Council, then chaired by Sweden, adopted it on October 29–30, 2009, and urged all actors to implement the
strategy as quickly as possible. This has been done with a number of
flagship projects that are of strategic importance not only for the Baltic
region as a whole, but also for particular regions, citizens, and enterprises. These include such measures as replacing phosphates in deter-

gents and decreasing nitrate discharges into the Baltic Sea. Others include the Baltic Energy Market Interconnection Plan (BEMIP), which will improve energy transmission among the Baltic states, and the maritime monitoring system already discussed. Some of these measures have already been implemented.

As of 2011, the European Council has been receiving annual reports on the implementation of the strategy. These show that the strategy has launched an impressive number of flagship projects, although they will take time to bear fruit. For example, the challenge of limiting the dumping of nitrates into the Baltic Sea is recognized in theory by the farming community. The latest pollution reports, however, have revealed that these effluents have not decreased as expected and the level of eutrophication is still unsatisfactory.[32] Despite these shortcomings, the Baltic Sea strategy offers the potential for overcoming the myriad problems that have plagued cooperation in the Baltic region in the past. And as the various actors and organizations work out a common agenda, it will be necessary to communicate this agenda to their members and their citizens in order to create regional awareness and consensus.[33]

If the Baltic Sea region is able to transform itself into a model region with competitive research and innovation, sustainable environmental policies, attractive conditions for international investors, and a high quality of life, the consequences will be enormous. In the era of globalization, such success would prepare the region to compete with those located outside of Europe. In addition, Europe as a whole, as well as other European regions, could both learn and benefit from the cross-border cooperation that made regional cohesiveness possible. To date, no other European region has been the focus of such intensive efforts based on cooperation among the European Commission, the states, and the regional stakeholders. These efforts could provide a model for regions throughout Europe as well as in Asia and elsewhere.[34]

Conclusion

THIS history of the Baltic Sea illustrates clearly that trade and cultural exchange initially constituted the Baltic Sea as a region, and that politics came to shape the region only later. Scandinavians, Slavs, Finns, and Balts took part in long-distance trade that was concentrated in multiethnic markets, with Frisian, Jewish, and Arab merchants establishing connections with the North Sea, the Mediterranean, the Near East, and even Central Asia. The wares in which they traded—whether utilitarian or cultural—contributed to the refinement of the lives of the elite. Regional power structures developed as a result of trade and theft, and, over time, trade came to be concentrated in the emerging princely residences. Merchants were persuaded to settle here and cities and towns were founded that urbanized the Baltic coast. From here, the Hanseatic merchants came to dominate trade by establishing relations with producers in the hinterland, either directly or by way of local middlemen.

Because an ecclesiastic infrastructure was built up at the same time, numerous economic, religious, and cultural networks were formed in and around the Baltic Sea, and to this day the architectural heritage that has survived attests to the effectiveness of the Hanseatic League as an organizational model.

The Nordic monarchies and personal unions under a single monarch, such as the Kalmar Union and the Kingdom and Grand Duchy of Poland-Lithuania, that came to power during the Late Middle Ages both cooperated and competed with the Hanseatic League. Among other things, they were dependent on Hanseatic monies in the pursuit of their political disputes. But increasingly, they attempted to share in the profits of the Hanseatic merchants, as happened when Denmark began to claim the right to control the Øresund and collect tolls from ships passing through it. Other mercantile nations, notably the Netherlands, exploited the weakened Hanseatic position and began to integrate the

Baltic Sea region into their increasingly global economic plans. The Dutch were greatly aided by the technical superiority of their trading techniques, shipping and shipbuilding, and craft. Their ability to finance trade and their cultural influence also added immeasurably to their success. Although the Baltic monarchies fought among themselves over a share of the trade and Sweden achieved a virtual monopoly during the seventeenth century, in practical terms all of these powers were dependent on the prowess of Dutch entrepreneurs and mariners. At the same time, Dutch and German architects created the representational pomp that demonstrated Swedish hegemony to the world.

The entire Baltic region followed the "Netherlands" model. Peter the Great's Baltic ambitions, for example, culminated in his drive to create a new Amsterdam—although St. Petersburg redounded primarily to the benefit of English merchants. The English now had access to a large expanse of relatively virgin Russian hinterland from which to extract shipbuilding materials and iron. The peasants in the Baltic hinterland never crossed the sea, and they dealt with the ports only to the extent that they ferried the wares and products of the manors to market. They were nonetheless affected in an immediate way by the trade and cultural exchange that the Baltic Sea made possible. Merchants exploited the seemingly inexhaustible resources of land and forest, with the peoples living along the shores of the Baltic supplying enormous quantities of grain, flax and hemp, wood and forestry products, and later leather to the world economy. The ready availability of land and the demand for grain caused the nobility to produce large quantities of grain on their own manorial farms. The peasants were forced to work on these farms, and their freedom of movement was severely restricted. They were reduced to serfs. Because cultural commodities could be acquired only for money or grain, the nobility, in its desire to emulate western European culture, increasingly exploited the peasants. This led to an "agrarian question," which was never fully resolved, even by the collectivization that took place after World War II. Even in Sweden and Finland, where the peasants were not serfs, social differentiation increased in the countryside such that the proportion of peasants who were land poor or landless increased dramatically.

While the Baltic constituted an economic region structured around agriculture, it was also a locus of communication. The lingua franca of the region was Low German, and the channels through which Hanseatic trade moved—aided by the invention of the printing press—spread the ideas of the Reformation far from their original sources. This also applied when the English and Scottish Enlightenment fell on fertile ground in Danzig and Königsberg and Adam Smith found his way into the curriculum of the University of Königsberg. Both the nobility and the middle class stayed informed by reading the *Gazette de Leyde* and the *Hamburgische unpartheyische Correspondent* and took their social and consumerist cues from the *Journal des Luxus und der Moden*. At the same time, scholars such as August Ludwig von Schlözer and Johann Gottfried Herder unearthed the history and popular culture of the smaller ethnic populations living in the Baltic region and made their findings known. They also provided a stimulus for collecting folk songs. The literature of Weimar classicism and Jena romanticism inspired numerous national poets in the region. By contrast, Nordic romanticism in painting was invented at the Copenhagen Art Academy, while students at the architectural academy in Berlin sought new urban solutions in keeping with the regional awareness that was developing. Painters such as Albert Edelfelt, Anders Zorn, and the painters of the Skagen group, who specialized in Baltic landscapes, were inspired by their studies in Paris. This appreciation of the Baltic, which had begun as an aristocratic or upper-class pleasure, was transformed in the twentieth century, when members of the middle class joined artists and writers and spent their summers on the Baltic Sea.

In the twentieth century, the new states in the Baltic Sea region were culturally caught between their desire to create a national identity and their relationship to the past. For example, the idealization of rural life in literature and the revival of brick Gothic architecture hearkened back to an earlier time in history, although the rediscovered materials also came to be used in the new functionalist buildings of architects such as Gunnar Asplund and Alvar Aalto. A similar dichotomy is found in politics as well—as can be seen in the desire to coordinate the foreign policies of the Scandinavian and Baltic states along with Poland in a "Baltic League," which fell apart because of the divergent interests of the various partners. Nonetheless, Poland and the Baltic states institutionalized research into their common Baltic past. The first conference of historians of the Baltic region, which took place in 1937 in Riga, was overshadowed by the expansionist policies of Germany and the Soviet Union, which changed the Baltic region permanently through their war, occupation, mass killings, deportations, and Sovietization.

Although connections such as those between the Soviet Union and Finland or Sweden never disappeared completely and eventually gained new life during the process of détente, the events of 1989 created new possibilities for the Baltic region, first as a transformation region (from socialism to capitalism, from party dictatorship to democracy) and then as a model region within the European Union. The states that surround the Baltic Sea have been supremely successful in reinventing themselves as a region. Under a single regional umbrella organization (Council of the Baltic Sea States), these states, substate organizations, and nongovernmental organizations are working together with private stakeholders to work out a Baltic future that makes sense to *them*.

At a time when international policies are defined less and less by nation-states and when states must share the political stage with other actors at the international, subnational, and supranational levels, the flat hierarchies in the Baltic Sea region provide an admirable model. They remind us of the horizontal structures that characterized the Hanseatic League, and they could well serve as a model, not only for other regions in Europe, such as the Mediterranean, but also for regions in Asia, such as the South China Sea.

Place Name Concordance

In naming places, we have mainly used the common English- or German-language variants or in some cases the spellings used in contemporary sources. The following concordance gives an overview of place names in the various languages, with the variant most frequently used in the book in bold.

English/German	Polish	Russian	Swedish/Danish	Estonian/Finnish	Lithuanian/Latvian
Altmark	Stary Targ				
Arensburg				Kuressaare	
Baltischport		Baltijskij Port	Rågervik	Paldiski	
Braunsberg	Braniewo				
Cammin	Kamień Pomorski				
Cracow/Krakau	Kraków				
Cranz		Zelenogradsk			
Culm/Kulm	Chełmno				
Danzig	**Gdańsk**				
Dorpat	Derpt Dorpat Dorpt	Derpt Jur'ev		Tartu	
Elbing	Elbląg				
Fellin		Vil'jandi		Viljandi	
Gedingen	**Gdynia**				
Gnesen	Gniezno				
Goldingen					Kuldiga (La)

Greifenberg	Gryfice				
Hapsal			**Hapsal**	Haapsalu	
Harrien				Harju	
Jerwen				Järva	
Kovno/Kauen	Kowno	Kovno			**Kaunas** (Li)
Kexholm/Kecksholm		Priosersk	**Kexholm**	Käkisalmi	
Kokenhusen		Kukeinos			Koknese (La)
Kolbatz	Kolbacz				
Kolberg	Kolobrzeg				
Königsberg	Królewiec		**Kaliningrad**		
Köslin	Koszalin				
Lemsal					Limbaži (La)
Libau		Liepaja			Liepāja (La)
Lissa	Leszno				
Marienwerder	Kwidzyn				
Memel	Klaipeda	Klaipeda			Klaipėda (Li)
Mitau	Mitawa				Jelgava (La)
Moscow		Moskva			
Narva		Narva		Narva	
Neidenburg	Nidzica				

(continued)

English/German	Polish	Russian	Swedish/Danish	Estonian/Finnish	Lithuanian/Latvian
Neustad			**Nystad**	Uusikaupunki	
Nöteburg / Schlüsselburg		Schlusselburg / Petrokrepost'	**Nöteborg**	Pähkinälinna	
Novgorod / Navgard / Naugard		**Novgorod**			
Nyenschantz		Nijenschánz	**Nyen** / Nyenskans		
Oliva					
Ösel				Saaremaa	
Osterode	Ostróda				
Pernau	Parnawa	Pernov		**Pärnu**	Pärnu (Li) / Piarnu (Li) / Pērnava (La)
Pilten	Piltyń				Piltene (La)
Pleskau	Psków	**Pskov**		Pihkva	Pleskava (La) / Pskovas (Li)
Pyritz	Pyrzyce				

Reval	Rewal	Kolyvan' Revel'		**Tallinn**	
Riga	Riga				Rīga (La)
Ribe/Ripen			Ribe		
Rügenwalde	Darłowo				
St. Petersburg **Petrograd** **Leningrad**					
Soldau	Działdowo				
Stargard	Stargard Szczeciński				
Stettin **Szczecin**	Szczecin				
Stolp	Słupsk				
Swinemünde	Świnoujście				
Thorn	Toruń				
Tilsit	Sovetsk				Tilžė (Li)
Viborg/Wiborg	**Vyborg**		**Viborg**	**Viipuri**	
Vilnius/Wilna	Wilno	Vil'na			**Vilnius** (Li)
Warsaw	Warszawa				

(*continued*)

Table (continued)

English/German	Polish	Russian	Swedish/Danish	Estonian/Finnish	Lithuanian/Latvian
Wenden/**Wendau**	Werki	Kes'		Cēsis	Võnnu (La) Verkiai (Li)
Wiek				Lääne	
Wierland				Virumaa	
Windau					Ventspils (Li)
Wolin	Wolin				
Wolmar		Volodimirets		Volmari	Valmiera (Li / La)
Zoppot	Sopot				
			Åbo	**Turku**	
			Brändö	**Kulosaari**	
			Gamlakarleby Karleby	Kokkola	
			Hangö	**Hanko**	
			Helsingfors	**Helsinki**	
			Tavastehus	Hämeenlinna	
			Uleåborg	Oulu	
			Vasa	**Vaasa**	

Notes

INTRODUCTION: TRADE AND CULTURES

1. F. Braudel (1972).
2. D. Kirby (1990); D. Kirby (1995); M. Klinge (1994); M. Klinge (2010); A. Palmer (2005).
3. K. Schlögel (2003), pp. 68–69.
4. For more on the Mediterranean and Braudel's approach, see also D. Abulafia in W. V. Harris (2005), pp. 64–94, here 65. For an understanding of the Baltic Sea as a natural environment, see H. Küster (2002).
5. *Mare Balticum remigans=traveling over the Baltic Sea.*
6. O. Holder-Egger, ed. (1911, reprinted 1965), p. 15.
7. W. Laur (2001).
8. *Nunc autem, . . . , aliquid de natura Baltici maris dicere . . . Sinus ille ab incolis appelatur Balticus, eo quod in modum baltei longu tractu per Scithicas regiones tendatur usque ad Grecium.* Schmeidler (1917), pp. 58, 237–238. ("Now, to say something about the nature of the Baltic Sea . . . this gulf is called Baltic by the inhabitants because it stretches like a belt to the regions of the Scythians and to Greece.") (Adam of Bremen).
9. M. Tamm, in Murray (2009), pp. 11–36; also M. Tamm, in Merisalo, ed. (2006), pp. 147–172.
10. For more on the concept of the Baltic Sea in the Middle Ages, see J. Svennung (1953); H. Ludat (1952), pp. 222–248.
11. *Codex Diplomaticus Lubecensis* (1976), pp. 92–93.
12. Letter of safe passage from Albrecht of Bavaria for the Hanseatic cities, April 10, 1401, in H. A. Poelmann, ed. (1917), p. 182. I thank my colleague Hielke van Nieuwenhuize for a list of the Dutch sources.
13. J. Hackmann, in H. Bosse, O.-H. Elias, and R. Schweitzer, eds. (2005), pp. 15–39, here 21.
14. Record from Amsterdam, October 20, 1493. Verein für Hansische Geschichte, ed. (1916) *Hansisches Urkundenbuch*, 11: 453–455.
15. Variants include: Oostersche Zee, Ostersche Zee, Oestersche Zee, Oistersche Zee. Oostzee appears in a description of the damage done to Bruges and Flanders, April 19, 1533. See R. Häpke (1913–1923), pp. 105–106; see also pp. 116–119: Der Hof von Holland und Statthalter Hoogstraten, June 18, 1533.
16. *Resolutiën der Staten-Generaal van 1576 tot 1609*, July 7, 1586, vol. 5, 1585–1587, RGP Grote Serie 47 (1921), p. 367.
17. *Resolutiën der Staten-Generaal van 1576 tot 1609*, February 24, 1600, vol. 11, 1600–1601, RGP Grote Serie 85 (1941), p. 329.
18. Multiple names are used in the sources. In addition to Merchants of Eastland, we also find Th'eastland Merchants and Company of Eastlande Merchants. See M. Sellers, ed. (1906).
19. *Resolutiën der Staten-Generaal van 1576 tot 1609*, February 28, 1590, vol. 7, 1590–1592, RGP Grote Serie 55 (1923), p. 290.

20. *Resolutiën der Staten-Generaal van 1576 tot 1609*, February 27, 1606, vol. 13, 1604–1606, RGP Grote Serie 101 (1957), p. 826.

21. A. Veen (1636).

22. J. H. Zedler, ed. (1733), pp. 289–290.

23. J. Hackmann, in H. Bosse, O.-H. Elias, and R. Schweitzer, eds. (2005), pp. 23–30.

24. M. Lehti (1999); M. Grzechnik (2012).

25. E. Maschke (1935); W. Hubatsch (1984).

26. M. Lehti (2003), pp. 11–49; M. Lehti (2006), pp. 494–510.

27. For more, see B. Turner (2010), pp. 317–326.

28. On the debate about cultural transfer and cultural exchange, see M. North, ed. (2009).

29. This is consistent with conceptualizations developed at the Mare Balticum postgraduate program at the University of Greifswald.

30. On the sea as a (selective) medium, see Y. Kaukiainen (1997), pp. 211–217; D. Kirby and M.-L. Hinkkanen (2000).

I. VIKINGS, SLAVS, AND BALTS

1. Schmeidler, ed. (1917), chapter 22, pp. 79–80.

2. J. Herrmann (1976), pp. 161–162. Contains the German translation of Adam's quotation.

3. D. Whitelock, ed. (1979), p. 842.

4. A good overview of the various regions of Viking expansion and control may be found in P. Sawyer, ed. (1997).

5. G. Hatz, in M. North, ed. (1995), p. 78.

6. J. Shepard, in S. Brink and N. Price, eds. (2008), pp. 496–516; F. Androshchuk, in S. Brink and N. Price, eds. (2008), pp. 517–542; F. Androshchuk (2013).

7. Quoted from C. Lübke (2004), p. 109.

8. Ibid.

9. J. Herrmann (1982), pp. 292–328.

10. B. Friedmann (1986).

11. C. Lübke, in R. Jaworski et al., eds. (2000), pp. 34–51.

12. H. Valk, in S. Brink and N. Price, eds. (2008b), pp. 485–495; M. Konsa et al. (2008), pp. 53–63.

13. A. Šne (2008), pp. 33–56; A. Šne, in A. V. Murray, ed. (2009), pp. 53–71; H. Valk (2008a), pp. 57–86.

14. A. Selart (2007), pp. 58–67.

15. J. Herrmann (1982), p. 125.

16. V. Hilberg, in S. Brink and N. Price, eds. (2008), pp. 101–111; S. Kalmring, in S. Sigmundsson, ed. (2011), pp. 245–259; K. Brandt et al., eds. (2002).

17. B. Ambrosiani, in S. Brink and N. Price, eds. (2008), pp. 94–100.

18. H. Steuer, *Zeitschrift für Archäologie* 12 (1978): 255–260; H. Steuer, in K. Düwel et al., eds. (1987), pp. 405–527.

19. D. Adamczyk, in I. Panic and J. Sperka, eds. (2007), pp. 15–27; D. Adamczyk, in A. Komlosy et al., eds. (2008), pp. 32–48.

20. G. Hatz (1974); G. Hatz, in K. Düwel et al., eds. (1987); G. Hatz, *Offa* 21/22 (1964–1965): 262; I. Leimus, *North Goes West* (2009): 7–34.

21. R. Hammel-Kiesow, in N. Angermann and K. Friedland, eds. (2002), pp. 25–68.

22. North (2012a), p. 366, defines villications as follows: "The feudal system was organized in *villicationes* or manors with scattered holdings, whereby the *villicatio* was composed of a demesne *(terra salica)*, which was worked by bonded farm labourers and dependent peasants, and peasant land (hide land)."

23. P. Sawyer (1982), pp. 39–64.

24. J. Peets (2003).

25. J. Herrmann (1976), pp. 202–204.

26. Ibid., pp. 206–208.

27. J. Herrmann (1982), pp. 24–32. Cf. also H. Janson, in J. Staecker, ed. (2009), pp. 171–191.

28. B. Sawyer (2000); Klinge (2010), p. 14; R. Bohn (1997), pp. 29–30.

29. J. Herrmann (1982), pp. 48–50.

30. Ibid., pp. 44–47.

31. Ibid., pp. 138–142.

2. THE CHRISTIAN MISSION AND THE SETTLEMENT OF THE LAND

1. J. E. Olesen, in O. Auge, F. Biermann, and C. Herrmann, eds. (2009), pp. 49–58; W. Schich, in O. Auge, F. Biermann, and C. Herrmann, eds., pp. 235–253.

2. R. Bartlett (1993); also A. V. Murray (2001), A. V. Murray (2009).

3. D. Harrison, in D. Harrison, ed. (2010a), pp. 120–121.

4. B. Sawyer and P. Sawyer (2003), pp. 147–159; D. Harrison, in D. Harrison, ed. (2010a), pp. 121–124.

5. S. C. Rowell (1994); W. Paravicini (1989, 1995).

6. D. Harrison, in D. Harrison, ed. (2010b), pp. 219–224.

7. A.-E. Christiansen (1980), pp. 109–117, 177–182; D. Harrison, in D. Harrison, ed. (2010c), pp. 449–452; J. Korpela, *Journal for Baltic Studies* 33/4 (2002): 384–397, here 386–387; K. Katajala, *Scandinavian Journal of History* 37/1 (February 2012): 23–48, 38.

8. R. Wittram (1954), pp. 28–30.

9. H. Boockmann (1999), pp. 181–191.

10. K. Militzer (2005), pp. 72–77.

11. H. Boockmann (1999), pp. 126–129.

12. Ibid., p. 126.

13. Ibid., pp. 112–113.

14. A. Šne, in A. V. Murray, ed. (2009), pp. 53–71, here 63–66.

15. Ibid., pp. 70–71.

16. P. Line, in A. V. Murray, ed. (2009), pp. 73–99.

17. A. Šne, in A. V. Murray, ed. (2009), p. 67.

18. F. Biermann, in O. Auge, F. Biermann, and C. Herrmann, eds. (2009), pp. 9–37; E. Badstübner, in H. Schwillus and A. Hölscher, eds. (2000), pp. 136–147.

3. THE HANSEATIC LEAGUE AND THE MONARCHIES

1. A. Schmidt, ed. (1962), p. 54.

2. W. Reisner (1903), p. 99; M. Scheftel (1988), p. 11.

3. V. Henn, in V. Henn et al., eds. (1989), pp. 15–21; review in R. Hammel-Kiesow (2008).

4. E. Hoffmann, in A. Graßmann, ed. (1988), pp. 79–340, here 134–150; E. Groth (1999); D. Harrison, in D. Harrison, ed. (2010b), pp. 198–200.

5. T. H. Lloyd (1991); S. Jenks, *Hansische Geschichtsblätter* 108 (1990): 45–86.

6. H. Wernicke (1983).

7. N. Jörn, R.-G. Werlich, and H. Wernicke, eds. (1998b); K. Fritze (1967).

8. P. Dollinger (1989), pp. 275–340; J. Bracker and R. Postel, eds. (1999), pp. 700–757; H. Samsonowicz, in S. Jenks and M. North, eds. (1993), pp. 23–30.

9. S. Jenks (1992); J. D. Fudge (1995).

10. D. Seifert (1997); J. Schildhauer, *Jahrbuch für Wirtschaftsgeschichte* 9/4 (1968): 187–211.

11. J. Bracker and R. Postel, eds. (1999), pp. 110–195.

12. T. Riis (2003).

13. N. Bracke (1999), pp. 19–39.

14. J. Rosén (1939); A.-E. Christensen (1980), p. 12.

15. J. E. Olesen, in K. Helle, ed. (2003), pp. 710–770, here 740.

16. J. E. Olesen (1980); J. E. Olesen, in W. Paravicini, ed. (1991), pp. 213–231.

17. N. Davies (2005), pp. 93–113.

18. K. Militzer (2005), pp. 143–156.

19. K. Baczkowski (1999), pp. 277–303.

20. O. J. Benedictow, in K. Helle, ed. (2003), pp. 237–249.

21. J. Kahk and E. Tarvel (1997).

22. J. E. Olesen, in T. Fischer and T. Riis, eds. (2006), pp. 167–180.

23. J. Vahtola, in K. Helle, ed. (2003), pp. 576–580.

24. K. Kasiske (1934); H. Wunder (1968).

25. H. Reincke, in H. Reincke (1951), pp. 167–200, here 170; W. Reisner (1903), p. 99; J. H. Ibs (1994), p. 136; B. Noodt, in R. Hammel-Kiesow and M. Hundt, eds. (2005), pp. 55–66, here 58; R. Hammel, in A. Falk and R. Hammel, eds. (1987), pp. 85–300, here 141.

26. S. Jenks, in M. North, ed. (2005), pp. 15–111; A. v. Brandt (1966), pp. 215–239.

27. S. Jenks (2005), pp. 63–64.

28. More recently, some architectural historians have begun to view the Lübeck Cathedral as a stylistic breakthrough because the Marienkirche was eventually rebuilt as a cathedral church. See E. Badstübner (2005).

29. N. Zaske and R. Zaske (1985), pp. 45–80.

30. J. von Bonsdorff (1993).

31. Now interpreted as representing the stalls of the traveling merchants to Riga instead of the Novgorod merchants. See T. Brück, in N. Angermann and P. Kaegbein, eds. (2001), pp. 97–136.

32. H. Bolte, *Jahrbuch für die Geschichte Mittel- und Ostdeutschlands* 52 (2006): 227–262.

33. S. Bagge (2001).

34. C. I. Ståhle, *Ny illustrerad svensk litteratur-historia* 1 (1967); V. Jansson (1945); R. Pipping (1943); H. H. Ronge (1964).

35. W. Ziesemer (1928).

36. M. Bentlin (2008).

37. J. Meier and D. Möhn, in J. Bracker, V. Henn, and R. Postel, eds. (1999), pp. 524–534; T. Behrmann, *Frühmittelalterliche Studien* 36 (2002): 343–467.

38. R. Hammel, in A. Graßmann, ed. (1988), pp. 50–76; E. Hoffmann, in A. Graßmann, ed., (1988), pp. 79–340, here 297–315; W. D. Hauschild, in A. Graßmann, ed. (1988), pp. 341–432, here 359–365.

39. H. Stoob, *Hansische Geschichtsblätter* 100 (1982): 87–109; J. Bugenhagen (1517–1518), 2008.

40. A. Tvauri and T.-M. Utt (2007), pp. 141–154.

4. THE REFORMATION AND THE NORDIC RENAISSANCE

1. M. North, in M. North (1996a), pp. 197–208.

2. E.-B. Körber, Nordost-Archiv. *Zeitschrift für Regionalgeschichte, Aspekte der Reformation im Ostseeraum*, N. F. 13 (2004–2005): 15–44.

3. J. Wächter, in H. T. Porada, ed. (1997), pp. 179–188.

4. P. D. Lockhart (2007), pp. 25–35.

5. J. E. Olesen, Nordost-Archiv. *Zeitschrift für Regionalgeschichte, Aspekte der Reformation im Ostseeraum*, N. F. 13 (2004–2005), pp. 75–119; M. Schwarz Lausten (2008).

6. B. Eriksson, in D. Harrison and B. Eriksson, eds. (2013), pp. 456–460.

7. M. Bogucka, in E. Cieślak, ed. (1982), pp. 208–259, here 233–247.

8. M. G. Müller (1997), pp. 41–49, 198–204; M. Kuleczka (2010).

9. J. Lavery (2002), pp. 103–144.

10. G. von Pistohlkors, ed. (1994); C. Schmidt (2000); V. Helk (1977).

11. K. Ciesielska, *Studia i materiały do dziejów Wielkopolski i Pomorza* 4 (1958): 219–256; H. Penner (1963); a new overview is provided by E. Kizik (1994).

12. M. Bogucka (1956); F. Gause (1965), pp. 310–312.

13. M. Bogucka, in W. J. Wieringa et al., eds. (1983), pp. 55–56; M. Bogucka, in J. P. S. Lemmink and J. S. A. M. van Koningsbrugge, eds. (1990), pp. 22–24.

14. M. North, in W. E. Minchinton, ed. (1988b); S. Murdoch (2006), pp. 84–124, 127–169.

15. W. P. Blockmans, in S. Jenks and M. North, eds. (1993), pp. 49–58; P. Hoppenbrouwers and J. L. van Zanden, eds. (2001).

16. George Downing in a letter to Clarendon, July 8, 1661, cited in C. Wilson (1957), p. 3.

17. The literature on Baltic trade in the early modern period is vast. The following anthologies contain the best overviews: W. J. Wieringa et al., eds. (1983); W. G. Heeres et al., eds. (1988); J. P. S. Lemmink and J. S. A. M. van Koningsbrugge, eds. (1990); M. North (1996c). For more on the Dutch trade specifically, see J. Israel (1989).

18. M. van Tielhof (2002). For Holland, see M. van Tielhof (1995), pp. 97–98.

19. M. North, in M. North (1996b), pp. 1–14.

20. M.-L. Pelus (1981), pp. 207, 220, 396–397. See also P. Jeannin, *Zeitschrift für Lübeckische Geschichte und Altertumskunde* 43 (1963): 19–67.

21. K. Kumlien, *Hansische Geschichtsblätter* 71 (1952): 14, table 1; E. F. Heckscher (1935), Bilaga V, S., p. 21, tables 3 and 4, and Bilaga VI, p. 30.

22. H. Wiese and J. Bölts (1966), p. 78, table 9.

342   NOTES TO PAGES 103–109

23. L. Beutin (1929); N. Jörn, *Zeitschrift des Vereins für Lübeckische Geschichte und Altertumskunde* 78 (1998a): 323–348, here 337; M. North, in M. Lanzinner and A. Strohmeyer, eds. (2006a), pp. 221–236.
24. M. North, *Journal European Economic History* 13 (1984): 117–127.
25. K. Zernack, in M. Biskup and K. Zernack, eds. (1983), pp. 1–20; M. Bogucka and H. Samsonowicz, *Studia nad gospodarką, społeczeństwem i rodziną w Europie późnofeudalnej* (1987): 139–151.
26. W. Rusiski, *Roczniki dziejów społecznych i gospodarczych* 39 (1978): 16–18; J. Topolski (1977), pp. 117–118.
27. M. North (1982), pp. 98–106. On the origins of the Amsterdam grain market, see M. van Tielhof (1995).
28. Compiled according to V. Arnim (1957); M. North (1990b).
29. W. Prange, in H. Patze, ed. (1983), pp. 519–553.
30. A. Wyczański, *Acta Poloniae Historica* 4 (1961): 119–132.
31. S. Mielczarski (1972), pp. 142–154; A. Wawrzyńczyk (1961), pp. 47–50.
32. M. North, *Zeitschrift für Ostforschung* 34 (1985): 39–47, here 43–44; A. Mączak (1962).
33. On the one hand, during the first two decades of the seventeenth century, when demand in the domestic market had decreased markedly, Osterode and Soldau delivered 71 percent and 65 percent of their rye, respectively, to Elbing. M. North (1985), p. 45; M. North (1982), pp. 34–36; M. North, *Zeitschrift für Historische Forschung* 26 (1999): 43–59.
34. H. Haack (1968), pp. 27–29; E. Münch, *Mecklenburger Jahrbücher* 112 (1997): 45–59, here 55–56.
35. P. D. Lockhart (2007), p. 85.
36. W. Prange (1971), pp. 26–28, 128–130, 592–594, 610–612; J. Jessen, *Zeitschrift der Gesellschaft für Schleswig-Holsteinische Geschichte* 51 (1922): 127–130; M. North, *Vierteljahrschrift für Sozial- und Wirtschaftsgeschichte* 70 (1983): 1–20, here 10–13, 18–19; M. North (1982), chapter 4, pp. 48–62.
37. H. Maybaum (1926), pp. 121–124; P. Steinmann (1960), p. 149; M. North (1982), pp. 79–82. Münch (1997), pp. 56–57, doubts the information given by Maybaum concerning the requirement of three days of corvée labor per week, since he found a case of six days per week of corvée labor in 1616. A. Wawrzyńczyk (1962), pp. 92–95, 121; W. Prange (1983), pp. 550–551; W. Prange, in C. Degn and D. Lohmeier, eds. (1980), pp. 63–64; M. North, in E. Schremmer (1994), pp. 77–89.
38. G.-E. Hoffmann and K. Reumann, *Geschichte Schleswig-Holsteins* 5 (1986): 189–190.
39. C. Schmidt (1997), pp. 29–30.
40. C. Schmidt (1997), pp. 54–56; M. Seppel, *Social History* 34/ 3 (2009): 284–300; M. Seppel, *Zeitschrift für Ostmitteleuropa-Forschung* 54/2 (2005): 174–192.
41. W. Prange, in H. Patze, ed. (1983), p. 249.
42. R. Hansen, in K. Friedland, ed. (1973), pp. 80–93, here 91: "Rantzovior[um] Insignia et Halle, Henricus Rantzovius, Johannis filius, Bredonis nepos, Caii abnepos, hoc predium cum circumiacentibus pagis a Frederico II rege Daniae

ac proceribus regni durante bello Svetico octenni sibi haeredibus, familiae ac posteris coemit et Ranzovisholmium appelari voluit. Anno Dni. MDLXVII, Anno suae aetatis XLIII."

43. D. Schleinert (1996), pp. 34–40.
44. F. Mager (1955), p. 108; T. Rudert, in J. Peters, ed. (1997), pp. 351–384.
45. W. Kula (1970). Cf. E. Melton, *Central European History* 21 (1988): 315–349; M. North, *Zeitschrift für Agrargeschichte und Agrarsoziologie* 36 (1988): 11–22. Cf. M. North, in E. Schremmer, ed. (1994), pp. 87–88.
46. J. Roding, in J. P. S. Lemmink and J. S. A. M. van Koningsbrugge, eds. (1996), pp. 95–106.
47. O. Koester (2000), pp. 8–10; O. Koester, in S. Heiberg, ed. (1988), pp. 301–302.
48. L. Müller (1988).
49. M. Bogucka, *Cahiers de Clio* (1984): 78–79, 14–16; M. Bogucka, in G. Labuda, ed. (1976), pp. 526–650, here 545–553, 561–571; Z. Nowak, in E. Ciéslak, ed. (1982), pp. 686–753, here 740–747, 750–753; M. Wardzyński, in M. Krieger and M. North, eds. (2004), pp. 23–50.
50. M. Wardzyński, in M. Krieger and M. North, eds. (2004), pp. 23–50.
51. A. Bartetzky (2000); H. Vredeman de Vries und die Renaissance im Norden (exhibition catalogue) (2002); Netherlandish Artists in Gdańsk in the Time of Hans Vredeman de Vries: Material from the Conference in Gdańsk, 20–21 November 2003, Gdańsk 2006.
52. For a review, see T. Hrankowska, ed. (1995).
53. M. Wardzyński (2004), pp. 23–50.
54. E. Kizik, in M. Krieger and M. North, eds. (2004), pp. 51–76, here 65–70.
55. Cf. M. North (2001a), pp. 79–100.
56. Ibid., pp. 100–122
57. A. Jolly, *Oud Holland* 113/1–2 (1999): 13–34.
58. H. D. Schroeder (2000).
59. M. Wisłocki (2005); B. Schmidt, ed. (2006); K. Kodres, in A. Schindling et al., eds. (2010), pp. 50–70.

5. SWEDISH DOMINANCE

1. T. Hall (2009), pp. 31–61; I. Svanberg, in G. Lindberg, ed. (1990), pp. 115–122.
2. N. E. Villstrand, in N. E. Villstrand, ed. (2013), pp. 90–92; M.-L. Rodén, in N. E. Villstrand, ed. (2013), pp. 178–184.
3. More on the innovations introduced by Dutch seafarers will be provided in the forthcoming Greifswald PhD dissertation of H. v. Nieuwenhuize: "Solche officiers die wohlerfahren, auch vaillante, courageuese und guthe solldaten seindh. Niederländische Seeoffiziere im schwedischen Dienst (1640–1660)."
4. M. Roberts, *Scandia* 48 (1982): 61–105; P. H. Wilson (2009), pp. 512–553.
5. For more on this and what follows, see R. L. Frost (2000), pp. 156–191.
6. Ibid. pp. 137–138.
7. N. E. Villstrand, in N. E. Villstrand, ed. (2013), pp. 134–141.
8. C.-J. Gadd (2000), pp. 81–82. For more on the reductions debate and the progress of reductions in Sweden and the reform of 1682, see A. F. Upton (1998), pp. 8–10, 51–70, 73–75.

9. H. Backhaus (1969); N. Jörn and M. North, eds. (2000); K. A. Modéer (1975); N. Jörn et al., eds. (2003).

10. For more on the situation in the Swedish Baltic provinces generally, see T. Jansson and T. Eng, eds. (2000).

11. H. v. z. Mühlen, in G. v. Pistohlkors, ed. (1994), pp. 195–202; A. F. Upton (1998), pp. 190–198.

12. P. D. Lockhart (2007), pp. 228–229.

13. K. J. V. Jespersen, in E. Kouri and T. Scott, eds. (1987), pp. 486–501; K. J. V. Jespersen (2004), pp. 40–48; R. Bohn (2001), pp. 69–77.

14. N. Davies (2005), pp. 246–283.

15. E. Cieślak, in E. Opgenoorth, ed. (1996), pp. 24–31; K. Friedrich (2000).

16. E. Opgenoorth, in E. Opgenoorth, ed. (1994), pp. 13–22.

17. E. Opgenoorth (1978), pp. 26–28, 113–115.

18. M. North, in A. Komlosy, H.-H. Nolte, and I. Sooman, eds. (2008d), pp. 132–147.

19. H. Brand, in L. Bes et al., eds. (2007), pp. 15–17.

20. J. A. Faber, in W. G. Heeres et al., eds. (1988), pp. 83–94; M. v. Tielhof (2002).

21. H. Kempas (1964), pp. 293–294; M. North, in W. J. Wieringa et al., eds. (1983b), pp. 73–83.

22. S.-E. Åström (1988), pp. 20–28; M. North, in M. North (1996b), pp. 1–14.

23. J. V. T. Knoppers and R. V. V. Nicholls, in K. Friedland and F. Irsigler, eds. (1981), p. 61.

24. J. T. Lindblad, in C. Lesger and L. Noordegraaf, eds. (1995), pp. 77–84.

25. E. Küng, *Forschungen zur baltischen Geschichte* 3 (2008): 87–102.

26. M. North (1982), pp. 114–118.

27. E. Waschinski (1959), pp. 211–213, 221; H. Wiese and J. Bölts (1966), pp. 233–335; M. North, *Blätter für deutsche Landesgeschichte* 126 (1990): 223–242, here 238–239.

28. J. Kahk (1999), p. 36; E. Cieślak, in G. Labuda, ed. (1984), p. 62; S. Hoszowski (1957), pp. 398–340.

29. M. North (2008b), pp. 58–59.

30. M. North, *Zeitschrift für Agrargeschichte und Agrarsoziologie* 36 (1988): 13–15; M. North, in E. Schremmer, ed. (1994), pp. 77–89, here 81–82.

31. W. Prange (1971), pp. 29–31, 267–269.

32. H. Plehn (1906), p. 88; R. Schilling (1989), pp. 38–40.

33. R.-A. d'Hulst, (1982), pp. 29–30; twenty-seven of these paintings were delivered in 1648 and 1649.

34. K. Neville (2009), pp. 3–10.

35. A. Mollet (1981).

36. K. Neville (2009), pp. 23–60.

37. B. Noldus (2004), pp. 73–77, 84–92.

38. Ibid., pp. 95–118.

39. L. Hansar, *Studies on Art and Architecture* 18 (2009): 72–77.

40. S. I. Karling (1936), p. 353.

41. A. Langer, in J. Harasimowicz, P. Oszczanowski, and M. Wisłocki, eds. (2006), pp. 203–215.

42. J. G. L. Kosegarten (1857), pp. 258–259, 265.

43. M. Bogucka, in W. J. Wieringa et al., eds. (1983), pp. 55–56.; M. Bogucka, in J. P. S. Lemmink and J. S. A. M. V. Koningsbrugge, eds. (1990), pp. 22–24.
44. M. Bogucka, *Cahiers de Clio* 78–79 (1984): 15; M. Bogucka, *Acta Poloniae Historica* 33 (1976): 23–41.
45. For more on the Netherlands and Amsterdam specifically, see P. Burke (1974).
46. E. Kizik, in M. Krieger and M. North, eds. (2004), pp. 65–70; B. Noldus (2004), pp. 102–104.
47. G. v. Rauch (1969).
48. J. Kreslins, in J. Hackmann and R. Schweitzer, eds. (2006), pp. 321–330.
49. H. W. Schwab, in S.-O. Lindquist, ed. (1989), pp. 141–160.
50. A. T. Kuster, ed. (2005), pp. xvi–xvii.
51. F. Krummacher, in E. Ochs, N. Schüler, and L. Winkler, eds. (1996), pp. 341–357; B. Przybyszewska-Jarminska, in E. Ochs, N. Schüler, and L. Winkler, eds. (1996), pp. 414–426.

6. THE RISE OF RUSSIA

1. C. Ahlström, in W. J. Wieringa et al., eds. (1983), pp. 153–160; H. Storch (1794).
2. H. Saarinen (1996), pp. 202–213.
3. R. I. Frost (2000), pp. 294–296.
4. N. Davies (2005), p. 408.
5. M. G. Müller (1984); N. Davies (2005), pp. 386–411.
6. G. v. Pistohlkors, in G. v. Pistohlkors, ed. (1994), pp. 265–278.
7. Ibid., pp. 266–294.
8. F. Terveen (1954); F. Terveen, *Zeitschrift für Ostforschung* 1 (1952): 500–515; W. Mertineit (1958); see also above, p. 130.
9. O. Büsch (1981).
10. F.-W. Henning (1964), pp. 142–146; V. Gropp (1967), pp. 37–45.
11. E. Cieślak (1962); E. Cieślak (1972), p. 26.
12. W. Gastpary (1969); J. Dygdała (1977), pp. 14–15, 20, 23.
13. C. Bussenius (1960).
14. C. Jany (1967), vol. 3, pp. 24–34.
15. E. Mansén, in E. Mansén, ed. (2013a), pp. 31–32.
16. N. Kent (2008), pp. 101–109; J. Nordin, in P. Ihalainen et al., eds. (2011), pp. 29–40; H. Tandefelt, in P. Ihalainen et al., eds. (2011), pp. 41–53.
17. L. Herlitz (1974), p. 74; U. Jonsson (1980), pp. 54–55; M. Olsson, *Economic History Review* 59/3 (2006): 481–497.
18. M. Bregnsbo, in P. Ihalainen et al., eds. (2011), pp. 55–65.
19. For more on the cultural development of Copenhagen and Denmark, see p. 202 in the German edition of this work.
20. J. A. Faber, in W. G. Heeres et al., eds. (1988), pp. 83–94, here 89–91.
21. D. Ormrod (2003), pp. 284–287.
22. H. C. Johansen, in W. J. Wieringa et al., eds. (1983), pp. 161–170. This may seem strange since a steep decline in Dutch trade and shipping is generally assumed after the Fourth Anglo-Dutch War; J. Vries and A. van der Woude (1997), p. 493.
23. P. Pourchasse (2006), pp. 99–110, 115–134.
24. J. de Vries and A. van der Woude (1997), pp. 498–503.

25. E. Mansén, in E. Mansén, ed. (2013b), pp. 70–71.

26. C. Koninckx, in J. R. Bruijn, ed. (1993), pp. 121–138.

27. M. Krieger (1998); O. Feldbaek (1997), pp. 63–131.

28. E. Cieślak and J. Trzoska, in E. Cieślak, ed. (1993), pp. 357–444, here 402–419.

29. S.-E. Åström (1988), pp. 99–103.

30. A. Attman (1983), pp. 65–66.

31. J. Knoppers (1976), pp. 146–155.

32. S.-E. Åström (1988), pp. 90–93.

33. A. Kahan, in A. C. Cross, ed. (1979), pp. 181–189.

34. A. Attmann (1973), pp. 45–47; M. North, in A. Komlosy, H.-H. Nolte, and
I. Sooman, eds. (2008d), pp. 141–142.

35. Cf. H. Bosse, in O.-H. Elias et al., eds. (1996), pp. 165–208.

36. W. Lenz (1953); H. Bosse, *Zeitschrift für Ostforschung* 35/4 (1986): 519–534.

37. U. Plath, in A. Bauerkämper et al., eds. (2004), pp. 43–69, here 45–46; U. Plath
(2011).

38. I. Jürjo (2006), pp. 27–32.

39. K. Deecke (2011).

40. H. Rietz (1977), p. 87.

41. Ibid., p. 91.

42. A. Sommerlat (2010), pp. 39–41.

43. Quotation from H. Ischreyt, *Deutsche Studien* 46 (1974): 116–126, here 116.

44. M. North, in G. Schmidt, ed. (2010b), pp. 83–96, here 94–95.

45. See A. Eberts (2009).

46. A. Önnerfors (2003); A. Muschik, *Baltische Studien* N. F. 93 (2007): 163–184.

47. A. Hillebrand (2009), p. 277.

48. Ibid., pp. 227–276.

49. H. Rietz, in G. Labuda, ed. (1984), pp. 764–820, here 803–811.

50. I. Jürjo (2006), pp. 192–194; H. von Wistinghausen, in O.-H. Elias, ed. (1996),
pp. 255–304; H. von Wistinghausen (1995).

51. A. Sommerlat (2010), pp. 60–68.

52. E. Mansén, in E. Mansén, ed. (2013c), pp. 370–372.

53. Continued as *Neue critische Nachrichten* (1765–1774) and *Neueste critische
Nachrichten* (1775–1807). A. Önnerfors (2003), pp. 70–83, 209–239; A. Önnerfors, in M. North and R. Riemer, eds. (2008), pp. 238–248.

54. H. Bosse, in L. P. A. Kitching, ed. (1997), pp. 105–122, here 109–111; M. North
(2008c), pp. 141–148.

55. H. Rietz (1977), pp. 50–53; J. Krämer (1998), pp. 859–868.

56. H. Bosse, in L. P. A. Kitching, ed. (1997), p. 117.

57. J. Ciechowicza (2004).

58. U. Ebel (1990), pp. 37–45. See also below (nineteenth century), pp. 218–219.

59. H.-E. Boedecker, P. Veit, and M. Werner, eds. (2002).

60. J. Müller-Blattau (1968), pp. 68–69.

61. A. Hodgson (1984), pp. 82–97.

62. M. North (2012b).

63. E. Korthals-Altes, *Simiolus* 31 (2004–2005): 216–250.

64. P. Hertz (1924), pp. 358–390, here 364–365; M. North (2012b), pp. 21–36.

65. K. J. V. Jespersen et al. (2010).

66. M. North, in A. Golahny, M. M. Mochizuki, and L. Vergara, eds., (2006b), pp. 301–331; M. North (2012b), pp. 55–72, 83–88.
67. K. Neville (2009).
68. E. Manikowska (2007); E. Manikowska, in M. Krieger and M. North, eds. (2004), pp. 109–128. For more on Katharina's acquisition of the Gotzkosky collection as the basis for a gallery, see C. Frank, in M. North, ed. (2002), pp. 117–194.
69. E.g., J. Bernoulli (1780).
70. C. Heß (2007); J. Driesner (2003); J. Driesner (2011).
71. A. Drost (2003); A. Drost, *Zeitschrift Barock Geschichte-Literatur-Kunst* (2006): 105–122; A. Drost, *Blätter für Deutsche Landesgeschichte* 139 (2003–2004): 301–320.
72. E. Donnert (2002), pp. 85–118.
73. J. Maiste (2007), pp. 395–411.
74. K. Polli and R. Raudsepp, eds. (2007).
75. S. Lorentz (1937).

7. NORDIC ROMANTICISM

1. M. Bell and M. Hietala (2002), pp. 18–30.
2. See above, pp. 157–158.
3. C. Hänsch et al., eds. (2008).
4. See above, pp. 151–152.
5. M. North and R. Riemer, eds. (2008).
6. E. F. Heckscher (1964), pp. 178–179.
7. F. Voeltzer (1924), pp. 37–41.
8. M. North, in H.-W. Hahn et al., eds. (2008a), pp. 101–122.
9. R. Glenthøj and M. Nordhagen Ottosen (2014).
10. S. Kinzler, ed. (2013).
11. F. Singleton (1998), pp. 61–67.
12. R. Jaworski, in R. Jaworski and M. Müller, eds. (2000), pp. 253–303.
13. E. Hoffmann (1985), p. 24; see also E. Hoffmann, *Zeitschrift der Gesellschaft für Schleswig-Holsteinische Geschichte* 111 (1986): 143–155.
14. Cf. F. C. Dahlmann, *Kieler Blätter* 1 (1815): 47–84, 245–303; N. N. Falck (1825), pp. 348–358.
15. R. Tuchtenhagen (2009b), pp. 103–107.
16. M. North, in D. Lohmeier and R. Paczkowski, eds., (2001b), pp. 79–89.
17. U. Lange, ed. (2003), pp. 440–448.
18. K. J. V. Jespersen (2004), pp. 61–64.
19. E. Mansén, in E. Mansén, ed. (2013d), p. 633.
20. K. J. V. Jespersen (2004), pp. 196–203.
21. See below, pp. 214, 217.
22. I. Bohn (2005), pp. 152–163.
23. A. Loit, in A. Loit, ed. (1985), pp. 59–81, here 74f.
24. E. Jansen, in A. Loit, ed. (1985), pp. 41–57.
25. J. Hackmann, in E. Fischer et al., eds. (2007b), pp. 293–320, here 306.
26. K. Wohlfahrt (2006); see also J. Hackmann (2007a), J. Hackmann, ed. (2012).
27. M. Garleff (2001), pp. 77–82; P. W. Werth (2014), pp. 79–81, 129–130.

28. C. Bjøern, *The Scandinavian Economic History Review* 25 (1977): 117–137; K. J. V. Jespersen (2004), pp. 132–139. For more on innovations in Schleswig-Holstein, Mecklenburg, and Brandenburg, see M. Cerman (2012), pp. 102–104.

29. W. Prange (1971).

30. C. Degn (1959–1969), pp. 247–264.

31. R. Bohn (2001), p. 85.

32. I. Bohn (2005), pp. 164–172.

33. J. Kahk, *Zeitschrift für Ostmitteleuropa-Forschung* 45/4 (1996): 544–555; K. Lust, *Zeitschrift für Ostmitteleuropa-Forschung* 55/4 (2006): 510–525.

34. F.-W. Henning (1964), pp. 142–146; V. Gropp (1967), pp. 37–45.

35. V. Gropp (1967), p. 51.

36. Ibid., pp. 163–164. The additional financial burdens are calculated only for the peasants working the demesnes.

37. On this and the following, see M. North (2008b), pp. 71–72.

38. P. Boje, in M. North, ed. (1993), pp. 21–38.

39. I. Buchsteiner (1993).

40. M. Fritz et al., in M. North, ed. (1993), pp. 79–93; B. Stråth, in B. Stråth (2012a), pp. 318–366.

41. D. Kirby and M.-L. Hinkkanen (2000), pp. 204–210, here 204–205; Y. Kaukiainen, *International Journal of Maritime History* 4 (1992): 175–191.

42. Y. Kaukiainen (1991), pp. 150–174; F. Hodne, in M. North, ed. (1993), pp. 39–58.

43. M. Garleff (2001), pp. 75–77.

44. N. Kent (2008), pp. 185–186; B. Stråth, in B. Stråth (2012b), pp. 367–382; B. Stråth, in B. Stråth (2012c), pp. 417–445.

45. G. Saetra, in P. van Royen et al., eds. (1997), pp. 173–210, here 178. See also the other Scandinavian articles in this volume.

46. H. G. Schröter (2007).

47. T. U. Raun, in G. v. Pistohlkors et al., eds. (1995), pp. 85–102, here 100–101; R. Pullat (1972), p. 60.

48. U. v. Hirschhausen (1999), pp. 521–523.

49. M. Bell and M. Hietala (2002), p. 30.

50. J. Maiste, K. Polli, and M. Raisma (2003); J. Maiste (1999), vol. 2.

51. J. Maiste (2007).

52. Arken Museum of Modern Art (2008), *The Skagen Painters: In a New Light.* In connection with the exhibition "The Skagen Painters—In a New Light."

53. T. Martin and D. Sivén (1996).

54. C. Lengefeld (2004).

55. Jānis Staņislavs Roze, Kārlis Hūns, and Jūlijs Feders should be mentioned in this context.

56. See I. Pujāte (1991); D. Lamberga, in G. Reineking-v. Bock, ed. (2007), pp. 145–167.

57. V. Landsbergis (1992); L. Laučkaite (2008), pp. 72–83. See below as well, p. 285.

58. F. Dahlström, in G. Andersson, ed. (2001), pp. 104–127, here 120–121. For more on the influence of the Leipzig Conservatory, see Y. Wasserloos (2004), pp. 65–69, 85–86.

59. F. K. Smith (2002), pp. 33–35, 39–45.

60. Ibid., pp. 37–39; B. Curtis (2008), pp. 132–133.

61. F. K. Smith (2002), pp. 35–37, 58–59.

62. E. Salmenhaara, in A. Kalevi et al., eds. (1996), pp. 21–76; D. M. Grimley, ed. (2011).

63. On the role of intellectuals in the national movement, see above, pp. 195–196.

64. F. J. Marker and L.-L. Marker (1996), pp. 96–161.

65. G. C. Lichtenberg, *Göttinger Taschen Calender* (1793): 109.

66. W. Karge (1993). A good overview of the origins of Bad Doberan and other seaside resorts are contained in the state examination thesis by A. Brenner (2010).

67. O. Kurilo, ed. (2009).

68. More on this and the following in M. Klinge (1994), pp. 130–133; M. Klinge (2010), pp. 164–167.

69. Cf. above, pp. 213–215.

8. REVOLUTIONS AND NEW STATES

1. U. v. Hirschhausen (2006), pp. 38–41; J. Hackmann, in E. Mühle and N. Angermann, eds. (2004), pp. 149–172.

2. H. Meinander (2013), pp. 117–123.

3. I. Bohn (2005), pp. 198–202.

4. R. Tuchtenhagen (2009b), p. 107.

5. G. Liulevičius (2000).

6. F. Singleton (1998), pp. 108–115.

7. T. U. Raun (2001), pp. 104–111; A. Plakans (1995), pp. 116–120; R. Tuchtenhagen (2009a), pp. 81–82.

8. M. Klinge (1994), pp. 140–141.

9. A. Palmer (2005), pp. 301–302.

10. R. Tuchtenhagen (2009a), pp. 84–86.

11. K. J. V. Jespersen (2004), pp. 162–165.

12. N. Kent (2008), pp. 219–221.

13. H. G. Schröter (2007), p. 68.

14. R. Tuchtenhagen (2008a), pp. 120–125; F. Bajohr and M. Wildt, eds. (2009); T. Etzemüller, *Mittelweg* 36/18 (2009): 49–63; Y. Hirdman, U. Lundberg, and J. Björkman, in Y. Hirdman, U. Lundberg, and J. Björkman, eds. (2012), pp. 200–231.

15. P. Wulf, in U. Lange, ed. (1996a), pp. 513–548.

16. M. North (2008b), pp. 81–82.

17. For more on the agrarian reforms of 1919, see T. Rosenberg, *Baltische Seminare* 14 (2009): 24–44.

18. W. Roszkowski (1995), pp. 91–103.

19. Ibid., pp. 128–132.

20. Ibid., pp. 141–143.

21. M. Hempe (2002); M. North (2008b), pp. 90–91.

22. K. Jandausch (2011).

23. J. Eellend, in P. Wawrzeniuk, ed. (2008), pp. 35–56.

24. T. U. Raun (2001), pp. 125–126.

25. H. G. Schröter, in M. North, ed. (1993), pp. 95–127.

26. R. Bohn (2001), p. 112.

27. H. G. Schröter (2007), pp. 78–82.
28. J. Valge, in A. M. Kõll and J. Valge, eds. (1998), pp. 95–135.
29. T. U. Raun (2001), pp. 126–128.
30. D. v. Nerée, in H. Wernicke and R.-G. Werlich, eds. (1996), pp. 363–377; M. North (2008b), pp. 91–93.
31. T. U. Raun (2001), p. 130; see also A. Kasekamp (2010), pp. 116–117.
32. T. U. Raun (2001), pp. 129–133.
33. C. Hasselblatt (1996).
34. M. Garleff, in G. v. Pistohlkors, ed. (1994), pp. 498–499; J. Hiden (2004).
35. D. Henning (1996), pp. 249–273.
36. T. U. Raun (2001), pp. 136–137; G. Kurman (1968); E. Nirk (1987), pp. 206–209; C. Hasselblatt (2006), pp. 449–469, 507–514.
37. D. Bleiere et al., eds. (2008), pp. 224–225; D. Bleiere (2006).
38. A. Plakans (1995), pp. 102–103, 106–107.
39. D. Bleiere et al., eds. (2008), p. 224.
40. E. Eriksson, in C. Caldenby et al., eds. (1998), pp. 46–79; E. Rudberg, in C. Caldenby et al., eds. (1998), pp. 80–108.
41. K. Kodres, ed. (2010b).
42. J. Hackmann, in B. Lichtnau, ed. (2007c), pp. 118–134.
43. D. Bleiere et al., eds. (2008), pp. 226–230; J. Krastiņš (1996).
44. P. Wulf, in U. Lange, ed. (1996b), pp. 553–589, here 549–550, 571–572.
45. J. Jacoby, in K. Ketting, ed. (1987), pp. 32–38.
46. J. Kask and G. Bergendal, in G. Bergendal, ed. (1998), pp. 11–15.
47. A. Kalevi et al., eds. (1996), pp. 65–77.
48. D. Bleiere et al., eds. (2008), pp. 233–238.
49. L. Fürman, in A. Žiūraitytė and K.-P. Koch, eds. (2003), pp. 43–50.
50. O. Narbutiene, in A. Žiūraitytė and K.-P. Koch, eds. (2003), pp. 175–184.
51. J. Kivimäe, Nordost-Archiv N. F. 4 (1995): 501–520; J. v. Hehn (1984).
52. R. Bohn (2000), pp. 383–452.
53. T. U. Raun (2001), pp. 139–146; A. Plakans (1995), pp. 143–148.
54. D. Bleiere et al., eds. (2008), pp. 263–266.
55. A. Plakans (2011), p. 351.
56. W. Wette, in A. Komlosy, H.-H. Nolte, and I. Sooman, eds. (2008), pp. 237–252, here 241–245; A. Bubnys (2005), p. 3; Y. Arad (2004), p. 177; C. Dieckmann and S. Sužiedėlis, eds. (2006); A. Ezergailis (1996), pp. 239–270.
57. T. Snyder (2010).
58. A. Plakans (1995), p. 152; A. Plakans (2011).
59. C. Pletzing and M. Pletzing, eds. (2007).

9. SOVIETIZATION VERSUS WELFARE STATES

1. A. M. Kõll, ed. (2003).
2. A. J. Prażmowska (2004), pp. 191–198; N. Davies (2005), vol. 2, pp. 417–431, 435–440; L. J. Gibianskij, in M. Lemke, ed. (1999), pp. 31–80.
3. M. North (2008b), pp. 97–101.
4. For more on resistance, see, e.g., A. Anušauskas (2006); J. Lukša (2009).
5. T. U. Raun (2001), pp. 170–174; W. Prigge, Journal of Baltic Studies 35/3 (2004): 211–230.

6. M. Klinge (1994), pp. 162, 165–166; F. Singleton (1998), pp. 134–146; for more on postwar Sovietization, see O. Mertelsmann, ed. (2003); O. Mertelsmann (2005).
7. D. Feest (2007), pp. 337–441.
8. H. Strods and M. Kott, *Journal of Baltic Studies* 33/1 (2002): 1–31.
9. D. v. Melis, ed. (1999); A. Bauerkämper (2005), pp. 31–34.
10. T. U. Raun (2001), pp. 175–176, 198–200; A. Plakans (1995), pp. 108, 165–166.
11. M. North (2008b), pp. 103–105.
12. N. F. Christiansen, *Scandinavian Journal of History* 26 (2001): 177–196; K. J. V. Jespersen (2004), pp. 76–78, 176–181.
13. H. G. Schröter (2007), pp. 100–106.
14. K. J. V. Jespersen (2004), pp. 172–177.
15. N. Kent (2008), pp. 249–252.
16. F. Singleton (1998), pp. 147–154.
17. O. Krantz, in W. Fischer, ed. (1987), vol. 6, pp. 222–292, here 279–288; U. Kivikari (1996), pp. 11–22.
18. K. J. V. Jespersen (2004), p. 179.
19. C. Hasselblatt (2006), pp. 582–596.
20. K. O'Connor (2006), pp. 131–139.
21. R. Kmita (2009).
22. S. C. Weber (2000).
23. R. Nugin (2009).
24. M. A. Svede, in A. Rosenfeld and N. T. Dodge, eds. (2002), pp. 17–24; E. Sepp, in A. Rosenfeld and N. T. Dodge, eds. (2002), pp. 43–140.
25. T. Hall (2009), pp. 128–168.
26. F. Singleton (1998), pp. 170–172.
27. K. Hallas-Murula, K. Kodres, and M. Kalm (2000).
28. O. Kautny (2002).
29. T. U. Raun (2001), pp. 217–218.
30. N. Davies (2005), vol. 2, pp. 469–501; A. J. Prażmowska (2004), pp. 200–210.
31. V. S. Vardys and J. B. Sedatis (1997), pp. 84–92.
32. K. Langer, in Landtag Mecklenburg-Vorpommern/Enquete Kommission, ed. (1997), pp. 9–196.
33. H. Vogt (2005), pp. 20–36.
34. K. Gerner and S. Hedlund (1993), pp. 83–93.
35. Ibid., pp. 93–100.
36. N. Davies (2005), vol. 2, pp. 501–504.
37. K. Langer, in Landtag Mecklenburg-Vorpommern/Enquete Kommission, ed. (1997), pp. 9–196; M. North (2008b), pp. 110–114. An agreement on currency, economic, and social union had already been concluded with the Federal Republic, which came into effect on July 1, 1990.
38. V. S. Vardys and J. B. Sedatis (1997), pp. 168–190; A. Kasekamp (2010), pp. 167–171.

10. TRANSFORMATION AND EU INTEGRATION

1. M. North, in M. Krieger and J. Krüger, eds. (2010a), pp. 47–55.
2. M. North (2008b), pp. 113–117.

3. N. Davies (2005), vol. 2, pp. 507–513. For more on Poland's transition diffi-
culties, see K. Ziemer, ed. (2000).

4. A. Kasekamp (2010), pp. 172–180.

5. W. Merkel, *Politische Vierteljahresschrift* 48 (2007): 413–433. For overviews,
see also D. Jahn and N. Werz, eds. (2002); D. J. Smith, in D. J. Smith et al.,
eds. (2002).

6. M. Lauristin and M. Heidmets, eds. (2002); D. Gruber (2008); L. Assmuth, in
A. Aarelaid-Tart and Li Bennich-Björkman, eds. (2012), pp. 107–124.

7. N. Davies (2005), vol. 2, pp. 505–506, 509–510.

8. A. Vonderau (2010).

9. A. Kasekamp (2010), pp. 181–184.

10. F. Singleton (1998), pp. 153–154.

11. J. Andersson and K. Östberg, in J. Andersson and K. Östberg, eds. (2013),
pp. 357–373.

12. C.-F. Laaser and K. Schrader (2002); Statistisches Bundesamt, Statistisches
Jahrbuch 2006 für das Ausland/International Statistical Yearbook 2006, EU-
Intrahandel, https://www.destatis.de/DE/Publikationen/StatistischesJahr
buch/Jahrbuch2006Ausland.pdf?__blob=publicationFile.

13. B. Auffermann, *Aus Politik und Zeitgeschichte* 43 (1992): 36–47; B. Auffermann (1999); R. Väyrynen, in T. Tiilikainen and I. Damgaard Petersen, eds.
(1993), pp. 43–63.

14. A. Kasekamp (2010), pp. 188–193.

15. http://www.pomerania.net/main.cfm.

16. F. Weymar (2010); D. Kuchenbrandt and M. Bornewasser, in K. Deecke and
A. Drost, eds. (2010), pp. 189–200.

17. For a good overviews of the state and nonstate organizations, see M. Karlsson
(2004); R. Bördlein, *Der Bürger im Staat* 54/2–3 (2004): 147–153; C. Gebhard
(2009).

18. D. Jahn and K. Kuitto, in M. Joas et al., eds. (2008), pp. 19–42.

19. Overview in B. Henningsen, ed. (2002).

20. S. Ewert (2012), p. 259.

21. D. Dusseault, *Asia Europe Journal* 8 (2010): 379–398.

22. http://helcom.fi/action-areas.

23. A. Erll, *Asia Europe Journal* 8 (2010): 305–315.

24. M. Mälksoo, in P. Ehin and E. Berg, eds. (2009), pp. 65–83; M. Lehti and
J. Hackmann, eds. (2010).

25. K. Jõesalu, *Asia Europe Journal* 8 (2010): 293–303.

26. G. Janauskas, *Asia Europe Journal* 8 (2010): 339–345.

27. On the history of, perspectives on, and critiques of the EU Baltic Sea strategy,
see M. Lehti (2009); P. Joenniemi, *DIIS Brief* (2009); C. Schymik and P.
Krumrey (2009); R. Bengtsson, in A. Kasekamp, ed. (2012), pp. 7–32.

28. Quoted in M. Lehti (2009), pp. 9–10.

29. For more on what follows, see Communication from the Commission to the
European Parliament, the Council, the European Economic and Social Com-
mittee and the Committee of the Regions concerning the European Union
Strategy for the Baltic Sea Region, Brussels 10. 6. 2009, COM (2009), 248 final.

30. S. Ewert (2012), pp. 260–261; Schymik and Krumrey (2009), p. 16.

31. See above.
32. European Commission, Commission Staff Working Paper, Brussels, 13.09.2011.
33. M. Lehti (2009), pp. 25–26.
34. A. Lindholm, K. Nygård Skalman, and C. H. M. Ketels (2009). See also the issue titled "The Baltic Sea and South China Sea Regions: Incomparable Models of Regional Integration?" *Asia Europe Journal* 8 (2010).

References

Abukhanfusa, K., ed. 1999. *Mare nostrum: Om Westfaliska freden och Östersjön som ett svenskt maktcentrum.* Stockholm: Västervik.

Abulafia, D. 2005. "Mediterraneans." In W. V. Harris, ed., *Rethinking the Mediterranean,* pp. 64–94. Oxford: Oxford University Press.

Adamczyk, D. 2007. "Od dirhemów do fenigów: Reorientacja bałtyckiego systemu handlowego na przełomie X i XI wieku." In I. Panic and J. Sperka, eds., *Średniowiecze polskie i powszechne* 4: 15–27. Katowice, Poland: Wydawnictwo Uniwersytetu Śląskiego.

———. 2008. "Friesen, Wikinger, Araber: Die Ostseewelt zwischen Dorestadt und Samarkand, ca. 700–1100." In A. Komlosy, H.-H. Nolte, and I. Sooman, eds., *Ostsee 700–2000. Gesellschaft—Wirtschaft—Kultur,* pp. 32–48. Vienna: Promedia.

Ahlström, C. 1983. "Aspects of Commercial Shipping between St. Petersburg and Western Europe, 1750–1790." In W. J. Wieringa et al., eds., *The Interactions of Amsterdam and Antwerp with the Baltic Region, 1400–1800,* pp. 153–160. Leiden, The Netherlands: M. Nijhoff.

Alexander, M. 2005. *Kleine Geschichte Polens.* Bonn, Germany: Reclam.

Alexander, M., and G. Stökl. 2009. *Russische Geschichte: Von den Anfängen bis zur Gegenwart.* Stuttgart: Kröner.

Ambrosiani, B. 2008. "Birka." In S. Brink and N. Price, eds., *The Viking World,* pp. 94–100. London: Routledge.

Andersson, J., and K. Östberg. 2013. "Sverige och Nittiotalskrisen." In J. Andersson and K. Östberg, eds., *Sveriges Historia 1965–2012,* pp. 357–373. Stockholm: Norstedts.

Andersson, L. I. 2003. *Sveriges Historia under 1800- och 1900-talen.* Stockholm: Liber.

Androshchuk, F. 2008. "The Viking in the East." In S. Brink and N. Price, eds., *The Viking World,* pp. 517–542. London: Routledge.

———. 2013. *Vikings in the East: Essays on Contacts along the Road to Byzantium, 800–1100.* Uppsala, Sweden: Uppsala Universitet.

Angermann, N., et al., eds. 2005. *Ostseeprovinzen, baltische Staaten und das Nationale* (Festschrift Pistohlkors). Münster: Lit.

Anušauskas, A. 2006. *The Anti-Soviet Resistance in the Baltic States.* Vilnius: Du Ka.

Arad, Y. 2004. "The Murder of the Jews in German-Occupied Lithuania, 1941–1944." In A. Nikžentaitis, S. Schreiner, and D. Staliūnas, eds., *The Vanished World of Lithuanian Jews,* pp. 175–203. Amsterdam: Rodopi.

Arken Museum of Modern Art. 2008. *The Skagen Painters: In a New Light.* Ishøj, Denmark: Arken Museum of Modern Art.

Arnim, V. 1957. *Krisen und Konjunkturen der Landwirtschaft in Schleswig-Holstein vom 16. bis zum 18. Jahrhundert.* Neumünster, Germany: Wachholtz.

Assmuth, L. 2012. "Rural Belongings: Baltic Russian Identities in Estonian and Latvian Borderlands." In A. Aarelaid-Tart and L. Bennich-Björkman, eds., *Baltic Biographies at Historical Crossroads*, pp. 107–124. London: Routledge.

Åström, S.-E. 1988. *From Tar to Timber: Studies in Northeast European Forest Exploitation and Foreign Trade, 1660–1860.* Helsinki: Societas Scientiarum Fennica.

Attman, A. 1973. *The Russian and Polish Markets in International Trade, 1500–1650.* Gothenburg, Sweden: Institute of Economic History of Gothenburg University.

———. 1983. *Dutch Enterprise in the World Bullion Trade, 1550–1800.* Gothenburg, Sweden: Kungl. Vetenskaps- och Vitterhets-Samhället.

Auffermann, B. 1992. "Finnland: Neuorientierung nach dem Kalten Krieg." *Aus Politik und Zeitgeschichte* 43: 36–47.

———. 1999. *Für eine "Nördliche Dimension" der EU-Politik: Eine Initiative im Kontext finnischer Außen- und Integrationspolitik.* Kiel, Germany: SCHIFF Institute.

Auge, O. 2009. *Handlungsspielräume fürstlicher Politik im Mittelalter: Der südliche Ostseeraum von der Mitte des 12. Jahrhunderts bis in die frühe Reformationszeit.* Ostfildern, Germany: Thorbecke.

Avtonomov, A. 2000. "The President and Parliament in Contemporary Russia." In M. Bowker and C. Ross, eds., *Russia after the Cold War*, pp. 50–68. Harlow, UK: Longman.

Backhaus, H. 1969. *Reichsterritorium und schwedische Provinz: Vorpommern unter Karls XI. Vormündern, 1660–1672.* Göttingen: Vandenhoeck & Ruprecht.

Baczkowski, K. 1999. *Dzieje Polski późnośredniowiecznej, 1370–1506.* Cracow, Poland: Fogra.

Badstübner, E. 2000. "Klöster der Zisterzienser in Nordeuropa und die Backsteinbaukunst an der südlichen Ostseeküste." In H. Schwillus and A. Hölscher, eds., *Weltverachtung und Dynamik*, pp. 136–147. Berlin: Lukas.

———. 2005. *Licht und Farbe in der mittelalterlichen Backsteinarchitektur des südlichen Ostseeraums.* Berlin: Lukas.

Bagge, S. 2001. *Da boken kom til Norge.* Oslo: Norsk Idehistorie.

Bajohr, F., and M. Wildt, eds. 2009. *Volksgemeinschaft: Neue Forschungen zur Gesellschaft des Nationalsozialismus.* Frankfurt: Fischer.

Baláz, S. 2011. "Die Integration der Russischsprachigen in die estnische Gesellschaft: Diskursanalyse der estnischsprachigen Tageszeitung Postimees, 1995–1999." PhD diss., University of Greifswald.

Bartetzky, A. 2000. *Das große Zeughaus in Danzig: Baugeschichte, architekturgeschichtliche Stellung, repräsentative Funktion.* Stuttgart: Steiner.

Bartlett, R. 1993. *The Making of Europe: Conquest, Colonization and Cultural Change, 950–1350.* London: Penguin.

Barton, H. A. 2009. *Essays on Scandinavian History.* Carbondale: Southern Illinois University Press.

Bauerkämper, A. 2005. *Die Sozialgeschichte der DDR.* Munich: Oldenbourg.

Behre, G., L.-O. Larsson, and E. Österberg. 2003. *Sveriges historia, 1521–1809. Stormaktsdröm och småstatsrealitet.* Stockholm: Liber.

Bell, M., and M. Hietala. 2002. *Helsinki, the Innovative City: Historical Perspectives*. Jyväskylä, Finland: Finnish Literature Society.

Benedictow, O. J. 2003. "Demographic Conditions." In K. Helle, ed., *The Cambridge History of Scandinavia I: Prehistory to 1520*, pp. 237–249. Cambridge, UK: Cambridge University Press.

Bengtsson, R. 2012. "The EU Strategy for the Baltic Sea Region: Golden or Missed Opportunity?" In A. Kasekamp, ed., *The Estonian Foreign Policy Yearbook 2011*, pp. 7–32. Tallinn: Estonian Foreign Policy Institute.

Bentlin, M. 2008. *Niederdeutsch-finnische Sprachkontakte: Der lexikalische Einfluss des Niederdeutschen auf die finnische Sprache während des Mittelalters und in der frühen Neuzeit*. Helsinki: Suomalais-Ugrilainen Seura.

Bergendal, G., ed. 1998. *Music in Sweden*. Stockholm: Svenska Bokforlaget.

Bernoulli, J. 1780. *Johann Bernoulli's Reisen durch Brandenburg, Pommern, Preußen, Kurland, Rußland und Pohlen, in den Jahren 1777 und 1778*, vol. 6, *Rückreise von St. Petersburg über Mietau und Warschau nach Berlin*. Leipzig: Caspar Fritsch.

Bertino, A. 2011. *"Vernatürlichung": Ursprünge Friedrich Nietzsches Entidealisierung des Menschen, seiner Sprache und seiner Geschichte bei Johann Gottfried Herder*. Berlin: de Gruyter.

Beutin, L. 1929. *Hanse und Reich im handelspolitischen Endkampf gegen England*. Berlin: Curtius.

Biermann, F. 2009. "Glaube, Macht und Pracht: Geistliche Gemeinschaften des Ostseeraums im Zeitalter der Backsteingotik—Einführung." In O. Auge, F. Biermann, and C. Herrmann, eds., *Glaube, Macht und Pracht: Geistliche Gemeinschaften des Ostseeraums im Zeitalter der Backsteingotik*, pp. 9–37. Rahden, Germany: Marie Leidorf.

Bingen, D. 1995. "Polen: Zwischen Restauration und Reform." In Bundesinstitut für Ostwissenschaftliche und Internationale Studien, ed., *Zwischen Krise und Konsolidierung: Gefährdeter Systemwechsel im Osten Europas*, pp. 122–133. Munich: Hanser.

Bjøern, C. 1977. "The Peasantry and Agrarian Reform in Denmark." *Scandinavian Economic History Review* 25: 117–137.

Bleiere, D. 2006. *History of Latvia*. Riga: Jumava.

Bleiere, D., et al., eds. 2008. *Geschichte Lettlands: 20. Jahrhundert*. Riga: Jumava.

Blockmans, W. P. 1993. "Der holländische Durchbruch in der Ostsee." In S. Jenks and M. North, eds., *Der hansische Sonderweg? Beiträge zur Sozial- und Wirtschaftsgeschichte der Hanse*, pp. 49–58. Cologne: Böhlau.

Blomkvist, N. 2005. *The Discovery of the Baltic: The Reception of a Catholic World System in the European North, AD 1075–1225*. Leiden, The Netherlands: Brill.

Boedecker, H.-E., P. Veit, and M. Werner, eds. 2002. *Le concert et son public: Mutations de la vie musicale en Europe de 1780 à 1914 (France, Allemagne, Angleterre)*. Paris: Éd. de la Maison des Sciences de l'Homme.

Bogucka, M. 1956. *Gdańskie rzemiosło tekstylne od XVI do połowy XVII wieku*. Wrocław, Poland: Zakład Narodowy im. Ossolińskich.

———. 1973. "Amsterdam and the Baltic in the First Half of the 17th Century." *Economic History Review* 26: 433–447.

————. 1976. "Kultura Pomorza wschodniego w dobie renesansu i baroku." In G. Labuda, ed., *Historia Pomorza*, II, 1: 1464/66–1648/57, pp. 526–650. Poznań, Poland: Edytuj książkę.

————. 1982. "Przemíany spoleczne i walki spoleczno-polityczne w XV i XVI w." In E. Cieślak, ed., *Historia Gdańska*, vol. 2, *1454–1570*, pp. 208–259. Gdańsk, Poland: Wydawnictwo Morskie.

————. 1983. "The Baltic and Amsterdam in the First Half of the 17th Century." In W. J. Wieringa et al., eds., *The Interactions of Amsterdam and Antwerp with the Baltic Region, 1400–1800*, pp. 51–57. Leiden, The Netherlands: M. Nijhoff.

————. 1984. "Les relations entre la Pologne et les Pays-Bas (XVIe siècle, première moitié du XVIIe siècle)." *Cahiers de Clio* 78–79:14–16.

————. 1988. "Die Kultur und Mentalität der Danziger Bürgerschaft in der zweiten Hälfte des 17. Jahrhunderts." In S.-O. Lindquist, ed., *Economy and Culture in the Baltic, 1650–1700*, pp. 129–140. Visby, Sweden: Gotlands Fornsal.

————. 1990. "Dutch Merchants' Activities in Gdansk in the First Half of the 17th Century." In J. P. S. Lemmink and J. S. A. M. v. Koningsbrugge, eds., *Baltic Affairs: Relations between the Netherlands and North-Eastern Europe, 1500–1800*, pp. 19–32. Nijmegen, The Netherlands: Institute for Northern and Eastern European Studies.

Bogucka, M., and H. Samsonowicz. 1987. "Struktury społeczne Gdańska w XV–XVII wieku na tle przemian w handlu bałtyckim." In J. Topolski, *Studia nad gospodarką, społeczeństwem i rodziną w Europie późnofeudalnej*, pp. 139–151. Lublin, Poland: Lublin Wydawnictwo Lubelskie.

Bohn, I. 2005. *Finnland: Von den Anfängen bis zur Gegenwart*. Regensburg, Germany: Pustet.

Bohn, R. 1997. *Gotland*. Kronshagen, Germany: Conrad Stein.

————. 2000. *Reichskommissariat Norwegen: "Nationalsozialistische Neuordnung" und Kriegswirtschaft*. Munich: Oldenbourg.

————. 2001. *Dänische Geschichte*. Munich: C. H. Beck.

Boje, P. 1993. "Denmark's Role in the World Economy, 1750–1950." In M. North, ed., *Nordwesteuropa in der Weltwirtschaft, 1750–1950*, pp. 21–38. Stuttgart: Steiner.

Bolte, H. 2006. "Der Greifswalder Jurist Johann Meilof und seine livländische Urkundensammlung." *Jahrbuch für die Geschichte Mittel- und Ostdeutschlands* 52: 227–262.

Bolton, T. 2009. *The Empire of Cnut the Great: Conquest and the Consolidation of Power in Northern Europe in the Early Eleventh Century*. Leiden, The Netherlands: Brill.

Bonsdorff, J. v. 1993. *Kunstproduktion und Kunstverbreitung im Ostseeraum des Spätmittelalters*. Helsinki: Finnische Altertumsgeschichte.

Boockmann, H. 1999. *Der Deutsche Orden: Zwölf Kapitel aus seiner Geschichte*. Munich: C. H. Beck.

Bördlein, R. 2004. "Regionale und transnationale Zusammenarbeit von staatlichen und nichtstaatlichen Organisationen." *Der Bürger im Staat* 54/2–3: 147–153.

Borggrefe, H., ed. 2002. *Hans Vredeman de Vries und die Renaissance im Norden* (Exhibition at the Weserrenaissance-Museum Schloss Brake, May 26–August 25, 2002, Koninklijk Museum voor Schone Kunsten, Antwerpen, September 14–December 8, 2002). Munich: Hirmer.

Borschberg, P., and M. North. 2010. "Transcending Borders: The Sea as Realm of Memory." *Asia Europe Journal* 8: 279–292.

Bosse, H. 1986. "Die Einkünfte kurländischer Literaten am Ende des 18. Jahrhunderts." *Zeitschrift für Ostforschung* 35: 519–534.

———. 1996. "Die Hofmeister in Livland und Estland: Ein Berufsstand als Vermittler der Aufklärung." In O.-H. Elias, T. Jansson, and I. Jürjo, eds., *Aufklärung in den baltischen Provinzen Russlands: Ideologie und soziale Wirklichkeit*, pp. 165–208. Cologne: Böhlau.

———. 1997. "Über die soziale Einbettung des Theaters: Riga und Reval im 18. Jahrhundert." In L. P. A. Kitching, ed., *Das deutschsprachige Theater im baltischen Raum, 1630–1918. The German-Language Theatre in the Baltic, 1630–1918*, pp. 109–111. Frankfurt: Lang.

Bracke, N. 1999. *Die Regierung Waldemars IV: Eine Untersuchung zum Wandel der Herrschaftsstrukturen im spätmittelalterlichen Dänemark*. Frankfurt: Lang.

Bracker, J., and R. Postel, eds. 1999. *Die Hanse: Lebenswirklichkeit und Mythos*. Lübeck, Germany: Schmidt-Römhild.

Brand, H. 2007. "Baltic Connections: Changing Patterns in Seaborne Trade, c. 1450–1800." In L. Bes, E. Frankot, and H. Brand, eds., *Baltic Connections: Archival Guide to the Maritime Relations of the Countries around the Baltic Sea (including the Netherlands), 1450–1800*, vol. 1, *Denmark, Estonia, Finland, Germany*, pp. 1–24. Leiden, The Netherlands: Brill.

Brand, H., and L. Mueller, eds. 2007. *The Dynamics of Economic Culture in the North Sea and Baltic Region*. Hilversum, The Netherlands: Verloren.

Brandt, A. v. 1966. "Die gesellschaftliche Struktur des spätmittelalterlichen Lübeck." In Konstanzer Arbeitskreis für Mittelalterliche Geschichte, ed., *Untersuchungen zur gesellschaftlichen Struktur der mittelalterlichen Städte in Europa, Reichenau-Vorträge, 1963–1964*, pp. 215–240. Konstanz, Germany: Thorbecke.

Brandt, K., M. Müller-White, and C. Radtke, eds. 2002. *Haithabu und die frühe Stadtentwicklung im nördlichen Europa*. Neumünster, Germany: Wachholtz.

Braudel, F. 1972. *The Mediterranean and the Mediterranean World in the Age of Philip II*. 2 vols. Trans. Siân Reynolds. Berkeley: University of California Press.

Bregnsbo, M. 2011. "Struensee and the Political Culture of Absolutism." In P. Ihalainen et al., eds., *Scandinavia in the Age of Revolution: Nordic Political Cultures, 1740–1820*, pp. 55–65. Farnham, UK: Ashgate.

Bregnsbo, M., and K. V. Jensen. 2004. *Det danske imperium: Storhed og fald*. Copenhagen: Aschehoug.

Brenner, A. 2010. "'Wenn jemand eine Reise tut, so kann er was erzählen . . .': Die Anfänge des Bädertourismus am Beispiel des ersten deutschen Seebades Doberan-Heiligendamm." Staatsexamensarbeit, University of Greifswald.

Brück, T. 2001. "Zur Geschichte der Stralsunder Rigafahrer von der Mitte des 14. bis zum Beginn des 17. Jahrhunderts." In N. Angermann and P. Kaegbein, eds., *Fernhandel und Handelspolitik der baltischen Städte in der Hansezeit*, pp. 97–136. Lüneburg, Germany: Institut Nordostdeutsches Kulturwerk.

Brüggemann, K., ed. 2004. *Narva und die Ostseeregion*. Narva: TÜ Narva Kolledž.

Bubnys, A. 2005. *The Holocaust in Lithuania between 1941 and 1944*. Vilnius: Genocide and Resistance Research Centre of Lithuania.

Buchsteiner, I. 1993. *Großgrundbesitz in Pommern 1871–1914: Ökonomische, soziale und politische Transformationen der Großgrundbesitzer*. Berlin: Akademie-Verlag.

Bugenhagen, B. 2008. "Die Musikgeschichte Stralsunds von der Einführung der Reformation bis zum Ende des 17. Jahrhunderts." PhD diss., University of Greifswald.

Bugenhagen, J. 2008. *Johannes Bugenhagen, Pomerania*. Facsimile edition and translation of the manuscript of 1517–1518. Schwerin, Germany: Helms.

Bünz, E. 2002. *Zwischen Kanonikerreform und Reformation. Anfänge, Blütezeit und Untergang der Augustiner-Chorherrenstifte Neumünster-Bordesholm und Segeberg (12. bis 16. Jahrhundert)*. Paring, Germany: Augustiner Chorherren.

Burke, P. 1974. *Venice and Amsterdam: A Study on Seventeenth-Century Élites*. London: Temple Smith.

Büsch, O. 1981. *Militärsystem und Sozialleben im alten Preußen 1713–1807: Die Anfänge der sozialen Militarisierung der preußisch-deutschen Gesellschaft*. Berlin: de Gruyter.

Bussenius, C. 1960. "Die preußische Verwaltung in Süd- und Neuostpreußen, 1793–1806." PhD diss., University of Heidelberg.

Cerman, M. 2012. *Villagers and Lords in Eastern Europe, 1300–1800*. Basingstoke, UK: Palgrave Macmillan.

Christensen, A.-E. 1941. *Dutch Trade in the Baltic around 1600: Studies in the Sound Toll Register and Dutch Shipping Records*. The Hague: Einar Munksgaard.

———. 1980. *Kalmarunionen og nordisk politik, 1319–1439*. Copenhagen: Gyldendal.

Christiansen, E. 1980. *The Northern Crusades: The Baltic and the Catholic Frontier, 1100–1523*. London: Macmillan.

Christiansen, N. F. 2001. "The Dynamics of Social Solidarity: The Danish Welfare State, 1900–2000." *Scandinavian Journal of History* 26: 177–196.

Ciechowicza, J. 2004. *200 lat teatru na Targu Węglowyn w Gdańsku*. Gdańsk, Poland: Nordbałtyckie Centrum Kultury, Wydawn. Uniw. Gdańskiego.

Ciesielska, K. 1958. "Osadnictwo 'olęderskie' w Prusach Królewskich i na Kujawach w świetle kontraktów osadniczych." *Studia i materiały do dziejów Wielkopolski i Pomorza* 4/2: 219–256.

Cieślak, E. 1962. *Walki społeczno-polityczne w Gdańsku w drugiej połowie XVII wieku. Interwencja Jana III Sobieskiego*. Gdańsk, Poland: Gdańskie Towarzystwo Naukowe.

————. 1972. *Konflikty polityczne i społeczne w Gdańsku w połowie XVIII w.—Sojusz pospólstwa z dworem królewskim.* Gdańsk, Poland: Zakład Narodowy im. Ossolińskich.

————. 1984. "Powojenne załamanie gospodarcze—pierwsze przejawy ożywienia gospodarczego w połowie XVIII wieku." In G. Labuda, ed., *Historia Pomorza, I: do roku 1815*, pp. 50–122. Poznań, Poland: Edytuj książkę.

————. 1996. "Verfassung, Verwaltung, Recht, Militär im Königlichen Preußen." In E. Opgenoorth, ed., *Handbuch der Geschichte Ost- und Westpreußens*, vol. 2, *Vom Schwedisch-Polnischen Krieg bis zur Reformzeit, 1655–1807*, pp. 24–31. Lüneburg, Germany: Institut Nordostdeutsches Kulturwerk.

Cieślak, E., and J. Trzoska. 1993. "Handel i żegluga gdańska w XVIII w." In E. Cieślak, ed., *Historia Gdańska*, vol. 1, *1655–1793*, pp. 357–444. Gdańsk, Poland: Wydawnictwo Morskie.

Čiurlionis, M. K. 1992. *Time and Content.* Vilnius, Lithuania.

Commission of the European Communities, Communication from the Commission to the European Parliament, the Council, the European Economic and Social Committee and the Committee of the Regions Concerning the European Union Strategy for the Baltic Sea Region, Brussels, June 10, 2009, COM (2009) 248 final. [http://ec.europa.eu/regional_policy/sources/docoffic/official/communic/baltic/com_baltic_en.pdf]

Curtis, B. 2008. *Music Makes the Nation: Nationalist Composers and National Building in Nineteenth-Century Europe.* Amherst, NY: Cambria Press.

Dahlbäk, G. 1988. *I medeltidens Stockholm.* Stockholm: Stockholmia förl.

Dahlmann, F. C. 1815. "Ein Wort über Verfassung." *Kieler Blätter* 1: 47–84, 245–303.

Dahlström, F. 2001. "Von der Hofkapelle zur Philharmonie: Die Stadt als Wirkungsfeld für Musiker." In G. Andersson, ed., *Musikgeschichte Nordeuropas: Dänemark, Finnland, Island, Norwegen, Schweden*, pp. 104–127. Stuttgart: Metzler.

Dalhede, C. 2001. *Handelsfamiljer på stormaktstidens europamarknad: resor och resande i internationella förbindelser och kulturella intressen. Augsburg, Antwerpen, Lübeck, Göteborg och Arboga.* Partille, Sweden: Warne Forlag.

————. 2006. *Viner kvinnor kapital. en 1600-talshandel med potential? Fjärrhandelsfamiljerna Jeronimus Möller i Lübeck och Sibrant Valck i Göteborg.* Partille, Sweden: Warne Forlag.

Davies, N. 2005. *God's Playground: A History of Poland.* 2 vols. Oxford: Oxford University Press.

Deecke, K., and A. Drost, eds. 2010. *Liebe zum Fremden: Xenophilie aus Geistes- und Sozialwissenschaftlicher Perspektive.* Cologne: Böhlau.

————. 2011. "'Staatswirtschaft vom Himmel herabgeholt': Konzeptionen liberaler Wirtschaftspolitik in Universität und Verwaltung 1785–1845: Ausprägungen und Brechungen am Beispiel Ostpreußens und Vorpommerns." PhD diss., University of Greifswald.

Degn, C. 1959–1969. *Die Herzogtümer im Gesamtstaat, 1773–1830.* Neumünster, Germany: Wachholtz.

Degn, O. 2010. *Tolden i Sundet: Toldopkraevning, politik og skibsfart i Øresund, 1429–1857.* Copenhagen: Told- og Skattehistorisk Selskab.

Dessau, C. 2008. *Nationale Aspekte einer transnationalen Disziplin zur rechtskulturellen Einbettung der Rechtstheorie in Finnland, Schweden und Deutschland zwischen 1960 und 1990.* Berlin: Duncker & Humblot.

Dieckmann, C., and S. Sužiedėlis, eds. 2006. *The Persecution and Mass Murder of Lithuanian Jews during Summer and Fall of 1941: Crimes of the Totalitarian Regimes in Lithuania, the Nazi Occupation,* vol. 3. Vilnius: Margi Raštai.

Dollinger, P. 1989. *Die Hanse.* Stuttgart: A. Kröner.

Donnert, E. 2002. *St. Petersburg: Eine Kulturgeschichte.* Cologne: Böhlau.

Dorošenko, V. V. 1985. *Targovlja i kupečestvo Rigi v XVII veke.* Riga: Zinatne.

Dreifelds, J. 1996. *Latvia in Transition.* Cambridge, UK: Cambridge University Press.

Driesner, J. 2003. "Materielle Kultur in Greifswald im 17. und 18. Jahrhundert." Master's thesis, University of Greifswald.

———. 2011. *Frühmoderne Alltagswelten im Ostseeraum: Materielle Kultur in Stralsund, Kopenhagen und Riga—Drei Regionen im Vergleich.* Cologne: Böhlau.

Drost, A. 2003. *Neustrelitz—eine frühmoderne Idealstadt. Ausdruck realer Machtverhältnisse oder städtebauliche Mode des Barock und Absolutismus in der ersten Hälfte des 18. Jahrhunderts?* Magisterarbeit, University of Greifswald.

———. 2003–2004. "Neustrelitz: Machtbewusstsein und Zeitgeist im Spiegel von Idealstadtkonzepten zu Beginn des 18. Jahrhunderts." *Blätter für Deutsche Landesgeschichte* 139: 301–320.

———. 2006. "Barocke Stadtpläne: Neustrelitz und sein idealer Stadtgrundriss im zeitgenössischen Vergleich." *Zeitschrift Barock Geschichte Literatur Kunst*: 105–122.

———. 2010. "Historical Borderlands in the Sea Area: Layers of Cultural Diffusion and New Borderland Theories: The Case of Livonia."*Journal of History for the Public* 7: 10–24.

Duchhardt, H. 1997. *Balance of Power und Pentarchie: Internationale Beziehungen, 1700–1785.* Paderborn, Germany: Schöningh.

Dusseault, D. 2010. "Europe's Triple By-Pass: The Prognosis for Nord Stream, South Stream and Nabucco." *Asia Europe Journal* 8: 379–398.

Dygdała, J. 1977. *Polityka Torunia wobec władz Rzeczypospolitej w latach, 1764–1772.* Warsaw: Państwowe Wydawnictwo Naukowe.

Ebel, U. 1990. *Konzepte einer nationalspezifischen Dramatik von Holberg bis Ibsen.* Metelen, Germany: Ebel.

Eberts, A. 2009. "Kristijonas Donelaitis und seine 'Metai': Eine Rezeptionsgeschichte." PhD diss., University of Greifswald.

Eckert, F. 2007. *Elitenwandel in Osteuropa: Die Auswirkungen des Systemwechsels auf die politische Führung.* Saarbrücken, Germany: VDM, Dr. Müller.

Eellend, J. 2008. "Agrarianism and Modernization in Inter-war Eastern Europe." In P. Wawrzeniuk, ed., *Societal Change and Ideological Formation among the Rural Population of the Baltic Area, 1880–1939,* pp. 35–56. Södertörn, Sweden: Södertörns högskola.

Ehin, P., and E. Berg, eds. 2009. *Identity and Foreign Policy: Baltic-Russian Relations and European Integration*, pp. 65–83. Farnham, UK: Ashgate.

Ehrensvärd, U., et al. 1995. *Mare Balticum: The Baltic—Two Thousand Years.* Helsinki: Otava.

Elsuwege, P. v. 2008. *From Soviet Republics to EU Member States.* Leiden, The Netherlands: Brill.

Eriksson, B. 2013. "Kyrka och reformation." In D. Harrison and B. Eriksson, eds., *Sveriges Historia*, pp. 456–460. Stockholm: Norstedts.

Eriksson, E. 1998. "Rationalismus und Klassizismus, 1915–1930." In C. Caldenby, J. Lindvall, and W. Wang, eds., *Architektur im 20. Jahrhundert: Schweden*, pp. 46–79. New York: Springer.

Erll, A. 2010. "Regional Integration and (Trans)cultural Memory." *Asia Europe Journal* 8: 305–315.

Etzemüller, T. 2009. "'Swedish Modern': Alva und Gunnar Myrdal entwerfen eine Normalisierungsgesellschaft." *Mittelweg* 36/18: 49–63.

European Commission. 2011. Commission Staff Working Paper on the Implementation of the European Union Strategy for the Baltic Sea Region, Brussels, September 13, 2011, SEC (2011) 1071 final. (http://www.europarl.europa.eu/registre /docs_autres_institutions/commission_europeenne/sec/2011/1071/COM _SEC%282011%291071_EN.pdf).

Ewert, S. 2012. *Region Building im Ostseeraum: Zur Rolle der Hochschulen im Prozess der Regionalisierung im Nordosten der Europäischen Union.* Wiesbaden: Springer.

Ezergailis, A. 1996. *The Holocaust in Latvia, 1941–1944: The Missing Center*, pp. 239–270. Riga: Historical Institute of Latvia.

Faber, J. A. 1988. "Structural Changes in the European Economy during the Eighteenth Century as Reflected in the Baltic Trade." In W. G. Hceres et al., eds., *From Dunkirk to Danzig: Shipping and Trade in the North Sea and the Baltic, 1350–1850*, pp. 83–94. Hilversum, The Netherlands: Verloren.

Falck, N. N. 1825. *Handbuch des Schleswig-Holsteinischen Privatrechts, 1.* Altona, Germany: Hammerich.

Feest, D. 2007. *Zwangskollektivierung im Baltikum: Die Sowjetisierung des estnischen Dorfes 1944–1953.* Cologne: Böhlau.

———, ed. 2010. *Von den Restgütern zu den Sowchosen in Estland, 1939–1953: Dokumentensammlung.* Berlin: Lit.

Feldbaek, O., ed. 1991–1992. *Dansk Identitetshistorie, 1536–1990.* 4 vols. Copenhagen: C. A. Reitzels Forlag.

———. 1993. *Danmarks økonomiske historie, 1500–1840.* Herning, Denmark: Nørhaven.

———, 1997. *Dansk Søfarts Historie*, vol. 3, *1720–1814: Storhandelens tid*, pp. 63–131. Copenhagen: Gyldendal.

Felder, B. M. 2009. *Lettland im Zweiten Weltkrieg: Zwischen sowjetischen und deutschen Besatzern, 1940–1946.* Paderborn, Germany: Schöningh.

Fiedler, S. 2009. "Museumsarchitektur und kulturelle Identität: Nordische Kunstmus een in der zweiten Hälfte des 20. Jahrhunderts." PhD diss., University of Greifswald.

Frandsen, K.-E. 2010. *The Last Plague in the Baltic Region, 1709–1713*. Copenhagen: Museum Tusculanums Forlag, Koebenhavns Universitet.

Frandsen, S. B. 2008. *Holsten i helstaten: Hertugdømmet inden for og uden for det danske monarki i første halvdel af 1800-tallet*. Copenhagen: Museum Tusculanums Forlag, Koebenhavns Universitet.

Frank, C. 2002. "Die Gemäldesammlungen Gotzkowsky, Eimbke und Stein zur Berliner Sammlungsgeschichte während des Siebenjährigen Krieges." In M. North, ed., *Kunstsammeln und Geschmack im 18. Jahrhundert*, pp. 117–194. Berlin: Spitz.

Friedmann, B. 1986. *Untersuchungen zur Geschichte des abodritischen Fürstentums bis zum Ende des 10. Jahrhunderts*. Berlin: Duncker & Humblot.

Friedrich, K. 2000. *The Other Prussia: Royal Prussia, Poland and Liberty, 1569–1772*. Cambridge, UK: Cambridge University Press.

Fritz, M., et al. 1993. "The Emergence of Swedish Multinationals." In M. North, ed., *Nordwesteuropa in der Weltwirtschaft, 1750–1950*, pp. 79–93. Stuttgart: Steiner.

Fritze, K. 1967. *Am Wendepunkt der Hanse*. Berlin: Deutscher Verlag der Wissenschaften.

Frost, R. I. 2000. *The Northern Wars, 1558–1721*. Harlow, UK: Longman.

Fudge, J. D. 1995. *Cargoes, Embargoes and Emissaries: The Commercial and Political Interaction of England and the German Hanse, 1450–1510*. Toronto: University of Toronto Press.

Fürman, L. 2003. "Deutsche Dirigenten am Rigaer Opernhaus zwischen 1919 und 1944: Zur Frage der Inszenierung von Leo Bleck." In A. Žiūraitytė and K.-P. Koch, eds., *Deutsch-baltische musikalische Beziehungen: Geschichte—Gegenwart—Zukunft; Bericht über die 35. Konferenz der Musikwissenschaftler des Baltikums in Vilnius 18.–20. Oktober 2001*, pp. 43–50. Sinzig, Germany: Studio.

Gadd, C.-J. 2000. *Den agrara revolutionen, 1700–1870*. Stockholm: Natur och Kultur/LTs förlag i samarbete med Nordiska museets förlag och Stiftelsen Lagersberg.

Galbreath, D. J. 2005. *Nation-Building and Minority Politics in Post-socialist States: Interests, Influence and Identities in Estonia and Latvia*. Stuttgart: Ibidem.

Garipzanov, I. H., P. J. Geary, and P. Urbańczyk, eds. 2008. *Franks, Northmen, and Slavs: Identities and State Formation in Early Medieval Europe*. Turnhout, Belgium: Brepols.

Garleff, M. 1994. "Die Deutschbalten als nationale Minderheit in den unabhängigen Staaten Estland und Lettland." In G. v. Pistohlkors, ed., *Deutsche Geschichte im Osten Europas: Baltische Länder*, pp. 452–551. Berlin: Siedler

———. 2001. *Die baltischen Länder: Estland, Lettland, Litauen vom Mittelalter bis zur Gegenwart*. Regensburg, Germany: F. Pustet.

Gastpary, W. 1969. *Spraw toruńska w roku 1724*. Warsaw: Chrześcijańska Akademia Teologiczna.

Gause, F. 1965. *Geschichte der Stadt Königsberg*, vol. 1, *Von der Gründung der Stadt bis zum letzten Kurfürsten*. Cologne: Böhlau.

Gebhard, C. 2009. *Unraveling the Baltic Sea Conundrum: Regionalism and European Integration Revisited*. Baden-Baden: Nomos.

Gerner, K., and S. Hedlund. 1993. *The Baltic States and the End of the Soviet Empire*. New York: Routledge.

Gibianskij, L. J. 1999. "Sowjetisierung Osteuropas—Charakter und Typologie." In M. Lemke, ed., *Sowjetisierung und Eigenständigkeit in der SBZ/DDR (1945–1953)*, pp. 31–80. Cologne: Böhlau.

Glenthøj, R., and M. Nordhagen Ottosen. 2014. *Experiences of War and Nationality in Denmark and Norway, 1807–1815*. Basingstoke, UK: Palgrave Macmillan.

Grambauer, S. 2009. *Erfolg personeller Integrationsmaßnahmen bei Unternehmensakquisitionen: Handlungsanweisung für die erfolgreiche Mitarbeiterintegration*. Saarbrücken: Südwestdeutscher Verlag.

Grimley, D. M., ed. 2011. *Jean Sibelius and His World*. Princeton, NJ: Princeton University Press.

Gropp, V. 1967. *Der Einfluss der Agrarreformen des beginnenden 19. Jahrhunderts in Ostpreußen auf Höhe und Zusammensetzung der preußischen Staatseinkünfte*. Berlin: Duncker & Humblot.

Groth, E. 1999. *Das Verhältnis der livländischen Städte zum Novgoroder Hansekontor im 14. Jahrhundert*. Hamburg: Baltische Gesellschaft.

Gruber, D. 2008. *Zuhause in Estland? Eine Untersuchung zur sozialen Integration ethnischer Russen an der Außengrenze der Europäischen Union*. Berlin: Lit-Verlag.

Grzechnik, M. 2012. *Regional Histories and Historical Regions: The Concept of the Baltic Sea Region in Polish and Swedish Historiographies*. Frankfurt: Lang.

Haack, H. 1968. "Die sozialökonomische Struktur mecklenburgischer Feudalkomplexe im 16. und 17. Jahrhundert, untersucht am Beispiel der Eigentumskomplexe der Familien Hahn und der Domanialämter Güstrow, Ivenack und Stavenhagen." PhD diss., University of Rostock.

Hackmann, J. 2004. "Architektur als Symbol: Nation Building in Nordosteuropa; Estland und Lettland im 20. Jahrhundert." In E. Mühle and N. Angermann, eds., *Riga im Prozeß der Modernisierung: Studien zum Wandel einer Ostseemetropole im 19. und frühen 20. Jahrhundert*, pp. 149–172. Marburg, Germany: Herder-Institut.

———. 2005. "Was bedeutet 'baltisch'? Zum semantischen Wandel des Begriffs im 19. und 20. Jahrhundert, Ein Beitrag zur Erforschung von Mental Maps." In H. Bosse, O.-H. Elias, and R. Schweitzer, eds., *Buch und Bildung im Baltikum* (Festschrift Kaegbein), pp. 15–39. Münster: Lit-Verlag.

———. 2007a. "Geselligkeit in Nordosteuropa: Studien zu Vereinskultur, Zivilgesellschaft und Nationalisierungsprozessen in einer polykulturellen Region, 1770–1950." Habilitation thesis, University of Greifswald.

———. 2007b. "Kennt Geselligkeit Grenzen? Beobachtungen zur historischen Dynamik von Vereinskultur und Zivilgesellschaft im multikulturellen Nordosteuropa." In E. Fischer et al., eds., *Chorgesang als Medium von Interkulturalität: Formen, Kanäle, Diskurse*, pp. 293–320. Stuttgart: Steiner.

———. 2007c. "Metamorphosen des Rigaer Rathausplatzes zwischen 1938 und 2003: Moderner Umbau versus historische Topographie." In B. Lichtnau, ed., *Architektur und Städtebau im südlichen Ostseeraum von 1970 bis zur Gegenwart: Entwicklungslinien—Brüche—Kontinuitäten*, pp. 118–134. Berlin: Lukas.

———, ed. 2012. *Vereinskultur und Zivilgesellschaft in Nordosteuropa: Regionale Spezifik und europäische Zusammenhänge.* Cologne: Böhlau.

Hackmann, J., and R. Schweitzer, eds. 2006. *Nordosteuropa als Geschichtsregion.* Lübeck, Germany: Schmidt-Römhild.

Hadenius, S. 2007. *Sveriges politiska historia från 1866 till vårå dagar: Konflikt och samförs.* Stockholm: Hjalmarson & Högberg Bokförlag.

Hall, T. 2009. *Stockholm: The Making of a Metropolis.* New York: Routledge.

Hallas-Murula, K., K. Kodras, and M. Kahn. 2000. *20th Century Architecture in Tallinn: Architectural Guide.* Tallinn: Museum of Estonian Architecture.

Hammel, R. 1987. "Hauseigentum im spätmittelalterlichen Lübeck. Methoden zur sozial- und wirtschaftsgeschichtlichen Auswertung der Lübecker Oberstadtbuchregesten." In A. Falk and R. Hammel, eds., *Archäologische und schriftliche Quellen zur spätmittelalterlichen und neuzeitlichen Geschichte der Hansestadt Lübeck. Materialien und Methoden einer archäologisch-historischen Auswertung*, pp. 85–300. Bonn: Habelt.

———. 1988. "Räumliche Entwicklung und Berufstopographie Lübecks bis zum Ende des 14. Jahrhunderts." In A. Graßmann, ed., *Lübeckische Geschichte*, pp. 50–76. Lübeck, Germany: Schmidt-Römhild.

Hammel-Kiesow, R. 2002. "Novgorod und Lübeck: Siedlungsgefüge zweier Handelsstädte im Vergleich." In N. Angermann and K. Friedland, eds., *Novgorod: Markt und Kontor der Hanse*, pp. 25–68. Cologne: Böhlau.

———. 2008. *Die Hanse.* Munich: C. H. Beck.

Hansar, L. 2009. "Plan Structure Typology of Old Estonian Towns in the 13th–17th Centuries." *Studies on Art and Architecture* 18: 72–77.

Hänsch, C., J. Krüger, and J. E. Olesen, eds. 2008. *Thomas Thorild, 1759–1808: Ein schwedischer Philosoph in Greifswald.* Greifswald, Germany: Ernst-Moritz-Arndt-Universität.

Hansen, R. 1973. "Vom Holmekloster zu Rantzausholm, 1566–1568: Geschichte und geschichtliche Bedeutung eines Gutskaufs." In K. Friedland, ed., *Stadt und Land in der Geschichte des Ostseeraums*, pp. 80–93. Lübeck, Germany: Schmidt-Römhild.

Häpke, R., ed. 1913–1923. *Niederländische Akten und Urkunden zur Geschichte der Hanse und zur deutschen Seegeschichte.* 2 vols. Lübeck, Germany: Borchers.

Harder-Gersdorff, E. 1978. "Lübeck, Danzig und Riga: Ein Beitrag zur Frage der Handelskonjunktur im Ostseeraum am Ende des 17. Jahrhunderts." *Hansische Geschichtsblätter* 96: 106–138.

Harnisch, H. 1977. "Die agrarpolitischen Reformmaßnahmen der preußischen Staatsführung in dem Jahrzehnt vor 1806 / 07." *Jahrbuch für Wirtschaftsgeschichte* 3: 129–153.

Harrison, D. 2002. *Sveriges historia medeltiden.* Stockholm: Liber.

———. 2010a. "Vikingatiden." In D. Harrison, ed., *Sveriges historia 600–1350*, pp. 92–146. Stockholm: Norstedts.

———. 2010b. "Sockenkyrkor, Stentorn och Småkungar." In D. Harrison, ed., *Sveriges historia 600–1350*, pp. 149–234. Stockholm: Norstedts.

———. 2010c. "Sverige." In D. Harrison, ed., *Sveriges historia 600–1350*, pp. 429–452. Stockholm: Norstedts.

Hasselblatt, C. 1996. *Minderheitenpolitik in Estland: Rechtsentwicklung und Rechtswirklichkeit, 1918–1995*. Hamburg: Baltos Lankos.

———. 2006. *Geschichte der estnischen Literatur*. Berlin: de Gruyter.

Hatz, G. 1964–1965. "Die Münzen von Alt-Lübeck." *Offa* 21–22: 261–267.

———. 1974. *Handel und Verkehr zwischen dem Deutschem Reich und Schweden in der späten Wikingerzeit*. Lund, Sweden: Almqvist & Wiksell.

———. 1987. "Der Handel in der späten Wikingerzeit zwischen Nordeuropa (insbesondere Schweden) und dem Deutschen Reich nach numismatischen Quellen." In K. Düwel et al., eds., *Untersuchungen zu Handel und Verkehr der vor- und frühgeschichtlichen Zeit in Mittel- und Nordeuropa*, vol. 4, pp. 86–112. Göttingen: Vandenhoeck & Ruprecht.

———. 1995. "Danegeld." In M. North, ed., *Von Aktie bis Zoll: Ein historisches Lexikon des Geldes*, p. 78. Munich: C. H. Beck

Hauschild, W.-D. 1988. "Frühe Neuzeit und Reformation: Das Ende der Großmachtstellung und die Neuorientierung der Stadtgemeinschaft." In A. Graßmann, ed., *Lübeckische Geschichte*, pp. 341–432. Lübeck, Germany: Schmidt-Römhild.

Hecker-Stampehl, J., et al., eds. 2004. *Perceptions of Loss, Decline and Doom in the Baltic Sea Region*. Berlin: Berliner Wissenschaftsverlag.

Heckscher, E. F. 1935. *Sveriges ekonomiska historia från Gustav Vasa I*, vol. 1, *Före Frihetstiden*. Stockholm: Bonnier.

———. 1964. *The Continental System: An Economic Interpretation*. Gloucester, MA: Smith.

Hedenborg, S. 2006. *Sverige: En social och ekonomisk historia*. Lund, Sweden: Studentlitteratur.

Heeres, W. G., et al., eds. 1988. *From Dunkirk to Danzig: Shipping and Trade in the North Sea and the Baltic, 1350–1850*. Hilversum, The Netherlands: Verloren.

Hehn, J. v. 1984. *Die Umsiedlung der baltischen Deutschen—Das letzte Kapitel baltisch-deutscher Geschichte*. Marburg, Germany: Herder-Institut.

Heiberg, S. 2001. "Art and the Staging of Images of Power: Christian IV and Pictorial Art." In B. Noldus and J. Roding, eds., *Pieter Isaacz (1568–1625), Court Painter, Art Dealer and Spy*, pp. 231–244. Turnhout, Belgium: Brepols.

Helk, V. 1977. *Die Jesuiten in Dorpat, 1583–1625: Ein Vorposten der Gegenreformation in Nordosteuropa*. Odense, Denmark: Odense University Press.

Helcom. The Helsinki Commission (http://helcom.fi/action-areas).

Hempe, M. 2002. *Ländliche Gesellschaft in der Krise: Mecklenburg in der Weimarer Republik*. Cologne: Böhlau.

Henn, V. 1989. "Was war die Hanse?" In V. Henn et al., eds., *Die Hanse: Lebenswirklichkeit und Mythos*, pp. 15–21. Lübeck, Germany: Schmidt-Römhild.

Henning, D. 1996. *Von der Oberschicht zur Minderheit: Die deutsche Minderheit in Lettland, 1917–1940*. Lüneburg, Germany: Institut Nordostdeutsches Kulturwerk.

Henning, F.-W. 1964. *Herrschaft und Bauernuntertänigkeit*. Würzburg: Holzner.

Henningsen, B., ed. 2002. *Towards a Knowledge-Based Society in the Baltic Sea Region*. Berlin: Spitz.

———, ed. 2005. *Changes, Challenges and Chances: Conclusions and Perspectives of Baltic Sea Area Studies*. Berlin: Berliner Wissenschaftsverlag.

Herlitz, L. 1974. *Jordegendom och ränta: Omfördelningen av jordbrukets merprodukt i Skaraborgs län under frihetstiden*. Gothenburg, Sweden: Institute of Economic History of Gothenburg University.

Herrmann, J. 1976. *Zwischen Hradschin und Vineta: Frühe Kulturen der Westslawen*. Leipzig: Urania.

———. 1982. *Wikinger und Slawen: Zur Frühgeschichte der Ostseevölker*. Neumünster, Germany: Wachholtz.

Hertz, P. 1924. *Den kongelige Malerisamlings tilblivelse*, pp. 358–390. Copenhagen: Statens Museum for Kunst.

Heß, C. 2004. "Mobiliar und Wohnungsauskleidung Danzigs im 17. und 18. Jahrhundert." In M. Krieger and M. North, eds., *Land und Meer: Kultureller Austausch zwischen Westeuropa und dem Ostseeraum in der Frühen Neuzeit*, pp. 129–152. Cologne: Böhlau.

———. 2007. *Danziger Wohnkultur in der Frühen Neuzeit: Untersuchungen zu Nachlassinventaren des 17. und 18. Jahrhunderts*. Berlin: Lit.

Hiden, J. 2004. *Defender of Minorities: Paul Schiemann, 1876–1944*. London: Hurst.

Hiden, J., and M. Housden. 2008. *Neighbours or Enemies? Germans, the Baltic and Beyond*. Amsterdam: Rodopi.

Hilberg, V. 2008. "Hedeberg: An Outline of Its Research History." In S. Brink and N. Price, eds., *The Viking World*, pp. 101–111. London: Routledge.

Hillebrand, A. 2009. *Danzig und die Kaufmannschaft großbritannischer Nation: Rahmenbedingungen, Formen und Medien eines englischen Kulturtransfers im Ostseeraum des 18. Jahrhundert*. Frankfurt: Lang.

Hirdman, Y., U. Lundberg, and J. Björkman. 2012. "Den utopiska refromismen." In Y. Hirdman, U. Lundberg, and J. Björkman, *Sveriges Historia 1920–1965*, pp. 200–231. Stockholm: Norstedts.

Hirschhausen, U. v. 1999. "Die Wahrnehmung des Wandels: Migration, soziale Mobilität und Mentalitäten in Riga, 1867–1914." *Zeitschrift für Ostmitteleuropa Forschung* 48/4: 475–523.

———. 2006. *Die Grenzen der Gemeinsamkeit: Deutsche, Letten, Russen und Juden in Riga, 1860–1914*. Göttingen: Vandenhoeck & Ruprecht.

Hodgson, A. 1984. *Scandinavian Music: Finland & Sweden*. Rutherford, NJ: Fairleigh Dickinson University Press.

Hodne, F. 1993. "Norway's Role in the World Economy, 1750–1950." In M. North, ed., *Nordwesteuropa in der Weltwirtschaft, 1750–1950*, pp. 39–58. Stuttgart: Steiner.

Hoffmann, E. 1985. *Niels Nicolaus Falck. 25.11.1784–11.05.1850. Ansprachen bei der Feier aus Anlass seines 200. Geburtstages am 17. November 1984 im Au-*

ditorium maximum der Christian-Albrechts-Universität zu Kiel, pp. 23–35. Kiel, Germany: Christian-Albrechts-Universität.

——. 1986. "Nicolaus Falck und die schleswig-holsteinische Frage." *Zeitschrift der Gesellschaft für Schleswig-Holsteinische Geschichte* 111: 143–155.

——. 1988. "Lübeck im Hoch- und Spätmittelalter: Die große Zeit Lübecks." In A. Graßmann, ed., *Lübeckische Geschichte*, pp. 79–340. Lübeck, Germany: Schmidt-Römhild.

Hoffmann, G. E., and K. Reumann. 1986. "Die Herzogtümer von der Landesteilung 1544 bis zum Kopenhagener Frieden von 1600." In G. E. Hoffmann et al., eds., *Geschichte Schleswig-Holsteins: Die Herzogtümer von der Landesteilung 1544 bis zur Wiedervereinigung Schleswigs 1721*, vol. 5, pp. 3–203. Neumünster, Germany: Wachholtz.

Högberg, S. 1969. *Utrikeshandel och sjöfart på 1700-talet: Stapelvaror i svensk export och import, 1738–1808*. Stockholm: Bonnier.

Holder-Egger, O., ed. 1911. *Einhardi Vita Karoli Magni*. Reprint: Hannover: Hahn, 1965.

Hoppenbrouwers, P., and J. L. v. Zanden, eds. 2001. *Peasants into Farmers? The Transformation of Rural Economy and Society in the Low Countries (Middle Ages–19th Century) in Light of the Brenner Debate*. Turnhout, Belgium: Brepols.

Hösch, E. 2009. *Kleine Geschichte Finnlands*. Munich: C. H. Beck.

Hoszowski, S. 1957. "Zniszczenia w czasie wojny szwedzkiej na terenie Prus Królewskich." In *Polska w okresie drugiej wojny pólnocnej, 1655–1660*, vol. 2, *Rozprawy*, pp. 398–400. Warsaw: Państwowe Wydawnictwo Naukowe.

Howard, J., and K. Hallas-Murula, eds. 2003. *Architecture 1900: Stockholm, Helsinki, Tallinn, Riga, St. Petersburg*. Tallinn: Kirjastus Eesti Arhitektuurimuuseum.

Hrankowska, T., ed. 1995. *Niderlandyzm w sztuce polskiej*. Warsaw: Wydawnictwo Naukowe.

Hubatsch, W. 1984. *Im Bannkreis der Ostsee: Grundriss einer Geschichte der Ostseeländer in ihren gegenseitigen Beziehungen*. Marburg, Germany: Elwert-Gräfe & Unzer.

Hübner, J. 2005. "Die Umbildung der Verwaltungsstrukturen in Polen: Ausgangssituation, Quellen und Ressourcen, Ergebnisse." In J. Suchoples and M. Kerner, eds., *Skandinavien, Polen und die Länder der östlichen Ostsee: Vergangenheit, Gegenwart, Zukunft*, pp. 104–139. Wrocław, Poland: Wydawnictwo Uniwersytetu Wrocławskiego.

Hughes, L., ed. 2001. *Peter the Great and the West: New Perspective*. Basingstoke, UK: Palgrave Macmillan.

——. 2002. *Peter the Great: A Biography*. New Haven, CT: Yale University Press.

d'Hulst, R.-A. 1982. *Jacob Jordaens*. Ithaca, NY: Cornell University Press.

Ibs, J. H. 1994. *Die Pest in Schleswig-Holstein von 1350 bis 1547/48: Eine sozialgeschichtliche Studie über eine wiederkehrende Katastrophe*. Frankfurt: Lang.

Ihalainen, P., et al., eds. 2011. *Scandinavia in the Age of Revolution: Nordic Political Cultures, 1740–1820*. Farnham, UK: Ashgate.

Ischreyt, H. 1974. "Ich bleibe aber gerne in Deutschland." *Deutsche Studien* 46: 116–126.

Israel, J. 1989. *Dutch Primacy in World Trade, 1585–1740*. Oxford: Oxford University Press.

Jacoby, J. 1987. "A Survey of Art Music." In K. Ketting, ed., *Music in Denmark*, pp. 32–38. Copenhagen: Danish Cultural Institute.

Jahn, D., and N. Werz, eds. 2002. *Politische Systeme und Beziehungen im Ostseeraum*. Munich: Olzog.

Jahn, D., and K. Kuitto. 2008. "Environmental Pollution and Economic Performance in the Baltic Sea Region." In M. Joas et al., eds., *Governing a Common Sea: Environmental Policies in the Baltic Sea Region*, pp. 19–42. London: Earthscan.

Jahnke, C. 2000. *Das Silber des Meeres: Fang und Vertrieb von Ostseehering zwischen Norwegen und Italien (12.–16. Jahrhundert)*. Cologne: Böhlau.

———. 2007. *Geld, Geschäfte, Informationen: Der Aufbau hansischer Handelsgesellschaften und ihre Verdienstmöglichkeiten*. Lübeck, Germany: Schmidt-Römhild.

Janauskas, G. 2010. "New Structures, Changing Identities: The Concepts of the Baltic Sea Region." *Asia Europe Journal* 8: 339–345.

Jandausch, K. 2011. *Ein Name, Schild und Geburt: Niederadlige Familienverbände der Neuzeit im südlichen Ostseeraum*. Bremen: Temmen.

Jansen, E. 1985. "On the Economic and Social Determination of the Estonian National Movement." In A. Loit, ed., *National Movements in the Baltic Countries during the 19th Century: The 7th Conference on Baltic Studies in Scandinavia, Stockholm, June 10–13, 1983*, pp. 41–57. Stockholm: Centre for Baltic Studies at the University of Stockholm.

Janson, H. 2009. "Pagani and Cristiani: Cultural Identity and Exclusion around the Baltic in the Early Middle Ages." In J. Staecker, ed., *The Reception of Medieval Europe in the Baltic Sea Region: Papers of the XIIth Visby Symposium, Held at Gotland University Visby*, pp. 171–192. Visby, Sweden: Gotland University Press.

Jansson, T., and T. Eng, eds. 2000. *Stat—kyrka—samhälle: Den stormaktstida samhällsordningen i Sverige och Östersjöprovinserna*. Stockholm: Studia Baltica Stockholmiensia.

Jansson, V. 1945. *Eufemiavisorna: En filologisk undersökning*. Uppsala, Sweden: A. B. Lundequistska Bokhandeln.

Jany, C. 1967. *Geschichte der preußischen Armee vom 15. Jahrhundert bis 1914*. 4 vols. Osnabrück, Germany: Biblio.

Jauhiainen, J. S. 2007. "Consolidated Local Governments in Partnerships: A Key to Promoting Economic Development in Estonia." In S. Giguere, ed., *Baltic Partnerships: Integration, Growth and Local Governance in the Baltic Sea Region*, pp. 131–157. Paris: OECD.

Jaworski, R. 2000. "Das geteilte Polen, 1795–1918." In R. Jaworski and M. Müller, eds., *Eine Kleine Geschichte Polens*, pp. 253–303. Frankfurt: Suhrkamp.

Jeannin, P. 1963. "Lübecker Handelsunternehmungen um die Mitte des 16. Jahrhundert." *Zeitschrift des Vereins für Lübeckische Geschichte und Altertumskunde* 43: 19–67.

Jenks, S. 1990. "Die 'Carta Mercatoria': Ein 'Hansisches' Privileg." *Hansische Geschichtsblätter* 108: 45–86.

———. 1992. *England, die Hanse und Preußen: Handel und Diplomatie, 1377–1474.* Cologne: Böhlau.

———. 2005. "Von den archaischen Grundlagen bis zur Schwelle der Moderne, ca. 1000–1450." In M. North ed., *Deutsche Wirtschaftsgeschichte: Ein Jahrtausend im Überblick*, pp. 15–111. Munich: C. H. Beck.

Jespersen, K. J. V. 1987. "The Revolution of 1660 and Its Precondition, the Tax-State." In E. Kouri and T. Scott, eds., *Politics and Society in Reformation Europe*, pp. 486–501. London: Macmillan.

———. 2004. *A History of Denmark.* Basingstoke, UK: Palgrave Macmillan.

Jespersen, K. J. V., C. Porskrog Rasmussen, H. Raabyemagle, and P. Holstein. 2010. *Moltke-Rigets mægtigste mand.* Copenhagen: G. E. C. Gad.

Jessen, J. 1922. "Die Entstehung und Entwicklung der Gutswirtschaft in Schleswig-Holstein bis zu dem Beginn der Agrarreformen." *Zeitschrift der Gesellschaft für Schleswig-Holsteinische Geschichte* 51: 127–130.

Joenniemi, P. 2009. "The EU Strategy for the Baltic Sea Region: A Catalyst for What?" In *DIIS Brief* August 2009. http://www.cespi.it/GOVMED/pjo_eu_strategy_balticsearegion.pdf.

Jõesalu, K. 2010. "The Meaning of 'Late Socialism': Analyzing Estonians' Post-Communist Memory Culture." *Asia Europe Journal* 8: 293–303.

Johansen, H. C. 1983. *Shipping and Trade between the Baltic Area and Western Europe, 1784–1795.* Odense, Denmark: Odense University Press.

———. 1983. "Ships and Cargoes in the Traffic between the Baltic and Amsterdam in the Late Eighteenth Century." In W. J. Wieringa et al., eds., *The Interactions of Amsterdam and Antwerp with the Baltic Region, 1400–1800*, pp. 161–170. Leiden, The Netherlands: M. Nijhoff.

———. 1988. *Industriens vaekst og vilkår 1870–1973: Dansk industrihistorie efter 1870.* Odense, Denmark: Odense University Press.

———. 1991. "Baltic Timber Exports in the Late Eighteenth Century." In *The Baltic as a Trade Road: Timber Trade in the Baltic Area Competition between Steam and Sails*, pp. 17–35. Porvoo, Finland: Uusimaa.

Johansen, P., and H. z. Mühlen. 1973. *Deutsch und undeutsch im mittelalterlichen und frühneuzeitlichen Reval.* Cologne: Böhlau.

Jolly, A. 1999. "Philip Brandin, ein niederländischer Bildhauer des 16. Jahrhunderts im Dienst der Herzöge von Mecklenburg." *Oud Holland* 113/1–2: 13–34.

Jonsson, L., ed. 1992–1994. *Musiken i Sverige.* 4 vols. Stockholm: Fischer.

Jonsson, U. 1980. *Jordmagnatar, landbönder och torpare i sydöstra Södermanland, 1800–1880.* Stockholm: Almqvist & Wiksell.

Jörn, N. 1998a. "Die Auseinandersetzungen zwischen Hanse und Merchant Adventurers von den obersten Reichsgerichten im 16. und 17. Jahrhundert." *Zeitschrift des Vereins für Lübeckische Geschichte und Altertumskunde* 78: 323–348.

Jörn, N., R.-G. Werlich, and H. Wernicke, eds. 1998b. *Der Stralsunder Frieden von 1370: Prosopographische Studien.* Cologne: Böhlau.

Jörn, N., and M. North, eds. 2000. *Die Integration des südlichen Ostseeraums in das Alte Reich, 1495–1806.* Cologne: Böhlau.

Jörn, N., B. Diestelkamp, and K. Å. Modéer, eds. 2003. *Integration durch Recht: Das Wismarer Tribunal, 1653–1806*. Cologne: Böhlau.

Jürjo, I. 2006. *Aufklärung im Baltikum: Leben und Werk des livländischen Gelehrten August Wilhelm Hupel, 1737–1819*. Cologne: Böhlau.

Jurkynas, M., and A. Romanaite. 2007. "Divergent Perceptions of Political Conflict in Lithuania." In M. Schartau et al., eds., *Political Culture and Identities in the Baltic Sea Region*, pp. 183–204. Berlin: Berliner Wissenschaftsverlag.

Juske, A. 2006. *Sailing and the Island of Saaremaa*. Tallinn: Infotrükk.

Kahan, A. 1979. "Eighteenth-Century Russian-British Trade: Russia's Contribution to the Industrial Revolution in Great Britain." In A. G. Cross, ed., *Great Britain and Russia in the Eighteenth Century: Contacts and Comparisons*, pp. 181–189. Newtonville, MA: Oriental Research Partners.

Kahk, J. 1996. "Die baltischen Agrarreformen des 19. Jahrhunderts in neuer historischer Perspektive." *Zeitschrift für Ostmitteleuropa-Forschung* 45: 544–555.

———. 1999. *Bauer und Baron im Baltikum: Versuch einer historisch-phänomenologischen Studie zum Thema "Gutsherrschaft in den Ostseeprovinzen."* Tallinn: Henning von Wistinghausen.

Kahk, J., and E. Tarvel. 1997. *An Economic History of the Baltic Countries*. Stockholm: Almqvist & Wiksell.

Kalevi, A., et al., eds. 1996. *Die finnische Musik*. Helsinki: Otava.

Kalmring, S. 2011. "The Harbour of Hedeby." In S. Sigmundsson, ed., *Viking Settlements and Viking Society: Papers from the Proceedings of the Sixteenth Viking Congress, Reykjavík and Reykholt, 16th–23rd August 2009*, pp. 245–259. Reykjavík: Hið íslenzka fornleifafélag.

Karge, W. 1993. *Heiligendamm: Erstes deutsches Seebad. Gegründet 1793*. Schwerin, Germany: Demmler.

Karling, S. I. 1936. *Narva, eine baugeschichtliche Untersuchung*. Tartu: Krüger.

Karlsson, M. 2004. *Transnational Relations in the Baltic Sea Region*. Huddinge, Sweden: Coronet.

Kasekamp, A. 2000. *The Radical Right in Interwar Estonia*. Basingstoke, UK: Palgrave Macmillan.

———. 2010. *A History of the Baltic States*. Basingstoke, UK: Palgrave Macmillan.

———, ed. 2012. *Estonian Foreign Policy Yearbook 2011*. Tallinn: Estonian Foreign Policy Institute.

Kasiske, K. 1934. *Die Siedlungstätigkeit des Deutschen Ordens im östlichen Preußen bis zum Jahre 1410*. Königsberg, Germany: Gräfe & Unzer.

Kask, J., and G. Bergendal. 1998. "Swedish Art Music: Openness and Synthesis." In G. Bergendale, ed., *Music in Sweden*, pp. 11–15. Stockholm: Svenska Institutet.

Katajala, K. 2012. "Drawing Borders or Dividing Lands? The Peace Treaty of 1323 between Sweden and Novgorod in a European Context." *Scandinavian Journal of History* 37/1 (February): 23–48.

Kaufmann, T. DaCosta. 1995. *Court, Cloister, and City: The Art and Culture of Central Europe, 1450–1800*. Chicago: University of Chicago Press.

———. 1998. *Höfe, Klöster und Städte. Kunst und Kultur in Mitteleuropa, 1450–1800.* Cologne: DuMont.

———. 2004a. "Der Ostseeraum als Kunstregion: Historiographie, Stand der Forschung und Perspektiven künftiger Untersuchungen." In M. Krieger and M. North, eds., *Land und Meer: Kultureller Austausch zwischen Westeuropa und dem Ostseeraum in der Frühen Neuzeit,* pp. 9–21. Cologne: Böhlau.

———. 2004b. *Toward a Geography of Art.* Chicago: University of Chicago Press.

———. 2011. "Reframing the Frames: The European Perspective." In M. Andersen, B. Bøggild Johannsen, and H. Johannsen, eds., *Reframing the Danish Renaissance: Problems and Prospects in a European Perspective; Papers from an International Conference in Copenhagen, 28 September–1 October 2006,* pp. 32–50. Copenhagen: National Museum of Denmark.

Kaukiainen, Y. 1991. *Sailing into Twilight: Finnish Shipping in an Age of Transport Revolution, 1860–1914.* Helsinki: SHS.

———. 1992. "Coal and Canvas: Aspects of the Competition between Steam and Sail, c. 1870–1914." *International Journal of Maritime History* 4: 175–191.

———. 1997. "Itämeri, pohjoisen Euroopan Välimeri." *Historiallinen Aikakauskirja* 95: 211–217.

Kautny, O. 2002. *Arvo Pärt zwischen Ost und West: Rezeptionsgeschichte.* Stuttgart: Metzler.

Kempas, H. 1964. "Seeverkehr und Pfundzoll im Herzogtum Preußen: Ein Beitrag zur Geschichte des Seehandels im 16. und 17. Jahrhundert." PhD diss., University of Bonn.

Kent, N. 2008. *A Concise History of Sweden.* Cambridge, UK: Cambridge University Press.

Kinzler, S., ed. 2013. *Der Kieler Frieden 1814.* Neumünster, Germany: Wachholtz.

Kirby, D. 1990. *Northern Europe in the Early Modern Period: The Baltic World, 1492–1772.* London: Routledge.

———. 1995. *The Baltic World, 1772–1993: Europe's Northern Periphery in an Age of Change.* London: Longman.

———. 2006. *A Concise History of Finland.* Cambridge, UK: Cambridge University Press.

Kirby, D., and M.-L. Hinkkanen. 2000. *The Baltic and the North Seas.* London: Routledge.

Kivikari, U. 1996. *Wirtschaftsraum Ostsee: Eine neue Zukunft für eine alte Region.* Helsinki: Otava.

Kivimae, J. 1995. "'Aus der Heimat ins Vaterland.' Die Umsiedlung der Deutschbalten aus dem Blickwinkel estnischer nationaler Gruppierungen." In *Nordost-Archiv N. F. 4:* 501–520.

Kizik, E. 1994. *Mennonici w Gdańsku, Elblągu i na Żuławach wiślanych w drugiej połowie XVII i w XVIII wieku.* Gdańsk, Poland: Wydawnictwo Gdańskie.

————. 2004. "Niederländische Einflüsse in Danzig, Polen und Litauen vom 16. bis zum 18. Jahrhundert." In M. Krieger and M. North, eds., *Land und Meer: Kultureller Austausch zwischen Westeuropa und dem Ostseeraum in der Frühen Neuzeit*, pp. 65–70. Cologne: Böhlau, pp. 65–70.

Klinge, M. 1994. *Die Ostseewelt*. Helsinki: Otava.

————. 2010. *The Baltic World*. Helsinki: Otava.

Klocker, G., ed. 2001. *Ten Years after the Baltic States Re-entered the International Stage*. Baden-Baden, Germany: Nomos.

Kmita, R. 2009. *Ištrūkimas iš fabriko: modernë janti lietuvių poezija XX amžiaus 7–9 dešimtmečiais*. Vilnius: Lietuvių Literatūros ir Tautosakos Institutas.

Knoppers, J. V. T. 1976. *Dutch Trade with Russia from the Time of Peter I to Alexander I*. Montreal: Interuniversity Centre for European Studies.

Knoppers, J. V. T., and R. V. V. Nicholls. 1981. "Der Ostseeraum und der Welthandel mit Pottasche: Die Bedeutung der Pottasche im Rahmen der chemischen Technologie, 1650–1825." In K. Friedland and F. Irsigler, eds., *Seehandel und Wirtschaftswege Nordeuropas im 17. und 18. Jahrhundert*, pp. 59–83. Ostfildern: Scripta Mercaturae.

Kodres, K. 2006. "Handwerker als Kulturvermittler am Beispiel des frühneuzeitlichen Reval in Estland." In B. Schmidt, ed., *Von der Geschichte zur Gegenwart und Zukunft: Mittelständische Wirtschaft, Handwerk und Kultur im baltischen Raum*, pp. 119–135. Hamburg: DOBU.

————. 2010. "Die kirchliche Kunst in den von Esten bewohnten Gebieten im Zeitalter der Reformation und der Konfessionalisierung." In A. Schindling, W. Buchholz, and M. Asche, eds., *Die baltischen Lande im Zeitalter der Reformation und Konfessionalisierung: Livland, Estland, Ösel, Ingermanland, Kurland und Lettgallen. Stadt, Land und Konfession, 1500–1721*, vol. 2, pp. 50–70. Münster: Aschendorff.

————, ed. 2010b. *Eesti kunsti ajalugu [History of Estonian Art]*, vol. 5, *1900–1940*. Tallinn: Eesti Kunstiakadeemia.

Koester, O. 1988. "Art Centers and Artists in Northern Europe, 1588–1648." In S. Heiberg, ed., *Christian IV and Europe*, pp. 301–305. Copenhagen: Council of Europe.

————. 2000. *Flemish Paintings, 1600–1800*. Copenhagen: Statens Museum for Kunst.

Kõll, A. M., ed. 2003. *The Baltic Countries under Occupation: Soviet and Nazi Rule, 1939–1991*. Stockholm: Almqvist & Wiksell.

Komlosy, A., et al., eds. 2008. *Ostsee, 700–2000: Gesellschaft, Wirtschaft, Kultur*. Vienna: Promedia.

Koninckx, C. 1980. *The First and Second Charters of the Swedish East India Company, 1731–1766*. Kortrijk, Belgium: Van Ghemmert.

————. 1993. "The Swedish East Indian Company (1731–1807)." In J. R. Bruijn, ed., *Ships, Sailors and Spices: East Indian Companies and Their Shipping in the 16th, 17th and 18th Centuries*, pp. 121–138. Amsterdam: NEHA.

Konsa, M., R. Allmäe, L. Maldre, and J. Vassiljev. 2008. "Rescue Excavations of a Vendel Era Boat-Grave in Salme, Saaremaa." *Archaeological Fieldwork in Estonia*, pp. 53–63.

Körber, E.-B. 2005. "Die Reformation im Ostseeraum als Kommunikations- und Verkehrsereignis." In R. Tuchtenhagen, *Aspekte der Reformation im Ostseeraum*, pp. 15–44. Lüneburg, Germany: Nordost-Institut.

Korpela, J. 2002. "Finland's Eastern Border after the Treaty of Nöteborg: An Ecclesiastical, Political or Cultural Border?" *Journal for Baltic Studies* 33/4: 384–397.

Korthals-Altes, E. 2004. "The Art Tour of Friedrich of Mecklenburg-Schwerin." *Simiolus* 31: 216–250.

Kosegarten, J. G. L. 1857. *Geschichte der Universität Greifswald mit urkundlichen Beilagen*. Greifswald, Germany: C. A. Koch's Buchhandlung.

Krämer, J. 1998. *Deutschsprachiges Musiktheater im späten 18. Jahrhundert: Typologie, Dramaturgie und Anthropologie einer populären Gattung*. Tübingen, Germany: Niemeyer.

Krantz, O. 1987. "Schweden, Norwegen, Dänemark, Finnland, 1914–1970." In W. Fischer, ed., *Handbuch der europäischen Wirtschafts- und Sozialgeschichte*, vol. 6, *Europäische Wirtschafts- und Sozialgeschichte vom Ersten Weltkrieg bis zur Gegenwart*, pp. 222–292. Stuttgart: Klett-Cotta.

Krastiņš, J. 1996. *Riga Jugendstilmetropole. Art Nouveau Latvia*. Riga: Baltika.

Kreslins, J. 2006. "Konfessionelles Engagement und historische Identität: Religion, Kommunikationskultur und 'Nordosteuropa als Geschichtsregion.'" In J. Hackmann and R. Schweitzer, eds., *Nordosteuropa als Geschichtsregion*, pp. 321–330. Lübeck, Germany: Schmidt-Römhild.

Krieger, M. 1998. *Kaufleute, Seeräuber und Diplomaten: Der dänische Handel auf dem Indischen Ozean*. Cologne: Böhlau.

Krieger, M., and M. North, eds. 2004. *Land und Meer: Kultureller Austausch zwischen Westeuropa und dem Ostseeraum in der Frühen Neuzeit*. Cologne: Böhlau.

Kroll, S., and K. Krüger, eds. 2006. *Städtesystem und Urbanisierung im Ostseeraum in der Frühen Neuzeit: Urbane Lebensräume und Historische Informationssysteme; Beiträge des wissenschaftlichen Kolloquiums in Rostock vom 15. und 16. November 2004*. Münster, Germany: LIT.

Krummacher, F. 1996. "Ein Profil in der Tradition: Der Danziger Kapellmeister Balthasar Erben." In E. Ochs et al., eds., *Musica Baltica; Interregionale musikkulturelle Beziehungen im Ostseeraum*, pp. 341–357. Sankt Augustin, Germany: Academia.

Kuchenbrandt, D. 2010. "Mehr als nur Musik! Auswirkungen von Emotionen, Kognitionen und Verhalten auf Intergruppeneinstellungen am Beispiel deutsch-polnischer Musikbegegnungen." PhD diss., University of Greifswald.

Kuchenbrandt, D., and M. Bornewasser. 2010. "Gemeinsames Musizieren: Affektive Einflüsse im deutsch-polnischen Kontext." In K. Deecke and A. Drost, eds., *Liebe zum Fremden. Xenophilie aus geistes- und sozialwissenschaftlicher Perspektive*, pp. 189–200. Cologne: Böhlau.

Kula, W. 1970. *Théorie économique du système féodal: Pour un modèle de l'économie polonaise, 16e–18e siècles*. Paris: Mouton.

Kuleczka, M. 2010. "Rozwój i poetyka dramatu protestanckiego w Prusach Krolewskich (Gdańsk, Toruń, Elbląg), 1550–1650: Humanizm i Reformacja." PhD diss., University of Cracow.

Kulik, A., and S. N. Pshizova, eds. 2005. *Political Parties in Post-Soviet Space: Russia, Belarus, Ukraine, Moldova, and the Baltics.* Westport, CT: Praeger.

Kumlien, K. 1952. "Stockholm, Lübeck und Westeuropa." *Hansische Geschichtsblätter* 71: 9–29.

Küng, E. 2001. *Rootsi majanduspoliitika Narva kaubanduse küsimuses: 17. sajandi teisel poolel.* Tartu, Estonia: Eesti Ajalooarhiiv.

———. 2008. "Die schwedische Ostseepolitik, die internationale Handelskonjunktur und die Entstehung der Narvaer Handelsflotte in der zweiten Hälfte des 17. Jahrhunderts." *Forschungen zur baltischen Geschichte* 3: 87–102.

Kurilo, O., ed. 2009. *Seebäder an der Ostsee im 19. und 20. Jahrhundert.* Munich: Meidenbauer.

Kurman, G. 1968. *The Development of Written Estonian.* Bloomington: Indiana University Press.

Kuster, A. T., ed. 2005. *Heinrich Schütz: Geistliche Chor-Music.* Ann Arbor, MI: Kuster.

Küster, H. 2002. *Die Ostsee: Eine Natur- und Kulturgeschichte.* Munich: C. H. Beck.

Kutter, U. 1996. *Reisen—Reisehandbücher—Wissenschaft: Materialien zur Reisekultur im 18. Jahrhundert.* Neuried, Germany: Ars Una.

Laar, M. 2006. *Estonia's Way.* Tallinn: Pegasus.

Laaser, C.-F., and K. Schrader. 2002. *European Integration and Changing Trade Patterns: The Case of the Baltic States.* Kiel Working Paper 1088. Kiel, Germany: Institut für Weltwirtschaft.

Laizáne-Jurkáne, M. 2005. "Development Trends of Regional Cooperation Organizations in the Baltic Sea Region: Latvia's Strategy." In Ž. Ozoliņa, ed., *Latvia in International Organisation, Commission on Strategic Analysis,* Research paper 4, pp. 133–154. Riga: Zinātne.

Lamberga, D. 2007. "Die Bildung des nationalen Selbstbewusstseins in der lettischen Kunst, 1880–1910." In G. Reineking-von Bock, ed., *Künstler und Kunstausstellungen im Baltikum im 19. Jahrhundert,* pp. 145–167. Lüneburg, Germany: Carl-Schirren-Gesellschaft.

Landsbergis, V. 1992. *M. K. Čiurlionis. Time and Content.* Vilnius, Lithuania.

Lane, T., ed. 2002. "Lithuania: Stepping Westward." In D. J. Smith et al., eds., *The Baltic States: Estonia, Latvia and Lithuania,* pp. 1–246. London: Routledge.

Lange, U., ed. 2003. *Geschichte Schleswig-Holsteins: Von den Anfängen bis zur Gegenwart.* Neumünster, Germany: Wachholtz.

Langer, A. 2006. "Die Hirschberger Gnadenkirche 'Zum Kreuze Christi' im künstlerischen Spannungsfeld von nordeuropäisch geprägtem Protoklassizismus und römisch geprägtem Barock." In J. Harasimowicz et al., eds., *Po obu stronach Bałtyku: Wzajemne relacje między Skandynawią a Europą Środkowa,* pp. 203–215. Wrocław, Poland: Via Nova.

Langer, K. 1997. "Vorgeschichte und Geschichte der 'Wende' in den drei Nordbezirken der DDR." In Landtag Mecklenburg-Vorpommern Enquete-Kommission, ed., *Leben in der DDR, Leben nach 1989: Aufarbeitung und Versöhnung,* vol. 9, pp. 9–196. Schwerin, Germany: Landtag Mecklenburg-Vorpommern.

Laučkaite, L. 2008. *Art in Vilnius, 1900–1915*. Vilnius: ART STOCK.

Laur, W. 2001. *Deutsche Orts-, Landes- und Gewässernamen in den baltischen Ländern*. Lüneburg, Germany: Nordostdeutsches Kulturwerk.

Lauristin, M., and M. Heidmets, eds. 2002. *The Challenge of the Russian Minority: Emerging Multicultural Democracy in Estonia*. Tartu: Tartu University Press.

Lavery, J. 2002. *Germany's Northern Challenge: The Holy Roman Empire and the Scandinavian Struggle for the Baltic, 1563–1576*. Boston: Brill Academic.

Lehti, M. 1999. *A Baltic League as a Construct of the New Europe: Envisioning a Baltic Region and Small State Sovereignty in the Aftermath of the First World War*. Frankfurt: Lang.

———. 2003. "Possessing a Baltic Europe: Retold National Narratives in the European North." In M. Lehti and D. J. Smith, eds., *Post–Cold War Identity Politics: Northern and Baltic Experiences*, pp. 11–49. London: Frank Cass.

———. 2006. "Paradigmen ostseeregionaler Geschichte: Von Nationalgeschichte zur multinationalen Historiographie." In J. Hackmann and R. Schweitzer, eds., *Nordosteuropa als Geschichtsregion*, pp. 494–510. Lübeck, Germany: Schmidt-Römhild.

———. 2009. "Baltic Region in Becoming: From the Council of the Baltic Sea States to the EU Strategy for the Baltic Sea Area." Lithuanian Foreign Policy Review 22: 9–27. http://www.lfpr.lt/uploads/File/2009-22/Marko%20Lehti.pdf.

Lehti, M., and J. Hackmann, eds. 2010. *Contested and Shared Places of Memory*. London: Routledge.

Leimus, I. 2009. "Millenium Breakthrough." *North Goes West*, special issue: 7–34.

Lemmink, J. P. S., and J. S. A. M. v. Koningsbrugge, eds. 1990. *Baltic Affairs: Relations between the Netherlands and North-Eastern Europe, 1500–1800*. Nijmegen, The Netherlands: INOS.

Lengefeld, C. 2004. *Anders Zorn: Eine Künstlerkarriere in Deutschland*. Berlin: Reimer.

Lenz, W. 1953. *Der baltische Literatenstand*. Marburg, Germany: Herder-Institut.

Lichtenberg, G. C. 1793. "Warum hat Deutschland noch kein großes öffentliches Seebad." *Göttinger Taschen Kalender*, p. 109.

Lindblad, J. T. 1982. *Sweden's Trade with the Dutch Republic, 1738–1795*. Assen, The Netherlands: Van Gorcum.

———. 1995. "Louis de Geer, 1587–1652: Dutch Entrepreneur and the Father of Swedish Industry." In C. Lesger and L. Noordegraaf, eds., *Entrepreneurs and Entrepreneurship in Early Modern Times: Merchants and Industrialists within the Orbit of the Dutch Staple Market*, pp. 77–84. The Hague: Stichting Hollandse Historische Reeks.

Lindholm, A., K. Nygård Skalman, and C. H. M. Ketels. 2009. "Section C: The EU Baltic Sea Region Strategy." In *State of the Region Report 2009*, pp. 103–115. Copenhagen: Baltic Development Forum.

Line, P. 2009. "Sweden's Conquest of Finland: A Clash of Cultures." In A. V. Murray, ed., *The Clash of Cultures on the Baltic Frontier*, pp. 73–99. Aldershot, UK: Ashgate.

Linz, J. J., and A. Stepan. 1996. *Problems of Democratic Transition and Consolidation: Southern Europe, South-America, and Post-Communist Europe*. Baltimore: The Johns Hopkins University Press.

Liulevičius, G. 2000. *War Land on the Eastern Front: Culture, National Identity and German Occupation in World War I*. Cambridge, UK: Cambridge University Press.

Lloyd, T. H. 1991. *England and the German Hanse, 1157–1611: A Study of Their Trade and Commercial Diplomacy*. Cambridge, UK: Cambridge University Press.

Lockhart, P. D. 2007. *Denmark 1513–1660: The Rise and Decline of a Renaissance Monarchy*. Oxford: Oxford University Press.

Loit, A. 1985. "Die nationalen Bewegungen im Baltikum während des 19. Jahrhunderts in vergleichbarer Perspektive." In A. Loit, ed., *National Movements in the Baltic Countries during the 19th Century: The 7th Conference on Baltic Studies in Scandinavia, Stockholm, June 10–13, 1983*, pp. 59–81. Stockholm: Centre for Baltic Studies at the University of Stockholm.

Lönnrot, E. 2008. *The Kalevala: An Epic Poem after Oral Tradition*. Translated from the Finnish with an introduction and notes by Keith Bosley. Oxford: Oxford University Press.

Lönnroth, L., and S. Delblanc, eds. 1999. *Den svenska litteraturen*. 3 vols. Stockholm: Bonnier.

Lorentz, S. 1937. *Jan Krzysztof Glaubitz: Architekt wileński XVIII wieku: materiały do biografii i twórczości*. Warsaw: Towarzystwa Naukowego Warszawskiego.

Lorenzen-Schmidt, K.-J. 1995. "Gutsherrschaft über reiche Bauern. Übersicht über bäuerliche Widerständigkeit in den Marschgütern an der Westküste Schleswig-Holsteins und Jütlands." In J. Peters, ed., *Gutsherrschaft als soziales Modell*, pp. 261–278. Munich: Oldenbourg.

Lübke, C. 2000. "Auf dem Weg zu einem Ganzen: Akkumulation und Expansion von Macht." In R. Jaworski et al., eds., *Eine kleine Geschichte Polens*, pp. 34–51. Frankfurt: Suhrkamp.

———. 2004. *Das östliche Europa*. Berlin: Siedler.

Ludat, H. 1952. "Ostsee und Mare Balticum." In H. Ludat, ed., *Deutsch-slawische Frühzeit und modernes polnisches Geschichtsbewusstsein*, pp. 222–248. Vienna: Böhlau.

Luks, L. 2000. *Geschichte Russlands und der Sowjetunion: Von Lenin bis Jelzin*. Regensburg, Germany: Pustet.

Lukša, J. 2009. *Forest Brothers: The Account of an Anti-Soviet Lithuanian Freedom Fighter, 1944–1948*. Budapest: Central European University Press.

Lust, K. 2006. "Die Innovationsbereitschaft der livländischen Bauern und die Agrarreformen im 19. Jahrhundert." *Zeitschrift für Ostmitteleuropa-Forschung* 55: 510–525.

Lutsepp, E., and M. Kahn, eds. 2010. *Eesti kunsti ajalugu [History of Estonian Art]*, vol. 5, *1900–1940*. Tallinn: Eesti Kunstiakadeemia.

Mączak, A. 1962. *Gospodarstwo chłopskie na Żuławach Malborskich na początkach XVII wieku*. Warsaw: Państwowe Wydawnictwo Naukowe.

———. 1972. *Między Gdańskiem a Sundem: Studia nad handlem bałtyckim od połowy XVI do połowy XVII wieku*. Warsaw: Państwowe Wydawnictwo Naukowe.

Mager, F. 1955. *Geschichte des Bauerntums und der Bodenkultur im Lande Mecklenburg*. Berlin: Akademie-Verlag.

Maiste, J. 1999. *Johann Wilhelm Krause, 1757–1828*. 2 vols. Tallinn: Eesti Keele Sihtasutus.

———. 2007. *Eesti kunsti lugu*. Tallinn: Varrak.

Maiste, J., K. Polli, and M. Raisma. 2003. *Alma Mater Tartuensis: Tartu Ülikool ja tema arhitekt Johann Wilhelm Krause*. Tallinn: Eesti Keele Sihtasutus.

Mälksoo, M. 2009. "Liminality and Contested Europeanness: Conflicting Memory Politics in the Baltic Space." In P. Ehin and E. Berg, eds., *Identity and Foreign Policy: Baltic-Russian Relations in the Context of European Integration*, pp. 65–83. Farnham, UK: Ashgate.

Manikowska, E. 2004. "Der Erwerb von Kunst und Luxusgütern für Stanisław August Poniatowski und das Danziger Netzwerk." In M. Krieger and M. North, eds., *Land und Meer: Kultureller Austausch zwischen Westeuropa und dem Ostseeraum in der Frühen Neuzeit*, pp. 109–128. Cologne: Böhlau.

———. 2007. *Sztuka—Ceremoniał—Informacja: Studium wokół królewskich kolekcji Stanisława Augusta*. Warsaw: Zamek Królewski w Warszawie.

Mansén, E. 2013a. "Krig och fred." In E. Mansén, ed., *Sveriges Historia 1721–1830*, pp. 19–61. Stockholm: Norstedts.

———. 2013b. "Resor, kolonier och handel." In E. Mansén, ed., *Sveriges Historia 1721–1830*, pp. 69–123. Stockholm: Norstedts.

———. 2013c. "Offentlig debatt." In E. Mansén, ed., *Sveriges Historia 1721–1830*, pp. 370–403. Stockholm: Norstedts.

———. 2013d. "Fred, frihet och förändring." In E. Mansén, ed., *Sveriges Historia 1721–1830*, pp. 630–633. Stockholm: Norstedts.

Marker, F. J., and L.-L. Marker. 1996. *A History of Scandinavian Theatre*. Cambridge, UK: Cambridge University Press.

Martin, T., and D. Sivén. 1996. *Akseli Gallen-Kallela: National Artist of Finland*. Sulkava, Finland: Watti-Kustannus.

Maschke, E. 1935. *Das germanische Meer: Geschichte des Ostseeraumes*. Berlin: Grenze u. Ausland.

Maybaum, H. 1926. *Die Entstehung der Gutsherrschaft im nordwestlichen Mecklenburg*. Stuttgart: Kohlhammer.

Meier, J., and D. Möhn. 1999. "Literatur: Formen und Funktionen." In J. Bracker, V. Henn, and R. Postel, eds., *Die Hanse. Lebenswirklichkeit und Mythos*, pp. 524–534. Lübeck, Germany: Schmidt-Römhild.

Meinander, H. 2013. *A History of Finland*. Oxford: Oxford University Press.

Melin, J., et al. 2006. *Sveriges historia: Koncentrerad uppslagsbok*. Stockholm: Prisma.

Melis, D. v., ed. 1999. *Sozialismus auf dem platten Land: Mecklenburg-Vorpommern, 1945–1952*. Schwerin, Germany: Helms.

Melton, E. 1988. "Gutsherrschaft in East Elbian Germany and Livonia, 1500–1800: A Critique of the Model." *Central European History* 21: 315–349.

Merkel, W. 2007. "Gegen alle Theorie? Die Konsolidierung der Demokratie in Osteuropa." *Politische Vierteljahresschrift* 48: 413–433.

Mertelsmann, O., ed. 2003. *The Sovietization of the Baltic States, 1940–1956: Papers Presented at the International Workshop in Haapsalu, Estonia: May, 9–11, 2003*. Tartu, Estonia: Kleio.

———. 2005. *Vom Hitler-Stalin-Pakt bis zu Stalins Tod: Estland, 1939–1953*. Hamburg: Bibliotheca Baltica.

———. 2006. *Der stalinistische Umbau in Estland: Von der Markt- zur Kommandowirtschaft*. Hamburg: Dr. Kovač.

Mertineit, W. 1958. *Die fridericianische Verwaltung in Ostpreußen: Ein Beitrag zur Geschichte der preußischen Staatsbildung*. Heidelberg: Quelle & Meyer.

Mielczarski, S. 1972. *Rynek zbożowy na ziemiach polskich w drugie połowie XVI i pierwszej połowie XVII: Próba rejonizacji*. Gdańsk, Poland: Gdańskie Towarzystwo Naukowe.

Militzer, K. 2005. *Die Geschichte des Deutschen Ordens*. Stuttgart: Kohlhammer.

Modéer, K. A. 1975. *Gerichtsbarkeiten der schwedischen Krone im deutschen Reichsterritorium*. Stockholm: Nordiska bokhandeln.

Moe, B. 2010. "Musikkulturel trafik i København og Rostock: Musikerrekruttering og repertoirefornyelse i første halvdel af 1600-tallet." PhD diss., University of Copenhagen.

Mollet, A. (1651) 1981. *Le jardin de plaisir*. Paris: Éditions du Moniteur.

Mörke, O. 2000. "Holstein und Schwedisch-Pommern im Alten Reich: Integrationsmuster und politische Identitäten in Grenzregionen." In N. Jörn and M. North, eds., *Die Integration des südlichen Ostseeraumes in das Alte Reich*, pp. 425–472. Cologne: Böhlau.

———. 2008. "Auf der Suche nach Europa: Schwedisch-niederländische Beziehungen in der Zeit Axel Oxenstiernas." In M. Engelbrecht et al., eds., *Rund um die Meere des Nordens* (Festschrift Rebas), pp. 209–220. Heide, Germany: Boyens.

Mühlen, H. v. z. 1994. "Das Ostbaltikum unter Herrschaft und Einfluss der Nachbarmächte, 1561–1710, 1795." In G. v. Pistohlkors, ed., *Deutsche Geschichte im Osten Europas: Baltische Länder*, pp. 195–202. Berlin: Siedler.

Müller, L. 1988. *The Merchant Houses of Stockholm, c. 1640–1800: A Comparative Study of Early-Modern Entrepreneurial Behaviour*. Uppsala, Sweden: Uppsala University Library.

Müller, M. G. 1984. *Die Teilungen Polens, 1772, 1793, 1795*. Munich: C. H. Beck.

———. 1997. *Zweite Reformation und städtische Autonomie im Königlichen Preußen: Danzig, Elbing und Thorn in der Epoche der Konfessionalisierung, 1557–1660*. Berlin: Akademie-Verlag.

Müller-Blattau, J. 1968. *Geschichte der Musik in Ost- und Westpreußen*. Wolfenbüttel, Germany: Möseler.

Münch, E. 1997. "Zu den mittelalterlichen Grundlagen der frühneuzeitlichen Adelsgüter Mecklenburgs." *Mecklenburgische Jahrbücher* 112: 45–60.

Murdoch, S. 2006. *Network North, Scottish Kin, Commercial and Convert Associations in Northern Europe, 1603–1746*. Leiden, The Netherlands: Brill.

Murray, A. V., ed. 2001. *Crusade and Conversion on the Baltic Frontier, 1150–1500.* Aldershot, UK: Ashgate.

———, ed. 2009. *The Clash of Cultures on the Medieval Baltic Frontier.* Aldershot, UK: Ashgate.

Muschik, A. 2005. *Die beiden deutschen Staaten und das neutrale Schweden: Eine Dreiecksbeziehung im Schatten der offenen Deutschlandfrage, 1949–1972.* Münster: LIT.

———. 2007. "Die Ideen der Französischen Revolution in Schwedisch-Vorpommern." *Baltische Studien N. F.* 93: 163–184.

Museum of the History of the City of Gdańsk. 2006. *Netherlandish Artists in Gdańsk in the Time of Hans Vredeman de Vries.* Material from the Conference Organized by Museum of the History of the City of Gdańsk and Weserrenaissance-Museum Schloß Brake Lemgo, Main City Town Hall, Gdańsk, 20–21 November 2003. Gdańsk, Poland: Museum of the History of the City of Gdańsk.

Narbutiene, O. 2003. "Litauische Komponisten an deutschen Musikhochschulen." In A. Žiūraitytė and K.-P. Koch, eds., *Deutsch-baltische musikalische Beziehungen: Geschichte—Gegenwart—Zukunft; Bericht über die 35. Konferenz des Musikwissenschaftlers des Baltikums in Vilnius 18.–20. Oktober 2001,* pp. 175–184. Sinzig, Germany: Studio.

Nawrocki, P. 2010. *Der frühe dänische Backsteinbau: Ein Beitrag zur Architekturgeschichte der Waldemarzeit.* Berlin: Lukas.

Nerée, D. v. 1996. "Industrie und Handwerk in Pommern in der Weimarer Republik." In H. Wernicke and R.-G. Werlich, eds., *Pommern: Geschichte—Kultur—Wissenschaft,* pp. 363–377. Greifswald, Germany: Ernst-Moritz-Arndt-Universität.

Neville, K. 2009. *Nicodemus Tessin the Elder. Architecture in Sweden in the Age of Greatness,* Turnhout, Belgium: Brepols.

Nicholas, D. 2009. *The Northern Lands: Germanic Europe, c. 1270–c. 1500.* Chichester, UK: Wiley.

Nikžentaitis, A., et al., eds. 2004. *The Vanished World of Lithuanian Jews.* Amsterdam: Rodopi.

Nirk, E. 1987. *Estonian Literature.* Tallinn: Eesti Raamat.

Noldus, B. 2004. *Trade in Good Taste: Relations in Architecture and Culture between the Dutch Republic and the Baltic World in the Seventeenth Century.* Turnhout, Belgium: Brepols.

Noodt, B. 2005. "Lübecker Quellen zur demographischen Wirkung der Pest im 14. Jahrhundert." In R. Hammel-Kiesow and M. Hundt, eds., *Das Gedächtnis der Hansestadt Lübeck* (Festschrift Antjekathrin Graßmann), pp. 55–66. Lübeck: Schmidt-Römhild.

Nordin, J. 2011. "The Monarchy in the Swedish Age of Liberty, 1719–1772." In P. Ihalainen et al., eds., *Scandinavia in the Age of Revolution: Nordic Political Cultures, 1740–1820,* pp. 29–40. Farnham, UK: Ashgate.

North, M. 1982. *Die Amtswirtschaften von Osterode und Soldau. Vergleichende Untersuchungen zur Wirtschaft im frühmodernen Staat am Beispiel des Herzogtums Preußen in der zweiten Hälfte des 16. und in der ersten Hälfte des 17. Jahrhunderts.* Berlin: Duncker & Humblot.

————1983a. "Untersuchungen zur adligen Gutswirtschaft im Herzogtum Preußen des 16. Jahrhunderts." *Vierteljahrschrift für Sozial- und Wirtschaftsgeschichte* 70: 1–20.

————. 1983b. "Waldwarenhandel und -produktion." In W. J. Wieringa et al., eds., *The Interactions of Amsterdam and Antwerp with the Baltic Region, 1400–1800*, pp. 73–83. Leiden, The Netherlands: M. Nijhoff.

————. 1984. "A Small Baltic Port in the Early Modern Period: The Port of Elbing in the Sixteenth and Seventeenth Century." *Journal of European Economic History* 13: 117–127.

————. 1985. "Getreideanbau und Getreidehandel im Königlichen Preußen und im Herzogtum Preußen: Überlegungen zu den Beziehungen zwischen Produktion, Binnenmarkt und Weltmarkt im 16. und 17. Jahrhundert." *Zeitschrift für Ostforschung* 34: 39–47.

————. 1987. "Miasto, domena i okolice w Prusach Książęcych: Na przykładzie miasta i domeny Ostróda w XVI i XVII wieku." *Zapiski Historyczne* 52/1: 69–78.

————. 1988a. "Lohnarbeit und Fronarbeit in der ostpreußischen Landwirtschaft vom 16. bis zum 18. Jahrhundert." *Zeitschrift für Agrargeschichte und Agrarsoziologie* 36: 11–22.

————. 1988b. "The Role of Scottish Immigrants in the Economy and Society of the Baltic Region in the Sixteenth and Seventeenth Centuries." In W. E. Minchinton, ed., *Britain and the Northern Seas: Some Essays; Papers Presented at the Fourth Conference of the Association for the History of the Northern Seas, Dartington, Devon, 16.–20. September 1985*, pp. 21–24. Pontefract, UK: Lofthouse.

————. 1990a. "Die frühneuzeitliche Gutswirtschaft in Schleswig-Holstein." *Blätter für deutsche Landesgeschichte* 126: 223–242.

————. 1990b. *Geldumlauf und Wirtschaftskonjunktur im südlichen Ostseeraum an der Wende zur Neuzeit, 1440–1570*. Sigmaringen, Germany: Thorbecke.

————. 1994. "Abgaben und Dienste in der ostdeutschen Landwirtschaft vom Spätmittelalter bis zur Bauernbefreiung." In E. Schremmer, ed., *Steuern, Abgaben und Dienste vom Mittelalter bis zur Gegenwart*, pp. 77–89. Stuttgart: Steiner.

————. 1996a. "Englische Reiseberichte des 17. Jahrhunderts als Quelle zur Geschichte der königlich-preussischen Städte Danzig, Elbing und Thorn, XIX." In M. North, *From the North Sea to the Baltic*, pp. 197–208. Aldershot, UK: Variorum.

————. 1996b. "The Export of Timber and Timber By-Products from the Baltic Region to Western Europe, 1575–1775." In M. North, *From the North Sea to the Baltic*, pp. 1–14. Aldershot, UK: Variorum.

————. 1996c. *From the North Sea to the Baltic: Essays in Commercial, Monetary and Agrarian History, 1500–1800*. Aldershot, UK: Variorum.

————. 1999. "Die Entstehung der Gutswirtschaft im südlichen Ostseeraum." *Zeitschrift für Historische Forschung* 26: 43–59.

————. 2000. "Integration im Ostseeraum und im Heiligen Römischen Reich." In N. Jörn and M. North, eds., *Die Integration des südlichen Ostseeraumes in das Alte Reich*, pp. 1–11. Cologne: Böhlau.

———. 2001a. *Das Goldene Zeitalter: Kunst und Kommerz in der niederländischen Malerei des 17. Jahrhunderts*. Cologne: Böhlau.

———. 2001b. "Von der nordeuropäischen Großmacht zum kleinen Nachbarn: Dänisch-deutsche Beziehungen im Wandel (17.–19. Jahrhundert)." In D. Lohmeier and R. Paczkowski, eds., *Landesgeschichte und Landesbibliothek. Studien zur Geschichte und Kultur Schleswig-Holsteins* (Festschrift Rothert), pp. 79–89. Heide, Germany: Boyens.

———. 2003. "The Hamburg Art Market and Influences on Northern and Central Europe." *Scandinavian Journal of History* 28: 253–261.

———. 2006a. "Reich und Reichstag im 16. Jahrhundert. Der Blick aus der angeblichen Reichsferne." In M. Lanzinner and A. Strohmeyer, eds., *Der Reichstag, 1486–1613: Kommunikation—Wahrnehmung—Öffentlichkeit*, pp. 221–236. Göttingen: Vandenhoeck & Ruprecht.

———. 2006b. "The Transfer and Reception of Dutch Art in the Baltic Area during the Eighteenth Century: The Case of the Hamburg Dealer Gerhard Morell." In A. Golahny, M. M. Mochizuki, and L. Vergara, eds., *In His Milieu: Essays on Netherlandish Art in Memory of John Michael Montias*, pp. 301–331. Amsterdam: Amsterdam University Press.

———. 2007. "Merchants and Credit in the Southern and Eastern Baltic." In P. L. Cottrell et al., eds., *Centres and Peripheries in Banking. The Historical Development of Financial Markets*, pp. 211–222. Aldershot, UK: Ashgate.

———. 2008a. "Die Auswirkungen der Kontinentalsperre auf das nördliche Deutschland und den Ostseeraum." In H.-W. Hahn, A. Klinger, and G. Schmidt, eds., *Das Jahr 1806 im europäischen Kontext: Balance, Hegemonie und politische Kulturen*, pp. 101–122. Cologne: Böhlau.

———. 2008b. *Geschichte Mecklenburg-Vorpommerns*. Munich: C. H. Beck.

———. 2008c. *Material Delight and the Joy of Living: Cultural Consumption in Germany in the Age of Enlightenment*. Aldershot, UK: Ashgate.

———. 2008d. "Ostseehandel. Drehscheibe der Weltwirtschaft in der Frühen Neuzeit." In A. Komlosy, H.-H. Nolte, and I. Sooman, eds., *Ostsee 700–2000, Gesellschaft—Wirtschaft—Kultur*, pp. 132–147. Vienna: Promedia.

———, ed. 2009. *Kultureller Austausch: Bilanz und Perspektiven der Frühneuzeitforschung*. Cologne: Böhlau.

———. 2010a. "Das Meer als 'Lieu de Mémoire': Der Öresund." In M. Krieger and J. Krüger, eds., *Regna firmat pietas: Staat und Staatlichkeit im Ostseeraum* (Festschrift Olesen), pp. 47–55. Greifswald, Germany: Ernst-Moritz-Arndt-Universität.

———. 2010b. "Nationale und kulturelle Selbstverortung in der Diaspora: Die Deutschen in den russischen Ostseeprovinzen des 18. Jahrhunderts." In G. Schmidt, ed., *Die deutsche Nation im frühneuzeitlichen Europa*, pp. 83–96. Munich: R. Oldenbourg.

———. 2012a. *The Expansion of Europe, 1250–1500*. Manchester: Manchester University Press.

———. 2012b. *Gerhard Morell und die Entstehung einer Sammlungskultur im Ostseeraum des 18. Jahrhunderts*. Greifswald, Germany: Ernst-Moritz-Arndt-Universität.

————. 2014. "Serfdom and Corvée Labour in the Baltic Area, 16th–18th Centuries." In S. Cavaciocchi, ed., *Schiavitù e servaggio nell'economia europea, Secc. XI–XVIII [Serfdom and Slavery in the European Economy, 11th–18th Centuries]*, pp. 147–154. Florence: Florence University Press.

North, M., and R. Riemer, eds. 2008. *Das Ende des Alten Reiches im Ostseeraum: Wahrnehmungen und Transformationen.* Cologne: Böhlau.

North, M., and B. Turner. 2010. "The Baltic Sea and South China Sea Regions: Incomparable Models of Regional Integration?" *Asia Europe Journal* 8: 271–277.

Nowak, Z. 1982. "Lata rozkwitu kultury, nauki i sztuki." In E. Cieślak, ed., *Historia Gdańska*, vol. 2, *1454–1655*, pp. 686–753. Gdańsk, Poland: Instytut Historii Polski Akademii Nauk, Zakład Historii Gdańska i Dziejów Morskich.

Nugin, R. 2009. *The Implementation of Stalinist Art Model in Estonia in 1945–1950: A Story of Defeat of Artists' Free Will.* Cologne: Lambert Academic.

Oberländer, E., et al., eds. 2001. *Autoritäre Regime in Ostmittel- und Südosteuropa, 1919–1944.* Paderborn, Germany: Schöningh.

O'Connor, K. 2006. *Culture and Customs of the Baltic States.* Westport, CT: Greenwood.

Olesen, J. E. 1980. *Rigsråd—Kongemagt—Union: Studier over det danske rigsråd og den nordiske kongemagts politik, 1434–1449.* Århus, Denmark: Universitetsforlaget.

————. 1983. *Unionskrige og staendersamfund: Bidrag til Nordens historie i Kristian I's regeringstid 1450–1481.* Århus, Denmark: Universitetsforlaget.

————. 1991. "Die doppelte Königswahl 1448 im Norden." In W. Paravicini, ed., *Mare Balticum. Beiträge zur Geschichte des Ostseeraums in Mittelalter und Neuzeit* (Festschrift Hoffmann), pp. 213–231. Sigmaringen, Germany: Thorbecke.

————. 2003. "Inter-Scandinavian Relations." In K. Helle, ed., *The Cambridge History of Scandinavia*, vol. 1, *Prehistory to 1520*, pp. 710–770. Cambridge, UK: Cambridge University Press.

————. 2004. "Die Reformation im Königreich Dänemark." *Nordost-Archiv: Aspekte der Reformation im Ostseeraum*, N. F. 13: 75–119.

————. 2006. "Die Verbreitung des Schwarzen Todes in Skandinavien und Finnland." In T. Fischer and T. Riis, eds., *Tod und Trauer: Todeswahrnehmung und Trauerriten in Nordeuropa*, pp.167–180. Kiel, Germany: Ludwig.

————. 2009. "Der Einfluß dänischer Klöster auf den Ostseeraum." In O. Auge, F. Biermann, and C. Herrmann, eds., *Glaube, Macht und Pracht: Geistliche Gemeinschaften des Ostseeraums im Zeitalter der Backsteingotik*, pp. 49–58. Raaden, Germany: Leidorf.

Olsson, M. 2006. "Manorial Economy and Corvée Labour in Southern Sweden, 1650–1850." *Economic History Review* 59: 481–497.

Önnerfors, A. 2003. *Svenska Pommern: Kulturmöten och identifikation, 1720–1815.* Lund, Sweden: Lunds universitet.

————. 2008. "Das Ende des Alten Reiches als Medienereignis in schwedischen und deutschen Zeitschriften und Zeitungen." In M. North and R. Riemer, eds., *Das Ende des Alten Reiches im Ostseeraum: Wahrnehmungen und Transformationen*, pp. 238–248. Cologne: Böhlau.

Opgenoorth, E. 1978. *Friedrich Wilhelm: Der Große Kurfürst von Brandenburg.* 2 vols. Göttingen: Musterschmidt.

———. 1994. "Politik, 'Verfassung,' Verwaltung, Recht, Militär." In E. Opgenoorth, ed., *Handbuch der Geschichte Ost- und Westpreußens*, vol. 1, *Von der Teilung bis zum Schwedisch-Polnischen Krieg, 1466–1655*, pp. 13–22. Lüneburg, Germany: Institut Nordostdeutsches Kulturwerk.

Ormrod, D. 2003. *Rise of Commercial Empires: England and the Netherlands in the Age of Mercantilism, 1650–1770.* Cambridge, UK: Cambridge University Press.

Pabriks, A., and A. Purs. 2002. "Latvia: The Challenges of Change." In D. J. Smith et al., eds., *The Baltic States. Estonia, Latvia and Lithuania*, pp. 1–169. London: Routledge.

Pagel, Oliver. 2014. "Finnische Touristen entdecken das sowjetische Tallinn." *Forschungen zur baltischen Geschichte* 9: 215–236.

Palmer, A. 2005. *Northern Shores: A History of the Baltic Sea and Its Peoples.* London: John Murray.

Paravicini, W. 1989, 1995. *Die Preußenreisen des europäischen Adels (two parts).* Sigmaringen, Germany: Thorbecke.

Peets, J. 2003. *The Power of Iron: Iron Production and Blacksmithy in Estonia and Neighbouring Areas in Prehistoric Period and the Middle Ages.* Tallinn: Ajaloo Instituut/Institute of History.

Pelus, M.-L. 1981. *Wolter von Holsten marchand Lubeckois dans la seconde moitié du seizième siècle: Contribution à l'étude des relations commerciales entre Lübeck et les villes livoniennes.* Cologne: Böhlau.

Penner, H. 1963. *Ansiedlung mennonitischer Niederländer im Weichselmündungsgebiet von der Mitte des 16. Jahrhunderts bis zum Beginn der preußischen Zeit.* Weiherhof, Germany: Mennonit. Geschichtsverein.

Petersohn, J. 1979. *Der südliche Ostseeraum im kirchlich-politischen Kräftespiel des Reichs, Polens und Dänemarks vom 10. bis 13. Jahrhundert: Mission, Kirchenorganisation, Kultpolitik.* Cologne: Böhlau.

Pfister, C. 1994. *Bevölkerungsgeschichte und Historische Demographie, 1500–1800.* Munich: R. Oldenbourg.

Pipping, R. 1943. *Den fornsvenska litteraturen.* Stockholm: Bonniers.

Pistohlkors, G. v., ed. 1994. *Baltische Länder.* Berlin: Siedler.

———, 1994. "Die Ostseeprovinzen unter russischer Herrschaft (1710/95–1914)." In G. v. Pistohlkors, ed., *Baltische Länder*, pp. 265–278. Berlin: Siedler.

Plakans, A. 1995. *The Latvians: A Short History.* Stanford, CA: Stanford University Press.

———. 2011. *A Concise History of the Baltic States.* Cambridge, UK: Cambridge University Press.

Plath, U. 2004. "Nichts neues im wilden Osten? Die baltischen Provinzen Russlands im Blick deutscher Reisender und Migranten um 1800." In A. Bauerkämper et al., eds., *Die Welt erfahren. Reisen als kulturelle Begegnung von 1780 bis heute*, pp. 43–69. Frankfurt: Campus.

———. 2011. *Esten und Deutsche in den baltischen Provinzen Russlands: Fremdheitskonstruktionen, Kolonialphantasien und Lebenswelten, 1750–1850.* Wiesbaden: Harrassowitz.

Plehn, H. 1906. "Zur Geschichte der Agrarverfassung von Ost- und Westpreußen." *Forschungen zur brandenburgischen und preußischen Geschichte* 18: 66–112.

Pletzing, C., and M. Pletzing, eds. 2007. "Displaced Persons: Flüchtlinge aus den baltischen Staaten in Deutschland." Munich: Meidenbauer.

Poelman, H. A., ed. 1917. *Bronnen tot de geschiedenis van den Oostzeehandel*, vol. 1, *1122–1499, eerste stuk.* Grote Serie 35. The Hague: Rijks Geschiedkundige Publicatiën.

Polli, K., and R. Raudsepp, eds. 2007. "Maarjamaa rokokoo: Rokoko in Estland; Gottlieb Welté, 1745 / 49–1792." Exhibition catalogue. Tallinn: Art Museum of Estonia—Kadriorg Art Museum.

Porskrog Rasmussen, C. 2003. *Rentegods og hovedgårdsdrift: Godsstrukturer og godsøkonomi i hertugdømmet Slesvig, 1524–1770.* 2 vols. Aabenraa, Denmark: Institut for Grænseregionsforskning.

———. 2004. "Ostelbische Gutsherrschaft und nordwestdeutsche Freiheit in einem Land: Die Güter des Herzogtums Schleswig, 1524–1770." *Zeitschrift für Agrargeschichte und Agrarsoziologie* 52/2: 25–40.

———, et al. 2008. *Die Fürsten des Landes: Herzöge und Grafen von Schleswig, Holstein und Lauenburg.* Neumünster, Germany: Wachholtz.

———, et al. 2010. *Moltke: Rigets maegtigste mand.* Copenhagen: Gads.

Pourchasse, P. 2006. *Le commerce du nord: Les échanges commerciaux entre la France et l'Europe septentrionale au XVIIIe siècle.* Rennes, France: Presses universitaires de Rennes.

Prange, W. 1971. *Die Anfänge der großen Agrarreformen in Schleswig-Holstein bis um 1771*, pp. 57–76. Neumünster, Germany: Wachholtz.

———. 1980. "Das adlige Gut in Schleswig-Holstein im 18. Jahrhundert." In C. Degn and D. Lohmeier, eds., *Staatsdienst und Menschlichkeit: Studien zur Adelskultur des späten 18. Jahrhunderts in Schleswig-Holstein und Dänemark*, pp. 57–76. Neumünster, Germany: Wachholtz.

———. 1983. "Die Entwicklung der adligen Eigenwirtschaft in Schleswig-Holstein." In H. Patze, ed., *Die Grundherrschaft im späten Mittelalter*, vol. 1, pp. 519–553. Sigmaringen, Germany: Thorbecke.

Prażmowska, A. J. 2004. *A History of Poland*, pp. 191–198. Basingstoke UK: Palgrave Macmillan.

Prigge, W. 2004. "The Latvian Purges of 1959: A Revision Study." *Journal of Baltic Studies* 35/3: 211–230.

Przybyszewska-Jarminska, B. 1996. "Musica moderna: The Ways of Dissemination in the Baltic Centres." In E. Ochs, N. Schüler, and L. Winkler, eds., *Musica Baltica: Interregionale musikkulturelle Beziehungen im Ostseeraum; Konferenzbericht Greifswald-Gdańsk 28. November bis 3. Dezember 1993*, pp. 414–426. Sankt Augustin, Germany: Academia.

Ptaszyński, M. 2011. *Narodziny zawodu: Duchowni luterańscy i proces budowania konfesji w Księstwach Pomorskich XVI / XVII w.* Warsaw: Wydawnictwo Naukowe Semper.

Pujāte, I. 1991. *Janis Rozentāls: Reprodukciju albums.* Riga: Liesma.

Pullat, R. 1972. *Eesti linnad ja linlased XVIII sajandi lõpust 1917. Aastani.* Tallinn: Eesti Raamat.

Raša, S. 2003. *Mihails Eizenšteins: Temas un simboli Rigas jugendstila arhi-tektura, 1901–1906*. Riga: Neptuns.

Rauch, G. v. 1969. *Die Universität Dorpat und das Eindringen der frühen Aufklärung in Livland 1690–1710*. Hildesheim, Germany: Olms.

———. 1976. "Die französische Revolution von 1789 und die baltischen Provinzen." *Zeitschrift für Historische Forschung* 3/1: 51–59.

Raun, T. U. 1995. "Social Change in Estland and Northern Livland, 1871–1897: The Limits and Uses of Census Data." In G. v. Pistohlkors et al., eds., *Be-völkerungsverschiebungen und sozialer Wandel in den baltischen Provinzen Russlands, 1850–1914*, pp. 85–102. Lüneburg, Germany: Institut Nordost-deutsches Kulturwerk.

———. 2001. *Estonia and the Estonians*. Stanford, CA: Stanford University Press.

Reincke, H. 1951. "Hamburgs Bevölkerung." In H. Reincke, *Forschungen und Skizzen zur Hamburgischen Geschichte*, pp. 167–200. Hamburg: Hoffmann & Campe.

Reisner, W. 1903. *Die Einwohnerschaft deutscher Städte in früheren Jahrhun-derten mit besonderer Berücksichtigung Lübecks*. Jena, Germany: Gustav Fischer.

Resolutiën der Staten-Generaal van 1576 tot 1609 (1921). N. Japikse, ed. Vol. 5, *1585–1587*. The Hague: Martinus Nijhoff.

Resolutiën der Staten-Generaal van 1576 tot 1609 (1923). N. Japikse, ed. Vol. 7, *1590–1592*. The Hague: Martinus Nijhoff.

Resolutiën der Staten-Generaal van 1576 tot 1609 (1941). N. Japikse, ed. Vol. 11, *1600–1601*. The Hague: Martinus Nijhoff.

Resolutiën der Staten-Generaal van 1576 tot 1609 (1957). H. H. P. Rijperman, ed. Vol. 13, *1604–1606*. The Hague: Martinus Nijhoff.

Rietz, H. 1977. *Z dziejów życia umysłowego Rygi w okresie oświecenia*. Toruń, Poland: Uniwersytet Mikołaja Kopernika.

———. 1984. "Prusy Zachodnie i Wschodnie—Kultura." In G. Labuda, ed., *His-toria Pomorza, II: Do roku 1815*, pp. 764–820. Poznań, Poland: Wydawnictwo Poznańskie.

Riis, T. 2003. *Studien zur Geschichte des Ostseeraumes, IV: Das mittelalterliche dänische Ostseeimperium*. Odense: University Press of Southern Denmark.

Roberts, M. 1982. "Oxenstierna in Germany, 1633–1636." *Scandia* 48: 61–105.

Rodén, M.-L. 2013. "Stormaktstiden." In N. E. Villstrand, ed., *Sveriges Historia 1600–1721*, pp. 178–184. Stockholm: Norstedts.

Roding, J. 1990. "The Myth of the Dutch Renaissance in Denmark: Dutch In-fluence on Danish Architecture in the 17th Century." In J. P. S. Lemmink and J. S. A. M. v Koningsbrugge, eds., *Baltic Affairs: Relations between the Netherlands and North-Eastern Europe, 1500–1800*, pp. 343–353. Nijmegen, The Netherlands: Institute for Northern and Eastern European Studies.

———. 1996. "The North Sea Coasts, an Architectural Unity?" In J. Roding and L. H. v. Voss, eds., *The North Sea and Culture, 1550–1800: Proceedings of the International Conference Held at Leiden, 21–22 April 1995*. Hilversum, The Netherlands: Verloren.

Ronge, H. H. 1964. *Rimlista till Konung Alexander*. Uppsala, Sweden: Almqvist & Wiksell.

Rosén, J. 1939. *Striden mellan: Birger Magnusson och Hans Bröder*. Lund, Sweden: A.-B. Gleerupska univ.-bokhandeln.

Rosenberg, T. 2009. "Nationale und ethnische Konflikte in Estland und Lettland während der Zwischenkriegszeit." *Baltische Seminare* 14: 24–44.

Ross, K., and P. Vanags, eds. 2008. *Common Roots of the Latvian and Estonian Literary Languages*. Frankfurt: Lang.

Roszkowski, W. 1995. *Land Reforms in East Central Europe after World War One*. Warsaw: Institute of Political Studies, Polish Academy of Sciences.

Roth, M. 2004. *Der Einfluss des Europarats auf die demokratische und menschenrechtliche Transformation der baltischen Staaten*. Frankfurt: Lang.

Rothacher, A. 1999. *Die Transformation Mittelosteuropas: Wirtschaft, Politik und Gesellschaft in Tschechien, Polen, Ungarn, Slowenien, Kroatien und Litauen*. Vienna: Österreichischer Wirtschafts.

Rowell, S. C. 1994. *Lithuania Ascending: A Pagan Empire within East-Central Europe, 1295–1345*. Cambridge, UK: Cambridge University Press.

Rudberg, E. 1989. *Sven Markelius, arkitekt*. Stockholm: Arkitektur förlag.

———. 1998. "Der frühe Funktionalismus, 1930–1940." In C. Caldenby et al., eds., *Architektur im 20. Jahrhundert: Schweden*, pp. 80–108. Munich: Prestel.

Rudert, T. 1997. "Grenzüberschreitungen: Frühformen der Gutsherrschaft im mecklenburgisch-pommerschen Grenzgebiet im 16. Jahrhundert." In J. Peters, ed., *Gutsherrschaftsgesellschaften im europäischen Vergleich*, pp. 351–384. Berlin: Akademie-Verlag.

Rusiński, W. 1978. "Kilka uwag o zróżnicowaniu struktury agrarnej w Europie środkowowschodniej w XVI–XVIII wieku." *Roczniki dziejów społecznych i gospodarczych* 39: 11–25.

Saarinen, H. 1996. *Bürgerstadt und absoluter Kriegsherr: Danzig und Karl XII. im Nordischen Krieg*. Helsinki: Suomen Historiallinen Seura.

Saetra, G. 1997. "The International Labour Market for Seamen, 1600–1900: Norway and Norwegian Participation." In P. van Royen et al., eds., *"Those Emblems of Hell"? European Sailors and the Maritime Labour Market, 1570–1870*, pp. 173–210. St. John's, NF: International Maritime Economic History Association.

Salmenhaara, E. 1996. "Entstehung einer nationalen Kultur und Musikkultur." In A. Kalevi et al., eds., *Die finnische Musik*, pp. 21–76. Helsinki: Otava.

Samsonowicz, H. 1993. "Die Handelsstraße Ostsee–Schwarzes Meer im 13. und 14. Jahrhundert." In S. Jenks and M. North, eds., *Der hansische Sonderweg? Beiträge zur Sozial- und Wirtschaftsgeschichte der Hanse*, pp. 23–30. Cologne: Böhlau.

Sandström, Å. 1990. *Mellan Torneå och Amsterdam: En undersökning av Stockholms roll som förmedlare av varor i regional- och utrikes varor i regional- och utrikeshandel, 1600–1650*. Stockholm: Stockholms stad.

Sawyer, B. 2000. *The Viking-Age Rune-Stones: Custom and Commemoration in Early Medieval Scandinavia*. Oxford: Oxford University Press.

Sawyer, B., and P. Sawyer. 2003. "Scandinavia Centers Christian Europe." In K. Helle, ed., *The Cambridge History of Scandinavia*, vol. 1, *Prehistory to 1520*, pp. 147–159. Cambridge, UK: Cambridge University Press.

Sawyer, P. 1982. *Kings and Vikings: Scandinavia and Europe, AD 700–1100*. London: Routledge.

———, ed. 1997. *The Oxford Illustrated History of the Vikings*. Oxford: Oxford University Press.

Scheftel, M. 1988. *Gänge, Buden und Wohnkeller in Lübeck*. Neumünster, Germany: Wachholtz.

Schich, W. 2009. "Der Beitrag der Zisterzienser zur Entwicklung der Kulturlandschaft und der Wirtschaft südlich der Ostsee." In O. Auge, F. Biermann, and C. Herrmann, eds., *Glaube, Macht und Pracht: Geistliche Gemeinschaften des Ostseeraums im Zeitalter der Backsteingotik*, pp. 235–253. Raaden, Germany: Leidorf.

Schildhauer, J. 1968. "Zur Verlagerung des See- und Handelsverkehrs im nordeuropäischen Raum während des 15. und 16. Jahrhunderts: Eine Untersuchung auf der Grundlage der Danziger Pfalkammerbücher." *Jahrbuch für Wirtschaftsgeschichte* 4: 187–211.

Schilling, H. 2007. *Konfessionalisierung und Staatsinteressen: Internationale Beziehungen, 1559–1660*. Paderborn, Germany: Schöningh.

Schilling, R. 1989. *Schwedisch-Pommern um 1700: Studien zur Agrarstruktur eines Territoriums extremer Gutsherrschaft; untersucht auf der Grundlage des schwedischen Matrikelwerkes, 1692–1698*. Weimar: Böhlau.

Schleinert, D. 1996. *Amt und Distrikt Loitz nach 1638. Untersuchungen zum Strukturwandel der landwirtschaftlichen und sozialen Verhältnisse in Vorpommern nach dem Dreißigjahrigen Krieg*. Magisterarbeit, University of Greifswald.

Schleinert, D. 2001. *Die Gutswirtschaft im Herzogtum Pommern-Wolgast im 16. und frühen 17. Jahrhundert*. Cologne: Böhlau.

Schlögel, K. 2003. *Im Raume lesen wir die Zeit*. Munich: Carl Hanser.

Schmeidler, B., ed. 1917. *Magistri Adam Bremensis Gesta Hammaburgensis ecclesiae pontificum*. Hannover: Hahn.

Schmidt, A., ed. 1962. *Aeneas Silvius Germania*. Cologne: Böhlau.

Schmidt, B., ed. 2006. *Von der Geschichte zur Gegenwart und Zukunft: Mittelständische Wirtschaft, Handwerk und Kultur im baltischen Raum*. Hamburg: DOBU.

Schmidt, C. 1997. *Leibeigenschaft im Ostseeraum: Versuch einer Typologie*. Cologne: Böhlau.

———. 2000. *Auf Felsen gesät: Die Reformation in Polen und Livland*. Göttingen: Vandenhoeck & Ruprecht.

Schmidt, G. 1998. "Städtehanse und Reich im 16. und 17. Jahrhundert." In A. Graßmann, ed., *Niedergang oder Übergang? Zur Spätzeit der Hanse im 16. und 17. Jahrhundert*, pp. 25–46. Cologne: Böhlau.

Schroeder, H. D. 2000. *Der Croy-Teppich der Universität Greifswald und seine Geschichte*. Greifswald, Germany: Rektor der Ernst-Moritz-Arndt-Universität.

Schröter, H. G. 1993. "Wirtschaftlicher Wettbewerb und Kartellierung als Indi-katoren für die 'Arbeitsweise der praktischen Vernunft' in Skandinavien, 1818–1939." In M. North, ed., *Nordwesteuropa in der Weltwirtschaft, 1750–1950*, pp. 95–127. Stuttgart: Steiner.

———. 2007. *Geschichte Skandinaviens*. Munich: C. H. Beck.

Schumpeter, E. B. 1960. *English Overseas Trade Statistics, 1697–1808*. London: Clarendon.

Schwab, H. W. 1989. "Zur Struktur der 'Musikkultur des Ostseeraumes' während des 17. Jahrhunderts." In S.-O. Lindquist, ed., *Economy and Culture in the Baltic, 1650–1700: Papers of the VIIIth Visby Symposium held at Gotland Fornsal Gotland's Historical Museum, Visby, August 18th–22th, 1986*, pp. 141–160. Visby, Sweden: Gotlands Fornsal.

Schwarz Lausten, M. 2008. *Die Reformation in Dänemark*. Gütersloh, Germany: Gütersloher-Haus.

Schymik, C., and P. Krumrey. 2009. "EU Strategy for the Baltic Sea Region: Core Europe in the Northern Periphery?" Working Paper FG1. Berlin: Stiftung Wissenschaft und Politik.

Seifert, D. 1997. *Kompagnons und Konkurrenten: Holland und die Hanse im späten Mittelalter*. Cologne: Böhlau.

Selart, A. 2007. *Livland und die Rus' im 13. Jahrhundert*. Cologne: Böhlau.

Sellers, M., ed. 1906. *The Acts and Ordinances of the Eastland Company*. London: Offices of the Royal Historical Society.

Sepp, E. 2002. "Estonian Nonconformist Art from the Soviet Occupation in 1944 to Perestroika." In A. Rosenfeld and N. T. Dodge, eds., *Art of the Baltics: The Struggle for Freedom of Artistic Expression under the Soviets, 1945–1991*, pp. 43–140. New Brunswick, NJ: Rutgers University Press.

Seppel, M. 2005. "Die Entwicklung der 'livländischen Leibeigenschaft' im 16. und 17. Jahrhundert." *Zeitschrift für Ostmitteleuropa-Forschung* 54: 174–192.

———. 2009. "The Landlords' Obligation to Maintain Their Serfs in the Baltic Provinces." *Social History* 34: 284–300.

Shepard, J. 2008. "The Viking Rus and Byzantium." In S. Brink and N. Price, eds., *The Viking World*, pp. 496–516. London: Routledge.

Singleton, F. 1998. *A Short History of Finland*. Cambridge, UK: Cambridge University Press.

Smith, D. J. 2002. "Estonia: Independence and European Integration." In D. J. Smith et al., eds., *The Baltic States. Estonia, Latvia and Lithuania*, pp. 1–196. London: Routledge.

Smith, F. K. 2002. *Nordic Art Music: From the Middle Ages to the Third Millennium*. Westport, CT: Greenwood.

Šne, A. 2008. "Stammesfürstentum und Egalität: Die sozialen Beziehungen auf dem Territorium Lettlands am Ende der prähistorischen Zeit (10.–12. Jahrhundert)." *Forschungen zur baltischen Geschichte* 3: 33–56.

———. 2009. "The Emergence of Livonia: The Transformations of Social and Political Structures in the Territory of Latvia during the Twelfth and Thirteenth Centuries." In A. V. Murray, ed., *The Clash of Cultures on the Medieval Baltic Frontier*, pp. 53–71. Aldershot, UK: Ashgate.

Snyder, T. 2010. *Bloodlands: Europe between Hitler and Stalin.* New York: Basic Books.

Sommerlat, A. 2010. *La Courlande et les Lumières.* Paris: Éditions Belin.

Soom, A. 1954. *Der Herrenhof in Estland im 17. Jahrhundert.* Lund, Sweden: Eesti Teaduslik Selts Rootsis.

Ståhle, C. I. 1967. "Medeltidens profana litteratur." In E. N. Tigerstedt, *Ny illustrerad svensk litteraturhistoria*, vol. 1, *Forntiden: Medeltiden, Vasatiden.* Stockholm: Natur och kultur.

Staley, E., ed. 1939. *Magistri Adam Bremensis Gesta Hammaburgensis Ecclesiae pontificum I, II.* Oklahoma City: University of Oklahoma Press.

Starościak, J. 1999. *The Council of Baltic Sea States (CBSS): Its Mandate and Working Procedures and Its Significance for the Baltic Sea Region.* Kiel, Germany: SCHIFF.

Steinmann, P. 1960. *Bauer und Ritter in Mecklenburg: Wandlungen der gutsherrlich-bäuerlichen Verhältnisse im Westen und Osten Mecklenburgs vom 12. / 13. Jahrhundert bis zur Bodenreform 1945.* Schwerin, Germany: Petermänken.

Steuer, H. 1978. "Geldgeschäfte und Hoheitsrechte zwischen Ostseeländern und islamischer Welt." *Zeitschrift für Archäologie* 12: 255–260.

———. 1987. "Gewichtsgeldwirtschaft im frühgeschichtlichen Europa: Feinwaagen und Gewichte als Quellen zur Währungsgeschichte." In K. Düwel et al., eds., *Untersuchungen zu Handel und Verkehr der vor- und frühgeschichtlichen Zeit in Mittel- und Nordeuropa, IV,* pp. 405–527. Göttingen: Vandenhoeck & Ruprecht.

Steuer, H., et al. 2002. "Der Wechsel von der Münzgeld- zur Gewichtsgeldwirtschaft in Haithabu um 900 und die Herkunft des Münzsilbers im 9. und 10. Jahrhundert." In K. Brandt et al., eds., *Haithabu und die frühe Stadtentwicklung im nördlichen Europa,* pp. 133–167. Neumünster, Germany: Wachholtz.

Stommer, M. 2011. "Europa-Skeptiker oder Europa-Pragmatiker? Die isländische Europapolitik zwischen Machtpolitik, nationalen Interessen und normativen Orientierungen." PhD diss., University of Greifswald.

Stoob, H. 1982. "Albert Krantz, 1448–1517: Ein gelehrter, geistlicher und hansischer Syndikus zwischen den Zeiten." *Hansische Geschichtsblätter* 100: 87–109.

Storch, H. 1794. *Gemälde von St. Petersburg.* 2 vols. Riga: Hartknoch.

Stråth, B. 2012a. "Industrins tillväxt och kriser." In B. Stråth, *Sveriges Historia 1830–1920,* pp. 318–366. Stockholm: Norstedts.

———. 2012b. "Fattighjälp mot Socialpolitik." In B. Stråth, *Sveriges Historia 1830–1920,* pp. 367–382. Stockholm: Norstedts.

———. 2012c. "Arbetsmarknadens konflikter." In B. Stråth, *Sveriges Historia 1830–1920,* pp. 417–445. Stockholm: Norstedts.

Strods, H., and M. Kott. 2002. "The File on Operation 'Priboi': A Re-assessment of the Mass Deportations of 1949." *Journal of Baltic Studies* 33/1: 1–31.

Sundberg, A. 1998. *Svenska krig, 1524–1814.* Stockholm: Hjalmarson & Hogberg.

Svanberg, I. 1990. "Holländarna på Södermalm." In G. Lindberg, ed., *Sicken turk! Om invandrarnas svenska historia*, pp. 115–122. Stockholm: Riksförb. för hembygdsvård.

Svede, M. A. 2002. "When Worlds Collide: On Comparing Three Baltic Art Scenarios." In A. Rosenfeld and N. T. Dodge, eds., *Art of the Baltics: The Struggle for Freedom of Artistic Expression under the Soviets, 1945–1991*, pp. 17–24. New Brunswick, NJ: Rutgers University Press.

Svennung, J. 1953. *Belt und baltisch: Ostseeische Namensstudien mit besonderer Rücksicht auf Adam von Bremen*. Uppsala, Sweden: Uppsala Universitets Årsskrift.

Tamm, M. 2006. "Les signes d'altérité: La représentation de la Baltique orientale dans le De proprietatibus rerum de Barthélemy l'Anglais (vers 1245)." In O. Merisalo, ed., *Frontiers in the Middle Ages: Proceedings of the Third European Congress of Medieval Studies*, pp. 147–172. Turnhout, Belgium: Fédération internationale des Instituts d'études médiévales.

———. 2009. "A New World into Old Words: The Eastern Baltic Region and the Cultural Geography of Medieval Europe." In A. V. Murray, ed., *The Clash of Cultures on the Medieval Baltic Frontier*, pp. 11–36. Aldershot, UK: Ashgate.

Tandefelt, H. 2011. "The Image of Kingship in Sweden." In P. Ihalainen et al., eds., *Scandinavia in the Age of Revolution: Nordic Political Cultures, 1740–1820*, pp. 41–53. Farnham, UK: Ashgate.

Tegborg, L., ed. 1999–2005. *Sveriges kyrkohistoria*. 8 vols. Stockholm: Verbum.

Terveen, F. 1952. "Das Retablissement König Friedrich Wilhelms. I. in Preußen-Litauen von 1714 bis 1740." *Zeitschrift für Ostforschung* 1: 500–515.

———. 1954. *Gesamtstaat und Retablissement: Der Wiederaufbau des nördlichen Ostpreußens unter Friedrich Wilhelm I, 1714–1740*. Göttingen: Musterschmidt.

Tielhof, M. v. 1995. *De Hollandse graanhandel, 1470–1570: Koren op de Amsterdamse molen*. The Hague: Stichting Hollandse Historische Reeks.

———. 2002. *The "Mother of All Trades": The Baltic Grain Trade in Amsterdam from the Late 16th to the 19th Century*. Leiden, The Netherlands: Brill.

Topolski, J. 1977. *Gospodarka polska a europejska w XVI–XVIII wieku*. Poznań, Poland: Wydawnictwo Poznańskie.

Troebst, S. 2002. " 'Intermarium' und 'Vermähung mit dem Meer': Kognitive Karten und Geschichtspolitik in Ostmitteleuropa." *Geschichte und Gesellschaft* 28: 435–469.

———. 2003. "Introduction: What's in a Historical Region? A Teutonic Perspective." *European Review of History* 10/2: 173–188.

Tuchtenhagen, R. 2008a. *Kleine Geschichte Schwedens*. Munich: C. H. Beck.

———. 2008b. *Zentralstaat und Provinz im frühneuzeitlichen Nordosteuropa*. Wiesbaden: Harrassowitz.

———. 2008c. "Zwischen Klasse und Rasse: Der europäische Nordosten beim Ertasten der Staatlichkeit 1918–1940." In A. Komlosy, H.-H. Nolte, and I. Sooman, eds., *Ostsee 700–2000. Gesellschaft, Wirtschaft, Kultur*, pp. 218–236. Vienna: Promedia.

———. 2009a. *Geschichte der baltischen Länder*. Munich: C. H. Beck.

————. 2009b. *Kleine Geschichte Norwegens*. Munich: C. H. Beck.

Turner, B. 2010. "The Construction of Spatial Regional Identities: The Case of the Baltic in a Global Context." *Asia Europe Journal* 8: 317–326.

Tvauri, A., and T.-M. Utt. 2007. "Medieval Recorder from Tartu, Estonia." *Estonian Journal of Archaeology* 11/2: 141–154.

Upton, A. F. 1998. *Charles XI and Swedish Absolutism*. Cambridge, UK: Cambridge University Press.

Utno, L. 2001. "Development of the Estonian Political Parties after Estonia Regained Independence." In L. Utno, ed., *10 Years of Reindependence of the Republic of Estonia, 1991–2001*, pp. 65–75. Tallinn: Institute of National Development and Cooperation.

Vahtola, J. 2003. "Population and Settlement." In K. Helle, ed., *The Cambridge History of Scandinavia*, vol. 1, *Prehistory to 1520*, pp. 576–580. Cambridge, UK: Cambridge University Press.

Valge, J. 1998. "The Case of an Export-Oriented Industry: The State Oil-Shale Industry in Estonia." In A. M. Kõll and J. Valge, eds., *Economic Nationalism and Industrial Growth: State and Industry in Estonia, 1934–1939*, pp. 95–135. Stockholm: Acta Universitatis Stockholmiensis.

————. 2006. *Breaking away from Russia: Economic Stabilization in Estonia, 1918–1924*. Stockholm: Department of Baltic Studies, Stockholm University.

Valk, H. 2008a. "Estland im 11.–13. Jahrhundert: Neuere Aspekte aus der Sicht der Archäologie." *Forschungen zur baltischen Geschichte* 3: 57–86.

————. 2008b. "The Vikings and the Eastern Baltic." In S. Brink and N. Price, eds., *The Viking World*, pp. 485–495. London: Routledge.

Vardys, V. S., and J. B. Sedatis. 1997. *Lithuania: The Rebel Nation*. Boulder, CO: Westview.

Väyrynen, R. 1993. "Finland on the Way to the European Community." In T. Tiilikainen and I. Damgaard Petersen, eds., *The Nordic Countries and the EC*, pp. 43–63. Copenhagen: Copenhagen Political Studies Press.

Veen, A. 1636. *Tabula exactissima Regnorum Sveciae et Norvegiae*. Amsterdam: Amstelodami Frederick de Wit.

Verein für Hansische Geschichte, ed. 1916. *Hansisches Urkundenbuch* 11: 1486–1500, pp. 453–455. Munich: Duncker & Humblot.

Verein für Lübeckische Geschichte und Altertumskunde, ed. 1976. Urkundenbuch der Stadt Lübeck. Abth. 1: Codex Diplomaticus Lubecensis (UBStL), 1. Reproduction. Lübeck, Germany: Asschenfeldt.

Vetik, R. 2004. "Barriers to Democratic Consolidation: The Estonian Case." In D. Pollack et al., eds., *Democratic Values in Central and Eastern Europe*, pp. 49–62. Frankfurt/Oder: Frankfurt Institute for Transformation Studies.

Villstrand, N. E. 2013. "Den Svenska militärstaten." In N. E. Villstrand, ed., *Sveriges Historia 1600–1721*, pp. 90–168. Stockholm: Norstedts.

Voeltzer, F. 1924. "Lübecks Wirtschaftslage unter dem Druck der Kontinentalsperre." PhD diss., University of Hamburg.

Vogt, H. 2005. *Between Utopia & Disillusionment: A Narrative of the Political Transformation in Eastern Europe*. New York: Berghahn.

Vonderau, A. 2010. *Leben im "neuen Europa." Konsum, Lebensstile und Körpertechniken im Postsozialismus.* Bielefeld, Germany: Transcript.

Vries, J. de, and A. v. d. Woude. 1997. *The First Modern Economy: Success, Failure, and Perseverance of the Dutch Economy, 1500–1815.* Cambridge, UK: Cambridge University Press.

Wächter, J. 1997. "Die Reformation in Pommern." In H. T. Porada, ed., *Beiträge zur Geschichte Vorpommerns: Die Demminer Kolloquien, 1985–1994.* Schwerin, Germany: Helms.

Wagensohn, T. 2001. *Russland nach dem Ende der Sowjetunion.* Regensburg, Germany: Pustet.

Wardzyński, M. 2004. "Zwischen den Niederlanden und Polen-Litauen: Danzig als Mittler niederländischer Kunst und Musterbücher." In M. Krieger and M. North, eds., *Land und Meer: Kultureller Austausch zwischen Westeuropa und dem Ostseeraum in der Frühen Neuzeit,* pp. 23–50. Cologne: Böhlau.

Waschinski, E. 1959. *Währung, Preisentwicklung und Kaufkraft des Geldes in Schleswig-Holstein von 1226–1864,* vol. 2. Neumünster, Germany: Wachholtz.

Wasserloos, Y. 2004. *Das Leipziger Konservatorium der Musik im 19. Jahrhundert: Anziehungs- und Ausstrahlungskraft eines musikpädagogischen Modells auf das internationale Musikleben.* Hildesheim, Germany: Olms.

Wawrzyńczyk, A. 1961. *Problem wysokości plonów w królewszczyznach mazowieckich w drugiej połowie XVI i pierwszej ćwierci XVII w.* Warsaw: Państwowe Wydawnictwo Naukowe.

———. 1962. *Gospodarstwo chłopskie w dobrach królewskich na Mazowszu w XVI i na początku XVII w.* Warsaw: Państwowe Wydawnictwo Naukowe.

Weber, S. C. 2000. *Verteidigung der Moderne: Positionen der polnischen Kunst nach 1945.* Bonn: Swiridoff.

Wenta, J., et al., eds. 2008. *Mittelalterliche Kultur und Literatur im Deutschordensstaat: Leben und Nachleben.* Toruń, Poland: Wydawnictwo Naukowe Uniwersytetu Mikołaja Kopernika.

Wernicke, H. 1983. *Die Städtehanse, 1280–1418.* Weimar, Germany: Böhlau.

———, ed. 2000. *Greifswald: Geschichte der Stadt.* Schwerin, Germany: Helms.

Werth, P. W. 2014. *The Tsar's Foreign Faiths. Toleration and the Fate of Religious Freedom in Imperial Russia.* Oxford: Oxford University Press.

Wette, W. 2008. "Juden, Holocaust und Widerstand im Ostseeraum." In A. Komlosy, H.-H. Nolte, and I. Sooman, eds., *Ostsee 700–2000: Gesellschaft, Wirtschaft, Kultur,* pp. 237–252. Vienna: Promedia.

Weymar, F. 2010. "Zum Zusammenhang von intergruppalen Freundschaften und der Favorisierung der Eigengruppe: Eine empirische Studie im deutschpolnischen Schulkontext." PhD diss., University of Greifswald.

Whitelock D., ed. 1979. *English Historical Documents,* vol. 1, c. 500–1042, p. 842. London: Methuen.

Wieringa, W. J., et al., eds. 1983. *The Interactions of Amsterdam and Antwerp with the Baltic Region, 1400–1800.* Leiden, The Netherlands: M. Nijhoff.

Wiese, H., and J. Bölts. 1966. *Rinderhandel und Rinderhaltung im nordwesteuropäischen Küstengebiet vom 15. bis zum 19. Jahrhundert.* Stuttgart: Fischer.

Wilson, C. 1957. *Profit and Power: A Study of England and the Dutch Wars.* London: Longmans, Green.

Wilson, P. H. 2009. *Thirty Years War: Europe's Tragedy*. London: Penguin.

Wisłocki, M. 2005. *Sztuka protestancka na Pomorzu, 1535–1684*. Szczecin, Poland: Muzeum Narodowe w Szczecinie.

Wistinghausen, H. v. 1995. *Die Kotzebue-Zeit in Reval im Spiegel des Romans "Dorothee und ihr Dichter" von Theophile von Bodis*. Tallinn: Tallinna Raamatutrükikoda.

———. 1996. "Die Kotzebue-Zeit in Reval im Spiegel des Romans 'Dorothee und ihr Dichter' von Theophile von Bodisco." In O.-H. Elias, ed., *Aufklärung in den baltischen Provinzen Russlands: Ideologie und soziale Wirklichkeit*, pp. 255–304. Cologne: Böhlau.

Wittram, R. 1954. *Baltische Geschichte: Die Ostseelande Livland, Estland, Kurland, 1180–1918*. Munich: Oldenbourg.

Wohlfahrt, K. 2006. *Der Rigaer Letten Verein und die lettische Nationalbewegung von 1868–1905*. Marburg, Germany: Herder-Institut.

Wulf, P. 1996a. "Revolution, Schwache Demokratie und Sieg in der 'Nordmark': Schleswig-Holstein in der Zeit der Weimarer Republik." In U. Lange, ed., *Geschichte Schleswig-Holsteins: Von den Anfängen bis zur Gegenwart*, pp. 513–548. Neumünster, Germany: Wachholtz.

———. 1996b. "Zustimmung, Mitmachen, Verfolgung und Widerstand: Schleswig-Holstein in der Zeit des Nationalsozialismus." In U. Lange, ed., *Geschichte Schleswig-Holsteins: Von den Anfängen bis zur Gegenwart*, pp. 553–589. Neumünster, Germany: Wachholtz.

Wunder, H. 1968. *Siedlungs- und Bevölkerungsgeschichte der Komturei Christburg, 13.–16. Jahrhundert*. Wiesbaden: Harrassowitz.

Wyczański, A. 1961. "Tentative Estimate of Polish Rye Trade in the Sixteenth Century." *Acta Poloniae Historica* 4: 119–132.

Zaske, N., and R. Zaske. 1985. *Kunst in Hansestädten*. Leipzig: Böhlau.

Zedler, J. H., ed. 1733. *Grosses vollständiges Universal Lexicon Aller Wissenschaften und Künste*, vol. 3. Halle, Germany: Zedler.

Zernack, K. 1977. *Osteuropa: Eine Einführung in seine Geschichte*. Munich: C. H. Beck.

———. 1983. "Der Ostseehandel der Frühen Neuzeit und seine sozialen und politischen Wirkungen." In M. Biskup and K. Zernack, eds., *Schichtung und Entwicklung der Gesellschaft in Polen und Deutschland im 16. und 17. Jahrhundert*, pp. 1–20. Wiesbaden: Steiner.

———. 1993. *Nordosteuropa: Skizzen und Beiträge zu einer Geschichte der Ostseeländer*. Lüneburg, Germany: Nordostdeutsches Kulturwerk.

Ziemer, K., ed. 2000. *Die Neuorganisation der politischen Gesellschaft: Staatliche Institutionen und intermediäre Instanzen in postkommunistischen Staaten Europas*. Berlin: Spitz.

Ziesemer, W. 1928. *Die Literatur des Deutschen Ordens in Preußen*. Breslau: F. Hirt.

Zubeck, R. 2006. "Poland: A Core Ascendant?" In V. Dimitrov et al., eds., *Governing after Communism: Institutions and Policymaking*, pp. 83–128. Lanham, MD: Rowman & Littlefield.

Żukrowska, K. 1995. "Poland: Changes for the Better." In B. Góralczyk et al., eds., *In Pursuit of Europe: Transformations of Post-Communist States, 1989–1994*, pp. 67–79. Warsaw: Institute of Political Studies, Polish Academy of Sciences.

Acknowledgments

This history of the Baltic Sea presents an account of the research that has been conducted over the past three decades. At the same time, it serves as a sort of final report for the Graduate Program "Contact Area Mare Balticum: Foreignness and Integration in the Baltic Sea Region" funded by the German Research Foundation (Deutsche Forschungsgemeinschaft) at the University of Greifswald. Between 2000 and 2010, doctoral students enrolled in this program have undertaken research in the areas of philosophy, psychology, law, history, linguistics, literature, and music. As such, this book is the result of the new understandings elaborated by up-and-coming scholars, and by colleagues from the Baltic region and distant lands, many of whom spent time with us in Greifswald. Some, like Rolf Hammel-Kiesow, Martin Krieger, and Olaf Mörke, read parts of the manuscript, which they enriched with their comments and corrections. I owe them my thanks, as I do to my Estonian colleague Anti Selart, who not only stood in for me in Greifswald while I was away, but also enriched my understanding of the eastern coast of the Baltic. Equally stimulating were my conversations with Astrid Erll about the memory debate and with Kristoffer Neville about the history of art and architecture. In Greifswald, my colleagues in the International Graduate Program "Baltic Borderlands" were always available for questions. In particular, the application for this project, largely advanced by Maria Moynihan and Alexander Drost, has expanded my perspective on the Baltic.

Colleagues at my chair of modern history bore much of the burden of producing the book, and while I served as pro-rector, they ensured that work on the book would not be interrupted for too long. Christine Zeile at Verlag C. H. Beck also provided friendly prods from time to time. Thilko Carstens, Sebastian Nickel, Arne Last, Ulrike Ide, and Jörn Sander together with Susanne Friebe undertook research and acquired the literature, which at this point is vast. Jörg Driesner and Hielke van Nieuwenhuize obtained sources from archives in both the North Sea and Baltic Sea regions. Kord-Henning Uber and Christian Fricke did targeted research at various stages of the manuscript, which as always was entrusted into the able hands of Doreen Wollbrecht. Robert Riemer designed the maps and provided final editing. He was assisted by Matthias Müller, Maik Fiedler, Lasse Seebeck, and Jens Leuteritz. I am very grateful for the support of all of these individuals.

The fact that this book could have been written within the expected time frame given my many obligations is the result of one happy circumstance: I was awarded the Fulbright Distinguished Chair in Modern German Studies at the University of California at Santa Barbara. While some of my students in California were hearing about the North Sea and the Baltic Sea for the first time, the multicultural surroundings, the exchanges with colleagues, and the vista over the Pacific Ocean turned my thoughts to the Baltic. This is especially evident in the choice of illustrations, many of which were suggested by Laura Dizerega.

Illustration Credits

Figure 1 Kulturhistorisches Museum der Hansestadt Stralsund; photograph: Jutta Grudziecki.

Figure 2 WikiCommons: b/bb/Kloster_Eldena_im_Mai.jpg.

Figure 3 Niguliste Museum, Art Museum of Estonia; photograph: Stanislav Stepashko.

Figure 4 R. C. Temple, ed., *The Travels of Peter Mundy in Europe and Asia, 1608–1667*, vol. 4 (London: 1907–1925).

Figure 5 Kungliga biblioteket – Sveriges nationalbibliotek, http://www.kb.ze /samlingarna/digitala/mecia/forsta-bandet/stockholm-oster/.

Figure 6 http://upload.wikimedia.org/WikiCommons/b/b5/Paterssen_View_Se nate_Square_with_Monument_of_Peter_the_Great_1799.jpg.

Figure 7 Der Nyländska Jaktklubben Hafen in Helsinki Ateneum Art Museum Finnish National Gallery, Central Art Archives, Hannu Karjalainen.

Figure 8 http://upload.wikimedia.org/wikipedia/commons/7/78/Riga_-_Alberta _Iela_2a%2C_1906.JPG.

Figure 9 Public Diplomacy Department, Estonian MFA.

Figure 10 Pierre Mens / Øresundsbron, Image ID: 2002112109, Date: N/A.

Index

Aalto, Alvar, 249, 284, 328
Aasen, Ivar, 195
Aav, Evald, 252
Aavik, Johannes, 245
ABBA, 287
Absalon of Lund, 83
Academia Pietrina, 168
Ackermann, Anton, 265
Ackermann, Konrad Ernst, 175
Adamkus, Valdas, 306
Adam of Bremen, 2–3, 9, 20, 337n8
Adolf Frederick I, Duke, 118–119
Adolf II, Count, 33, 44
Adolf Frederick II, Duke, 148
Aeneas Silvius, 52
Aepinus, Johannes, 91
Agrarian reforms. *See* Agriculture
Agricola, Michael, 90
Agriculture: of Balts and Finns, 18–19;
    land settlement, 40–43; manorial
    economy, 132–135, 327; agrarian
    reforms, 199–205, 234–238, 243;
    increased productivity following
    WWI, 236–237; as factor in emerging
    identities in interwar years, 237–238;
    collectivization, 270–272; German
    economic transformation following
    fall of Soviet bloc, 308–309; Lithu-
    anian economic transformation
    following fall of Soviet bloc, 311;
    three-field crop rotation system, 47,
    200–201, 204. *See also* Grain
Åhrén, Uno, 248
Aircraft industry, 242, 273
Åland Islands, 189, 206, 226, 229, 231
Albert I, Count, 3
Albert I, Duke, 3
Albert III, King, 65
Albert of Prussia, Duke, 93, 95, 112
Albert of Riga, 35–36
Albert I, the Bear, Margrave, 32, 33
Albert V, Duke, 80
Albinus, Johan Tobias, 138
Alcohol, Nordic policies regarding,
    232
Alcuin of York, 10–11
Alexander I, Czar, 151, 183, 190, 198

Alexander III, Czar, 220
Alexander of Novgorod (Nevsky), 37–38
Alexis, Czar, 122
Alfvén, Hugo, 252
Algirdas, Grand Duke, 71
Alksnis, Ādams, 214
Alksnis, Jānis, 222
Allgemeine Deutsche Bibliothek (ADB),
    168
Alliance for Germany, 297–298
Alliksaar, Artur, 280
Alver, Betti, 245
Amandi, Johannes, 91
Amber trade, 19–20, 60
Ancher, Anna, 212
Ancher, Michael, 212
Andersen, Hans Christian, 217
Andersson, Benny, 287
Andreae, Laurentius, 90
Andrzejewski, Jerzy, 281, 282
Angerdorf-type village layout, 47
Animal motifs, 26
Anna of Pomerania, 114
Ansgar, 2, 30–31
Antwerp, 63, 103, 111, 113–114, 116, 136,
    212
Appelboom, Harald, 138
Arab world, trade with, 12–13, 19–21,
    326
Arbujad, 245–246
Architecture: medieval, 50–51; brick
    Gothic, 77–79, 328; Renaissance,
    110–115; Netherlandish and German
    cultural influences, 137–140; Vasa
    baroque tradition, 142; eighteenth-
    century, 180–182; in Helsinki,
    183–184; neoclassical, 211–212; Art
    Nouveau, 222, 223*fig.*; interwar,
    247–250; postwar, 284–285
Ardre stone, 25
Aristocratization, 141–142
Armfelt, Gustaf Mauritz, 190
Arndes, Stephan, 85
Arndt, Ernst Moritz, 171
Arneberg, Arnstein, 249
Arnold, Carl, 216
Art Nouveau, 214, 217, 222, 223*fig.*

Art(s): music, 24, 86, 142–144, 176–177,
    215–217, 251–253, 285–287; in
    Lübeck, 52–54; commissioned for
    cathedrals, 79–80; literature, 82–86,
    89–90, 195–197, 245–247, 279–281; in
    Danzig, 88; Renaissance, 110–116;
    Netherlandish and German cultural
    influences, 136–137, 141–142; theater,
    174–176, 217–218, 246; art collections
    and palaces, 177–182; nineteenth-
    century, 211–218; film, 282; postwar
    visual, 282–284; history of, 328
ASEA, 240
Ash, 59–60, 99–102, 130–131, 162–163,
    188
Asia, 8, 22, 25, 159, 161, 324–326, 329
Aspazija. See Rozenberga, Elza
Asplund, Gunnar, 248, 249, 328
Atterberg, Kurt, 252
Augustus II, the Strong, King, 146–147,
    149
Augustus III, King, 149
Augustus the Strong. See Augustus II,
    the Strong, King
Austria, 149–151, 185, 188, 190, 192, 194,
    231, 296, 314; Seven Years' War, 150;
    partitioning of Poland, 150–151;
    opposes Poland's May Constitution,
    185; in war against France, 188; and
    fall of GDR, 296; membership in
    European Union, 314
Automatic Identification System (AIS),
    321
Axel, Gabriel, 282

Bakst, Léon, 213
Balakauskas, Osvaldas, 286
Balcerowicz, 307, 308
Baltic, and construction and perception
    of Baltic region, 6
Baltic arts exhibits, 213
"Baltic Borderlands: Shifting Boundaries
    of Mind and Culture in the Border-
    lands of the Baltic Sea Region"
    graduate studies program, 319
Baltic Energy Market Interconnection
    Plan (BEMIP), 325
Baltic League, 6, 229, 328
Baltic Sea, 1–8, 11, 14, 19, 37, 50, 58, 63,
    67, 99, 110–119, 122, 145, 206,
    218–219, 302, 313–329

Baltic Sea States Subregional
    Cooperation (BSSSC), 318
Baltic Sea strategy, 1–2, 7, 314–315,
    323–325
Baltic studies, 1–2, 5–6
Baltic tribal society, 17–18
Balts, 1, 12–13, 17–19, 24, 326
Banaitis, Kazimieras Viktoras, 253
Bar Confederation, 150
Barisien, F. H., 182
Barlach, Ernst, 250–251
Barnim I, Duke, 42, 44
Barons, Krišjānis, 247
Barrel stave export, 100, 130, 163
Barroso, José Manuel, 322
Bauer, Friedrich Wilhelm, 175
Beck, David, 136
Beckmann, Johann, 167–168
Belbuck Abbey, 90–91
Belševica, Vizma, 280
Benois, Alexandre, 213
Bentzon, Jørgen, 251
Berchem, Nicolaes Pieterszoon, 178
Bergen, 56, 61, 63, 68, 73, 77, 79–80, 83,
    206, 217
Bergman, Ingmar, 282
Berklāvs, Eduards, 269
Berlin Bauakademie, 183, 211
Berman, Jakub, 265
Bermondt-Avalov, Pavel, 228
Bernadotte, Jean Baptiste, 189
Bernoulli, Johann, 168
Bernstorff, Andreas Peter, Count, 157,
    200
Berringer, Gustav Wilhelm, 250
Bertuch, Friedrich Justin, 171
Berwald, Christian Friedrich Georg, 177
Berwald, Franz, 177, 216
Berwald family, 177
Berzins, Boris, 283
Bible, translations of, 90
Bierut, Bolesław, 265
Birger Jarl, Duke, 38, 64
Birger Magnusson. See Birger Jarl, Duke
Birka: as commercial center, 19, 20;
    Christian influence in, 30, 31
Birkavs, Valdis, 305
Biron, Ernst Johann von, Duke, 149, 181
Bismarck, Otto von, 194, 275
Bjørnson, Bjørnstjerne, 217–218
Black Death. See Plague

Blumbergs, Ilmars, 283
Boeckel, Peter, 114
Bogislav I, Duke, 35
Bogislav X, Duke, 82
Bogislav of Pomerania, Duke, 66–67.
    See also Eric of Pomerania, King
Bohemia, 16, 59, 70, 73, 118, 168; Slav
    alliance with, 16; trade with, 59;
    Casimir the Great and, 70
Bokmål, 196
Boldewan, Johannes, 91
Bolesław I, Chrobry, King, 17
Bolesław III, Wrymouth, Prince, 34
Bolsheviks, 227, 228, 244
Bonaparte, Napoleon, 151, 186, 188
Borchgrevinck, Melchior, 143
Borwin, 33
Borwin, Dorothea, 114
Bothmer, Hans Caspar von, 180
Bourdon, Sébastien, 136
Brabant, 60–61, 63
Brahe, Tycho, 111
Brandenburg, 15, 32, 35, 37, 41–42, 48–49,
    120–122, 124, 128–129, 147–148,
    316–317
Brandenstein, Joachim Freiherr von,
    234
Brandin, Philipp, 114, 116
Brandis, Lucas, 85
Brandis, Matthäus, 85
Branting, Hjalmar, 231
Brass, 61, 79, 132
Brazauskas, Algirdas, 294, 305–306
Bremer Vulkan AG, 309
Breweries, 59, 107, 133, 205
Brick architecture. *See* Architecture
Bridget of Sweden, 84, 86
Bruges, 57–58, 60–61, 63
Brunward of Schwerin, 41
Bubonic plague. *See* Plague
Bubyr, Alexey, 217
Bugenhagen, Johannes, 85, 88, 90, 92,
    115
Bull, Ole, 216, 217
Bürger, Kurt, 267
Burial, 19–20, 50, 114, 290
Burspraken, 85
Busch, Johann Joachim, 180
Busoni, Ferruccio, 215
Butkevičius, Algirdas, 306
Buxtehude, Dieterich, 143, 176

Byzantium, 13, 34, 32; embraces trade
    with Varangians, 13; Orthodox
    influence of, 32

Cameron, Charles, 181, 183
Cantonal system, 154
Canute Lavard, Duke, 32
Canute the Great, King, 31
Capitulation of Estonia and Livonia
    (1710), 151–152
Carl XVI Gustav, King, 301
Carl of Denmark, Prince, 226
"Carta mercatoria," 56–57
Cartels, and industrialization during
    interwar years, 239–240
Casimir III, the Great, King, 70
Casimir IV, King, 72
Cathedrals, 77–80, 86, 114, 137, 142,
    182–183, 251, 340n28
Catherine I, Empress, 152
Catherine II, the Great, Empress, 150,
    179, 181
Catholic Church, 70, 290. *See also*
    Protestant Reformation
Cattle, 18, 23, 60, 70, 102, 107–108, 133,
    202–205, 290
Cekanauskas, Vytautus, 285
Chapel of St. Casimir, Vilnius
    Cathedral, 142
Charles VIII, King, 67–68
Charles IX, King, 121
Charles X Gustav, King, 121, 123
Charles XI, King, 123, 125, 146
Charles XII, King, 146, 147, 155
Charles XIII, King, 189
Chieftains, 11, 13, 15, 23–24, 32, 37
Choral music, 252, 286
Christburg Peace, 36
Christian I, King, 67, 68
Christian II, King, 69, 92
Christian III, King, 92–93
Christian IV, King, 111–112, 118–119,
    126, 142–143
Christian VI, King, 178
Christian Democratic Union (CDU),
    266–268, 297–298, 303–304
Christianity: Slav conversion to, 15;
    Christian mission, 28, 29–40;
    pagan religion and, 48, 50–51;
    Protestant Reformation, 88–97,
    115, 327–328

Christian Louis I, Duke, 148
Christian Ludwig II, Duke, 178
Christiansborg Palace, 178
Christiansen, Godtfred Kirk, 277
Christina, Queen, 120, 136–137, 140, 144
Christina of Stommeln, 84
Christopher III, King, 67
Chronicon terrae Prussiae (Chronicle of the Prussian land), 84
Church decoration, Renaissance, 115–116
Cities: founding of, 43–46, 54; influence of, over cooperative associations, 58. *See also* City planning
Citizenship rights, 46, 97, 117, 306–307
City planning, 111–113, 137–139, 180–184, 247–250, 284–285
Čiurlionis, Mikalojus Konstantinas, 214–215, 253
Class-based society, shift from estate-based to, 208–211
Clausen, Mads, 277
Cohesion Fund, 316
Coins, 11, 16, 19–23, 66, 164
Cold War, 263, 269
Collective farms, 270, 311
Collectivization. *See* Agriculture
Combs, 21, 26–27
Comédie en langue danoise, 175–176
Comenius, John Amos, 140
Committee of 48, 91
Communication, 85, 88–97
Communication space, 1–2, 164–177, 327–328
Communism. *See* Eastern bloc; Sovietization
Communist parties, 230, 233–234, 244, 256, 263–269, 285–286, 288, 292–293
Communist Party (KPD), 263–267
Communist Party (Latvian), 269
Company of Eastland Merchants. *See* Eastland Company
Compass Society, 52, 77
Confederation of Tarnogród, 149
Confederation of the Rhine, 185
Conrad I, High Duke, 36
Constantine, Grand Duke, 190
Constitutionalists (Revolution of 1905), 224–225

Constitution(s), 64, 124, 149–150, 153, 185, 228–230, 233–234, 243–244, 268, 294, 298, 304–306
Cooperation, 315–321, 317, 322, 324–325
Cooperative agreements, 240
Cooperative associations, 54, 58
Cooperatives, 231, 247, 272, 274, 308
Copenhagen, 76, 78, 92–101, 110–111, 122, 126, 143–145, 157–158, 164, 171, 175–180, 188–189, 193, 206, 212, 215, 217, 238, 247, 287, 301
Copenhagen Accord, 317
Copernicus, Nicolaus, 86
Copper, 56, 59–60, 102, 117, 131–132, 188, 207, 255
Cornelis Floris. *See* De Vriendt, Cornelis Floris
Corvée labor, 107–110, 133–135, 154, 157, 199–204, 342n37
Cotters, 200, 201, 203, 209, 235, 237
Council of the Baltic Sea States (CBSS), 7, 317–318, 323, 329
Council of the Realm, 66, 68–69, 155–156
Courland, 6, 17, 19, 39, 95, 108, 130, 146, 149, 152, 168, 172–173, 181, 227, 258; Viking attacks, 18; Bishopric, 39; cremation and burial, 50; Russian influence, 149; censorship, 168; periodicals, 172–173; German occupation, 227
Cracow, 59, 70, 80, 85–86, 112, 142, 146, 190, 192, 282, 285, 289
Cranach, Lucas, the Younger, 115
Cremation, 50
Cronica regni Gothorum (Chronicle of the Reign of the Goths), 83
Crop rotation, 47, 200–201, 204
Croy Tapestry, 114–115
Culm, 36, 39, 42, 45, 70, 84, 151
Culm law, 42, 45–46
Cultural exchange, 1, 8, 25–26, 50, 79–80, 135–144, 164, 326–327
Cultural heritage, 286, 293, 317, 321
Cultural memory, 301–322
Cultural space, establishment of, 164–177, 219
Czartoryski, Adam, 190
Czechoslovakia, 239, 288
Czech Republic, 314

Dähnert, Johann Carl, 170, 174
Dairy farming, 98, 133, 204–205
Dance of Death (Notke), 79
Danegeld, 12, 22
Danfoss Group, 277
Danske Lov (1683), 127
Dansk Socialdemokratisk Partiet, 209
Dantiscus, Johannes, 85–86
Danzig, 23, 34, 37, 58–59, 63, 70, 72,
    76–79, 81, 85, 87–89, 93–95, 97–98,
    100–105, 110–113, 121, 128, 130–131,
    141, 143–145, 147, 150–151, 158,
    161–164, 171, 175–176, 180, 187, 207,
    220, 228, 241, 259–260, 328
Danziger Anzeigen, 171
Dargezin, 47
Dargun monastery, 28, 35, 41
Dassow, Nicolaus, 141
Davidsen, Leif, 281
De Besche, Willem, 132
Decembrist Revolt (1825), 192
De Gaulle, Charles, 278
De Geer, Louis, 117, 131–132, 138, 140
De Heem, Jan Davidsz, 178
Deif van Brugge (The Thief of Bruges), 85
Deindustrialization, 239
De la Gardie, Magnus Gabriel, 137, 143
De Laval, Gustav, 205
De la Vallée, Simon, 137–138
Delblanc, Sven, 281
Demesne farms, 105–110, 127, 133–135,
    154–155, 200, 202, 271, 339n22
Democratization, 301–307, 329
Deniers, 22–23
Denmark, 4–5, 7, 12, 14–15, 28, 30–35,
    37–38, 48, 51–52, 56, 58, 60, 63, 65–69,
    73–74, 77, 81, 86, 92, 94–96, 98t., 102,
    107–108, 110, 112–113, 118, 122,
    126–127, 134, 136, 140, 143, 146–147,
    157, 162, 167, 173, 175–176, 178,
    187–189, 191–195, 199–200, 204–205,
    208–209, 212, 215–217, 229, 231–234,
    238, 240, 243, 248, 251, 253, 255,
    260–261, 263, 269, 275–278, 281,
    284, 287, 301, 312–314, 317, 319,
    326; control over Øresund, 4–5, 67,
    95, 118, 301, 326; battles for do-
    minion over Baltic Sea, 4–5, 122;
    danegeld, 12; Obotrite alliances,
    15; monasteries, 28, 51; Christian
    mission, 34–35, 37–39; trade, 56, 60,
    95–96, 102, 313; challenges Hanse-
    atic League, 58; monarchy, 63–66;
    Nordic Union, 67–68; population,
    73, 208; Black Death and population,
    74–75; Reformation, 92–93; freedom
    of movement in, 108; artistic
    influences, 111–112, 178, 212; rivalry
    with Sweden, 118; estates, 126–127;
    Great Northern War, 147; adminis-
    trative reform, 157–158; theater,
    175–176; Napoleonic Wars, 188–189;
    structural changes, following
    Napoleonic Wars, 191; nationalist
    movement, 192–194, 195; agrarian
    reform, 199–201, 234; agricultural
    productivity, 204; industrialization,
    205; urbanization, 208; socialist
    parties and unions, 209; music
    education, 215; cooperative initiatives
    with Russian Empire successor
    states, 229; internal politics
    following WWI, 231; foreign policy
    disagreements, 232; Great Depression,
    240; World War II, 253, 255; as welfare
    state, 263, 275–276; innovation, 277;
    admitted to European Economic
    Community, 278; postwar literature,
    281; postwar architecture, 284; jazz,
    287; Council of the Baltic Sea States,
    317. See also Nordic countries;
    Scandinavia
Denner, Balthasar, 178
Descartes, René, 140
Deutsche Seereederei, 309–310
De Vriendt, Cornelis Floris, 112
De Vries, Adriaen, 111
De Vries, Hans Vredeman, 110, 112,
    113
Dickmann, Ägidius, 112, 141
Directie van de Oostersche Handel en
    Reederijen, 4–5
Dittersdorff, Carl Ditters von, 174
Dmitry, Donskoy, Grand Prince, 71
Dombrovskis, Valdis, 305
Dominium maris Baltici, 4, 67, 95,
    118–122, 326
Domizlaus, 34
Domnérus, Arne, 287
Donalitius, Christian, 169
Donnersmarck, Guido Henckel von,
    207

Dorpat, 18, 46, 59, 86, 96, 121, 140, 142, 149, 165, 168, 197–198, 201–211, 224. *See also* Tartu
Dorpat court, 125, 139. *See also* Tartu
Dou, Gerrit, 178
Downing, George, 99
Drew, Kenny, 287
Düben, Andreas, 143
Dulon, Friedrich Ludwig, 176
Dury, John, 140
Dvarionas, Balys, 253
Dziady (Mickiewicz), 288

Earrings, and cultural exchange, 26
Eastern bloc, 265, 288–307, 329
Eastern Pomerania, 17, 120, 124, 189, 203, 259, 260, 271
East Germany. *See* German Democratic Republic (GDR)
Eastland Company, 5, 103–104, 337n18
East Prussia, 17, 129, 150–151, 153, 155, 199, 203, 205, 227, 233, 259–260; Russian occupation, 150; bubonic plague, 153; administrative reform, 155; agriculture, 199, 205; land transfer, 203; Russian invasion, 226–227; Sovietization, 259, 260
Economic transformation: during medieval times, 46–48; following fall of Soviet bloc, 307–313
Edda, 82
Edelfelt, Albert, 184*fig.*, 212, 213, 221, 328
Education, 168, 190, 195, 198, 209, 234–235, 243–244, 246, 252, 304, 317–319, 324
Edward I, King, 56
Edward III, King, 56–57
Edward VII, King, 220
Eesti Aleksandrikool, 198
Eglons-Lams, Visvaldis, 280
Ehrenstrahl, David Klöcker, 136
Ehrenström, Johan Albrecht, 183
Eider-Danish doctrine, 192–194
Eigtved, Nicolai, 176
Eisenstein, Mikhail, 222, 223*fig.*
Elbing, 36, 56, 63, 72, 94, 103–104, 106, 113, 128, 130, 140, 147, 150, 155, 175, 342n33
Elblag. *See* Elbing
Eldena, 28

Eldena Abbey, 28, 29*fig.*, 35, 47
Elections, 193, 209, 225–226, 229–231, 233–234, 238, 243, 256, 264, 267–268, 295–298, 303–306, 323
Electoral capitulation, 64
Elisabeth of Denmark, 114
Elksne, Arija, 280
Ellemann-Jensen, Uffe, 7
Elley Palace, 211
Emigration. *See* Migration
Energiewerke Nord, 310
Energy, 222, 277, 291, 310, 313, 317, 319–321, 324–325
Engel, Carl Ludwig, 183, 211
Engelbrekt Engelbrektsson, 67
Engholm, Björn, 2, 7
England, 5, 12, 20, 25–26, 31–32, 56–57, 60, 62, 73, 77, 103–104, 136, 145, 147, 150, 164, 168, 177, 186–188, 190, 204–205, 219–220, 301; trade interests in Baltic region, 5; German trade, 56–57; Hanseatic trade, 60, 62, 103; textile exports, 103–104; impedes Dutch shipping, 130; Seven Years' War, 150; eighteenth-century trade with Baltic region, 158, 159, 161; provenance of imports, 1701–1800, 160*t.*; continental blockade declared against, 186–188; seaside resorts, 219; conflict over Øresund, 301. *See also* Great Britain
Environmentalism, 232, 292–293, 317–321, 323–325
Epitaphs, 114, 116
Eric V, King, 64
Eric IX, King, 38
Eric XIV, King, 95
Eric Magnusson, 65
Eric of Pomerania, King, 66–67, 75
Ericsson, L. M., 205
Erlendsson, Eystein, 77
Ernesaks, Gustav, 286
Estlink, 320
Estonia, 6, 18, 22, 35, 37, 39, 43, 64, 86, 95, 121, 125, 139, 147, 149, 151–153, 165, 168, 172–173, 175, 181, 197–199, 201, 211–212, 227–229, 235–236, 239–240, 244–246, 249, 253, 255–259, 269–273, 280, 282–284, 286–287, 291, 293–294, 298, 300, 305–307, 310–311, 313–315, 318–319, 322; medieval

Estonians, 17, 18; Christianization, 35, 37, 39; settlement, 43; founding of cities, 46; manor reductions, 125, 126; Russian administrative reforms, 151–153; *Hofmeister*, 165; periodicals, 172–173; Italian baroque architecture, 181; nationalist movement, 197–198; agrarian reforms, 199, 201–202, 235, 236; nineteenth-century art, 212; World War I, 227, 228; cooperation, 229, 322; internal politics following WWI, 229–230; deindustrialization during interwar years, 239; industrialization during interwar years, 240–241; social and ethnic structure during interwar years, 243–244; interwar literature, 245–246; interwar architecture, 249; interwar music, 252; foreign policy during WWII, 253; World War II, 254, 255–256, 257, 258, 259; Sovietization, 262, 268–269; collectivization, 270–271; post-WWI industrialization, 272–273; postwar visual arts, 282, 283; postwar music, 286; political awakening, 290–291, 293–294, 298; autonomy and democratization, 298, 300; democratization, 305; stability, 306; citizenship rights, 306–307; economic transformation following fall of Soviet bloc, 310, 311, 313; membership in European Union, 314; adoption of euro, 315
Estonian Knights, 125
Estonian language, 84, 90, 94, 198, 246, 262, 287
Estonian-language lyceum, 198
Estonian song festivals, 198, 262, 263*fig.*, 285–286, 293–294
Estonia Theater, 217, 246, 252
Ethelred of Northumbria, King, 10
Ethnic assimilation, 48–51, 75
Eugenics, 232–233
Euro, adoption of, 314–315
European Economic Community (EEC), 278, 314
European Free Trade Association (EFTA), 278
European Regional Development Fund (ERDF), 316
European Social Fund (ESF), 316

European Union, 1–2, 7–8, 277, 301–302, 311, 313–324; Baltic Sea strategy, 7, 323, 324–326; and formation of Council of the Baltic Sea States, 7; preparation for membership in, 302; requires liberalization of citizenship rights, 306–307; economic transformation following fall of Soviet bloc, 313; incorporation of Baltic states, 313–317, 321–322; cooperation in, 322
Ewald, Klaus, 296

Faber, Joop, 129
Faehlmann, Friedrich Robert, 197
Falck, Jeremias, 112, 141
Fältskog, Agnetha, 287
FDP, 303–304
Federal Republic of Germany, 278, 289, 291, 298, 303, 308; foreign trade, 278; relationship with Poland, 289; GDR foreign debts, 291, 308; merged with GDR, 298; incorporation of German federal states, 303
Ferber, Johann Jacob, 168
Feudal system. *See* Agriculture
Film. *See under* Art(s)
Filosov, Dmitry, 213
Finland, 35, 38–39, 43, 50, 65, 69, 73–75, 86, 90, 131, 139, 149, 163, 183, 189–190, 195–197, 199, 201, 205–206, 208–209, 212, 215, 217, 220, 225, 227–229, 231–232, 235, 238–239, 243, 249, 252, 254–255, 258–260, 263, 269–270, 278, 281–282, 284, 311–314, 316, 319–320, 322, 327, 329; Christianization, 35, 39, 50; ethnic assimilation, 50; Black Death and population, 74; settlement, 75; Netherlandish cultural influences, 139; folk songs and poetry, 169; history of Helsinki, 183; structural changes following Napoleonic Wars, 190; nationalist movement, 195–197; agrarian reform, 199, 201, 235; industrialization, 205–206; population growth, 208; shift to class-based society, 209; socialist parties and unions, 209; nineteenth-century art, 213; nineteenth-century music, 216–217; seaside resorts, 220; Revolution of 1905, 225–226; World

Finland *(continued)*
War I, 227–228; cooperation, 229, 316, 322; democratization, 229; territorial disputes over Åland Islands, 229; foreign policy disagreements, 232; internal politics following WWI, 232–233; interwar music, 252; World War II, 254–255, 258–259; Sovietization, 263–270; postwar literature, 281; postwar architecture, 284–285; economic transformation following fall of Soviet bloc, 311–312; trade following fall of Soviet bloc, 313; membership in European Union, 313–314; Nord Stream project, 320; trade by sea, 320. *See also* Nordic countries

Finnish language, 84, 90, 196–197, 225, 243, 245

Finnish War (1808–1809), 183

Finnomania, 196

Finns, medieval, 12–13, 17–19, 32, 38, 50, 326

Fishing industry, 59, 74, 98, 310. *See also* Herring

Flachsbinder, Johannes. *See* Dantiscus, Johannes

Flanders: Hanseatic trade with, 4, 41, 48, 56–57, 60–61; settlers from, 41; German trade with, 56–58

Flax, 59, 98–99, 101–102, 130–132, 163, 240–241, 327

Flurzwang, 47

Fly-ship, 100–101

Folk songs, 169, 197, 247, 328

Fontainebleau Decree (1810), 188

Food industry, 59, 204–205, 240–241, 274, 277, 310

Forsskål, Peter, 167

France, 61, 117, 121, 129, 136, 138, 145, 150, 157–158, 168, 185–186, 188–189, 202, 211, 231, 255, 313; Seven Years' War, 150; revolution and Napoleonic Wars, 184–189. *See also* Frankish Empire

Francis II, Emperor, 185

Franck, Kaj, 285

Frankish Empire, 15, 26; Viking incursions in, 11, 12; Slavs and, 14; and Christianization of Vikings, 29–30. *See also* France

Frederick I, Duke, 69

Frederick I (Prussia), King, 147

Frederick I (Sweden), King, 155

Frederick II, Duke, 180

Frederick II (Denmark), King, 95, 109, 114

Frederick II (Prussia), King, 150

Frederick III, Emperor, 68

Frederick III, King, 122, 126–127

Frederick IV, King, 146

Frederick VI, King, 157

Frederick Francis I, Grand Duke, 219

Frederick William, Duke, 148

Frederick William I, the Great Elector, King, 122, 128–129

Frederick William I, King, 129, 148, 153–154

Frederiksborg Palace, 111

Freedom of movement, 107–108, 197, 199–200, 327

Freedom Union (Unia Wolności), 304

Freemen, 42–43, 49, 75

French Revolution, 167, 170, 173, 184–185, 192

Fresendorf variant, 26

Friedrich, Caspar David, 28, 212, 218

Frisian trade, 11, 19–20, 26–27, 326

Functionalism, 248–249, 285

Fur, 12–13, 55–56, 59, 88, 102

Für Geist und Herz (For spirit and heart), 172

Gade, Niels, 216

Gallen-Kallela, Akseli, 213

Galli, Giovanni Maria, 142

Ganelin, Slava, 287

Gazprom, 319

Gdańsk. *See* Danzig

Geda, Sigitas, 280

Genscher, Hans-Dietrich, 7

German Bridge, 56, 61, 63, 76

German Confederation, 191–192, 194

German Democratic Party (DDP), 233, 234

German Democratic Republic (GDR), 268, 274, 278, 288, 291–292, 295–298, 303, 308–309; elections, 268; industrialization following WWII, 274–275; foreign trade, 278; opposition in, 291–292; fall of Soviet bloc, 288, 295–298; democratization,

303–304; economic transformation following fall of Soviet bloc, 308–310

German Empire, 6–7, 20, 22–23, 39, 57, 61, 75–76, 85, 88–89, 92, 117–118, 120, 138, 151, 166, 168, 172–175, 177, 185, 187, 193–194, 204, 213, 215–216, 218–219, 228–229, 231–232, 234, 238–239, 241–242, 250, 252–255, 257–258, 260, 263, 265, 267–268, 275, 278, 289, 291, 299, 310, 313, 317, 319, 322, 329; Precursor, 14; Christian mission, 32–33; land settlement, 40, 43; end of the second, 233

German language: sanctioned in Russian states, 152; theater, 174

German nationalist movement, 192–194

German National People's Party (DNVP), 233

German People's Party (DVP), 233–234

German-Polish Nonaggression Pact (1934), 254

Germans: 1, 28, 40, 43, 48–50, 54, 76, 145, 151, 191, 197–198, 201–211, 214, 227, 235, 243–244, 254–255, 257, 260, 291, 297, 321

German-Soviet Nonaggression Pact (1939), 254

Germany: agrarian reforms, 204, 238; Baltic art exhibits, 213–214; World War I, 226–228; internal politics following WWI, 233–234; industrialization during Great Depression, 241–242; rearmament policy, 242; interwar architecture, 250; World War II, 253–255, 257–258, 259–260, 329; Sovietization, 265–268; democratization, 303–304; economic transformation following fall of Soviet bloc, 308–310; trade following fall of Soviet bloc, 313; Council of the Baltic Sea States, 317; Nord Stream project, 319–320; cooperation, 322. See also Federal Republic of Germany; German Democratic Republic (GDR); German Empire

Gero, 16

Gesewitz, Jürgen, 138

Gesta Danorum (Deeds of the Danes), 83

Gierek, Edward, 289

Glaubitz, Johann Christoph, 182

Glistrup, Mogens, 276

Godmanis, Ivars, 298

Gods, 24–25, 50

Gomolka, Alfred, 304

Gomułka, Władysław, 265, 273, 288–289

Gorbachev, Mikhail, 292–294, 299

Gothenburg, 161–162

Gotland, 19–21, 25–26, 46, 54–56, 58, 63, 65, 67–69, 78, 95, 122, 320; as commercial center, 19, 20, 54–56; cultural artifacts, 26; conquered by Denmark, 58; conflicting claims to, 67, 68

Gotland Travelers Association, 55

Gottfried of Ghemen, 84

Gotthard Kettler, Duke, 95

Göttrik (Gudfred), King, 30

Gottschalk, Prince, 15

Grain, 21, 47, 56, 59–61, 87, 98–101, 104–107, 121, 129–130, 132–133, 135, 149, 162, 188, 204, 206–207, 231, 327

Grave plates, 79

Great Britain, 10–12, 31, 103, 157–158, 161, 164, 183, 185, 187–189, 213, 215, 228, 231, 241, 255, 277–278, 319, 322; Viking incursions, 10–12; Christian mission, 31; cultural exchange, 164; Napoleonic Wars, 188–189; World War I, 228; admitted to European Economic Community, 278; cooperation, 322. See also England

Great Depression, 232, 238–242

Great Northern War (1700–1721), 5, 126, 146–149, 155, 179

Gregorian calendar, 96

Greifswald, 28, 45, 47, 56, 62, 78, 80–82, 85, 91–92, 98, 110, 115–116, 120, 134, 166, 169–170, 176, 180, 212, 242, 260, 292, 296–297, 310, 317, 319

Grétry, André, 174

Grieg, Edvard, 216, 218, 251

Grosvalds, Jāzeps, 250

Grünberg, Gottfried, 266

Grundtvig, Nikolai Frederik Severin, 195

Gruodis, Juozas, 253

Guido, 3

Guilds, 49, 77–79, 94, 101, 113, 136

Gustav I Vasa, King, 69, 93

Gustav III, King, 156, 184

Gustav IV Adolf, King, 185, 189

Gustav Adolph, Duke, 148

Gustavus Adolphus, 117, 120–121, 136, 142
Gustav Vasa (Naumann), 177
Güstrow Palace, 114

Haakon IV, King, 83
Haakon V, King, 83
Haakon VI Magnusson, King, 65
Haakon VII, King, 226, 255
Haakon Haraldsson, the Good, King, 32
Haavikko, Paavo, 281
Hack-silver, 22
Hagenhufendorf-type village layout, 47
Hager, Kurt, 295–296
Hall churches, 78–79
Hallén, Andreas, 216
Hamann, Johann Georg, 166
Hamburg, 2, 4, 9, 30–31, 58, 61, 63–64, 76, 79–81, 91–92, 98*t*., 101–103, 136, 143, 159, 164, 175–176, 178, 186–187, 200, 204, 212–214, 216, 241, 250
Hamburg-Bremen, Archbishopric of, 2, 30–31
Hamburger Patriot, 171
Hamburgische unpartheyische Correspondent, 171
Hamsun, Knut, 238, 245
Håndfæstning, 64
Hanse associations, 54–55, 58, 77, 79
Hanseatic League, 7, 52–63, 85, 103, 120, 322, 326–329
Hanseatic merchants, 44–46, 48, 52–55, 61–64, 69, 76–77, 79–80, 85, 91–92, 102–103
Hanserezesse, 84–85
Hansson, Per Albin, 232
Harald Gormsson, Bluetooth, King, 31
Harald Halfdansson, Klak, King, 30
Harthacnut III, King, 31
Hartlib, Samuel, 140
Hartmann, Johan Peter Emilius, 216
Hartung, Johann Heinrich, 172
Hats, 156, 179
Häusser, Elias David, 178
Headmasters, *Hofmeisters*, 164–167, 197
Hedeby, 19–20, 22–23, 26–27, 31
Heiberg, Johan Ludvig, 217
Heiligendamm, 219
Heimskringla, 83
Heinkel, Ernst, 242
HELCOM, 318, 321, 324

Helldén, David, 284
Helsinki, 167, 183–184, 190, 196, 211, 214–215, 220, 225, 227, 229, 252, 284, 320
Helsinki Commission (HELCOM), 318
Helsinki Convention, 318
Helsinki Music Institute, 215
Hemp, 59, 99, 101–102, 130–132, 163, 327
Henry, King, 15–16
Henry III, the Lion, Duke, 33–35, 45, 54–55
Henry Borwin I, Lord, 45
Henry Borwin II, Prince, 114
Henry of Latvia, 49
Herbert, Zbigniew, 281
Herder, Johann Gottfried, 166, 169, 197, 328
Hermann of Gleichen, 42
Heroldt, Johann Georg, 139
Herring, 56, 59–60, 98–100, 104–105, 130, 158
Hessen, Friedrich Karl von, 228
Hexaemeron, 84
Heydemann, Güstrow Heinrich, 266
Heymans, Peter, 114–115
Hiddensee Treasure, 20–21
Hide system, 41–42, 46–47. See also *Hufen*
High Altar (St. Nikolai), 80
Hildebrandt, Friedrich, 238
Hilger, Wolf, 116
Hiller, Johann Adam, 174
Hilltop fortifications, 18
Hindemith, Paul, 251, 253
Hindenburg, Paul von, 227
Hitler-Stalin Pact, 254, 262, 290, 293, 295, 306
Höcker, William, 265, 267
Høeg, Peter, 281
Høffding, Finn, 251
Hofmeister, 164–167, 197
Hogensee, Jakob, 91
Holberg, Ludvig, 175
Holmberg, Johann Christoph, 173
Holmekloster manor, 109
Holstein, 14–15, 35, 40–41, 48, 68–69, 105–109, 136, 143, 146, 191, 193–194, 201; Oldenburg Obotrite mission, 15; monarchy, 68–69; manorial economy, 105–106, 107, 109; freedom

of movement, 108; constitution, 191.
See also Schleswig-Holstein
Holstein, Jakob Staël von, 139
Holsten, Wolter von, 102
Holsti, Rudolf, 229
Holy Roman Empire. *See* German
Empire
Hondius, Willem, 110
Honecker, Erich, 291, 297
Horic I, King, 31
Horn, Arvid Bernhard, 155–156
Hosius, Stanislaus, 94
Hotels, 220, 273
Housing areas, 247–248, 262, 273
Housing boom, 311
Hufen, 106, 129, 153
Humanism, 85–86
Hungary, 22, 59, 70, 72–73, 168; and fall
of GDR, 296; membership in
European Union, 314
Hupel, August Wilhelm, 165–166, 169,
172–173

Ibn Ja'kub, Ibrahim, 16
Ibn Rustah, 12–13
Ibsen, Henrik, 217–218
Iffland, August Wilhelm, 174–175
Igor I, Prince, 12–13
IKEA, 277
Iltnere, Ieva, 283
Individual memory, 321–322
Industrialization, 153, 205–208, 222,
265, 272–273, 292; and shift to
class-based society, 210; of Riga, 222;
during interwar years, 239–242; and
Sovietization of Poland, 265; and
Sovietization following WWII,
272–275; and social planning in
Sweden, 276; and German economic
transformation following fall of
Soviet bloc, 309–310; and Estonian
and Lithuanian economic transfor-
mation following fall of Soviet bloc,
311
Intellectuals. *See* Scholars
Intelligenzblatt, 171, 179
Interior design and decor, 179–180
International Monetary Fund (IMF),
307, 310–311
INTERREG, 316
Iris, 172

Iron, 20, 40, 56, 60, 102, 117, 131–132,
161, 164, 188, 205, 207, 255, 327
Italian architecture, 110–111, 114–115,
142, 181, 184, 211
Italian musicians, 142, 144, 177
Ius indigenatus, 123, 128
Ivan III, Grand Prince, 62, 69
Ivan IV, the Terrible, Czar, 95, 96

Jacobsen, Arne, 284–285
Jaczo of Salzwedel, 41
Jadwiga, Queen, 70–71
Jagiełło, Grand Duke, 70–71
Jakobson, Carl Robert, 198
Jakubėnas, Vladas, 253
Jannsen, Johann Voldemar, 198
Janszoons, Willem, 5
Jaromar of Rügen, Prince, 28, 33
Jaruzelski, Wojciech, 289–290, 295
Jazz, 286–287, 323
Jensen, Johannes V., 281
Jesuits, 96, 142
Jewelry, 26
Jewish merchants, 19, 326
Jews, 87, 156, 210t., 227, 243–244, 255,
257; minority, during interwar years,
244–245; refuge for, during WWII,
255; pogrom against Lithuanian and
Latvian, 257; Polish anti-Semitic
campaign, 288
Job creation: during global economic
crisis, 240, 323; under Nazi Party, 242
Johann of Posilge, 84
Johansen, Viggo, 212
Johanson, Herbert, 249
John, King, 69
John II Casimir, King, 121–122
John IV, Duke, 80
John Albert I, Duke, 113–114
John Albert II, Duke, 118–119
John Frederick, Duke, 115
John Paul II, Pope, 289
Johnson, Eyvind, 281
Jordaens, Jacob, 136
Journals, eighteenth-century, 164,
170–174, 179
Juel, Jens, 212
Juškaitsi, Jonas, 280
Jutland, 11, 22, 29, 31, 74, 123, 194, 200,
226, 240; Black Death and population
of, 74

Kabakov, Ilya, 283
Käbin, Johannes (Ivan), 268–269
Kaczyński, Jarosław, 305
Kaczyński, Lech, 305
Kalanta, Romas, 290
Kalckstein, Christian Ludwig von, 129
Kalevala, 169, 196, 213, 217
Kaliningrad. *See* Königsberg
Kalmar Cathedral, 137
Kalmar Union, 66, 326
Kalniņš, Alfrēds, 253
Kalniņš, Jānis, 253
Kangro, Bernard, 245–246, 279
Kanter Johann Jakob, 172
Kantor, Tadeusz, 282
Kantzow, Thomas, 48
Kaplinski, Jaan, 280
Karelia, 38, 50, 69, 75, 121, 131, 149, 196, 229, 254–255, 258, 316; ethnic assimilation, 50; settlement, 75; World War II, 254–255; cooperation, 316
Karelians: medieval, 17; Christianization, 38
Karg-Elert, Sigfrid, 253
Karl, Xaver, 266–267
Karlfeldt, Erik Axel, 245
Karl Knutsson, 67–68
Karlskröniken, 83
Karotamm, Nikolai, 268
Kaspar of Minckwitz, 96
Kaunas, 227–228, 249, 257, 322
Kaurismäki, Aki, 282
Kaurismäki, Mika, 282
Kazaks, Jēkabs, 250
Kegel, Philip, 142
Keisri hull (Kross), 280
Kekkonen, Urho, 269
Kellgren, Johann Henric, 173
Kernave, Lithuania, 18
Keskküla, Ando, 283
Ketelhot, Christian, 90, 116
Keyser, Hendrik de, 111
Khrushchev, Nikita, 265
Kiel, 193, 220, 226, 226, 233
Kiev, 13, 16, 32, 71
Kilpinen, Yrjö, 252
Kirby, David, 1–2
Klami, Uuno, 252
Klinge, Matti, 1–2
Klinkāvs, Aleksandrs, 249

Klucis, Gustavs, 250
Knipstro, Johannes, 91–92
Knopke, Andreas, 91, 94
Knox, John, 97
Knýtlinga saga, 83
Köhler, Günter, 297
Koidula, Lydia, 286
Kokorinov, Alexander, 181
Kolbatz Abbey, 28, 35
Kolberg, 42, 44, 79, 91
Kolding, Niels Mortensen, 143
Köler, Johann, 198, 212
Kölner, Johann, 141
Komitet Obrony Robotników (KOR, Committee for the Defense of Workers), 289
Komorowski, Bronisław, 305
Königsberg, 56, 63, 88–89, 91, 94, 97, 100–102, 112–113, 128, 130–131, 143–145, 158, 162, 166, 171–172, 175–177, 187, 207, 259
Kontor: Peterhof as, for Hanseatic trade with Russia, 55; German Bridge as, for Hanseatic trade with Scandinavia, 56; establishment of German system, 57; trade organization formed by, 61–62; closing of Novgorod, 62; function of, 62; Antwerp, 63; decline of German Bridge, 63
Konungs skuggsjá, 83
Korobov, Ivan, 180
Kościuszko, Tadeusz, 151, 185
Kosegarten, Ludwig Gotthard, 218
Köslin, 42, 237
Kotli, Alar, 285
Kotzebue, August von, 172, 174–175
Kramer, Hans, 112
Krantz, Albert, 85
Kraus, Jakob, 166
Krause, Johann Wilhelm, 211–212
Kremer, Gidon, 286
Krenz, Egon, 297
Kreuger, Ivar, 240
Kreutzwald, Friedrich Reinhold, 197
Krėvė- Mickevičius, Vincas, 247
Krohg, Christian, 212
Krone (Estonia), 310
Krone (Sweden), 277
Kross, Jaan, 280
Krøyer, Marie, 212

Krøyer, P. S., 212
Kuhlau, Friedrich, 216
Kukk, Juhan, 230
Kulmer Handfeste (Culm law), 45
Kureke, Johann, 90
Kuroń, Jacek, 288
Kvarken Council, 316
Kwaśniewski, Aleksander, 304

Laar, Mart, 305
Labor movement(s), 208–209, 211, 231, 240, 265, 289
Lācis, Vilis, 279
Laganovskis, Jezups, 280
Laidoner, Johan, 228, 230, 256
Landkasten, 124
Landsbergis, Vytautas, 305
Land settlement, 40–43, 75, 237
Landsmål, 195
Lansere, Eugene, 213
Lapin, Leonhard, 283
Late romanticism, 251
Latgallians, 17–18
Latin chronicles and religious literature, 2–3, 9, 38, 83–85, 169
Latvia, 6, 17–18, 96, 151, 165, 169, 197–199, 202, 210–211, 225, 227–230, 235–236, 241, 243–244, 246–247, 250, 253, 255–259, 268, 271, 280, 283, 294, 298–300, 305–307, 310–311, 313–315, 320, 322; nationalist movement, 197–198; Revolution of 1905, 225; World War I, 227, 228; cooperation, 229, 322; internal politics following WWI, 229, 230; agrarian reforms, 235, 236; interwar exports, 241; social and ethnic structure during interwar years, 244; establishment of national culture and identity, 246–247; art, 250; foreign policy during WWII, 253; World War II, 255–256, 257, 258, 259; Sovietization, 268–269; collectivization, 271; postwar literature, 280; postwar visual arts, 283; autonomy and democratization, 294, 298, 299, 300; political awakening, 294; democratization, 305; stability, 306; citizenship rights, 306–307; economic transformation following fall of Soviet bloc, 310–311; trade

following fall of Soviet bloc, 313; membership in European Union, 314; adopts euro, 315; renewable energy, 320
Latvian artists, 214, 283–284
Latvian Communist Party, 269
Latvian language, 96, 246, 269
Latvians, as dominant nationality in Russian Baltic states, 210–211
Latvian Society, 198
Latvijas Sociāldemokrātiskā Strādnieku Partija (Latvian Social Democratic Workers Party), 225
Laube, Eižens, 222, 249
Lauw, Woldemar Johann von, 181–182
LDP, 267
Le Blon, Michel, 138
Leibeigene, 108
Lenin, Vladimir, 227
Lenngren, Carl Peter, 173
Lepper, Andrzej, 304, 307
Leptzow, Hennig, 80
Leszczyński, Stanisław, 147, 149
Lex Regia, 191
Liberalized pass ordinance (1863), 197
Liber daticus Lundensis, 86
Lichtenberg, Georg Christoph, 219
Lichtwark, Alfred, 214
Lidman, Sara, 281
Lindgren, Armas, 217
Lindgren, Astrid, 281
Lindgren, Torgny, 281
Linna, Väinö, 281
Literacy, in Estonia during interwar years, 246
Literat, 164–167
Literature: of Middle Ages, 82–86; of Reformation, 89–90; and nationalist movements, 195–197; during interwar years, 245–247; postwar, 279–281
Lithuania, 17–18, 37, 69–72, 95, 102, 121, 127, 142, 145, 150, 182, 199, 207, 225, 227–230, 235–236, 241, 244, 247, 249, 253–259, 269, 271, 281–284, 287, 290, 294, 298–299, 305–307, 310–311, 313–316, 319–320, 322, 326; settlement, 17; hilltop fortifications, 18; relations with Casimir the Great, 70; Christianization, 70–71; alliance with Poland, 70–72; agrarian reforms, 199,

Lithuania *(continued)*
202, 235, 236; nationalist movement, 199; industrialization, 207; Revolution of 1905, 225; World War I, 227–228; cooperative initiatives with Russian Empire successor states, 229; internal politics following WWI, 229, 230; interwar exports, 241; social and ethnic structure during interwar years, 244–245; national culture and identity, 247; interwar architecture, 249; interwar music, 253; foreign policy during WWII, 254; World War II, 255, 256–257, 259; Sovietization, 268–269; collectivization, 271; postwar literature, 280–281; postwar visual arts, 282, 283; jazz, 287; political awakening, 290, 294; autonomy and democratization, 294, 298, 299; democratization, 305–306; stability, 306; integration of Russian and Polish minorities, 307; economic transformation following fall of Soviet bloc, 310–311; trade following fall of Soviet bloc, 313; membership in European Union, 314; adopts euro, 315. *See also* Poland-Lithuania
Lithuanian Crusades, 37–38
Lithuanian language, 90, 199, 223
Livestock, 107, 205
Livonia, 6, 35–37, 39, 43, 46, 49–50, 59, 71, 82, 94–96, 98t., 118, 120–122, 124–126, 134, 139, 146–147, 149–153, 165–166, 168, 172–173, 197–199, 201, 211–212; Christian mission, 35–36, 37, 39; settlement, 43; founding of cities, 46; ethnic assimilation, 49–50; sacral architecture, 51; Reformation, 94–96; serfdom, 108; Truce of Altmark, 121; land registration, 124–125; manor reductions, 125–126; peasant ordinances, 134; Russian administrative reforms, 151–153; *Hofmeister*, 165; periodicals, 172–173; nationalist movement, 197–198; agrarian reforms, 199, 201–202
Livonian Brothers of the Sword, 35, 36, 37, 39, 49–50, 94–95
Livonian Knighthood, 125–126
Livonians, medieval, 17, 18

L. M. Ericsson (LME), 240
Location, process of, 44
Locher, Carl, 212
Lohse, Hinrich, 257
Lönn, Wivi, 217
Lönnrot, Elias, 169, 196
Lothar of Supplinburg, 32
Louis I, King, 70
Lovisa Ulrika, Queen, 156, 176
Low German language, 89, 327–328
Lübeck, 3–4, 15, 44–46, 52, 54, 56–58, 60–64, 66, 76–79, 81, 85–87, 89, 92, 95, 98, 98t., 101–103, 108, 114–115, 131, 143, 158, 164, 176, 186–187, 207
Lübeck Cathedral, 79, 86, 340n28
Lübeck law, 42, 45–46, 56
Lubmin nuclear power plant, 274, 292, 310
Lubomirski, Jerzy, 127
Ludwigslust palace, 180
Lund Cathedral, 77
Luther, Martin, 88–92, 94, 115
Lutheranism, 93–94, 96
Lutici Federation, 15, 32–33
Lutosławski, Witold, 285
Lutter am Barenberge, 119
Lyngstad, Anni-Frid, 287

Madsen, Karl, 212
Magdeburg rights, 44
Magnus, Olaus, 3–4
Magnus VI, the Law mender, King, 83
Magnus Eriksson IV (Sweden)/VII (Norway), King, 65, 75
Magnus of Holstein, Duke, 95–96
Malmö, 67, 78, 92, 193, 301
Malmström, Cecilia, 323
Mander, Karel van, 111
Manner, Eeva-Liisa, 281
Mannerheim, Carl Gustaf Emil, 227
Manorial economy. *See* Agriculture
Manor reductions, Swedish, 123–126
Mara, Elisabeth, 177
Mare Balticum, 2–5, 8
Mare Gothicum, 3–4
Mare occidentale, 3
Mare orientale, 3
Mare Sveticum, 3
Margaret I, Countess, 55, 57
Margaret I, Queen, 65–66
Margrethe II, Queen, 301

Maria Eleonora of Brandenburg, 136
Maria of Saxony, 115
Marienkirche (Danzig), 79, 143–144
Marienkirche (Greifswald), 45, 78–79
Marienkirche (Lübeck), 78–79, 86, 143, 176, 340n28
Marienkirche (Rostock), 45
Marienkirche (Stralsund), 92
Markelius, Sven, 248, 249
Marshall Plan, 269, 273
Martinson, Harry, 281
Maschke, Erich, 6
Al-Masudi, 13
Mathias Övedsson, 84
Mathias-Thesen shipyard, 274, 309
Maucourt, Charles, 178
May Constitution (1791), 185
Mazepa, Ivan, 147
Mazovia, 70, 106, 150
Mazowiecki, Tadesuz, 295, 304
Mecklenburg, 15, 26, 33, 35, 40–41, 45, 48–49, 65, 81, 90, 107–108, 113–116, 118–120, 123, 134, 148, 178, 180, 185–189, 201, 203–205, 233, 237–238, 241–242, 250, 259–260, 265–266, 268; Christianization, 15; Niklotides as ruling dynasty, 33; settlement, 41; ethnic assimilation, 48–49; Dutch art, 113–114; Thirty Years' War, 118–119; peasant ordinances, 134; Great Northern War, 148; Napoleonic Wars, 187–188; agrarian reforms, 201, 203–204, 237; livestock as source of agricultural income, 205; internal politics following WWI, 233–234; industrialization during Great Depression, 241, 242; interwar architecture, 250; World War II, 260; Sovietization, 265–268. See also Mecklenburg-Western Pomerania
Mecklenburg-Western Pomerania, 266, 271–272, 274, 298, 303, 308–309, 316
Medem, Jeannot, 211
Meder, Johann Valentin, 143
Meilof, Johannes, 82
Meinhard, 35
Meissen porcelain, 26
Memel, 113, 162–163, 163t., 187, 228, 239, 259
Memory, 2, 151, 232, 301, 319, 321–322
Mennonites, 97, 141

Menshikov, Aleksandr, 152
Menzlin, 19
Mer baltique, 5
Merchant Adventurers, 103
Merchants, 2–5, 8–9, 11, 13, 19–20, 21, 26–27, 36, 38, 44–46, 48, 52, 54–64, 69, 76–77, 79–80, 85, 87, 91–92, 95, 97, 101–104, 117, 126, 132, 138, 140–141, 149, 154–157, 161, 163–164, 176, 179, 184, 187, 198, 206, 210, 222, 326–327
Merchants of Eastland. See Eastland Company
Mer de hoost, 4
Mer d'oost, 4
Mer d'Oostlande, 4
Meri, Lennart, 305, 321
Merikanto, Aarre, 252
Metsu, Gabriel, 178
Mevius, David, 141
Michael I, Czar, 121
Michaelis, Johann, 141
Michetti, Nicolai, 181
Mickiewicz, Adam, 288
Middle Low German language, 48, 84–85
Mieszko I, King, 16–17, 34
Mieželaitis, Eduardas, 280
Migration, 1, 14, 49, 76, 97, 201–204, 208, 210, 244, 272, 276, 287
Migration Period, 14
Milius, Matti, 283–284
Miłosz, Czesław, 279
Mindaugas, Prince, 37
Mindaugas II, King, 227–228
Minorities. See Multiethnicity
Mir Iskusstva, 213
Moczar, Mieczysław, 288
Model region, Baltic region as, 322–325, 329
"Modern Hanseatic Days," 322
Modrow, Hans, 296
Modzelewski, Karol, 288
Moeller, Richard, 266
Møller-Maersk, 277
Mollet, André, 136–137
Molotov, Vyacheslav, 255
Moltke, Adam Gottlob von, 179
Moltmann, Carl, 266–267
Momma, Jakob, 117, 132, 138
Monarchies, 63–73, 326–327
Monasteries, 10–11, 15, 28, 34–35, 48–51, 78–79, 96

Monopolies, 4, 60–61, 81, 99, 131, 133, 156, 161, 205, 232, 239–240, 327
Montaigu, René, 175
Montgomery, Bernard, 260
Morell, Gerhard, 178–179
Mrożek, Sławomir, 281
Müller, Joachim, 91
Multiethnicity, 97, 191, 210–211, 243–245, 277, 306–307
Mundy, Peter, 87, 88*fig.*
Muscovy Company, 5, 337n18
Music. *See under* Art(s)
Music societies, 176, 215
Mylius, Christian G. J., 165–166
Myrdal, Alva, 233, 248
Myrdal, Gunnar, 233, 248

Napoleonic Wars, 184–189
Narva, 95, 101–102, 130, 132, 139, 146, 149, 162, 163*t.*, 207, 258–259, 273
National identity: through national movements, 194–195; Finnish, 196; Lithuanian, 209; Nordic labor movement, 209; and relationship to past, 328
Nationalist movements, 192–199, 211
National Pension Act (1913), 209
National Socialists (NSDAP), 232, 238, 242, 250–251, 254–255, 257, 271
NATO, 261, 306, 315
Naugard, 42
Naumann, Johann Gottlieb, 177
Navakas, Mindaugas, 283
Nazis. *See* National Socialists
Neoclassicism, 211–212, 245, 248
Neptun shipyard, 241, 242, 274
Nesselmann, Georg Heinrich Ferdinand, 6
Netherlands, 3–4, 60, 63, 69, 81, 84, 87, 97, 98*t.*, 102–104, 110, 112, 117–118, 122, 129, 131–132, 136–137, 139–142, 145, 147, 162*t.*, 164, 167, 301, 319, 326; trade interests in Baltic region, 3–5; battle for dominion over Baltic Sea, 4; Hanseatic trade, 60–63, 98; exports and industries, 98; expansion of trade, 98–101; grain trade, 104–105; influence in architecture and arts, 110–114; dominance in trade, 129–132; cultural influence on Sweden, 135–144; eighteenth-century trade
with Baltic region, 158–159; 1770s imports, 161, 162*t.*; dominance of Riga trade, 163; cultural exchange, 164; periodicals, 173; Dutch art collections, 177–178; conflict over Øresund, 301; integrates Baltic region in economic plans, 326–327
Netscher, Caspar, 178
Nettelbladt, Christian, 169–170, 174
Neubrandenburg, 41–42, 242, 259, 268, 275
Neuenkamp, 92
Neuenkamp Abbey, 41
Neustrelitz, 180
Nevsky, Alexander, 37
New East Prussia, 151
Newspapers, 171–175, 196–199, 258, 291, 293, 320
Nexø, Martin Andersen, 281
Nicholas I, Czar, 192
Nicholas II, Czar, 220, 226
Nicolai, Friedrich, 168, 171
Niebuhr, Carsten, 167
Nielsen, Asta, 243
Nielsen, Carl, 251
Niklot, Prince, 32–33
Niklotides, 33
Nikolaikirche (Stralsund), 78, 91
Nikolaus of Jeroschin, 84
Nobel, Alfred, 205
Nobility: as tribal authorities, 23; Old Prussian, 43, 49; Slavic, 48; weakness of Danish monarchy, 64; Polish, 70; Reformation and Swedish, 93; increased agricultural production, 107; freedom of movement of peasantry, 108; residences of Renaissance, 115; privileges, 123, 126, 152–154, 157; revolt in Poland-Lithuania, 127; Prussian, 128, 202; Russian administrative reforms, 152, 153–154; under Danish absolutism, 157. *See also* Agriculture
Nobles' Republic of Poland-Lithuania, 121–122, 127, 146, 182
Nokia, 277–278
Nordic countries, 73–74, 215, 232, 239, 263, 300, 311, 318–319; population, 73; foreign policy disagreements, 231–232; internal politics following WWI, 232; threat potential, 232;

public health programs, 232–233; Great Depression, 238; industrialization during interwar years, 239; membership in European Union, 313–314; education and scholarship, 318. *See also* Denmark; Finland; Norway; Sweden

Nordic romanticism, 183–221, 328

Nordic Union, 67–68

Nordische Miscellaneen, 169, 172

Nord Stream project, 310, 319

Nordström, Karl, 213

Norman, Ludvig, 216

Norsemen. *See* Vikings

Det Norske Arbeiderparti, 209

Det Norske Teater, 217

North European Pipeline. *See* Nord Stream project

North Sea, resorts by, 219

North Sea region, eighteenth-century trade with Baltic region, 159–161

Norway, 12, 31–32, 52, 56, 60, 64–65, 68, 73–74, 76–79, 81, 84, 86, 147, 189, 191, 194–195, 200–201, 205–206, 207–209, 215–217, 226, 229, 231–232, 239, 249, 255, 259, 261, 269, 287, 309, 314, 317, 323–324; Christianization, 32; German trade, 56; Hanseatic trade, 60; monarchy, 65–67; conflicting claims to, 68; Nordic Union, 68; Black Death and population, 73–74; population, 73–74, 208; structural changes following Napoleonic Wars, 191; nationalist movement, 195–196; agrarian reform, 201; industrialization, 205–206; urbanization, 208; shift to class-based society, 209; socialist parties and unions, 209; nineteenth-century music, 216; nineteenth-century theater, 217–218; Revolution of 1905, 226; cooperative initiatives with Russian Empire successor states, 229; foreign policy disagreements, 232; internal politics following WWI, 232–233; interwar architecture, 248–249; World War II, 255; jazz, 287; membership in European Union, 314; Council of the Baltic Sea States, 317. *See also* Nordic countries; Scandinavia

Norwegian language, 195–196, 217

Notke, Bernt, 54, 79

Novgorod, 9, 13, 18, 22–23, 32, 38, 50, 55–56, 59, 61–63, 65, 75, 77, 145

Nyrop, Martin, 247

Oberpahlen, 166, 181–182

Obotrites, 14–15, 23, 32–35, 40. *See also* Slavs

Odin, 24–25

Oehlenschläger, Adam, 195, 217

Oeseler, Christoph Otto, 141

Oil crisis of 1973–1974, 276

Olaf II Haraldsson (St. Olaf), King, 32

Olaf IV, King, 64

Olaf Tryggvason, King, 32

Olai, Ericus, 83

Old Prussian language, 90

Oleg, Prince, 13

Olga, Regent, 12–13

Olof Skötkonung, King, 32

Oostersche Zee/Oostzee region, 4

Oostland, 4

Oostzee, 4–5

OPEC (Organization of Oil Exporting Countries), 276

Order of Teutonic Knights (Teutonic Order, Teutonic Knights), 36–39, 42–46, 49, 59–60, 64, 67, 70–72, 75, 79, 81–82, 84, 93–95; Christian Mission, 36–40; settlement of Prussia, 42–43; settlement of Livonia, 43; founding of Thorn and Culm, 45–46; service system, 49; trade regions controlled by, 59–60; conflict with Eric III, 67; possessions recognized under Treaty of Kalisz, 70; uniting of Piast petty principalities, 70; Polish-Lithuanian alliance, 71–72; Reformation, 94–95

Øresund: Denmark claims right to control, 4–5, 67, 95, 118, 326; tolls for passage, 67, 122; passage through, in eighteenth century, 158; ships passages through, 1503–1845, 159g.

Øresund Bridge, 301, 302fig.

Øresund region, 316, 321

Øresund University, 301

Organization of Oil Exporting Countries (OPEC), 276

Organs, 86

Ørsted Pedersen, Niels Henning, 287

OSCE (Organization for Security and Cooperation in Europe), 314
Oslo, 69, 83, 215, 232, 248–249
Östberg, Ragnar, 248
Osterode, 106
Ostindiska companiet, 161
Otto Adelheid pfennigs, 22
Otto I, Emperor, 14–15
Ottonians, 14
Otto of Bamberg, 33–34
Oudry, Jean-Baptiste, 178
Ovens, Jürgen, 136
Oxenstierna, Axel, 120, 123, 137, 140

Paasikivi, Juho Kusti, 269
Pabriks, Artis, 322–323
Pacius, Fredrik, 216
Pact of Vilnius and Radom (1401), 71
Paganism, 29–40, 48, 50–51, 70
Palaces, 114–115, 117, 137–139, 177–182
Palladius, Peder, 93
Palmer, Alan, 2
Pan-Scandinavianism, 195
Parliamentary system, 225–226, 229–231, 295
Parr, Franz, 114
Pärt, Arvo, 285–286
Patersen, Benjamin, 146fig.
Patkul, Johann Reinhold, 126, 147
Päts, Konstantin, 230, 256
Paul I, Czar, 153
Peace groups, 292
Peasantry: land settlement, 40–43, 50; economic transformation during middle ages, 47–48, 49; population, 73, 75–76; Reformation, 96, 97; products of Dutch, 98; manorial economy, 106–110, 127, 132–135; administrative reform, 123–124; granted right to own property, 156, 157; revolts and uprisings, 184–185; granted freedom of movement, 197; agrarian reforms, 199–204, 234–237; shift to class-based society, 208–211; Revolution of 1905, 225; collectivization, 271–272; exploitation, 327
Peasants Mutual Aid Association, 267
Pedersøn, Mogens, 143
Pēkšens, Konstantīns, 222
Pelše, Arvīds, 269

Penderecki, Krzysztof, 285
People's Chamber of the German Democratic Republic, 268, 297
Periodicals, eighteenth-century, 171–172
Perti, Giovanni Pietro, 142
Pesne, Antoine, 178
Pēterburgas Avīzes, 198
Peterhof, 55
Peter I, the Great, Czar, 145–146, 152, 180–181, 327
Peter of Dacia, 84
Peter of Dusburg, 49, 84
Peter of Ravenna, 82
Peterson-Berger, Wilhelm, 251
Petersons, Ojars, 283
Petri, Laurentius, 90, 93
Petri, Olaus, 90
Petrograd, 226–227. See also St. Petersburg
Pfennig, 22
Philipp I, Duke, 115–116
Piasts, 14, 34, 70
Pietism, 167
Piłsudski, Józef, 230
Pingoud, Ernest, 252
Piracy, 18, 20, 33, 67
Pitch, 99, 101, 130–131, 163
Pius II, Pope, 52
Place names: and construction and perception of Baltic region, 2–8; concordance, 331–336
Plague, 73–76, 147, 153–154
Pliekšāns, Jānis, 246
Poland, 4, 6, 14–16, 22, 59, 63, 69–75, 93–97, 106–107, 112, 118, 120–122, 126, 128, 133, 146, 149–151, 155, 172, 185, 187, 189–190, 192, 225, 228–231, 235–236, 238, 254, 257, 260–261, 263–264, 269, 271, 273, 278–279, 282, 287–290, 295, 298, 301–302, 304–308, 313–317, 319–321, 326, 328; battle for dominion over Baltic Sea, 4, 121–122; Polish state federation, 16; commercial products, 59–60; monarchy, 63, 69–73; manorial economy, 106, 107, 133; freedom of movement, 108; Dutch architecture, 112; Truce of Altmark, 121; Swedish invasion, 126; Netherlandish cultural influences, 142; Great Northern

War, 146–147; territorial transformation, 149; Seven Years' War, 150;
partitioned among Russia, Prussia,
and Austria, 150–151; administrative reform, 155; May Constitution,
185; Napoleonic Wars, 189; structural
changes following Napoleonic Wars,
190; World War I, 228; cooperation,
229, 317; internal politics following
WWI, 229, 230–231; agrarian
reforms, 235–236; social and ethnic
structure during interwar years,
245; foreign policy during WWII,
254; World War II, 254, 260, 261;
Sovietization, 263, 264–265;
collectivization, 271; post-WWI
industrialization, 273; postwar
literature, 281; postwar visual
arts, 282; economic decline and
anti-Soviet protests, 288–290;
autonomy and democratization,
294; political awakening, 295;
conflict over Öresund with Denmark,
301; democratization, 302, 304–305;
stability, 306; economic transformation following fall of Soviet bloc,
307–308; membership in European
Union, 313, 314, 315; trade following
fall of Soviet bloc, 313; NATO
membership, 315; Nord Stream
project, 320; Baltoscandian
Confederation, 328. See also
Poland-Lithuania
Poland-Lithuania, 71–72, 95, 121, 145,
182, 326; monarchy, 71–72; Reformation, 95; battle for dominion over
Baltic Sea, 121; administrative
reform, 127; Netherlandish and
German cultural influences, 142;
recedes as power, 145; territorial
transformation, 149; competition
and cooperation with Hanseatic
League, 326
Polans, 14, 16
Polański, Roman, 282
Polish United Workers Party (Polska
Zjednoczona Partia Robotnicza),
264–265, 295
Põllu, Kaljo, 283
Pollution, 321, 325
Poloni/Polani, 16

Põltsamaa. See Oberpahlen
Polyphony, 86
Pomerania, 14, 26, 28, 33–35, 40–41, 45,
48–49, 78, 80, 82, 85, 90–92, 107–108,
113–116, 118, 120, 124, 134–138,
169–170, 199, 203, 205, 233, 237–238,
241–242, 260, 316; Polish annexation,
14; Dutch settlement, 28; Christianization, 33–34; settlement, 41; ethnic
assimilation, 48–49; architectural
influences, 78–79; freedom of
movement, 108; Thirty Years' War,
118, 120; as object of contention for
Sweden, 120–121; Swedish estates,
124; peasant ordinances, 134;
scholars, 169–170; newspapers,
173–174; agrarian reforms, 199,
237; agriculture, 205; internal
politics following WWI, 233;
industrialization during Great
Depression, 241; job creation, 242;
cooperation, 316–317. See also
Eastern Pomerania; Mecklenburg-
Western Pomerania; Swedish
Pomerania; Western Pomerania
Pomerelia, 37
Popiełuszko, Jerzy, 290
Pop music, 287
Popular Front of Estonia (Rahvarinne),
293, 298
Popular Front of Latvia (Latvijas Tautas
Fronte), 294
Porthan, Henrik Gabriel, 169
Post, Pieter, 139
Postimees, 224
Potash, 101, 131, 162, 188
Potter, Paulus, 178
Pötter-Lillienhoff, Joachim, 138
Pottery, 26
Poulsson, Markus, 249
Pribaltijskij, 6
Pribislav, 32
Privilege of Koszyce (1374), 70
Product Decree, 156
Prohibition, 232
Project Balticness, 323
Property rights, granted to peasantry,
156, 157
Protestant Reformation, 88–97, 115,
327–328
Prunskiene, Kazimiera, 298

Prussia, 16, 35–36, 39–40, 42–43, 49, 72, 75–76, 93–94, 98*t*., 106–107, 122–123, 127–129, 131, 134–135, 147–148, 150–151, 153–155, 169, 185–187, 189, 193, 199, 202–203, 205, 233, 259–260; Christian mission, 36–37; Teutonic Order, 39–40; settlement and population, 42–43, 75–76; assimilation and discrimination, 49; Reformation, 93–94; grain production, 106; battle for dominion over Baltic Sea, 122; estates, 127–129; Seven Years' War, 150; partitioning of Poland, 150–151; Russian administrative reforms, 153; administrative reform, 154–155; opposes Poland's May Constitution, 185; Napoleonic Wars, 185–186, 189; continental blockade against England, 187; intervention in Denmark, 193; agrarian reforms, 199, 202–203; agriculture, 205; World War II, 259, 260. *See also* East Prussia; New East Prussia; Royal Prussia; West Prussia
Prussian Confederation, 72
Public health programs, Nordic, 232–233
Pufendorf, Samuel, 140
Purvītis, Vilhelms, 214
Putin, Vladimir, 306
Putrams, Juris, 283

Quandt, Bernhard, 267
Quarenghi, Giacomo, 181, 183, 211
Quellinus, Artus, 136
Quisling, Vidkun, 255

Racial hygiene, 232–233
Radauskas, Henrikas, 279
Rahe, Horst, 309–310
Rail Baltica, 324
Railroad, 204, 207, 222, 274, 324
Rainis. *See* Pliekšāns, Jānis
Raitio, Väinö, 252
Ralswiek, 19–20
Rani, 14, 33
Rantzau, Heinrich, 109
Rantzausholm, 109
Rastrelli, Bartolomeo Francesco, 180–181
Ratzeburg, 40–41
Raudsepp, Hugo, 246

Reformation. *See* Protestant Reformation
Region and regionalism, new historical perception of concept, 2
Reichskommissariat Ostland, 257
Reißiger, Friedrich August, 216
Religion, 24, 29–40, 96. *See also* Catholic Church; Christianity; Protestant Reformation
Religious literature, 84
Renaissance, 110–116
Repin, Ilya, 212
Reric, 19, 20
Rethra, temple at, 15
Reuter, Bjarne, 281
Reuter, Johan, 139
Reval, 35, 46, 56, 58–59, 62, 76–77, 79, 94–95, 102, 108, 125, 139, 143, 147, 149, 164, 172, 174–175, 181, 207, 210–211, 214, 217, 220, 239, 246, 257. *See also* Tallinn
Revelationes (Bridget of Sweden), 84
Reventlow, Christian Ditlev, 157, 200
Reventlow, Johann Ludwig, 157, 200
Revolts and uprisings, 184–185, 192–193, 223–226, 227, 262
Revolution of 1905, 223–226
Revolution of 1917, 227
Reymont, Władysław, 237–238, 245
Richolff, Georg, 85
Rieben, Achim von, 116
Riel, Alex, 287
Riga, 17, 35, 37, 39, 46, 56, 58–59, 62, 76–77, 79–80, 82, 91, 94–96, 100*g*., 101–102, 108, 113, 121–122, 125, 130–131, 139, 143, 145, 147, 149, 152–153, 162–166, 169, 171, 174, 176, 180–182, 198, 207, 210–211, 214, 217, 222, 223*fig*., 225, 227, 239, 244, 246, 249, 252–253, 256–257, 269, 272, 295, 315, 318, 329
Riisager, Knudåge, 251
Rimkrønike, 83–84
Rinaldi, Antonio, 181
Ristikivi, Karl, 279
Rock Temple, 284
Rode, Hermen, 52–54
Rokossovsky, Konstantin, 260
Roman, Johan Helmich, 177
Romanticism, 195–196, 212, 216, 249, 251, 328

Roon, Albrecht von, 194
Rosen, Axel von, 139
Rosenberg, Alfred, 257
Rosenhane, Schering, 117, 137
Rostock, 45, 56, 62, 76, 80–82, 85, 98,
    115–116, 207, 241–242, 250–251, 259,
    266, 268, 275, 296–298, 304, 309
Roth, Hieronymus, 128–129
Rothko, Mark, 250
Royal Prussia, 72, 93, 97, 106, 112,
    127–128, 133, 150–151, 154–155, 172
Royal Swedish Opera, 176
Rozenberga, Elza, 246
Rozentāls, Jānis, 214, 222
Różewicz, Tadeusz, 281
Rubenow, Henrich, 80–81
Rühs, Friedrich, 171
Runeberg, Johan Ludvig, 196
Rune stones, 24–25
Runge, Jacob, 116
Runge, Philipp Otto, 212
Rurik, 13
Rus', 12–13
Russia, 5–7, 9, 17, 19–20, 22, 50, 54–57,
    69, 72, 75, 94–96, 101–102, 117,
    121–122, 145, 147, 149–152, 156,
    163–164, 168–169, 173, 177, 182–183,
    185, 187–190, 192, 199, 202, 207, 209,
    212–213, 220, 225–229, 232, 246, 254,
    258–260, 268–269, 272–273, 284, 294,
    296, 301, 306, 310, 313, 315–317,
    319–320, 323–324; construction
    and perception of Baltic region,
    6; subjugation of Estonians, 18;
    colonization efforts, 75; Reformation
    in Livonia, 95–96; resources of
    hinterlands, 101; battle for dominion
    over Baltic Sea, 122; territorial
    transformation, 145–151; constitution
    and administrative reforms, 151–158;
    important Baltic ports, 161; estab-
    lishment of cultural and communi-
    cation space, 164–177; Sweden's
    Finnish territories ceded to, 183;
    opposes Poland's May Constitution,
    185; Napoleonic Wars, 189; conces-
    sions offered to Finland and Poland,
    190; revolutionary movements, 192;
    Lithuanian nationalist movement,
    199; agrarian reform, 201–202;
    industrialization, 207; shift to

class-based society, 210–211;
    nineteenth-century art, 213; seaside
    resorts, 219–220; Revolution of 1905,
    223–226; World War I, 226–227, 228;
    foreign policy disagreements, 232;
    deindustrialization, 239; conflict
    over Øresund, 301; relationship with
    Baltic states, 306–307; trade following
    fall of Soviet bloc, 313; NATO
    membership as perceived threat,
    315; cooperation with Finland, 316;
    Council of the Baltic Sea States, 317;
    Nord Stream project, 319–320.
    See also Soviet Union
Russian early classicism, 181
Russo-Japanese War (1904–1905), 223
Rüütel, Arnold, 293
Ruysch, Rachel, 178
Ruysdael, Jacob, 178

Saarinen, Eliel, 249
Sadolin, Jörgen Jensen, 93
Saftleven, Herman, 178
Sagas, 24, 82–83, 218
Sailing, 20, 104, 159, 205–206, 220, 262
Sailing ships. See Ships
St. Marien parish church, 78
St. Nikolai (Stockholm), 79
St. Nikolai (Stralsund), 80, 116
St. Petersburg, 101, 145, 146fig., 153, 158,
    161–164, 167, 169, 174–175, 179–181,
    183, 190, 198, 207, 211–214, 220, 239,
    252–253, 327. See also Petrograd
Sajudis, 294, 305
Salt, 21, 59–61, 99, 102, 104–105, 158, 219
Saltsjöbaden Agreement, 240
Sarpaneva, Timo, 285
Savisaar, Edgar, 293, 298
Saxo Grammaticus, 83
Saxony, 3, 9, 14, 35, 89, 115, 126, 143,
    146–147, 150; Swedish invasion, 126;
    music, 143; Great Northern War,
    146–147; Seven Years' War, 150
Scacchi, Marco, 144
Scandinavia, 7, 11, 13, 20–22, 26, 56, 66,
    74–79, 81, 83–86, 88, 195, 208, 240,
    242–243, 281–282, 317; Viking
    expansion, 11; trade, 13, 20–21, 56,
    62, 76; religion, 24–25; cultural
    exchange, 26; united under single
    monarch, 65–66; agriculture, 74;

Scandinavia *(continued)*
    settlement, 75; architecture, 77–78,
    79; literature, 83; eighteenth-century
    trade with Baltic region, 158;
    pan-Scandinavianism, 195–196;
    Baltoscandian Confederation, 229,
    328; interwar standard of living,
    242–243; minority conflicts, 243;
    World War II, 253; as welfare state,
    275–276; postwar literature, 281;
    film, 282; membership in European
    Union, 302; long-distance trade, 326.
    See also Denmark; Norway; Sweden
Scandinavian defense union, 260–261
Scania: trade, 19, 56, 58, 65–66, 75, 77,
    118, 121, 140, 157, 195, 301, 317;
    conquered by Denmark, 58; Swedish
    claims to, 65; Black Death and
    population, 75
Schabowski, Günter, 297
Scheel, Heinrich, 222
Scheffel, Friedrich, 222
Schengen Accord, 314–315
Schiemann, Paul, 244
Schimmelmann, Ernst Heinrich von,
    Graf, 157, 200
Schlegel, Gottlieb, 166
Schleswig, 9, 23, 31, 68–69, 146, 177,
    191–194, 229, 243; integration into
    Danish kingdom, 193–194; territorial
    disputes over, 228–229. *See also*
    Schleswig-Holstein
Schleswig-Holstein, 7, 68, 76, 98*t.*, 107,
    133–135, 189, 191–194, 199–200, 204,
    208, 233, 238, 250, 259–260, 263, 270,
    287; division of, 68–69; agriculture,
    107, 199, 200, 204; crisis in manorial
    economy, 133, 134–135; rights of
    estates, 191; nationalist movement,
    192–193; population, 208; autonomy,
    233; architecture, 250; interwar
    architecture, 250; World War II, 260;
    collectivization, 270; Jazz Baltica
    Festival, 287
Schleswig-Holstein Question, 191–192
Schlözer, August Ludwig von, 168–169,
    328
Scholars: recruited to Sweden, 140–141;
    eighteenth-century, 164–170; critical
    of aristocratic rule, 184–185
Scholarship. *See* Education

Schönberg, Arnold, 253
Schreker, Franz, 253
Schroetter, Friedrich Leopold von, 155
Schröder, Paul, 234
Schröter, Georg, 114
Schröter, Simon, 114
Schuch, Caroline, 175
Schües, Nikolaus W., 309–310
Schultz, Daniel, 113
Schultz, Johann, 181
Schulz, Albert, 266
Schütz, Heinrich, 143–144
Schwerin, 33, 41, 45, 78, 80, 114, 118,
    177–178, 180, 188, 242, 266–268, 292,
    297–298, 304
Schwerin Castle, 114
Science(s): Swedish, 169–170; journals
    published in, 171
Seaside resorts, 218–219
Second Schleswig War, 194
Seite, Berndt, 304
Selonians, 17
Semigallians, 17–18, 37
Sepmann, Henno, 285
Serfdom. *See* Agriculture
Seven Years' War, 150, 176–177
Severing, Carl Theodor, 219
Shipbuilding, 99–101, 130–131, 158, 205,
    207, 239, 241, 273–274, 278, 308–310,
    327
Shipping. *See* Ships; Trade
Ships, 4–5, 12, 61, 63, 95, 98*fig.*, 99, 104,
    122, 130, 132, 147, 158, 159*fig.*,
    161–164, 187, 188, 206–207, 220, 226,
    241, 274, 301, 309, 320–321, 326;
    sailing, 20, 104, 159, 205–206; traffic,
    98, 101–102, 132, 156, 158, 161–163,
    187–188, 209, 255, 277, 309, 320–321,
    324, 327; steam, 204, 206
Shipyards, 101, 207, 241, 273–274, 289,
    309
Sibelius, Jean, 217
Siefert, Paul, 144
Siemysl, Prince, 34
Sigismund I, King, 93–94
Silesia, Swedish cultural influences in,
    42, 59, 70, 76, 113, 140, 211
Sillanpää, Frans Eemil, 238, 245, 281
Sinclair, Friedrich Carl, 170
Singing Revolution, 262, 286
Skagen painters, 212–213, 328

Skalbe, Kārlis, 247
Skandia Theater, 248
Skaumand, Duke, 49
Skeppsbron, 117
Skomand, Dietrich, 49
Skujiņš, Frīdrihs, 249
Slaves, 17, 19–20, 22–24, 73
Slav rebellion (983), 15, 32
Slavs, 9, 12–18, 20, 24–25, 28, 32–34, 41, 169, 326
Slovakia, 59, 314
Slovenia, 314
Small Catechism (Luther), 89–90
Smetona, Antanas, 230
Smith, Adam, 116, 328
Smuggling, during Napoleonic Wars, 187–188
Snake motifs, 26
Snellman, Johan Vilhelm, 196
Sniečkus, Antanas, 269
Snorri Sturluson, 82–83
Sobottka, Gustav, 265
Social Democratic Party (SPD), 209, 233–234, 238, 265–267, 297–298, 303–304
Socialdemokratiska Arbetarepartiet, 209
Socialism: following World War I, 275–277; decline of, 288–300, 329. See also Welfare states
Socialist parties, 209–210, 230–231, 275
Socialist Unity Party of Germany (Sozialistische Einheitspartei Deutschlands, SED), 267–268, 271, 291–292, 296–298
Society, 17, 23–27, 47, 165, 167, 208–211, 233, 242–245, 275–276, 286, 307
Society for the Preservation of the Estonian Cultural Heritage (Eesti Muinsuskaitse Selts), 293
Söderman, August, 216
Söerikastaja (Kross), 280
Soldau, 106, 342n33
Solidarity Union (Solidarność), 289, 304
Solzhenitsyn, Alexander, 270
Somov, Konstantin, 213
Songaila, Ringaudas, 294
Song festivals, Estonian, 198, 285–286, 293–294
Sooster, Ülo, 283
Soviet bloc. See Eastern bloc
Sovietization, 1, 6–7, 262–275, 311, 329

Soviet Military Administration of Germany (SMAD), 265–267
Soviet Union, 67, 228, 231–232, 242, 250, 253–258, 260, 262–265, 268–274, 278, 285–288, 290, 292, 294–295, 298–299, 307, 309, 311–313, 329; Sovietization of Baltic region, 6–7, 263–270; World War II, 253–260, 329; Sovietization of Tallinn, 262; collectivization, 270–272; industrialization, 272–275; Finnish trade, 278; postwar visual arts, 282; postwar architecture, 285. See also Russia
Spas, 218–219
Special-interest societies, 198
Spierinck, Peter, 138
Spitsbergen, 231–232
Stalin, Josef, 265
Stanisław August (Poniatowski), King, 150, 179
Stargard, 92
Stargard Land, 41
Starov, Ivan, 181
Stazewski, Henryk, 282
Steamships. See under Ships
Stech, Andreas, 113
Steenwinckel, Hans van, the Elder, 111
Steenwinckel, Hans van, the Younger, 111
Steenwinckel, Lourens, 111
Stelling, Johannes, 234
Stenbock, Magnus, 147
Stender, Gotthard Friedrich, 169
Stenhammar, Wilhelm, 251
Sten Sture, 4, 68–69, 79
Stephan Báthory, King, 96, 103–104
Stettin, 10, 23, 34–35, 44, 81, 91–92, 96, 108, 114–115, 120–121, 147–148, 158, 163t., 187, 207, 241, 259, 317
Stockholm, 56, 65, 68, 76, 101–102, 117–118, 131–136, 140, 143–145, 156, 158, 161, 164, 168, 173, 176–177, 181, 190, 206, 213, 215–217, 220–221, 248–249, 284, 312, 323
Stockmann, Rudolf, 116
Stoewer, Bernhard, 207
Stolp, 90–92
Stralsund, 21, 45, 56, 58, 62, 64, 76, 78–81, 90–92, 98, 116, 120, 137, 147, 169–170, 173, 176, 180, 187, 242, 274, 309

Stralsund altar, 79–80
Straujuma, Laimdota, 305
Strindberg, August, 218
Structural Funds, 316
Struensee, Johann Friedrich, 157
Stuchs, Lorenz, 89
Suffrage, 208–209, 225
Summer vacationing, 218–221, 238
Sunesen, Andreas, 35, 83–84
Suomalainen, Timo, 284
Suomalainen, Tuomo, 284
Suomen Työväenpuolue, 209
Surveillance Cooperation Baltic Sea
   (SUCBAS), 321
Suta, Roman, 250
Svantevit, 14, 24, 33
Svear, 12, 20, 30
Sviatoslav, 12–13
Swecomanes, 197
Sweden, 1, 4–5, 9, 12, 19, 21, 32, 35, 38,
   50–52, 56, 58, 60, 64–69, 75–77,
   81–84, 86, 93–96, 98t., 101–102,
   112–114, 117–118, 120–127, 130–132,
   135–140, 142, 145–149, 153, 155–156,
   163, 167–171, 173–175, 177, 179,
   183–185, 187–189, 195, 199, 201, 205,
   208–209, 212, 214, 217, 220, 226, 229,
   231–232, 240, 243, 248, 251, 255, 258,
   260–261, 263, 269–270, 275–279, 281,
   284, 301, 312–314, 319–320, 322–324,
   327, 329; battle for dominion over
   Baltic Sea, 4, 118–122; fur trade,
   12–13; Christian mission, 32, 38–39;
   expansion into Finland, 50; monasteries, 51; German traders, 56;
   exports, 60; monarchy, 64–65, 68–70;
   Nordic Union, 67–68; population, 73,
   208; Black Death and population, 74;
   literature, 83, 84; Reformation, 93;
   trade, 95–96, 102, 313; Dutch
   architecture, 112; administration
   and estates, 123–129; Dutch trade
   dominance, 129–132; crisis in
   manorial economy, 132–135;
   Netherlandish and German cultural
   influences, 135–144; Great Northern
   War, 146–148, 149; administrative
   reform, 155–157; scholars and
   intellectualism, 169–171; newspapers,
   173–174; theater, 175–176; cedes
   Finnish territories to Russia, 183;
   Napoleonic Wars, 185, 189; continental blockade against England,
   187; declares trade blockade against
   Mecklenburg ports, 187–188;
   nationalist movement, 195; agrarian
   reform, 199, 201; industrialization,
   205; urbanization, 208; shift to
   class-based society, 209; socialist
   parties and unions, 209; nineteenth-
   century music, 216; cooperative
   initiatives with Russian Empire
   successor states, 229; territorial
   disputes over Åland Islands, 229;
   internal politics following WWI,
   231–233; foreign policy disagreements, 232; Great Depression, 240;
   interwar music, 251–252; World War
   II, 255; as welfare state, 263, 275–276;
   influence on Sovietized Finland,
   270; innovation, 277–278; postwar
   literature, 279, 281; postwar
   architecture, 284; ABBA, 287;
   conflict over Øresund, 301; economic
   transformation following fall of
   Soviet bloc, 312; membership in
   European Union, 313–314; rediscovery and acceptance of past,
   322. See also Nordic countries;
   Scandinavia
Swedish East India Company, 156
Swedish language: Bible translated into,
   90; and nationalist movements, 197
Swedish Pomerania, 121, 124, 134–136,
   138, 173, 184–185, 188–189, 203
Sweyn Forkbeard, King, 31
Swidde, Willem, 118fig.
Swords, 24
Sydow, Max von, 282
Szczecin. See Stettin

Tallinn, 35, 246, 249, 252, 257, 262,
   278–279, 283, 285, 287, 290, 293, 295,
   298–299, 320–321, 324. See also Reval
Talvik, Heiti, 245–246
Tammsaare, Anton Hansen, 246
Tankar om Borgerliga Friheten
   (Thoughts on civil liberty) (Forsskål),
   167
Tapiola, 284
Tar, 59–60, 99, 101–102, 130–132, 161,
   163, 188, 205–207

Tartu, 246, 252, 280, 283, 293, 318–319.
  See also Dorpat
Tatars, 71
Tavastians, 38
Taxation, 70, 123–124, 126–129, 152–153,
  275–276
Tegnér, Esaias, 195
Telemann, Georg Philipp, 176
Temppeliaukio Church, 284
Tencalla, Constantino, 142
Tengbom, Ivar, 248
Teniers, David, 178
Ter Borch, Gerard, 178
Terboven, Josef, 255
Tessin, Carl Gustaf, 179
Tessin, Nicodemus, the Elder, 137–138
Tetra Pak, 277
Teuffel, Georg, 139
Teutonic Order. *See* Order of Teutonic
  Knights
Textiles, 57, 59, 62, 97–98, 102–105,
  129–130, 158, 241
Theater. *See* Art(s)
Third Order, 94, 154–155
Thirty Years' War, 105, 118–121, 132,
  135, 140, 148
Thorild, Thomas, 170, 184
Thorn, 36, 45, 53, 63, 72, 86, 93–94, 113,
  128, 147, 150–151, 155, 172
Thorvaldsen, Bertel, 212
Tillbergs, Oleg, 283
Tilo of Culm, 84
Timber, 59, 100–101, 104, 130–132, 158,
  162–163, 188, 205–207, 231, 233–241,
  277
Timm, Ernst, 296
Tithes, and land settlement, 40–41
Tolts, Andres, 283
Tõnisson, Jaan, 224, 229
Tönning, 187
Toruń. *See* Thorn
Tourism, 243, 275, 310, 324
Towns and cities. *See* Cities; City
  planning
Trade, 1–5, 7–9, 11–13, 16, 18–23, 26, 33,
  44–46, 50, 52, 54–65, 67, 75, 78, 80,
  84, 87, 89, 95, 97–104, 123–130, 132,
  139, 141, 145–146, 149, 152–154,
  156–159, 161–164, 173–174, 186–188,
  206–207, 210, 213, 239, 241–244, 278,
  289, 313, 320, 324, 326–328

Tramp trade, 206
Transportation, 317, 324
Travel destination, Baltic Sea as,
  218–221
Treaty of Andrusovo (1667), 122
Treaty of Brest-Litovsk (1918), 228
Treaty of Brömsebro (1645), 122
Treaty of Copenhagen (1660), 122
Treaty of Kalisz (1343), 70
Treaty of Lisbon (2008), 315
Treaty of Nöteborg (1323), 38
Treaty of Nystad (1721), 149, 162
Treaty of Oliva (1660), 122
Treaty of Partition (1797), 151
Treaty of Ribe (1460), 68, 191
Treaty of Roskilde (1658), 122
Treaty of Stettin (1570), 96
Treaty of Stralsund (1370), 58, 64
Treaty of Utrecht (1474), 62
Treaty of Westphalia (1648), 120, 123,
  124
Treptow an der Rega, 88, 90, 92
Tretter, Martin, 89
Treuhandanstalt, 308, 309
Trianon Decree (1810), 188
Trier, Lars von, 282
Trondheim cathedral, 77
Trotzig, Peter, 139
Truce of Altmark (1629), 121
Truce of Yam-Zapolsky (1582), 96
Turner, Samuel Wilhelm, 171
Tusk, Donald, 305
Tuxen, Laurits, 213

Ueckermünde, Georg von, 90
Ulbricht, Walter, 265
Ullmann, Liv, 282
Ulmanis, Kārlis, 230, 246
Ulrich, Duke, 114
Ulrichshusen, 115
Ulrika Eleonora, Queen, 155
Uluots, Jüri, 258
Ulvaeus, Björn, 287
Undén, Östen, 260
Under, Marie, 245
Undset, Sigrid, 245
Union of the Baltic Cities (UBC), 318
Union(s), 1, 7, 66, 72, 128, 183, 189, 209,
  225–226, 228–232, 242, 248, 250,
  253–258, 260, 262–274, 277–278,
  285–290, 292, 294–295, 298–300,

Union(s) (continued)
302, 304–309, 311–315, 317–319,
321–322, 326, 329; Danish-
Norwegian, 67–68; Nordic Union,
67–68; and expansion of mandatory
education, 209; socialist parties
and, 209–210; in Sweden following
WWI, 231; during Great Depression,
240; Polish, 289, 295; and monarchies, 326–327
Universities: founding of, 80–82;
Gymnasia, 94; Dutch professors
recruited by, 140–141; Jesuit
influence, 142; eighteenth-century,
167–168; and educational communi-
ties, 318–319
University of Åbo, 141, 169, 173, 183
University of Copenhagen, 93, 11
University of Cracow, 86
University of Dorpat, 141–142, 168,
210–211, 214. See also Tartu
University of Göttingen, 167
University of Greifswald (Baltic
Borderlands), 80–82, 90, 115, 141,
170, 173–174, 319, 397
University of Helsinki, 183, 196, 216
University of Königsberg, 94
University of Latvia (Riga), 246
University of Lund, 140, 195
University of Rostock, 80–82
University of Tartu, 246, 280, 283.
See also Dorpat
University of Turku, 196
University of Uppsala, 167
University of Vilnius, 96, 142
University of Wittenberg, 82
Unt, Mati, 280
Upits, Andrejs, 279
Uppsala cathedral, 77
Urach, Wilhelm von, 227–228
Urbanization, 117, 141, 207–208
Urban society, 73–77, 141–142
US-Baltic Charter, 315

Vacietis, Ojars, 280
Vaičiūnaitė, Judita, 280
Vaičiūnas, Petras, 247
Valdemar II, King, 35, 63–64
Valdemar IV, King, 58, 64–65
Valters, Jānis, 214
Vanags, Aleksandrs, 222

Van Amsterdam, Reinier, 113
Van den Blocke, Abraham, 87, 110, 112
Van den Blocke, Isaak, 110
Van den Blocke, Willem, 87, 110, 112
Van der Gucht, Maximilian, 142
Van der Heide, Henning, 54
Van der Schardt, Jan Jorisz, 110–111
Van de Velde, Adriaen, 178
Van Ghetelen, Hans, 85
Van Hoove, Paul, 115
Van Huysum, Jan, 178
Van Mieris, Frans, 178
Van Mieris, Willem, 178
Van Obbergen, Anthonis, 110–112
Van Ostade, Adriaen, 178
Varangians, 12–13, 18, 22
Vartislav III, Prince, 45
Vartislav IV, Duke, 33–34
Vartislav IX, Duke, 80–81
Vasa baroque tradition, 142
Vasilyev, Nikolai, 217
Vasks, Pēteris, 286
Veleti, 14–15, 23–24
Venclova, Tomas, 280
Venstre Party, 234
Vermordsen, Frands, 93
Veski, Johannes Voldemar, 245
Viborg, 38, 102, 134, 141, 162, 249, 255.
See also Vyborg
Viborg, wood exports from, 1787, 163t.
Vietinghoff, Otto Hermann von, 174
Vikings, 1, 8–12, 18, 20, 22, 24–25, 29,
31, 73, 252
Viking style, 25–26
Vilks, Ēvalds, 280
Villications, 23, 339n22
Vilnius, 17, 71, 96, 112, 142, 182, 214,
225, 227–229, 245, 259, 285, 295, 318
Vilnius Cathedral, 142
Vingboons, Justus, 137
Vingboons, Philip, 139
Visarid, 283
Visby, 23, 46, 55–56, 58
Visscher, Claes Jansz. (Piscator), 110
Vītols, Jāzeps, 252
Vitslav I, 41, 45
Vitslav III, 33
Vogel, Samuel Gottlieb, 219
Voght, Caspar, 200
Vogler, Abbé, 177
Voldemaras, Augustinas, 230

Volkswerft shipyard, 274
Vom Rode, Paul, 91
Vyborg, 310, 319. *See also* Viborg
Vytautas, Grand Duke, 71–72

Wackenitz, Jacob, 109
Wagenschoss, 130
Waghenaer, Lucas Janszoon, 5
Wajda, Andrzej, 282
Walentynowicz, Anna, 289
Wałęsa, Lech, 289–290, 304
Wallander, Sven, 247
Wallenstein, Albrecht von, 119
Wall epitaphs, 116
Waltari, Mika, 281
Warnke, Hans, 266
Warriors, upper-caste, 24
Wax, 21–22, 59–60, 102
Weckmann, Matthias, 143
Weenix, Jan, 178
Wegelius, Martin, 215–216
Weinreich, Hans, 89
Welfare states, 275–277
Welté, Gottlieb, 182
Wendorff, Hugo, 233, 234
Wend paragraphs, 49
Western Pomerania, 120, 124, 147, 203,
    260, 265–266, 271, 274, 298, 303,
    308–310, 316–317; Great Northern
    War, 147–148; agrarian reform, 203;
    support for Nazi Party, 238; World
    War II, 260; Sovietization, 265–266;
    collectivization, 271–272; economic
    transformation following fall of
    Soviet bloc, 310; cooperation,
    316–317
West Francia, 12
West Germany. *See* Federal Republic of
    Germany
West Prussia: administrative reform,
    155; agriculture, 205; German
    occupation, 254
Wiek, 28
Willer, Peter, 113
William II, Emperor, 220
William of Brandenburg, 95

Wismar, 45, 56, 62, 76, 78, 80, 98, 114,
    120, 147–148, 185, 187–188, 207, 242,
    259–260
Wismar Tribunal, 124–125
Witten coins, 66
Władysław I, Łokietek (the Elbowhigh),
    King, 37, 70
Władysław III, King, 72
Władysław IV, King, 121
Władysław IV Vasa, King, 142
Wojtyła, Karol Józef, 289–290
Wolgast, 90, 115, 147, 212, 309
Wolgast Palace, 115
Wolin, 9, 14, 16, 19–20, 23, 34, 92, 120,
    148
Wolinians, 16
Wolter von Plettenberg, 94–95
Women's suffrage, 208–209
Wood and wood products, 59–61, 78, 99,
    101, 158, 162
World Bank, 307
World War I, 6, 209, 220, 222, 226–227,
    231, 234, 239, 241, 248–249
World War II, 6, 253, 260, 275, 303,
    327
Wouwerman, Philips, 178
Wrangel, Carl Gustaf, 136, 138
Wranitzky, Paul, 174
Wrymouth, 34

Yacht clubs, 220
Yeltsin, Boris, 294, 299
Yeropkin, Pyotr, 180

Zacharias, Justus Friedrich, 167
Zālīte, Māra, 280
Zamoyski, Jan, 109
Zanussi, Krzysztof, 282
Zaor, Jan, 142
Zarina, Aija, 283
Zebrzydowski, Mikołaj, 127
Zeelanders, 62, 98
Zemtsov, Mikhail, 180
Zhdanov, Andrei, 256
Zorn, Anders, 213–214, 221, 328
Zuiderzee, 58